Charles Fraser-Mackintosh

Antiquarian Notes, Historical, Genealogical, and Social

Second series: Inverness-shire, parish by parish

Charles Fraser-Mackintosh

Antiquarian Notes, Historical, Genealogical, and Social
Second series: Inverness-shire, parish by parish

ISBN/EAN: 9783337428525

Printed in Europe, USA, Canada, Australia, Japan

Cover: Foto ©ninafisch / pixelio.de

More available books at **www.hansebooks.com**

ANTIQUARIAN NOTES,

HISTORICAL, GENEALOGICAL, AND SOCIAL

(SECOND SERIES):

INVERNESS-SHIRE PARISH BY PARISH.

BY

CHARLES FRASER-MACKINTOSH, F S.A. Scot.,

AUTHOR OF "DUNACHTON PAST AND PRESENT"; "ANTIQUARIAN NOTES"; "INVERNESSIANA"; "LETTERS OF TWO CENTURIES"; "THE LAST MACDONALDS OF ISLA"; ETC., ETC.

―――

INVERNESS: A. & W. MACKENZIE.

PREFACE.

THE title of this work, which has been appearing for a couple of years in the columns of the *Scottish Highlander* under the heading of "Old Yet New," has been selected on the suggestion of some friends and well-wishers as more appropriate.

The idea of dealing with ancient history and story by Parishes is a sound one, and has been admirably carried out by Mr William Mackay in his elaborate and carefully worked out *History of Urquhart and Glenmoriston*. It might be held as overloading to deal with each Parish in the same comprehensive manner, while on the other hand one volume might be quite inadequate for a whole County. It certainly would for such a County as Inverness.

I have to thank several gentlemen for information and hints; Mr Alexander Mackenzie for the handsome way in which he has printed and issued the volume; as also his son, Mr Thomas Mackenzie, for preparing such a full and accurate index.

C.F.-M.

BOURNEMOUTH,
1st February, 1897.

CONTENTS.

———:o:———

	PAGE.
PREFACE	v.
LIST OF SUBSCRIBERS	xii.

PARISHES—

   I. KILMORACK—
      Glenstrathfarar   1
   II. KILTARLITY—
      Janet Ross, Lady Dowager of Lovat, 1544-65 ...   13
   III. KIRKHILL—
      The Mackintoshes in the Fraser country ...   17
   IV. BONA—
      Interesting Historical Incidents   25
      Dochcairn and Dochfour   33
      The Macleans of Dochgarroch   38
      Abriachan   56
   V. DORES—
      Its old Possessions and Divisions   60
      The Macbeans of Kinchyle   63
      Present and Past Valuation   69
      A Stirring Runaway Romance   71
   VI. BOLESKINE AND ABERTARFF—
      The Origin of Fort-Augustus   76
      The Village   83
      Incidents in John Mackay's, Inchnacardoch, career   86
      The Gwynne Family and Mrs Grant of Laggan,
        1827   89
      Abduction by William Fraser, merchant, Fort-
        Augustus, 1744   92
      Dalcattaig and Portclairs   98
      The Earl of Selkirk and the Stratherrick Emi-
        grants in 1803   107
      The People of Abertarff, and the Canal, in 1808   108
   VII. URQUHART AND GLENMORISTON—
      The Grants of Glenmoriston   110

VIII. KILMONIVAIG—

Blar-nan-Leine, in 1544	113
Glengarry—State of Affairs in 1762	120
Do. do. do. 1762-1788	124
Condition of its People	126
State of Affairs in 1788-1808	128
Condition of the People, and other Grievances, in 1793, etc.	133
The Glengarry Trials of 1798 and 1807	137
Glengarry and his Tenants	142
Glengarry and the Old Stone Bridge of Inverness	145
Glengarry's Piper, and the Canal Commissioners in 1807, etc.	149
Coll Macdonald of Barisdale	152
Ronald Scammadale	155
Brae Lochaber—Old and New Rentals—Old Places and People	158
Keppoch	174

IX. KILMALLIE—

Fort-William and the Gordon Lands	179
Camerons v. Macdonalds, et e contra	191
Regarding An Old Map of Mamore	195
Old Rights of Fishing and Floating on the Lochy	196
Lochaber Literary Men—Past and Present	199
Dismemberment of Inverness-shire in Lochaber	201
Tenants and Rentals of Glenluie and Loch Arkaig in 1642	202
Eilean-'ic-an-Toisich, and the Clunes Lands	204
Loss of Glenluie and Loch Arkaig by Mackintosh	205
Lochiel—Enormous Increase of Rent	207
Consolidation of Sheep Farms	213
Church Site Refusal in 1843	217
Present Rental and other Details	219
The True History of Miss Jeanie Cameron	227
Miscellaneous	230

X. GLENELG—

The Glenelg men Ferociously attack a Lochalsh Funeral Party	233
A Macdonell-Macleod Marriage Contract	236
Leases, Roads, Railways, and Recruiting	239
The Frasers of Lovat and the Macleods	242
North Morar	245

XI. ARDNAMURCHAN—

Arisaig and South Morar—Modern Evictions and Last Century Rentals	248

Eilean Tioram Castle and Lands	254
Glenaladale and Prince Charles	256

XII. SMALL ISLES—
Canna and Eigg—Old Tenants and Rentals	260

XIII. SLEAT—
The Macdonalds	263
Property left by Sir Alexander—Inventory	264
Roderick Macdonald of Camuscross and his son James	272
Marshal Macdonald's visit to Skye—a curious salutation	448

XIV. STRATH—
The Mackinnons of that Ilk	276
The Elgol and Camusunary Tenants in 1785	278
The Mackinnons of Corry and others	280
The Farmer-Minister and the Publican	280
The MacAllisters in Strath	283

XV. PORTREE—
Malcolm Nicolson, Scorrybreck	284
How a French Invasion was repelled	449

XVI. KILMUIR—
Duntulm Castle and the Duntulm Centenarian	286

XVII. SNIZORT—
Its Past and Present—A contrast	288

XVIII. DUIRINISH—
Lieutenant-Colonel Macleod's appointment to the 42nd Highlanders	290
Macleod of Bay	291
Glengarry hounded out of Skye	292
Macleod of Bay assaulted by an Irishman	293

XIX. BRACADALE—
The Parish Minister and his wife	296

XX. HARRIS—
St. Kilda—Its Owners and Tenants since 1805	299

XXI. NORTH UIST—
Removal of Maclean of Hosta in 1780	301

XXII. SOUTH UIST—
The Macdonalds of Belfinlay, now of Waternish	305
Do. do. do.	449
The Clanranalds in South Uist and Benbecula	311
Their Tenants and Rentals in Benbecula in 1798	311
Do. do. in South Uist in 1798	313
The Estates sold	320
The Macdonalds of Bornish	320
The Macdonalds of Boisdale	322

Present and Past distribution of the Land	326
A South Uist Centenarian	328

XXIII. BARRA—

The MacNeills of Barra and the People	331

XXIV. LAGGAN—

Its Gordon, Grant, Macdonald, Mackintosh and Macpherson Proprietors...	334
The Gordon Rentals in 1677...	342
Do. do. in 1829..	344
Heads of Families in 1679	345
The Macphersons appear as Land Owners, and their after succession	346
John Gordon of Glenbucket as Gordon Factor...	350
Evan Macpherson of Cluny of the 'Forty-five, and the Management of his estate	352
Cluny Castle and the War Cry of the Clan	359
The Macphersons of Breackachie	361
The Macphersons of Ovie and MacCoul	364
The "Gentlemen" of Badenoch, their Feuds and Fracas	364

XXV. KINGUSSIE—

Ruthven Castle—Its ancient and Modern Possessors	369
Names of Householders in the Parish in 1679	372
The Gordon Rentals and Feus in 1667	373
Do. do. do. in 1828	374
The Macphersons of Phoness	375
The Ossian Macpherson Purchases and Evictions	380
One of the "Three Curses" of Badenoch—Violent Proceedings	382
Invertromie, Etterish, Invernahaven, etc.	385

XXVI. ALVIE—

The Invereshie Macphersons	390
The Gordon Rentals and Removals	394
Jane Maxwell, Duchess of Gordon and her Doings before and after the Evictions	395
The Inscription on her Tomb	398
The Ossian Macphersons	399
Their Alvie Evictions—List of Names	450
The Dr Johnson Correspondence	400
Traces of the Ossianic "Originals"	403
James Macpherson's Morals, Successors, and Fortune	404
The Mackintoshes, and the Duchess of Bedford's Glenfeshie Huts	407

XXVII. ROTHIEMURCHUS—		
The Mackintoshes, Shaws, and Grants	...	411
XXVIII. KINCARDINE AND ABERNETHY—		
The Stuart Barons, John Roy, and the Count of Maida	... ...	416
The Abernethy Removals		420
XXIX. DUTHIL—		
John Beg MacAndrew and his Exploits	...	422
XXX. MOY AND DALAROSSIE—		
The MacQueens of Pollochaig	... ...	427
An Ancient Deer Forest		428
Mackintosh Anecdotes		429
XXXI. DAVIOT AND DUNLICHITY—		
The Mackintoshes of Aberarder		431
Tenants and Rental, Aberarder Estate in 1797		434
XXXII. CROY—		
The Dallasses of Cantray and Budgate	...	435
Dalcross Castle and Lands		436
XXXIII. CAWDOR—		
The Campbells of Cawdor, and Condition of the Estate in 1796		438
XXXIV. ARDERSIER—		
The Erection of Fort-George, etc.		442
XXXV. PETTY—		
Its Original Owners	...	444
Modern Changes ...	...	445
ADDENDA ET CORRIGENDA ...	...	447
INDEX—		
NAMES OF PERSONS		457
NAMES OF PLACES		471

LIST OF SUBSCRIBERS.

———:o:———

Aberdeen University Library, per P. J. Anderson, Esq.
Abinger, Right Hon. Lord, Inverlochy Castle, Fort-William
Anderson, John N., Esq., Stornoway
Atholl, His Grace the Duke of,
Barron, James, Esq., *Courier* Office, Inverness
Berthon, Raymond Tinne, Esq., Beckenham, Kent
Blair, Sheriff, Inverness
Brown, William, Esq., bookseller, Edinburgh (4 copies)
Burgess, Peter, Esq., banker, Fortrose
Burns, William, Esq., solicitor, Inverness
Calder, A., Esq., Tombain, Grantown
Cameron, Allan, Esq. of Lundavra, Athlone, Ireland
Cameron-Swan, Donald, Esq., Holland Park, London
Cameron, D. M., Esq., merchant, Inverness
Cameron, John, Esq., bookseller, Inverness
Cameron, P., Esq., solicitor, Alexandria, Dumbartonshire
Cameron, P., Esq., Corrychoillie, Edinburgh
Cameron Robert F., Esq., C.A., Inverness
Campbell, Donald Stewart, Esq., solicitor, Montrose
Campbell, J. L., Esq., Dalmally, Argyleshire
Campbell, Sheriff, Stornoway
Chisholm, Archibald A., Esq., Procurator-Fiscal, Lochmaddy
Chisholm, James, Esq., East Croydon
Chisholm, Joseph, Esq., Ballifeary, Inverness.
Chisholm, The, London (Large Paper)
Clarke, Lieutenant-Colonel Cumming, Ballindown
Cowan, George, Esq., Edinburgh
Cran, John, Esq., Kirkton, Bunchrew
Davidson, Ben., Esq., New York, U.S.A.
Douglas & Foulis, Messrs, booksellers, Edinburgh (4 copies)
D'Oyley, Madame la Marquise, Paris

Dunbar, Archibald H., Esq., Yr. of Northfield, Bournemouth
Ewart, General Sir John Alexander, K.C.B., Longholm, Dumfries-shire
Finlayson, John, Esq., Caledonian Bank, Inverness
Fraser, Alexander, Esq., Union Street, Inverness
Fraser, Alexander, Esq., solicitor, Inverness
Fraser, Alexander, Esq., Motherwell
Fraser, Edmund, Esq., Secretary of Her Majesty's Legation, Brussels (Large Paper)
Fraser, J. Leslie, Esq., dentist, Inverness.
Fraser, R. B., Esq., London (Large Paper)
Gillespie, C. G. Esq., Meoble Lodge, Fort-William
Grant, Donald, Esq., solicitor, Grantown
Grant, Dr Ogilvie, Inverness
Grant, Francis W., Esq., Maryhill, Inverness
Grant, J. P., Esq. of Rothiemurchus
Gray-Buchanan, A. W., Esq., Polmont
Gray, George, Esq., Clerk of the Peace, Glasgow
Holland, Richard D., Esq. of Kilvean, Inverness (Large Paper)
Innes, Alexander Lee, Esq. of Milnfield, Inverness
Innes, Charles, Esq., solicitor, Inverness (Large Paper)
Inverness Public Library
Joass, Rev. Dr J. M., Golspie
Johnston, George P., Esq., bookseller, Edinburgh
Kemble, Major, Knock, Skye
Livingston, Duncan, Esq., Portsmouth, Ohio, U.S.A.
Lochiel, Achnacarry Castle
Lovat, the Right Hon. Lord, Beaufort Castle (Large Paper)
Macandrew, Sir H. C., Inverness
Macbain, Alexander, Esq., M.A., Raining's School, Inverness
Macbean, Lieutenant-Colonel Forbes, Dover
Macbean, W. Charles, Esq., solicitor, Inverness
Macdonald, Admiral David Robertson, of Kinlochmoidart
Macdonald, Alexander, Esq., Antigonish Co., Nova Scotia
Macdonald, Colonel Alexander, Portree
Macdonald, Allan, Esq., LL.D., Glenarm, Ireland
Macdonald, Allan, Esq., M.A., LL.B., solicitor, Inverness
Macdonald, C. Donald, Esq., Rosario de Sta Fe, Argentine Republic
Macdonald, Captain Allan of Waternish (1 and 1 Large Paper)

Macdonald, Duncan, Esq., Edinburgh (Large Paper)
Macdonald, Harry, Esq. of Viewfield, Portree
Macdonald, H. L , Esq. of Dunach, Oban (Large Paper)
Macdonald, Hugh, Esq., solicitor, Aberdeen
Macdonald, J. M., Esq., London
Macdonald, John, Esq., merchant, Inverness.
Macdonald, John, Esq., Nevis Bank, Fort-William
Macdonald, Keith Norman, Esq., M.D., Edinburgh
Macdonald, Kenneth, Esq., Town-Clerk, Inverness (Large Paper)
Macdonald, Lachlan, Esq. of Skeabost (Large Paper)
Macdonald, Malcolm N., Esq., Nairn
Macdonald, Rev. D. J., Killean, Kintyre
Macdonald, William, Esq., M.D., Glasgow
Macdougall, E. A., Esq., Westminster
Macdougall, John, Esq., Tomatin
Macdonell, Eneas R., Esq. of Morar (2 copies)
Macewen, William C., Esq., W.S., Edinburgh
Macgillivray, Alexander, Esq., Arlington Road, London
Macgregor, John, Esq., Bearsden, Elgin
Mackay, Captain A. Leith-Hay, Inverness
Mackay, Eneas, Esq., bookseller, Stirling
Mackay, John, Esq., *Celtic Monthly*, Glasgow (36 and 3 Large Paper)
Mackay, John, Esq., C.E., J.P., Hereford
Mackay, Thomas A , British Linen Bank, Inverness
Mackay, William, Esq., solicitor, Inverness
Mackenzie, Alexander, Esq , Park House, Inverness (Large Paper)
Mackenzie, Alexander, Esq., Walton Lodge, Bath
Mackenzie, Donald, Esq., Inland Revenue, Bonar-Bridge (Large Paper)
Mackenzie, Dr F. M., Inverness
Mackenzie, Hector Hugh, Esq., Balelone, Lochmaddy
Mackenzie, John, Esq., factor, Uig, Skye
Mackenzie, John, Esq., Kirn
Mackenzie, N. B. Esq., Fort-William
Mackenzie, Rev. C. H., Bristol
Mackenzie, Sir Kenneth S. of Gairloch, Baronet
Mackenzie, Sir James D., Baronet, Redcliffe Square, London
Mackenzie, Thomas, Esq. of Dailuaine (Large Paper)
Mackenzie, Thomas William, Esq., Park House, Inverness

Mackenzie, William, Esq., clothier, Inverness (Large Paper)
Mackenzie, William, Esq., Secretary, Crofters Commission
Mackenzie, Wm. Dalziel, Esq. of Farr (Large Paper)
Mackinnon, Alexander K., Esq., London
Mackinnon, Duncan, Esq., London (2 copies)
Mackinnon, John, Esq., London
Mackinnon, John, Esq., Walsall
Mackinnon, Sir W. A., K.C.B., London
Mackintosh, Æneas, Esq., The Doune, Inverness (Large Paper)
Mackintosh, Alexander, Esq., Forfar
Mackintosh, A. Mackintosh, Esq., London
Mackintosh, Angus, Esq., Hatfield, Herts
Mackintosh, D. A. S., Esq , Shettleston
Mackintosh, D., Esq., Roseheath, Inverness
Mackintosh, Duncan, Esq., Bank of Scotland, Inverness
Mackintosh, ex-Bailie John, Inverness
Mackintosh, John, Esq., Tickhill, Yorkshire
Mackintosh of Mackintosh, Moy Hall (Large Paper)
Mackintosh, Rev. Alexander, Fort-William
Mackintosh, William, Esq., J.P., Drummuir
Maclaren, Thomas, Esq , bookseller, Inverness
Maclean, Alexander Scott, Esq., M.I.M.E., Greenock
Maclean, Councillor Roderick, Inverness
Maclean, Daniel, Esq , junior, Greenock
Maclean, Lieutenant Hector F., Yr. of Duart
Maclean, Rev. A. M., Yr. of Dochgarroch, Dudley
Macleod, A. W., Esq., Glasgow (Large Paper)
Macleod, N., Esq., Raasay
Macleod, Norman, Esq., bookseller, Edinburgh (3 copies)
Macleod of Macleod, Dunvegan Castle
Macleod, Reginald, Esq. (of Macleod), Queen's Remembrancer
Macleod, Wm. Bowman, Esq., Edinburgh (Large Paper)
Macpherson, A., Esq., solicitor, Kingussie
Macpherson, A. J., Esq., Newtonmore
Macpherson, Lieutenant-Colonel Lachlan, of Glentruim, Kingussie
Macpherson-Grant, Sir George, Baronet, of Ballindalloch
Macrae-Gilstrap, John, Esq., Newark-on-Trent (Large Paper)
Macritchie, Andrew J., Esq., solicitor, Inverness

Malcolm, George, Esq., Invergarry.
Martin, Murdoch, Esq., Glasgow
Matheson, John, Esq , M.D., Gibson Square, London (Large Paper)
Matheson, Sir Kenneth, Baronet, of Lochalsh (Large Paper)
Maxwell, Sir John Stirling, Baronet, M.P., Pollokshaws
Melven Bros., Messrs, booksellers, Inverness (2 copies)
Menzies, Colonel D., Blarich, Sutherland
Mitchell Library, Glasgow, per F. T. Barrett, Esq.
Munro, David, Esq , Annfield, Inverness
Munro, Henry, Esq., Nessmount, Inverness
Munro, Sir Hector, Baronet, Fowlis Castle (Large Paper)
Murray, Francis, Esq., of Drummond Park, Inverness
Nairne, David, Esq., *Northern Chronicle*, Inverness
Noble, John, Esq., bookseller, Inverness (15 and 2 Large Paper)
Public Library, Toronto, Canada, per James Bain, Esq.
Ramsden, Sir John, Bart. of Ardverikie (2 and 2 Large Paper)
Reid, Sir Hugh Gilzean of Warley Abbey, Birmingham
Ross, Councillor A. M., Editor of the *Star*, Dingwall
Ross, ex-Provost Alexander, LL.D., Inverness
Ross, James, Esq., Broadford Hotel, Skye
Ross, John M., Esq., 2 Devonshire Gardens, Glasgow (Large Paper)
Sinclair, Allan J., Esq., Town Hall, Newport
Sinclair, Rev. A. Maclean, Prince Edward Island
Sinton, Rev. Thomas, The Manse, Dores
Smith, George, Esq., journalist, Inverness
Smith, Bailie W. J., Inverness
Stewart, & Son, Messrs, booksellers, Forres
Stewart, Rev. Alexander, LL.D., Nether-Lochaber
Stuart, ex-Bailie W. G., Nethy-Bridge
The Librarian, St. Benedict's Abbey, Fort-Augustus
Thin, James, Esq., bookseller, Edinburgh (3 copies)
Thomson, County Councillor Robert, Kinmylies, Inverness
Thomson, James, Esq., gas manager, Inverness
Warrand, Colonel, A. J. C. of Ryefield (Large Paper)
Wilson, P. G., Esq., court jeweller, Inverness
Wilson, Thomas, Esq., solicitor, Lochmaddy
Young, David, Esq., Caledonian Bank, Inverness
Yule, Miss A. F., Tarradale House (2 copies)

ANTIQUARIAN NOTES:
SECOND SERIES.

THERE is not a mountain or glen, lake or river, in the Highlands without its own tradition and story, and whether bright or dark, humorous or pathetic, they are all to us, in this present age of research, full of speculative interest. But their real history, and that of the people since the 'Forty-five, concerns Highlanders so closely that authentic and hitherto unpromulgated information, cannot be too widely made known. With this object in view, I have selected for the first of this series of Notes one of the largest artificial Saharas in the North.

I.—PARISH OF KILMORACK.
GLENSTRATHFARAR.

At the period of the final disjunction of the county of Ross from Inverness-shire, the Earl of Seaforth and Mackenzie influence was all powerful. Most of the Seaforth estates were made part of Ross, however arbitrary the bounds and wanting in natural division. For instance, the disjunction of Lewis, if divided at all, ought to have been at Tarbert; and nearer Inverness, the whole upper waters of the Morriston, the Affaric, the Cannich, and the Farar belonged naturally to Inverness, although assigned in every case, but that of the Affaric, to Ross. Again Corriecharrabie, whose waters run into the Orrin, should belong naturally to Ross. The name of "Glenstrathfarar" is modern and, the two first syllables being synonymic, should be limited to "Strathfarar." Of old the whole of it belonged to the Earldom of Ross, and the first time any part of the Inverness-shire portion has been noted is on 3rd March, 1416, in the contract of marriage betwixt Janet Fenton, sister of William Fenton of that Ilk, and Hugh Fraser of Lovat. In this contract it is stated that Fenton gives *inter alia* with his sister the two Buntaits, of the value of ten merks of old extent, under this condition that what time the lands of "Uchterache" be recovered, the said Hucheon and the said Janet shall receive these lands in joint infeftment to the extent of ten merks, and if the same lands of Uchterache be not found of the extent of ten merks land of old extent, Fenton shall make it up and shall receive back the two Buntaits.

Lovat seems to have got Uchterache, but did not give back Buntait. The name of Uchterache was general, and being supposed to be of the value of ten merks of old extent, probably included all the Lovat portion of Glenstrathfarar, with the exception of Inchvuilt, afterwards referred to. Prior to 1416 it seems to have been part of the Fenton portion of the Barony of Aird, and been impignorated by the family. By charter dated Beauly, 2nd May, 1607, Simon, Lord Lovat, grants *inter alia* the lands of Bencharran, lying within the Barony of Aigais, Forestry of Brewlin and Sheriffdom of Inverness, in wadset to James Fraser, first of Phopachy, and Elizabeth Fraser his spouse, daughter of William Fraser of Struy. The Forestry of "Brewlin" is thus found at an early date, subsequent scribes changing the word to "Beauly," although the Barony of Beauly, which extended from Tarradale to the Burn of Breachachy, never had a forest. On referring to my Belladrum collections I find that Ochtero (the old Uchterache) and others came into possession of the Belladrum family in 1636, remaining with them about a century and a half. By charter dated at Lovat 26th November, 1636, Simon, Lord Lovat, grants *inter alia* to Hugh Fraser of Belladrum, the town and lands of Bencharran, the town and lands of Muilzie, the town and lands of Ochtero, and the easter half of the town and lands of Brewling, extending to a half davoch and an eighth part of old extent, lying within the Barony of Aigais, Forestry of Brewlin, Lordship of Lovat, and Sheriffdom of Inverness. Upon the same date Lovat empowers Belladrum out of the price, to redeem three wadsets over the lands. In 1637 three other names appear, viz., Inchvuilt, Inchlochell, and Inchvallagan. George, Earl of Seaforth, grants a charter of the above three lands, described as lying within the Earldom of Ross and Sheriffdom of Inverness, dated at Brahan, 16th August, 1637, in favour of Colin Mackenzie of Kincraig and Colin, his eldest son. One of the witnesses to the sasine following, passed 3rd March, 1638, is "William Vic-Homas in Inchlochell." Colin Mackenzie, the younger, now of Kincraig, gives a blench charter of these three subjects as possessed by himself and his tenants, and described as lying within the parish of Kilmorack, Earldom of Ross and Sheriffdom of Inverness, in favour of Hugh Fraser of Belladrum, dated Inverness, 30th June, 1656. The reddendo to the superior is 13s 4d Scots with 3s 4d of augmentation. In 1661 Hugh, Lord Lovat, with consent of the Earl of Rothes and Sir George Mackenzie of Tarbat, his curators, and others, grant a precept of Clare Constat in favour of Hugh Fraser of Belladrum of the lands contained in the charter of 1634. In 1691, when the Cess Roll for Inverness-shire was made up, Fraser of Belladrum is valued in Kilmorack for Glenstrathfarar for the sum of £296 Scots, all his other lands lying within the parishes of Kiltarlity and Wardlaw. In 1711 James Fraser, now of Belladrum, is infeft in Belladrum as heir of his grandfather Hugh, by Roderick Mackenzie of Prestonhall, superior, and in 1756, James Fraser, then of Belladrum, makes up titles to the Kilmorack lands as heir of his great-grandfather, Hugh of 1661. In 1767 Captain James Fraser of Belladrum, on the narrative that though he was still fully assessed according to the Roll of 1691, he and his predecessors had been really denuded of the whole Kilmorack lands in favour of the family of Lovat, except Easter Muilzie and Muilzie-reoch, which still belonged to him, at least in mid-superiority, prayed the Commissioners of Supply for modification and relief.

The description of some of the Monar shielings was—"All and whole the lands and grazings of Luipinvir of Monar, as also the lands and grazings of Mulchullinish, and the lands along the middle division of Luipinvir of Monar, as also the lands and grazings of Luiptiltrails of Monar." The upper part of Strathfarar, as also Corrycharrabie, was almost entirely forest, and pleasant indeed must have been the great forest hunts, which often lasted for a whole week. From morning to evening the woods, thickets, and recesses, for miles around were beaten inwards. At night the numerous company feasted and danced, and "high politics" were discussed by the leaders, forming not infrequently the basis of great public movements. The minister of Wardlaw, apparently from personal observation, narrates the details of one at Monar, attended by Lord Lovat, Lord Seaforth, and other prominent men, and it was while hunting in Corriecharrabie that the ill-fated Master of Lovat, in consequence of the taunts of his stepmother, hurriedly departed in July 1544, to meet death at Blarnan-leine. An old account of this battle, purporting to give Lord Lovat's stirring appeal and address before the fight commenced, hitherto unpublished, will be given later on.

Strathfarar in its entirety, including the portion belonging to Sir Kenneth Matheson, and Fairburn, from the head waters of Loch Calavie, the river Strathmore and their respective tributaries, includes some of the finest scenery in the Highlands, combined with excellent fishings and grazings. Many years ago in conjunction with a valued friend, now no more, it took me eight hours to walk from Craig in Loch Carron, to Loch Monar side, and until our arrival we saw neither house nor person.

Having given a brief account of the early history of the ownership of Strathfarar, Inverness-shire, I will next deal with the occupation, beginning with the townships and names of the tenants as in 1767. The tenants in the Strath in that year were as follows:—

At Bencharran—Neil Maclean, Katharine Macdonald, Thomas Fraser, Duncan Macdonell, Mary Macfarquhar, and Peter "Greumach."

Wester Muilzie—Robert Fraser.

Easter Brewlin—John Fraser.

Ochtero—Donald Chisholm, John Chisholm, Elspet Fraser, and Alexander Macdonald.

Ardchuilck—James Fraser, Mary Fraser, Duncan Forbes, and Thomas Fraser.

In all 15 heads of families, with cottars and dependants, probably over 100 souls. The rent paid was £40 1s sterling.

It was to an island in Loch Muilzie that Lord Lovat was carried for safety after the battle of Culloden, prior to setting out for the West Coast. He left Gortuleg House early on the morning of 17th April, 1746, was taken across Loch Ness to Glenurquhart, thence up the valley into Strathglass. The English were too much occupied that day in the Aird looting and burning, and many of Prince Charles' soldiers had time to escape. The plunder gathered in the Aird and brought to Inverness for sale and shipment was enormous. My earliest recollections are connected with an old man who died in Ballimore of Dochgarroch fifty years ago, at a very advanced age, and understood to have been born the very day Culloden was fought. One of the old man's, by name Alister Roy Macdonald, stories was that his father, when ploughing at Dunballoch two days after the battle, was with his horses impressed into carrying valuables from Castle Dounie ruins to Inverness, for which he got neither pay nor thanks.

It will be observed that in Wester Muilzie Robert Fraser was tenant. He also held a wadset from Belladrum, of Easter Muilzie, and Muilzie-reoch, was a man of considerable note, married to Culbokie's eldest daughter, and paying a rent of 184 merks. Even at that period rents were rising, for the wadset being redeemed at Whitsunday, 1766, the lands were let of new at 300 merks. Regarding

Muilzie, I have a note that "he perished in the storm which happened in February, 1768." His effects when rouped fetched nearly £400 sterling, and while £1 17s sufficed for the undertaker, no less than £6 16s 2d was expended "in wine and other necessaries," and £12 16s 8d for spirits, bread, and cheese, at the funeral on 18th February.

As showing the class of people who lived in Strathglass at one time, it may be mentioned that Hugh Fraser of Aigais, who lived in the beginning of last century, known as "Old Father Aigais," was thrice married. His first wife, daughter of the Rev. Donald Fraser, brought him one son, Thomas. He married, secondly, the daughter of Fraser of Teanacoil, with issue—(1) Hugh Fraser, whom his father settled in Muilzie, father of Robert Fraser above referred to; (2) Alexander Fraser, whom his father settled in Eskadale, father of Captain Hugh Fraser of Eskadale; (3) James Fraser, settled by his father in Polmon; (4) and (5) James and Simon Fraser, settled in Inchlair. He married, thirdly, the daughter of Fraser of Dunballoch, with issue—William, Robert, Andrew, Margaret, Isobel, Mary, and Amelia, in all thirteen children, most of whom were married and had issue, and in consequence almost all the Frasers in Strathglass of the better class towards the end of last century, were cousins.

The means of the tenants may be illustrated by the case of John Macdonald of Brewlin, whose stocks after his death were rouped at Torrankenlia on 11th June, 1789, and consisted of 3 horses, 1 bull, 18 cows, comprehending milk cows, heifers, and stirks, 34 goats, and 35 sheep.

The Commissioners on the Forfeited Estates, or more properly their factors, were the first evictors in the Highlands, and they were guilty of favouritism to such a degree in favour of strangers that many of the tenants emigrated voluntarily. A gentleman in Inverness, writing to his relative serving in the East Indies, under date of 16th April, 1775, makes the following remarks:—

"The spirit of emigration to America still continues in the Highlands, and is daily spreading and gaining strength. Many hundreds are going over this year from the Aird, Urquhart, Glenmoriston, Glengarry, Kintail, and other parts, besides many in the south-west parts of Scotland, which is very strange, considering the present confusion in America. The Provinces of New England and Virginia are actually in rebellion, and have an army in the field, and the whole Continent seems to have united in an attempt to throw off their dependence on Great Britain. Government is sending over eight regiments to reinforce the army there, and a large fleet to block up their harbours and bring them into order. What the event will be God knows, but I am afraid a good deal of blood will be spilled before matters are settled."

Simon, Lord Lovat, was by no means a bad landlord, being not only an improver of land, but of a kindly and courteous demeanour towards the very lowest. He never stirred about without a bag of farthings for beggars and others, a coin at that time, it has to be recollected, which would purchase a needful article. Lord Lovat turned out no people, but, as I have said, gave encouragement for reclaiming land. The Commissioners' leases cannot be found fault with on the score of the conditions as to farming, housing, and enclosing, and the period of endurance was exceptionally long. Their rule terminated in 1774, and during General Fraser's possession, up to 1782, the same humane feeling towards the people prevailed. Many of the General's old soldiers were settled in Strathfarar, and it may be said that during the time of the administration of General Fraser's trustees, up to 1802, the people had greatly increased in numbers and were generally well off, and undisturbed. Such of them as did emigrate departed in good spirits, to the only lively tune emigration has produced—

"'Sa null air na h-eileanan,
Dh' America gun teid sinn;
'S thall rathad Shasuinn,
Sid a rathad theid sinn."

The time was coming, however, when eviction preceded emigration, and the unhappy emigrant's departure was under the wail—

" Cha till, cha till, cha till sinn tuilleadh,
An cogadh no sith cha till sinn tuilleadh,

> Cha till sinn gu brath
> Gu latha mor na cruinne."

> "We have gone to the shore,
> With those who no more
> Shall see their loved isle for ever,
> For ever."

The doom of Strathfarar was arranged in 1802 to take effect at Whitsunday 1803, and it is but fair to the memory of the Hon. Archibald Fraser to enquire whether he was justified by way of necessity, or otherwise, in the steps he took. In 1742, Lord Lovat having by that time settled with Hugh Fraser of Fraserdale, executed an entail of his estates in favour of his eldest son, Simon Fraser, and the other heirs male of his body. Had Lord Lovat and his eldest son not been forfeited, the estates would under that entail have devolved on the successor free of encumbrance. The Crown took steps to set aside the entail, and by a majority of one voice in the Court of Session was successful, and the Lovat estates were annexed to the Crown. Simon Fraser, being himself attainted, could not succeed and had no status to object to the Crown's contention, while Lord Lovat's two younger sons, Alexander, who died without issue in 1762, and Archibald had the strongest possible interest. Although an appeal to the House of Lords was competent, this was not taken, and Archibald Fraser in one of his numerous private prints complained that his interests were purposely unattended to at the time. The Lovat estates were restored to Simon Fraser in 1774, free and unfettered, save with a burden of £20,000 odds incurred by the Commissioners. During his possession he not only, according to his brother, paid none of this debt but incurred a good deal more in the purchase of North Morar, etc. Further, he executed a new entail of the Lovat estates, altering the old order of succession, and left a trust settlement whereby his trustees were to retain the possession and management until the whole debts were paid off. Archibald Fraser complained that though he was called to the succession in 1782 as institute of entail, under his brother's deed, yet he never received a farthing of the rents, which were barely sufficient to meet the interest of debts and burdens, and after this went on for several years the trustees had to obtain an Act of Parliament to enable them to sell several lands and valuable superiorities. Morar was scheduled for sale, but the very high prices obtained for the superiorities obviated its being exposed. In a sentence, Archibald complained that while he ought to have succeeded unencumbered, he stood deprived for many years of any income, and was ultimately denuded of a considerable portion of the Lovat estates and had to develop what remained as best he could. On the other hand; it must not be forgotten that Government departed from its large claim, the importance of which is indicated by the Duke of Gordon in a letter dated London, 7th March, 1785, from which the following is an extract. "At the same time he (Lovat) told me that he must necessarily delay for a few days till he had concluded a transaction with Government, now in agitation, which is of the utmost importance to his family."

When the trust virtually came to an end Archibald Fraser's position was thoroughly substantial.

The clearance of Strathfarar was the work of Highlanders of fair standing. Many such, alas, tempted by the prosperity of the Lowland sheep-men followed their example. Two of old "Father Aigais'" descendants, Hugh Fraser, Achnacloich, who married Eskadale's daughter, an heiress, and Robert Fraser of Aigais, who married one of the Borrodale ladies, entered into a partnership to lease the whole, except Corriecharrabie, at a tremendous increase of rent over that for 1767, which was only a trifle over £40. The new rent was £600 and the lease was signed at Beaufort on the 29th December, 1802. It seems to be recorded in the Sheriff Court books in the month of October, 1804, and is a singular though short production, with several marginal additions as if haggled over at the last moment. I call it a singular document, for while stipulating that assignees and sub-tenants are excluded, yet the tenants "may retain and accommodate in spots least fit for sheep farming, such of the present inhabitants of the said lands as they shall specify in writing." It is quite certain that the arable lands of the people were very well fitted for sheep farming, and so what was intended for the poor remnant of the people was land unfit for beasts. This really was a worse fate than that of the West Coast and Isles men, who, driven to the shores, had some chance of subsistence from the sea. The tenants, by a marginal note, had also power to subset to each of twelve cottars a croft not exceeding in value five pounds a year, apparently an afterthought of compunction, and the lease was to terminate at Whitsunday, 1821. Here follows the tenants as on 13th May, 1803, a few days before the clearance was carried out, and it will be seen that the numbers had more than doubled since 1767—

Luibreoch--Allan Cameron, Charles Cameron.
Inchvuilt—James Michael, Rory Macdonald, Alexander Macdonald, Hugh Macdonald.
Brewlin—Duncan Turner, servant to General Fraser; Angus Chisholm, do.; Donald Fraser, do.; Simon Cameron, do. and mailer; Alexander Chisholm, do., do.
Uchanro—Thomas Fraser, a servant.
Ardchuilck—Hugh Forbes, a servant; Hugh Macgillivray.
Inchvlair—Rory Buie, a servant.
Muilzie-reoch—John Fraser, tenant; Hugh Fraser, John Forbes.
Muilzie nan Clach—Hugh Fraser, Simon Fraser, his son; Robert Chisholm, Rory Forbes, John Macra.
Bencharran—Alexander Fraser, Hugh Maclennan, Donald Macdonald, Rory Maclean.
Deanie—Hugh Fraser, Thomas Fraser, Donald Macrae, Thomas Fraser, Alexander Fraser, piper and mailer.

There were in all 32 heads of families. Aigais appears to have had some special claim to Deanie and Bencharran, and at his own instance warns out the five tenants of Deanie, with this variation that while Hugh Fraser is omitted, having probably died, the name of Mary Forbes, a widow, is included. From Bencharran Aigais warns out the four tenants before named, with the addition of John

Maclennan and Janet Stewart, a widow. In 1803 Allan Cameron, and Hugh Maclean, Craigscorry, whose mother was one of "Father Aigais'" descendants, are ejected from Luibreoch. The tenants lost no time in stocking their new possession, and under date of 17th June, 1803, Eskadale writes—"Aigais and myself have now arrived at Inchlochell with betwixt 500 and 600 hoggs from the West Coast," and complains "they are not put in full possession, and that the grass of Gleninchlochell is being eaten up and destroyed." In 1806 Lovat ejects from Deanie the poor piper, Alexander Fraser, who seems to have escaped this doom in 1803. In this last year he has a separate summons for himself, instigated by Eskadale, whose ill doings as an evictor are well known in Strathglass. In 1805 some of the Brewlin tenants, who had been left in a semi-starving state under the new conditions were finally removed and got value for timbers, etc., to the extent of £40 19s 8d. Besides their own houses, barns, and byres, reference is made to servants' houses, milk houses, dairymaids' store places, sheep cotes, etc., showing that the people must have at one time at least been well off. The after history of Glenstrathfarar is of little interest, being a mere shifting and displacement of large sheep tenants, Highland and Lowland, as they became bankrupt, or fell out of the race, or had their rents unduly raised. Some little credit is due for the accommodating of a portion of the people who had been removed from Glencannich and Glen Affric, but this relief was never intended to be permanent, and did not stop that total afforestation which was approaching as steadily and inevitably as death.

The grazing of Corriecharrabie was counted the finest in Strathglass or Strathfarar, and consequently had been frequented, like Killin, as summering from far and near. I have spoken to old men who in their youth not only shielled but smuggled there, and it was delightful to listen to their enthusiastic accounts of those days and of the gatherings at Tigh Corriecharrabie, pleasantly situated on the banks of the Orrin.

Having given the names of the inhabitants of Glenstrathfarar in 1767 and 1803, it may be interesting to give the names of the inhabitants of Beauly who were the founders of that village in the latter year. In the atest rolls the number of tenementers in Beauly exceeds over 300, and many will no doubt recognise the names of their predecessors. In special, my valued friend Mr Joseph Chisholm, Cannich Cottage, Ballifeary, will find the names of his father and grandfather. John MacCallum, innkeeper; James Fraser, farmer; Simon Fraser, servant; Alexander Finlayson, merchant; Donald Mackenzie, tenant; William Fraser, tenant; William Thomson, tenant; Alexander Calder, tenant; Alexander Fraser, smith and tenant; John Mackenzie, pensioner; James Macdonald, ground-officer; William Chisholm, carpenter; John Chisholm, carpenter; Alexander Chisholm, carpenter; William Chisholm, tenant; Joseph Chisholm, his son; Hugh Fraser, tailor; John Mackenzie, flesher; Hugh Allan, ship builder; John Mackinnon, baker; John Campbell, shoemaker; Alexander Fraser, weaver; Thomas Fraser, day-labourer; Hugh Wishart, day-labourer; Alexander Michael, blacksmith; John Macdonald, wheelright; Alexander Mackenzie, merchant; James Fraser, mason; John Mackenzie, shoemaker; William Chisholm, innkeeper; Malcolm Morrison, weaver; Rory Maclean, tenant; Andrew Fraser, soldier, Hugh Fraser, mason; James Ross, weaver; Thomas Stewart, day-labourer; Christopher Urquhart, coppersmith; James Clough, coppersmith; Thomas Mackenzie, shoemaker; Alexander Macra, flax dresser; and William Macdonald, wheelright—41 heads of families of the total 245 then on all the Lovat estate in the parish of Kilmorack.

II.—PARISH OF KILTARLITY.

JANET ROSS, LADY DOWAGER OF LOVAT, 1544-1565.

LORD LOVAT at his death in 1544 was in his 55th year, and the Master of Lovat 19 years old. The MS. history says that Dame Janet Ross—her eldest son being between 16 and 17 years old at his father's death and no near male of age to take charge—herself "undertook the management of her son's affairs, which she executed with great fidelity and address," and the historian praises her in other respects, she having leaned early to the Reformed Faith, and after the Reformation becoming a violent partizan.

The charge of the education of the youthful Alexander, Lord Lovat, was entrusted to the well-known Robert Reid, who united in his person the offices of Bishop of Orkney, Abbot of Kinloss, and Prior of Beauly. The Bishop had under his education at one time, Lord Lovat, his brother William, afterwards of Struy, the sons of the Lairds of Kintail, Fowlis, Balnagown, and the Sheriff of Murray, and kept a pleasure barge plying between Beauly and Kinloss.

After Alexander, Lord Lovat, attained majority he married Janet Campbell of Calder, and died young in 1557. His mother and he had several litigations, and she was constantly in Court, as I notice from the Inverness-shire Records, with her tenants and others; nor was her daughter-in-law, Janet Campbell, a whit behind in this respect. She is found litigating with John Vic Ranald, Andrew Vic Homas Roy, Thomas Vic Hamish, John Vic Horkill, and Struy, her brother-in-law, for keeping her out of her Terce of Aigais, and with all the tenants of Dalcross. Janet Ross's latest litigation seems to have been in objecting to the service of her grandson Hugh, as heir to his father

Alexander, on 2nd May, 1560. When Alexander died his brother William, first of Struy, became Tutor to his nephew Hugh, Lord Lovat, and appears to have done his best to make things agreeable for the two Dowagers. Dame Janet Ross lived at Kirkton of Pharnaway with her children, her son Alexander having built her there a comfortable house, and the Tutor allowed Alexander's widow to keep her court at Lovat. This did not last many years, for Janet Campbell soon married for the second time, Donald Gorm's son of Sleat, a widower. The following singular narrative is taken from the MS. history and shows beyond all doubt the masculine character of Janet Ross. Bean "Cleireach" who had been rewarded for his treachery by the Bailieship of Stratherrick had just died at Dalcrag. "Cleireach" here means a cleric or scribe, not that Benjamin or Bean's surname was Clark. I refrain from giving the wretch's real surname, as he was a "Mac" of one of the tribes of Clan Chattan. The narrative proceeds:—

"In the end of May, 1559, the Tutor of Lovat made a tour through the different parts of the estate to administer justice. He fixed John Fraser of Farraline Bailie of Stratherrick. He made an appointment with the two ladies dowager to meet them at Kilichuiman, now Fort-Augustus, where, having prepared everything for their reception, they went up by boat on Loch-Ness.

"The Lady Dowager Janet Ross expressed a great desire to see the field at Lochy, where her husband was slain. Her son, the Tutor, immediately convocates 100 men of a convoy, and attended his mother to the field.

"After their return, the Tutor left the ladies in the Fort at Kilichuiman, and went himself to Glenelg, where he settled affairs, and returned to the ladies, who all arrived safe in the Aird in the month of September. The ladies sailed down Loch-Ness, and the Tutor went by Stratherrick, the Leys, and Dalcross to Inverness.

"There is a memorable event which happened these ladies as they were sailing home by Loch Ness, which I would not mention, but that the country people firmly believe it still, and I have seen them send six miles for the water of the lake to their cattle. The story is—The ladies had ordered the bell of Kilichuiman to be put in the boat, to be set up in Glenconventh. When they were about the middle of the lake they were overtaken with a violent tempest, so that they could neither sail nor row. One of the men (wiser it seems than the rest) desired to throw out the bell into the loch, since they could not carry it back. This was accordingly done, and presently followed a calm, so that the ladies got safe to shore. From that time the waters of Loch Ness, or according to others who are more wise, the water below where the bell was cast became medicinal. Superstitious people call it wine, and send it from a great distance to their cattle when they are sick."

Lady Lovat's double performances above recorded may be fairly characterised as "a sin and a shame."

There is some dubiety as regards the children of Hugh, Lord Lovat, by his two marriages. Both the MS. history and Mr Anderson say that by his first marriage with Miss Grant of Grant Lord Lovat had one son, the Master of Lovat, killed at Blar-nan-leine, and one daughter. They differ as to names, however, and otherwise. The MS. calls the mother Katherine; Mr Anderson says Anne Grant of Grant. The MS. says the daughter's name was Katherine, who married John Rose of Kilravock, while Mr Anderson calls her Janet and that she died young. I do not find any John Rose of Kilravock at this period. The MS. history and Mr Anderson agree that by the second marriage with Janet Ross Lord Lovat had two sons, Alexander and William, also two daughters, but differ as to the names of the daughters and number of sons—the MS. giving a third son Hugh, dying unmarried in his eighteenth year, and the names of the daughters as Agnes and Marjory, who it is said died unmarried. Mr Anderson on the other hand calls the eldest Ann, and the second Katherine, who married Rose of Kilravock without giving his Christian name. With reference to Lord Lovat's daughters the one styled by Mr Anderson Ann was undoubtedly Agnes, for her contract with William Macleod, apparent of Macleod, has her own signature. But the question is, was she by the second marriage as both the MS. and Mr Anderson say? If so, she must have been very young at the time of her first marriage, for her contract is dated at Lovat 15th April, 1540, and the marriage is stipulated to take place before 1st July of that year, so it was not a contract as between children brought about by parents as a matter of policy. Now, her brother, Alexander, Lord Lovat, was only between 16 and 17 in July, 1544, four years later.* Agnes Macleod had but one child, Mary, the wealthy heiress of Dunvegan, and after a lengthened widowhood she married on 2nd May, 1562, designing herself Lady Terciar of Dunvegan, Alexander Bayne of Tulloch, with issue. Then as to the second daughter, sometimes called Catharine, sometimes Marjory, said to have been married, and not to have been married, I have to observe that at Kirkton of Pharnaway on 26th March, 1562, a contract of marriage is entered into between Margaret Fraser, daughter of Dame Janet Ross, Lady Lovat, with her mother's consent on the one part, and Allan Macranald of the Leys on the other part. By Lady Lovat's will in 1565 she specially bequeaths to Agnes and Margaret her daughters, "her clothing and ornaments of her body," while of their tocher a balance remained of £93 6s 8d Scots due to Leys, and £66 13s 10d to Tulloch.

By Allan Macranald, Margaret Fraser of Lovat had a son Allister, who was slain in a brawl by Angus Williamson of Termit, otherwise "Angus of the Brazen Face" of Kellachie, in the year 1599. Young Easter Leys was the unfortunate man whom Angus referred to in his celebrated conversation with James VI. Angus readily got pardon for "whipping of a man's bonnet" and then assumed that the pardon covered an incident omitted to be mentioned as going too much into details, viz., that there was "a head in the bonnet" so whipped off.

* As Hugh, Lord Lovat, then a widower, was in June 1527 upon terms of marriage with the widow of Lachlan Mackintosh of Mackintosh, which fell through, it is almost certain that his daughter Agnes, married in 1540, could not have been by his second marriage with Janet Ross.

III.—PARISH OF KIRKHILL.

THE MACKINTOSHES IN THE FRASER COUNTRY.

AFTER their forfeiture, the great possessions of the Bysets in the Aird, comprehending, with the exception of ecclesiastical property, the whole of the present parishes of Kirkhill, Kiltarlity, and Kilmorack, became much subdivided. A perusal of the Cess Rolls of 1644 and 1691 will show, however, that with trifling exceptions they fell into the hands of the Frasers and Chisholms and their cadets. During the seventeenth century the Frasers lost ground considerably. Amongst those who strove to obtain a footing in the Aird were the Earls of Argyll—the second Earl in 1497, receiving large portions from Sir David Lyndsay of Beauford, while other lands were also acquired.

The first Mackintosh who obtained land there was Farquhar Roy Mackintosh, son of Dougall Mor Mac Gillie Callum, which Malcolm was youngest son of Malcolm Beg Mackintosh, tenth of Mackintosh. Malcolm Mackintosh was slain at the battle of Craigcailleoch in 1441, leaving a very young family, of whom the eldest, Dougall above mentioned, was reckoned one of the greatest warriors of his day. At Edinburgh, on the 16th of October, 1511, Archibald, 2nd Earl of Argyll, by charter of taillie and donation, for the homage and service manifoldly rendered and to be rendered to him and his, by Farquhar Mackintosh, son of Dougall Mor Mackintosh, granted, to be held ward and relief, all and whole the lands of Kirkton and Inchberry, with their pertinents, lying within the Sheriffdom of Inverness, to the said Farquhar Mackintosh and the heirs male of his body lawfully procreated or to be procreated, whom failing to Donald Mackintosh his brother-german and the heirs male of his body lawfully procreated or to be procreated, whom failing to the heirs male of the body of the foresaid Dougall, their father, lawfully procreated or to be procreated, whom all failing, fully to return to the said noble Earl and his nearest heirs male whomsoever. The charter was confirmed by James IV. at Edinburgh on 27th February, 1512. Unfortunately Dougall Mor in his old age, instigated by the evil advice of relatives, turned against his Chief, and with his two sons was killed in an attack on the Castle of Inverness in 1521. Failing lawful heirs male, Kirkton and Inchberry reverted to Argyll in terms of the charter, and the Earl's son, Colin third Earl, after serving heir to his father in 1526, feued the lands the following year to Hugh, fifth Lord Lovat, and they have since remained with the Lovat family, although the superiority continued for a considerable time in the Argylls. The first Mackintosh acquisition was thus of brief duration.

The Fentons of Ogill were descended of the same family that owned much of the Aird. In 1475 Alexander Fenton of Ogill is found, and on 6th December, 1507, the before mentioned Archibald, Earl of Argyll, for an onerous consideration sells and alienates to Thomas Fenton of Ogill, his heirs and assignees, the lands of Beaufort with the pertinents. Seventeen years later, James Fenton of Ogill, styling himself lord of the lands of Beaufort, by charter dated Edinburgh, 13th December, 1524, granted to honourable persons, Lachlan Mackintosh of Dunachton and Jean Gordon, his spouse, and the longest liver of them in conjunct fee, all and sundry, his lands of Beaufort, with tenants, tenancies, and services of free tenants of the same and their pertinents, lying within the Sheriffdom of Inverness. The holding was—the parties and longest liver in fee, and their heirs, whom failing the nearest and lawful heirs of Janet—of the King in fee and heritage, and doing to the King the service used and wont only. The charter, which is witnessed by Master John Irwine, Rector of Benholme, Sir David Edward, Sir Robert Gordon of the Glen, Walter Chessman, Sir Walter Fairweather, and others, is confirmed by James V. at Edinburgh of same date. From the destination being to Jean Gordon's heirs, failing children of the marriage, it is probable the price paid to Fenton was part of her own fortune. There were three children of the marriage—William, who succeeded, Margaret and Muriel—and after the cruel murder of her husband Lachlan Mackintosh, the hand of Jean Gordon, heiress of Lochinvar, a young, wealthy, and accomplished widow, was eagerly sought. I observe that on 25th June, 1527, at Darnaway, an agreement for her marriage was entered into between her brother James Stuart, "the little Earl of Moray," and Hugh Fraser, fifth Lord Lovat, then a widower. The marriage was to be solemnized as soon as a dispensation was obtained, and in the first instance Master Gilbert Strachan, or any other that had power to dispense within the degrees of consanguinity or affinity the parties stood to each other, was to be applied to, and failing in this, the parties to "send to the Court of Rome, with all diligence for hamebringing of the same dispensation." The Earl was to give 1200 merks in money, and Lovat 40 merks of land furth of the Barony of Dalcross, as a jointure. Either the dispensation was refused, or the contemplated marriage broken off for other causes, somewhat hastily, for it is recorded that Jean Gordon married, the same year (1527), James Ogilvie of Cardale, laird of Findlater. Curiously Jean Gordon's son, William Mackintosh above mentioned, fifteenth of Mackintosh, afterwards married Margaret Ogilvie, sister of James, his step-aunt.

The lands contained in Mackintosh's charter, under the general title of "Bewfurde," comprehended—

I. The Barony of Drumchardiny, in the parish of Kirkhill, which apparently included all the present Newton and Lentran estates, with the exception of Kingillie, and extended to three davochs land of old extent, ultimately sub-divided as follows :—Holm and Rhinduie, one davoch ; Cragach, one half davoch ; Drumchardiny, one and a half davoch.

II. The half davoch land of old extent of Easter Eskadale in the parish of Kiltarlity, and

III. The half davoch land of old extent of Kinnairies, also in the parish of Kiltarlity—the whole lying within the ancient Barony of Beaufort; and in 1617 of the value of £7 old extent, and £35 new extent.

William, son of Lachlan Mackintosh and Jean Gordon, does not seem to have made up titles to these Aird lands, as his son Lachlan Mackintosh is retoured thereto as heir of his grandfather Lachlan, on 9th June, 1567. Lachlan conveys the fee of the lands to his eldest son Angus, by charter dated at Inverness, 15th June, 1568, confirmed by James VI. at Dalkeith, 1st January, 1574. On the 21st of January, 1617, Lachlan, afterwards Sir Lachlan Mackintosh, eldest son of Angus, is served heir to his grandfather Lachlan in the whole lands.

The lands being distant from the chief Mackintosh estates, it would appear that they were dealt with in form of wadset, and not set to tenants in the usual way. As regards the Kirkhill lands, Lachlan Mackintosh in 1570 wadsets Drumchardiny to Hugh, Lord Lovat, for £500 Scots, Lovat granting at the same time a letter of reversion, and in 1583 his Lordship's chamberlain gives an acquittance for the teinds of Drumchardiny for crop 1583. It would appear that the lands remained under wadset to the Lovat family up to 1617.

On 31st October, 1576, Mackintosh, in respect of a sum of 200 merks, wadsets Cragaig to Allister Vic Homas Fraser, who grants letter of reversion the same day. On 2nd June, 1598, a contract is entered into between Lachlan Mackintosh and James Vic Allister Fraser anent the wadset of the half of Cragaig, and on the following day James grants Mackintosh a letter of reversion on the repayment of 700 merks. On the 23rd July, 1593, Thomas Fraser of Moniack and spouse, get a wadset of the half of Cragaig, and a letter of redemption on payment of 400 merks is granted by them of same date. A similar obligation by Moniack is granted on 5th August, 1598. Mackintosh wadsets the half of Cragaig to Andrew Vic Coul Fraser, and on 3rd June, 1598, Andrew grants letter of reversion on payment of 500 merks and 50 merks.

The lands above mentioned appear to include the whole one and a half davoch of old extent of Holm, Rhinduie, and Cragach, and to have remained with these families, after Lachlan Mackintosh's death, and during the minority of his grandson and successor, up to 1617.

The Mackintosh lands in Kiltarlity were held as follows—

1. *Easter Eskadale.* On the 21st September, 1570, Mackintosh wadsets the lands of Eskadale to William Fraser of Struy for 500 merks, and Struy grants a letter of reversion on the same day subscribed with his hand. On 26th June, 1585, the wadset is renewed between the parties. The Struy family continued in possession until 1618. The necessities of the family of Mackintosh compelled the sale of their Aird estates, and I find that on 10th of March, 1618, there is a Crown charter by James VI. on the resignation of Lachlan Mackintosh of Dunachton, of the lands of Eskadale, extending to half a davoch of land of old extent, with shielings, ale house, and crofts, in favour of Thomas Fraser of Struy and Elizabeth Dunbar his spouse.

2. *Kinnairies.* On the 11th May, 1569, Mackintosh wadsets the half davoch lands of Kinnairies to Alexander Chisholm of Comar, for five hundred merks, and the Chisholm grants a letter of reversion of the same date signed with his own hand. The wadset and redemption are renewed by the parties on 11th June, 1585, and again on the penult of May, 1589—Chisholm dying within a couple of months or so thereafter. He appears to have left Kinnairies to a younger son, whose Christian name, though I have not observed it, I apprehend was Allister, called "Mor." It is certain that in 1618, there were two Johns Chisholm, one John Chisholm of Comar and the other John Chisholm of Kinnairies, cousins-german in the first and second degree. On the 22nd April, 1618, James VI., upon the resignation of Lachlan Mackintosh of Tor Castle, grants a charter of the lands of Kinnairies, extending to one half davoch land of old extent of the value of 17s 6d,

in favour of John Chisholm, styled of Kinnairies, and the heirs male of his body, whom failing to Thomas Chisholm, second son of John Chisholm of Comar and his nearest and lawful heirs whomsoever. John Chisholm of Kinnairies was succeeded by his only son Alexander, upon whose death, without male issue, Thomas Chisholm, second son of Comar, in 1634, serves as heir male of taillie and provision to Alexander, as his (Thomas') father's brother's son. Thomas Chisholm of Kinnairies sold the lands shortly after to Colonel Hugh Fraser, the first Fraser of Kinnairies, and in the Valuation Roll for 1644 Colonel Fraser is assessed at the large sum of £626 in Kiltarlity. In the same year Thomas Chisholm, described as of "Wester (Lovat's) Eskadale," is assessed at £261, while as "Thomas Chisholm of Kinnairies," he is assessed in Kilmorack at £40. From this Thomas was descended the late Mr Colin Chisholm of Inverness. The half davochs of Easter Eskadale and of Kinnairies adjoined. It will have been noticed that for some time the Lovat family had been, as wadsetters, possessors of one and a half davochs of Drumchardiny. It is recorded by Mr Anderson in his History of the Frasers, apparently on good authority, that "the family of Mackintosh held large possessions in the Aird which this Lord Lovat (Simon, the eighth Lord), of whom we now speak, was very anxious to get into his own hands. With this view he employed Fraser of Belladrum and Fraser of Culbokie to purchase the lands of Drumchardiny, Holm, and Cragach, but they over-reached him and purchased for themselves. This was soon after 1617, and chagrined his Lordship not a little." It was natural that Lovat should desire these lands, for he was proprietor (excluding the island of Merkinch) of the whole country from the River Ness to the Burn of Rhinduie, comprehending Kinmylies, Bunchrew, Englishton, Kirkton, Phopachy, and Inchberry on the one side, with the properties or superiorities of Moniacks, Achnagairn, etc., on the other. The character of this Lord, although counted extravagant and a dilapidator of his estates so far as regards his successors, is thus kindly noticed in the history—

"This nobleman has been represented in very different lights, for while he was generally surnamed Simon 'Mor,' or the Great, other called him 'Shim Gorrach,' *i.e.*, Simon the Fool. He surely had several laudable qualities. He was one of the best of landlords or masters. He never would remove a tenant that paid his rents for any grassum or bribe. He could never be prevailed upon to set a price upon the River of Beauly, or to give a tack for a liquidate value on the fishing of it, for he said that fishing was a casual, a contingent thing, depending upon a special Providence, and that the over-rating a thing so casual might provoke God to blast the common blessings. For the same reason he would not set any of his orchards in tack, though he had several of them, and a prodigious quantity of fruit in them. From the orchard of Beauly alone he had usually six chalders of good fruit, apples and pears. He had another excellent quality, that he could not endure to hear an absent person run down by any present. It was a maxim of his, that as receipts made thieves so a credulous receiver made the liar. This noble lord excelled in hospitality, and was generous, liberal, and charitable—his house was an open harbour for good men, and his heart was no less open to entertain and receive them. The door of his house was seldom shut, and yet such regularity was observed that none was ever seen drunk at his table."

By charter dated 1st November, 1616, Lachlan Mackintosh of Dunachton, with consent of John Grant of Freuchie and James Grant of Ardnill, interdicting creditors, sold to Hugh Fraser of Belladrum, his heirs male and assignees whatsoever, all and whole the town and davoch lands of Holm and Rhindowie, the town and half davoch land of Cragach, with the ale house and ale house croft of the same, with fishings and grazings, together also with half of the miln of Holm, half of the multures, sequels, and knaveships of the towns and lands of Drumchardiny, Holm, Rhindowie, and Cragach, lying within the barony of Drumchardiny and Beaufort and Sheriffdom of Inverness. James VI., at Edinburgh, on 20th December, 1616, ratifies the above sale, and of new granted the above-mentioned lands to the said Hugh Fraser of Belladrum, together with half of the yair called Carriencoir, pertaining to the said lands of Holm and Cragach, and to the lands of Drumchardiny adjacent to them, with fishings of salmon and other white fish in the sea, and in pools of which the tenants and possessors of Holm and Cragach were formerly in use and possession, and incorporated all into the free Barony of Holm.

On the 14th of November, 1616, Lachlan Mackintosh of Dunachton with consent foresaid sells to Hugh Fraser of Culbokie, his heirs male and assignees whomsoever, the town and lands of Drumchardiny extending to one and a half davoch land of old extent, with the ale house and ale house crofts of the same with fishings and grazings, half of the miln of Holm, half of the multures, sequels, and knaveship of the town and lands of Drumchardiny, Holm, Rhindowie, and Cragach in the barony of Drumchardiny and Beaufort, and Sheriffdom of Inverness. James VI., at Edinburgh, on 20th December, 1616, ratifies the above sale, and of new granted the above-mentioned lands to the said Hugh Fraser of Culbokie, together with half of the yair called Carriencoir pertaining to the said lands of Drumchardiny, and to the lands of Holm and Cragach adjacent to them, with fishings of salmon and of other white fish in the sea and in the pools of which the tenants and possessors of Drumchardiny were formerly in use and possession, and incorporated the whole into the free Barony of Drumchardiny. The value of these lands were about equal—Belladrum in the Roll for 1644 being assessed at £573 and Culbokie at £567 Scots. The hill lands and Baronies of Holm (now Lentran) and of Drumchardiny, incorporated out of the old Barony of Drumchardiny as above in 1618, were not formally divided as late as 1790.

Thus passed away the hold of the Mackintoshes in the Aird, which lasted from 1524 to 1618.

IV.—PARISH OF BONA.

INTERESTING HISTORICAL INCIDENTS.

THE parish of Bona was perhaps the smallest in the county of Inverness, extending only to twelve ploughs, or three davochs of land. It extended from the parish of Urquhart at the south-west to Inverness at the north-east, and comprehended the separate estate of Abriachan, Dochnacraig or Davochdearg, Dochcairn, Dochfour, and Dochgarroch. The boundary to the East was Loch Ness, Little Loch Ness, and the river, and on the West the hills and grazings of Caiplich. The church probably stood at Killionan of Abriachan, or at Cladh Uradain of Lochend. In pre-Reformation times the only name of an officiating ecclesiastic found is that of Elias, vicar of Bona, in 1233. After the Reformation the name of William Simpson is found as a "Reader" in 1567. Thomas Innes, whose stipend was less than that of the vicar of Wakefield, is found in 1584. The self-aggrandizing Thomas Fraser, first of Knockie, but better known as the first Fraser of Strichen, busied himself in acquiring rights and tacks of teinds of parishes, and amongst others those of Boleskine, Abertarff, and Bona. On the 18th of April, 1584, the said Thomas Innes with consent of George, Bishop, and the Dean and Canons of Moray gave in tack to Thomas Fraser of Strichen and Isobel Forbes his spouse for 19 years the teinds of Bona, burdened with payment of £20 Scots to the minister annually. On the 8th July, 1618, the Commissioners for the plantation of Kirks united Bona with Inverness, and in respect of an augmentation of £40 Scots to the minister of the United parish, eiked to the endurance of the tack three nineteen years, and in 1634, Strichen agreed to a second augmentation of money and victual. The family either by express grant, or by use, became patrons of Bona, as well as tacksmen of the teinds, and after the Revolution by the Act of 1690 patrons came to have absolute right of teinds, subject to a competent stipend to the minister. In this way Strichen, and afterwards in his place Lovat, had alternate right with the Crown to present to the Collegiate Church of Inverness.

The uniting of the two parishes was a grievous wrong, for it was almost impossible for the people of Abriachan and the Caiplich to attend public worship at Inverness. This was afterwards remedied in part by the erection of a meeting-house, used also as an adventure school. This building, the ruins of which I well remember, stood on the site of the lodge now on the Inverness side of the burn, which is the march between Dochnacraig and Dochcairn, and between the public road and the loch. A croft, until lately called the Meeting House Croft, was attached to the house and school, and the whole was part of the Dunain estate and contiguous to the burial ground. During last century the present channel of the march burn was formed in a straight line through the meeting house croft to the loch, the old channel taking a straggling course north-eastwards, and joining the loch where a road to Bona ferry by the bank of the loch presently leaves the Urquhart road, and by inattention or acquiescence a few acres of the Dunain estate thus fell to Dochfour.

As far back as 1455, after the forfeiture of the Earl of Moray, there were *inter alia* the two Baronies of "Boniche," and of "Binochare" reserved to the Crown, and it is now almost impossible to define their limits further than this, that Dunain proper, between Dochgarroch and Kinmylies, which does not lie in Bona parish, is part of the old Barony of Banquhar. Probably Banquhar included all the Castle lands in the parishes of Inverness and Bona, as these were granted to the family of Huntly.

There were two schools in Bona—one at Abriachan of old standing, the office of schoolmaster during part of the last half of last century being filled by Mr Lachlan Maclachlan. I give a letter of Mr Maclachlan's when at the Bona meeting house school, not that it is of much value, but as a memento of the worthy teacher of Abriachan, father of an honourable clergyman, Mr James Maclachlan, of Moy, and grandfather of the eminent Celtic scholar, the late Rev. Dr Thomas Maclachlan. The letter refers to some document thought to be of importance in a question of hill marches between Borlum and Essich, at one time in possession of a member of the Dochgarroch family, tenant of the mains of Borlum—

"Sir,—The bearer lately put me in mind of some paper that I happened to see with Hugh Maclean, son to Robert Maclean, when he resided in Borlum, concerning the marches thereof. I must own I did see such, which was written in Clerk William Baillie's time. If it is of any service to you, I cannot deny but I have seen them, and taught the boy to read them. All that I can tell about them you will know, providing Robert Maclean denies to tell anything he knows; but I am sure, though I cannot remember what is contained in them, that they are said and mentioned in the said papers to be registered in Inverness. This is all until you further inform yourself by Robert Maclean, or charge me to tell what I know, from sir, your most humble servant,

(Signed)   L. MACLACHLAN.

"Dochfure, 13th Sept., 1763.

"P.S.—I do not want to be put to any trouble."

The inhabitants at the North end were much inconvenienced, and, wishing something permanent, petitioned the Society for Propagating Christian Knowledge in the terms annexed, with success. The school, called a General Assembly school, was established at Dochgarroch. The first erection, in which for some time I was a pupil, was replaced about 1838, and used until after the passing of the Education Act. A half-holiday was always given on the occasion of the preachings by the Rev. Alexander Clark by the burn side of Dochnacraig, and by the Rev. James Kennedy, of Inverness, on the river side at Dochgarroch locks. Crowds assembled, and the scholars were happy enough to exchange these pleasant outside gatherings, though they lasted two good hours, for the irksomeness of the indoor grind. The meeting house having fallen into decay, service was occasionally held in the old school of Dochgarroch, in which a loft was fitted up to accommodate hearers. A raised platform at one end had an arm chair for the minister in the centre, while on the right and left there were pews for the Dochgarroch and Dochfour families, while Dochnalurg had the front seat in the loft. The first christening I ever witnessed was after a Gaelic evening service in the old school, Mr Clark officiating. He was rather deaf that night, and could not catch the name given by the father in a subdued tone, really a whisper, though repeatedly asked. The ears of the young people in the gallery were sharp enough, and heard "Yosé" without difficulty. At last one of the christening party interfered and shouted the name loud enough. In after years I chaffed Joseph more than once, his career being rather off the square, that this was to be accounted for, by the difficulty of making a Christian of him at the outset,—

"Unto the Honourable the Society in Scotland for Propagating Christian Knowledge,

"The petition of the gentlemen and heads of families in Dochfure with the concurrence of the ministers of the Gospel at Inverness,

"Humbly Showeth,—That whereas that part of the united parish of Inverness and Bona called Dochfure, lying at the distance of four miles from any school, as also Dunain and Dochgarroch, which are contiguous to Dochfour, labour under very great hardships and disappointments in not having a schoolmaster to teach and instruct their children, are under the necessity to apply to the Honourable Society that they may be pleased to consider the great loss they sustain thereby.

"The different parts above mentioned have no less than 40 children, who are all fit to attend school, besides a number of children daily increasing;

"May it therefore please the Honourable Society to consider the condition of the above named places and in their wonted goodness and clemency to grant the petitioners their desire in appointing a schoolmaster for the instruction of their children, And your petitioners will ever pray."

"*N.B.*—The ministers will attest the truth of the above, and recommend the prayer of the petition to the committee."

DOCHNACRAIG.

The two ploughs of land sometimes called Davochdearg, and Davochnacraig, and in later years more commonly called Lochend, appear for the first time in the enumeration of the lands granted to the Earl of Huntly for the keeping of the Castle of Inverness. These lands in old titles are called the Barony of the Castle lands, and frequently described as situated within the Barony of Banquhar. Dochnacraig extends from the burn of Altdearg on the South, to the burn of Altdochcairn on the North, the leading feature within its bounds being Castle Spiritane. Much tradition regarding this ancient structure exists of a hazy character, but all combining in connecting it with that branch of the Maclean family which settled in the North. About 1420 Sir Charles Maclean, it is said, built the castle which was practically destroyed in the time of his son Hector by the Camerons. To Sir Charles Maclean and his descendants the Clan Tearlaich I will allude more particularly when Dochgarroch is reached.

No more beautiful valley than that of the Ness, from Loch Ness to Inverness, could be found in the Highlands. It has been sadly disfigured in various places by the formation of the canal which also caused the removal of the Castle.

The Castle, commonly called "Spirital"—I give as "Spiritane," finding it so called in a deed of 1671.— occupied a very strong position on a promontory naturally surrounded on three sides by water and with the artificial moat surrounded on all sides. Fortunately an outline of the remains of the castle, as these existed a hundred years ago has been preserved, showing the ruin, the moat, and over two acres of the adjoining land, including the garden of one rood, thirty-seven poles, Scots measure. At present the direct road to Bona Ferry leaves the Glenurquhart road below Dochfour gardens, keeps by the loch and river side, and may be driven over, but formerly the body of water now surrounded by trees and separated from the river, commonly called "The Abban," was an inlet covering ten acres, so that the bye-goers had to ford it some distance from the castle. When the canal was taken in hand it was at first intended not to utilise the river as it emerged from Loch Ness to Bona Ferry, but to cut a new straight channel to the North or West, from Loch Ness, into Little Loch Ness, as it was called of old, some hundred yards south of the Cladh Uradain. The expense of deepening and widening the river was great, yet the danger of high wind acting on the enormous surface of the waters of Loch Ness, straight upon unprotected locks, was considered too dangerous, and the scheme was abandoned. All that need be said here is, that had the decision been otherwise Castle Spiritane would have been saved.

In 1805 the question of assessing the compensation to be made by the Canal Commissioners came on. The Dunain family, who had been long owners, were most averse to the castle being interfered with, and in this they had the strong sympathy of Dochgarroch, whose predecessors had been owners long before the Baillies. A jury sat at Inverness on the 5th October, 1805, presided over by Duncan George Forbes of Culloden as Chancellor, who valued Castle Spiritane and the two acres of adjoining ground at one hundred and eleven pounds, but as the line of the canal had not been finally settled upon and the Dunain family so anxious to retain the castle, the following words were by consent inserted in the judgment—"and these subjects are to remain the property of the claimant, Mr Baillie, unless hereafter required for the purposes of the canal, and in the event the same shall be so required, the proprietor shall be bound and obliged to give them up to the said Commissioners at the foresaid value now ascertained by the jury."

Other objects of interest in Dochnacraig were a cairn to the South of the burial ground, the burial ground itself, the hollow of Ossian, the seat of Uradan, the burn of Alt Tuarie, and the magnificent Carn Dearg rising almost precipitously from Loch Ness to the height of 1600 feet. It is matter of tradition that a good part of the southern portion was under heavy wood, according to what the late Colonel Maclean of Dochgarroch had been told in his youth (a hundred years ago), and this is so far corroborated by the southmost town and grazings being called Woodend. The southern portion has been planted within the last twenty-five years, and is doing well. Prior to the acquisition of Dochnacraig by Alexander Baillie of Dunain in 1619, I have not observed any charters to previous owners, except the grant to the family of Huntly. The Baillies allege that they take their name from the town of Bailleul in French Flanders, now the Department of the North, and claim that their predecessor came over with William the Conqueror. In the roll of William's companions prepared by M. Leopold Delisle, member of the Archæological Institute of France, with the approval of the Bishop of Bayeux, will be found the names "Gŭillame Belot," "Renaŭd de Bailleul," and "De Bailleul," without Christian name. In the roll of Battle Abbey appear Bellet and Bailif, and subsequently under the name of Bailiol, the family come much to the front.

John de Baliol, grandfather of King John Baliol, who had married Devorgilla of Galloway, founded Baliol College, Oxford, chiefly for the education of Scottish students. Through Sir Alexander de Baliol, uncle or grand uncle of King John, proceeded the Scottish Baillies whose head, William, is in 1357 styled "Sir William Baillie of Lamington." Alexander, son or grandson of the above Sir William, settled in the North, and, according to the MS. of Colonel John Baillie of Dunain, was the first Baillie of Dunain. In time we come to Alexander, counted as seventh of Dunain, in great favour with the Huntly family, and for some time their Chamberlain of Lochaber, with the farms of Inverlochy in Lochaber, and Crathie Croy in Badenoch, free of rent as part of his fee. The Baillies possessed Dochnacraig on redeemable right before 1619, but their first indefeasible right was granted in that year by charter of George Earl of Enzie, and Anna Campbell his spouse, with consent of the Marquis of Huntly, dated at Bog o' Gight, 25th and 28th November, 1619. The subjects granted were Dochnacraig, consisting of two ploughs of old extent (with the exception after noticed), comprehending the shielings of Freichorrie, Ruinataink, Ruinachorrie, and Ruiclachnagrane; as also the lands of Davochcairns, extending to one plough of old extent, and infeftment followed on 11th December, 1619, the witnesses thereto being John dhu Baillie in Lagnalien, Alexander Vic Phadrig in Davochnacraig, William Baillie in Davochfour, William Baillie in Davochnacraig, Hector Vic Allister in Davochcairne, Farquhar Vic Eachin, his son, etc.

Of the same dates the Earl and Countess of Enzie, but without consent of the Marquis of Huntly, as in the charter of Dochnacraig and Dochcairn, granted to Alexander Baillie the alehouse and alehouse croft of Davochnacraig, with pasturages and grazings in common with the other occupants; and also "the salmon fishings upon the lake and water of Ness, appertaining to the lands of Beandcher, with their pertinents, lying within the castle lands of Inverness and Sheriffdom thereof." This appears to be the original right to salmon fishings, and as the Dunain family exercised the right from Clachnahalig to the Black Stone of Abriachan, it would appear that latterly, and from 1619 at least, the Barony of Benchar comprehended all the lands from Dunain at the North to Abriachan at the South.

Alexander Baillie gave a wadset of Dochnacraig to his third son, Captain James, and appears to have lived there, probably at Castle Spiritane, part of which was inhabited as late as 1671. Several letters of Alexander, particularly the famous one addressed to the Lady Inshes of the day in which he calls her "My Flower of the Forest," are dated from Dochnacraig, and at the same place he grants a disposition of moveables to his son David Baillie, dated 22nd January, 1658. In June, 1671, this David Baillie, first of Dochfour, who will be afterwards referred to, was in pecuniary embarassment, and a messenger's expected call was prepared for. The messenger narrates that having proceeded to the manor place of Castle Spiritane, where the said David Baillie had his usual and actual residence, together with his wife, children, and servants; and getting no access, he gave six audible knocks on the principal gates or doors of the castle, and without response or opening of doors, he left his paper in the keyhole. I find no other after reference to Castle Spiritan until the canal was resolved upon.

Dochnacraig was under wadset at different times, and though the involvements consequent on the sudden death of Colonel John Baillie in 1797 necessitated its scheduling, with a view to a judicial sale, the handsome price got from the canal commissioners saved it to the Dunain family until the death of the last Dunain in 1869; when falling to three heiresses portioners the whole estate was sold to Sir John Ramsden, and exchanged by him for lands belonging to the late Evan Baillie of Dochfour in Badenoch.

DOCHCAIRN AND DOCHFOUR.

It would have been observed that a charter of Dochcairns had been granted in 1619 to Alexander Baillie of Dunain. In his time the family obtained its highest standing, but having a large family he gave off portions in wadset and otherwise. Dochcairns consisted of a plough of land, extending from Dochnacraig at the South to the half davoch of Dochfour at the North, and divided therefrom by a small streamlet, now from drainage and otherwise at times hardly discernible, and of old entering Loch Dochfour or little Loch Ness, near the boat-house. Upon Dochcairns the present house, or rather the first of it, was erected by Alexander Baillie, fourth of Dochfour, about 1770. There must have been a house there at an earlier period, for I have seen a deed bearing to be signed at Dochcairn in 1698. Before the grounds were set out and the present ornamental and kitchen gardens extended and formed, a small clump of old trees, half way between the house and burn of Dochcairn, was well known as the "Fairy Knowe" of Dochcairn, an object of much interest and speculation with the young. In 1657 Easter and Wester Dochcairns were disponed by Alexander Baillie to his second son,

David Baillie, therein described as "of Dochfour," with their shielings and grazings, and the salmon fishings upon Little Loch Ness and the River Ness from the burn of Wester Dochcairn to the march with Dochfour, reserving the superiority and a feu of 4 bolls. The shielings of Dochcairns were Rui-na-Ceardich, Rui-na-Sunderrie, Rui-ic-Gillie-Chrom, and Rui-na-Clerich, and it will be seen that the rights of grazing on these shielings, and the contiguous ones of Dochnacraig, gave rise afterwards to questions and litigation. Dochfour and Dochcairns being thus conjoined in the year 1657, they will now be treated of as one.

It seems probable that all the land from Kinmylies to Abriachan had been occupied by the two families of Baillie and Maclean upon redeemable rights or tacks under the Gordons, ever since they acquired the Castle lands. It is certain that Alexander Baillie of Dunain possessed Dunain, Lagnalien, half of Dochgarroch, Dochcairn, and Dochnacraig, but I have not observed that he or his predecessors had any right to Dochfour, which remained on wadset from the Gordons down to 1770, when it was first feued. The exact period of its acquisition by David Baillie above mentioned, the first of the present family of Dochfour, I have not observed, but it was after 1644 and prior to 1657.

In 1632, the then wadsetter of Dochfour was Alexander Baillie (no doubt of the Dunain family) who, designed "of Davochfour, is granted on 2nd October of that year a receipt and discharge by the Earl of Enzie for sixteen bolls of victual for his "occupancy and possession" for crop 1631. It would thus seem that the rent or feu for each plough of the Castle lands was eight bolls. Alexander Baillie, described as "of Dochfour" in a deed of 1623, was succeeded by his son William Baillie, who married Marion Maclean of Dochgarroch. This William, described in 1637 as portioner of Dochfour, and in 1644 as heritable proprietor, seems to have fallen into difficulties, for in 1637 he, with consent of his wife, grants a wadset of the half of Dochfour to Alexander Fraser, son to umquhile Malcolm Fraser of Culduthel, which Alexander Fraser was the then tenant under Baillie of the lands so wadsetted. The wadset right is dated at Inverness 22nd August, 1637, and registered 14th June, 1644. After 1644 I find no further reference to the old Baillies of Dochfour. David Baillie was thus in 1657 wadsetter of Dochfour and feuar of Dochcairn, having right of salmon fishing *ex adverso* of Easter and Wester Dochcairns. Naturally, when Dochfour was a separate tenement, the dwelling-house would be upon it, and so it was, at a pretty spot on the terrace of the Dochfour Burn at Balnacruik. When rebuilding, either David Baillie or his son Alexander, removed the dwelling-house to Dochcairn as being their irredeemable property. Vestiges of the original house at Balnacruik, afterwards converted into a barn, remained within my recollection. David Baillie lived at Castle Spiritan and a good deal at Kinmylies. He and his son Alexander continued Catholics, and his evidence was refused in the Court of Session in 1673 as being "unrelaxed" for some eight years by the Presbytery of Inverness. He married first, in 1629, Janet, daughter of William Paterson, burgess of Inverness, without male issue, which marriage is not referred to in the Dochfour genealogy; second, Janet Fraser. This marriage is stated in the genealogy to be with "Margaret, daughter of the Lord Lovat." No date is given, and no such marriage is to be found in the Lovat histories, and the name certainly was not Margaret. True, Simon Lord Lovat in 1737 calls Hugh Baillie, third of Dochfour, grandson of Janet, "his relation," but it must be remembered that with Lovat every Fraser was "his cousin." There was a disposition of Dochcairn granted by David Baillie in 1659 in favour of Janet Fraser and himself in life-rent and their only son Alexander in fee. Alexander Baillie, second of Dochfour, married first, about 1689, Mary, daughter of Alexander Grant, in Milntown of Ballachastell, and Catharine Ogilvie, with issue—one son, William, who died young. This marriage is omitted in the Dochfour genealogy. He married, secondly, Hannah Fraser of Reelig, with issue—Alexander, living in 1711, who predeceased his father; Hugh, who succeeded; Evan of Abriachan; William of Rosehall; James; and David. Born prior to 1659, Alexander, blind for many years, was living in 1737, a prominent man in his day. The address to the Chevalier St. George, originated by Glengarry, was carried through the Highlands for signature by Campbell of Glendaruel and Dochfour, and several important meetings took place in the House of Dochfour. This I give on the sworn affidavits of Castleleathers, the minister of Boleskine, and the catechist of Dores, emitted for a special purpose in 1759. In 1709 Dochfour buys his feu over Dochcairns from Dunain, but astricts the lands to the mill of Tor, or Dunain mill, having previously in 1692 adjusted and settled all questions between them. Dochfour was not in a hurry paying his stipend. Crop 1720 would be due in spring 1721, and the Rev. Robert Baillie has to take a bill dated 1st March, 1723, payable at the Martinmas following for $88\frac{1}{2}$ merks, of balance of the stipend, crop 1720. Even then he does not get payment and he records the bill on 28th April, 1724. Alexander Baillie of Dochfour was succeeded by his eldest surviving son, Hugh, third of Dochfour, who, with his wife Emilia Fraser, also of the family of Reelig, was infeft in Dochcairn in 1733. He is chiefly known by his duel in the Caiplich with the Chamberlain of Urquhart, so graphically narrated by Lord Lovat in his letter to the Laird of Grant, 15th December, 1737. At this time the family was numerous but scattered, Hugh and James occupying some lands in Urquhart, their father still living. His son Alexander was entered in Dochcairn by Alex. Baillie of Dunain in 1751. Besides Alexander Hugh Baillie had sons, James, Evan, Duncan, and several daughters. The sons sought fortune abroad, and the three elder were all very successful. Alexander, fourth of Dochfour, returned about 1770, living at Cradlehall while the new house on Dochcairn was being built. He planted the hills of Dochcairn and Dochfour and greatly improved the place.

On the return home of Colonel John Baillie of Dunain in 1784, the lairds of Dochfour and Dunain, near neighbours, and no very distant cousins, fell out, particularly about their grazings in the Caiplich, and landed in Court, the name of the deceased Evan Baillie of Abriachan being severely reflected on by Dunain, while as warmly defended by Dochfour, Abriachan's nephew. The Duke of Gordon, who was then selling the superiorities of the Castle lands, intervened. Dochfour was desirous of peace, Dunain was immersed in the formation of the Inverness Fencibles, and in 1794 matters were adjusted in this way. The Duke sold the superiorities of Dunain, Dochgarroch, and Dochnacraig to Dunain, thereby constituting him a freeholder, and he sold the superiority of Dochfour and Dochcairns to Dochfour. Dochfour gave up to Dunain all the Dochcairn shielings west of the burn and in the heights of Caiplich; while Dunain gave to Dochfour the salmon fishings opposite to or *ex adverso* of the lands of Dochfour proper, the want of which had been a sore subject with the Dochfour family all along, not only as *in emulatione vicini* but comprehending the pool of Carn Robbie, well known as one of the surest in the river. Upon Alexander Baillie of Dochfour's death in 1799, without lawful issue, he, ignoring the sons of his deceased immediate younger brother James, left a settlement in which his trustees are directed to offer Dochfour at the sum of £10,000 to his third brother Evan, who had by this time acquired the barony of Kinmylies, and if he declined, to hold the estate until the majority of his, Alexander's, illegitimate son Alexander. Evan accepted the offer, and he and his successors have since, though not the elder branch, possessed Dochfour. Evan's eldest son, Peter, having predeceased his father, the succession opened to Peter's eldest son Evan in 1835, who, dying a few years ago, was in turn succeeded by his grandson, the present James Evan Bruce Baillie of Dochfour, M.P. for the County of Inverness,

From 1820, when the last Baillie of Dunain's brothers died, and he himself had become incurably insane, it became a paramount object with the Dochfour family to acquire Dunain whenever the opportunity offered, and how this and the estate of Dochgarroch fell ultimately into their hands will be afterwards told.

THE MACLEANS OF DOCHGARROCH.

The family of Maclean of Dochgarroch stood as one of the oldest resident heritors in the now united parishes of Inverness and Bona. Unfortunately accounts differ as to their genealogy, and though naturally quite disposed as grand nephew of the last Dochgarroch to accept the longest pedigree, I content myself at present with going back for the trifling period for a Maclean of 450 years, and mentioning those regarding whom there can be no doubt. Between the years 1580 and 1640 one name is frequently referred to in the records of the parish, viz., that of Alexander Maclean of Dochgarroch, commonly styled "Allister-Vic-Coil-Vic-Ferquhar." He is once or twice found with the two additional patronymics of "Vic-Eachin-Vic-Harlich." I therefore start with

I. CHARLES, Constable of Urquhart and Castle Spiritan, of whom the race of Clan Thearlaich. He is found, together with his son Hector, witnessing charters by John, last Earl of Ross and Lord of the Isles. Mr William Mackay in his valuable work, published in 1893, identifies Hector with the well-known lands now called Balmacaan, but really Balmaceachainn, in Urquhart.

II. HECTOR married, said to be his second wife, Margaret, third daughter of Malcolm, tenth of Mackintosh, under whom the above Charles Maclean described as "Tearlach Vic Eeachin Vic Wolan" had taken protection for himself and his successors. Mr Mackay explains very clearly the origin of the questions between the Mackintoshes and the Kilravocks anent the possessions of the crown lands of Urquhart and Glenmoriston, arising out of the above marriage, and it is matter of regret to the descendants of Maclean and Mackintosh that, while too weak to retain them himself, Kilravock was the means whereby the lands were lost to both families. Hector Maclean was ultimately succeeded by his son,

III. FARQUHAR, in whose time, driven out of Urquhart and having no certain standing elsewhere, the fortunes of the family were at a low ebb. It is certain however that at this period the Dochgarroch family were closely connected with Farquhar Maclean, Bishop of the Isles, and with Agnes and Marion Maclean, Prioresses of Iona. Indeed by some the two Farquhars have been held as one and the same person. Farquhar was in turn succeeded by his younger son,

IV. DONALD, who is the first I find in Dochgarroch, and styled "Donald Farquhar's son in Dochgarroch." He serves at Inverness as a juryman on the 3rd of July, 1557, in the service of Lachlan Mackinnon of Strathwordell as heir to his father Ewen Mackinnon. Donald's name is found in the Sheriff Court records of the period both as pursuer and defendant. Although the family possessed no indefeasible title to Dochgarroch until the year 1623 they, from 1557 downwards, kept possession, and Donald himself, at least nominally, was proprietor of Raasay and part of Trotternish. This is proved by a Precept of Clare Constat by John, Bishop of Sodor or the Isles, perpetual commendator of the Monastery of St. Columba in Iona, with consent of his Archdeacon and other Canons chapterly assembled, dated Edinburgh the 10th January, 1631, in favour of Alexander Maclean, who is therein described as son of the late Donald Maclean, son of Ferquhard, son of Hector, which Donald was last vest and seized in the lands, comprehending the 8 merks of Raasay and three merks in Trotternish. It is to be feared that Dochgarroch was proprietor only in name, for Archdeacon Monro in 1549 describes Raasay as pertaining to MacGillechallum by the sword, and to the Bishop of the Isles by heritage. The Archdeacon was a cousin of Dochgarroch, the latter no doubt getting Raasay from the Bishop, his relative, with the view of expelling MacGillechallum. It is said that Donald lived to 1622, but this, though not impossible, is unlikely, seeing he is found filling the responsible position of juryman in 1557, and though there are several documents extant from and after 1606, no reference is made to his being then in life. Donald had a younger son, styled Hector Vic Coil Vic Ferquhar, who resided chiefly at Culcabock and married Margaret, daughter of Paul Macpherson of Lonnie. He is found at Culcabock 1614-1621, and on 31st May in the latter year he discharges his brother Alexander of 1000 merks which Alexander had bound himself to settle on his brother at his marriage. Donald Maclean was succeeded by his eldest son,

V. ALEXANDER who, described as "Alexander Vic-Coil Vic Ferquhar," is mentioned in 1611 as a creditor of Rose of Kilravock for 2000 merks. It is said that Alexander was thrice married, and that his first wife was a daughter of Kilravock. I have found no verification of this statement, nor any other connection between the families other than the above, which shows that Dochgarroch was a man of considerable means. That he was a man of integrity is shown by his having been entrusted with the Kingairloch charters which he delivered back to Donald Maclean, Hector's son, apparent of Kingairloch, on 6th December, 1609. He was certainly twice married, first to Margaret Grant, a daughter of Glenmoriston or Corriemony, and I infer of the former because in the marriage contract of their son, John Maclean, with Agnes Fraser of Struy, in 1629, John Grant of Glenmoriston is mentioned as one of the friends. Although Allister Maclean was in possession of Dochgarroch, the lands seemed to have been under wadset by the Gordons to Dunain. On the 3rd of April, 1605, Alexander Baillie of Dunain grants receipt for 900 merks to Allister Vic Coil Vic Ferquhar "in" Davochgarroch in full payment of the sum contained in a contract and appointment for the sale of Dunain's rights over Dochgarroch, dated 28th March, 1605. On the 7th of June, 1606, Dunain grants disposition to Dochgarroch of the lands of Dochnalurg, extending to a quarter davoch of old extent, upon which Dochgarroch was infeft on the 19th of June, 1606. In these two deeds Allister is styled "of Dochgarroch." On the 17th June, 1606, there is another contract between Dunain and Dochgarroch, showing that Dunain's rights were redeemable, and giving power to Dochgarroch to transact with the Earl of Enzie. Sasine followed on the 19th of June. In 1615 Dochgarroch deals with the Gordons, and in implement of an agreement and the payment of large sums, the Earl of Enzie, Anna Campbell his spouse, and the Marquis of Huntly grant a charter of Dochgarroch and Dochnalurg, dated at Inverness and Aboyne on the 4th and 15th July of the above year. This right was redeemable and it was not until 1623 that an indefeasible title was obtained by Alexander Maclean. On the 12th May that year at Inverness a contract is entered into between the Gordons and Alexander Maclean and his son John, whereby the Macleans on the one hand renounce all present rights, discharge 3000 merks of wadset monies and pay 2000 merks further, and on the other hand the Gordons agree to give a feu charter of Dochgarroch, a half davoch, and of Dochnalurg, a quarter davoch lands, with a feu of two chalders, and personal obligations as to hoisting and hunting, attending the superior courts, etc. A charter in these terms is granted on the same day by the Earl of Enzie with consent of the Marquis of Huntly, directed to Alexander Baillie of Dochfour as bailie, on which infeftment followed also same day. Among the witnesses were Allister-Mor-Vic-Iain-Vic-William, in Lagnalien; Duncan Vic-Coil-dhu, in Davochgarroch; Donald Vic-Andrew there, and others. This charter was confirmed by Charles I. at Edinburgh on the 2nd February, 1635.

Having got Allister Vic Coil Vic Ferquhar at length fully vested in the estates I turn to a description of the lands and some events in their history.

The following is the description and boundaries of Dochgarroch and Dochnalurg, as contained in the feu charter by the Earl of Enzie with consent of the Marquis of Huntly, in favour of Alexander Maclean of Dochgarroch and his eldest son John, in life rent and fee respectively, dated 12th May, 1623—

"All and whole the lands of Dochgarroch, extending to half a davoch of land of old extent, and also the town and lands of Dochnalurg extending to a quarter of a davoch of land of old extent, with power of building a miln, with the sheillings in the Hill of Caiploch called Rui-Cruinn, and Rui-Blar-na-Cailleach, which lands of Dochgarroch and Dochnalurg lie contiguous limited and bounded as follows, viz.:—Beginning at the Eastern boundary at the stream descending from the Hill of Caiploch, which is called the burn of Dochgarroch, and separates said lands of Dochgarroch from the lands of Lagnalian, and thereafter said burn descending to a loch called Lochan Shan Vall, and from thence stretching to the summit of Tormore and even to the Gob which leads in to the water of the Ness at the East ; and bounded by the burn of Dochfour, and a stone wall which leads to the water of Ness and separates said lands of Dochnalurg from the lands of Dochfour at the West ; the water of Ness at the South ; and stretching themselves in the Hill of Caiploch until they reach to the common pastures of the lands of Moniack, Holme and Craggach in the North."

This is an unusually clear delimitation, and upon the Dunain, River, and Dochfour sides little change of marches has since taken place. There were questions with Dunain, however, at the East, properly North. From the source of the Dochgarroch Burn the line was clear, but higher up towards the Caiplich there was no definition. In June, 1652, the questions of marches between Dunain and Dochgarroch were referred to Hugh Fraser of Struy and John Forbes of Culloden, who set up a cairn near the head of Alt Dynack (which is the chief source of the Burn of Bunchrew), and from thence to the source of the Burn of Dochgarroch, as the march. This decision was not satisfactory. Both parties issued letters of lawburrows against the other, and both were harrassed by the town people cutting peats. To defeat the common foe, John Maclean of Dochgarroch and William Baillie of Dunain agreed again to arbitrate, and on the 27th of June, 1659, an imposing gathering, indeed it may be called a court, was held "at or near the place called the Head of Auldynak," in the Caiplich. Dochgarroch, with his son Alexander, and Dunain were personally present, together with numerous followers as witnesses; also Lieut.-Colonel Miles Man, Deputy Governor of Inverness; Hugh Fraser of Belladrum; Lachlan Mackintosh, brother german to the Laird of Mackintosh; John Forbes of Culloden; Hugh Fraser of Struy; and Alexander Mackintosh of Connage, Justices of Peace of the Sheriffdom of Inverness. The Justices heard parties, and the testimony of Belladrum and Culloden, the arbiters of 1652, and of David Baillie of Dochfour, also present then and now, and adhered to the line then fixed, adding to and enlarging the cairn at Alt Dynack, and placing fifteen other cairns along the line to the head of the Burn of Dochgarroch. The decision was without prejudice to the protests of the town of Inverness and others then made, and the written decision was ordered to remain in possession of Connage, whose clerk, William Cumming, was to give transumpts to all concerned. Lochan Shan Val, along the Dunain march, has from drainage operations disappeared. It lay immediately to the right of the present road to Glenurquhart, where going from Inverness the house of Dochgarroch first comes in sight. The Tormore, or Hill o' Torr, is the highest wooded ground near the river, but the "Gob," described as running into the river disappeared during the Canal operations, having together with a good deal of the Tormore, been utilized for its clay in puddling the Canal sides and bottom. Before the final raising of the level of the Canal there were two solitary alder trees, ordinarily a few inches from the Canal waters, slim, but of some height, so close that they appeared as if springing from the same root, one being situated on Dochgarroch and the other on Dunain.

It has been repeatedly told me that prior to the Canal operations, the river from its emerging at Little Loch Ness down to the famous pool, "Poll an Laggan," was a perfect dream of beauty. It spread widely opposite Dochnalurg, and flowed peacefully by various channels along several islands, attractively and variedly wooded, while the steep slopes of Borlum were one thick mass of green firs. The march with Dochfour was unaltered, except that the burn, having occasionally altered its course, was not actually the march towards the river. The burn, with its chief source, the Tuarie, having a long course, the Dochgarroch hill lands not only entirely overlapped Dochfour and Dochcairn but also a part of Dochnacraig. The estate lost heavily at its North and West march. Dunain claimed the old Urquhart road as the West march but Dochgarroch claimed the watershed with the Aird, and all lands draining into the Alt Tuarie and Dochgarroch burns, which left quite enough to Craggach, Holm, and Moniack, of the hill grazings and pasturages proper to them, facing the Beauly Firth and draining thereunto. As matters stood until the sale of Dochgarroch in 1832, this question was debated, but in 1835, soon after the accession of the late Evan Baillie of Dochfour, he entered into an arbitration, foolishly referring it to a person closely connected with one of the Aird proprietors, who gave to the Dochgarroch estate a mere stripe West of the old Glenurquhart Road, and cut off a large portion of muir and valuable peat ground actually watered by an affluent of the Tuarie, giving it to Reelig. Here the parish of Bona lost largely to the parish of Kirkhill.

A portion of Dochnalurg towards the hill is called "Iss-a-chath" or Battlefield. This is the way it is pronounced but I presume the right spelling is "Innis," used as "place," or "Ionnsaidh," "attack," or "assault." Here was fought over 400 years ago the battle thus described in the MS. History of the Frasers—

"In the minority of James III. Donald of Isles broke out into insurrection and was partly checked by Lord Lovat. He was so incensed that he left his brother, Alexander, and a considerable body of men to harass Lord Lovat's country, and to prevent his pursuing the rear of the main force; and their numbers daily increasing, they had at last laid siege to Lovat. Hugh Lord Lovat ordered his clan and vassals to assemble, and having sallied out, he attacked the Macdonalds briskly on the side of Lovat, while the country people having notice thereof, killed all that straggled from the main body, and then attacked the Macdonalds in flank, so that they were soon obliged not only to raise the siege but to retreat. Lord Lovat pursued them to the Caiploch, about four miles West of Inverness, and there fought the battle of Mam-Cha, where the Macdonalds received such a total overthrow that they made no more attempts in Lovat's country."

There is a famous iron spring near the head of Ault Tuarie, called the "Fuaran Dearg," of old held in great repute for its strengthening power, also several fine springs, notably one at the Blackfold, another below Easter Ballimore, and another below Battlefield. A mile to the south of the Fuaran Dearg is the the well-known Fuaran-na-Baintighearna, or the Lady's Well, where three properties meet. The most picturesque object is the Burn of Dochfour, which has three fine falls within short distances, with its pool above the most dangerous, inhabited in my youth by the *each uisge*. It is beautifully wooded, contains wild fruit in abundance, with numerous specimens of rare flora, and altogether, though 54 years have passed since I left Dochnalurg, the burn has so impressed and interwoven itself into my early life, that in Dreamland, associated with youthful sports and researches, it frequently appears, and for the moment I am young again.

Having got Allister-Vic-Coil-Vic-Ferquhar vested in the estates, I shall continue Alexander's own history, who is reported to have fought at Glenlivat; and this is possible, although I find no verification of it, nor of the allegation that he went in force to recover Raasay. That he was killed and buried in Kilpheder in 1635 is not correct, as I have a discharge in his favour by Effie Macbean, goodwife of Essich, dated the 24th May, 1640. In a deed of 31st July, 1641, his son John is designed as apparent of Dochgarroch; and it is not until 8th July, 1644, that I find John Maclean designed "of Dochgarroch." Alexander's father Donald must have been in a very humble position at his son's birth, seeing that he was unable to give him such an education as would enable him to sign his name. Notwithstanding his inability to write, Alexander raised his family to a position and influence not maintained by his successors.

In 1609 he renews his dependence on Mackintosh for himself and his race of Clan Tearlaich, which brought him into trouble afterwards. The extraordinary antipathy of James, Earl of Moray, to the Clan Chattan which involved not only other families, but the town of Inverness, is well depicted by Spalding. Among others, Alexander Maclean was charged by David Stewart, Procurator-Fiscal for Lord Moray, with "resetting, supplying, and inter-communing with the name and rebels of Clan Chattan, their associates, followers, and dependers." Dochgarroch evidently thought discretion the better part of valour, and he appeared at a court held at Elgin on the 6th November, 1629, and "confessed his guiltiness"; and throwing himself on the Earl's clemency was fined. The amount is not stated, and probably all the Earl wanted was submission. Four days later, on 10th November, he remits the fine and discharges Dochgarroch.

Alexander got into serious involvement with the Earl of Enzie, by having along with Alexander Baillie of Dunain granted as cautioners a bond for 3300 merks to James Cuthbert of Drakies, dated 10th June, 1626. The Earl having failed to pay, all kinds of diligence were taken against Dunain and Dochgarroch in 1633, which so alarmed Thomas Fraser of Struy, whose daughter had married Alexander's son John in 1629, as to necessitate his taking steps against Dochgarroch to protect his daughter's interest. Alexander had at least three daughters, (1) Agnes, who married William, younger brother of Alexander Baillie of Dunain, contract dated 11th March, 1614—tocher 1000 merks, discharged 10th November the same year, two of the witnesses being John Grant of Glenmoriston and Alexander Baillie of Dunain. (2) Marion, who married William Baillie of the old Baillies of Dochfour, and is referred to in 1637. (3) Janet, who married first, as his second wife, James Cumming of Delshangie, on 27th October, 1625. Dochgarroch settles 1000 and Delshangie 2000 merks upon

Janet; and among the witnesses to the contract are Mr Alexander Grant, minister of Urquhart, and Alexander Baillie of Dunain. This Janet lived to a good age, being found in 1674 as then wife of James Grant of Sheuglie. From Delshangie sprung the Cummings, writers in Inverness, between whom and the Macleans several marriages took place. Lasting over 200 years, the race terminated in the person of Alexina, commonly called "Lexy" Cumming, who died at Inverness about fifty years ago, reputed to be a hundred years of age, daughter of James Cumming, writer and messenger in Inverness. I recollect being introduced as a cousin to this venerable lady, whose masculine features and huge silver snuff box made a deep impression upon me. The Hogarth portraits of Simon Lord Lovat have taken such a hold on the public mind and become so numerous that it can hardly be credited that his Lordship, as late as the period of his being Governor of Inverness, was a remarkably fine looking man. Miss Cumming was the possessor of a really fine portrait by Zell, which still exists. The insignificant little representation given in the edition of Major Fraser of Castle Leathers' Manuscript published a few years ago, attributed to Zell, while it has the same dress and pose, is not only an inadequate representation but changes the whole expression. Alexander's first contract of marriage is not preserved; the second, with Annabella Munro of Daan, dated at Inverness in 1628, is in fair condition. Alexander was succeeded by his eldest son,

VI. JOHN, who in 1629, married Agnes Fraser, daughter of Thomas Fraser of Struy, who survived her husband and eldest son Alexander. It will be recollected that by the feu charter of Dochgarroch, the feu duty stipulated was two chalders, or 32 bolls, and man service in "hoisting" and "hawking" or a suitable man in place. All the Dochgarroch accounts, traditional and otherwise, speak of the feu being doubled on account of some old failure in duty on the part of Maclean. So far as can be seen, the ordinary feu was 8 bolls per plough, or 32 for the davoch. Dochgarroch and Dochnalurg consisted of three ploughs, so that upon it was placed an additional burden of 8 bolls, and thus some foundation for the tradition. Serving in "hoisting" meant to rise in arms with the superior, and there has most fortunately been preserved a formal receipt to John Maclean for a sufficient well mounted trooper, which I give in full. Such an acknowledgment is rare, and the granter's designation reminds us at once of the famous Dugald Dalgetty, whom Sir Walter Scott calls "Rit Master." The word is, of course, German, but is spelt "Rute" in this document—

"I, Alexander Gordon of Birsmoir, Rute Master of Horse under the Marquis of Huntly, grants me to have received from John Maclean of Dochgarroch ane sufficient trooper well mounted, with horse, saddle, clothes with trappings, as becomes ane trooper to have, whereof I grant the receipt and that for his usual lands as weel hadden as not hadden of the said Marquis of Huntly, and discharges the said John Maclean of Dochgarroch, his heirs, executors, and assignees thereof, for now and ever, obliging the said Alexander Gordon, Rute Master of Horse aforesaid, to warrant this my discharge, good, valid and effectual, to the said John Maclean and his forsaids at all hands and against all mortals, and that conform to a warrant granted by his Majesty to warrant him as ane servitor, and likeways discharges all officers and soldiers from any quartering of the said John Maclean of Dochgarroch his lands within the Parochin of Inverness and Castle lands thereof, and these presents shall be your warrant. Dispensing by these presents with his own personal forthcoming, whenever the same is presented to you by these presents, subscribed with my hand at Inverness, the twelfth day of July, sixteen hundred and fifty-nine years. (Signed) A. GORDON of Birsmore."

John Maclean's eldest son,

VII. ALEXANDER, married on the 28th of November, 1656, Agnes, daughter of Alexander Chisholm of Comar. He predeceased his wife, father, and mother, dying in the month of September, 1671, leaving two children at least—John and Allan, the eldest of whom succeeded his grandfather John, in October, 1674, Agnes Fraser, his grandmother, dying six years later, in 1680. Curiously, every account erroneously states that Alexander died without issue, thereby, if true, cutting off from all the subsequent Macleans the honourable blood of the Chisholms. But in Alexander's will, dated the 3rd of August, 1671, he nominates his brother John as tutor to his "eldest son." Another brother of Alexander's named Donald, upon the 2nd of June, 1685, grants a discharge to John Maclean, then of Dochgarroch, "as oye to John Maclean, sometime of Dochgarroch," and *in gremio* discharges John Maclean of all he can ask of him for himself, or by or through the decease of Alexander Maclean, his father, or John Maclean, his goodsir, his (Donald's) father and brother. The other children of John Maclean of Dochgarroch and Agnes Fraser whom I have noticed were John, described as in Leys; (2) Hector, in Dochnalurg; (3) Donald, merchant burgess of Inverness; (4) Farquhar, in Kinmylies; (5) Elspet, described as eldest daughter, married prior to 1657 Angus MacQueen in Inshes, of the Corrybrough family; (6) Catharine, married, first to Donald Munro, in Culcabock; second, to Duncan Macpherson, in Daltochy of Ardclach, contract dated penult January, 1669; and (7) Janet, who married Malcolm, younger son of William Mackintosh of Holme, contract dated, 19th May, 1665. Alexander's eldest son,

VIII. JOHN, married on the 23rd December, 1682, Margaret, daughter of David Fowler, Bailie of Inverness. Upon the narrative that he was "presently going to His Majesty's Host," John Maclean granted a factory to his brother german, Allan Maclean, dated Inverness, 19th October, 1688. He was present at Killiecrankie. This step was ruinous to Dochgarroch, and from this time embarassments arose. John left several children; his daughter Margaret married—contract dated Gartallie, 28th November, 1705—William Grant, younger son of Corriemonie. The deed is written by John Maclean, younger of Dochgarroch, and among the parties' cautioners and witnesses are John Grant, elder of Corriemonie; John Maclean, elder of Dochgarroch; James Cumming, younger of Delshangie; Master James Stewart, schoolmaster at

Urquhart; Alexander Baillie of Dochfour; and Robert Grant in Buntait, brother german to Corriemonie. Another daughter, Janet, married—contract dated 26th December, 1723—William, son of Duncan Mackintosh, and grandson of the late William Mackintosh of Borlum, my great grand parents. John, eighth of Dochgarroch, died before 1710, his widow living until 1724. Besides the two daughters above named John and Margaret Fowler left several sons, of whom I have noted Alexander, Donald, David, and Lachlan.

Here it will be convenient to refer to a distinguished descendant of this John Maclean, known as John "Og," whose benefactions are destined to prove of inestimable value to the name of Maclean. John Og's third son, Donald, served James VII. and after the Revolution settled in Argyleshire. From him through his son Lachlan derived Lieutenant-Colonel Alexander Maclean, some time of the 3rd West India Regiment. Colonel Maclean, by his settlement, dated 1857, ordered a sum of £20,000 to be set apart and administered by the Lord Provost and Magistrates of Glasgow for the support and education of a certain number of boys named Maclean. The fund was so administered until the passing of the Education Act, which so much interfered with such bequests, that for a time the scheme was practically in abeyance, much to the regret of the numerous Macleans in Glasgow and elsewhere. But a few of the most energetic of the name, including in particular Mr Walter Maclean, President of the Clan Maclean Association; Mr C. J. Maclean, Treasurer; and Mr John Maclean, one of the Vice-Presidents, the latter being of the Dochgarroch family, bestirred themselves to adapt the bequest to the altered circumstances, and still secure all the advantages intended by the testator. The Lord Provost and Magistrates gave their cordial concurrence, and ultimately, though not without great pertinacity and determination, a new scheme suitable to the altered state of the law, and to include girls, was agreed upon, and received the sanction of the legal authorities. The scheme so approved of and now in operation is as follows—

The interest of £20,000 capital is applied to—(1) Maintenance of bursaries of the value of £5 per annum, open to boys or girls between the ages of seven and fourteen years of the name of Maclean in attendance at any public or State-aided school, available for two years, but may be renewed. (2) School bursaries of the value of not less than £10, or more than £15 per annum, open to boys or girls of the name of Maclean who have passed the Fifth Standard for one year at any public or State-aided or technical school or classes for technical or manual instruction approved of by the Governors, but these also may be renewed. (3) University bursaries of the value of not less than £25, or more than £30 per annum, open to male or female candidates of the name of Maclean to be awarded by competitive examination in such manner as the Governors shall determine, and tenable for four years at any Scottish University. It should be further mentioned that Colonel Alexander Maclean left a sum of £1500, to be set apart for the establishment and support of a church to the memory and honour of the Macleans and their close connection with Iona, to be called *Relig Orain nam Braithrean*, the sittings to be free, especially to soldiers, sailors, and pensioners, who understand Gaelic. This sum having been found insufficient, was increased to £5000, and the interest—£150—is now divided between the Church of Scotland and the Free Church for the support of Gaelic missionaries in Glasgow, each receiving £75.

IX. JOHN, ninth of Dochgarroch, succeeded his father, and in 1710—contract dated 30th January, 1710—married Christian Dallas, eldest daughter of the deceased Alexander Dallas, with consent of her brother, William Dallas, then of Cantray. This was a fortunate marriage. The lady was of excellent descent, clever and prudent. Her temper was not of the best, and when provoked by the indolence or neglect of servants, and others, she used to break into fits of anger, insisting on being obeyed, and adding, "You forget who I am. I am daughter of Cantray Doun and Cantray Dallas—("*Is mis nighean Cantra Doun's Cantra Dallash*")—a saying afterwards proverbial in the family, and meaningly thrown at the Maclean ladies by their male relatives when they showed temper. Dochgarroch went out in the 'Fifteen, escaped attainder, but was in concealment for some time, during which he killed a soldier at Dochnalurg who had misbehaved himself. His affairs were unsatisfactorily administered by his brother, Alexander, a writer in Inverness. John Maclean had two sons, Charles, who succeeded, and William; and although the different accounts speak of another son John, said to be the eldest and to have fallen at Culloden, I have found no verification, and the fact that in William's contract of marriage he is called *second* lawful son of the deceased John Maclean, late of Dochgarroch, with consent of Charles Maclean of Dochgarroch, his elder brother-german, would indicate that there was no older brother called John. William married Marie Mackintosh, second daughter of Lachlan Mackintosh of Knochnageal, second brother of Brigadier Mackintosh, by his first wife Mary Lockhart, contract dated at Nether Cullairds on the 6th of November, 1751, and it is rather singular in respect that Marie marries with consent of her eldest sister Janet, who signs the deed. This Janet afterwards married the "strong" minister of Moy, Mr Leslie. The date of John Maclean's death is uncertain. He was succeeded by his son,

X. CHARLES, an officer in the Black Watch in 1745. He married Marjorie, second daughter of Angus Mackintosh of Drummond, contract dated 22nd of November, 1753, and left four sons and three daughters, John, Phineas, Angus, William, Janet, Marjory, and Barbara. Mrs Maclean died before her husband, and he died in 1778.

XI. JOHN, the eldest son, a young man of promise, was seized when in Grenada with a stroke in 1777 which deprived him of reason—he died in 1826. Phineas died young. Angus obtained the rank of Captain in the East Indian Army and died at Calicut in 1794. Janet married her cousin once removed, Captain Alexander Mackintosh, only son of William Mackintosh and Janet Maclean formerly referred to—contract dated 23rd October, 1779. They were my grandfather and grandmother. Marjory married Bailie Alexander Lee of Inverness, whose eldest daughter, Jean, married Bailie Hugh Innes of Inverness; and Barbara died unmarried.

XII. WILLIAM, youngest son of Charles, succeeded his eldest brother John. He served in various regiments and in different parts of the world, and married Elizabeth Maclean of Rochester. He was of an easy temper and involved himself and his family deeply. The money received from the Canal Commissioners, over £2000, postponed the evil day. It was only a question of time and whether John would outlive his brother, William. If so, the estate had been safe. But John died in 1826, and then Dochfour knew he would succeed, which he did in 1832, getting the estate for £10,000, when 92 years of age.

According to general belief, it was said that Dochfour had set apart under trustees large sums lent to the Earl of Cawdor for the acquisition of Dunain when it came into the market, as was pretty certain, and this is so far corroborated by the fact that large sums amounting to over £50,000 were lent to Cawdor between 1810 and 1827, called up however in 1840. William Maclean was an old man at the time of the sale, and it was promised him that after a lease then current of the mansion house and mains to his son expired he should not be removed. When the lease expired however, in 1839, Dochgarroch was removed, and Mrs Mackenzie, housekeeper at Dunain, writing to Miss Anne Baillie of Dunain, then in Edinburgh, under date May, 1839, well expresses the feeling in the district, when she says, "There is the greatest sympathy with Dochgarroch in his having to leave the old place." He died in October, 1841. How well I recollect the gathering in December, 1838, when for the last time Dochgarroch and his son had their near relatives from Dochnalurg at the usual Christmas dinner at Dochgarroch. William left three sons, Allan, Charles, and William, all deceased.

XIII. ALLAN died at the Old House of Drummond,

unmarried. Charles, Lieutenant-Colonel in the army, retired after 47 years' active service, and died at Woodside, Fortrose, in December, 1864, leaving one daughter, Charlotte Amelia. William, the youngest son, left by his wife, Elizabeth Henderson, four children. The second son,

XIV. ALLAN, succeeded his uncle, and has by his wife Marion, daughter of the late Rev. Edward Guilie, vicar of St. Lukes, Jersey, two sons and one daughter—Allan Mackintosh, Hector, and Jessie. He lives at Brighton.

The population of Bona has greatly diminished within the last fifty years. Abriachan remains much the same, and the people have been kindly treated by the Seafield family. The tenants of Dochnacraig in 1799 were:—Bona—Donald Taylor; Lurgmore—Donald Fraser Vic Hamish; Ballabarron—Alexander Macandrew, Angus Cameron; Midtown—George More Ferguson, Widow Ferguson, Christian Elder; Meeting-House—Widow Macallan; Uppertown—Thomas Vic Huistean's widow, Widow Alexander Mackenzie; Woodend—Donald Dallas, Alexander Macdonald, John Macqueen; Caiplich—John Fraser's widow, in all fourteen families, or about 100 souls. This list may be compared with the Roll for 1894. The names of Ferguson and Dallas have long been connected with Dochnacraig. Upon Dochcairn, Dochfour, Dochnalurg, and the low lands of Dochgarroch, there are no tenants, crofters, cottars, nor any except the employees of the estate, with one or two exceptions. In my recollection there were two cottars at Dochcairn, three at Balnacruik, and one in the hill, called "Iain-mor-a-chraggan." Upon Dochnalurg there were four cottars at the roadside, and three at Battlefield. Upon Dochgarroch there were three tenants in Ballimore; four tenants and cottars at Gortan-nan-gour, including a tailor and a weaver; three cottars above the Caiplich road; five cottars near the Canal, including a public-house and a smithy; five tenants at Ballindarroch; and two at the Snuff Mill, in all about 42 "smokes," which, overshadowed by the great house of Dochfour, begun about 1838, has ended in their displacement, and the removal of old boundaries and landmarks to such an extent that a new carriage approach runs through the sites of the houses of Gortan-nan-gour. The beauty of Little Loch Ness was destroyed by a new road formed through it, necessitating the removal of a pretty little islet, and the public inconvenienced by having to use this new exposed road for nearly a mile, instead of the old sheltered avenued road. Further, rights-of-way through Dochnalurg, Gortan-nan-gour, and Dochgarroch, from the public road to the Hill of Caiplich were obliterated, and lost to the public. None living in Scotland, so far as I am aware, is responsible for these acts, yet it is right they should be held in remembrance, occurring as they did within sound of the church bells of Inverness.

Before parting with this portion of the parish I give a view, looking northwards, of Castle Spiritan ruins and garden. To the right at the top is part of the lands of Glac-na-madaidh of Borlum. The water to the right is the river, of old called Bona Narrows, that at the top is Little Loch Ness, and to the left the inlet of Abban. The water between the castle and garden was the moat, of which a portion to the left is yet distinguishable.

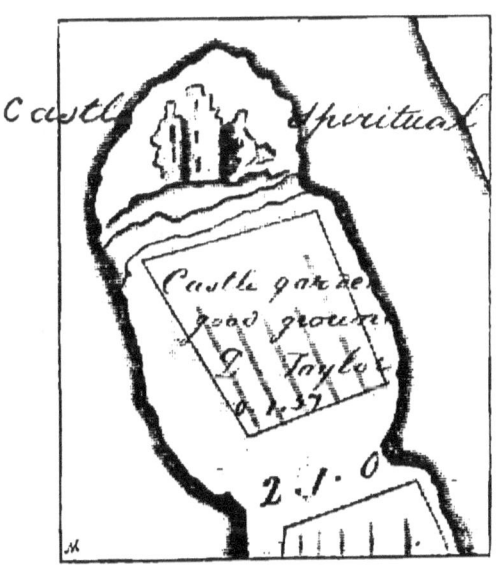

ABRIACHAN.

The lands of Abriachan extending to a davoch, or four ploughs, were gifted at an early period to the Bishopric of Moray, and consisted of two portions, Wester and Easter Abriachan, with the shielings of Corryfoness. The division doubtless was Loch Lait, and the burn of Abriachan, running out of the loch, falling into Loch Ness.

On the 6th December, 1334, John, Bishop of Moray, granted charter of a half davoch of his lands of Abriachan, described as lying between the barony of Bonach in the East, on the one side, and the barony of Urquhart on the West, to Sir Robert de Lauder, Knight, for payment of an annual feu of four merks Scots, together with other prestations. Sir Robert was Governor of the Castle of Urquhart, and the whole lands in the neighbourhood belonging to his successor having been resigned, Alexander, Bishop of Moray, of new granted the half davoch of Abriachan above referred to to Alexander Stewart, the Wolf of Badenoch, on 3rd February, 1386. The two Abriachans are lost sight of for about one hundred and fifty years, until 1544, when, described as lying within the barony of Kinmylies, and lordship of Spynie they are feued *inter alia* by the Bishop of Moray to Hugh Lord Lovat by charter dated 13th May, 1544. They remained with the Lovat family until 1647, when they were sold to Colonel Hugh Fraser of Kinnairies, whose son Alexander Fraser re-sold them to Ludovick Grant of Grant. The sale bears to be by Alexander Fraser (with consent of David Polson of Kinmylies), including all the rights of the said Alexander, of Katharine his spouse, of his deceased father, and brother, and Agnes and Christian, grandchildren of the deceased Colonel Hugh Fraser of Kinnairies, of the towns and lands of Easter Abriachan and Wester Abriachan, grazings and shielings thereof called Corryfoness, and Corriehulachie. Grant relieved Kinmylies, which was henceforward to be disunited from Abriachan, of 20 merks of the feu to superiors and 130 merks of minister's stipend. The deed of sale is dated the 11th of June, 1695.

The lands were in 1704 put under wadset for 10,000 merks to James and Alexander Fraser, elder and younger of Reelig, who conveyed the wadset in 1730 to Evan Baillie, younger son of Alexander Baillie, second of Dochfour, from whose representatives the wadset was redeemed by Sir James Grant of Grant, and the lands have since been in the actual possession of the family. From a fragmentary sketch, neither signed nor dated, an unknown writer refers to Sir James in these terms:—
"To his tenants Sir James was ever kind and at the commencement of this century, during the years of famine, he prevented many of them, especially the inhabitants of Glenurquhart, from emigrating to America. He not only reduced but in many instances discounted the rents altogether."

The extent of Abriachan to the West in Caiplich, and consequently the Parish of Bona, was greatly increased about 150 years ago. The right to cut peats in the Mount of Caiplich was the subject of much controversy between the owners and the Burgh of Inverness, which had by its charter of 1591 such right conferred on the inhabitants, and many acts of violence occurred. The Baillies of Dunain being nearest to Inverness suffered most, and the extent of muir attached to Dunain proper, was, further, of small extent, being confined to one shieling called Ruy-Sluggan. The Baillies maintained that the old Urquhart road was the march between the castle lands and Abriachan on the one hand, with Lentran, Newton, Reelig, Lovat, and Belladrum on the other, the proprietors of these estates concurring with Dunain. As a rule when properties lie in distinct watersheds the sky-line is the true boundary. As now determined, neither the watershed nor Urquhart road forms the march between Inverness and Bona parish and the parish of Kirkhill. In or about 1792 matters came to a crisis. Abriachan claimed the burn of Caiplich, which in its course becomes the burn of Moniack, as its West march, while the Lovat Trustees and Belladrum claimed the old road as their East march. Further, Colonel

John Baillie of Dunain and Sir James Grant differed as to the marches towards the West, behind Easter Abriachan and Dochnacraig. Various actions were raised, thereafter conjoined, and ultimately in 1795 an arbitration by Mr Adam Rolland, advocate, was agreed upon. Surveyors were appointed; the arbiter spent days on the ground; old witnesses were called up from all quarters, and eight years after taking up the business Mr Rolland in 1803 gave his decision. This was entirely in favour of Abriachan, on the ground mainly of more regular and actual possession of the subjects in dispute and the behaviour of one person. This was Mr Evan Baillie, writer in Inverness, long a confidential agent of Simon Lord Lovat, who acted for the Trustees and Commissioners after the forfeiture, and necessarily had much influence in the district. But Mr Baillie was wadsetter of Abriachan, and as early as 1751 had frightened the occupants, the tenants of Lovat and Belladrum, and obtained some kind of decree against them, the Crown Commissioners taking no interest in the matter. Nothing could be more dangerous for two conterminous proprietors than to have the same tenant of lands immediately adjoining, unless the marches were absolutely defined in writing or by plan. The decision of the arbiter as between Dochnacraig and Abriachan was absurd even for a lawyer. Colonel Baillie had the shieling of Treachorry in his titles, which is a small valley watered in its centre by the burn of the same name, and claimed the whole valley. Abriachan claimed one half, to the burn, with nothing to support but acts of occasional possession. The arbiter in one place distinctly discerns in favour of Colonel Baillie's contention, and in another place as distinctly decides that the burn of Treachorry is to be the march. This left matters as they were, and Colonel Baillie having died pending the reference, while up to 1869 the estate of Dunain was under curatory, the question remained in abeyance. It was finally settled in 1871 between the representatives of the Earl of Seafield and Sir John Ramsden by mutual concession and an agreement to plant on either side of the march, here bleak, exposed, and much wanting ornamentation. This decision and work I look back upon with pleasure, with this drawback, that the last time I was in the Caiplich the plantation on Treachorry seemed much inferior to those on Renudin of Abriachan.

There was a track, almost impassable for carts, along the loch side when it reached the Ault Dearg. Consequently, as the great bulk of the houses in Abriachan are situated well up the hill, and some, such as Balnagriasaichean, Tomcon, etc., actually to the West of the old Urquhart road, the people with loads as a rule travelled to Inverness by the old road, descending at first by the Leachkin and latterly by the Lagnalien connection. As matters now stand, the loch-side road is an excellent one. There is the great convenience of a pier, where the steamers regularly call, but the ascent from the loch is very severe.

In no part of the Highlands was smuggling carried on with greater vigour than in Abriachan, which from the fine water, its unapproachableness in some parts, its natural hiding places in others, rendered the pursuit of the business a secure one.

The modern tombstones at Killionan contrast most unfavourably with the few unique, ancient memorials; and with regard to the great stone adjacent and the time-honoured tradition that water never fails in its cup, it is to be feared that it must be set down as a myth.

V.—PARISH OF DORES.

ITS OLD POSSESSORS AND DIVISIONS.

THE whole of this parish, formerly called Durris, was included in the grant of the Earldom of Moray to Sir Thomas Randolph and, probably forming a Barony, continued in great part with the family until the forfeiture and death of Archibald Douglas, who had married the heiress of the Dunbars. Prior to this period, 1454, no subsidiary grant, except that to Lovat of the barony of Stratherrick, which lay partly in Dores and partly in Boleskine, has been noted. The widowed Countess of Moray lived to a great age, and her brother, Sir Alexander Dunbar of Westfield, hereditary Sheriff of Moray, whom some consider to have been properly heir, received in 1468, *inter alia*, a large part of the parish thereafter styled the barony of Durris. Sir Alexander Dunbar gave Durris to his fifth son David, who was succeeded by Alexander, and he in turn by Robert, father of David Dunbar, who was proprietor of Durris in 1569. David was succeeded by Mark Dunbar, who in 1608, with consent of Ninian Dunbar his son, sold parts of the barony of Durris, and specially Lopan, Balblair, Drummond, Little Ballichernoch, and Tirchurachan to Sir John Campbell of Calder.

The Mackintoshes had their eye upon Durris as far back as 1492, but a promising agreement then entered into between the Dunbars and Mackintoshes fell to the ground.

Another part of the parish was granted in 1507 to Alexander Ogilvie, styled of Far, by whom it was incorporated into the barony of Cardale. Alexander Ogilvie was succeeded by his son, James Ogilvie, whose title, made up in 1534, was confirmed in 1557. James Ogilvie sold his part of Durris to the Regent Moray, whose grandson, James Earl of Moray, disponed Borlum, Cullairds and Kinchyle to

Calder on 31st October, 1608. Calder also acquired the Church lands of Dores, including Daars and others from the then lay holder of the Priory lands of Urquhart. Calder thus became proprietor of all the lands of Dores fronting Loch Ness and the river Ness, from Holme to Inverfarigaig, with the exception of Erchitt and Meikle Ballichernoch, acquired by the Lovats under a title different from the barony of Stratherrick.

A third portion of Dores, consisting of Bunachton, the three Duntelchaigs, and Bochrubin, were included in the grant of the Castle lands to the Earl of Huntly.

The remainder of the parish belonged to Lovat. It may be said that in 1610 the whole parish belonged to Calder and Lord Lovat, with the exception of Bunachton, belonging to the Marquis of Huntly, and the Duntelchaigs and Bochrubin, acquired in 1568 by the Mackintoshes in part assythment for the murder of William Mackintosh of Mackintosh by Huntly in 1550. Feuing on the part of Calder proceeded rapidly, chiefly with the Clan Chattan. In 1610, William Mackintosh, second son of Lachlan Mor Mackintosh of Mackintosh, feued Borlum ; and in the same year Angus Macphail vic Phoil vic Gillies Macbean feued Kinchyle and, in 1614, the Church lands of Daars and others. Alexander Mackintosh, son of Kellachie, feued Aldourie, including Balblair and Drummond. Alexander Mackintosh of the Kellachie family feued one half of Holme within the parish of Inverness ; Kellachie feued Dalmigavie ; and Dunmaglass was feued by Ferquhar vic Allister. All these grants flowed from Calder, so that the influence of the Clan Chattan in the parishes of Inverness, Dores, Dunlichity and Dalarossie, practically at one and the same period, was greatly extended. The Frasers also flourished in Dores, Farraline, Balnain, Gortuleg, Leadclune, Errogie, and others starting up—good shoots of active frame and warlike spirit.

The new road formed by General Wade from Inverness to Fort-Augustus opened up Strath Dores greatly. The old road for wheel traffic stopped at Milton of Holme, the main road to the West and South going by Drummond Brae, of old the Gaick Roy, and thence until it divided, one road going by Essich and Achnabat—"Rathadan-Druim;" and the other by Torbreck, passing by the front of the old house. This was found very inconvenient, and Alexander Fraser of Torbreck, whom Bishop Forbes, a frequent guest, styles "honest Phopachie," made the present divergence, starting at the entry of the avenue, and joining the old road, behind the present Torbreck house. Thence the road passed through the woods, emerging at Cullairds, and from thence to Scaniport. At Scaniport the road again divided; one led to the Castle of Borlum, and from thence through the woods of Ballindarroch to Bona Ferry, and from thence past the house of Aldourie, until it came to the Church of Dores; the other road kept the valley, passing by Balnafroig, the house of Kinchyle, Antfield, and Daars, to the Church, where it met with the other road, above mentioned, by Borlum, Bona, and Aldourie. The present road is much shorter, but has the inconvenience of a sharp rise beyond Milton. Another after leaving Scaniport went with a more rapid descent by the Crask of Durris to Alt Duarak.

The parish of Dores has gained a small portion of land at the expense of the parish of Inverness, beyond Milton of Holme. Between the Dores Road and the River Ness there is a pendicle of land, called of old "Easter Dowinsche," now the property of Mr C. Walker of Ness Castle. The original charter describes the land as "that piece of waste land of Easter Dowinsche, a part and pertinent of the lands of Torbreck lying within the castle lands of Inverness," and it is well-known that Torbreck lies within the parish of Inverness. Why the Dunain family did not take possession of it cannot be accounted for, but it is clear they did not, and in 1523 it would seem as if it were vacant. William Mackintosh of Borlum had, as above stated, feued Borlum and Cullairds from Calder in 1610, his North march at the river being "Wester Dowinsche." By charter dated at Inverness, 30th April, 1623, George Earl of Enzie, feued the lands described as above to Borlum, the feu being 3s 4d Scots, on the narrative that Borlum had paid a price, and the lands were convenient to Wester Dowinsche belonging to him. Infeftment followed on the 24th of June, 1627, one of his witnesses being William Vic Angus Vic Phoil in Kinchyle, and another Borlum's son, Robert Mackintosh.

Probably because all Borlum's lands, with this small exception, lay in Dores, it came in course of time to be held and considered as part of that parish. Thus instead of the march between the two parishes being as now from a point where a dyke running westward towards the river joins the present Dores road, then follows the road in a northerly direction until the lands of Milltown are met, when the westerly direction towards the river is resumed, the old and real boundary between Inverness and Dores at this point is by superintending and continuing the dyke before referred to straight to the river.

The handsome trees on Dowinsche, the beginning of the fine garden, and of the cottage, afterwards burnt about the year 1837, were all laid down by Mr John Young of the "Inverness Journal," under a lease which inadequately protected his great expenditure. Mr Young was removed and complained with reason of his harsh treatment by the then owner.

There is a fine Druidical circle in a wood a little to the left of the Dores road beyond Scaniport, and before the road to Ballindarroch is reached. It was by the Dores road that Dr Johnson travelled in 1773 from Inverness to the West coast, and it is recorded that Boswell and he halted to examine this circle.

THE MACBEANS OF KINCHYLE.

According to Shaw the first of the Macbeans of Kinchyle, by origin a Macgillonie, came from Lochaber with Eva, the heiress of Clan Chattan, and settled near Inverness. According to the Mackintosh History in the time of Angus, sixth of Mackintosh, "Bean Vic Coil Mor (of whom the Clan Vean had their denomination) lived in Lochaber, and was a faithful servant to Mackintosh against the Red Cumming who possessed Inverlochie and at that time was a professed enemy of Mackintosh;" and again in the time of the next Mackintosh it is said that "Mulmoire or Myles Vic Bean Vic Coil Mor, and his four sons Paul, Gillies, Myles, and Ferquhar, after they had slain the Red Cumming's steward, and his two servants Paten and Kissen, came to William Mackintosh, seventh of Mackintosh, in Connage in Pettie, where he then dwelt, and for themselves and their posterity took protection and dependence of him and his as their chief." This would have been about 1334, and establishes the Macbeans as one of the oldest branches of the historic Clan Chattan. The Clan Vean suffered severely, it is said, at the battle of Harlaw. There is no authentic deduction however until 1500, when Gillies Macbean may have lived, succeeded by William, he by Paul, and he by Angus in 1609, when we arrive on firm historical ground. In 1609

I. ANGUS MACBEAN, for himself and his race, signed the Bond of Union amongst the Clan Chattan. There were three other heritors in the county of the name, at Faillie, Tomatin, and Drummond, but all writers who treat of the matter place Kinchyle at the head of the tribe.

Campbell of Calder had only acquired the lands of Kinchyle on 31st October, 1608, yet as early as April, 1609, he is found contracting with Angus Macbean for a feu. By feu contract dated at Auldearn, 18th May, 1610, Sir John Campbell of Calder feus Kinchyle to Angus vic Phail vic William vic Gillies, described as "in Kinchyle," the feu duty being £10 Scots, and with power to Angus to build a miln, and other privileges, one of the witnesses being William Mackintosh of Benchar, afterwards of Borlum, and another, Alexander Campbell, brother-german to Calder. Infeftment duly followed upon the feu charter. By another feu charter Calder feued to Angus Macbean styled "of Kinchyle" the church lands of Durris, called Daars, and others lying within the barony and regality of Urquhart (in Moray) and Sheriffdom of

Inverness. The feu was fixed at £6 2s Scots and the charter, dated at Calder 26th May, 1614, was followed by infeftment. Upon 27th May, 1626, having lent the Earl of Enzie two thousand merks, the Earl gave a wadset of the half davoch land of old extent of Bunachton to Angus vic Phail of Kinchyle. Upon the 10th of November, 1631, Angus of Kinchyle with consent of his eldest son, John, entered into an adjustment of marches with his neighbour to the South, Alexander Mackintosh of Aldourie. The transaction was entirely for the benefit of Aldourie, whose house was so close to the burn of Alt Dourak (the march), that when the burn was in spate the house was endangered, and Aldourie desired to cut a new and straight channel a little to the North and further away from his house. Kinchyle, who had but a trifle of frontage to Loch Ness, lying between the above burn and Borlum's lands at Bona, agreed to Aldourie's request, and got in exchange a deal of hill land by Loch Ashie. Angus Macbean was succeeded by his eldest son,

II. JOHN, who did not make up a title to the estates. He had a brother named William, found in 1627. John was succeeded by his son,

III. PAUL, who on 11th May, 1664, received a precept of Clare Constat from Sir Hugh Campbell of Calder, for infefting him as heir of his grandfather Angus, dated at Invermoriston. It would appear that Calder and Glenmoriston were great friends, for in a letter by John Forbes second of Culloden to Calder, dated in August, 1664, Culloden begs of Calder to use his influence to settle the serious differences between Inshes and Glenmoriston. Upon this precept Paul Macbean was infeft, but he seems to have fallen into such great difficulties that he had to resign all the lands into the superior's hands, on the narrative of his embarassments, by deed dated 10th of April, 1685. Upon a long preamble of the prior state of possession, Sir Hugh Campbell of Calder feued out the whole lands to "William Macbean in Kinchyle" (who raised money to pay off the old debts), by charter dated 25th November, 1685. The old feu, it will be noticed, was £10 Scots for Kinchyle and £6 2s for the Church lands, but in the charter of 1685 the total feu is a single sum of £20 Scots. Infeftment followed upon the charter on 19th June, 1686. Among the witnesses were William Mackintosh, son of Donald Mackintosh of Kellachie and also of Aldourie, Angus Macbean, writer in Inverness, and Lachlan Macbean, brother-german to William Macbean. There was also another brother, the well-known Mr Angus Macbean, minister of Inverness. Paul Macbean of Kinchyle, is one of the 28 signatories to the bond by the minor heads of the Clan Chattan to Mackintosh as their chief, dated at Kincairne the 19th November, 1664. This bond has the signatures of John Macpherson of Invereshie, and John Macpherson of Pitmean, the respective heads of the important houses known as Sliochd Gillies vic Ewen, and Sliochd Iain vic Ewen.

The propinquity of William Macbean to Paul is not stated by Calder, but there is no doubt they were father and son, for in 1692 William is found styled "younger of Kinchyle," though he had purchased the lands as above mentioned in 1685. The latest date in which I observed Paul's name was in 1691.

The Kinchyles and Borlums at first were great allies as well as neighbours. It has been observed that the first Borlum was witness to the first charter to Kinchyle, and when Borlum was first infeft in 1610, Angus Macbean of Kinchyle acted as his Procurator at the taking of infeftment. William the third Borlum and Paul the third Kinchyle fell out greatly, however, about their marches and the right of casting peats, and the matter on one occasion was settled by the sword at considerable loss to both parties. The fight took place at Tom-na-miol-choin, or the Greyhound's hillock, on the borders of Keanpoul and Easter Kinchyle.

IV. WILLIAM married, contract dated 23rd December, 1688, Jean, second daughter of Donald Mackintosh of Kellachie, who was also proprietor of Aldourie, which he sold to his son-in-law, John Barbour, and by her he had at least two sons, Eneas or Angus and Gillies. The Farr Collections bear that Jean Macbean was grandmother of the first Charles Grant, and that "the Macdonalds of Dalness are of the Macbeans of Kinchyle." William was succeeded by his eldest son,

V. ENEAS, who in 1711 married Isobel, eldest daughter of Roderick Mackenzie of Redcastle, whose tocher was 5000 merks. No contract was entered into prior to the marriage, and the defect was remedied by a post nuptial contract between the parties dated 9th and 10th January, 1718. From its terms there would appear to have been "a Catholic debt" of ten thousand merks upon Kinchyle, then standing in name of John Barbour of Aldourie, and the lady's tocher was to be imputed in part payment of this debt. Borlum had lent old Kinchyle 2000 merks in 1708 ; and Mackintosh of Culclachy 5000 merks to William and Eneas Macbean in 1718. Among the stipulations in the contract was one that if Isobel Mackenzie survived her husband, she had right to stay at the mansion house.

VI. GILLIES, who was one of the witnesses to his brother's post nuptial marriage contract in 1718. I find him described as "in Bunachton," and latterly "in Dalmagerry," but not at any time either "at or of Kinchyle." Gillies was a man of great note and strength, and was appointed Major of the Clan Chattan Regiment in 1745. He greatly distinguished himself at Culloden. Lord Archibald Campbell, in his recent work, "Notes on Swords from the Battlefield of Culloden," does Kinchyle full justice, but makes a woful hash of his name. "What men could do in the days of Culloden is well illustrated, and can be judged from the following. *Gillie* Mac Bean, perceiving the Campbells had thrown down a wall and were attacking the Highland army in flank, placed himself opposite the breach formed, and killed fourteen men before he himself fell leaving an undying name for heroism." In the Farr Collections, it is said that Major Gillies Macbean was killed at the first dyke west from the field. He married one of the Misses Macpherson of Lonnie in Petty, and was succeeded by his son,

VII. DONALD, a minor. In 1750 the estate was in the hands of creditors, and a process of judicial sale at the instance of William Macgillivray of Dunmaglass and Hugh Fraser of Bochrubin was instituted. Donald Macbean was afraid to serve heir, and an attempt to make up a title by Trust Bond and adjudication in favour of Lieutenant Alexander Macbean, sometime of the Regiment of Foot commanded by Lord John Murray, a cousin of Donald's, failed. A few years later, when General Simon Fraser of Lovat was raising his first regiment, Donald Macbean was appointed Lieutenant, and on the narrative that he was ordered abroad, Lieutenant Donald granted on the 5th of April, 1757, a commission to William Macbean, Attorney at Law, London, and Captain Lieutenant Forbes Macbean of the Royal Artillery, sons of the late Rev. Alexander Macbean of Inverness, Evan and Donald Macbean, writers in Inverness, and Robert Macpherson tacksman of Lonnie, his uncle, to manage his affairs. Donald was served heir to his uncle Eneas, on the 16th October, 1759, describing himself as eldest son of Gillies Macbean, sometime tacksman of Dalmagarry, second lawful son of William Macbean of Kinchyle. A charter by Pryse Campbell, younger of Calder, was granted on the 14th January, 1760, and the commissioners sold the estates to Simon Fraser, sometime commissary at Gibraltar, for £2200 sterling, with entry at Whitsunday, 1760. Donald Macbean retired from the army, and, described as "late Captain of the 10th Foot," married Anne, second daughter of James Mackintosh, commonly described as of Wood End, grandfather of Sir James Mackintosh of Kellachie. Captain and Mrs Macbean are found in 1780 living at Teary, near Forres, the last of the Macbeans of Kinchyle who possessed that property. The distinguished military race of "Forbes Macbeans," now in the third generation, descended from the Rev. Alexander Macbean, of Inverness, are cadets of Kinchyle, if not the representatives of the family.

The old mansion family house was a ruin in 1791, but had some fine old trees about it, alas removed by an incoming tenant. Simon Fraser the proprietor, writes under date of 10th December in that year from London—" I was exceedingly angry at finding the fine trees round the old ruins of Kinchyle House cut down."

The modern mansion is pleasantly situated, and to the late Mr Alexander Burnett is, I believe, due the planting so judiciously of the clumps of larch, which now give the place so much shelter and adornment.

PRESENT AND PAST POPULATION OF THE PARISH.

Dores is a pretty and fertile parish, and at one time contained a large population. It has been dwindling for many years, and poor rates have been much in excess of the average. Any one may take up the Valuation Roll for the year ending Whitsunday, 1894, and see for himself how few tenants are on the larger estates. I will take Borlum as my text, not including Kinchyle. The Mackintoshes parted with Borlum at Whitsunday, 1759, and however unfortunate and thriftless themselves, they were not evictors. A judicial rental was taken by the purchaser on 20th October, 1759, when it was found that there were the following tenants. I need not give their rents, but may observe that in most cases they were instantly and largely increased—as, for instance, the Mains from 44 bolls and 132 merks to 60 bolls and 202 merks. In the Mains of Borlum—Robert Maclean, with sub-tenants William Fraser, Angus Macbean, William Noble, Malcolm Mackenzie, John Macdonald, and Alexander Maclean. Alexander Maclean was son of Dochgarroch and father of Robert, and is described as at Ach-a-Chaisteal of Borlum—in all in the Mains 7 heads of families. Nether Cullairds—Alexander Mactavish; Upper Cullairds—Donald Maclean and James Yeaman; Knockfrangaich—Alexander Macdonald and William Mackinnon; Midtown—William McWillie and Donald Clark; Balroick of Oldtown—William Macbean; Oldtown—Thomas Fraser; Scaniport—William and Angus

Mackintosh; Laggan — Andrew Forbes; Druiminure—
Angus Macdonald; Dowinische or Milltown of Borlum
—William Gordon, corn and waulk miller; Ballindarroch—
John Mackintosh; Bona—John Maclennan, in all 23 tenants.
Crofters, 1st, in and about Bona, Donald Matheson, John
Mackay, Sween Macqueen, ferryman, Neil Cameron, and
Mary Macdonald or Maclennan; and 2nd, in the Hill in
Feabuie four crofters, whose names seemed not worth
mentioning, or that of 9 crofters and mailers, the gross total
being 32 heads of families, or say 150 to 200 souls.

The following list is highly instructive. By the Act
38, George III., Chapter 27th, a return was ordered of
all the men between 15 and 60, such was the pressure
for soldiers. At Scaniport on 26th May, 1798, the estate
representative, and Captain Thomas Fraser, of the Leadclune family, late of the 78th, Justice of the Peace, then
tenant of the Mains of Borlum, made a return for Borlum
of those fit to carry arms or act as drivers. Mains of
Ness Castle—Captain Thomas Fraser, Donald Falconer,
John Macbean, James Mackintosh, Malcolm Macbean,
arms, Andrew Macpherson, cart driver—in all, 6; Ballindarroch—Francis Macbean, John Macdonald, Alexander
Macdonald, all arms, 3; Scaniport—Donald Urquhart,
Duncan Fraser, James Sween, William Chisholm, Donald
Macbean, William Rose, arms; Alexander Urquhart, cattle
driver—in all, 7; Laggan—John Macdonald, George Fraser
—both arms, 2; Milltown—John Dunbar—arms, 1; Lower
Cullaird—John Mackintosh, Lachlan Macqueen, Alexander
Macqueen—all arms, 3; Upper Cullaird—John Rose,
Donald Grant, cattle drivers; John Fraser, William Grant,
arms—in all 4; Knockfrangaich—Andrew Macgillivray,
arms, 1; Balmeanach—William Falconer, Alexander Mac-
gillivray, arms, Donald Mackenzie, cattle driver—in all, 3;
Tominteomar—Donald Macdonald, arms, 1; Balnaroig—
William Macbean, Alexander Fraser, James Fraser, Robert
Fraser, Angus Macbean, arms, John Macbean, James
Fraser, John Fraser, cattle drivers —8 in all; Bona—Thomas
Wilson, Robert Fraser, arms, David Sween, pioneer—3 in

all; Hill—John Fraser, Donald Fraser, John Mac Omie, Alexander Mac Omie, William Macgillivray, arms—6. Total arms, 38. Drivers, etc., 9. "Memorandum. The estate commands three roads of communication between the East and West sea, has encampment grounds to any extent, and abounds with material for erecting field fortifications for offence or defence, particularly Fascines, Hurdles, Gabions, and Epaulment Frames, etc."

The church manse and churchyard of Dores are pleasantly situated, with beautiful surroundings. An examination of the churchyard shows how predominating was the name of Macbean. The parish has given birth to many eminent men—the first Charles Grant and Sir James Mackintosh, at Aldourie; the well-known family of Gortuleg, in whose old house Prince Charles rested after his flight from Culloden; Brigadier-General Simon Fraser, who fell at Saratoga, and many others.

A STIRRING RUNAWAY ROMANCE.

In connection with Bona and the inn kept by the Mac-lennan family a bit of romance may be narrated. Some time before the close of the last century several Macphersons who had been dispossessed in Badenoch came to Boleskine Parish, and amongst others Lieutenant Evan Macpherson of the Ovie family took Cullachy. Mr Alexander Macpherson, writer, who had been deprived of his office of Procurator-Fiscal went to Faicham of Glengarry. He was a son of Bailie Donald Macpherson senior, of Inverness, who died at Drumgalvie in the parish of Kingussie in the month of January 1802 aged 77, and who had fought for Prince Charles in his youth. The two Macphersons, who were nearly connected, were close allies and both impecunious. The well-known and respected messenger-at-arms, John Mackay at Innis-na-cardoch, was entrusted with a caption against the gallant officer. Escape, whether from an officer or from prison entailed responsibility for the debt, and Mr Mackay was a responsible man. From his own story, it would appear that Mackay, upon the instructions of Alexander Stewart, writer in Edinburgh, did

"Upon the 20th day of March, 1795, by virtue of letters of caption dated and signeted the 24th day of December, 1793, raised at the instance of John Archibald, and William Duff, children of the deceased Major Alexander Duff, late of the 89th Regiment of Foot, and Robert Donaldson, writer to the Signet, their curator, against Lieutenant Evan Macpherson, late of the 16th Regiment of Foot, and others therein named and designed for not making payment to the said complainers of the principal sum of £1000 sterling, £200 like money of liquidate or penalty incurred through failure, and the legal interest of said principal sum from and since the 11th of November, 1792, all contained in and due by the Bond therein narrated, bearing date the 21st and 22nd days of November, 1791, and payable against the term of Whitsunday then next to come, he, John Mackay, messenger-at-arms, passed to the dwelling-house of Thomas Clark, vintner, at Fort-Augustus, having and holding in my hands the said letters of caption, with my blazon displayed on my breast, in His Majesty's name and authority, I lawfully apprehended him the said Lieutenant Evan Macpherson my prisoner, by touching him on the shoulder with my wand of peace, and required him to obey the said letters and go along with me as a prisoner, which apprehending the said Lieutenant Evan Macpherson received with the greatest satisfaction and pleasure, and told me that it was nothing but what he looked for and that it was the only thing that detained him so long in the country so as to give every manner of satisfaction to his creditors, and added that he was very sorry they should have put themselves to any expense by employing a messenger because he would go to jail at the desire of any single creditor, and that he wished they had ordered him to jail earlier. I hired a boat and hands to bring us to Bona at Lochend, and a little before eight o'clock we set sail and arrived at Bona foresaid about one o'clock next morning, when we sat up warming ourselves till after two o'clock of said morning, when the said Lieutenant Evan Macpherson had occasion to go to the door, and of his own accord called my servant along with him, and returning both in the course of a few minutes, but while the said Lieutenant Evan Macpherson was out, his genteel behaviour was remarked and spoken of by the boatmen and several other passengers then present, setting forth that his learning and education afforded him the knowledge of the laws of his country and made him submissive thereto. This genteel behaviour, together with the calm resignation to which he appeared from the time I apprehended him, and Mrs Macpherson expressing herself in a similar manner, made me satisfied in my own mind that even should I grant him a Parole of Honour that he would deliver himself in jail. About half-past two o'clock of the morning foresaid, he the said Lieutenant Evan Macpherson and I went both to the said bed, putting off our coats and shoes only. From the circumstances above expressed I thought it very unnecessary to order a guard upon the door. He soon fell sound asleep, and in a short time thereafter I also fell asleep. About half-past three o'clock of said morning he got out of bed and made his escape to the thicket of oak wood which is quite close to the house in which we slept. I immediately pursued after him, and made every search that I thought might be of service; but all in vain, as he had some miles of wood on every side."

Mackay says that it was not easy to describe his feelings on this occasion, or the unhappy and distressed state into which this conduct of Lieutenant Macpherson threw him. He was led from motives of humanity to treat him with a degree of lenity which, though upon similar occasions he had shown to persons he considered less worthy to be entrusted, where honour and character were at stake, he had never any reason to repent. The apparent composure of Lieutenant Macpherson, and the implicit resignation to his fate which he evinced, with the conduct of his wife and his other friends, satisfied him that he had no danger to fear; and he must indeed have had more than human foresight upon whom the artful design and duplicity of his conduct from the time of his apprehension until he effected his escape would not have imposed in some degree.

The messenger used every exertion to retake the fugitive. For that purpose he engaged every man he could trust for fifty miles around him, and offered very high rewards for success. He laid people in wait upon all the avenues he suspected, and he himself along with a strong party traversed night and day the country from Inverness to Fort-William, but to no purpose. All his efforts were unsuccessful, nor could he possibly obtain the least information as to Lieutenant Macpherson's course. By this time it was intimated that some of his creditors and their commissioners had expressed it as their opinion that Mackay had made himself and his cautioners liable in the debt upon the diligence on which Lieutenant Macpherson was apprehended. Though no circumstance could occur which could increase his distress or add to the exertion which Mackay made to remedy his misfortune, it could not but affect him that a conduct should be imputed to him which those acquainted with him knew he was incapable of. Writing to a messenger in Elgin, he says under date 6th April, 1795—

"This infamous rascal is a Lieutenant in the 100th Regiment, namely the Marquis of Huntly's, a detachment of which is now lying in Fort-George waiting transports to bring them to Gibraltar, and the transports is daily expected there, but to guard this post there is a messenger employed at Inverness, but my dread is that he will attempt to get on board from Garmouth or some other place upon that coast, but your plan will be to get yourself informed if he is about Gordon Castle, or perhaps about Mr Tod, the factor's, and the only method of securing this plan is to find out the day the transports sets off, and guard the coast, that is to say if you cannot procure information otherwise."

Not being able to procure any intelligence of Macpherson in the North, Mackay suspected that he might have formed a plan of leaving the country entirely. Impressed with this opinion, he set out with an intention of going to London, and if necessary to follow him to Gibraltar, where his regiment lay, or to any other part of the world he could trace him to, determined that he would rescue himself from every reflection at the hands of his employers by lodging the fugitive in jail or perish in the attempt. In prosecution of this intention Mackay arrived in Edinburgh on the 13th of April, without obtaining any account whatever of Lieutenant Macpherson, and while he was preparing advertisements for the newspapers describing the runaway and offering very large rewards for leading to his discovery, and providing himself with the necessary warrants and information to take with him to London, he discovered and apprehended him in the Abbey of Holyrood House, and immediately lodged him in Edinburgh Jail, having been advised that the

Sanctuary could afford him no protection, having been before legally made prisoner, as stated in the execution above set forth.

Macpherson's creditors were satisfied that Mackay had done his duty, but being themselves heavy sufferers they were unable to reimburse him for his great outlay. His conduct to Mackay was shabby while of no use to himself, for being lawfully apprehended the Abbey was no Sanctuary, and he could have been brought back even from Gibraltar. One or two curious incidents in Mr Mackay's eventful career will be given later on under Fort-Augustus in the combined Parishes of Boleskine and Abertarff.

VI—PARISH OF BOLESKINE AND ABERTARFF.

THE ORIGIN OF FORT-AUGUSTUS.

UPON the appointment towards the close of last century of George Brodie as Governor of Fort-Augustus, he took steps to reclaim the properties of the villagers who had been encouraged to settle in the neighbourhood of the Fort. This was highly resented and ended in litigation. Governor Brodie's pleas were rejected. The history of extra mural Fort-Augustus prior to 1799 will, I think, be found interesting although houses and owners have much changed.

The fort of Fort-Augustus was originally built in the beginning of the 18th century and was afterwards rebuilt at the Rising of 1745. It was very small and insignificant at first and from its situation was evidently intended not so much for a place of strength which could resist the regular attack of an enemy as a convenient station for the accommodation of troops in marching from the East to the West coast. Another object Government had in view in erecting Fort-Augustus was the civilization, according to their views, of that part of the Highlands. These different objects it is evident would be materially assisted by the erection of a village near the Fort; and accordingly, here, as in many other parts of the Highlands, Government gave great encouragement to the inhabitants in the neighbourhood to come near the Fort and form a village.

With this view Government about the year 1715 purchased from the family of Lovat a piece of barren waste ground contiguous to the Fort. The boundaries of this purchase were up to 1799 perfectly known and easily distinguished from the ground which the Government originally possessed and on which they built the Fort.

This new purchase being destined for a village, every encouragement was given by the different Governors of Fort-Augustus to the inhabitants of the county to come and settle on it by building houses and making gardens. The plan succeeded; a very considerable village came to be erected, beneficial to the country around and of peculiar importance to the fort and garrison of Fort-Augustus by the accommodation it was always capable of affording to His Majesty's troops.

The value of this piece of barren heath purchased by Government was so exceedingly small that when it came to be portioned out into small lots for building on by the Governors of Fort-Augustus in fulfilment of the intentions of the Government, no written title was given to the inhabitants that came to settle on that piece of land and to form the village. The whole value of none of the lots was worth the expense of a disposition and sasine, titles which the inhabitants, when the village was first begun, could neither read nor be made to understand.

Whether anything was originally exacted by way of feu duty or ground rent is unknown, but it is certain that in process of time when the village began to progress the Governors bargained for a feu-duty, which seldom exceeded 5s per annum for each lot, and which feu duties the Governor for the time being was allowed to draw and retain to himself in addition to his pay as Governor.

On the faith of this agreement on the part of Government the inhabitants made their gardens and built houses, and when at any time the demands of Government rendered it expedient to acquire the possession of any of the village property, which sometimes happened, then a fair and equitable price was paid by the authorities to the village proprietor for what was taken from him. So universally was this good faith attended to that in the whole history of the village there did not occur a single instance where the inhabitants were disturbed in the peaceable possession of their property by the Governors, who on the contrary uniformly gave every encouragement in their power to new settlers coming to build on the Government ground. The inhabitants were taught to believe that the right to their houses and gardens were indubitable, although they had no written title flowing from Government, and ever since the erection of the village they had been allowed without any interruption to transmit their village property to their children and dispose of it at pleasure to third parties for a fair and equitable price.

So much for the general custom. I now propose to deal with an individual case, that of Mr John Mackay, messenger-at-arms, whose acquaintance the reader has already made, and who will be again referred to later on. Trusting to the inveterate practice of the village for near a century, Mr Mackay was induced to make purchases and to acquire property in the village of Fort-Augustus. One of the subjects acquired by him was possessed in 1748 by Mr Dallas, as schoolmaster. Dallas sold the house to Andrew Stark. Stark sold it to Alexander Chisholm, and Chisholm conveyed it to Donald Macdonald at Cairngoddy, a farmer living some miles from Fort-Augustus. This Macdonald again sold the house to the mother of the pursuer. The conveyance proceeds on the narrative that " I, Donald Grant, residing in Aberchalder (which is four miles distant from the village), heritable proprietor of the house and yard after mentioned, for a certain sum of money instantly advanced and paid to me by John Mackay, messenger in Fort-Augustus, as the agreed price and worth thereof, the receipt of which I hereby acknowledge therefor, etc."

After acquiring it in this manner, Mr Mackay improved it at considerable expense, and when the Society's school was withdrawn from Fort-Augustus he converted it into a schoolhouse, for which he secured an adequate rent. Mr Mackay's own house, though not within the bounds of the village of Fort-Augustus or upon the Government ground, was yet within ten yards of the schoolhouse, and the education of his children at a school so near and convenient for them was a powerful motive for his letting it to the village schoolmaster.

Mr Mackay acquired another possession in the village at the end of his own house, and just within the march of the piece of land that had been purchased from Lovat by Government for erecting a village. This second property was, about thirty years before, possessed by Donald Macdonald. From him it was purchased by the late Governor Trapaud, from whom Mr Mackay acquired it. But the subject being then in bad repair, Mr Mackay rebuilt and converted it into a peat barn, on account of its contiguity to his own dwelling-house, and in that manner it had been possessed by him for nine or ten years. The garden and crofts which were attached to these houses were used and occupied from time to time by him as his conveniency required.

Mr Mackay and other two villagers, viz., Thomas Clarke, innkeeper, and Donald Grant, King's mason, erected a kiln for drying corn, etc., in the village. This was for the convenience of the surrounding country, and the late Governor Trapaud not only encouraged the undertaking but also agreed to contribute a sum of money towards the expense, though his death soon after prevented the fulfilment of that intention. So the whole expense was defrayed by the three men named.

Mr Mackay possessed these three properties within the village in 1797, when the then Lieutenant-Governor of Fort-Augustus was appointed to succeed Governor Trapaud. Being a stranger in that part of the country and particularly to the practice, customs, and privileges of the villagers, and being misinformed as to the particulars by interested persons, the Governor was induced to suppose that as the whole houses and gardens of the inhabitants of the village had been erected and laid out on the Government ground; and as Government had never granted any disposition or written conveyance for these lots of land to any of the inhabitants, the ground and all the buildings upon it must still be held to be the property of the Crown, and that the inhabitants might be removed from their possessions by the Governor of Fort-Augustus without any remuneration or recompense whatever for the sums which, trusting to the good faith and encouragement given them by Government, they had expended on their possessions.

The Governor was pleased to try the experiment with Mr Mackay, and for this purpose commenced an action of removing against him before the Sheriff of Inverness, to remove from the three properties he had acquired in the village by the progress already described, and from the land occupied by him.

Mr Mackay did not wish to enter into an expensive litigation in opposing the removing, because the Governor might say he wanted the property for the uses of the garrison, and when that was the case it had always been the practice of the inhabitants to give up their property on being fairly indemnified for the loss. On this account Mr Mackay gave no opposition to the removing but he insisted that upon being removed he was entitled to the value of the subjects from the Governor, and for that purpose brought a counter action against that Officer concluding for the appraised value of the houses, dykes, and improvements. Against this action the Governor pleaded that neither the pursuer or any of the villagers had right to the value of their houses, as they had no charter from the Crown but paid rent for their possessions to the Governor, and that he was not bound by the transactions of the late Governor or his predecessors. The Governor likewise gave in a separate paper stating that it escaped him in his defences to mention that Mr Mackay was at "full liberty to carry off the Government ground the materials of the houses or huts except in so far as it may appear that the few stones used in the building these huts on Government property being as is supposed found upon the Government ground." To these defences, answers were lodged in which Mr Mackay stated the practice of the village and the encouragement that had been uniformly held out by the different Governors on the part of the Government to the inhabitants settling and building in the village, and he further stated that it was the uniform practice, as should be afterwards shown, for the Governors to pay for any of the houses they might have occasion to take from the inhabitants for the uses of the garrison.

The Governor, aware of the force of this inveterate practice on the part of the preceding Governors, with which it was understood he had been but little if at all acquainted, betook himself to a specialty in the case, and maintained that Mr Mackay at that time living and having his dwelling house without the Government ground, though within a few yards of it, was not entitled to any of the privileges of a villager. On advising the case the Sheriff pronounced the following interlocutor :—

"19th April, 1790, The Sheriff-Depute having considered the lybell, defences, answers, replies, duplies, and writs produced finds that as the pursuer had not his house on the Government lands, but on a neighbouring tenement, the erecting the peat barn, schoolhouse and kiln must be presumed to have been for his own accommodation as inhabiting said tenement and does not fall under any general rule applicable to the villagers. Finds that the pursuer as a tenant without lease having built the dyke lybelled without any covenant for meliorations, his claim on that account cannot be sustained, therefore, and in respect of the offer by defender to allow the pursuer to carry away the materials of the houses, sustains the defences, and assoilzies the defender from the conclusions of the lybell, reserving to the pursuer his claim of one-third of the materials of the kiln from Thomas Clarke and Donald Grant or others who may be in possession of said kiln and decerns."

To this interlocutor the Sheriff adhered upon advising a petition, and the cause having been afterwards advocated it was upon the 28th November, 1801, by a majority of the judges, decided in favour of Mr Mackay.

The following cases of free and recognised sales of village lots in Fort-Augustus were founded upon against the Governor. In 1760 Dugald Mactavish, merchant, built a house close to the old fortification and sold it to Angus Macdonald, whose daughter was in occupation in 1799, for 100 guineas. Mactavish bought the stances of other houses, and erected a good and substantial house which was purchased in 1777 by Government for £160, and a title taken from Mactavish, although he had none himself. George Beverley sold a house for £40 to Peter Macdonald, who resold to Thomas Gillespie at Glen Quoich on behalf of one Murray in Perthshire for £100, and finally sold to Thomas Clark; and lastly a house belonging to Elgin, a square wright, was purchased from him for the Government at a fair price.

The West boundary of the Government lands was the River Oich, the lands immediately beyond having for a considerable time been held in feu or in wadset from the family of Lovat by that of Culduthel, and it is understood included all the Lovat lands west of Oich and Loch Ness, from the Glenmoriston lands to those of Glengarry.

Alexander Fraser of Culduthel seeing the thriving condition of the village of Fort-Augustus, about 1779, encouraged settlers to come to the opposite side of the river, opposite to Fort-Augustus, in order to form a village there. In consequence of this encouragement, a village was actually built called Bunoich, in which among others, Dugald Mactavish built a small house.

There were no written titles to these houses to Mactavish or to any of the villagers from the proprietor. The estate was afterwards sold to the family of Lovat, and Mactavish having incurred the displeasure of the managers of the Lovat estate, they brought an action of removing against him in which they succeeded. But he afterwards brought an action against the Lovat trustees concluding for the value of the houses he had built, and after a keen litigation the Court, by two consecutive interlocutors on the 13th and 29th May, 1790, found the trustees liable in terms of the libel, notwithstanding that they judicially offered to allow Mactavish to carry away the materials of his houses.

When the Hon. Archibald Fraser came into possession, he called Bunoich "Balfrishel," and there was quite a rivalry between the dwellers on either side of the Oich. It would appear that the allottees were subject to billet when the

Fort was inadequate for holding passing troops, that Government had first claim upon their horses and carts for transport, and the "pride and pomp of war" attracting many recruits from the village youth, Government benefited greatly by the village.

FORT-AUGUSTUS.

Mr Malcolm Maclachlan declared in 1799, that he was a resident in the village of Fort-Augustus ; that about 1750, he, the said Malcolm, being a "macanical" man, and versant in the knowledge of the management of a garden, and vegetables being very scarce in this part of the Highlands, the late Governor Trapaud, with the approbation and consent of many of the commissioned officers then in Fort-Augustus, encouraged the said Malcolm to come to a part of the extremest of the garrison ground at Fort-Augustus, and gave him the stance for a house and for an extensive garden, upon which he built a good and sufficient house and garden, the remains of the latter was entire, except some lately destroyed by the late Lieutenant Stuart of the Invalids, but the house being coveted by the clergy then of the place, namely, Mr James Grant, now of Laggan, and Dougald Mactavish, the principal elder, for a schoolhouse much wanted in the place, he, Malcolm, sold the house and garden to them at a certain price. The said Malcolm was in possession for about eight years, during which time the late Governor Trapaud and the officers for the time being visited the said Malcolm's garden and house and told him many times, from his dexterity in cultivation and serving people in so remote a part of the country with vegetables, that he must go to Laggan-a-bhan to labour and raise crops for the distressed in or coming over Corryarraik. The said Malcolm further asserted that when he entered to the foresaid place, he had no other method than to dung or bring the spots to be of any service to himself or the proprietor but by force of dung, and then there were a number of old huts or houses that had been feued before or about the year 1745 that were going into ruins, and in particular he bought one of them from one Barbara Gollan, another from Alexander Fraser, *alias* " Ucky," and another from John Bàn Maclean. The said Malcolm Maclachlan declared he has been acquainted with the village for upwards of 60 years (since 1739) and recollected Governor Caulfield, who only cessed in his short time the inhabitants 6d a year each. Collingwood, who succeeded, cessed them a shilling, and Trapaud, who followed, did not raise the rent at once, but brought it on gradually; but it consisted with his, Malcolm's knowledge, that none of these Governors ever removed any person without being found guilty of a flagrant fault or treasonable crime, and even they were allowed to dispose of their property to the best advantage, and it consisted with his knowledge that during the whole troublous times "by the name of the forty-five" that the whole houses in the village was upon the extreme parts of the garrison ground, and the first commencement of these buildings were erected by the then troops that could not be accommodated in the garrison and thereafter disposed of by them at their removal to the inhabitants, who have since continued in possession without interruption.

The succession of Governors in last century—Caulfield, Collingwood, Trapaud, and Brodie—is important, and of Trapaud it may be noted that, though an Englishman and without family connection of any kind with Scotland, it was found after his death that from his long residence at Fort-Augustus, extending over sixty years, he be deemed legally domiciled in Scotland.

Another formal declaration, by Donald Macdonald in Carngoddie, may be given as illustrating the ancient history of Fort-Augustus. Donald says in 1799, that he was 80 years of age, and born in Fort-Augustus, and that the inhabitants in it were since he knew the first house of it in the practice of buying and selling, that he left 30 years ago when Governor Trapaud bought his house from him. He was acquainted with Finlay Macmillan afterwards in Urquhart, Lachlan Macqueen in Glenmoriston, James Fraser in Glendo, Malcolm Maclachlan above alluded to, Mrs Corbat, Alexander Bàn, piper in Glenmoriston;

also that Donald Macdonald's house was on the very spot where the peat barn is. Recollects when Mr Dallas was schoolmaster about fifty years ago he was a great favourite of Duke William's, and had his schoolhouse on the very spot where Mr John Mackay's house is. Dallas sold to Stark, Stark to Chisholm, Chisholm to Donald Macdonald, and Macdonald to John Mackay. Mackay rebuilt it for his mother, and then gave it to Grant, his brother-in-law, who, upon settling at Aberchalder, resold to Mackay. Macdonald further states that about 35 years ago (1764), Angus Macdonell, *alias* "Innore," bought a large house from Dugald Mactavish at £60, which was on the same line of road as those of Mr Mackay's, and was called, from a large sign at the door of it, "The Figure of Four"; and he could point out other houses bought and sold.

The references by Macdonald show how the Highlanders designated the Duke of Cumberland, and the curious name of the house reminds one of the singular novel published a few years ago, "The Sign of Four."

It would seem that the village was not only populous but patriotic. A writer says that "their zeal and loyalty towards Government has always been found true, and one instance of it is that upon the 10th March last they assembled for the purpose of raising a Volunteer company, and a suitable number enrolled themselves for that purpose, which was laid before the Duke of Portland, to which a favourable answer was made. But Governor Brodie's proceedings against the village had so far damped the ardour of the people, that I suppose it would now be in vain to attempt any such measures where Governor Brodie would have the smallest jurisdiction over them."

One of Governor Brodie's high handed proceedings may be noted. William Fraser was owner of a house and some ground in Fort-Augustus, which, on enlisting in Sir James Grant's Fencibles, he let to a tenant recognised by Governor Trapaud. Brodie, however, turned the tenant out by the strong hand, as it is termed, and allowed the house to fall into decay out of mere wantonness. When

Fraser returned he found his house a ruin, and before he was permitted to repair or occupy, he had to pay back rent for all the years since the Governor's appointment.

The opening up of the Canal made a great change in Fort-Augustus. By and bye it will have a railway, and it has considerable expectations in the future.

INCIDENTS IN JOHN MACKAY'S CAREER.

I give a memorial prepared for Mr John Mackay and Mr George Urquhart in 1816, illustrative of certain inns and innkeepers of the time. Outrageous as were the proceedings the criminal authorities declined interfering, and Mr Mackay, from kindly feeling to Mrs Macrae, contented himself with bringing the matter under the notice of the proprietrix of Seaforth, who administered a severe reproof to this "wild Macraw of the West." Mr Mackay says he was at the time turned 70 years of age, but in the notice of his death, 4th January, 1821, he is described as 73 years old.

Mr Mackay first stayed in Fort-Augustus, afterwards had a lease of Ardochy from General Hastings Fraser, and finally resided at Innisnacardoch. He had a large family, and some of my readers will, like myself, entertain a pleasant recollection of one of his sons, Alexander, so long a respected, genial, and popular Inspector of Taxes at Inverness. Mr Mackay's clerk, Mr William Mackinnon, whom I recollect 50 years ago as Sheriff-Clerk Depute at Fort-Augustus, was in his day a well-known character of picturesque appearance. Here follows the document—

"Memorial for John Mackay, tacksman of Inishnacardoch and head constable of the county of Inverness, and George Urquhart, publick carrier, residing in Inverness.

"The first of these gentlemen travelled the North of Scotland for these forty years, and the second for these twenty years, and are well known on the road for their attention. In the line between Inverness and the West sea at Kyle Rea and other parts of the Western Isles, there is a fine road carried on till within a few miles of its interior extent. On the line of this road at Cluny there is a place of resort for travellers going by the name of an inn, which is in the possession of Alex. Macrae, a sheep farmer of that place. This miserable inn has neither a comfortable stable, no hay, has no beds, and the whole accommodation is some whisky and potatoes, with some of the mutton which Macrae rears upon his farm. Upon the 23rd day of August last, the memorialists were travelling that country with their horses and came there upon that day, where they met Captain Macdonell of Faicham, and in the course of the evening there were joined by Mr Garve, inspector of roads, where they took some supper and drink and retired to rest in such beds as they had in the place, and in this way were they disposed of.

"Their horses were put into a kind of a dirty house, full o *cow dung*, where they could not lye, and their fare were alone confined to a capfull of natural grass which was cut by the river side, without a manger, so that for that night they were upon this wet grass. Next morning when the memorialists got up they asked for corn, and then only got three lippies, but no place to hold the corn, which of necessity was placed on an old blanket on the roadside. After breakfast the bill was demanded from a girl who had charge of the house, but she being unable to make up the bill, and Macrae, the landlord, residing in another house at a distance, they had recourse to William Mackinnon, Mr Mackay's clerk, as the girl directed, and the share of each person divided, and there was included in this bill the three lippies of oats given the horses, and the girl being asked if there was anything and what to pay for the wet grass, the girl answered that she supposed that there was nothing to pay.

"By this time the horses were taken out of the house they were lodged in, and the memorialists were upon their backs, when Captain Macdonell insisted that they would take a dram before parting, and while so employed, the boy who attended the stable, and whose province it was to detail the price of the corn asked of Mr Mackay's clerk two shillings for each horse for the wet grass given the horses the preceding night, on which Mr Mackay's clerk desired him to go to the servant girl, and ask her what was to pay, which he did and returned for answer that the sum demanded was wanted and coming to Mr Mackay's ears he told him that he had no change and would pay him the next time he would return to that place, or, if he, the boy, had change that he would instantly pay for it, altho' he thought that one shilling for each horse was sufficient for the accommodation that was afforded them.

"That upon this Mr Mackay's clerk went into the house and desired the girl to get change, but no change being at hand the whole went away, saying they would pay when he, Mackay, came again.

"They were not long upon the road when they observed a boy accompanied with a man having a large cudgel, and on coming up to the memorialist, Urquhart, he laid hold of the bridle of his horse and stops him. Mr Mackay was behind, and having enquired what he was about and to go about his business, he then returned and said that they had not yet reached Cruachan, a place so called at some distance, and then observed two more and Mr Macrae, the landlord, traversing the meadows below them. Upon which Mr Mackay asked what was meant by such proceedings, to which he answered that it was on account of the grass given the horses not being paid, upon which Mr Mackay having borrowed two shillings from one of those in company, which was offered to the man who seized upon Mr Urquhart's horse, but he refused them, and upon this the money was thrown down upon the road. This man came again, being encouraged by Macrae the landlord, who took hold of the bridle of the horse belonging to the memorialist, Mr Urquhart, and swore that he would bring his cudgel red from Mr Urquhart's skull, upon which Mr Urquhart dismounted and this man took away the horse.

"Soon thereafter a second man came and by directions from Macrae, the landlord, who stood at the opposite side of the road, seized upon the bridle of the horse belonging to Mr Mackay, upon which he asked if he was the person that employed those men so to use the memorialists, to which he answered that he was, and that it was on account of not paying their fare before they went away, upon which Mr Mackay alighted from his horse, and the said man took it away with him, which appeared extremely strange as Mackay was the intimate of Macrae his father and mother for upwards of twenty years, and had occasion to be in their house at least four or five times each year, where he had liberally spent his money and regularly paid them except as happened here for the want of change, but always paid them on his return back.

"Mr Macrae being possessed of the horse, he was not therewith satisfied, but observing four cow beasts brought by the memorialist Mr Mackay from Glenelg driven by a servant, he caused some of the banditti seize upon them, and brought them also at the same time with him, proposing to Mr Mackay's servant to turn out and fight, but the poor man was afraid of his life and declined it. Being thus deprived of the horses and the cows, the memorialists were under the necessity of walking all the way to Fort-Augustus, upwards of twenty-five miles of very bad road, and the memorialist Mackay was a very unfit subject for this travel, being heavy in boots, and turned of seventy years of age.

"Next morning Alexander Macrae or some one of those who were his companions sent the horses to Fort-Augustus, and being ridden the whole night they were very much destroyed, and the evening of the following day they were followed by the said four cows.

"The facts can be easily instructed by those whose names are annexed and the tendency of it is most apparent.

"The want of police will render this useful and necessary road of no avail, for while this road is infested with such barbarism it will deter travellers from frequenting it, but from the conduct of Macrae it is humbly submitted that he has subjected himself to punishment for his conduct, and it is humbly apprehended that the county as police should take it up and give instruction to their Procurator-Fiscal to investigate it and bring the necessary prosecution. For although it might be justifiable the insisting of payment even at the most entravagant rate after the girl declared that she thought there was nothing to pay for the grass there, certainly some politeness ought to be adopted when she who kept the inn had no change, but surely no apology can possibly be made for forcibly depriving the memorialists of their two horses, of the four cow beasts, which had no concern with the squabble, and in afterwards sending them back after their wrath was appeased and the injury accomplished, but the memorialists leave their case with the county in the hopes that they shall see it necessary to place a regular man upon the road ; to punish Macrae for his conduct as an example to others, for unless this is done the road may in a great measure be abandoned.

"Note of the names of the persons that can prove the outrage alluded to—Captain Alexander Macdonell of Faicham, and Mr Garve, inspector of roads and bridges, saw all that was done or said in the house, which was civil and discreet in all points, but after going away therefrom and when followed by Macrae and his banditti there was none present but William Mackinnon, clerk to Mr Mackay, and Archibald Macdonald, tenant in Carnagoddy, near Fort-Augustus, who was driving the four cow beasts.

"The horses and said four beasts were, as mentioned in the memorial, brought from Cluny to Fort-Augustus by Ranald Macdonell, son to John Macdonell, senior, cattle dealer at Fort-Augustus, and by him driven to Mr Mackay's residence at Inshnacardoch, with a letter accompanying the same from Mrs Macrae, mother to the said Alex. Macrae."

THE GWYNE FAMILY AND MRS GRANT OF LAGGAN, 1827.

The story of the Gwyne family, as narrated hereafter, is described by the accomplished Mrs Grant of Laggan, as one that would be hooted at as exaggerated and improbable fiction if told in a work of imagination.

The use of Loch-Ness as a means of communication with Inverness and the sea was early recognised, and its free navigation, as well as that of the River Ness, declared by law. During the Usurpation, specially constructed boats plied on the loch, and after Fort-Augustus was erected in 1729, Government maintained a regular service of boats called "galleys." The story of the commanders of the galleys is given in the following papers, and some old people of Killichuiman will recollect some if not all the members of Captain Mark Gwyne's family, on whose behalf the petition was presented. Their house was the nearest to the Loch, between the Canal and River Oich, with some fine old trees in the grounds, and with the exception of the old inn, the King's House, partly remodelled, probably the oldest house in the village.

Mrs Grant, as is well known, spent her youth at the Fort, her father, Duncan MacVicar, having been appointed barrack master in 1768, and eleven years afterwards she married the Rev. James Grant of Laggan. Mrs Grant, who survived until 1838, recollected Dr Johnson's visit to the Fort in 1773. She had just before interesting herself in the Gwynes received a pension of £50 through the intercession of Sir Walter Scott, and it may be observed that in one of his letters Sir Walter seems slightly huffed that, though it cost him a deal of trouble and importunity, the lady was somewhat offended by the smallness of the amount. Mrs Grant's letter shows her character as kindly, amiable, and affectionate.

"Brae House, Tuesday, February, 1827.

"Dear Sir,—The ornaments of Style are now become so cheap and common that it requires no great power of mine to embellish an affecting story. I think however extreme history in one respect resembles beauty, that it's most adorned when adorned the least. Flowers of Rhetoric would merely destroy the simplicity that best recommends a state of real woe. This being the case I think the plain statements in your sketch is sufficient. The trifling alterations I have made go merely to substantiate and place as it were in clear light facts and dates which my age and long intimacy with the family have made more familiar to me than perhaps to any other now remaining of their friends.

"This case requires no exaggeration. So much do the strange incidents and deep afflictions of real life exceed all the paintings of fancy, that if the story of this family and its disaster made part of a work of imagination it would be looked at as an exaggerated and improbable fiction.

"God grant that the prayer of these orphans, poor in mind, body, and estate, may meet attention. This is one of the few occasions which tempt me to committ the sin of wishing myself rich. I am, however, rich in good wishes, and of this wealth no one can deprive me. Farewell, dear sir.—I am yours truthfully,
(Signed)   ANNE GRANT."

Follows the memorial and petition of the family of the now deceased Captain Mark Gwyne, to the Right Honourable the Secretary at War, 1827 :—

"The late Capt. Gwyne, who for fifty years commanded the Government sloop employed in carrying stores from Loch Ness for the garrison at Fort-Augustus, entered as midshipman in the navy when he was twelve years old, and was above eighty at the time of his decease. Having thus been about 70 years in what may be properly styled the Naval Service, and being considered as one of the Government officers and under the command of the Government, receiving a salary of about £130 per annum. In this situation he supported respectably the character of a British officer for about fifty years and was much esteemed for the candour, benevolence, and spotless integrity of his character in private life. His family under their present circumstances have a more than common claim upon the beneficence of Government. His father, who was a man of superior abilities and a thoroughbred seaman, having a large family growing up, was at his own request transferred from the navy, in which he had served from a boy, to the command of the above mentioned sloop, so that for a hundred years this family have been in the service of their country. The father of the deceased was about the year 1773 engaged in superintending the building of a new sloop at the lower end of Loch Ness which obliged him often in stormy winter weather to go up and down from his home at Fort-Augustus in an open boat.

"On one of these occasions, in the month of December, the boat in which he was returning home was cast away and every one on board perished. His eldest son, John, was at this time a lieutenant on board a man-of-war then stationed on the coast of North Carolina, and was in the same month and year with several others drowned by the upsetting of a boat as he was returning from the shore to his ship. The second son, Jaspar, was purser in different King's ships and was lost on board the "Repulse," which foundered in the West Indies when making a part of the fleet which returned from America about the year '78. Thus three individuals of this family lost their lives in the service of their country, all being of worth, bred to the naval service almost from infancy.

"It remains to finish the calamitous history of this deserving family by stating the present circumstances of all that remains of their representatives. Captain Gwyne, marrying late in life was left with the charge of a young motherless family, when his health and spirits were declining. A long protracted illness and the expense of rearing and educating his children entirely exhausted any little matter saved from his income as a provision for them. Two sons and two daughters are thus left utterly destitute, all so feeble in constitution and so liable to ill health that they are unable to work for their bread; some of them are deficient in intellect and one has been for years bedrid. So helpless a family having so many claims on public compassion may, it is thought, hope for some share of the liberality of that Government which their predecessors have served faithfully and honourably. So many of them dying in the service of their country that the family is so far extinct, that they have not a relation left to pity and assist them. If a case so very singular and so clamant on different accounts shall engage the attention of your lordship, it is the humble petition of the orphan family above described that either a continuance of their father's salary, or assistance from some other public fund may be afforded to prevent their suffering the extremity of want."

ABDUCTION BY WILLIAM FRASER, MERCHANT, FORT-AUGUSTUS, 1744.

Towards the end of January, 1744, a great sensation was caused in Inverness and neighbourhood by the abduction of Miss Jean Fraser, only daughter of the deceased Bailie William Fraser of Inverness, and of Mrs Jean Kinnaird. The young lady was a desirable match, having a fortune of 5000 merks. The abductor was William Fraser, then merchant in Fort-Augustus, a member of one of the most respectable families in Stratherrick. If the lady herself was willing, her friends were not, and the circumstances may be so far gleaned from the following letter by the Town Agent in Edinburgh, to Provost Hossack, dated 1st February, 1744, kindly communicated to me by the present Town Clerk:—

"Edinr., 1st February, 1744.

"Dear Sir,—Last night about six aClock the Bearer with the Magistrates letter and precognitions anent the Insult and Ryot committed on my good old friend Baillie Fraser's daughter found me in the Excheqr. Court where I was detained till betwixt eight & nine aClock at night upon closs bussiness. But as soon as I got free I went down to Mr Robert Dundass, His Majestie's Solicitor-Generall

& consulted him upon the affair, & after reading over the precognitions and coppies of letters, &c., he drew a petition to the Lords of Justiciary in name of Mrs Fraser, the mother, & her son, and by six aClock in the morning I got the Justiciary Clerk Dept. and . . . . . had the petition transcribed over, and a proper warrand write out ready agt nine aClock to get signed by a Lord of Justiciary. But haveing got as much time as to wait upon my Lord President & acquaint him of the affair, he was of opinion that as the thing was so very atrocious that the petition should be in name of the Lord Advocat & be signed by Mr Solicitor. Accordingly, when I came back to the Parliament House about ten aClock I first acquainted the whole Lords of Justiciary of the affair, and they thought as the President did, that the King's Advocat should give his countenance so far as to take the precognition for his own information and then sign the petition himself. Thereupon I got the petition write out of new & and the warrand made out upon it. I waited till the Lords rose & then got the Justiciary Lords to meet, and they ordered the warrand, which is signed by Lord Roystoun, & you have it inclosed. As it is now half ane hour after two, I doubt much if the bearer can overtake the tyde at Leith. However, to show you that I have been diligent, & not neglected a moment, I have despatched the bearer before I sat down to dinner. As for the assistance of the military, the Lords would not allow it except that they heard the Civill Magistrat was deforced, in which case proper application may be made, & assistance will be given. There is one thing that you must get done and that is to get a letter from Mrs Fraser and her son directed to Mr Robert Dundass, His Majestie's Solicitor, acquainting him that they have sent to me the precognition and proper information anent the Insult and Ryot committed by Wm. Fraser on their daughter and sister, & begging his countenance and assistance to get justice, which you'll send me any time with your conveniency that it may lye with the precognitions. This I undertook for, or I would not got the Solicitor to sign the petition. I received the five guineas you sent me. —I am, Dr Sr, your most obedient sert. (Sgd.) WILL. FORBES."

"There are two persons complained on that are not right designed & yrfor no warrand could be got agt them. (Addressed on the back) to Mr John Hossack, Provost of Inverness."

I now follow up the matter from information in my own possession.* It would appear that Lord Lovat was applied

---

* Printed Papers in the Justiciary Case were recently offered for sale in an Edinburgh Second-hand Catalogue, but unfortunately for me, were sold before my attention was directed to the matter.

to by William Fraser and his friends, but his Lordship absolutely declined, and the following letter addressed to Hugh Fraser, younger of Foyers, shows Lord Simon's views of abduction in old age, different probably from what he would have written fifty years earlier. Be that as it may, the letter is highly proper and becoming in one holding Lord Lovat's high position. The letter is illegible in several parts, and I do not guarantee its literal correctness :—

"Beaufort, 25th January, 1744.

"Dear Hughie,—Your letter of this day's date from Gortuleg came to my hand just now twixt 6 and 7 o'clock at night. Though it be not uncommon to see two or a few men of a county distracting and misleading others near the brink of Darkness, yet I own what you write is beyond comprehension, surprising and astonishing. That a small number of people, and some as I know intelligent enough countrymen, should carry off and violate all duties, and run on as if they were destinate to ruin and destruction, which the unhappy affair they have in hand must certainly entail upon them yet I hope in God what I write to you to the people who should lead and conduct that country under me, and what will come to the others concerned if any vestige of judgment remains with them, will give them a better turn to this unhappy affair and by some measure prevent what must be a fatal blow to all of them if things go on according to the strain of your letter. I can do no more at this distance than desire that you, or should this not find you in the country, one of the others to whom it is addressed, make public to the gentlemen of the country who are embarked in this unlucky business, of any discretion or sagacity, and tell them as I have maturely considered the consequences that must attend such a mad and unjustifiable conduct by them against the country and against my family and character, that I desire and order as they shall be answerable, and upon their duties and allegiances sacred and civil, to put a stop to their madness, and proceed no further in their outrageous and unhappy measures, and to convey the poor injured girl in the most safe and convenient manner to the town of Inverness, to the mother and the Guardians of the peace. And if this they refuse or delay to comply with, I must look upon as stating themselves aliens to me, showing all disregard to my orders, and doing me and my family all the hurt in their power. You may assure them, and they may read in this letter, that the resentment of the relations of the poor girl and of the town of Inverness, cannot be so implacable against them as mine will justly be. I desire that you or those to whom this shall come to lose no time in making the best use of those orders they can.—Dear Hughie, yours, (Signed) LOVAT."

"As to the letter which it seems the girl has wrote to Inverness, in order to 'appease the Magistrates," I can assure you neither that nor all the declarations that she can make, while her liberty is restrained will avail or better the case a single farthing. These proceedings can have no other effort but to aggravate the crime and to inflame the resentment to it and nothing but sending the girl immediately to Inverness, whether married or unmarried, can save every man that has been in this affair from ruin and destruction, the whole name of Fraser from eternal shame, and my person and family from hurt and trouble."

A paper dated 1779 bears that this "William Fraser, merchant in Fort-Augustus, thereafter vintner in Inverness, having under cloud of night, with a band of men, forcibly entered the house in the month of January, 1744, of Mrs Jean Kinnaird, relict of Baillie William Fraser, merchant, in Inverness, and thence carried off Jean Fraser, only daughter of the said Baillie William Fraser, and brought her to Stratherrick, where he married her, the Magistrates of Inverness, entered a criminal prosecution against him and his accomplices before the Court of Justiciary."

The criminal proceedings were likely to be attended with very serious consequences to William Fraser, and Lord Lovat having failed them as just mentioned, William Fraser and his friends applied to Norman Macleod of Macleod to intercede with the Magistrates of Inverness to withdraw the prosecution. Macleod was then member for the county, and possessed great influence therein, and also with the Magistrates, and the Hanoverian Government. His private character was bad, and this coupled with his conduct towards Prince Charles, has given him an unenviable position in the history of his honourable house. But he did exert himself in a matter probably congenial, though considerable time elapsed before an arrangement could be made, and it was not until the 17th of June, 1745, that the proceedings were stayed by Macleod accepting a bill, payable on the 2nd of November, 1745, to Mr William Forbes, Writer to the Signet, Agent for the town, for the very considerable sum, at that period, of £70 sterling, being the expenses of the criminal process up to that date.

William Fraser's outrageous proceedings appear to have arisen from his impecuniousness, and as early as 1745, the portion of his wife, Jean Fraser, of 5000 merks was assigned by them to Thomas Fraser of Garthmore.

Owing to the troubles in the country in '45-46, no demand was made upon Macleod's bill until 1754, and the further steps which took place under it, and William Fraser's ungrateful conduct, may now be recorded. Macleod naturally applied to Fraser, by this time settled as a vintner in Inverness, to relieve him, and that as he declined to do so, a process was instituted against him in the Sheriff Court at Inverness.

As soon as the first interlocutor was pronounced, William Fraser advocated the case. In the meantime letters of inhibition at Macleod's instance were raised in 1758; and in the month of January, 1760, after a long proof and keen contest, decree was given against William Fraser for the said sum of £70, with interest from 2nd November, 1745, as also for £83 5s 11d of expenses, and £17 1s 3d expenses of extract. In July, 1761, Macleod took a process of adjudication against Fraser, adjudging a tenement of land or dwelling-house in Inverness, which he had himself acquired under adjudication, containing the following reference to the Burgage land west of the River Ness, having a description with which I am not familiar, viz, "Little Inverness." The description is as follows:—" All and haill that house or tenement of Burrow bigged land lying in that part of the town of Inverness, which lies on the north side of the water of Ness, commonly called little Inverness, formerly possessed by Alexander Chisholm, cooper in Inverness, and his sub-tenants, and now by his widow, with the yeard, area, and pertinents thereto belonging, if any be." Macleod at the same time adjudged an heritable bond over the lands of Erchitt for £220 sterling of principal and annual rents, granted by Fraser of Erchitt to the said William Fraser.

At the date of this adjudication in July, 1761, the

original debt of £70 had run up to £224 sterling. Macleod finding that the bond over Erchitt had been previously validly conveyed to Dr James Fraser of London, and William Fraser having died insolvent, was glad to get rid of the business even at a considerable sacrifice, and upon the 28th April, 1767, assigned the debt to trustees for behoof of Ann Fraser, relict of the deceased Simon Fraser, merchant in Inverness. Ann Fraser and her trustees now took up the running with vigour, and in the first place obtained decreets of constitution and of adjudication against William Fraser, son and heir in general of the deceased William Fraser, and his tutors and curators.

Ann Fraser's advisers discovered that the deceased William Fraser had a debt against John Macdonell of Ardnabi, against whom he had obtained a decreet of adjudication on the 15th June, 1752.

She also was confirmed executor creditor to William Fraser, giving up on inventory Jean Fraser's 5000 merks before referred to; as also £43 16s 9d, the amount of a bill drawn by the deceased William Fraser and accepted by Simon Fraser, brother to Hugh Fraser of Foyers. It would appear that on the 3rd November, 1761, there was a post nuptial contract of marriage between William Fraser and Jean Fraser. With regard to the debt against Ardnabi, James Fraser of Gortuleg, Writer to the Signet, offered Ann Fraser £60 for her rights, which she accepted on 31st May, 1776.

At Whitsunday 1779 the original debt of £70, which, with interest and expenses amounted, as before mentioned, in July 1761 to £224, had now reached with further interest the enormous sum of £424 sterling. Of this sum Ann Fraser had received the Ardnabi debt of £60, and she considered the Foyers bill with accumulated interest amounting to £80, good, thus leaving a deficit of no less than £282. To meet this there was only the adjudication against the property in Little Inverness, and as there was a competition by other creditors, I fancy Ann Fraser did not make much of her speculation, although I am unable positively to say how the matter terminated.

The business of vintner was a profitable one, and people of fairish position took up the calling. I have mentioned that William Fraser was of a respectable Stratherrick family, and the well known Major James Fraser of Castle Leathers, younger son of Culduthel, for some time "kept a Public" in Inverness, of which, however, he was rather ashamed.

Jean Fraser, the heroine of my story, lived into this century. I find a receipt dated at Inverness, the 27th May, 1803, wherein, "I, Jean Fraser, relict of the deceased William Fraser, vintner in Inverness, acknowledge to have received from James Fraser, vintner in Inverness, the sum of £60 sterling to account of the furniture sold him by contract."

DALCATTAIG AND PORTCLAIRS.

The fine estate of Glenmoriston, extending to 70,000 acres, watered by its beautiful river, is incomplete however at top and bottom. Originally the whole top belonged to other families, but by the acquisition of Glen Loyne from the Laird of Grant, the lands watered by the river Loyne, which falls into the Moriston, forming the upper boundary at this part, is complete to the watershed. The boundary at Cluanie is arbitrary, and the lands in the parish of Glenshiel must at some remote period have been lost or dissevered from the remainder of Glenmoriston. The original barony as bestowed on the Grants, on the other hand, consisting in whole of a £27 land of old extent, included the forty shilling land of Culnakirk, and the twenty shilling land of Clunemore in Glenurquhart. Glen Loyne was probably got in exchange for Culnakirk and Clunemore, parted with in 1696.

That Dalcattaig and Portclairs, really forming for several miles one side of the Glen, prominent and imposing from all quarters, did not originally form part of the Glenmoriston estate, seems so surprising and unnatural that various accounts are given for the anomaly. I will first give the version told me in the Glen many years ago, and follow it up by narrating the real history, with some account of the long continued struggle on the part of the Grants to acquire these lands. The popular tradition is that the lands were of old really part of Glenmoriston, that on one occasion on a windy stormy day Lovat and Glenmoriston were out hunting, having, as they started, their plaids fastened, as was customary, with valuable brooches. Lovat was prudent, and carried a large common pin in reserve. As the wind increased Lovat, afraid of loosing his brooch, took it off, substituting the pin. Glenmoriston unfortunately lost his brooch, which, in consequence of the high wind and storm, could not be found. Starving with cold and labouring under the inconvenience of carrying his plaid, now merely an encumbrance, he begged Lovat to lend him his brooch. This Lovat, who had a particular regard for his brooch, was unwilling to do and wished to be excused. At length, under importunity, he gave the brooch to Glenmoriston, and to impress due caution said, "If you lose my brooch, you must replace it by Dalcattaig and Portclair." This Glenmoriston in his need agreed to, and alas by and bye, a furious gust striking him, the fastening gave way, and the brooch disappeared for ever, although searched and searched for, for months; and thus the lands were lost to Glenmoriston. So far the tradition.

Now for the real state of matters, as these have come under my observation. In 1691, when the Cess Roll was made up for Inverness-shire, John Doun, fifth of Glenmoriston, is entered in the parish of Boleskine and Abertarff, as heritor of Dalcattaig and Portclair. In 1693, when Iain-a-Chraggain, sixth of Glenmoriston, accompanied by Donald Macdonell of Lundie, his friend and supporter, came to Dunain, courting Janet Baillie, sister of William Baillie, then of Dunain, Iain, with consent of his father, agreed to settle upon her seven hundred merks per annum of a jointure out of his lands of Inver and Glenmoriston, and of Dalcattaig and Portclairs. But it would appear that the last mentioned lands at these periods were only held in wadset of Lovat.

Patrick Grant, seventh of Glenmoriston, after the death of his elder brother John in 1735, entered into a submission with Simon Lord Lovat, regarding the lands of Meikle Portclair. The paper prepared for Glenmoriston now given has no date, but it would be between 1735 and 1745, and is most interesting.

"Information for Patrick Grant of Glenmoriston—

"The deceased John Grant of Glenmoriston, grandfather to the said Patrick Grant did settle seven thousand merks in the hands of the deceased Hugh Lord Lovat, for which he got the lands of Dalcaitag and Portclaires in wadset, by which wadset right Glenmoriston was obliged to pay off a surplus duty as the customs of the said lands eighty pounds Scots or thereby yearly to the family of Lovat as ye said wadset right in itself more fully purports. Some years after obtaining of the said wadset, these customs did run on unpaid; and for recovering of the same the deceased Thomas Fraser, Lord Lovat, then Beaufort, father to the Right Honourable Simon Lord Fraser, now of Lovat, being then a young valiant and forward gentleman, was appointed and commissioned to march with two or three hundred men in order to take possession of a part of the said wadset lands violently, if no other accommodation could be made with Glenmoriston in friendly manner to that effect, which accordingly he did, and after coming to those bounds with the foresaid number of men, he and Glenmoriston did meet, and after a long communing it was unanimously agreed that the town of Meikle Portclare should be always sequestrate and allow'd in the possession of the family of Lovat during the non-redemption of the said wadset for making full payment and satisfaction of the said customs and superplus duty, to prevent any further demur or disorder that might arise in case of any bad payments of this subject matter in time coming, and to that effect there was a settlement made in writing twixt the said Beaufort and Glenmoriston; but among other misfortunes in the year 1689 the castle of Invermoriston, being the house of Glenmoriston's residence, was burnt by the Earle of Sutherland, where all Glenmoriston's papers with everything else were entirely destroyed, excepting his charters and other rights, which were hid under ground, among which this agreement and writing was cut off, so that it cannot now be further evidenced, whereby the attestation of some old honest men who are yet living in the country, and knows the premises to be all of verity, and further can attest that alwayes since the commencement of the said wadset right, anterior to the above agreement, Glenmoriston has been in possession of the said lands of Meikle Portclare.

"The late Mr John Grant, younger of Glenmoriston, brother to the said Patrick Grant did purchase the said lands of Dalcaitag and Portclare with the rest of the estate of Glenmoriston (which were forfeited) from the hands of the publick, and to pay off the price of his estate, was obliged to borrow money from this present Lord Lovat, for which he did renounce his right of the said lands of Dalcaitaig and Little Portclaire, but always excepted in the renunciation the lands of Meikle Portclaire on which the former wadset right stands good for two thousand marks, being the balance unpaid of the moneys settled in that manner with the family of Lovat, and as this Lord Lovat through ignorance that Glenmoriston was ever in possession of the said town of Meikle Portclaires and that consequently he believed Glenmoriston had no just title or right to the two thousand marks unpaid, on that account and to remove all disputes 'twixt my Lord Lovat and Glenmoriston, a submission was formally extended 'twixt them, to be determined by the final sentence and decision of Evan Baillie of Abriachan and Alexander Munro, Commissary of Inverness, arbitrators, but ere anything was or could be done in relation to the said submission, Glenmoriston died. But now with the same view the like submission is renewed betwixt my Lord Lovat and the said Patrick Grant of Glenmoriston, to be determined by the decision of Mr Robert Craig and Mr William Grant, advocates, arbiters mutually chosen by the said parties who are to have their instructions from this information and other writs herewith given."

Patrick Grant was most anxious to have a commission to examine aged witnesses, many of whom were 90 years of age and upwards, as to his grandfather's originally possessing Meikle Portclair. The proceedings fell to the ground, however, in consequence of Lord Lovat's forfeiture, and seem to have dropped thereafter.

Iain-a-Chraggain having been forfeited for his accession to the Rising of 1715, his estates fell under charge of the Commissioners on Forfeited Estates. Glenmoriston was sold at a public roup on 24th of November, 1730, and was purchased by Ludovick Colquhoun of Luss for the sum of £1086 sterling, and under burden of paying all wadset moneys thereon. The whole rental in 1725 and 1726, was only £60 8s 4d sterling, whereof £26 8s 10d represented wadsetted lands, leaving of surplus for the laird and the

Forfeited Estates Commissioners in his stead £33 9s 6d. In 1725 the accounts stood thus, on the one side the rents as above, £60 8s 4d; on the other, cash paid Edmund Burt, Esq., £8 8s 0d; the wadsetted lands, as above, £26 18s 10d; stipend, £3 14s 1d; arrears, £21 7s 5d; total, £60 8s 4d. And in 1726, the rent £60 8s 4d; the arrears, £21 7s 5d; total, £81 15s 9d; on the other side, cash paid Edmund Burt, Esq., £9 9s 0d; the wadsetted lands, £26 18s 10d; stipend, £3 4s 11d; arrears, £41 13s 10d; total, £81 15s 9d. In a minute of sale, dated 3rd December, 1730, Sir John Clerk, Baronet, George Dalrymple, and Thomas Kennedy, Esquires, Barons of Exchequer, declared that they sold to Ludovick Colquhoun, all and haill the lands of Glenmoriston, and "also the lands of Dalcattaig with its parts and pendicles as the same were possessed by John Grant, late of Glenmoriston, and his predecessors heretofore," as also all other lands and estates, though not named, which might have belonged to the said John Grant. The price of £1086 sterling, Luss bound himself to pay. The purchase was a friendly one, and in course of time Colquhoun and his successors resold at different times the property and superiority of Glenmoriston to the Grants. Luss did not convey Dalcattaig and Little Portclair included in the sale to him, because, as mentioned in Patrick Grant's memorial, Lovat lent money to Patrick, on condition of being allowed to have these lands, but first John Grant, and thereafter his brother Patrick Grant, claimed from Lovat Meikle Portclair, as I have said, in virtue of the old wadset moneys not having been fully paid. Simon Lord Lovat, thus became interested in the lands of Dalcattaig and Little Portclair though sold by the Forfeited Estate Commissioners to Luss, as is more fully set forth in an application by Colquhoun in 1750, making a claim on Lord Lovat's estates. After narrating the sale to him in 1730, Colquhoun of Luss, then Sir Ludovick Grant of Grant, states that "Simon, late Lord Fraser of Lovat, being desirous to purchase that part of the estate of Glenmoriston called Dalcattaig, and Little Portclair, which would not be separately sold by the Barons of Exchequer, did prevail with him to grant an obligation whereby, upon payment of 5500 merks with interest from the time of attaining possession, he, Grant, became bound to grant a sufficient and solid disposition of the premises to Lord Lovat and his heirs male, or to any person or persons he should appoint by a writing under his hand. That the obligation if extant was supposed to be among the other writings of the said Simon, late Lord Fraser of Lovat. That Lord Lovat, by obligation signed by him at Edinburgh, on 24th November, 1730, before William Drummond of Balhaldie and John Macfarlan, Writer to the Signet, bound himself to pay Grant the sum of 5500 merks, with interest from the date of his being put in possession of Dalcattaig and Little Portclair. But Lord Lovat, without paying the price, or demanding a disposition of the lands, did at his own hand assume and enter upon possession of the lands, and continued therein until his death, without making any satisfaction either of principal or interest. That after Lord Lovat's death and forfeiture, his estates were surveyed, and amongst other lands those of Dalcattaig and Little Portclair were included, but in reality they formed no part of the Lovat estates, as he, Grant, had never been denuded thereof." Grant accordingly entered claim upon Lord Lovat's estates for the said sum of 5500 merks, with annual rent since 1731, if the Crown desired to keep the lands, or otherwise that he would resume possession thereof, and merely claim the annual rent, in satisfaction for the period he was out of his lands.

Land was rising rapidly in value, so the Crown kept these lands, and they remained as part of the estates of Lovat which were restored to General Simon Fraser.

It was necessary towards the end of last century for the trustees of General Simon Fraser to sell lands and superiorities to pay off debts, and having procured an Act of Parliament to effect this, the trustees proceeded to a cognition and sale, scheduling several lands and superiorities as the most convenient for disposal and least hurtful to the estate of Lovat generally. Amongst others the 11th lot was "the lands of Wester Eskadale and Wester Main, lying in the parish of Kiltarlity, and in the district called Strathglass. These lands lie detached at the other extremity of the estate, and being adjacent to the property of Captain Fraser of Eskadale, there is reason to believe he will give a suitable price." Objections were called for by any of the heirs of entail, and *inter alia* Captain Simon Fraser of Foyers and Major Archibald Fraser, late of the Glengarry Regiment of Fencibles, appeared and stated *inter alia* "that certain parts of the estate of Lovat called the lands of Dalcattaig and the two Portclairs, lying in the parish of Abertarff, or Stratherrick, and on the north side of Loch Ness are not included in the condescendence of the pursuers. The reasons given for the sale of Eskadale above mentioned, apply with far greater force to these lands, as they lie discontiguous to the estate of Lovat, under the Act of Parliament. The lands of Dalcattaig and Portclairs lie contiguous to Glenmoriston, and there is every reason to suppose he will give a suitable price for them, and indeed he has already signified his intention of offering fifty years' purchase for them, and will readily give the full value of the same, when the real value is ascertained and made known." This was in 1798, and no doubt Foyers, who had married one of the Glenmoriston ladies, was put in motion by that family. It was unsuccessful, however, for the Lovat trustees declined to consent, and the matter again fell to the ground.

When Colonel John Grant of Glenmoriston died he left considerable means, part of which was invested in the name of Patrick, Colonel Grant's eldest son, in 1804 in the purchase of the Estate of Scotos, forming portion of the Barony of Knoydart. Ronald Macdonell of Scotos, was married to one of the Glemoriston ladies, which may have led to the purchase, for it was never in itself a success, being detached from Glenmoriston, and scattered through the remainder of Knoydart. Glengarry gave much trouble in the matter of boundaries, marches, accesses, etc., and finally he bought Scotos, which was again re-incorporated with Knoydart, and so continues till this day. Scotos was sold in the time of James Murray Grant, who had succeeded his elder brother Patrick. The late Glenmoriston, who was long a prominent man in the North, took great interest in county and public affairs, filled the offices of Convener and vice-Lieutenant, and being a constant resident, had a thorough knowledge of his family history, and a just pride in its honourable traditions. The family was the first to support the Charles Grants for the representation of the County, and adhered to father and son to the last. Later on, when Thomas Alexander Fraser of Lovat attained his majority, he also became a leading supporter, and it might be said that no two gentlemen in the Highlands were more intimate or disposed to favour the other. After the passing of the Reform Bill, when the suffrage was thrown open to tenants paying £50 and upwards, Charles Grant the younger's position became weaker in the County, until at length his defeat became inevitable, and he took refuge in a Peerage, the Government desiring to appoint another to his office. The Whig party fought desperately to maintain Grant in his position, Glenmoriston being ever in front. The election literature of 1830-1836, is full of wit, one of the most celebrated productions being the rhyming verses commencing with the words

> There was a committee,
> Composed of twenty three,
> Of the wisest men of Inverness, Ness, Ness,
> Etc., etc., etc.

These twenty-three were the leading Whigs whose respective shortcomings and foibles were cleverly and accurately hit off. The author was reputed to be Macleod's sister, he himself being called to account as responsible for her by an irate officer, one of the twenty-three, of whom it was suggested that he did not possess even

> "The *little* learning which is a dangerous thing,"

for it was said

> " The Colonel at school could never learn, learn, learn."

Charles Grant had become Lord Glenelg; his party was still in power, and the county representation having gone for ever from the Northern aristocratic Whigs, all began to press for rewards and acknowledgments. Specimens of the stupid, shrewd, and clever, had their reward, but amongst them was not to be found the name of "honest Glen" as he was called, though he was, as I said, always in front, and stood one contest in person. This overlooking of him was much commented upon. I have, however, wandered from Dalcattaig. No laird felt the annoyance of vicinity so much in his younger days as the late laird, all his frontage to Loch Ness being comprised within the river Moriston and the burn of Ault Sigh. He knew he could not purchase the lands, as they were under strict entail, but he naturally thought that his most intimate friend would oblige him without hesitation by agreeing to an advantageous exchange.

The lands of Knockie and Delchapple, being in the market, were purchased by Glenmoriston with the view of exchange with Dalcattaig and Portclairs. Knockie lay very convenient to Lovat's Stratherrick estates, but on being approached, Lovat positively declined to negotiate; and so Knockie remains with Glenmoriston of no particular value to him except that it stretches out pleasantly in view of Invermoriston House on the other side of the Loch. Miss Maria H. Grant in one of her charming novels alludes to one of the pleasures of life at Invermoriston, consisting of the frequent visits paid to and received from Knockie while tenanted by a worthy but tedious soldier, now deceased, known as the "Great Bore," the mutual invitations being through smoke raised by the lighting of fires on particular eminences.

The adjoining lands of Innisnacardoch and Achterawe would have changed hands years ago, unless prevented at great cost by the late Lovat, which would have left Dalcattaig and Portclairs isolated from other Lovat lands. In these changing times it would be rash to say that there is no chance of their ever becoming part of Glenmoriston.

THE EARL OF SELKIRK AND THE STRATHERRICK EMIGRANTS IN 1803.

Lord Selkirk's emigration scheme met with much opposition from Highland landlords, and though unsuccessful was in every sense a great undertaking, promulgated before the proper time. The different publications on the subject, his own defences, the observations and strictures of Brown and others, the accounts of the desperate struggles with the Fur Companies, ending in the Earl's retirement from the contest, are full of interest, and it is a pity no historian like Washington Irving in his entrancing story of "Astoria" has as yet depicted in an equally graphic manner the history of the Selkirk Settlement in these days, at present to a great extent occupied by a large and thriving population.

How the enclosed letter from Lord Selkirk came into my possession I cannot say, it being lately discovered tied up in a bundle connected with Stratherrick, nor do I know anything of Mr James Stewart, to whom it was addressed, described as "late Fraser F. Regiment, Foyers, by Inverness." It is not in good preservation, has several markings, the only complete one, however, being "Doctor John Macra, Ardintoul, Kintail, by Loch Carron." The letter is entirely in the Earl's handwriting, small, neat, and distinct. The Earldom of Selkirk has lately merged into one of the minor titles of the Duke of Hamilton.

"London, January, 16th 1803.

"Sir,—I lately received yours of the 3rd, in reply to which I have to observe that I have already engaged the full number of people whom I intend to take out to America in my own employment, and also the persons whom I wish to superintend them, so that I have not at present any situation vacant of the nature you refer to. If, however, it is in any event your intention to go to America, I would incline to suggest your joining the Stratherrick people who are going this season. If you have sufficient influence with them to induce them to settle in the situation I shall point out to you, I can put you on a way of rendering the business very lucrative to yourself, while it will at the same time be advantageous to the people, provided they are able to lay out something on the

purchase of land after their arrival.   I am, sir, your obedient servant.
(Signed)   "SELKIRK."

It is well known that many of the original Frasers, Mactavishes, Macgillivrays, and others, the real heads of the North West Company, went from Stratherrick.

THE PEOPLE OF ABERTARFF, AND THE CANAL, IN 1808.

From the annexed petition it would appear that the population between Loch Lochy and Loch Ness in 1808 was very considerable, while the season was unfavourable and employment scarce. The Fort-Augustus market of old was an important one. "All the gentry in the country are generally present" writes an inhabitant, quarrels were renewed and fought out, and it was at one of them, I rather think about 1806, that Dr Macdonald of Fort-Augustus was severely beaten, said at the time by instigation of Glengarry, who owed him a grudge. Glengarry was held responsible, and had to pay £2,000 damages, besides the Court calling the attention of the Lord Advocate to the propriety of his being removed from the Lieutenancy and Magistracy of the county. Times are changed in the parish, for ecclesiastics not lairds, are now both dominant and militant in and about Fort-Augustus. Follows the petition—

"Unto the Right Honourable the Commissioners for the Caledonian Canal, etc., etc. The Petition and Memorial of the persons hereto subscribing, tacksmen, tenants, cottars, and labourers residing in that part of the Great Glen of Scotland, situated between the eastern end of Loch Lochy and western end of Loch Ness.

"Humbly Sheweth,—That the formation of Highland roads and bridges in the north of Scotland and the Caledonian Canal, held up to the memorialists a source of industry which would put an end to the apparent necessity of emigration among the lower classes of society in the district of the country where the memorialists reside, as well as in many other districts to the north and south of this line.

"This hope so sanguinely entertained was realised by the memorialists in the commencement of the Glengarry line of road from the Military road at Aberchalder towards Loch Urn. In forming this beneficial road many of the memorialists derived very considerable benefit, as no person could work but had it in his power to do so, near his own house, and a variety of the articles of consumpt in the country received a ready market from the influx of money occasioned by this public undertaking.

"This road being now completed from Aberchalder many miles westward induced the contractor to commence forming the road this season at Lochurn Head, as he finds labourers from that district of country, and that it lessens considerably the expense of carriage, whereby the numerous inhabitants in and about the foresaid Great Glen of Scotland and in Sleismine and Sleisgarve of Glengarry, are laid idle.

"In this very severe year, the memorialists feel much the want of public employ and many of them may be obliged to seek for subsistence at a distance, and thereby induced to desert their native country.

"As one object which the nation had in view in those public employs, was to find labour for the lower classes of the community which is amply supplied on the east and west end of the Canal (as well as the improvement of the country at large) it would afford the greatest relief to your memorialists if the central district of the Canal was commenced so as to find labour for them and others in its contiguity. For having already reaped the benefit of public employ they feel the want thereof, particularly in so severe a season as the present, more than if they had never tasted of its sweets. Under such distress as the generality of your memorialists labour, they look forward with confidence in the benevolent interest of the Right Honourable Commissioners to direct such measures to be taken as in their wisdom they shall see proper.

"May it therefore please the Right Honourable Commissioners to take the premises under their consideration and to do therein as to them shall appear proper and thereby afford to the memorialists such relief as to them the justice of their case may require. And the petitioners shall ever pray."

VII.—UNITED PARISH OF URQUHART AND GLENMORISTON.

THE GRANTS OF GLENMORISTON.

THIS parish has been so exhaustively dealt with by one of its distinguished sons, Mr William Mackay, that I have little to say. If each parish within the great county of Inverness produced such a worthy and capable historian, the county so rich in story, poetry, and song, would indeed be admirably represented.

The connection of the Lairds of Grant with the parish is a gloomy reminiscence, if not now a standing menace. Founded, if not on fraud, patently on Royal favouritism, it has run what can hardly be termed an honourable course of four hundred years, culminating in depriving the people of any rights to the greater part of the lordship. The expropriation of the old families of Corrimony, Sheuglie, Achmony, and others has been most prejudicial to the Glen and put an end to that independent feeling so necessary and beneficial in a district where one family is territorially supreme.

Although Glenmoriston has during the last fifty years fallen sadly back in population and importance, yet there is still a very kindly feeling held towards the family, who at an early period broke off from the continuous mean and time-serving traditions of its head.

The Grants of Glenmoriston never sided with the Grants of Grant, but not being sufficiently numerous to form a regiment, allied themselves to the Macdonells of Glengarry, and in another place I have mentioned the quota of Glenmoriston officers in the conjunct regiment.

This brought out a warm and lasting friendship, of which perhaps no better illustration could possibly be given than the contract between John Macdonell of Glengarry and John and Patrick Grant, elder and younger of Glenmoriston, dated Invergarry, 1st November, 1735. It was probably executed in duplicate (being referred to in Sir William Fraser's *Chiefs of Grant*.) I possess one if not the only principal. It is now given—

"Att Invergarry. The first day of November One thousand Seven Hundred and Thirty-five years. It is contracted, agreed and finally ended betwixt the parties after mentioned, viz., The Honble John McDonell of Glengary, and John and Patrick Grants of Glenmoristone, elder and younger, with the speciall advices and consent of Alexander Grant of Craskie younger, and Angus Grant of Dalldragon on the one and other parts, In manner following, That is to say, The said John McDonell, and the saids John and Patrick Grants with consent forsaid Hereby Bind and Oblige themselves and their heirs whatsomever, strictly to maintain betwixt the foresaid families of Glengarie Glenmoristone, such Kindness and Friendship as was formerly keeped and observed by their predecessors, and that they shall joyn with one another (In so far as is lawful and just) against any opposition or encroachments or unlawfull attempts to be made against any of the saids families (The family of Grant being always excepted by the saids John and Patrick). And the saids John and Patrick Grants Doe by these presents and with consent forsaid, Bind and Oblidge them and their forsaids That They nor any of their family shall not at any time hereafter maintain, Harbour or resett The person of Allan Grant, son to the said John Grant, or Travell with, or assist him, or any of his followers directly or indirectly any manner of way. And the fornamed parties contractors, with consent forsaid, Bind and Oblidge them and their forsaids to obtemper, perform, and fulfill their respective parts of this contract to others, under the penalty of Two Thousand pounds Scots money of failtie to be payed to the party performers or willing to perform the promises by and attour performance of this present contract. And that these presents may be registered in the Books of any Judicatory competent, That upon a decree of the Judges thereof Letters of Horning on ten days and other Execution in form as effeirs may pass hereupon, They constitute Their prors, &c. In witness whereof the above contractors with consent foresaid have subscribed these presents (written on stamped paper by

James Stewart, sometime Baillie of Maryburgh). Day, place, month, and year of God above written before these witnesses, Ronald Mc Donell of Shian, John McDonell of Drynachan, and the said James Stewart, writer hereof.

     Signed) "JOHN McDONELL of Glengarry.
      „   "JO. GRANTT.
      „   "PAT. GRANTT.
      „   "RANALD MACKDONELL, Witness.
      „   "JOHN McDONELL, Witness.
      „   "JAS. STEWART, Witness."

 This is one of the most curious papers I ever came across, shewing as it does that apparently for some slight or injury done by Allan Grant, fourth son of Iain a' Chraggain, fifth Laird of Glenmoriston according to the genealogy, Allan's father and brother repudiated and disowned him. The genealogy mentions Allan's name but nothing else regarding him. It may have been for a disgraceful cause similar to that which occasioned a sudden and deadly quarrel between two Badenoch proprietors bearing the same name and formerly great allies and cronies.

 For years I was in ignorance of the cause of this Badenoch feud until a chance reference in a gossiping letter in 1772 from a lady to her brother in the East Indies cleared the matter up.

 The concurring Grants of Crasky and Dundreggan were descended of John the Tutor, and Duncan Caum, second and third sons of Iain Mor a Chaisteil, the third Laird of Glenmoriston.

VIII.—PARISH OF KILMONIVAIG.

BLAR-NAN-LEINE, FOUGHT IN 1544.

HAVING lately come across a copy of an old Manuscript History of the Frasers prepared between 1740 and 1750, I have extracted all essential references to this famous fight—the portions omitted being chiefly comments by Buchanan and Arthur Johnston, which, although couched in elegant Latin, do not add to the facts.

Bishop Leslie in his History regrets the death of the Master of Lovat, with whom he was acquainted in France, and he tells us that the Master had his education in the University of Paris under the best masters, and that he would have proved an honour to his country as well as to his illustrious family had he not been cut off untimely in the very blossom of his youth. The chronicler's comments upon "Bean Cleireach's" conduct is as follows:—

"Lord Lovat had detached his Tutor or Bean Clerk with 100 men to secure a pass with orders not to go out of sight, but to come to their relief if he found it necessary. Every one of the gentlemen present absolutely refused to leave their chief, and so none of them went on that command. Whether it was owing to cowardice, inadvertency, or treachery, he kept out of sight, and came not to the field till all was over, yet it seems it was no treachery, otherwise Lord Alexander would not have given him an honourable discharge for his intromissions, as he did for thirteen years after the battle."

Really this meant nothing, for though Lord Alexander may have been sorry for his father, yet he knew his mother's conduct towards her stepson, the Master of Lovat, resulted as she hoped in her own son succeeding; and it may be taken for granted that the lady and the "clerk" perfectly realised the situation. Some particulars regarding this Lady Lovat will be given later on. Follows the manuscript account—

"There was indeed a rancour of some standing betwixt Lord Lovat and the Captain of Clanranald that looked likely some time or other to break out into a flame that might occasion much bloodshed. The occasion and rise, as it is still reported, and handed down in the family by uninterrupted tradition, and likewise by those who have committed it to writing was this—

"Lord Lovat had a sister who was married to Clanranald, by whom he had only one son, called by the Highlanders, Ranald Oig, young Ranald, and because he was educated at Lovat they called him Ranald Galda, *i.e.* Lowland Ranald, for upon the death of his mother, while he was but an infant, he, according to a custom that then and still somewhat prevails in the Highlands, was taken by Lord Lovat, his uncle, and educated with the Frasers, his mother's relations.

"The father, Clanranald, after the death of his first lady, married a daughter of Torcal Macleod of the Lewis, by whom he had many children, so taking an unreasonable and unaccountable fondness for the son of the second marriage, he resolved to disinherit his eldest son by his former wife, Lord Lovat's sister, and to settle the succession and clanship on the younger brother.

"This design could not but be considered by Lord Lovat and his friends as a very high indignity and affront on every gentleman of the family, and the late depredations they had committed in some parts of Lord Lovat's estate inflamed the resentment to a degree that was not easy to be quenched. The Regent, being resolved at any rate to suppress those insolencies and depredations, gives a commission to the Earl of Argyle to pursue them from the south, and at the same time wrote to Lord Lovat that, in virtue of his commission as the King's Lieutenant in these parts, he should convocate the whole country and march at their head against these lawless ravagers, till he met Argyle.

"George, Earl of Huntly, was highly incensed at the honour King James 5th conferred on Lovat in making him his Lieutenant in those parts, and was no less vexed that he exerted himself with such activity that he kept all within his jurisdiction so long in perfect tranquility, which Huntly looked upon as an eclipsing of him and rendering him insignificant.

"And now, when the Regent and Council sent him their orders to raise the neighbouring clans and march at their head himself to join the Earl of Argyle, the Earl of Huntly looked upon himself not only as eclipsed but highly affronted, and therefore employed his emissaries among the Macdonalds, and especially the Clanranalds, to seek to cut off Lord Lovat.

"This noble lord raised about 400 men, consisting mostly of the gentlemen of his name, and with these he marches through Urquhart and Glenmoriston to Chilichuiman, now Fort-Augustus, where he encamped till the other clans joined him. He with great difficulty commanded his son Simon, Master of Lovat, who had come the preceding year from France to stay at home, to take care of the country.

"When the Grants, Clan Chattan, and others had joined Lord Lovat at Chilichuiman, they all marched in a body through Abertarff, Glengarry, and Lochaber, meeting with no opposition, and found the Earl of Argyle and his forces at Inverlochy. For the Highlanders no sooner understood that an army was marching against them than they scattered and retired to their inaccessible mountains and hidden recesses, so that it was not easy either to follow or attack them.

"The Earl of Argyle and Lord Lovat having concerted measures for preserving the peace and tranquility of the Highlands and stayed for some time at Inverlochy, Lord Lovat put his nephew, Ranald, in peaceable possession of Muidart, and all his forces were ordered to return home.

"When Lord Lovat was on his way home at Letterfinlay, he was informed that the Macdonalds were gathering together to obstruct his passage, upon which his brother-in-law, the Laird of Grant, Mackintosh, and others advised him to alter his route and march another way to disappoint these miscreants who would lie in ambush for him, or if he intended to march straight forward, they would convoy him to his own country. It is probable this kind offer would have been accepted of, but James Fraser of Foyness, a headstrong, obstinate man, dissuaded his chief from it, protesting it would be reckoned cowardice in Lord Lovat and an indignity done to offer him a convoy; that they were able enough themselves for any that could pretend to obstruct their passage. Upon this, all these chieftains and their men took leave of him, and parted with him.

"He marched down directly the south side of Loch Lochy, and about half way he sent one, Bean Clerach or Clerk, with 100 bowmen to guard a pass that was before them, with a charge to keep in sight of the main body, and if he saw danger to come to their assistance. Bean Clerk sets off, but mistaking his orders, kept out of sight on the other side of Drumglach, and so was of no use to the rest, nor any of the 100 men he carried with him.

"When Lord Lovat and the 300 men that were with him came to Lagan-ach-an-Druim near the end of the loch, they observed the Macdonalds coming down the north side of the loch, with 7 displayed banners in 7 battalions of about 600 or 700 men, to secure the pass at the end of the loch."

While it is absolutely certain that the combatants were limited to the Frasers on the one side, and the Macdonalds on the other, with their proper followings, an assertion has lately been made which cannot be overlooked in dealing with the subject.

Mr Alexander Macpherson, factor for Cluny, and who must be held as writing with authority from his constituent, whose papers he has examined, published, in 1893, a book called *Glimpses of Church and Social Life in the Highlands in Olden Times, and other papers.* At page 289 in a foot note, referring to Macpherson of Cluny, he says—" On this banner are emblazoned the arms of the chief, being the coat granted in 1672 by Sir Charles Erskine, Lord Lyon, King-at-Arms. The supporters are two of the clansmen as they appeared in 1455, at Blar-nan-leine, or the famous 'Battle of the Shirts' on which occasion they threw aside their belted plaids, etc., and fought in their shirts and jerkins. In the family charter chest is an extract of his blazon from the books of the Herald College at Edinburgh, but which it seems do not now exist. This extract was made under the superintendence of James Cuming,. keeper of the Lyon Records, by whom it is signed."

As a Fraser, with a deal of Macdonald blood, I take exception to this extraordinary assertion, and cannot—having no ill will towards the Macphersons—but regret observing the persistent efforts of their historians to foist pretentions, and claim, at the expense of others, honours not their due.

1. There is not the shadow of pretence for alleging that two Macphersons fought at Blar-nan-leine, or if they did, that they distinguished themselves in such a way as to justify the Lord Lyon in assigning them such an acknowledgment of pre-eminence, to the detriment of the Frasers and Macdonalds.

2. Mr Macpherson says "two of the clansmen as they appeared." I observe in the coat attached to an authorised portrait of the late Ewen Macpherson of Cluny that, while carrying enormous shields by way of defence, the supporters carry no arms of offence, and if this was the form of their " appearance," of what use could they have been ? The old authoritative description of the supporters has these words " their shirt tied between them," but in the coat above referred to, alas! the shirts have disappeared.

3. The date of the battle given as 1455 is wrong by 89 years, but as the Macphersons by their own accounts seem to be dogged by the errors of printers or transcribers, perhaps Mr Macpherson really wrote 1544.

Follows the continuation of the account of the battle:—

"Lord Lovat immediately calls a council of war, and having all resolved to engage, he encourages his men in a short harangue to this purpose—

"Gentlemen, you are my guard-de-corps, whom I have chosen out of many to accompany me in this honourable expedition for the services of my Sovereign. You are most of you my flesh and blood, the offspring of those heroes who signalised themselves so often in the defence of their country. Remember the honour of your noble ancestors, of whom you are descended, some of which will be for ever on record as illustrious examples of Scotland's pristine bravery. The several branches of our ancient family have upon all occasions distinguished themselves, and to this day never brought the least stain upon the name they bear. The time is short to speak of each of them in particular; methinks I see them all alive in you, and that they have transmitted their courage and bravery as well as their blood and name to you. You are indeed but a handful to encounter yonder formidable crew, but consider the difference in other respects. They are rebels, you are loyal subjects; they outlaws, you are free subjects. I go on before you. I will hazard my life with you and for you. I by far prefer a noble death to an inglorious retreat, or anything that sullys the glory of my house; and are not you as much concerned in its glory as I am? We have from others the character of men of fortitude and resolution; we carry our lives on the point of our swords. Let us act as men. Fall on, and refer the event to Almighty God; 'for the battle is the Lord's, who can save with few as with many.'

"He had scarcely ended when the enemy came close to them at the end of Loch Lochy. Hereupon ensued a most fierce and bloody conflict, fought more like tigers than men. The Frasers threw aside not only their plaids, as has been the common practice with the Highlanders, but threw off their very short coats and vests, and engaged in their shirts, with their two-handed swords and Dane axes.

"This conflict is still called by the country people Blar-an-lein, i.e., the Battle of the Shirts. The fronts of both armies engaged so closely without either sides yielding or giving way, that they were felled down on each side like trees in a wood till room was made by these breaches on each side, and at last all came to fight hand to fist. There was none there but met with his match to encounter him; many were seen to fall, but none to fly; they all fought for victory, which still remained uncertain.

"There is one remarkable passage which I cannot omit. I told you above that Lord Lovat had with difficulty prevailed on his son, the Master, to stay at home to take care of the country. He had been on a day's hunting for his diversion in the forest of Corricharbie, and having taken home great plenty of vension, his step-mother, Lady Lovat, told him with a sneer, that it was fine amusement for young men to be chasing birds and beasts, and then to sleep soundly in their beds, when old men were fighting in the fields. This sarcasm touched so sensibly this noble youth that instantly he takes a dozen resolute fellows with him, and sets out resolving to find his father and friends, and accordingly he joined them at Loch Lochy a little after the conflict began, and fell in where the battle was hottest. The first sight of him quite dispirited and confounded his father. All was now at stake, they fought in blood and gore, and when many of them wearied with their two-handed swords and the heat, they went into the loch in couples and struck each other with their dirks. The Master acted like a hero, and each of the men he brought with him was worth many.

"Lord Lovat fought so gallantly, hewing down all that came in his way, that his enemies called him a "Cruaidh Choscar," *i.e.*, the hardy slaughterer, and when they observed him to fall in the field, it inspired the few that remained of the Clanranald with fresh vigour, crying out with great joy "thuit a Cruaidh Choscar, thuit," the hardy cutter is fallen, is fallen, and as they cried they were knocked down, yea, even those who lay as dead in the field, when an enemy came by would lay hold of a sword and endeavour to cut off a leg or an arm. This they continued from noon till the darkness surprised them, when very few from either side were left alive, and the victory to this day uncertain. The Mac Ranalds as they were more numerous, so more of them fell in proportion. It is certain that only four of the Frasers came alive out of the field, and not double that number of the Mac Ranalds and their adherents. But the loss on the side of the Frasers was incomparably more regretted, for Lord Lovat himself, and his eldest son, the Master of Lovat, and 300 gentlemen of his name were slain. So that there was not one of the name of Fraser of the quality of a gentleman that was come to the state of manhood left alive. I have seen an account of this unhappy conflict by one who was on the field in a few days after it happened and was affected by the elegant, lively, and pathetic manner in which he lamented Lord Lovat and his son's fall in the words of David for Saul and Jonathan (2 Sam. i. 17 to 26).

"History (so far as I heard) does not parallel this unhappy conflict, which was remarkable in many respects. About 1000 men were engaged, of which 12 did not come alive from the field of battle. The Master of Lovat was the last who came to the field of battle and was the first who was slain, which put his father into such a fury, that his death was revenged by the destruction of many.

"There were 80 gentlemen of estates who were killed on the spot, who all left their wives pregnant, and every one of them brought forth a male child, and each of these children arrived at the age of man, so that the over-ruling providence of the wise Disposer of all events did very signally at this time interpose in preserving this family.

"The Macdonalds chose the flower of their numerous clan and yet were defeated in respect of credit and conduct and the number killed. They acknowledge in their poems made on this occasion that they fought with gentlemen, whom they surprised unawares, having no design to fight. 'Cha be clann imme a bh' ann ach clann sgoltag cheann.' That is they did not meet with cowards but with cleavers of heads. Fraser of Foyers was the only gentleman who came alive out of the field of battle. He was miserably mangled and wounded, but being in life was carried by his foster-brother on his back all the way home for which he got free the crofts that he then laboured, and his posterity enjoy it still.*

"When the news of this unhappy conflict came to Lord Lovat's country, all who stayed at home, men and women, went to the field of battle, from whence they carried the bodys of all their principal gentlemen. Andrew Roy of Kirkhill, who was uncle to Lord Lovat, was so like him that in a mistake they carried his body instead of My Lord's till they came to Cilliwhimman, where Lord Lovat's nurse met them and found it was Andrew Roy, upon which they buried him there, as they did most of the gentlemen they brought out of the field of battle, and returned, bringing Lord Lovat's body with them, who with his son and Ronald Galda† were interred

---

* Foyers must have died a few days after as proved by the service of his son Hugh wherein it is proved that he died "in the month of July, 1544."

† Ronald Gallda, by the testimony of the Macdonalds, fought like a hero. His death was caused by a Strontian man called "Mac Dhonuill Ruadh Beg," who, happening to be singled out by Ronald, teacherously called out, "Look behind you," which Ronald incautiously doing, he was instantly pierced in the side and fatally wounded. Ronald, by a supreme effort, dealt a tremendous back stroke, his last, on his assailant's skull. The Moidart people were not at all proud of their neighbour's after boasting of his part at Blar-na-Leine. Father Charles Macdonald in his charming book on "Moidart," published in 1889, says that this man was buried in Eilean-Finnon, the sacred isle of Loch Shiel, and the skull, with other bones lying under the altar slab, used to be examined with interest for the purpose of showing the mark of Ronald Gallda's sword, and by one man, among others, living as late as 1889.

at Beauly. The inscription on his tomb was legible till the year 1746. *Hic jacet Hugo Dominus Fraser de Lovat qui fortissimi pugnans contra Reginalinos occubuit July, 17, 1544.* Here lies Hugh, Lord Fraser of Lovat, who fell fighting gallantly against the Clanranalds, 17 July, 1544."

The real date was the 15th of July.

GLENGARRY.—STATE OF AFFAIRS IN 1762.

Alexander Macdonell of Glengarry died at Invergarry House on the 23rd of December, 1761, being succeeded by his nephew, Duncan, a minor, son of Lieutenant-Colonel Angus Macdonell, who was accidently killed at Falkirk in 1746. Alexander Macdonell was closely mixed up with the Rising of 1745, and though his father John was then living, having survived until 1st September, 1754, Alexander took the leading part. He made his will on the 29th of April, 1761, leaving his sister, Isabella Macdonell, a lady ignored in histories of the family, as his sole executrix. Alexander left to his brother, Captain James Macdonell of Glenmeddle, his French rifle gun ; to Alexander Macdonell of Wester Aberchalder, his own Fusee ; to Duncan Macdonell, his nephew and apparent heir, the arms belonging to him at Edinburgh, in the custody of Alexander Orme, Writer to the Signet, being family arms ; requests his said sister to call for and recover his trunk at Mrs Foster's in Beaufort Buildings, London, and deliver the sword therein and his picture to the heir male of the family, and to deal with the rest of the contents in the manner he had verbally directed her. The most significant direction is in these words—" I further recommend to my said sister, immediately on my decease, to seal up my cabinet and take care that the same shall not be opened until the friends of the family meet, and then I direct Angus Macdonell of Greenfield, John Macdonell of Leek, and Allan Macdonell of Cullachie, or the survivor of them then present, to see all the political and useless letters among my papers burnt and destroyed, as the preservation of them can answer no purpose." Why Glengarry, who lived several months after the execution of his will, did not himself destroy the papers above alluded to can be conjectured by people for themselves—all that need be said here is that their destruction was a pity, and the reason given unsatisfactory.

After Alexander Macdonell's death in 1761, his affairs were found to be in a deplorable state, as will be immediately seen by the particulars now given, enabling us to trace the subsequent unprecedented emigrations and clearances to their origin. At this period the Glengarry estates extended not only from the Loch and the River of Oich north westwards to the watershed and the upper sources of the Quoich, but across to the west main coast, having the south or east side of Loch Hourn as the north boundary, both sides of Loch Nevis, with the river and Loch of Morar, as the south boundary.

The rental of the lands unburdened by wadset was as follows—

I. Sliesmein a twenty penny land comprehending Faichamiosal, Faichimard, Munerigie, Daigen, grazing and forest of Glen Quoich, £625 16s. Item £12 super plus rent payable by Donald Macdonell, of Lundie—total £637 16s Scots as the rental of Sliesmein.

II. The twelve penny land of North Morar, comprehending Breckharrerusich, Breckgrannautor, Buorblach, Glasnacardich, Brinacorries, Stoul, Finisgaig, Ardnante, Swordland, Kinlochmorar, Camusnabraan, Romisaig, Culnamuck, Ardmurrach, Mallaigmore. Rental, £116 0s 4d. Surplus from Kyllis, £6 Scots. Total of Morar, £122 0s 4d Scots.

III. Achadrom, comprehending Glasterbeg, Killeonan, Carnaculross, Keanloch, Pitmaglaster, and Laggan. Rental, £713 16s. Feu-duty of Shian, £15 6s 8d. Total of Achadrom, £729 2s 8d Scots.

IV. Sliesgarve, comprehending Invergarry and Letterfearn, with the miln of Invergarry and salmon fishing on Loch Oich, Glenlie, Boline, Laddy, Ardochie, Garrygullach, Ballachan, and Badentoig, and part of the forest of Glen Quoich annexed thereto, Frenchorrie grazing, part of said forest. Rental, £1161 14s 8d Scots.

V. Knoydart. Feued to Scotos numerous lands. Duty, 1d Scots, and to pay the Duke of Argyll over Superior's feu for the whole of Knoydart. The two penny half penny land of Barisdale; the five penny land of Sandaig; the grazing of Corryyorchkill, Kilchoan, comprehending Scottary, and Glenmeddle, Dalardespig and garden thereon, grazings of Glenflatter. Rent, £654 13s 4d, Scots.

VI. Lands in the parish of Abertarff. The four merk land of Wester Aberchalder; Alexander Macdonell, wadsetter, who was in use, to pay Glengarry yearly £20 Scots of goodwill; the six merk land of Middle Aberchalder, £270 4s Scots; Easter Aberchalder, Angus Macdonell, wadsetter, paid of surplus rent £13 6s 8d; the six merk land of Kytrie, £304 8s, but deduct £72 Scots for a merk and a half value occupied by James Macpherson, Killyhuntly, at least until he be legally dispossessed thereof; the merk land of Culnaloch and pendicle of Saunachan. Rent, £94 5s 4d. The grazing of Derachorry and miln of Abertarff. Rental £144 6s 8d. Total in Abertarff, £774 10s 8d, Scots.

To sum up, Glengarry's free rental stood thus—

1. Sliesmein	Scots £637	16 0
2. North Morar	122	0 4
3. Achadrom	729	2 8
4. Sliesgarve	1161	14 9
5. Knoydart	654	13 4
6. Abertarff Parish	774	10 3
	Scots £4079	17 9

In sterling money, a little over £330.

The wadset lands, which brought in nothing to the chief, were exceedingly numerous, involving large sums.

I. Sliesmein. 1. Drynachan, John Macdonell of Leek, wadset for £1333 6s 8d. Rent uplifted by him, £72 Scots. 2. Lundie and Delchionie, Donald Macdonell of Lundie, principal £1666 13s 4d. Rent, £116. 3. Achluachrach, the said Donald Macdonell, principal £1333 6s 8d. Rent, £104 4s. 4. Ardnabie and Inchlaggan, John Macdonell, principal 4400 merks, and 5. Ardachie with Easter half of Derrylochie, principal 2000 merks. Rental of the various possessions £330 6s 8d Scots. 6. The other half of Derrylochie, John Macdonell of Leek, principal 500 merks, rental, £16 13s 4d. Total wadset monies over parts of Sleismein, £4333 6s 8d, and 6500 merks Scots. Total rental uplifted by the wadsetter £612 Scots.

II. Morar. 1. Mallaig beg, wadset to Barisdale for 1000 merks, rent, £60 6s 8d. 2. Beoraid, wadset held by John Macdonell in Sandaig for 3000 merks, rent, £146 6s 8d. 3. Kyllis Morar, wadset to Randolph Macdonell of Kyllis for 4000 merks, rent £32 13s 4d. Total wadsets over Morar 8000 merks, and total rentals uplifted by the wadsetters, £239 6s 8d Scots.

III. Achadrom. No wadset.

IV. Sliesgarve. 1. Achaunie. Angus Macdonell of Greenfield,

wadsetter for 2000 merks   Rent uplifted by him, £116. 2. The grazing of Lecknafearn, part of the forest of Glen Quoich, Malcolm Macleod of Raasay, wadsetter for 1200 merks, rent uplifted by the wadsetter, £40 Scots. Total wadsets over Sleisgarve, 3200 merks ; total rents uplifted by the wadsetters, £156 Scots.

V. Knoydart.   1. The farthing land of Skiarie, the half-farthing land of Caolasbeg, the halfpenny lands of Munial and Camusdown, the penny land of Lee, the halfpenny land of Souriais, the town and lands of Inverie Mor, Milliarie ,and Brechachy, the halfpenny land of Groab, the town and lands of Riquell, the halfpenny land of Culnacarnich, comprehending the pendicle of Cuilvane, the halfpenny land of Sallachrie, the halfpenny land of Carnachray, the town and lands of Brunsaig and Glaschyle, the town and lands of Ridarroch and Torcruine, and part of the lands of Inverguseran and glen thereof, the three and a half farthing land of Achglyne and halfpenny land of Gorton, all wadset to Barisdale for 27,000 merks. Rent, £123 3s 5d sterling. 2. The two and-a half penny lands of Newgart, the penny land of Sandliman, the penny land of Scammadale, all wadsetted to Macdonell of Scotos for £4666 13s 4d Scots. Rental uplifted by Ronald Macdonell, then of Scotos, £237 13s 4d Scots. 3. The twopenny land of Crowlin, wadset held by John Macdonell of Crowlin for £2000 Scots, rent worth to him £143 6s 8d. 4. Kinlochourn, Angus Macdonald wadsetter thereof for £666, 13s 4d, rent worth to him £63 6s 8d.   5. The ten farthing land of Inverguseran, wadset to Macdonell of Inverguseran for £1460 13s 4d. Rent uplifted by the wadsetter, £133 6s 8d. 6. The six farthing land of Ardnaslishnish, Allan Macdonell, wadsetter for (sum left blank) his rent £62 Scots. 7. Airor, wadset to John Macdonell for £1000, rental, £90 Scots ; 8. Kyllis, wadset to Randolph Macdonell for £2666 13s 4d Scots, and worth to him in rent £133 6s 8d Scots. Total wadsets over Knoydart (excepting that over Ardnaslinish, blank as before mentioned) 27,000 merks and £12,460 13s 4d Scots, and the rental, £863 Scots, and £123 3s 5d sterling.

VI. Abertarff.   1. The four merk land of Wester Aberchalder, wadsetted to Alexander Macdonell for 2000 merks, rent £148 ; 2. Easter Aberchalder, wadsetted by Angus Macdonell for £1333 6s 8d, rent, £151 6s 8d ; 3. The eight merk land of Cullachie, wadsetted orignally to Donald Macdonell of Lochgarry for 8000 merks, rent, £314 13s 8d Scots ; 4. The twelve merk land of Easter and Wester Achteraw, wadsetted to Alexander Macdonell of Achteraw, for £8000, rental, £472 Scots ; 5. The three merk lands of Pitmean, wadset to Alexander Macdonell for £2000, rental, £118 Scots ; 6. The merk and a half land of Leek, and town and lands of Invervigar and Auchindarroch, wadsetted to John Macdonell of Leek, for 3000 merks Scots, rental, £136 13s 4d Scots. Total wadsets over Abertarff parish lands, 13,000 merks, and £11,333 6s 8d ; total rental, £1340 13s 8d Scots. Again to sum up—

	Merks.	Debts. Pounds Scots.	Sterling.	Rents to Wadsetters. Pounds Scots.
1. Sliesmien ...	£6500 0 0	£4333 6 8		£672 0 0
2. Morar ...	8000 0 0			239 0 0
3. Achadrom ...		No Wadset		
4. Sliesgarve ...	3200 0 0			156 0 0
5. Knoydart ...	27,000 0 0	£12,460 13 4	£123 3 5	863 0 0
6. Abertarff ...	13,000 0 0	£11,333 6 8		1340 13 8
	£57,700 0 0	£28,127 6 8	£123 3 5	£3270 13 8

The rental uplifted by wadsetters may be taken at £4750 Scots, which was considerably more than Glengarry's own free rent.

GLENGARRY.—STATE OF AFFAIRS IN 1762-1788.

The amount of the heritable debt on Glengarry has been already stated, while the personal debts, on the death of Alexander Macdonell in 1761, were large. The wadsets were old and lucrative, but where was the money to pay them off. The next heir was a minor, and his affairs fell into the hands of the lawyers and the courts, resulting in a process of ranking and sale which lasted over several years. Under it North Morar was sold in 1768 to General Simon Fraser of Lovat, and as Morar held of the Crown as part of the lordship of Gartmoran, the price paid for it was considerable. As this occurred prior to the restoration of the Lovat estates, Morar was the first land possessed by General Fraser. The price paid for it relieved the Glengarry personal debts, and for a few years things moved quietly on until 1772, when an event occurred which initiated changes, the effects of which remain to the present day. This was the marriage of Duncan Macdonell of Glengarry in the end of that year to Marjory Grant, eldest daughter of Sir Ludovick Grant of Dalvey. Her fortune was £2000 sterling, whereof one half was paid at the time, the remainder payable at Sir Ludovick's death, who did not long survive, with interest at the rate of 5 per cent. till paid. Duncan Macdonell was a weak man ; his wife the very reverse, and her great rise in social importance moved her at once to strive with success but regardless of sufferings to clear off the debts, to raise the rents, and generally to aggrandise the position of the Glengarry family.

The first step was to give notice to the wadsetters, every one of whom, it would have been noticed, were Macdonells and connected more or less with the chief. Being of old date and prices advancing rapidly their position was excellent, for it may be taken as certain that, besides sitting in their own personal occupancies free, the interest of the wadset monies was more than paid by their numerous sub-tenants, crofters, and cottars. Further, being men of education with an assured position in the country, it was galling for them to think of subsiding into the new position of tenants, burdened with a large increase of rent, and hence they nearly all emigrated, taking along with them the choicest of their followers. The emigration, which was to the New England States, was the wisest step for them to pursue, and proved beneficial to them, but it drained the cream of manhood of Glengarry, to the great detriment of the district. Some of the chief men remained, in particular Lundie and Barisdale.

Lundie was unwilling to move, and this is how he had to settle. Glengarry gave him a bond for £250 sterling at five per cent., getting the wadsets discharged, but his rents were fixed at £20 4s 5d for Inshlaggan, a fat cow for Glengarry's table, or £3 15s sterling, and £38 for Faicham, Lundie, and Dulochus, or say, in all £62 sterling, which may be contrasted with his former position. For a time Lundie did well, but times were unpropitious. In 1784 he is described as "late of Lundie," his place being taken at Faicham, etc., by Alexander Macpherson, writer, at a rent of £84, instead of the prior rent of £38. The last I observe of Lundie is in 1785, when in possession of a stock of 110 goats, 2 horses, and 89 sheep, but without land, he is pursued by Glengarry for statutory trespass moneys on his old holding. I have been informed that he emigrated in poverty shortly after, and this was the end of the historic family of Lundie, who as far back as 1644 were heritors valued at the respectable figure of £933 6s 8d Scots. I have collected some materials for a brief account of this family which may be utilised some day.

I next refer to the other of the two largest wadsetters who remained, viz., Barisdale. Archibald, the third, who was attainted, tried, and condemned to death many years after Culloden under very strange circumstances, and after his long imprisonment, entered the Government service. Barisdale itself was only leased by him, the wadset lands of the family being seized by the Crown, and restored at the general giving back of such forfeited estates as remained under charge of the Commissioners. Archibald and his famous son, Coll, fourth Barisdale, maintained their position and came to terms under a reference whereby the wadset was cancelled, when the Barisdales sank to the position of tenants. Coll Barisdale lived chiefly at Auchtertyre in Lochalsh, holding under the Seaforths, and though in his letters, when he has occasion to refer to private affairs, he says he was never very sure what Alexander Macdonell of Glengarry might do, he held his own with credit, being indeed in appearance, education, and ability a clansmen of whom any chief might be proud. His son Archibald, fifth and last Barisdale, continued in occupation.

THE CONDITION OF THE PEOPLE.

I shall now refer to the condition of the people. Burdened with the enlarged rents, they struggled on, but as early as 1780 they were much behind. The year of scarcity, 1782, finished them, and the hornings and poindings in 1783 and 1784 for arrears bulked largely. One special burden, viz., services for carriages, peat cutting, fowls, etc., was converted into a serious money payment, apparently quite disproportionate and oppressive. For instance, in the case of Dugald Cameron, late cowherd to Glengarry, afterwards tenant of Boline, while his rent was £11 4s 3d, the converted services amounted to £3 2s 8d, and in other cases the proportion appear to be the same, or about one-third additional.

In 1782, the first sheep farmer from the Borders appeared

in Glengarry. I observe by a letter from Messrs Thomas Gillespie and Henry Gibson, to a friend who had recommended them, dated Caplegill, April 16th, 1782, they say—"Mr Gillespie and I return you our joint thanks for the kindness and civility shown to Mr Gillespie, junior, in recommending him in such strong terms to Mr Macdonell of Glengarry, with whom he has made a bargain—the articles transmitted to us for our approbation which we have agreed to and wrote Mr Macdonell so, begging of him to write us as soon as he receives our letter, that we may take the proper measures for building houses for the reception of our herds against Whitsunday first, which is the term of entry." The lands thus taken were the forest of Glen Quoich, etc., then in the proprietor's hands.

In 1785 I find that the following 55 tenants, crofters, and cottars were warned and the decree of removal and ejection promptly extracted, viz., Donald Scott, Donald Macdonell, senior; Angus Macphee, Donald Macdonell, junior; Duncan Kennedy, Donald Macdonell, Donald Cameron, Archibald Macdonell, Archibald Scott, Allan Macdonell, Neil Kennedy and Angus Macdonell, from Laggan, 12; Donald Maclellan, Angus Maclellan, Charles Stewart and Ewen Macdonell, from Glenline, 4; Donald Cameron, from Boline, 1; Alexander MacCalkan, Angus Macdonell, John Kennedy, Katharine Macdonell, from Laddy, 4; Duncan Macmillan, Donald Macmillan, Angus Macmillan, tenants in Battenteog and possessors of Pollarie, 3; Margaret Macmillan, Myles Macmillan, Alexander Macmillan, and John Macdonell in Inshlaggan, and possessors of the grazing of —————, 4; Ranald Macdonell, John Kennedy, Duncan Kennedy, Donald Gillies, from Ardnabi, 4; John Campbell, Donald Kennedy, Angus Macdonell, senior; Angus Macdonell, junior; Alexander Macdonell and Donald Macdonell from Dangin, 6; Angus Mackintosh, John Mackintosh, John Macdonell, Katharine Macdonell, Donald Macdonell, Donald Kennedy, Duncan Macdonell, and Allan Macdonell, from Achnaclerach, 8; John Macdonell, Duncan Macdonell, senior; Duncan Macdonell, junior; John Macphee, Widow Janet Macdonell, Anne Macdonell and Alexander Macdonell, from Munerigie, 7; John Macdonell, tenant in Lundie, 1. The total as above mentioned is 55 heads of families, say 300 souls.

In 1786 the four above-named tenants of Ardnabi are warned out of Ardachy, as also James Macdonell, Duncan Gillies, Angus Gillies and John Kennedy, their sub-tenants, 4; Roderick Kennedy, from Munerigie, 1; John Macphee, John Mactavish, and Alexander Mactavish from Achlnaclerach, 3. Total, 8 heads of families, say, 40 souls. In this year, as will be afterwards noted, 500 emigrated from Knoydart under their priest, Mr Alexander Macdonell of the Scotos family.

In 1787 Ranald Macdonell, Alexander Macdonell, James Macdonell, and Duncan Kennedy were warned out of Dirriwargal, Balearie, and Arriurian, 4; Dougal Cameron, Evan Gillies, and Duncan Macdonell, from Boline, 3; Total 7 heads of families, say 35 souls.

GLENGARRY.—STATE OF AFFAIRS IN 1788-1808.

In 1788, Glengarry again warned out some of the people warned in former years but afterwards permitted them to remain on a precarious footing; and of new people, John Macphee, from Poulnonachan; John Macdonald and Duncan Kennedy, from Laggan; Alexander Macpherson, from Shian; and Duncan Macgillies, from Inshavoilt and Breallagie. In the midst of these distresses, Duncan Macdonell somewhat suddenly died, a comparatively young man, at Elgin on the 11th of July, 1788, on his way for the benefit of his health to the waters, then in some repute, of Peterhead, leaving his widow principal trustee of the estate and guardian of her son, Alexander, then in his fifteenth year. No great regret seems to have been felt. A kindly disposed clergyman, the Rev. Patrick Grant of Boleskine, when referring to Glengarry's death, merely says to a friend, under date of 22nd July—" I intended writing you on Monday of last week, but accompanied Glengarry's corpse that day, and only came home Sunday morning." His widow, however, went to considerable expense in restoring the mausoleum at Killionan. In Duncan's time, North Morar was lost, but all the wadsets were redeemed, and progress was made towards the reclamation of Shian and the Aberchalders, while the rental had been increased enormously since 1772.

The Glengarry claims to the representation of the Lords of the Isles, first openly asserted by Lord Macdonell and Aros, was revived in Duncan Macdonell's time. His son, in 1798, desires to recover some family papers which were in possession of a lawyer deceased, "from the period the late Lord Macdonald of Sleat thought proper to dispute my father's right to the Chieftainship of the Clan and Arms of the ancient Lords of the Isles and Earls of Ross. And though that matter is decided, it is far from pleasant to lose a thing of the kind, and therefore I depend on your steady exertions to find them." Duncan's widow, who managed matters with a high hand, ignoring her co-trustees, and in one letter asserting most indignantly that "Factor Butter" was no trustee of her son, continued the same course until her death at Inverness on the 1st of October, 1792. Her eldest son had been alternately crossed and petted, so that before his mother's death, and especially thereafter before attaining his majority, young Glengarry's temper and disposition showed itself as most overbearing. The old and valued friend of the family, Mr William Macdonald of St. Martins, Clerk to the Signet, who had often come to its assistance from the time of John of the '45, though left a trustee, was never consulted. He says in a letter of 13th July, 1793, referring to the young Chief—" I dread his getting into bad hands. Perhaps he may pull up and come to reason, for it grieves me to see the representative of that family running into folly, and must soon involve him." The raising of the Glengarry Fencibles and consequent demand for men had put a stop for a time to removals, and I have not observed any subsequent to those already described, prior to 1800, except in 1797, when two tenants in Glashchoyle, three in Leachaultnakure, and one in Tororay, all in Knoydart, were summoned, but they escaped through the folly of the Sheriff-officer in calling as his witnesses his own two sons, both under 14 years of age. Those families which did not contribute all their available men were severely dealt with, and in one case a poor widow was oppressed because she did not give her two sons. She was warned out, though resident on the Lochiel estate, under pretence that her cattle trespassed. Widow Kennedy was, in reality, a cottar under the Achnasaul tenants, and she gave a son to Glengarry on the promise that she would get an independent croft from him, which he not only did not give but, because she declined giving another son, he warned her, as if she were within his bounds. A clansman of Lochiel was very indignant and intervened with effect, observing in reply to the further accusation that the Kennedys were idle and disorderly, that it was not true, "but if Glengarry himself were less so, he would not be obliged to abscond at this date (12th of June, 1798) from the laws of his country"—a reference to the Macleod duel.

The Fencibles being disbanded, pressure was again felt, and in 1802 the second great emigration occurred. In the transactions of the Celtic Society of Montreal, published in 1887, Professor Bryce of Winnipeg says—

"In 1802 three vessels sailed from Fort-William, in Scotland, to Quebec, laden with Highlanders. Many of these were Macdonell's Highlanders—a regiment largely of Glengarry men—who had served in repressing the Irish rebellion of 1798. There were among these people colonists from Glenelg and Kintail, and elsewhere in the Highlands. There were some thousands of these settlers, who chiefly settled in Glengarry County, Ontario, and they have given a backbone to that part of Canada at the very crisis in its history, since their arrival."

In the same volume of Transactions, Mr John Maclennan, of Lancaster, Ontario, whose father was a Kintail man, thus refers to the emigration—

"In 1802 three vessels came from Fort-William to Quebec emigrant laden. Among them were the disbanded soldiers of the Glengarry Fencibles Regiment that had been raised by Alexander Macdonell, chief of Glengarry, for service in Ireland in the repression of the Rebellion of 1798. They were granted free land, and were accompanied by their chaplain, the Reverend Alexander Macdonell, afterwards Bishop of Kingston, and the first in the Province, and who lived to the age of 80, much esteemed by all classes. The influence over the men who were his clansmen as well as his flock, was deservingly great. They formed a compact colony in the centre of the country, and built the fine church of St. Raphaels."

I refer to Bishop Macdonell later on.

The rental this year, 1802, was as follows, an enormous rise since 1768, when it was only a little over £700 0s 0d sterling.

		£	s	d
Skiary ... ... Sterling		40	0	0
Barisdale		105	0	0
The two Crowlins and Scamadale		160	0	0
Lee and Munial		140	0	0
Ardnaslishinish		12	0	0
Newgart of Inverguseran...		197	0	0
Samdallan		65	0	0
Airor		57	0	0
Down		68	0	0
Rhiedarroch		52	10	0
Glaschoil		35	0	0
The two Inveries and Dale		105	0	0
Glenmeddle		300	0	0
Kyles and Bruinsack		164	14	0
Salachary and Torcruin		55	6	0
Kinloch Nevis		315	0	0
Millary, Lochourn, Glenquoich, Pollary and Inshlaggan		970	0	0
Ardochie and Ardnabie		98	0	0
Daingan		55	0	0
Achaluachrach		62	0	0
Faicham and Munerigie		126	0	0
Leek		40	0	0
Invervigar		40	0	0
Easter Aberchalder		280	0	0
Wester Aberchalder		240	0	0
South Laggan		230	0	0
Kinloch and Culross		140	0	0
Killionan		320	0	0
North Laggan West		40	0	0
Glenline and Boline		112	0	0
Laddymore		35	0	0
Laddybeg and Ardochy		60	0	0
Carried forward ...		£4719	10	0

	Brought forward	...	£4719 10 0
Greenfield	... ...	...	70 0 0
Garryguallach	... ...	...	250 0 0
Faicham Iosal	... ...	...	31 10 0
Crofters this year	... ...	...	19 0 0
	Total	... ...	... £5090 0 0

Those marked in the rental as crofters were those who paid direct to the proprietor—the numerous body known as crofters and cottars as a rule being sub-tenants of the principal tacksman contributing generally the whole rent, leaving the tacksman to sit rent free.

The great emigration of 1802 did not stop removals, which still continued on a modified scale. In 1803 Mr Donald Macleod of Ratagan is evicted; and in 1806 from Pollary, the two Arriveans, and Derryverigyle, Knoydart, John Mackinnon, ground officer, an old retainer of the family, is removed. In 1804 there were warned out, and decrees extracted against them, the following in Knoydart—Ewen Macdonald, John Macdonald, and Alexander Macpherson from Rhiedarroch, 3; James Macdougall, Donald Macdougall, and Evan Ban Cameron, from Doun, 3; Archibald Kennedy, Donald Macdonald, and Lachlan Mackinnon from Airor, 3; Duncan Kennedy, and James Kennedy from Kyles, 2; in all eleven heads of families.

In 1806, the following were warned out and the decrees against them extracted :—Angus Gillies, Angus Kennedy and Donald Macdonell, from Auchagirnack and Shean-Taller, 3; John Hall and William Macdonell from the change-house of Portbain, being part of Letterfearn, 2; William Robertson, from the change-house of Laggan, a part of North Laggan, 1; Alexander Breack Kennedy, Angus Kennedy, Alexander Macdonell, junior; Alexander Macdonell, senior; Angus Macdonell and Paul Macdonell from Leek, 6; John Macdonell, Angus Macdonell, Donald Macdonell, John Kennedy, Ewen Kennedy, Angus Kennedy and Widow Flora Macdonell or Macrae from Invervigar, 7; in all not less than nineteen heads of families.

In 1808, the following were similarly treated. John Fraser from Portbain of Letterfearn, 1; John Roy Macdonald, Alexander Gillies, John Macdonald, from Laggan, 5; John Cameron, Evan Macdonald and Evan Macphee, from Shian, 3; James Macdonell and John Stewart from Auchgirnach, 2; Donald Macdonald and Donald Macdonell from Old Ground, 2; Alexander Mactavish from Mandally, 1; John Stewart from Invergarry, 1; Donald Buie Macdonald from Skiary, 1; Donald Roy Macdonell from Sandaig, 1; Angus Mackinnon, John Mackinnon, James Macdonell, Angus Macdonell, Ranald Macdonell, Donald Maclellan or Maclennan, and Neil Macphail from Airor, 7; and Donald Macdonell, from Soerges, 1; in all twenty-four heads of families.

GLENGARRY.—STATE OF THE PEOPLE—THEIR
GRIEVANCES, IN 1793, ETC.

Colonel Alexander Macdonell was killed in 1828, leaving much debt, which resulted in Glengarry being sold some years after to the Marquis of Huntly. Alexander's son, Eneas Ronaldson Macdonell, emigrated about 1839 with a number of his people to Australasia, but being unsuccessful he returned to Knoydart, where he died. After his death, that estate fell under trustees, who sold it in 1853 to the late Mr James Baird of Cambusdoon. Part of the bargain included the removal virtually *in toto* of such of the people as still remained, and the hardships and cruelties of this the last eviction are so fresh and known to so many living, through Mr Alexander Mackenzie's *History of the Highland Clearances* and otherwise, that it is needless to refer to them.

I have thus in outline shown step by step, when, by whom, and why, these most unhappy evictions and emigrations occurred. It will have been observed that all the wadsetters of 1768 were Macdonells and of the Chief's house, and though a century has passed it is impossible without emotion even now to think of the numerous Macdonells, tenants and sub-tenants, cottars and dependents, who in turn were dispossessed, a noble race whose predecessors, by their labours, exertions, and services, often to death, were the means through which the House of Glengarry had its renown. But it was all in vain. Rents rose prodigiously, yet the family decayed, lost and lost every acre except the "Craggan an Fhithich" and mausoleum of Killionan, and there is not now a living male descendant of Duncan Macdonell of Glengarry. It is a fact not less painful than preposterous that at the present day (1894) some dozen crofters (all remaining) cannot get sufficient land of the tens of thousands acres of Knoydart to maintain them without the intervention of the Crofters Commission.

The introduction of sheep farmers was most harassing to the people. When not removed, their rents were raised, their grazings curtailed, actions for trespass frequent; in short, ultimate removal through harassment and insolvency became certain. One of the minor grievances was fox hunters' dues, of which I give a specimen, being a dignified remonstrance by the old Knoydart people to the factor on the estate, enclosing a summons to the Fort-William Court served on one of their number for £1 4s 9½ for fox hunters' dues, and £1 11s 8d, proportion of his maintenance—a document well worthy of preservation. Here it is—

"Knoydart, 12th February, 1793.

Sir,—We the under written antient tenants of Glengarry in the country of Knoydart, and remains of the former inhabitants, do acquaint you as factor and doer for Glengarry, do acquaint you we say, and remonstrate, how that the farmers who have sheep stock in this country, and particularly from other gentlemen's properties, are daily harassing any who have only black cattle, and charging us with daily pleas and disputing unreasonable as we judge it, so that it will be absolutely impossible for any to stand, unless a step is efficaciously put to their encroachments. In particular one of a very disagreeable nature is started against us presently, with regard to the expense of a fox hunter. In order to which we inform how that at getting our late tacks, no mention was made of any such particular, so that we judged ourselves totally exempt from any such burden. Secondly, last spring they agreed with a fox hunter for five quarters of a year at thirty-three pounds sterling. They pretended that as always so likewise for these space of time we should pay as much as themselves though our proportion of sheep is only a mite to thousands. Neither had they our consent or approbation at the time of feeing a fox hunter, nor did they await for it. Upon our refusal to pay we have all been charged with summons, tho' very ill executed. We beg therefore, that you undertake not only our cause but as we think it that of justice, bring our law plea to Inverness, where you are yourself, and also represent our situation to our master, who we hope will take pity upon, and repell the presumption of such individuals as think to take advantage, not only of our weakness, but his homage, and turn into their private interest and purses, these pennies we would more cheerfully reserve for his—not only but also his agents and attendants, we would not chose to complain of them in the tone of incomers or intruders, though we were the first servants and guardians of the family, if they behaved discreetly to any of, particularly some others intermixed with them. But these grievances are such as scarcely one brother would bear from another.

"In order, however, to spare ourselves and them too, the expense of law, we appointed a meeting with them, and agreed to pay a competency, provided they would give us in write their obligation of giving us no further trouble. This they refused, and the agreement was knocked up. Herein, for a specimen, we have enclosed one of the summones :—

"From Killichoan (signed)—John Macdonell, John Macdonell, Angus Macdonell, Angus Macdonell, senr., Donald Maclellan, Donald Macdonell, Angus Mackinnon.

"From Inverie Mor (signed)—Donald Macdonell, John Macdonell, Rory Macdonell.

"From Brionsaig (signed)—Angus Macdonell, Allan Macdonell, Ronald Macdonell.

"From Glaschoile (signed)—Angus Maclachlan, Dugald Maclachlan, John Macdonell.

"From Riharroch (signed)—John Macdonell, Angus Macdonell, Malcolm Macaulay, Alexander Macdonell, Rory Macdonell.

"From Scammadale (signed)—Ranald Macdonell.

"P.S.—We wrote to Glengarry and we hope you will take the trouble to forward it when you receive it, and give it the proper direction wherein we represented to our master our grievances and the encroachments and daily harrassments given us by the subtenants of other heritors such as Barisdale, Sandaig, and Donald Strome."

Before concluding my remarks on the Glengarry Emigrations, the account would be incomplete without referring to the two Alexanders Macdonell, clergymen, so intimately connected therewith.

The first Alexander Macdonell, of the Scotos family, went out to Canada in 1786. Of him Mr J. A. Macdonell of

Greenfield, in his most interesting sketches of Glengarry in Canada, published at Montreal in 1893, says—

"Shortly after the close of the Revolutionary war in 1786, a large emigration of Highlanders, numbering, I believe, some five hundred souls, took place, principally from that part of the Glengarry estates known as Knoydart, under the leadership of the Rev. Alexander Macdonell, who settled with their clansmen and kinsfolk in Glengarry. The following extract, taken from Neilson's *Quebec Gazette*, relates to the immigration:—

"'Quebec, 7th September, 1786.

"'Arrived ship "Macdonald," Captain Robert Stevenson, from Greenock with emigrants, nearly the whole of a parish in the North of Scotland, who emigrated with their priest (the Reverend Alexander Macdonell, Scotos), and nineteen cabin passengers, together with five hundred and twenty steerage passengers, to better their case, up to Catraqui' (Kingston.)

"This priest was one of the earliest Catholic priests or missionaries, other than French, in Upper Canada. He was born at Scotos House in Knoydart, Glengarry, Scotland, I believe, in 1750. He was educated in France, and ordained priest in Paris in 1778. He was founder of the parish of St. Raphael's, the pioneer parish not only of Glengarry, but of all Upper Canada, where he built the first church known in its day as the "Blue Chapel," and which was succeeded by the present large edifice, erected by Bishop Macdonell. He died at Lachine on his way to Montreal on 24th May, 1803."

The second Alexander Macdonell was born at Inshlaggan in 1762, educated at the Scots College of Paris, afterwards at Valladolid, and there ordained in 1787. He was subsequently missionary in the Brae of Lochaber, and Chaplain of the Glengarry Fencibles. After the emigration of 1802 and his settlement in Glengarry, he, in the words of Greenfield, p. 323—

"Was for 36 years a notable figure in the Province. He possessed an influence over his Highland fellow countrymen, which was exerted without stint for their temporal welfare and advancement, without distinction of creed, and for the furtherance of those sound and loyal principles which were so dear to his heart."

Upper Canada having been united into a Bishopric by Leo XII. in 1826, Alexander Macdonell was appointed its first Bishop. He visited Scotland for the last time in 1839, and was in the Highlands in the autumn of that year. He died early in 1840 in his 80th year and was interred in Edinburgh, but in 1861 his remains were removed to their final resting place at Kingston, Ontario.

I have the pleasure of giving a letter, written in 1837, from the Bishop to the then Chisholm, which well illustrates his benevolent disposition. With The Chisholm's mother, afterwards Lady Ramsay, sister of Colonel Alexander Macdonell of Glengarry, the Bishop would have been well acquainted prior to 1802—

"Kingston, Upper Canada, 26th May, 1837.

"My dear Chisholm,—Lady Ramsay will not be surprised that I should feel interested in the welfare and prosperity of her son, whom she educated with such care and attention, and whose talents improved and developed by education, hold out such high expectations not only to an affectionate parent, but to all his friends and indeed to his country.

"Little did I think when I had the pleasure of seeing you last, at St. John's Wood, near London, on reading a noble specimen of your improvement in your education, which you wrote for the perusal of your worthy uncle, the late Sir Alexander Grant, and myself, that I should have to address you to-day as the representative of the county of Inverness, an honour which has fallen to the lot of very few of the natives of that county since the union of England and Scotland. Although this be the first step of your political career, I hope it will not be the last, and, old as I am, I do not despair of your holding one of the most distinguished situations in the Government of the British Empire.

"This will be handed to you by Major Bonicastle of the Royal Engineers, a particular friend of mine, who will be able to give Lady Ramsay, if in London, every information she may wish to know concerning me, and, if not, I would be greatly obliged to you by mentioning my name to her ladyship when you write to her, and also to your uncle the General, and to say that I am well and in the enjoyment of good health.—I have the honour to be, my dear Sir, your most devoted humble servant.

(Signed) "ALEXANDER MACDONELL,
"Bishop of Kingston."

THE GLENGARRY TRIALS OF 1798 AND 1807.

The late Abertarff used to say that from the time of his birth, and he feared until his death, he would never be "out of law," to use a common expression. The same may be said of Alexander Macdonell of Glengarry, with this difference, that while Abertarff was the victim of circumstances over which he had no control Glengarry as a rule brought all his legal troubles on himself.

Let me take two of his trials. In the case of Lieutenant Macleod Glengarry was the wrongdoer, but conscious of this, he did all he could to effect an honourable arrangement, in which he was supported by his second, Major Macdonald. Macleod on the other hand was headstrong himself, and had an unsuitable second in the person of Captain Campbell, as obstinate as his principal. It is generally supposed that the original offence was committed at a Northern Meeting ball, but it was really at a Fort-George officers' and county gentlemen's ball held in April, 1798. Miss Forbes of Culloden, a great beauty, who afterwards married Hugh Robert Duff of Muirtown, having agreed to dance with Lieutenant Norman Macleod, grandson of Flora Macdonald, Glengarry spoke and behaved rudely, claiming her hand for the same dance. In consequence a hostile meeting took place near Fort-George on the 3rd of May, Macleod being wounded, but not at the moment thought dangerously. The combatants shook hands and parted. In a few days Macleod died, and in August following Glengarry was tried in the High Court of Justiciary. The prosecution was conducted with virulence, and not a stone was left unturned to press home the capital charge. The trial excited immense interest in the country, and particularly in the North, all the Northern lawyers and Advocates in Edinburgh being present. I have three letters on the subject. James Horne, W.S., writing on the 7th August, merely says in a P.S.—" Glengarry has just been acquit;" James Fraser of Gortuleg on the same day says—"Altho it will probably reach you otherways, I cannot avoid congratulating you on Glengarry's escape, which was narrow indeed, since the chancellor of the jury declared it arose only from the tendency to conciliation in the course of the day anterior to the fatal meeting. I sincerely wish he may make a good use of the hairbreadth escape. He must certainly pay a handsome assythment." The fullest account is that given by Coll Macdonell of Dalness, C.S., Glengarry's agent, who thus expresses himself on the 14th of August, 1798—

"I have yet scarcely recovered from the fatigues of Glengarrie's trial. You would have several public as well as private accounts of it, but none can give an adequate idea of the whole of what appeared in the course of it. The Lord Advocate exerted the utmost pitch of his abilities, and the verdict returned does not meet with the general approbation of the public, though I for one am convinced that it is a proper verdict, warranted by the evidence adduced. The public voice was so much against Glengarry, that not a single one among his friends thought that he would have been acquitted by a unanimous verdict. If you compare the *Mercury* and the *Advertiser* account, it will convey a tolerable good criterion of the import of the evidence, though several material things are omitted in both— particularly no notice is taken of a letter signed "Neill Campbell, Captain, 79th Regiment," which Captain Campbell denied to be his subscription. It was wrote to the publisher of the *Courant*. The evidence of Mrs Duff is the subject of general talk; without doubt you will hear it. She remained in Court to the last. The Lord Advocate paid very many compliments to her beauty, etc., in the course of his speech, but the chancellor of the jury said she was the best evidence for Glengarry of all that had been adduced."

Another serious trial in which Glengarry was chiefly interested, was that of Dr Donald Macdonald, Fort-Augustus, concluded in 1807.

Dr Macdonald was a man of dogged and obstinate temper and disposition. He was tenant in the first decade of the century of the sheep farm of Scotos proper, and the ill-feeling beteween him and Glengarry dated back to 1798, when at the birthday entertainment of that year at Invergarry House, Dr Macdonald assaulted the Macdonell Chief, or at least seized and threatened him. An attempt to adjust matters was afterwards made by the Rev. Dr Thomas Ross of Kilmonivaig, Mr Macdonell, Greenfield, and Mr John Mackay, Innis-na-cardoch, who all begged of Dr Macdonald to apologise to Glengarry for what had taken place, but the Dr would make none, considering himself not in fault. The ill-feeling remained, but did not come to any head until 1805, when according to himself the

Doctor was assaulted, threatened, and severely beaten by some of Glengarry's people at a market held in Fort-Augustus on the 30th of September in that year. There was a good deal of general turmoil and disturbance in the place at the time, apart from this particular squabble. The charges made ultimately resolved into a process of injury, oppression, and damages before the Court of Session, and the defenders called were Alexander Macdonell of Glengarry, Alexander Macdonell, at Kinloch, factor for Glengarry; John Macdonell, junior, piper to Glengarry; Ranald Macdonell, tacksman of Glenline; Angus Kennedy, commonly called Angus Bàn Kennedy, at Invervigar; and Allan Kennedy, brother to the said Angus Bàn Kennedy. Proof was led in Edinburgh at great length, and the proceedings lingered until the 23rd of June, 1807, when a decision was given. Sufficient details will be found in the following two letters from Glengarry's agent, and interlocutor pronounced by the Court:—

"Edinburgh, 23rd June, 1807.

"The fate of Dr Macdonald's case against Glengarry has been determined, and determined with a vengeance. The Lords awarded £2000 sterling of damages, besides expenses, and they also recommended to the Lord Advocate to prosecute criminally. The public expectation was high on account of prejudice, but the decision outstripped the public expectation, at least two-thirds in magnitude. The Court agreed that their opinion should be delivered by the Lord Justice Clerk. He made a very long speech, but even at the funeral of Balnatua, he imputed the blame, and the whole blame to Glengarry.

"To advise Glengarry to acquiesce in the judgment is so very repugnant to my feelings that I will not do it, let the consequences be what they may. Mr Blair, the most eminent lawyer at the Scots Bar, while he gave it as his opinion that damages would be awarded, and that we ought to prepare for it, considered that they would be small, and that the case was not by any means so bad as he had reason to believe, or cause to expect. Mr Erskine was of the same mind. On the opinion of the former I would place the greatest reliance, but in a matter of this kind where evidence is to be judged of too, according to the laws of common law, I do not apprehend that a judgment dictated by prejudices (for such I must consider it) is to be acquiesced in without an endeavour to overturn it in a place where that prejudice has no room to operate. You will perceive that my meaning is the House of Peers, for I expect no reversal here, though

Counsel were so astonished at the decision that they could not bring their mind to say one thing or other."

"Edinburgh, 24th June, 1807.

"Though not recovered from the dismay of our discomfiture, I think it right to communicate a copy of the interlocutor. . . . The malicious are now making an attack on Sir James Montgomery for not taking it up criminally, and to every one concerned a certain share of censure is allotted in the conversation of the Parliament House. In particular, the ladies took a great interest for the doctor. . . ."

The following is the interlocutor of the Court:—

"Edinburgh, 23rd June, 1807.

"The Lords having considered the state of the process, writs produced, testimonies of the witnesses adduced, and heard counsel for the parties in their own presence, they find that the hail defenders, on the 30th day of September as libelled, on the market day of Fort-Augustus, and at or near that place, were guilty of a violent and atrocious assault on the person of the pursuer, Mr Donald Macdonald, to the effusion of his blood and danger of his life. Find that the said assault did not originate in a sudden quarrel, but was the result of long premediated resentment and a deliberate purpose of revenge, and was attended with many circumstances of great barbarity and peculiar aggravation, especially on the part of the defender, Alexander Macdonell of Glengarry. Therefore finds the hail defenders conjunctly and severally liable to the pursuer in damages; modify the same to two thousand pounds sterling and decern. Find the defenders conjunctly and severally also liable in the expenses of process, and ordain an account thereof to be given in, and remit the same to the Auditor to tax, and report to the Court. And further in respect that the defender, Alexander Macdonell, was at the time of the above assault a Justice of the Peace, and Deputy-Lieutenant for the County of Inverness, and was not only the aggressor in the above assault, and did not interfere to preserve the peace, but did by imprecations and outrageous threats of personal violence, deter and prevent John Mackay, head constable of the County of Inverness, from interfering to assist, and rescue the pursuer when officially called on by him so to do, thereby openly aiding and abetting the other defenders in their attack on the pursuer, and did likewise endeavour to prevent the Military Guard when called for, when coming to the pursuer's relief; the Lords remit this point to His Majesty's Advocate with the view that he may consider how far it is proper that the said Alexander Macdonell of Glengarry, should any longer be continued in the Commission of the Peace and Lieutenancy for the County of Inverness, and in respect of the ungovernable resentment and violence manifested by the said defenders, also to consider whether it would not be proper that they should all of them be laid under proper security to keep the peace."

GLENGARRY AND HIS TENANTS.

Glengarry was a man of undoubted talent and fair business capacity. His extreme sense of this capacity led him to interfere and make, as he thought, complete arrangements which led him into no end of trouble. One of his tenants and factors says of him when called to strict account—

"The truth is that upon these vast estates of Glengarry, he Glengarry, had factors enough; he himself was Primus; his wife was Vice; his agent at Inverness Deputy; and the defendant was merely a Substitute, and for all his intromissions as such substitute he had most faithfully accounted."

He could be bitterly satirical when he chose. An unfortunate clansman with whom he had fallen out and been taken into Court, complains that "he had already such examples of Glengarry's friendship and feelings as to make him not surprised at anything that happens wherein the pursuer is concerned," and he further styles himself "Captain Alexander Macdonell." This title of Captain was strongly objected to by Glengarry, alleging that he "raised him from a private to an ensign in his regiment; that on the reduction of that regiment he made him his factor and entrusted him with the collection of his whole rents of from five to six thousand a year—that he gave him the adjutancy of his Volunteer battalion and afterwards of his local Militia regiment, equal to £150 a year, which he has enjoyed for about ten years." In another place an accusation is made against the poor Captain by Glengarry that one of his petitions "is couched in the same dignified strain which has characterised him for a course of years, and *has brought him to a level with his ancestors.*" In a dispute with Mr Alexander Cameron, tenant of Inverguseran, who complains of having been wantonly brought into court, after doing in his day much for Glengarry, including, according to his own words in 1819,

"In the first place, before I had any holding from Glengarry, and when I had the subset of Inverguseran from Strone and Maclachlan,

Glengarry raised his regiment, leaving a great many of the friends of his recruits on every farm in the country, and it happened there was a very good many of them between Newgart and Inveriemor, and after I paid Strone and Maclachlan my rents, they would not pay Glengarry unless he was to take these crofters in part payment of his rent. At last Maclachlan went to Invergarry with the rent, and brought a man of business with him, little Archibald Maclachlan, writer in Fort-William, to take a protest, unless the crofters were to be taken in part payment, so that Maclachlan came back with the rent without paying it. When I heard this, I went to Fort-William and desired Maclachlan to give me the rent, and that I would go to Invergarry with it. I went and paid Glengarry the rents and the crofters out of my own pocket and ever since till the regiment was disbanded, no less than five, six, or seven crofters with a cow or two each."

This letter throws some light on the inducement given to recruit. Of old, military service was the chief equivalent for rent, and suited to the times. Glengarry had all the honour and glory of command, and also drew high rents from his tenants, but nevertheless he attempted to throw the heavy additional burden on them of supporting the recruits' families. The following observations on the foregoing letter are in his own handwriting. He says:—

"While Cameron was only sub-tenant his ambition led him naturally to be obliging, and it was by such conduct alone he could cherish the hope of such success as afterwards attended him on being received as tenant, and being the resident on these lands he could not help complying with the rules laid down for other occupants. This was merely a hoax in order to make a virtue, if he could, of necessity. Accordingly, when he saw the matter was overdone, he made the best of it, by submitting to the general rule observed by all the other tenants, even those on the forfeited lands. This system of giving house stances, etc., to his relatives, was the line struck out by me in preference to taking recruits from my tenants, the usual mode adopted by neighbouring proprietors, and certainly the easiest for tenants."

In other litigations, important decisions were given against him. With a large sheep farmer Glengarry fell out, and attempted to stop him from heather burning because likely to kill the fibres and roots of natural woods such as birch and oak, and he failed. He was also unsuccessful in stopping a ploughing up at outgoing of land in cultivation at entry, though not since turned over. Again, in absence of express stipulation, it was decided against him that a sheep farmer was not bound to deliver the stock at outgoing by valuation. A parish clergyman, rather pressing for his stipend, is termed an "Eyterkin." A border sheep farmer, supposed to have greatly prospered, and become purse-proud and arrogant, is reminded that his first appearance in Inverness-shire was bare-footed, in "moggans," and that for three years he had consorted with the common fox-hunter, "taking his porridge out of the same cog."

A somewhat interesting point in reference to rights of moss arose in 1813. Prior to the sale of North Morar in 1768, the tenants on both sides of Nevis were in use to cut their peats, on the Knoydart side, at Kyles Knoydart, and this had continued ever since. Latterly, owing no allegiance to Glengarry, the Morar people cut as they liked. Prescription had not run, in consequence of Glengarry's years of minority having to be taken into account. The disposition of Morar was believed to include mosses, muirs, etc., but I was told that it was found that there being an intervening arm of the sea, though narrow, where Kyles Knoydart and Kyles Morar face—the possession must be held to have been *ex gratia.*

Lastly, I will refer to the case in which a well-known and respected townsman, Mr Neil Maclean, land surveyor, who died not many years ago, was in the execution of his duty as Glengarry's factor, faced with gun and broadsword. This occurred in 1817, and I will give the particulars in Glengarry's own words, dated the 19th of July. Archibald Dhu Macdonald, commonly called "Archie-du-na-Bitaig," being dispossessed from Riefern of South Morar in 1815, and according to Glengarry, "in consequence of his possessing an uncommon address," he got a share in the large farm of Kinloch Nevis, but unable to pay his rent, renounced his rights upon certain conditions. Archie had six or seven sons, all worthy chips of the old block, Glengarry says—

"I am bothered with Bitag; I gave him the grass of four cows in Sourchaise for this year by missive, when he renounced by comprisement the sheep stock of Kinloch Nevis, still far short of his debt to me, but he keeps in his sons' names or his own four more milkers, and I believe a young horse without authority or right of any kind. Can I not seize these in part payment of his debt still due to me, and remove him off the farm which he surrendered to me—I mean to its extremity Sourchaise, where his sons live, by my own authority, or am I necessarily to have him ejected, and go otherwise more formally to work. When Mr Maclean and the ground officer went to move him the other day, he ran into the house for a gun, loaded it in their presence, and cocked it, and then taking out an old broadsword worn by his grandfather at Culloden, and backed by his sons with oak sticks, they outnumbered and browbeat the factor and his adherents, and so maintain illegal and unwarrantable possession of my property by violence alone."

Archie and his sons were afterwards ejected, but the subsequent fate of the broadsword used in 1746 and again unsheathed in 1817 is to me, alas, unknown.

GLENGARRY AND THE OLD STONE BRIDGE OF INVERNESS.

One incident in Glengarry's life connected with the old Stone Bridge of Inverness is worth recalling. He had attended a county meeting, at which he presided, on the 25th of November, 1819, and being detained later than he anticipated had to remain in Inverness all night. It appeared that he expected company to dinner on the following day, and making the best of matters, sent on his own horses to Invermoriston, intending to post thither from Inverness early next morning, so as to arrive at Invergarry in time for dinner.

The following extract from a complaint to the Justices, at Glengarry's instance and that of the Procurator-Fiscal, shows what befel him at the bridge :—

"That by the law of this, and all other civilized realms, impeding and interrupting of a public high road, or a road upon a bridge, by means of lockfast or closed gates whereby the lawful traveller in a cold frosty morning is prevented from going alongst the bridge upon payment of the lawful dues, is severely punishable. Yet true it is and of verity, that Donald Macdonald at Burnside of Holm, now in Inverness, tollman, bridgeman, or tacksman of the Petty Customs on the Stone Bridge of Inverness, and Margaret Macdonald, his sub-tenant, are both and each or one or other of them guilty thereof or actors, art and part. In as far as the said Donald Macdonald having become tacksman of the Petty Customs levied at the Old Bridge of Inverness for the last and current year, whereby he became legally entitled to draw from the passengers the accustomed rates, and thereby became bound to serve at all hours of the day and night the passengers, and to attend that they were to receive free egress and regress at all hours of the day and night for payment of the accustomed dues. But notwithstanding thereof, the said Donald Macdonald sublet the toll of the said Old Bridge of Inverness to the said Margaret Macdonald, or set her there as his servant; the said Donald Macdonald or Margaret Macdonald, or one or other of them wilfully neglected to attend on and at the said Bridge, and upon the morning of the 26th day of November last or upon one or other of the days of that month, or of the month of October immediately preceding, the private complainer had occasion to pass alongst the said bridge having a four-wheeled carriage and two horses with his lady therein, and when he came with the said carriage to the summit of the said bridge, he then found that the gates on the said bridge were shut against him without a tollman or bridgeman or the tacksman of the said Petty Customs, as is usual, in attendance to open the same. That the private complainer repeatedly called for the said tollman, bridgeman or tacksman to come and open the said gates and allow the said carriage with the said private complainer and his family to pass, but he received no answer, nor was the said gates opened. That the private complainer having thereupon alighted from the carriage and knocked, assisted by his servant, against the gates on the said bridge or on the end of the said bridge, he for about half an hour received no answer, but at length the tollman or tacksman or sub-tenant, sub-tacksman or servant who was substitute by the said Donald Macdonald as tollman or bridgeman, was found in a neighbouring whisky house or retail house of spirituous liquors drinking at spirituous liquors, from whence he or she was brought, and the said gates opened. That in this detention the pursuer and his wife and family were upon the bridge for a period of about 30 minutes on a cold frosty morning, and their horses having in the meantime got restive, they ran off on the gates being opened, and the lives of the occupants of the said carriage were thereby in danger."

The tollman had to make a suitable apology and give compensation to the justly offended and aggrieved Chief.

Glengarry was very hospitable and a model in family life. He and his wife were a most affectionate and attached couple, and both very proud of their eldest son and successor, Eneas Ronaldson, who seems to have been an excellent scholar and at the head of his classes when at Perth Academy. Of the daughters, Marsali appears to have been the favourite, a girl of high spirit and lively temperament; and the letters I have seen give one a pleasing idea of the family life. Glengarry was a great sportsman of the old school, and as early as 1802, I observe him strictly observing the 12th of August, "in the hills." For many years he lived at Garry Cottage, Perthshire, and Invergarry House and shootings were let as early as 1810, to the then Lord O'Neill. He kept up pleasant relations with the Antrim family, sending the Countess pieces of the finest woods of Glengarry to be worked into articles of furniture. He sends young deer to the Duke of York, and imports pheasants. Sir Henry Vane Tempest and he interchange of their choicest herds, for the improvement of their breeds of cattle. He gives balls at Inverness, and for that held in July 1813 the famous fiddler, Donald Davidson, acknowledges payment of two pounds seven shillings sterling, being at the rate of one guinea for each of two violin players, and five shillings for the bass. In 1806 he is in London making a stir, and very particular as to his appearance in the Highland dress. "I ordered a pair of brogues in Fort-William to be sent after me, as I peak (pride) myself while mingled with strangers, on being the truest Highlander." Politically, he was not a strong partizan. A rather extreme address to King George IV., having been proposed to be sent from the county of Inverness, Glengarry addressed a sharp letter to the Preses of the meeting, held on the 4th of January, 1821, through the late Mr John Macandrew, solicitor, as he was himself unable to be present:—

"To the Preses of the County Meeting called for the 4th instant.
"Perth, 2nd Jany., 1821.

"Sir,—Altho' I am not aware of any particular emergency in the internal state of the country or its relations abroad, which at the present crisis calls forth a special declaration of loyalty or attachment to the Throne, sentiments universally known to pervade the whole population of the Highlands of Scotland in a degree nowhere surpassed! yet, as it is impossible for me to attend the meeting called by the Convener, on what for an extensive county I conceive *far too short notice*, if it was the object to obtain the real sentiments of its proprietors, I deem it proper to declare that in loyalty, pure *constitutional feelings* and attachment to the Throne I will yield to no man; and that I know this sentiment to be shared by those of *all ranks* with whom it has pleased Providence to connect me by relations, which it is my pride to avow and my particular anxiety to cherish. I feel it incumbent upon me as an extensive proprietor in Inverness-shire to state, that I will *not* consider myself a party to what may be done at a meeting so hastily called together, at a season when of all others *more than ordinary premonition should have been given* by the Convener, if it was not wished to pass off for the feelings and sentiments of the county at large, the opinions, interested or otherwise, of those who reside in and near the county town, situated *as Inverness is* upon its very eastmost extremity; nor will I acquiesce in the resolutions of that meeting as the sense of the county of Inverness.

"I beg also to remark, in opposition to what seems to be implied in the requisition, that in our county nothing of irreligion or sedition is known. The whole population of the Highlands are remarkable for zeal in religion generally and, comparatively speaking, for observance of *moral precepts*, and certainly to be surpassed by none in their devoted attachment to the *Throne, the constitution*, and the constituted authorities of the land, while the spirit and principles of Radicalism are *incompatible with* and *diametrically opposite to* every feeling of true Highlandism, nay, without a total demoralization of the Highland character or an extinction of the genuine race, *that Exotic* can never take root amidst Caledonia's mountains.

"A Highlander is naturally generous as well as brave and an enemy to everything wearing the semblance of oppression, and tho' his principles of attachment to those immediately placed over him will necessarily go far to influence his conduct, there is a pitch *beyond which* (in my opinion) even that may become ineffective, and there is no true son of the mountains *in an unbiassed state*, who has not regarded all the measures recently adopted against Her Majesty the Queen with *keen regard*, approaching closely to jealousy, however unwilling they may be to speak out *unnecessarily* in such delicate circumstances.—I have the honour to be, Sir, your obedient humble servt., (Signed) "A. MACDONELL.

"To be delivered in Court to the Preses by Jno. McAndrew, solicitor, Inverness, as Glengarry's agent there."

This letter is much in advance of the general views politically of that day, and it was supported by Rothiemurchus and others, while the resolution was only carried after some amendments.

Glengarry, it is well known, was an enthusiast for Gaelic, and did a great deal to have Mr Ewen Maclachlan transferred to Inverness. His children were taught Gaelic by Mr Alexander Campbell, afterwards minister of Croy.

Taking him all in all, faults and virtues, "we will never see his like again."

> "'S ann na laidhe 'n Cill Ionain,
> Dh'fhag sinn biatach an fhiona,
> Lamh a b' urrainn a dhioladh,
> 'S cas a shiubhal na frithe,
> Bu tu sealgair na sithne,
> Le d' chuilbheir coal direach ;
> 'S bho na thainig a chrioch ort
> Gheibh na lain-dhaimh an siochaint,
> Cadal samhach 's cha dirich an namhaid."

GLENGARRY'S PIPER AND THE CANAL COMMISSIONERS IN 1807, ETC.

It was an old and general accusation against Highlanders that they did not see the difference between "meum and tuum" when it became a question of taking the property of another. The following papers are given on account of the curious defence broadly stated in a legal paper, signed moreover by a procurator, not a Highlander, though subsequently his descendants became prominently connected with Inverness and the Highlands.

Telford, in bitterness of heart, from his being so often crossed and fleeced during the Canal operations, declared that Highland landlords were the most rapacious in Europe, but it is possible those whom he employed under him, chiefly aliens, did not make things as agreeable as they might, and in this instance John Telford endeavoured to make a mountain of a mole hill.

The Canal Commissioners, and John Telford, residing at Corpach, their manager, with concourse of the Procurator-Fiscal, state to the Sheriff of Inverness-shire in March,

1807, that the Commissioners some time ago purchased from Alexander Macdonell of Glengarry a large quantity of birchwood for the use of the said Canal, part of which was carried to Corpach, but a considerable part of it in the course of conveyance lay on the lands of Laggan and at the west end of Loch Oich, and the Commissioners erected on the said lands of Laggan a saw pit, which they covered with timber. That, regardless of all honesty, John Macdonald, piper, Alexander Gillies, Alexander Macdonell, Alexander Mor Macdonell, John Roy Macdonell, Paul Macdonell, and John Kennedy, all tenants in North Laggan, did not only strip the aforesaid saw pit of its roof, but carried it away, as also forty trees of birch or birch timber, which they disposed of for their own use, whereby they subjected themselves in damages. Service being ordered, answers were given in, in which the allegation of having in any way interfered with the saw pit or its roof is denied, and the respondents say they are most wrongously accused and unjustly charged with a crime which they did not commit. The reply as to the birch trees is given in their own words—

"In regard to the charge of carrying away forty birch trees, they most readily acknowledge that they found a few trifling sticks on the banks of Loch Oich, which the lake had seemingly cast on shore, but they were only fit for firewood, and were applied to that purpose, and whether they belonged in property to the complainers, the respondents knew not. They would be exceedingly sorry to deprive the complainers or any person of their property; but it is a well attested fact that a Highlandman is not accustomed in practice to such refined notions of property as to lead him to suppose he is committing the crime of theft, when he finds a stick of little value seemingly neglected by everybody, and kindles it into a flame to warm his naked limbs during a winter's storm or a spring frost. The respondents would indeed be sorry to consume a tree of any value in whatever state they found it, but they humbly submit if they have committed a crime the damage done is moderate indeed, as the few sticks which they burnt were only fit for firewood, and not known by them to be the property of the complainers."

The complaint was abandoned, but the following much more serious one, in which the Canal Commissioners were also concerned, cost Glengarry a good deal before it was settled. The public prosecutor complains—

"That a breach of the public peace, as also obstructing a public national work and carrying away the boats and vessels used for carrying on that work to a distant part of the country, are crimes severely punishable. Yet Colonel Alexander Macdonell of Glengarry was guilty actor or art and part, in so far as on the morning of 3rd September, 1816, he, accompanied by several persons all armed with fire-arms, saws, hatchets, or axes, proceeded to the East End of Loch Oich, where the Canal workmen were preparing to begin work for the day, and he, the said Alexander Macdonell, aided and assisted as aforesaid, seized upon and violently and forcibly carried away a boat employed on the said loch up to Invergarry House, and from thence placed her (sic) in a cart and carried her up to Lochgarry. Further, the said Colonel Alexander Macdonell, aided as aforesaid, threatened the workmen that their lives would be taken away if they did not desist from carrying the said Canal through Loch Oich, and the workmen were so intimidated that they did desist, and the Canal operations were stopped by the lawless behaviour of the said Colonel Alexander Macdonell."

Apropos of the view of the Glengarry Highlanders regarding stray wood such as that above referred to, the following humourous reference by William Macpherson of Invereshie anent the views of the men of Badenoch as to the "right of prey" upon the district of Moray, is well expressed and gives a good idea of the "chaffing" between Highland gentlemen and those in the Lower districts, when they met or corresponded. The letter was written while the effects of the dreadful harvest of 1782 were still being felt:—

"Invereshie, 10th May, 1783.

"We now begin to feel in this country the sad effects of the last bad harvest. Nothing but hope, the last friend to all in distress (though sometimes a deceitful one), could support our spirits. The present prospect of plenty against next harvest is a comfortable reflection, but I am afraid after every possible exertion is made, that numbers will be in a bad way before the crop in the ground can afford them relief. We are in this end of Badenoch in a much better situation than our neighbours. Either above us or below us we have several farmers who will buy no meal, nay some that have sold, but we have too many that want and must be supplied . . . The moment Burnside's business is over, I shall move towards Moray land, where in former days, *all men took their prey*. It would not surprise me if in this season of general distress, some of my countrymen should follow the laudable practice of their worthy predecessors. And if they are driven to it by starvation, what can they help it? The lives of Highlanders are too precious to be lost, nor will they lose them by famine as long as Lowland bodys have a cow or a boll of meal to spare."

GLENGARRY—COLL MACDONELL OF BARISDALE.

I have written at length elsewhere about the Macdonalds of Barisdale, but in giving an account of Glengarry and Knoydart it is impossible to overlook that branch.

The members of the family were as a rule extremely tall, fine-looking men. The coffin of Coll, the second, took six men to raise and carry it. Alexander, the third, is described by Knox as tall, while Coll, the fourth, of whom I am now to speak, was described as standing six feet four inches. The questions with Glengarry and his father were not finally settled under arbitration, until 1790, after the death of both the submitters. From 1788 Coll held a commission to regulate the fisheries. This, in the height of the fishing season, was no easy task and required a firm hand. Not only were there disputes between the fishermen themselves, but apparently thieves made it a regular trade to attend and pick up what they could. On the 6th of November, 1809, Barisdale writes to an official at Inverness—

"This will be handed to you by Sergeant Donald Macdonell who I have sent with a party to convey one Archibald Macphail to the jail at Inverness. I have also inclosed a line for our good Sheriff, and if matters are not so regular as they ought, I hope he will forgive me.

"Enclosed are the oaths of the witnesses against him with his own declaration, and that of his brother, taken at Ardhill before Mr Downie. It is absolutely necessary an example should be made of him in some way, for there is more depredations this year among the fishermen than has been for many preceding years. We have now sixty to seventy boats on the coast this season from the south that did not use to frequent our lochs, and they are very much suspected by all the fishermen for stealing and destroying of nets. If this man is made an example of, it will secure the property of honest men to themselves, at least for some time. He ought at least to be banished to Botany Bay, or to send him on board one of Her Majesty's ships, which last punishment is too good for him. Whatever apology those people may plead, whose greath is taken away by some other rascals, he has nothing to plead of that sort, having neither nets or anything else on board, or no ways concerned with the fishing, except to go about and rob as he found convenient. It is not often these things can be brought home to these sort of depredators, which makes it the more necessary to make an example of this man. I hope his being sent to prison will have some good effect on the coast for some time. I shall only mention to the Sheriff that such a man is sent, and you can convey to him my sentiments on the subject, which are entirely for the good of the public."

Another year, on the 27th of August, Barisdale writes—

"I came home from Loch Hourn yesterday and found your letter before me. I wish I had your Sheriff and all his officers for a week among the different tribes who have gathered there. We had no less than one thousand coasting boats there last week, and every vessel on the fishing. After all a bad fishing in general, and there is not as yet the appearance of a herring anywhere else. I wish you had been with me to see the procedures of my Courts, short and substantial, always decisive. . . I forgot to mention that I perceive I am charged £2 8s for a four-wheeled carriage. What is the meaning of that? I never had any, nor never will I am afraid, and as to a riding horse, my volunteer commission exempts me from that tax—at the same time I never kept one."

The poor fishermen now suffer from piracy in another form. If there were officials like Barisdale armed with sufficient powers, trawling within the limits would soon be extirpated.

These letters deal with his public duties. Let us now get his views of men and things, and have a look into his family life. On the 2nd of February, 1814, he says—

"We had Parson Rory Macra last night and the dames were highly entertained with his dancing. . . . I had a letter by the post before last from my Chief. He writes in good spirits. I am happy to see that he is better. He must now be convinced that much depends on himself, and surely he will go on with caution. What signifies estates without health. We are like to be swallowed up with snow—such frost and snow we have not seen for thirty years. The perennial bestial will I am afraid get fewer in number, and this year in many respects is hard upon the Highlands—no fishing, potatoes lost with the frost, and cattle will run away with the little crop."

As regards Glengarry, Barisdale writes on the 16th of April, 1814—

"By what I can understand I am very much afraid my Chief is in a poor way. I feel for him from all my heart. With all his faults he is a sincere and most strenuous advocate for his friends, and, had he been independent, had the heart of a prince."

Glenelg had been sold to Mr Bruce, and there was a "shaking of Macleod bones." Norman Macleod of Eilean Reach, who had long ruled as factor, found his position unbearable. Barisdale says on the 12th of February, 1814—

"Eilean Reach goes to Knock at Whitsunday; he gives Mrs Col Macdonald £300 sterling and takes all the stock at comprisement. She has only three years to run. He pays high for the farm, but is glad to be free of Mr Bruce. Ratagan is still unprovided for, the brother is still in London going fast, I fancy, down *snow hill*."

Barisdale took charge of Mrs Coll Macdonald of Knock's outgoing in a thorough business like way, and prepared the following advertisement for the *Inverness Journal*, which throws some light on the manner of rouping of the time—

"BLACK CATTLE.—To be sold by public roup at Knock, on Tuesday the 17th day of May, 1814.—The whole stocking of black cattle on the farm of Knock, parish of Sleat, consisting of upwards of 30 milch cows, with their rearing of different ages. The cattle which were put on the farm were taken from some of the best stocks in the Highlands, and as they are now to be sold without reserve such another opportunity may not occur for years, for people who wish to be served with a true genuine Highland breed of cattle. Credit will be given on good bills for twelve months."

Barisdale married Helen Dawson, of Graden, Roxburgh, and her house and that of her sister, Mrs Jeffrey, of New Kelso, were perfect seats of hospitality. She died in 1805, barely reaching middle age. Just about the time Barisdale lost his venerable mother, his father-in-law, Mr Dawson also died, leaving considerable means. On the 24th of February, 1815, Barisdale says—

"My late worthy friend and good honest man, will be missed by all his friends. He left considerable legacies among his family and the descendants of his daughters, from four to two thousand pounds according to the number of their children. Of course I fell into the lowest class. Still it is more than I expected or had a right to, so that I ought to be as well pleased as those that get most. There is no saying when we get the cash as the estate must first be sold, but it will always be of service when it comes."

The male line of Barisdale terminated in the person of Archibald, fifth and last of the family, which is now represented in the female line by Mrs Head of Inverailort, great grand-daughter of Coll, fourth Barisdale.

GLENGARRY.—RONALD SCAMMADALE.

In no part of the Highlands could there be found better specimens of the real representative Highlander than in the west mainland of Inverness-shire, from Lochalsh to Loch Moidart. I select a specimen, Ronald Macdonell of Scammadale and Crowlin, commonly called "Raonull Mor a' Chrolen," several letters of his being in my possession. Father Charles Macdonald, my late worthy friend, whose death I much regret, in his *Moidart; or among the Clanranalds*, says, page 5—

"When George III. expressed, on a certain occasion, a strong desire to see some of the surviving Highlanders who had been out in the '45 a certain number were brought forward, and among them a grim old warrior from Knoydart, named Raonull Mor a Chrolen. After putting some questions to the latter, the King remarked that no doubt he must have long since regretted having taken any part in that *Rebellion*. The answer was prompt and decisive—'Sire, I regret nothing of the kind.' His Majesty, for an instant, was taken aback at such a bold answer, but was completely softened by the old man adding—'What I did then for the Prince I should have done as heartily for your Majesty, had you been in the Prince's place.'"

This is very much the same feeling that animates all true Highlanders of the day.

Coll, fourth of Barisdale, writing of Ranald's latest marriage, on the fifth May, 1815, states that he was then in his 95th year, which would make the date of his birth 1720, but in the obituary notice, after referred to, of his death on 27th November, 1815, he is described as in his 91st year, making the date of his birth 1724. Ranald is described as natural brother to Coll Macdonald, the second Barisdale, and was thus a son of Archibald, the first Barisdale, who was at Killiecrankie, was out in 1715, took a part in the Rising of 1745; his son living, as already stated, down to 1815. Ranald saw the whole five generations of Barisdale —Archibald, first, Coll, second, Archibald, third, Coll, fourth, and Archibald, the fifth.

One of his most praiseworthy acts was his severe punishment of that obnoxious person known as "Allan of Knock," over whose remains there was placed an inscription not less fulsome than false.

Father Charles says that Ranald in his visits to his half sister, Mrs Macdonald of Rhu, used to be so tiresome in old age, usually speaking of Prince Charles and his own prowess, that his sister would lose patience and take him down somewhat, which raised him to such fury that his forehead would swell, his lips tremble, and his features, at all times harsh and sinister, would assume a ferocious, vindictive look.

Ranald lived latterly at Crowlin, he and his son Captain James having a lease of the two Scammadales and the two Crowlins. In 1809 his affairs became so embarrassed that the lease was renounced, and poor Ranald, like his relative and namesake, old Scotos, was in danger of being a wanderer without any fixed home. In one of the processes against Ranald and his son, Captain James, they say ironically that "in this case the defenders have only a corroboration of the friendly disposition of Glengarry to his grand uncle and cousin." Coll Barisdale, his great nephew interested himself, as I observe by a letter dated the 28th of February, 1810, in which he says—"I hope you will consider the case of the old gentleman. Viewing his own situation as he does at the age of 85, his greatest wish is to die in the country, and as I wrote you already, I am certain it will hurt Glengarry to see him obliged to leave the country."

Not only did he not leave, but he actually married Miss Macdonell of Slaney on the 5th of May, 1815. His object was no doubt to enable the lady to enjoy his pension. It is well known that old officers on their death-beds frequently married on this account. One case was much spoken of in and about Inverness and the Strathglass district—that of the excellent and respected Mrs Colonel Chisholm of Fasnakyle, whose husband died, I think, the very day of the marriage. Becoming a scandal, the War Office prohibited pensions to widows, unless they had been married for a certain stated period. The following discriminating notice appeared after Ranald's death—

"At his house in Knoidart (29th November, 1815), Mr Ranald Macdonell, Skamadale, Ensign on the Retired List of Captain Rose's Independent Company of Veterans, in the 91st year of his age, respected and admired as a genuine Highlander of the old school, and quite unmatched in the very general circle of his acquaintances. He followed the fortunes of Prince Charles Stuart from Prestonpans to Culloden, and served with distinguished zeal in both these actions, for which he afterwards suffered banishment to India for seven years, during which period he served in the hussars; and when returning to England, the vessel in which he sailed happening to be boarded by a French man of war before Ranald was aware of what was passing on deck, and had furnished himself with a cutlass; he, darting like an eagle among the victors, actually retook the British ship, killing single handed all the astonished Frenchmen who attempted to withstand his athletic rage, and driving the rest over the vessel's broadside into the sea. His retentive memory and mental faculties were spared him until within a few days of his last, and till above ninety he had the use of his powerful limbs. His father, his brother, and his nephew, as well as himself, all served the Prince at the same time, and were personally known to His Royal Highness; the father, however, had drawn his first sword with his chief Glengarry, under Viscount Dundee, in the battle of Killiecrankie, who had the Royal standard entrusted to his care, and commanded the whole of the "Clan donall," drawn up as of old on the right of the army, which was composed almost entirely of the Highland clans. The mortal remains of this hero of the last century were deposited with the dust of his fathers in "Killichoan" on Friday the 1st of December, leaving a wife, three daughters, many grand-daughters and several great grand-children, to bewail his death, exclusive of sons who had fallen in the service of their country, two of whom had followed the young Macdonell in the year 1792 into the first fencible regiment, thence into the Glengarry or the first British fencibles, and from thence into the line."

Alluding to Ranald's funeral, Father Charles Macdonald says—

"It was perhaps rather in keeping that a stormy life like this should in its close involve the nearest friends in something of a family disaster. It was while on his way to attend Ranald's funeral that the late Lochshiel (Alexander, nephew of Ranald) was nearly lost off the coast of Morar. The boat was struck by a sudden squall, capsized and, filling rapidly, went down, the whole crew, three in number, going down with it. It was almost by a miracle that the survivor after a hard struggle, reached the shore, but throughout the rest of his life, which was a long one, he never fully recovered from the effects of the shock received in this lamentable occasion. The old warrior's sword, a true Andrea Ferrara, was supended for years among other interesting memorials at Dalilea House. It was sold at the dispersion of the late Miss Jane Macdonald's effects a few years ago (1889), but as to where it went, or what became of it since, the writer has been unable to ascertain."

Surely it is not too late to have such an interesting relic of a prominent Knoydart Highlander recovered.

BRAE LOCHABER.

The south-west of the mainland of Inverness-shire of old consisted of three lordships, comprehending all the lands whose waters flow into the Atlantic. These were—1st, The lordship of Lochaber, which contained the whole of the present parish of Kilmonivaig, including a great part of Kilmallie, from Glengarry to the head of Lochiel; 2nd, the lordship of Mamore, which contained that part of Kilmallie west and south of Kilmonivaig, between Lochs Linnhe and Leven; and 3rd, The lordship of Gartmoran, which included Ardgour in Kilmallie, Sunart, and Ardnamurchan, and the parish of Small Isles, with all the present west mainland of Invernes-shire from Moydart to Knoydart and Glenelg. I shall here speak more particularly of the lordship of Lochaber, which for a time was possessed, or rather swayed, by a branch of the powerful family of Comyn. These Comyns were aliens and, differing from those of Badenoch, taking no great root in the territory. In the chartulary of Moray, under date 1234, there is a deed witnessed *inter alia* by Ferquhar, Seneschal of Badenoch, and by Edward, Seneschal of Lochaber. The former was undoubtedly the predecessor of The Mackintosh, and I identify Edward above-named as Farquhar's younger brother, afterwards predecessor of the Toshachs of Monzievaird. Ferquhar's nephew and in time sucesssor, also named Ferquhar, married Mora, daughter, according to the Mackintosh Latin History, "of Angus Oig Macdonald of the Isles, who was son to Angus Mor Macdonald-vic-Railt vic-Soirle-vic-Gilliebride." This connection with the Macdonalds and the subsequent marriage of Angus Mackintosh, only child of the above Ferquhar Mackintosh and Mora Macdonald, with Eva, heiress of the Clan Chattan, in 1291, formed the bases of that close communing and intercourse between the Mackintoshes and Lochaber which has now subsisted for upwards of six hundred years without a break.

After the battle of Bannockburn and the expulsion of the Comyns, the heriditary foes of Bruce, from Lochaber, the lands then in the hands of the Crown were granted to the Macdonalds, the Brae of Lochaber, including the whole parish of Kilmonivaig east of Lochy, being thereafter gifted by John Lord of the Isles to his son, Alexander Carrach, first of Keppoch. Alexander probably had a charter, but his estate being forfeited it fell back to the Lords of the Isles, and powerful, *quasi* independent as they were, and able for centuries to remain in the Brae in direct descent up to about 1790, leaders of a valiant branch of the Clan Donald, the Macdonells of Keppoch had no indefeasible titles, and were merely tenants or wadsetters of the Mackintoshes and the Gordons. This says much for their indomitable pluck and tenacity.

The Lords of the Isles showed great unfriendliness to the Keppochs, and also to the Clan Cameron, but they were most friendly with the Mackintoshes. The latter were in constant trouble with the Camerons as to their lands in Glenlui and Loch Arkaig in Kilmallie, which they inherited through the above Eva; and Alexander of Yle Earl of Ross and Lord of the Isles, in reward of past services and to strengthen the Mackintoshes, in 1443 renewed the grant of Glenlui and Loch Arkaig, and gave the Brae of Lochaber to Malcolm, tenth of Mackintosh.

This estate of over 30,000 acres comprehends one side of Glen Spean, and both sides of Glen Roy, with the exception of the upper part of the latter, namely, the farms of Glenturrett, Leckroy, and Annat, all now called Braeroy.

Further, in 1447 the above Alexander, whose sister Florence had married Duncan, son and heir of Malcolm Mackintosh, granted the bailliarie or stewarty of all Lochaber to Malcolm in perpetual fee and heritage. The office of bailie, particularly of a lordship, was much sought after in old times, being an office not only of emolument, but in every probability leading to better things. Even the powerful Earls of Argyll got their first hold of Tyree as bailies thereof under the Macleans, who had acquired from Iona. This grant of bailliarie of Lochaber is in splendid preservation, as is also the huge seal of the Earl. It was registered at Edinburgh on the 23rd August, 1781. Translated from the Latin, it is as follows, being the earliest original Lochaber charter I have seen, except the one dated 1443 above referred to :—

"To all who may see or hear this charter, Alexander de Yle, Earl of Ross, and Lord of the Isles, wishes eternal salvation in the Lord. Know ye that we have given, granted, and by this our present writ have confirmed to our most trusty cousin, Malcolm Mackintosh, in recompense of his assistance, all and whole the office of bailliarie or stewardship, of all and sundry the lands of our lordship of Lochaber, to be held and possessed the said office with all and sundry pertinents to the said office belonging, or can partly in future in any way belong, by the said Malcolm Mackintosh, and all his heirs-male, begotten, or to be begotten, of us and all our heirs, in fee and heritage for ever, as freely peacefully well and in quiet, as any office of bailliarie or stewardship granted for ever in a charter of confirmation, to any other Bailie in the whole kingdom of Scotland. Which office as aforesaid we, Alexander Earl and Lord aforesaid, and our heirs, to the aforesaid Malcolm and his heirs as foresaid against whatsoever mortals, shall warrant as just and forever defend. In testimony of all the premises we have caused our seal to be appended to these presents, at our Castle of Dingwall, the thirteenth day of the month of November, in the year of the Lord one thousand four hundred and forty-seven, these being present as witnesses Torquil Macleod, Lord of the Lewes, John Macleod, Lord of Glenelg, Celestine of the Isles, my natural son (*filio meo naturali*), Nigel Flemyng my secretary, and Donald my Justiciar, with divers others."

It has to be kept in mind that after the forfeiture of the Lords of the Isles, both the lordships of Mamore and Lochaber fell to the Crown. Mamore sunk and was absorbed into the lordship of Lochaber, which about 1500 was granted to the Earl of Huntly. Mackintosh, having after the forfeiture, been wise enough to get Glenluie, Loch Arkaig, the Brae, and the bailliarie, confirmed to him by the Crown by charter dated 14th July, 1476, was not only entirely free of the Gordons as the new Lords of Lochaber, but had the power, and exercised it, of bailliarie over the whole of Gordon's Lochaber estates. The title of Seneschal or Steward is to this day acknowledged in the Crown charters, for all it is worth since the abolition of Heritable Jurisdictions. Lochiel frequently attempted to stop Mackintosh by force of arms from holding Courts. I have read the minutes of several, the last which I recollect being held at Leckroy by Murdo Macpherson of Clune as Depute Steward in 1677, when, among other business, the escheat of those concerned in the murder of Keppoch is dealt with. When Mackintosh, by the armed interference of Breadalbane, had to sell Glenluie and Locharkaig, the bailliarie of these lands was included in the sale.

In the old times rights were not safe until confirmed by the superior for the time, so Malcolm Mackintosh, under the hands of a Procurator, insisted that John, third and last Lord of the Isles, should enter him, which John accordingly did by a precept furth of his own chancellarie, dated 14th June, 1456, on which Malcolm was infeft on the 18th July, 1456. Duncan Mackintosh, Malcolm's son and successor, who, I have said, took the precaution of being entered with the Crown in 1476, had previously entered with John, Lord of the Isles, by charter dated the 14th November, 1466. No doubt the Camerons were in possession of lands long before the Gordons, but latterly all Lochaber in Inverness-shire, with the exception of Mackintosh's lands, was held of the Gordon's, such as Lochiel, for his part of

Mamore, Letterfinlay, Glenevis, Callart, Kinlochleven, etc.

As their lands in Lochaber lay at a considerable distance from where the Mackintoshes finally took up their abode at the Isle of Moy, it followed that old neigbours, or the actual possessors, coveted their ownership. The well-meant action of Alexander, Lord of the Isles, in his grant of the Brae, greatly helped Mackintosh in his contests with Lochiel, but at the same time had the effect of raising a new enemy in the Macdonalds of Keppoch, who, whatever their feuds among themselves, always united against Mackintosh. Pride, family and clan importance, revenge for frequent slaughters, harryings, and slights, combined in a determination by the Mackintoshes never to part with or relinquish the possession of these lands. In 1547, Mackintosh made his most successful attack and succeeded in getting the heads of both Lochiel and Keppoch struck off. The countenance of Huntly, rarely given to Mackintosh, granted for his own ends on this particular occasion, was soon withdrawn, and the struggles were renewed. But it would be out of place here to enlarge upon them.

Besides leasing practically the whole of Brae Lochaber, Keppoch leased or wadsetted from the Gordons the whole of what was lately known as the Loch Treig and Inverlochy estates, and was entered for £400 of cess in the valuation roll of 1691.

The present inhabitants of the Brae are amongst the very few in the Highlands who are the direct representatives of those who have held the same possessions for centuries. Even some of the Keppoch family are still there, and I have a distinct recollection of one of the Inveroy tenants, at Achnacroish, several years ago, giving me the names of his seven predecessors until the line ran into that of the Chief. Under the circumstances, so honourable to the Mackintoshes and their tenants, it may interest at least the latter to know the names of some of the chief tenants in 1655, held bound for their sub-tenants, cottars and dependents. These were, the minors Alexander and Ranald

Macdonell of Keppoch, sons of Donald Glas, and their uncle Alexander Macdonald Buidhe, their "pretended" tutor, for Keppoch, Inveroybeg, Achaderry, Bregach, Tollie, Uracher, and Almie ; the tutor personally for Bohuntin, Kinchellie, Auchavaddie and Bohinie ; Alastair-vic-Aonas-oig for Bohuntin Ville, Crenachan, Brunachan, Achluachrach and Kilchaoril ; Allister vic Allister, and his sons Allister and Donald, for Reanach ; Allan-vic-Coil-roy-vic-Coil-vic-Allan for Bochasky ; Donald vic Robert, and his sons John, Allan, and Donald, for Murligan and Glen Glaster ; Allister-vic-Aonas-vic-Ian dhu, for Tulloch and Dallindundearg ; Allister-vic-Aonas-roy for Blarnahinven ; and Donald Gorme Macdonald for Inveroymore. At a later period in 1728, the tenants in Inveroymore and Inveroybeg, Keppoch, Acaderry, Bohinie, Crenachan, Blarnahinven, Bochaskie, Reanach, and Brunachan, were as follows, but I much regret that the remaining tenants of the Brae at that period cannot be given. Inveroymore—John Macdonald, tacksman ; Alexander Macdonald, Duncan Maclachlan, Duncan vic Iain, Duncan dhu vic Ewin, vic Iain, John Vic Walter, Duncan Mac Iain Oig, *alias* Cameron, John Macdonald, son to Inveroy. Inveroybeg—Donald Mac Dugald vic Glassich, Angus Mac Harlich, Angus Mac Soirle vic Iain reach, Dugald Mac Aonas vic Glassich, and Donald Maclachlan. Keppoch—Ewen Mac Eachen, John Mac Eachen, Angus Mac Dougall, Archibald vic Ewen, Duncan Mac Iain vic Iver, Angus Mac Coil Oig, Donald Mac Gillespick, *alias* Macdonald, Kenneth Ferguson, Kenneth Mackenzie, and Alexander Macphadrick. Achaderry—Donald Mac Ewen, John vic Conchie mor, Alexander Beaton, John Beaton, Donald Beaton, and Donald-vic-Iain-vic-Coil-roy. Bohinie—John vic Conchie vic Iain, Farquhar vic Conchie vic Iain, Angus vic Glassich, Donald Mac Allister, John Macdonald vic Allister, and Allan Macdonald vic Allister. Crenachan—John Macdonald, Angus Cameron, Donald Mac Arthur and Angus Mac Iain. Blarnahinven—Alexander Macdonald, tacksman ; Angus Macdonald and John Macdonald. Bochaskie—Angus Macpherson, Donald Macpherson, Donald Macpherson, and

Paul Macpherson. Reanach—John Macdonald, and Allan Roy. Brunachan—Alexander Mac Arthur, Donald Mac Arthur, Charles Mac Arthur, Alexander Mac Arthur, and Archibald Mac Arthur.

It was the policy of successive Mackintosh chiefs to give a prominent position to their loyal people in every district, and at an early period the honourable position of hereditary standard-bearer was conferred upon the family of Macdonald of Murligan. It did not necessarily follow that the standard-bearer was of the same name as the chief, and I observe, for instance, that when the Macgregors appeared before George IV. in Edinburgh in 1822, under Sir Evan Murray Macgregor—from long established friendship and succour in the time of need, the Macphersons becoming hereditary standard-bearers of the Macgregors—Captain Mungo Macpherson of the 42nd Highlanders, and Mr Duncan Macpherson, of Kingussie, carried the banner of Clan Gregor.

In Sir Eneas Mackintosh's memoirs, written *circa* 1774-1784, he says—"the hereditary standard-bearer to Mackintosh is Macdonald, whose descendants live in Glenroy and speak nothing but Gaelic." I have seldom seen a more curious paper than that now to be given. In a period of transition, though some time before the passing of the abolition of Heritable Jurisdictions, it serves to illustrate the views then held by a great chief as to dealing with one of his important office-bearers. The paper is docquetted "Obligation and Declaration. Angus Macdonell of Muirlaggan, to the Laird of Mackintosh, 1727," and is as follows :—

"Be it known to all men, by these presents, me, Angus Macdonell of Murligan : Forasmuch as the Honourable Lachlan Mackintosh of that ilk, Captain of Clan Chattan, my master, has at the date hereof, recognised and preferred me to be his Ensign and Banner Bearer, which my predecessors have always been these three hundred years and upwards—except since the eighty-eighth year of God— (1688) for which service and towards the support of my family, the said Lachlan Mackintosh has at the date hereof allowed me twenty merks Scots yearly of the sum of two hundred merks money foresaid

of yearly rent due and payable by me to him for my possession of the
lands of Murligan and Glen Glaster, as also upon my granting
and performing of this present obligation containing the conditions and
provisions after mentioned. Therefore to be bound and obliged,
likeas I, the said Angus Macdonell, bind and oblige me, my heirs,
executors and successors whomsoever, not only to continue true
and faithful to the said Lachlan Mackintosh as his and their Ensigns
and Banner Bearers, and to answer and attend him and his forsaids,
to perform the said office at all their honourable and lawful occasions
when called thereto, but likewise that I and my forsaids, during
our possession of the said lands of Murligan and Glen Glaster
shall serve and attend the said Lachlan Mackintosh and his above
written, with all the fencible men living on the said lands, and all
the other fencible men descending of my family (commonly called
Sliochd-Donull-vic-Aonas) whom me or mine can stop or lett, in
all their reasonable and lawful affairs—except carriages and ariages
and such like slavish services as are commonly called and required of
common small tenants, always when required thereto upon due and
competent premonition—as also to make good and punctual payment
of the sum of nine score merks Scots duty yearly for my tack and
possession of the said lands of Murligan and Glen Glaster. And
in case it shall happen that the said Angus Macdonell of Murligan or
my forsaids do prove disobedient, or deficient in performance of
the conditions as above, then and in that case, I bind and oblige me
and mine above mentioned, to make full payment and satisfaction
to the said Lachlan Mackintosh and his above expressed of the said
twenty merks allowed me yearly as above, and that for all the terms
and years from the date hereof to the next term of Whitsunday
or Martinmas after our disobedience, if the same shall ever happen,
and to forfeit our pretension of bearing the said banner, or receiving
any good therefor in all time coming thereafter. And for the said
Lachlan Mackintosh and his foresaids their further security in the
premises I bind and oblige me and my foresaids to fulfil, implement,
and perform all the conditions and provisions above written under the
penalty of five hundred merks Scots money by and attour performance,
consenting to the registration hereof in the Books of Council and
Session or any other Judges books competent, therein to remain for
preservation, and if need be that letters of Horning, and all other
executorials needful, pass hereon in form as effeirs and to that effect
constitute my Procurators. In witness whereof, written by Angus Shaw,
factor to the Laird of Mackintosh on this and the preceding page
of stamped paper, these presents are subscribed by me at Moyhall,
this fourth day of March, one thousand seven hundred and twenty
seven years before these witnesses, James Macqueen, younger of
Corribrough, and the said Angus Shaw, writer hereof (Signed)

"A. McD" being Angus Macdonell, his ordinary mark. Ja. Macqueen, witness, Ang. Shaw, witness."

The croft of Lochaber appertaining to the bards of the ancient possessors was at Clachaig, in the midst of the lands granted to Mackintosh and on the West side of the River Spean shortly after it is joined by the River Gulbin. From inattention, neglect, or sufferance in demanding no rent or acknowledgment, when the lordship of Lochaber was afterwards granted to the Gordons Clachaig was held to be included. Here Iain Lom, the immortal bard of Keppoch, lived and died, his remains resting peacefully in the picturesque Dun Aingeal of Kilchaoiril. The whole of Clachaig was only about 150 acres, and being a constant sore to the Mackintoshes, repeated efforts to purchase it were made, but in vain until in 1816, when a sale was effected.

Any one passing through this district by the Fort-William coach will observe the remains of old cultivated land near Clachaig, now part of the splendid farm of Tulloch, and I have in my day wondered who occupied the land, and why it was vacated. There were two traditions regarding Urachar and other townships—one, that there being of old no proper road, and the climate severe, the people had voluntarily left; the other, that the last occupants were such a wild turbulent set that their neighbours in Moy, Torgulbin, Tulloch, and others, demanded their expulsion. Lately I have seen papers which seem to favour the latter view, and they are given to show the lawless disposition of certain Brae Lochaber men, not much more than a century ago, who apparently lived in such comfort as could be afforded by the produce of muir and river, eiked out by thieving.

Donald Macdonell in Daldundearg of Tulloch states that in September, 1779, he had some words with Donald Macdonell, son of Archibald Macdonell in Tulloch, as to hained grass lands, and without provocation was struck in the head with a "naked" dirk, whereby he was wounded and his life endangered. That no sooner was this cruel and barbarous wound given than the said Donald Macdonald ran into the house of the said Archibald Macdonell, his father, and

arming himself and his brother Alexander with two guns
or firelocks, they threatened to shoot any person who would
attempt to assist the complainer. That the complainer being
a poor man, with a numerous family, was under the necessity
of compromising matters by receiving payment of six pounds
sterling, for the expense of medicine, doctor's bills, etc.

This story is taken up among other charges by Ronald and
Archibald Macdonald's tenants in Moy, and John Macdonald
in Torgulbin, in 1781, and thus referred to. After narrating
the stroke in the head with the dirk, Donald Macdonell
"entered his father's house in Tulloch, and having fully
armed himself with two loaded firelocks or guns, in order
to defend himself from being apprehended and brought
to justice—as he has good cause and reason to believe that a
party would be sent after him for that purpose—and
accordingly while Donald Macdonell was in danger of life,
Alexander Macdonell, tacksman of Tulloch, his master, with
Donald Macdonell, his son, and others, having gone as a
party near to the house of the said Donald Macdonell, the
culprit, he, the said Donald Macdonell and Alexander Macdonell, his brother, kept off the said party with the said
two loaded guns, threatening to kill the party therewith,
before they would allow themselves to be apprehended, or
if they, the party, would attempt to come on one step
further towards them." Besides the above Donald and
Alexander, Archibald had another son, John, and all four
kept their neighbours in hot water with their nefarious doings.

Donald Macdonell sold at the Fortingall Fair, November,
1780, two goats, one white with a black head, the other
grey; and the sale of the goats being there challenged by
Donald Macnab in Inverlair, alleging they had been stolen
from him, he, Donald Macdonell, to hush up the matter,
paid Macnab more than their value. Archibald Macdonell
had no sheep of his own, yet was seen driving several from
the farm of Aberarder, tenanted by Mr Mitchell, and both
Aberarder and Moy had lost many sheep in an unaccountable manner. Archibald Macdonell was in use of prow-
ling about lands where he had no right, carrying a gun

and bag of swan shot, and it was believed he used to shoot and carry away sheep, and more than once sheep were found dead with swan shot in their body. Donald Mackillop, junior, son of Donald Mackillop, a sub-tenant in Tulloch, was told in the hill by Alexander Macdonell to keep his dog tied up, and if not "that the third part of his body would not go home," a curiously expressed threat. Young Mackillop, was however, of a fighting race, and having words on another occasion with Alexander, who snapped his gun at him, Mackillop grappled with him successfully, and deprived him of his gun. Alexander on another occasion, threatened to shoot old Tulloch, his master, if he interfered with him. Mr Macdonell, Aberarder, having to go to the house of the Macdonells, and the interview not being satisfactory, was abused and threatened by Archibald, the father, armed with a dirk; by Alexander, first with a large knotted stick, thereafter with a loaded gun, and Donald with a cocked pistol, John being present, but not interfering. The meanest of all the charges, with which I conclude, was one by Alexander, who pressed a poor neighbour for repayment of sixpence which he had to reborrow from another neighbour. Not satisfied with the sixpence, Alexander demanded interest, and the debtor saying he had the loan of the sixpence only for a short time was told interest would be taken out of his skin, and he was instantly struck to the ground by a blow in the temple from a stone taken up for the purpose. These Macdonells were in league with one Archibald Bàn Kennedy in Greenfield of Glengarry and they worked into each other's hands, and it is not at all improbable that they were cleared out according to one of the traditions, and no new people substituted.

General Wade chose his route between Lochaber and Badenoch, along the Spey and the Roy, and before his time this was the chief access. It was finished by him up the Roy to the lower marches of Annat and Glenturret, and although he is known to have lived at Leckroy, and probably built the present house, the communication, as a good driving road, was never completed between Dalrioch and Meal Garve. This was an easy road, and for opening up the country, though perhaps not the readiest for passengers, is the best way for a railway between Fort-William and Kingussie. No doubt the making of Loch Laggan coach road was of great importance, and reflects much credit on the three proprietors who made it —the Duke of Gordon, Mackintosh, and Cluny; but there was no road to Loch Laggan of old, properly speaking. At the north, the Drove road from Dalwhinnie passed through Strathmashie, skirted Brae Laggan, and, passing to the south of Loch Cruineachan, joined the Corryarraick Road before it reached Garvamore. At the south, the road from Rannoch passed Corrour, Fersit, and by Tulloch, keeping close to the bank of the Spean, to Keppoch and High Bridge. There was, as mentioned by Colonel Thornton, an exceedingly bad track as far as the houses of Tullochcrom and Aberarder from the north, but how people got, except on foot, to Maggach, Kyleross, and Moy on the west side of Loch Laggan, and to Inverwidden and Luiblia on the east side, unless by boat, can only be conjectured.

Some particulars of old places, rents, people, and traditions of the Brae will now be given.

First.—*Old Rentals.*—The whole of Kilmonivaig, east of Loch Lochy, was the property of Mackintosh, the Duke of Gordon, and Letterfinlay, with its cadets of Ratullichs and Annat. I am not able to give any old rental of the latter, only the old rentals of Mackintosh and the Gordons. That of the former for the year 1650 was—

1. Keppoch, Inveroybeg, Achaderry, Bregach, Tollie, Urachar, and Altmie, £756 13s 4d Scots money, 18 custom wedders, 12 stones of butter, and 12 stone of cheese at converted prices, £96 Scots. Total, £852 13s 4d.

2. Bohuntin, Kinchellie, Achavaddy, and Bohinie, £280 Scots money; 8 custom wedders, 4 stone butter, 4 stone cheese at converted prices, £36 Scots. Total, £319 Scots.

3. Bohuntinville, Crenachan, Brunachan, Achluachrach and Kilchaorill, £130 Scots; item 12 custom wedders, 8 stone butter, 8 stone cheese at converted prices, £64 Scots. Total, £494 Scots.

4. Reanach, £66 13s 4d Scots; item, 2 custom wedders, 1 stone

of butter, and 1 stone of cheese at converted prices, £9 Scots. Total, £75 13s 4d Scots.

5. Bochasky, £40 Scots; item, 2 custom wedders, 1 stone butter and 1 stone cheese at converted prices, £9 Scots. Total, £49 Scots.

6. Murligan and Glenglaster, £210 Scots; item, 5 wedders, 3 stones of butter, and 3 stone of cheese at converted prices, £25 Scots. Total, £235 Scots.

7. Tulloch and Dalindundearg, £210 Scots; item, 5 wedders, 3 stones of butter and 3 stones of cheese at converted prices, £25 Scots. Total £235 Scots.

8. Blarnahinven, £80 Scots; item, 2 custom wedders, 1½ stone butter, and 1½ stone cheese at converted prices, £11 10s Scots. Total, £91 10s Scots.

9. Inveroymor, £33 6s 8d Scots.

Total of the Brae, £2382 3s 4d Scots, or about £200 sterling.

It may be mentioned that the present land rent is not more than that paid at the beginning of this century.

I now give the Marquis of Huntly's rental, as settled by him "with the men of Lochaber in anno 1667." The Marquis styles the Lochaber occupants as "the men of Lochaber," distinguishing them from those of Badenoch, whom he describes in the lett of 1677 as "the inhabitants of Badenoch." The Marquis' total rent in Kilmonivaig and Kilmaillie was 3535½ merks, whereof in Kilmonivaig—

1. Letterfinlay of feu	Merks—£76	13	4 Scots.
2. Annat and Ratullichbeg of feu	32	16	8
3. Inverlochy of Rent	200	0	0
4. Blarour	50	0	0
5. Inch and Blarourbeg	220	0	0
6. Auchicar	80	0	0
7. Auchinech	35	0	0
8. Tirindish	31	0	0
9. Killichonate and Unachan	125	0	0
10. Corriechoillie, Coireon, and Lecknaprech, (partly in Kilmallie)	230	0	0
11. Leanachan Mor and Achnashine	300	0	0
12. Auchindaul	160	0	0
13. Lindallie and Camusky	200	0	0
14. Torlundie	260	0	0
15. Tomcharrich	120	0	0
16. Torleck	100	0	0
17. Dounie	120	0	0

The above included many smaller possessions, as will be

known to those acquainted with the parish, and who will miss such old names as Fersit, Clionaig, Achnacoichan, and others. The present rental of the Gordon lands in Kilmonivaig shows an enormous increase on the foregoing, chiefly sporting rents from forest, muir, and river.

Second.—*Old Places and People.*—Many old places where important transactions occurred have even in name been forgotten, through merging in others, and the adding of farm to farm. Sheep were fatal to personal occupation, and Brae Roy has suffered, it may be said, extinguishment. What was doing in Annat on 20th October, 1673? The ambitious and no less astute Lord Macdonell and Aros, who had to content himself with that title after having striven in vain for the Earldom of Ross, going to meet the new and equally ambitious Lochaber Chamberlain, fools him bravely, and hails, pen in hand but tongue in cheek, Duncan Macpherson of Cluny, the grandson of Andrew Macpherson, who was happy to act as Mackintosh's forester over his part of the forest of Ben Alder forty years previously, as "Chief and principal man of the haill Macphersons and some others called old Clan Chatten." At Leckroy, on 8th January, 1712, Coll Macdonell of Keppoch, keen, shrewd, and an able penman, completes a transaction for the purchase of twelve mares, eight years old, with six foals, and a stallion, at the price of one thousand merks, from Donald MacAllister Mor, *alias* Macdonell, in Cullachy of Abertarff. Keppoch draws out a bond, which is all in his own handwriting, giving John Macdonell of Inveroy and Ronald Macdonell, younger of Clionaig, as his cautioners, having Ronald Macdonald of Gellovie and Archibald Macdonald of Tullochcrom witnesses. General Wade lived for some time and wrote letters from Leckroy. Towards the end of last century the well-known Donald Mor Og Cameron was tenant, betwixt whom, supported by the Duke of Gordon, there was a series of frightful litigations and criminal charges with George Cameron of Letterfinlay, and Fiscal Macpherson. Donald Mor Og, I have often heard, was a grand specimen of the old Highlander, and from its size, his coffin had to be put in and taken out by the window. Coming to Glenturret, so long occupied by a fighting race of Macdonells, it was also the scene of gentlemanly hospitality, terminating with Captain Ranald Macdonell, who had married Marcella Maclean of Pennycross. Of the many Glenturrett letters and papers I have, an interesting circumstance consists in the selection of executors by old Glenturret, Alexander Macdonell, who was at first known as "Blarour," showing how little difference in religious views entered at the time into people's heads. Macdonell selected the parish clergyman and the priest, who acted most harmoniously. These were the well-known Dr Thomas Ross of Kilmonivaig, and Father Ranald Macdonell of Leek, afterwards the well known priest of Uist.

Coming down to Glenroy, Reanach will ever be remembered for its having sheltered Alexander Stuart, Earl of Mar, after his disastrous defeat at Inverlochy, but it and Brunachan are now practically desolate. John Scott, tenant in Brunachan, seems to have been fairly well off, for on 28th April, 1803, he writes that he had at the place 700 sheep, and he sold 100 lambs at 8s 9d each. At Blarnahinven there is now hardly a vestige of former occupation, save a few trees; but let us view it on the second of August, 1679. Then we shall find a comfortable house and a well-to-do tenant of the old stock, in some perplexity as to how to procure the needful for completing a lucrative purchase of cattle, rather beyond his means. At last he makes up his mind to apply to his master, who, though much troubled by refractious tenants, has always shown him kindness, and so he writes to "The Right Honourable Lachlan Mackintosh of Torcastle," for the loan of 511 merks, and offers as his securities Ranald Macdonell of Lethindrie, in Duthil parish —a son, I think, of "Iain Lom"—and Gorrie Macdonell of Glenturrett. The application was favourably received, and Donald Macdonell *alias* Mac-Allister-vic-Aonas-roy, went to Dunachton, and got the money on the 26th of August in presence of Lachlan Mackintosh of Strone. If there were people at any time in Glenglaster, I do not know. Bochasky is also forsaken. In Glen Spean on both sides there is hardly any population until you come to Inverlair and Tulloch respectively; upon the Gordon side, Fersit, the Loch of the Swords, Bean-a-Bhric, etc., were well-known places, as also the little island at the foot of Loch Treig, the abode of the famous "Owl." Around these localities poetry has left its mark and fancy woven many a pleasing tradition which cannot now be lost, penetrated even as they are by the iron horse with its materialism. There are at present 17 tenants in common in Murligan, Achluachrach, and Glenglaster, etc., which goes by the general term of "Gaelmore." In 1797 there were just 18, and it may interest the men of the Brae to have an authentic list of the joint tenants of that year. The poor people were sadly involved by the failure of one John Macdonell, drover in Dalindundearg, a man of repute and extensive transactions, to whom their stock sales of that year had been given. The others were—Donald Mackillop, and Donald Rankin, managers, Dougald Macintyre, Dougald Rankin, Angus Macgillies, John Rankin, Donald Stalker, Finlay Beaton, Alexander Beaton, John Rankin, Duncan Mackillop, Ewen Cameron, Alexander Maciver, Angus Cameron, Donald Boyle, Donald Beaton, and John Macarthur.

I observe a singular letter, dated 12th November, 1803, from Donald Mactavish, Achaderry, uncle of a boy John Mackintosh, only son to the deceased John Mackintosh, in Easter Bohuntin, complaining that a few days before, the boy, herding in the hill of Bohinie, was fired at without provocation, by "Colin Campbell, son to Duncan Campbell, Strontian, and Ewen Macdonald, son to Glencoe, who were looking for game." Young Glencoe fired the shot, which struck the boy in the face and head, wounding him to the danger of life. The offenders would appear to be both youths, and Campbell instigated the other. The uncle, saying that "he is not able for to keep law with Glencoe," wishes the Procurator-Fiscal to do so. The matter was hushed up and it is likely young Glencoe took warning, for he turned out an honourable man and a distinguished physician in the East India Company's service.

KEPPOCH.

Much has been written, and much more could be written, regarding the family of Keppoch, but here I can only give the barest outline. Alexander Carrach, youngest son of John, Lord of the Isles, had in all probability the whole of Lochaber from his father. He was held in high repute by Highlanders, notwithstanding his burning of the Cathedral of Elgin. His estate was forfeited, and it does not seem as if his son and successor, Angus Macdonald, had any further right than the possession of Fersit, by which title he is known. At all events, by 1443, if not earlier, Alexander, Earl of Ross and Lord of the Isles, deals with the Brae as his uncontrolled property and gives a charter of it to Mackintosh, without money feu. The Earl's son John being forfeited, Mackintosh thereafter held the Brae, as well as Glenluie and Loch Arkaig—a hundred thousand acres—direct from the Crown. The Macdonalds, however, never lost sight of any chance to recover the lands of Alexander Carrach, and were much aided, in so far as the Brae was concerned, by the Gordons ever since they acquired the lordship of Lochaber about 1500. The Macdonalds were granted tacks by the Gordons to the whole of Kilmonivaig east of the Spean, for some time called "Gergawache"—lands of the value of 40 merks of old extent. The Macdonalds and the Camerons, supported by the Gordons, kept Mackintosh in constant trouble, until in 1547, both having given offence to the Earl of Huntly, the latter called in the help of William Mackintosh, who was lucky enough to apprehend both Ewen Allanson of Lochiel and Ronald Mor of Keppoch, and delivered them to Huntly at Elgin, who caused their immediate execution. How foolishly these chiefs acted, and how well Huntly played them off against each other, as circumstances emerged! These and such chiefs were the real fighting men and bore the brunt not only of every battle of their own, but also those of their superiors and over lords; whereas, had the chiefs joined amongst themselves, these lords would soon have been cleared out. But no—their own clan and family feuds, notwithstanding marriages of convenience—were their uppermost thought, and they fought the real battles of the over lords, who seldom faced danger themselves, and when they did made but a poor figure, sinking, like Huntly at Corrichie, under the over-protecting weight of their armour, or executing a rapid retreat—some would call it flight—like Argyll at Glenlivet and Inverlochy.

The riddance of Ronald Mor Macdonald, counted as eighth of Keppoch, did not end Mackintosh's troubles, for his successor was concussed by the Regent Moray in 1569 to grant an obligation to come to an arrangement with Keppoch, which would involve his feuing the lands, in all probability for an annual trifling money payment only. The carrying out of this fraudulent design was fortunately stopped by Hamilton's shooting the Regent, known (doubtless as a nickname) as the "Good," in quit of some cruel wrongs.

A temporary truce was patched up (been) between Mackintosh and Keppoch, in 1572, as will be seen by the following, one of the oldest documents I have observed connected with the Brae—

"Be it known to all men by these presents,—Me Ranald vic Donald vic Coil Glass of Gargawache in Lochaber, to be bound and by the tenor hereof, binds and obliges me, my heirs and assignees hereof to serve leally and truly an honourable man, Lachlan Mackintosh of Dunachton and his heirs, by myself, kin and friends, assisters, partakers, and allies, and to take his and their fauld and plain part, assist and concur with him and his heirs, in all and whatever his and their actions, causes, questions, quarrels, and debates which he and his heirs shall happen to have to do with, contrary all mortals, the king's duty and my Lord of Athole allenarly excepted ; and that neither I nor my heirs hear or see of his or her, heirs, kin, or friends, evil or skaith, but that I or my heirs shall advertise him and his heirs of the same, and shall give him and his heirs my leal and true counsel in all his actions and causes, As he and they shall require ; and shall serve him and his heirs leally and truly when and where he or his shall require me or my heirs to do the same, conform to the tenor of the contract made betwixt the said Lachlan and me of the date at Inverness, the 7th June, 1572, under the pains of perjury and inhability and violation of my faith, lealty and honour for ever. In witness whereof to this my bond of manrent subscribed with my hand at the pen led by the nottar under written at my command specially required by me hereto, my proper seal is affixed at the Isle of Moy the 12th June, 1572, before these witnesses, honourable men, James vic Coil Glass of Gask, John Forbes of Tollie, William Cuthbert and John Kerr, burgesses of Inverness; Neil vic Coil vic Neil, servitor to the said Ranald; Donald Dhu vic Homas vic Allister in Badenoch, and Sir John Gibson, parson of Urquhart; Nottar Public with other diverse. . . ."

The well-known Keppoch, Alexander Macdonald (Allister nan Cleas,) gave a similar bond to Mackintosh and his eldest son, Angus, signed at Dunkeld on the 25th January, 1589, before Sir John Stewart of Gartentulich, John Stuart vic Andrew of Inverchynachan, James Stuart of Tillyfourie, William Mac Eachan Macqueen of Corriebrough, and Thomas Gow, Nottar. Keppoch signs with his own hand.

After Glenluie and Loch Arkaig had to be parted with, more determined efforts than ever were made to make the Brae usless to Mackintosh. In these, Keppoch was supported by all the Camerons, except Glenevis—Sir Ewen Cameron personally, as an honourable man, keeping in the back ground. Alister Buidhe, uncle, and reputed murderer and instigator of the assassination of the Keppoch boys, Alexander and Ronald, began the contest, his son Archibald, who died about 1682, keeping it up well. It was reserved, however, for Coll Macdonell, fifteenth of Keppoch, known as "Coll of the cows," to come to the front victorious at the battle of Maolroy, where Mackintosh was ignominiously defeated, with the additional pangs of regret for the prior burning by Keppoch of the old castle of Dunachton, not long rebuilt, with its grounds planted and beautified. Smarting under his treatment, for Government did not bestir itself as wished, Mackintosh declined all Lord Dundee's efforts to get him to rise in 1689, although Lord Dundee was his near relation. In his distress Mackintosh implored and petitioned King William—fortunately in vain—to take the Brae off his hands at £5000 sterling.

The Duke of Gordon offered him £3000 sterling and the superiority of all his lands in Badenoch, but this was also fortunately declined. It was about this time that the fortification near the house of Keppoch called the "Sconce" was erected, from which every stone has been removed for the Keppoch buildings.

There are several very handsome larches, which may be 150 years old, and though the railway is too near, even yet the place, if the huge steading were removed, a new house suitable to the importance of the estate erected, and the surroundings laid out and beautified, Keppoch might be made as fine as any place in Lochaber. Coll Macdonell was finally brought to book at Fort-William on the 23rd of May, 1700, and new arrangements being made, both he and his son, the gallant Alexander Macdonell, continued for fifty years, not mere tenants but firm allies and friends of the Mackintoshes. Coll Keppoch's letters are well written, displaying a good knowledge of legal affairs. Alexander the son had a pension of 100 merks from Mackintosh, and this is one of his acknowledgments for his "gratuity," as he terms it, dated Keppoch, 13th January, 1735 :—

"I Alex. Macdonell of Keappoch grant me to have received from Angus Shaw, factor to the Laird of Mackintosh, the soum of one hundred marks Scots money as the said Laird of Mackintosh his gratuity to me for Martinmas one thousand seven hundred and thirty-four years, of the which soum forsaid I grant receipt. In witness whereof I have written and subscribed those presents at Keappoch the 13th of January, one thousand seven hundred and thirty-five years.   (Signed)   ALEX. MCDONELL."

Alexander Macdonell of Keppoch married Jessie Stuart of Appin, leaving two sons—Ranald his successor ; Alexander ; and five daughters, Clementina, Anne, Barbara, Jessie, and Catharine. The eldest son, Ranald, married Sarah Cargill, with issue—two sons who died young, when the male representation devolved upon the above Alexander, afterwards Major Macdonald, who had managed his nephew's affairs. Of haughty spirit and temperament, he could not get on with Sir Eneas Mackintosh, who after years of wrangling and difference resolved at last to remove him, and it would seem as if Keppoch and the Macdonells were for ever parted. Major Macdonell removed to Inch, and thereafter to Ireland, and there are descendants in the female line. Mr Alexander Mackintosh, a thriving merchant in Fort-William, was settled in Keppoch, but his circumstances giving way, he had to leave in a very few years. At the beginning of the century, Keppoch was let again to one of the clan Donald, namely, Alexander Macdonald of Glencoe, and later on Mr Angus Macdonell of the family of Keppoch became tenant. He married Miss Christina Macnab, in her own right lineally descended of the old Lords of the Isles. This excellent specimen of the old Highland lady, after the death of her only son, had to relinquish Keppoch and now lives in London with her accomplished daughters. There are still Macdonalds in Keppoch, but Inch, long their habitat, knows them not. The following pathetic notice appeared in the newspapers in 1850 :—

"Died at Keppoch on the 25th March 1850, aged 83, John Macdonell, Esq., the grandson of Keppoch who fell at Culloden and the last Highlander who could say he had the honour of kissing the hand of Charles Edward—Righ nan Gael."

Faithful and true the Keppochs have ever been.

IX.—PARISH OF KILMALLIE.

FORT-WILLIAM AND THE GORDON LANDS.

To all descended of the house of Mackintosh, the parish of Kilmallie will, as the birthplace of Eva, the honoured mother of Clan Chattan, ever be interesting. Fifty-one years ago, 1844, I paid it my first visits, two expeditions remaining indelibly fixed in my memory. One of these was a drive to Glenfinnan to see the monument to Prince Charles, and the other, crossing Lochiel and Loch Linnhe, accompanied by a friend, to see Inverlochy Castle and Fort-William, and on our return nearly drowned in a sudden storm, whence we had to run for several hours into the shelter of Camusnagaul. The day's misfortunes did not end there, for being dark by the time we left the bay, we went aground on a bank, since, I think, removed, not far from Corpach Heads, where we had to remain in the cold and darkness for some time, until the tide had sufficiently advanced to float us off. All this was in the month of January. My recollections of Fort-William were therefore of a mixed character, in consequence of the after proceedings, but I well recollect its streets as being very dirty and the extraordinary number of public-houses it contained. Fort-William is now the growing place of the West Highlands, and is entering on what I trust and am almost certain will be a long reign of prosperity—a West Highland emporium—having, or to have by and bye, outlets in every direction of the compass.

I wish it, as I have already publicly wished it, every prosperity, and desire that its appearance from the sea may in time be much improved by a carriage marine parade, while the water power available quite at hand should be utilised for electric purposes, and thereby the gas-works and other objectionable smoky erections done away with. The houses if white-washed, rising tier by tier from the sea, would look grand.

It would be idle as well as unprofitable to speculate on the condition of the people in prehistoric times, or even when in possession of the Comyns. The latter left little record and did not perpetuate their name. How different from the Macdonalds? Their possession was not much over 150 years—four generations exactly—yet how the actions of the Lords of the Isles pervade the whole district—and as for the people, then and now, and now as then, the surname of Macdonald dominates and predominates.

The old castle of Inverlochy, of which there are some remains, was no doubt erected in the time of the Comyns, and it is a great pity that such alien names as Fort-Augustus and Fort-William have come in place of the dignified and euphonious Gaelic Killiwhimen, and Inner-lochie. When about 1500 the Earl of Huntly got the lordship of Lochaber, he was bound to maintain the Castle of Inverlochy for the King's service, but just as occurred in the case of the Castle of Inverness, the obligation was, on the Earl's supplication shortly after, either modified or practically departed from.

Cromwell fortified and extended the defences of Inverlochy, keeping there a considerable garrison, who, judging from documents preserved, amused themselves, when left alone by Lochiel and others, in framing addresses of that snivelling cant so congenial and natural to the crop-eared Saxon Roundhead. After the restoration the place fell into decay, but after the Revolution, Government saw the prudence of having proper fortifications in this locality; and early in William and Mary's reign the fort of Fort-William was erected nearer the sea than Inverlochy, and was maintained until well on in the present century. A village sprung up around the Fort, in honour of the Queen called Maryburgh. No regular title seems to have been granted by the Duke of Gordon, but a money payment of £70 a year was made by the Board of Ordnance, for at least 30 years prior to 1787, for the site of the Fort and certain grounds adjoining, occupied for the accommodation of the garrison. The village was a Burgh of Barony, with right to hold a weekly fair. Matters so remained until 1787, when the Duke, desiring to have things put on a permanent footing, entered into a submission with the Board of Ordnance, to Mr David Young of Perth, and Mr Angus Macdonald of Achtriachatan, as valuators. The grounds desired by the Board were found to extend to 53 Scots acres, whereof it may be mentioned 4 acres, 2 roods, 20 poles, represented the Fort; 1 acre, 2 roods, 12 poles, the esplanade; 2 acres, 2 roods, the burial ground; 15 acres, the Point of Claggan in Kilmonivaig, the remainder being accommodation land. The arbiters fixed the annual value at £70, instead of £81 claimed, but declined giving an opinion on the forty years' purchase asked by the Duke, £4240. Ultimately his Grace accepted £2100, and the necessary writ was granted, referring to a plan prepared by Major Andrew Fraser, chief engineer for North Britain, and reserving to the Duke the salmon fisheries of the rivers and the coast adjoining, rights of anchorage for accommodating the trade and intercourse of the village, as also to the inhabitants and villagers, the use and privilege of the burial ground.

Major Fraser's plan, which was signed in duplicate, went amissing, and in 1820 the Board of Ordnance wished the grounds inspected, measured, and substantial march stones put up. This the Duke agreed to, but the local representatives differed greatly, while the principals also were not at one. The Duke maintained that the fort and esplanade were included in the 53 acres, while the Board held that they were not, the matter ending in the latter acquiescing in the Duke's views.

That "Queen Anne was dead" became proverbial, and as it was also certain that her sister Queen Mary was also dead for many years, the Gordons thought the keeping up the name of Maryburgh inconsistent with their dignity and so altered it to Gordonsburgh. Not to be outdone,

Sir Duncan Cameron, who succeeded the Gordons in the Burgh of Barony of Inverlochy, called the village Duncansburgh. It would be difficult, perhaps, to decide which of the two names was the ugliest; nor is that of Fort-William, which has supplanted both, a whit less objectionable.

The old rights in the town were merely entries in the Superior's rent rolls, as so much in name of "feu," while others were by way of "rent," and considerable trouble arose after Sir Duncan Cameron's purchase of Inverlochy in adjusting matters. These have, it is understood, been settled in course of time, while the new feus of Lochiel and Glenevis, are outwith the old settlements in Achintore-beg.

There are now only two proprietors in Kilmallie east of Loch Linnhe, Lochiel and Mrs Cameron Campbell. The former has a magnificent sea frontage from Fort-William to Ballachulish, but it must have been a very severe wrench for him to part with his portion of Ben-a-bhric and its shielings on the upper waters of Loch Leven, even though they never adjoined to or included Lochan-a-Chlaidhe, or the "Fuaran Ard," or the "Cailleach Mhor." Having already given the Gordon rental of Kilmonivaig, that for Kilmallie in 1677 is now given. I regret I cannot give the rentals of the other old heritors—those of Glenevis, Callart, Kinlochleven, and Lochiel's part of Mamore—

	Merks.		
Kinlochleven, (presumed feu) rent	110	0	0
Callart, feu	81	0	0
Lochiel, do.	20	0	0
Glenevis, do.	10	0	0
Blarachine and Tolly, rent	215	0	0
Inchrie and Sallachell	140	0	0
Blarmacfoildeach	200	0	0
Clashfern and Drumarban	160	0	0
Drumfour and Auchantor-beg, partly in Kilmonivaig	200	0	0
Corrichoillie, Corrieon and Leaknapreac, partly in Kilmonivaig	230	0	0
Carachanbeg, ...	160	0	0

One good point is cheerfully put to the somewhat meagre credit side of the Gordons in Lochaber during their three hundred and fifty years' possession, viz., that in 1800 the farm of Drumarban, within two miles of Fort-William, having fallen into the Duke's hands, it was broken up and let into crofts, chiefly for old soldiers of his own fencibles.

So long as there were soldiers at Fort-William and a staff kept up, there was a good deal of stir in the place. The markets were generally well attended. The resident gentry, it might be said, whereof Fort-William was the centre, were, though scattered, fairly numerous, while many of the larger farms were occupied by officers on half pay or retired. Gradually, after the close of the Peninsular War, the strength of the garrison was reduced, the local resident gentry decayed, the old officers died out, and stagnation prevailed. Yet at its best, Fort-William society was not altogether harmonious. Militarism with its parasite train, is ever exclusive, and the West Highland world whereof Fort-William was the centre was a century ago rent in twain by a bitter yet most ridiculous warfare over the Fort-William dancing master, one Kennedy, who had set up in the place a dancing school in 1802, which was attended by those who considered themselves the elite.

Of old Highlanders did not need to be taught, their steps being adapted to the music and its time, and thus perfectly in harmony. Times were changing, however, and so this school was opened in Fort-William. Fired with an emulation rather unsuited to his years and situation in life, Mr J. Macmillan, of the somewhat mature age of 22 for beginning this kind of schoolery, whose daily occupation was while by no means dishonourable 'yet of an humble nature, viz., that of strapper, presented himself for admission, which the poor dancing master, glad of support, did not hesitate to give him. The rest of the scholars, young ladies and others, with their parents and friends were furious, and insisted that if the objectionable person whose activity when on the floor was rather dangerous to others' limbs were not excluded, they would all leave. This put the poor dancing-master in much distress, and he offered to instruct Macmillan alone for nothing. Backed up by some "friends of man," and "universal brothers," not unknown even in the present day, Macmillan declined, and was in consequence dismissed. He thereupon raised an action of declarator against the dancing master, maintaining that so long as he kept open school he was bound to receive the petitioner in common form with others on payment of the usual fees, and that if he declined he should be found liable in heavy damages. This ridiculous case, after going through the Sheriff Court, was debated at great length in the Court of Session, talented advocates gravely debating the pros and cons as if important issues depended upon it. Local feeling was much embittered, and large sums were foolishly subscribed to carry on the proceedings.

Alexander Macdonald, son of Charles Macdonald in the Clachan of Aberfoyle, practised for some years in Fort-William as a doctor, and afterwards in Knoydart, but he must not be confused with the well-known surgeon in Knoydart, Alexander Macdonald, *alias* Maceachin, called the "Doctor Roy." The first-named Alexander Macdonald served his apprenticeship with Dr Robert Graham of Stirling, and his articles were discharged on the 9th of November, 1761. Like many budding surgeons, Alexander was glad to accept an appointment on a Greenland whaling ship, starting on his first voyage early in 1762, as seen by the following certificates:—

"I, Thomas Gairdner, merchant in Edinburgh, one of the owners of the ships employed from this port on the Greenland, and as an acting manager for the other partners, do certify that the bearer, Alexander Macdonald, surgeon, was by my appointment examined by a physician of skill, and recommended to be employed as a surgeon in our ship "The Campbelltown," on the voyage to Greenland this season, and the commander and crew have reported to me their entire satisfaction with his care and skill in his profession, and constant application when necessary in the way of his business; and, therefore in justice to his merit, I presume to recommend him to any one that shall have occasion to employ him. Given under my hand at Leith, August 10th, 1762. (Signed) "THOS. GAIRDNER."

"I, Commodore Dirck Janson, commander of the ship "Campbelltown" of the Edinburgh Whale Fishing Company, in the voyage this season, do certify to the owners of my ship and all whom it may concern, that Alexander Macdonald, surgeon on the voyage this season, has performed his duty with diligence, care, and as far as I know, with skill in his profession. Certified by me at Leith, August, 11th, 1762. (Signed) "COMMANDR. DIRCK JANSON."

By November, 1763, and probably at an earlier date, Dr Macdonald had settled at Fort-William in fairish practice. Among his patients were Lieutenant John Macdonald of Auchachar; Angus Macdonald of Achnacoichan; Lieutenant Donald Macdonald in Maryburgh; Donald Cameron in Boluick; Duncan Macpherson in Maryburgh; Donald Maclachlan in Coruanan; Ewen Macphee in Glendessary; Allan Cameron at Blairmachdrine; John Stewart of Forleck; Captain Alexander Cameron, at Auchnacarrie; Duncan Cameron, at Muick; Donald Macphee, in Glendessary; James Thomson, merchant in Maryburgh; Marion Wilson, residing in Maryburgh; Mary Cameron, relict of Donald Cameron, tacksman of Drumarban; Donald Mackinnon, at Moy; and Donald Cameron, tenant in Achnasaul.

It will be noticed that the Captain and Commander, whose name strongly reminds one of a famous character in "Guy Mannering," does not certify to Macdonald's skill from personal experience, probably being strong enough to dispense with any medical assistance, but the doctor's operations on the crew needed in all likelihood a heavy hand, which unfortunately stuck to Dr Macdonald. Auchachar and Achnacoichan considered his treatment and physics improper and dangerous, and being taken into Court for his account, the former stated in defence that in the autumn of 1764 there was a severe flying distemper over the country, and that he got alarmed by the appearance of certain blotches. Dr Macdonald undertook the cure, and dosed him with drugs and physic, so that from August 1764 to May 1765, he was unable to leave his room, became emaciated to a skeleton, "more like a ghost than a corporate body"; that Dr Macdonald ultimately acknowledged he did not understand the case, and on being challenged for charging at the rate of 1200 per cent. for his drugs he answered that it was on account of "his straitened circumstances."

Upon proper advice Auchachar, by drinking goat whey and "Trefoil" tea, gradually recovered. Achnacoichan's defence was that his son Angus, a boy of twelve at school at Fort-William, caught the prevailing distemper, which the father intended to have dealt with according to a recipe he possessed of his late brother, Dr John Macdonald, but meeting Dr Alexander Macdonald, the latter offered to treat him gratis, and applied mercurial and other drugs to such a degree that the boy became "so enervate and feeble that a kind of paralytic disorder occurred." Thoroughly alarmed, Achnacoichan consulted the garrison surgeon, who said that the drugs supplied were too much for the strongest man, and ordered a radical change. In 1767 Dr Macdonald removed to Knoydart, where I find him practising in 1771. The last notice of him is a letter in a shaky hand, and denoting an old, unpopular, and irascible man, dated, Knoydart, 4th January, 1790. He had apparently assaulted a neighbour, and I give part of his explanation. He says—

"I can prove 1st, that the stroke I aimed at him he never received, so consequently did him no injury; 2nd, that it was by his repeated endeavours to traduce my character and his insulting language when I desired to know his reasons for traducing my character that I made a stroke at him, not with an oak bludgeon but with an ash stick, which stroke he never received; 3, that he is of a bad character I can easily establish, and that he committed theft and depredations on my own property I can make clear, and that it was after he was found in my garden burthened with my onions,' I said that if I caught him in repetitions of the kind I would shoot him in the act as soon as a muir cock."

From Fort-William hundreds of emigrants sailed at different times. Mr Flyter, the well-known lawyer, writing on the 27th June, 1801, says—

"Your friend Mr Denoon left this on Wednesday for Nova Scotia on board the Sarah of Liverpool. The Aberdeen vessel sailed eight days before then, and I hope they will have a pleasant voyage. Both vessels were as full as they could hold of emigrants, and many who wished to go could not be received."

In 1805 the state of the earlier Fort-William Sheriff Court

Records was very unsatisfactory, as may be seen from Mr Flyter's letter now given. It is hoped that the old papers were at least to some extent recovered. Mr Flyter's letter dated Fort-William, 18th April, 1805, is as follows :—

"I cannot give any account whatever about old processes *or any other Records* of this Court preceding the beginning of February, 1799, the time I came to this country. It defied me to get a paper except few trifling processes then in dependence from my predecessor, Bailie Cameron. I often applied both to him and my constituent for possession of the Records of Court, but neither paid the least attention to the business. Any process that occurred in my own time I can easily put my hand on, but further I cannot go."

A Custom House had been established for some time at Fort-William with success. Upwards of a hundred years ago Mr Colin Campbell, one of the most influential men of the district, and much respected, was collector. The estate of Ardnamurchan having changed hands, and the new proprietor, being energetic and having the ear of those in high places, took it into his head to try and get the Custom House removed to the Bay of Kilchoan, and managed to carry matters so far as to enlist the sympathies of the Board of Customs at Edinburgh. The Duke of Gordon was furious, and with the Duchess, who took the matter up warmly, stopped the removal for a time. The natural shelter and other advantages of Tobermory, though like other Government fishing villages, failing as a permanently successful fishery establishment, were such as to give it the preference. Thus, while Riddell failed in his main object, Fort-William was ultimately sacrificed, having in its present prosperity, perhaps some consolation in the thought that its old opponent's descendants have been cleared out of their temporary possession of Ardnamurchan.

The annexed letter from the Board of Customs and the report by the Fort-William authorities may be read with interest at this day. It appears from Mr Tod's letter that Collector Campbell furnished him with early information, seeing with his usual sagacity that in Tobermory lay the danger. I observe that the Duchess at once applied to

Lord Adam Gordon, who then held a high military position in Scotland, and also to Mr Dundas :—

"Number Forty-six.

"Gentlemen,—Being informed that in the west side, about two miles from the point of Ardnamurchan, there is a natural wet harbour, that can be made perfectly safe against all winds at a small expense ; we direct you to report whether it would not be more for the benefit of the Public and Revenue to remove the Custom House from Fort-William to that station, notwithstanding the objections made by you to Kilchoan, and in particular whether the officers would not have it more in their power to check smuggling, especially if a small Boat or Vessel were provided, to be stationed near the place now proposed, and employed under your direction.

"We being perfectly satisfied of your impartiality and that no interested motives will have any weight with you for this information, which is to be transmitted with all possible dispatch.—We are, your loving friends,

      (Signed)   "J. H. COCHRANE.
       "   "DAVID REID.
       "   "ROBT. HEPBOURN.

"Custom Ho., Edinburgh,
 "13th June, 1787."

"Number Forty-nine.

"Honble. Sirs,—Agreeable to your Honours' orders of the 13th June instant, we beg leave to report that none of the officers of this Port, tho' acquainted by frequently sailing the Sound of Mull, either observed, heard, or had any knowledge of such a natural wett harbour, as your Honours' mention, previous to the above Order ; further than a late addvertizement in the Edinburgh newspapers by the Proprietor of his intentions to lett his Estate of Ardnamurchan, pointing it out, nor is it laid down, as such in any map, chart, or survey of the coast, known or seen by us. On inquiry we are however since informed by some countrymen ; That a Rocky Bank or Island across the Beach of the Bay of Kilchoan of Ardnamurchoan and about two miles from the point, forms a Gutt or Strand that with the highest Spring Tides admitts Boats and small craft below six to seven foot Draught of Water within that Bank. That the Bank at present is no security to even these Boats, as a low Land that near by overflows, without drawing such Boats above water mark on Land, when they touch the Shore of that Beach, that Bank being open on both sides at full sea. We are also assured by several shipmasters well-known on that Coast, and from our own knowledge believe it to be so, That the whole Bay of Kilchoan of which the foresaid Strand forms a part, is neither a safe or commodious Harbour for shipping, known or frequented as such. With several sunk Boats in that Bay it is exposed to near one half the points of the Compass as a Lee Shore, particularly to the due South, South East, and South West Winds, nor is it a Roadsted or proper Inlett or Outgoing that Shipping frequent or touch at in passing the Sound of Mull, or the Point of Ardnamurchan; in such circumstances, or meeting with Contrary Winds in the Sound, or off the Point, all vessels make for the safe and commodious harbour of *Tobermory* in the Sound of Mull, if be South the point, and when be North the point, for the Harbours of the Island of *Canay* (tho' about ten leagues Distant), Isle Oransay in Skye, or other harbours in that neighbourhood, and so far as we can learn there is no safe harbour known even for small craft, on either side of the Mainland of Ardnamurchan within many miles of the point thereof. On that footing we humbly apprehend engineers or professional men in such undertakings can only say the expense of making such a wett harbour perfectly safe, or estimate the sums necessary for quays or such artificial bulwarks on that beach as will effectually secure it a safe harbour for shipping.

Referring to our former report to your Honors of the 19th December last, stating our opinion of the advantages or disadvantages to the public of establishing a Custom House at Kilchoan. The trade and business at Fort-William, and our sedulous endeavours to check smuggling from thence, are so well-known to your Honors and appearing by our various quarterly and yearly returns to the respective offices under your Honourable Board, it does not become us, so nearly interested in the issue, to press our opinion further, how far it would be more for the benefit of the public and revenue to remove the Custom House from Fort-William to any part of the Sound of Mull. We entreat your Honors to refer to others not concerned in the proposal from views of interest, private motives or local attachments, impartially to certify that point. We trust it will thereby appear to your Honours, on every prospect and view of the case, that the Port of Fort-William should not be totally abandoned, or the whole offices thereof removed to a station about 40 miles distant from so large a tract of country as lyes behind, that has now, and of a long time, felt the benefit of that establishment. But we pray leave to declare it as our avowed and decided opinion, that if, it is thought fitt to be so removed to any part of the Sound of Mull, Tobermory should be the station as most eligible in every respect for every purpose of the Publick and Revenue, and not the Bay of Kilchoan or any part of the country of Ardnamurchan where from what we have already stated, we assuredly apprehend it could answer no publick view whatever.

"We submit to your Honours what services a few Custom House Officers could render the public, stationed on a Point of land surround by the Ocean, without a Harbour on that land, secluded by inaccessible roads for about 24 Scots Miles from even the small village of Strontian, as the nearest post-office of a Weekly runner ; where neither the Proprietor, a Civil Magistrate, or other man of business at least known in Trade, Manufacturer, or Merckantile line, presently reside, without troops nearer than Fort-William to assist them, and tho' a vessel was provyded to check smuggling under such Officers' Directions as that vessel could only in moderate weather touch at, or near the Station of these Officers, and in our opinion, should more properly be stationed or lye at Tobermory with any view of success. It does not occur to us that under these circumstances, the Officers at Kilchoan or such vessel could easily give the necessary intelligence or assistance. And we have said in our former report how unfitt in our idea, a small open Boat is to navigate those Seas for the use of the Revenue but in Moderate or Summer weather.

"In a case of this importance to the public we humbly conceive it to be our Duty to state fully the facts as strike us, and humbly hope they will be confirmed to your Honors as such by the impartial Public at large, and more particularly we beg leave to appeal as to the grounds on which we found our Observations to Captains Crawford, Campbell and Hamilton as Commanders of the Revenue Cutters on that Station and professional gentlemen best informed on the Coast, and to the fishing Traders of Greenock, Campbelltown, and Oban, who had every access to consider the case with attention which is humbly submitted.

"We have the Honour to be with much respect, Honoured Sir, Your very Obedient hum. Servants,   (Signed)   "COLIN CAMPBELL.
                                                     "   "DUN. M. BAILLIE.

"Customs Ho., Fort-William,
    "26th June, 1787."

"Fochabers, 4th July, 1787.

Sir,—As I am uncertain at present where to address a letter to the Duchess I beg you will take the trouble of forwarding to Her Grace the enclosed copy of a late correspondence between the Board of Customs and the officers of the Custom House at Fort-William, concerning the removing of the Custom House from that place to Ardnamurchan.

"As the very existence of the village of Gordonsburgh depends upon the Custom House being continued there, please inform Her Grace of the necessity of her making every possible exertion immediately to prevent Sir James Riddell's plan from being carried into execution. And it will also be proper while Her Grace has access to the Treasury Board and the several gentlemen of the Customs about Edinburgh, that she enter a *caveat* against the removing of the Custom House at any future period from Fort-William to any of the intended fishing towns, particularly to this same *Tobermory* which perhaps there is some reason to be afraid of as the rival of Gordonsburgh.

You know what steps it may be necessary to take at Edinburgh to prevent the Board of Customs and the Exchequer from coming to any decision till Her Grace arrives.—I am, sir, your most obedient servant,

(Signed) " WILL TOD.

To Cha. Gordon, Esq. of Cluny, etc., etc.

CAMERONS *v.* MACDONALDS, *et e contra*.

The hereditary ill-feeling between those surnamed Cameron and Macdonald is well-known. It is not, however, often mentioned in black and white. Before giving the instance after referred to, I may refer to the claim preferred by the Camerons to be placed on the right at Culloden. This was directed against the Macdonalds and is thus alluded to in an exceedingly modest but clear account of the Rising of '45 written by Lieutenant-Colonel Donald Macdonell of Lochgarry. It will be recollected that John Macdonell, then of Glengarry, was an old man, and his eldest son Alexander being taken captive before the Rising actually took place, and detained prisoner until it was over, was prevented from taking the field. The clan was therefore in two divisions, led, the one by Lochgarry, old Glengarry's near relation, and the other by the latter's younger son, Angus, accidently killed at Falkirk.

I have recently been favoured by my highly valued friend and ancient ally Mr Macdonell of Morar, with the perusal of an old manuscript bearing to be a "Memorial by Lochgarry for Glengarry." It gives a full account of all that occurred to Lochgarry, one of Prince Charlie's earliest supporters, up to his embarkation for France. The MS. is not only signed by Lochgarry but is apparently in his handwriting, and is of such value as calls for its separate publication. The Northern Macdonalds had become divided into four distinct families, Glengarry, Clanranald, Sleat and Keppoch, who, though sharply divided among themselves, had been up to this period steady loyalists. Now alas! for the first time the house of " Donald Gorm, *Clann Domhnuill nan Eilean*," appeared not with their brethren. Lochgarry, it will be observed, according to the after-quoted narrative, refrained from giving Lord George Murray's reasons for his unfortunate determination, as if Lord George desired the place for his own men. These reasons, however, have been given by himself. He could have had no object except to what was right, unless high expediency. The major blame undoubtedly lies at the door of Lochiel, who asked what he was not justified in asking, and that too at a very critical moment; while on the other hand Lord George was by this time well aware of the extreme jealousy and exalted punctilio that existed between the Highland chiefs, amounting almost to religious fanaticism. Lochgarry says—

"The Macdonells had the left that day, the Prince having agreed to give the Right to Ld. George and his Atholmen, upon which Clanronald, Keppoch and I spoke to his R.Hs. upon that subject, and begg'd he would allow us our former Right; but he intreated us for his sake we wou'd not dispute it as he had already agreed to give it to Lord George and his Atholmen, and I heard H.R.Hs. say that he repented it much and wou'd never doe the like if he had occasion for it. Your Regmt that I had the Honr. to command at this battle, was about 500 strong, and that same day your People of Glenmorrison were on their way to join us, and likewise about 100 Glengarry men were on their march to join us on the other side of Lochness. Att this unlucky battle, we were all on the left, and near on our Right, were the brave Macleans who wou'd have been about 200, as well looked men as ever I saw, commanded by Maclean of Drumnine, ane of the principal gentlemen of that Clan; he and his son were both kill'd on the spot, and I believe 50 of their number did not come off the field. Their leader waited of the Prince on his landing, with a commission from most of the principal Gentlemen of that Clan, who were always known to be among the first in the field when the Royl family had to doe, and wou'd have been all in arms at this time, had not been the unlucky accident of their Chief's being in the Government's hand, which was a cruel loss to the cause, and occasion'd that this brave Clan were not all in the field; they live likewise under the jurisdiction of the Duke of Argile, since the Forfeiture of their great Estates, occasioned by their constant attachment to the Royll. Family so consequently live in the neighbourhood of the numerous Clan of the Campbells, who were always dissatisfied to the Royll Cause, and if they had all arisen in arms their familys wou'd have been ruin'd by them, but if their Chief had been at their head, this they wou'd have little regarded. However, I'm sure, including the 200 at Culloden and those Lochiel had out of Swynart, and other parts, with several other young gentlemen that had joined the severall Regmts. of the Macdonells, wou'd have compleated twixt four and five hundred men of that Clan."

Lochgarry's reference to the gallant Macleans, though it does not bear upon what I am writing about will, I know, be excused.

The object of the memorial was, no doubt, to let Glengarry the younger have a full and direct account of the behaviour of the clan.

Barisdale was so unpopular with the Camerons that, without the slightest warrant or authority, they took it on themselves to deport Coll Macdonell, third Barisdale, and his son Alexander to France.

My immediate illustration relates to people, who, though in a humble position, may be expected to throw greater keenness and personality into a struggle than their superiors.

There were two small possessions in Kilmonivaig, Donie and Auchcar, names fallen into desuetude, on the old road by the water of Lundy, passing Lienachan and others, which joined the Glen Nevis road at Poulin More before it reached Loch Treig. Upon the 1st of April, 1780, Donald Macdonell, late volunteer in his Grace the Duke of Gordon's North Fencibles, now tacksman of the fifth part of the farm of Auchcar, his said Grace's lands in the lordship of Lochaber, says that he had the honour of his Grace the Duke of Gordon's acquaintance and his good countenance, for whom he had recruited for his regiment five men, four being Macdonalds of his own friends, and the fifth an Irishman, and that he, Donald, having a throng family of six "wake" children, had to give up soldiering, when he was discharged by his Grace, and a letter of tack for the fifth part of Auchcar given him.

A minute account is then given by Donald of his enjoyment with friends of his pipe and glass in the house of Donald Kennedy, in Maryburgh, on the evening of Friday, 24th March, 1780, when the company were intruded upon by Donald Cameron, tenant in Donie, who used violent

language and assaulted them, threatening Donald thus :—
"Donald Duke, for all your great friends, Duke of Gordon
and Macdonells, if I get you by yourself, sooner or later,
I'll beat you so that you will not be able to travel the road.
The principal charge against Cameron is given in Donald's
own words. It is—

"That on Saturday the twenty-fifth day of March last, being
the day following the encounter in Kennedy's house, when the
memorialist and a neighbour were upon the road to Inverness,
and had gone about three miles out of Maryburgh, the memorialist
having looked behind him he observed the said Alexander Cameron
and Donald Cameron, his brother, coming after him with a speedy
pace, and the memorialist then dreaded, from the hurry and appearance they had and from the information he, the memorialist, had
got the night before, that the said Alexander Cameron was threatening
to use him ill, and putting him from walking the road, the memorialist
and his neighbour having got into a hollow part, they went off the
road and shifted their course so as to avoid the said Alexander
Cameron and Donald Cameron, and having gone round a knowe, the
memorialist was greatly surprised to see the said Alexander and
Donald Cameron take a short cut and run both up towards the
memorialist, and no sooner had the said Alexander come up to him,
but he drew his large oak staff and made a stroke at the memorialist's
head, which, if he had received, would have undoubtedly killed
him, but was avoided by the memorialist running off, and the stroke
only touched him in the heel. The said Alexander then pursued and
struck the memorialist with his staff on the crown of the head, cutting
him desperately, whereupon the memorialist, seeing he could not then
escape, grappled with Alexander Cameron, and they two were allowed
a considerable time to pull, haul, and strike at one another—the memorialist had no staff, and received many strokes from Alexander Cameron
on the head with his staff, the marks of which are still visible—the
memorialist having then by chance got above Alexander Cameron,
was seized by the two legs by the said Donald Cameron in Donie,
the said Alexander's brother, trailed off him, and Alexander put
above him, and the said Alexander having kneed the memorialist, who
was all covered over with blood, was allowed to get up with life only in
him, being by this time much hurt and faintish ; that the said
Alexander is a bad member of society, and universally known in
the country as a quarrelsome and disorderly person, much given to
fighting."

Donald concluded by alleging that the attack was premeditated, and occurred upon the farm of Torlundy, at a place called Glackvirran, and he being "a poor man with a throng family, of the family of Keppoch," trusts that all well disposed persons will contribute to see that he gets justice, seeing the said Alexander and Donald Cameron have expressed no regret for their conduct and no excuse, except that the memorialist "was a Macdonell, to whom they seem to have an utter aversion." The Camerons were bound over to keep the peace in the sum of one hundred merks each.

AN OLD MAP OF MAMORE.

In 1803 there was prepared for the Duke of Gordon a hand map of Lochaber for convenient use and reference. It was drawn out by a Mr Clinkscale, either connected with the garrison, or more probably a schoolmaster. It is not to any scale, but being only a few inches square, it is very handy and useful, containing the names and situations of every place on the Gordon estates, as well as the roads.

These may first be referred to, and are of a twofold character. "The dotted lines .... are all good and passable roads. The roads denoted by single lines, ———, are generally footpaths, but may be travelled on horseback." So the plan states. Taking Fort-William as the centre, a good road follows the shore of Loch Linnhe as far as Inshrigh, and Ardgour Ferry. The old King's road to Glasgow still remains as it then was, by Achintore Mor, and Blarmafoldach to the head of Loch Leven. Before reaching the house of Kinlochleven, a minor road struck off to the northeast, by the foot of Loch Eilt to the north of Loch Treig, and to Fersit, while the Glenevis road followed the water until it emerged beyond Craiguanach and joined the last mentioned road north of Loch Treig.

The main road from Fort-William to the east and north, by Inverlochy and Torlundy, made for High Bridge, then divided into two branches, one continuing in the same direction to Low Bridge and the Ratulichs, where it again divided, one branch leading by the sides of Loch Lochy and Oich to Fort-Augustus, the other through Glengloy to Leckroy. The other branch of the main road from High

Bridge passed the two Blarours, Tirindrish and Achaneich, making for Glenroy, but for some time keeping a considerable distance from the water, and then joining the Glengloy road at Leckroy. No other road of any kind is shown except the above two, north of the Spean. A minor road led from Torlundy by Leanachan and Corrichoille, ultimately at Poulinmore, joining the Glenevis road before mentioned, and, finally, there was a minor road westward south of the Spean beginning at Inverlochy, keeping close to the River Lochy by Camisky and Lindallie to the old church of Kilmonivaig, at the junction of the Rivers Spean and Lochy, thence by the Spean to High Bridge, Unachan, Killichonate, Inch, Clinaig, Monessie, Achnacoichan, and Inverlair to Fersit. There is not a vestige of road shown on Mackintosh's side of Glen Spean, and of course Roy Bridge did not then exist. There was a ford over the Roy, just as it fell into the Spean, and another across the Spean at Inch, both very dangerous. At the former, Juliet or Shiela Macdonell, the Keppoch poetess, was drowned.

Mr Clinkscale was evidently a man of taste, and denotes the natural woods, in particular "the fine oaks" of Tirindrish. Other wooded places marked are above Leckroy, to the east of Loch Treig, Achnacoichan, Inchrigh, and Culchenna.

Centuries ago the sea washed the walls of Inverlochy Castle, and I possess a fine engraving showing a galley of some size swinging at anchor below the castle, having one prospect of still waters—the sea. At one time the huge moss of Corpach must have been covered with water, partly by the sea and partly by the overflows and siltings of the Lochy.

OLD RIGHTS OF FISHING AND FLOATING ON THE LOCHY.

I have frequently alluded to the beauty of the valley of the Ness before the Canal operations, and I can imagine the valley of the Lochy must have been at one time equally peaceful and beautiful. The River Lochy before the Canal was made, flowed easily and naturally, by the plain of Dalmacomer,

soon after joined by the Spean. On its south side, the
ancient Church of Kilmonivaig, on a fine terrace, looked
down upon the plain, the meeting of the waters, and the picturesque old burial place of the Macmartins—Cill-'ic-Comer.
Now matters are entirely changed ; the surface of the loch
has been much heightened, and the Canal itself, except for
the masts and sails of vessels or the cheerful funnels of
steamers, is by no means an object of beauty. The fishings
in the Lochy have been greatly interfered with, and the
three " F's," so much in evidence recently, were not unknown
in Lochaber 70 years ago, when Lochiel claimed from the
Canal Commissioners compensation for fishing, floating,
and ferrying disturbances on the Lochy.

Before referring to these, I wish to notice the cruives in
the river which had been set up by the Duke of Gordon
and Lochiel, then for a wonder, in alliance as regards their
rights of fishing. In 1797 Alexander Macdonell of Glengarry alleged that these two gentlemen had established
cruives in the river Lochy, and interdict was sought
against him to deprive him of his rights as an upper
heritor and user of the river for floating timber and other
purposes.

Glengarry taunts the Duke for his ignorance of the law,
as brought home to him in the case of the upper heritors
of the Spey, where his Grace's obstacles to navigation
or floating were declared illegal, and also that it had
been similarly decided in the case of the Ness. One
or two points of interest came up in course of the
proceedings—

"That while yet the manufacture of wood in the country was in
its infancy, the firwoods of Glengarry attracted the attention of
strangers, more than a century ago a smelting furnace was erected
near Invergarry on account of the quantity of charcoal which the
wood afforded, and the transportation of timber to the West Coast was
carried on upon a large scale. There is yet the trace of the Canal
which was then formed betwixt Loch Oich and Loch Lochy for the
conveyance of the timber, etc., which afterwards was floated down the
river to the sea. The practice which has taken place since, is
comfortable to it, for not only has the firwood of Lochiel been in use

of being floated down the river Lochy, but also the firwoods of Glengarry without interruption. For instance, the only ship built at Fort-William was made from the Glengarry firwoods, and was called 'The Lady Glengarry' on that account, and most of the houses at Fort-William are built of timber from the same woods. The river Lochy is well calculated for the purpose of water carriage from the interior into the sea. On Loch Lochy itself there are several large boats, and it has depth enough for the Royal George to swim in. The proprietors of Kilmonivaig have been in the use of keeping a boat upon the river below the Loch, and there are many instances of boats even going up the river, much more coming down, for different purposes of utility to the inhabitants, so that it is much more calculated for use than the river Spey, whose rapidity renders it less capable.'

Glengarry was successful, and the cruives, apparently more insisted on by the Stevensons, the salmon fishing tenants, than the proprietors, were discontinued. The opening of the Canal changed the question of floating, and Lochiel, in 1834, appears on a different tack. He could of course get his woods carried to Fort-William but he must pay at least dues, if not also freight. Some of the farms along the course of the Canal were deprived of access to wonted roads, banks leaked, culverts became choked, and over all grounds were permanently flooded by the raising of the level. Lochiel accordingly claimed large compensation. Hugh Robertson, wood merchant, stated in support of the loss of floating, that he paid not only canal dues, but that for pulling floats through by boat he got 3s a ton more than he used to receive as a floater, and that the new cut of the river at Gairlochy practically prevented floating, except at special times. As to the claim for loss on fishings Mr Charles Cameron, at Culchenna, stated that salmon did not now go up the new cut at Gairlochy, that he had seen numbers trying to get up, but were unable to get over the fall. That Lochiel's fishing was an excellent one, the witness having frequently killed two or three salmon before breakfast. The salmon spawned in Loch Arkaig, and went up the rivers at the head of the lake. That by the fish not getting up to the spawning ground, loss has arisen, not only to the Lochy but to the Arkaig fishings. Other witnesses stated that the ferry rents fell off greatly since the canal was formed, as there was no crossing the Canal formerly except at Banavie. The sum ultimately agreed upon and paid in name of damages and compensation was close upon £5000. This was over and above the large sums originally paid at the formation of the Canal.

LOCHABER LITERARY MEN, PAST AND PRESENT.

No part of the country has during the present century more steadily produced its quota of literary men than Lochaber. During the early part Mr Maclachlan was pre-eminent. After him may be mentioned Mr James Munro, and Dr Macintyre of Kilmonivaig, Dr Clerk of Kilmallie, and ahead of all others stands the evergreen Dr Alexander Stewart of Nether-Lochaber.

"May he live a thousand years."

Mr Maclachlan was fortunate in being warmly supported by the influential county gentlemen of his day. He had the knack of pleasing them and exciting the affection and attention of their children, his students. I have many of his letters and some of his Gaelic books, including his copy of Alexander Macdonald's Gaelic Dictionary of 1741, with copious notes. From his papers I select part of an elegy on a young student, Alexis Sinclair, as a fair specimen of his style. It has not, I think, been published, though not having a copy of his works beside me, I cannot be certain. The death would have been about 1806, and the youth was probably a Caithness boy. It is as follows—

AN ELEGY UPON ALEXIS SINCLAIR.

What solemn sounds from yonder hoary spire
Along the void in circling billows roll?
Be hushed my fears; tumultous thoughts retire;
Fate's awful heralds! Ah! they thrill the soul.
To youth and age they speak the warning strain;
Prepare, ye careless! for the approaching doom!
Turn from the toys of this sublunar scene,
And mark the world that lies beyond the tomb!
Thus, Wisdom slighted by the young and gay,
Knocks for admission at the human heart;
Alas! strong passions guard th' obstructed way,

And frowningly bid the heav'nly guest depart.
O dreadful spoiler of the Works of God!
Why not on woe-worn age exhaust thy store,
Which fourscore years had cours'd the toilsome flood,
Now longing sighs ! to gain the destin'd shore !
Why not make age thy prey ? tremendous king !
Ah ! why for youth thy fatal nets display !
Ah ! why deface the tender germs of spring,
But just expanding to the orient ray?
This flower whose beauties charm'd the lonely wild
So late transplanted from it's native plain,
To climes where science's fost'ring sunbeams smil'd
And shed new charms o'er all her flow'ry reign.
This flower that rose so lovely to the view,
Wav'd in Hope's eye, the large autumnal store ;
O ! heav'n the killing blast of winter flew,
And nipp'd the foliage, lovely now no more.
Late in the day I sought the pillar'd strand,
For one sweet hour t' indulge the social flow,
Where music wont to rouse the sprightly band,
And youthful hearts with genuine friendship glow.
No sprightly music wak'd th' accustom'd ball,
Nor shook the dome beneath the bounding throng ;
A mournful silence hush'd the spacious hall
And deep funereal echoes roll along.
Stretch'd on the bed of death Alexis lay.
All felt the once lov'd friend ; his heart was cold !
They found him pale inanimated clay ;
And saw the winding sheet his face infold !
But who yon weeping stranger's grief can tell?
See ! down his cheeks the copious torrents roll,
Inclining o'er the face he knew so well,
While all the sorrowing Parent melts his soul—
" My son ! my son ! my sweetest dearest care !
How art thou ever gone my hapless boy !
Ah ! my fond schemes were propp'd on fleeting air,
And now a long farewell to earthly joy.
O ! did we part my child, to meet no more,
But in the realm beyond the dreary grave,
God's will be done !   May I that will adore !
T'was God who took ; he took but what he gave."
Impetuous bursted from his high swol'n heart,
The too big glut of grief *his voice* suppress'd ;
Beneath the burden of th' oerwhelming smart,
He sinks !—Ye feeling fathers, know the rest.

THE DISMEMBERMENT OF INVERNESS-SHIRE IN LOCHABER.

The county of Inverness, and particularly the parish of Kilmallie, has suffered much from the high handed dismemberment effected by Lord Lorne in 1633, cutting off from Inverness-shire the districts of Ardgour, Kingairloch, Morven, Sunart, Ardnamurchan, and their isles.

At that time the Argyll family seem to have been superiors of what may be strictly termed the barony of Lochiel, reputed a £30 land. Not only was the dismemberment objectionable, but it was gone about in an extraordinary manner. Attempts have been made of late years to rectify some of the absurdities, and even at this moment there is a point as to the proper designation of proposed new parishes, North and South Kilmallie being suggested, though geographically incorrect. Perhaps the best solution would be to have Kilmallie in Inverness-shire alone, the remainder to be called Ardgour.

The barony of Lochiel extended from Glenfinnon at the south west to Banavie at the north east; the towns of Banavie and Corpach being the last enumerated in the older titles. This is a fine stretch of water frontage, but, except at Fassifern, is narrow and overlapped at the back by Glen Pean, which stretches almost to the head of Loch Morar. Lochiel estate proper was small in comparison with Glenluie and Loch Arkaig, and it was little wonder the Camerons struggled hard for possession of the latter. As it now stands, extending from Loch Eil to Loch Quoich and to the upper waters of the Garry, no finer estate is found in the Highlands.

If one looks at the ordnance sheets he will find that the boundaries in Lower Glenluie have been fixed arbitrarily, absurdly, and with disregard to all natural rules. The important township of Musherlich, with its adjunct of Tor Castle, was detached from the county of Inverness and the property of Mackintosh, who in vain protested against the spoliation. This proceeding was acquiesced in by Lochiel, being a handle against Mackintosh. After the enforced sale, when Argyll and Lochiel well knew that their acts would be closely scrutinised and advantage taken of any flaw, they were in a dilemma as to how Musherlich would be treated in the deed of conveyance. If inserted with Mackintosh's other lands, it would be tantamount to an admission that all the actings since 1633 had been tainted and vitiate; while if not inserted, it would be open to Mackintosh to raise the question that Musherlich was not included in the sale, and that he was entitled to reclaim it. The Argyll lawyers dealt with the point very judiciously. Musherlich was included in the disposition as for greater security only, the Earl alleging that it was already his property, and it was further conditioned that the then Mackintosh should retain the designation of "of Tor Castle," which he was then known by, during his life. Lachlan Macdonald the last designed of Tor Castle died in 1702.

RENTALS OF GLENLUIE AND LOCH ARKAIG IN 1642.

I now give a rental of Glenluie and Loch Arkaig in 1642. First the tenants' names, and second the rents—

NAMES.

1. Ewen Cameron of Lochiel in Moy.
2. Donald Cameron, Tutor of Lochiel.
3. Ewen Cameron, *alias* Bodach in Erracht.
4. Ewen Vic Allister More.
5. Donald Vic Coull Vic Allister in Barr.
6. John Dhu Vic Coil Oig in Strone.
7. John Vic Coil Vic Iain Vic Conchie in Inveruiskavullen.
8. Duncan Macmartin of Letterfinlay in Kyleross.
9. Duncan Vic Allan Vic Ewen in Clunes.
10. Duncan Roy Vic Iain Vic Allister in Inverarkaig.
11. Iain Vic Conchie Vic Ewen in Achnasoul.
12. Allister Vic Conchie Ban in Criew.
13. Ewen Oig Vic Conchie Vic Ewen in Muick.
14. Mulmor Vic Iain Vic William in Caillach.
15. Lachlan Vic Coil Vic Gillonie in Keandpol.
16. John Vic Coil Vic Allister in Invermaillie.
17. Ewen Vic Conchie Vic Iain in Lagganfearn.

18. Duncan Vic Ewen Vic Aonas in Glendessarie.
19. Donald Vic Iain Dhu Vic Gillony in Glen-Pean.
20. John Vic Ewen in Murlaggan.

They are described as "kinsmen and followers of the said Evan Cameron, and principal tenants, occupiers, and inhabitants by themselves and others in their names of Glenluie and Loch Arkaig, and particular towns thereof respective."

RENTS.

Moy.—40 bolls farm bear, at fiars' prices, £6 4s or £248. Silver duty, £20. Custom butter 12 stone, converted at £3 6s 8d—£40. 24 stone cheese, converted at £1 13s 4d—£40. 24 beds kids, converted at £1 6s 8d—£32. Total, £380 Scots.

Erracht.—£53 6s 8d silver duty, one mart £16, 4 wedders at £2 each—£8, 2 stones butter, and 4 stones cheese.

Barr.—£33 6s 8d silver duty, one stone butter, 2 stone cheese, and 2 wedders.

Strone, Achnaherry Interuiche.—£53 6s 8d silver duty, 1 custom mart, 2 stone butter, 4 stone cheese, and 4 wedders.

Inveruiskavullin and part of Glenmaillie.—£33 6s 8d silver duty, 1 stone butter, 2 stone cheese, 2 wedders.

Kyleinross.—£33 6s 8d silver duty.

Clunes and Glastermore.—£53 6s 8d silver duty, a custom mart, 2 stone butter, 4 stone cheese, and 4 wedders.

Inverarkaig and Keandmore.—£33 6s 8d silver duty, 1 stone butter, 2 stone cheese, 2 wedders.

Achnasaul, Glendessarie, and part of Salachan.—£53 6s 8d silver duty, 2 stone butter, 4 stone cheese, 4 wedders, and a custom mart.

Criew and part of Salachan—£33 6s 8d silver duty, 2 stone butter, 4 stone cheese, 4 wedders.

Muick and part of Arc.—£33 6s 8d silver duty, 1 stone butter, 2 stone cheese, 2 wedders.

Caillach.—£33 6s 8d silver duty, 1 stone butter, 2 stone cheese, 2 wedders.

Invermaillie, Walwart, Ardindische, and part of Glenmaillie.—£33 6s 8d silver duty, 1 stone butter, 2 stone cheese, 2 wedders.

Lagganfearn and part of Kinneach.—£33 6s 8d of silver duty, 1 stone butter, 2 stone cheese, 2 wedders.

Glen Pean.—£133 6s 8d silver duty.

Murlagan and part of Arc.—£33 6s 8d silver duty, 1 stone butter, 2 stone cheese, 2 wedders.

Total, £1029 13s 4d, Scots exclusive of collected customs, or about £90 sterling.

EILEAN-'IC-AN-TOISICH, AND THE CLUNES LANDS.

The following is an extract from the Mackintosh History:—

"In the year 1580 Mackintosh, for curbing the insolency of the Lochabrians, caused build a little island in the wester end of Loch Lochy, which was called Eilean Darroch, or the Oaken Island, for that it was built on oaken jests within the water. He had 2500 men for 3 months' time in Lochaber while the island was a building, and by means of this island (wherein he kept a garrison) he brought the Lochabrians in subjection to their superior; but how soon that island was surprized and demolished, the country people brake forth again to their wonted rebellion."

Having frequently tested without blot the accuracy of this history, I many years ago, when I had occasion to be frequently in Lochaber, enquired as to this island, but without any result. One day, however, the late Colonel Cameron of Clifton Villa, Inverness, of the historic family so long in Clunes, asked me if I ever heard of Eilean-an-Toisich, or sometimes called Carn-'ic-an-Toisich, to which I replied that I had not only heard of it, but had been long in search of it, and hoped now to know where it was.

Colonel Cameron then informed me that in his youth, on a remarkable clear day, being in a boat in the Bay of Clunes along with a very elderly man, full of tradition, the old man bade him look closely towards the bottom, when he observed several large hammer-dressed stones, as also logs of timber like joists. He was further told, that before the canal operations these remains were often visible on calm days, but since then only occasionally, and the old man had himself been informed by older people, that that was all now remaining of an artificial stronghold put up by the Mackintoshes to keep the people in order, hence, Eilean or Carn-an-Toisich. Colonel Cameron told me that the wood he saw was very likely oak. He farther stated that as the level of the loch had been much raised since the occasion, he doubted whether now it was possible even on a calm day, and otherwise suitable, to see anything. Finding that I was much interested and that he himself had for the first time learned the object of the structure, Colonel Cameron was good enough to say that perhaps some day we might make a pilgrimage to the spot, for he thought he could come very near it. Though not the eldest son of Allan of Clunes, his father had put the Colonel's name into the lease along with his own at the settlement with Lochiel in 1834, and were it not that the Colonel was on active service when the lease expired in 1853 he would never have given up the place to which he and his family were passionately attached.

I have now almost given up any hope of examining the Bay of Clunes, and indeed without the local knowledge of Colonel Cameron, any search for the remains of the island would probably be unavailing.

The raising of the loch has caused the disappearance of many other landmarks on the shores of Loch Lochy, and notably much of the road on its west side. Being now chiefly forest, neither Lochiel nor Glengarry have any interest in its maintenance or in re-forming it where submerged, but it long served the extensive and once populous territory from Laggan Achindrom to Inverie prior to 1834.

LOSS OF GLENLUIE AND LOCH ARKAIG BY MACKINTOSH.

Allan Cameron of Clunes stated that "from the river Arkaig to Goirtean-na-Croigh, including all the arable land in that space, viz., 12 acres at Bun Arkaig; 15 at Clunes, viz., Clief, Inverbuiebeg, Inverbuiemore, and Goirtean-na-Croigh, and about twenty-three acres of pasture, in all about 50 acres, had been submerged, besides a space of about 4 miles, averaging 30 yards in breadth to the Lochiel and Glengarry march at Derragalt, with stumps of trees standing out of the water. It was along this road that the Macdonalds marched on their way to the battle of Blar-nan-leine, and that Prince Charles two hundred years later, after a few hours' rest at Invergarry Castle, moved westward the day after Culloden. By this road also Mackintosh, for the last time, marched in force to Lochaber to meet Lochiel, who was waiting in arms to stop his passage across the Arkaig. A few words from a contemporary writer, personally present on the occasion, may not be without interest. Mackintosh had rendezvoused in Stratherrick and—

"On Saturday, 16th September, 1665, marched through the wood of Glastermore to the Clunes, a room belonging to Mackintosh, and upon their approach Lochiel and his kin drew themselves and all their cattle and goods to the south side of the water of Arkaig, a great water, not possible to get over but by boat and one ford which the enemy had guarded, resolving to keep the water between Mackintosh and his forces, and them. Now you are to know that the water of Arkaig being a mile long, which runs out of a loch that is 12 miles in length called Loch Arkaig, into another loch called Loch Lochie, and this water not being passable but by one ford, as said is, it behoved Mackintosh, who had no boats, to march about both sides of Loch Arkaig, 24 miles, before he could come at the place where the enemy was encamped."

They proceeded as far as Achnasaul, but in the meantime communings took place and Mackintosh and his people fell back on 18th September, encamping before the island of Loch Arkaig. The writer continues that upon the 19th of September—

"Mackintosh marched to the Clunes where there was a minute of contract drawn up and subscribed by both parties wherein Mackintosh was obliged to sell his lands of Glenluie and Loch Arkaig to Lochiel or any other person he would nominate, and Lochiel did engage himself and six of the specials of his friends under great penalties to pay to Mackintosh the sum of 20,500 merks on the 12th day of January next thereafter, within the town of Perth, and on the aforesaid day also to secure him sufficiently for the remainder of the sum (72,500 merks) to the satisfaction and content of any such persons of Mackintosh's own choosing, and the terms of payment to be Martinmas 1666 and Martinmas 1667. Upon the 20th September, 1665, Lochiel having crossed the water of Arkaig, Mackintosh and he met (24 men on each side) upon the lands of Clunes, and having drunk together in a friendly manner, in a token of perfect reconciliation, exchanged swords and so departed, having in all probability at that time, taken away the old feud which, with great hatred and cruelty continued betwixt their forbears for the space of 360 years. That afternoon Mackintosh and his people marched in order from Clunes to Laggan Achindrom, where after many friendly embracings, the forces of Badenoch and Braemar take leave of Mackintosh and the rest of the friends, and that friendly little army disbanded in peace."

The feud was ended, but naturally there was but little friendliness on either side, and for upwards of 200 years—

until 1869—no Mackintosh visited at Achnacarry, nor did a Lochiel set foot within Moyhall.

LOCHIEL.—ENORMOUS INCREASE OF RENT.

The subsequent history of Glenluie and Loch Arkaig, subsequent to the purchase by Lochiel, is little known. After the forfeiture of 1715 they were claimed under the Superiors Act by Argyll, but were afterwards restored to Donald Cameron the younger, who in 1745 was the undisturbed owner. Circumstances and the popular verdict have been very favourable to the character and position of the Lochiels since then.

The estate and clan are inseparably mixed up with Prince Charles, but there is no denying that to the heroism and devotion of the people is due the high place acceded to the family ever since and now. The estates were administered by the Forfeited Estates Commissioners until 1784, and though their factors were partial and biassed against the smaller occupants, upon the whole the rents were moderate. It is said that, like other chiefs, the Lochiels when exiles regularly received part of the rent. When such conduct is reported, it is always commented on as extremely honourable to the tenants. So it was, but let it be recollected that in former times, rent in the form of money was a minor, easy consideration—the real burden or tax being services, especially the liability to be called out to fight at any moment. And this burden, so often involving the lives of the bread winners, had become almost intolerable. Therefore the continuous absence or exile of the chief, after the law became generally operative and protective of the people, was really no hardship to them—rather the contrary—and this enabled them to pay a double rent now and then with comparative ease.

There is every reason to believe that the Commissioners did not overburden the tenants of Lochiel in the matter of rent, and of this Mr Alexander Mackenzie in his *History of the Camerons* gives a strong illustration in the case of Erracht. In 1779, a few years only of the current lease at a rent of £22 10s, remained. The elder Erracht, Donald

Cameron, second in command in the '45, applied for a renewal, and this was agreed to, at a rent fixed by the estates factor, Mr Henry Butter, who fixed the new rent at £48 9s 9d, but on a strong remonstrance from the tenant the increase was restricted by £3 9s 9d, with a 41 years' lease, whereof the rent for the first 21 was to be £25, and for the remaining 20, £45, beginning as at Whitsunday, 1781. By this time the craze for sheep farms had set in, and at the restoration of the estate to Donald Cameron of Lochiel, in 1784, was in full force.

I shall now give the rental of Lochiel in 1788 from Mr Mackenzie's History, distinguishing Glenluie and Loch Arkaig from the other lands. The total is there said to be £1212 9s 0½d sterling, which Lieutenant Cameron of Lundavra thinks too low, and says, giving farm by farm, that the estate was worth £2665, or more than double, and in token of his sincerity he more than doubles his own rent.

I. BARONY OF LOCHIEL.

	£	s	d
Drunnasallie—John Cameron	33	0	0
Kinlochiel—Donald Cameron	11	0	0
Stronlia—Two Camerons	17	6	8
Corrybeg—4 Macmasters and 3 Camerons	14	0	0
Fassiefern—Ewen Cameron	34	11	4
Mill of Fassiefern—Do.	8	6	8
Achdalieu—John Cumming	15	14	8
Annat—Collector Colin Campbell	22	10	0
Corpach—Alexander Macdonald of Glencoe	120	0	0
Fishing of do.—Do.	2	5	0
Banavie—Mr Fraser, minister, and P. Mackinnon	7	7	7
Corpach Public-House—Archibald Butter	3	10	0
Church Seat Rent	0	6	9½
Fishing of Lochy—Duke of Gordon	29	0	0
Ferry of Lochy—Alexander Robertson	3	8	8
	£302	7	4½

In all £302 7s 4½d of rent paid by 20 tenants.

II. GLENLUIE AND LOCH ARKAIG.

	£	s	d
Muirsherloch—8 Camerons and 1 Mackintosh	24	13	4
Strone—John Cameron	26	13	4
Carried forward	£51	6	8

Brought forward ...	£51	6	8
Barr—5 Camerons	25	6	8
Inveruiskavullin—2 Camerons	24	2	4
Erracht—Allan Cameron	25	0	0
Two Moys—12 Mackinnons and 4 Camerons ...	57	6	8
Achnacarry—Ewen Cameron, Fassiefern ...	26	5	0
Clunes—Donald Cameron	48	0	0
Achnasaul—8 Camerons	35	0	0
Crieff—John Macphee	12	0	0
Salachan—Cameron and Macphee	10	13	4
Muick and half Kenmore—Ewen Cameron ...	20	0	0
Half Kenmore—John Cameron	4	0	0
Coanich—3 Camerons, 1 Macphee	4	4	0
Caillach—Donald Macmillan, John Macphee ...	14	13	4
Murlagan—Macmillan, Mackintosh, Maclachlan	27	18	8
Kelenmore, a Shealing—Alex. Macmillan ...	8	15	0
Invermaillie—Alex. Cameron	16	13	4
Kinloch Arkaig—3 Camerons	13	15	4
Glenpeanbeg, ¾th ; Laganfearn, ¼th.—O'Kane Cameron	32	17	7
Glenpeanbeg, ¼th.—2 Camerons, 2 Macmillans	5	18	2
Glenpeanmore—Allan Macmillan	32	0	0
Glendessarie—10 Macphees, 4 Macmillans, 4 Camerons	90	0	0
	£585	16	1

In all £585 16s 1d of rent paid by 87 tenants.

III. MAMORE.

Achintore—Lieut. Donald Cameron	£40	0	0
Croft of Do.—Thomas Malcolm	2	7	3
Coruanan—Alexander Maclachlan	46	10	10
Corrycherichan—Mrs Cameron, a widow ...	17	6	8
Culchenna and Mill Croft—John Cameron ...	53	6	8
Lundavra—Allan Cameron	18	13	8
Ballachulish—6 Mackenzies	57	6	8
Do. Ferry—John Rankin	10	0	0
Onich—4 Mackenzies ; 4 Camerons	41	12	0
Culchenna Mill—Duncan Macinnes	6	1	4
	£293	5	1

In all £293 5s 1d of rent payable by 22 tenants.
Making a grand total rent of £1181 8s 6½d, payable by 129 tenants.

The rentals of 1642 and 1788 may be contrasted with advantage and the rise was by no means high, while the number of tenants holding direct of the landlord had increased. It has been said that the increase of rent was owing to the late Mr Belford, but this is quite erroneous. Mr Belford has enough to answer for in his dealings with the Dochanassie people in Glenfintaig. The mischief was done in the time of the restored Donald Cameron of Lochiel, and at an early period in his career. Mr Belford only acted as factor for but a very few years for this Donald, his chief sway being from 1833 to 1859, in the time of the second Donald Cameron, a very different man from his father, as will be hereafter seen. It would be going into invidious detail perhaps, not the object of these papers, to give farm by farm, the oppressive doings on the estate after its restoration.

Its restoration, under burden of debt of £3433 9s 1d 5-12ths, though humanely meant in this and other instances, in the case of Lochiel, the object being personally unworthy, proved fatal to the people. At the restoration Donald Cameron was only 15 years old, had been loosely and and extravagantly brought up, trained abroad, in habits and feelings having no sympathy with or pride in the family traditions or the prosperity of his people. Indeed he never visited Lochaber until 1790. He was much in debt before his majority, and deeply involved in connection with the Erracht sale and subsequent reduction. Ewen, afterwards Sir Ewen Cameron of Fassiefern, fought his battle with skill and determination, continued by his son Sir Duncan, up to Lochiel's death in 1832. But what could Fassiefern do? Money had to be found, and as early as 1793, by a new set of the estates, the rental was grievously increased. Heritable debt, family provisions, and the expense of building Achnacarry House mounted up to so large a figure that the trustees justly became alarmed, and the estate, already under trust, was put under entail and thus saved from extinction.

At the first set most of the old Cameron tenants became bidders, many of them officers on half-pay, who, by taking advantage of high prices, and changing the old system into sheep farming, were for a time enabled to pay their large rents. But what about the people, the life blood of the clan! They were no longer wanted. On the contrary, they were in the way, and, practically starved out, were glad in large numbers to enlist in Erracht's regiment. The sheep farms wanted but few hands, old cultivation fell out, and houses fell into decay. The people gladly enlisted with Erracht, but it was necessity, which has no law, that compelled the balance of the people to enlist and serve in the Lochiel Fencibles in 1799-1802.

All his life Lochiel was in straits, selling his woods to that extent that Sir Duncan Cameron had to save the woods on Fassiefern by paying for them, leaving them to stand, for which he was repaid by the next Lochiel, a most honourable man.

Soldiering was over in 1815; then the Canal operations began and for some years gave employment, when many of the people got lots at Corpach, Banavie, on the mosses of Caol, Lochyside, etc., where they still are, and this was the fate of the descendants of the gallant and warlike supporters of Lochiel! Starved out of their valuable farms and grazings in Glenkingie, Glendessary, Glen Pean, and others, most of the warlike and spirited race, the followers of Lochiel who remained in the country had to take up their home in the moss of Corpach, and in future, in the circumstances, to depend on mere casual manual labour for subsistence. That there was, at the time, fair demand for labour was most fortunate.

A few instances of the rise in rent will suffice—

I. Clunes.—By the rental of 1788, Donald Cameron, a most worthy Highlander, paid a rent of £48. Allan Cameron of Lundavra, values Clunes at £180. Now at the first set in 1793, the rent of Clunes was pretty stiffly raised from £48 to £110 7s 4d, upon one of the finest and oldest clansmen of Lochiel. He was on half-pay, and thereby, with close attention and natural cleverness, was able to exist and show that hospitality so peculiar to the family of Clunes, having had the special honour of Prince Charles as his guest. Before his lease expired, there being five years to run, Lochiel and Clunes bargained for a new lease for 19 years from Whitsunday 1815, at the enormous rise of treble the old rent, or £300. A favourite plan of Lochiel's was to ask a grassum, and allow for it in the rent, and here Clunes paid £1000 of grassum, getting the actuarial value in the reduction of rent, while the years to run of the old lease were also taken into account. Nothing but the tenant's intense attachment to the home of his forefathers justified such a rent, and when the place came to be re-set in 1834 to Allan Cameron and his son Captain John, the rent had to be reduced to £200. It may be said that none of the tenants was able to stand the increased rents, and large and regular abatements had to be made yearly.

II. Moy.—The old rent of the two Moys was £57 6s 8d, payable by 16 tenants. Allan Cameron valued the place at £70. Hugh Robertson, Lochiel's factor, became tenant, and in 1823 got a 19 years' lease at a rent of £120, burdened also with rates of 1s per £ and half the expense of a considerable fence with Erracht.

III. Annat.—The old rent was £22 10s, and Allan Cameron's valuation, £60. In 1815 it is set to John Kennedy of Kirkland for 19 years at a rent of £240, so enormous that at the renewal of 1834 the place only fetched £150, and in 1853, although Achdalew was conjoined to it, both places only fetched £200, from Lieutenant-Colonel John Cameron, Lienassie.

The total rental in 1788, shortly after Donald Cameron's restoration, was £1181 8s 6½d, while at his death in 1832 and for some time before it was not less than £6661 9s 6d, not a shilling of which was shooting rent.

Upon the accession of the late Donald Cameron of Lochiel in 1832, the estate was in debt to the amount of £33,000, burdened at the same time with handsome family provisions, and having a rack-rented tenantry, with a fluctuating surplus of some £1600 a year.

The house of Achnacarry had not yet been finished, and

thus the younger Lochiel, though a frequent visitor to Lochaber in his father's lifetime, and well acquainted with the people, had no home in the North. His position was a most unhappy one, having every wish to do what was right and proper to one in his position, but possessing insufficient means.

Not a sixpence was left to the late Lochiel from his father's executry, which included the considerable unsettled claim against the Canal Commissioners, and all the woods on the estate, but much to his credit he fought as it were against fate, struggling to do justice to his tenants, even beyond his means. When sheep farming was flourishing, the pinch was not so much felt. South country tenants cropped up, and took the farms and valuations. Later on, however, the demand fell off, and the question of valuation began to be serious, even in the late Lochiel's time. Landlords to a great extent are to blame for having in those days winked at the pernicious valuation system, not in the beginning affecting themselves directly.

It may be interesting to know who, out of the whole Highlands, the late Lochiel singled out as the most reliable valuators, and to be depended on, viz.—Thomas Gillespie of Ardochy, and Coll Macdonell of Inch.

I have said that Mr Belford was not to be blamed for the rise of the Lochiel rents and starving out of the people, but he is to blame for another phase of sheep farming, viz., that of consolidating farms. To landlords, who by the sheep farming system got rid of the people, it was further most advantageous to be freed from the cost of buildings, fences, etc. Hence, even shepherds' houses, fanks, fences, stells, etc., involved on every farm a certain expense which might be greatly reduced by consolidation.

CONSOLIDATION OF SHEEP FARMS.

This in time became serious, but I can only give one illustration of how sheep farming grew, extending within itself like a cancer. I do not blame those who, paying enormous rents of necessity, strove to extend their borders and curtail their outlay. "More land and no people" was their object and cry. Alexander Macdonald, of Glencoe, and John Campbell, Younger of Glenmore, were great monopolists on Lochiel, and other estates. Upon their downfall a shrewd careful shepherd, known at first as "John Cameron, drover, Corrychoillie," appears, afterwards becoming one of the most noted men of his day. His first place on Lochiel was the small farm of Coanich and Kenmore, which he entered in 1824 on a lease of ten years from Whitsunday 1824, the rent being £70—superseding the old tenants, "Ewen Cameron and others." During the currency of this lease Corrychoillie had added considerably to his possessions, viz., Murligan and Caillich, part of Glenkingie and Glen Pean; while in 1834 his farms culminated in his obtaining a lease of—1. Munquoich; 2. North Side of Glendessary, both as possessed by the heirs of Alexander Cameron; 3. Crieff; 4. Salachan; 5. Muick; 6. Half of Kenmore, all as possessed by the heirs of Lieutenant-Colonel John Cameron; 7. Murligan; 8. Caillich; 9. Grazings of Glenkingie; 10. Coanich; 11. West Kenmore, with the part of Glenkingie attached to Coanich; 12. Glen Pean More; 13. Glen Pean Beg; 14. Coull; and 15. Glaickfearn, all as possessed by Corrychoillie himself. The rent, with 1s per £ for rates and taxes, was £1430, on a lease of 19 years from Whitsunday, 1834, with a break in favour of either party in 1845. Large as this rent was it was not equal to the old rents exacted by the restored Lochiel, which came to £1700; thus—Glendessary, £590; Glen Pean, £960; Crieff, etc., £150—total, £1700. Lochiel himself did not expect this sum, but would have been contented with £1490. Corrychoillie, whose original offer was £1400, increased it to £1430, which offer, as he would not move further, Lochiel accepted, and in doing so on the 6th of January, 1834, wished the acceptance to be accompanied by these words—

"The gratification I experience at the near prospect of having a tenant of my own name, who by his activity and enterprise has been enabled to hold of his landlord and chief farms of greater value and extent than are in the possession of any one individual in the West Highlands."

This good feeling did not last long, not even to the break in 1845, and the cause of difference singularly was the well-known Ewen Macphee, afterwards called the "Outlaw of Loch Quoich," regarding whom so much was written and said fifty years ago. Macphee had been resident on Glenkingie, by Loch Quoich side, and left undisturbed by the previous tenants. Corrychoillie, a busy man, could not endure idlers, particularly such as inclined to go about with a gun in place of labouring or shepherding. The two met in a hostile manner on several occasions, one of the encounters ending in a threat on the part of Macphee to shoot Corrychoillie. Lochiel tried to mediate, taking up a very proper and considerate position. Upon the 27th of March, 1835, he writes—

"Let me have a particular account of Macphee's proceedings, his manner of life, and what his family consist of. My feeling with regard to this man is that having been so long unused to habits of industry or occupation of any kind, that when turned adrift he may have recourse to lawless proceedings for his support. Men of his stamp are sometimes reclaimed by kindness, when severity might drive them to desperation. On this principle, if I thought the man had any of the better principles of Rob Roy, I would endeavour to provide for him myself. In the meantime there can be no doubt that I am bound to clear the farm of him at the insistence of the tenant."

Again, fifteen months later, on the 23rd of March, 1835, Lochiel writes—

Corrychoillie made repeated complaints to me of the conduct of Macphee, and of loss he has sustained by him, both of which I cannot but think are somewhat exaggerated, as were he really the desperate character represented, surely Alexander Cameron, Inverguseran, and Thomas Macdonald (former tenants) would neither of them have suffered him to remain on the farm. As to the threat of shooting Corrychoillie, I think he is more likely to do so if he and his family are turned adrift at his instance. I should have thought that to a man of Corrychoillie's immense possessions, an acre or two of potato ground would be unworthy of consideration."

Ultimately the question came into Court. Macphee retired to the islet on Loch Quoich, claiming that it was part of Glen Quoich estate, in which he was supported by

Glengarry and his successors in that estate. Though the islet lies close to the Lochiel shore, it was found to lie in the parish of Kilmonivaig. Ewen Macphee, who was known as "Ewan-ban-Choribin," rests peacefully in Kilfinan of Glengarry, with his mother's connections, the famous Kennedys of Glengarry, but of this once numerous family I now only know Ewen's nephew, Mr Alexander Macphee, Newtonmore, my trusty ally and friend of thirty years' standing.*

At the break, in 1845, Corrychoillie either did not wish to continue, or was removed, and in any case the next tenants, the Cunninghames, according to the rent roll of 1845-6, paid for farms, with others, the enormous rent of £1698 18s, while Kennedy, for Fassiefern and others, paid a rent of £1803 11s. So much for consolidations. Besides abatements, some tenants had allowances made to them for disturbance. In 1820 Alexander Cameron, Inverguseran, then tenant of Bun Quoich and the North side of Glendessary, gets an abatement of £50 a year during the remainder of his lease in respect of his being "illegally deprived of the use of certain accustomed roads and privileges of old pertaining to the farm of Glendessary."

Between 1810 and 1825, Glengarry was busy asserting ancient rights of way through Lochiel to Kylerea and Skye, and stopping exits by the Quoich and Garry. It was about this time, it is understood, that it was found that Lochiel, though owning one side of Loch Quoich, had no right to land on the Glen Quoich side, or use the high way along it to the bridge of Quoich, and the North West, or towards Invergarry, as formerly.

No shooting rents were exacted until 1838 when General Cameron, Clunes, rented the lands north of Arkaig for the sum of £15 15s. Next year, Captain Peter Cameron, Fassiefern, rented the same lands for £110. The Marquis of Douro subsequently paid £400, and after him the Earl Malmesbury was tenant for many years and gave the place its high reputation. In his memoirs, Lord Malmesbury makes repeated references to Achnacarry, of which he

* Alexander Macphee died since the above was written, early in 1896.

seems to have been very fond. He had at first all the land west of the Canal, paying £400, but later was restricted to the lands north of the Luie, for which the rent was £300. The forest and shootings are of great value, but the stake fishings in Lochiel, and the fishings in the Lochy and Arkaig, have not hitherto proved of much consequence.

Colonel Donald Cameron re-built, as stated, the house of Achnacarry, but did not finish it, the other additions to the estate by him being the purchase of the patronage of Kilmallie and the right of superiority over Glenluie and Loch Arkaig and the Gordon lands.

The late Lochiel, with Sir Duncan Cameron, divided the Gordon Kilmallie lands. He built the Lochy Bridge and a fairish inn at Banavie. He took little part in public or local affairs and, I think, never appeared in print except as a site refuser.

CHURCH SITE REFUSED AT THE DISRUPTION.

In 1843 the Rev. Thomas Davidson, minister of Kilmallie, went out, followed by most of the people. The poor Highlanders entered heart and soul into the movement and have paid dearly for it since. No wonder that they now feel humiliated and hurt by the "opportunism" of their leaders, Principals, Professors, and Doctors, trampling under foot their cherished beliefs.

In the present day the idea of site refusing seems so preposterous that it appears almost incredible that such could have occurred within the last fifty years. The following is Lochiel's letter of refusal, shortly after cancelled and a site granted, preceded by a note of what the people, who were very keen, were doing prior to the disruption:—

"Corpach Cottage, 1st February, 1842.

"I beg leave to inform you that a meeting was held yesterday on the subject of Non Intrusion in the Church of Kilmallie and after a lecture from the Rev. Mr Macrae of Ross-shire on that subject, an association was formed favourable to these principles, and to whom from two to three hundred appended their names before leaving the church, and are to have monthly meetings or oftener, as the Reverend

Mr Davidson, shall see cause, and lectures on that question are to be given or delivered at these meetings."

It may be interesting to recall the names of Mr Davidson's chief supporters. They were, Donald Cameron, tacksman of Strone; John Cameron, tacksman of Drumsallie; Duncan Cameron, crofter, Banavie; Donald MacCulloch, schoolmaster, Muirsherloch; Alex. Ross, mason, Canal Bank, Alexander Fraser, lock-keeper, Corpach; Alexander Cameron, crofter at Achaphobuill; and Hugh Maclean, crofter, Blaich.

Lochiel's answer to the petition of his tenants for a site to build a "Free" Presbyterian Church was in the following terms—

"My good Friends and Tenants,—I have received your Petition, which has been forwarded to me by your Minister, praying that I would grant a Site on my property for building a New Church, as it is your determination to separate yourselves from the Established Church of Scotland. To the prayer of that Petition, though signed, as I am informed, by nine tenths of the adult male population of the Parish, I regret to say, I cannot, under present circumstances, accede.

"I have no wish, and certainly no right, to interfere with your liberty of conscience; at the same time I consider myself justified in acting in this matter to the best of my judgment, and in conformity with those views which nothing that has recently occurred has in any degree tended to change.

"Although not myself a member of the Established Church of Scotland, I am not the less alive to the many—very many—blessings she has conferred on our country; therefore to turn round now, and say that you will sacrifice everything hitherto held most dear, because it has pleased certain members of the Church to designate her as 'Erastian,' and as such no longer entitled to the love and respect of every true Presbyterian, is what I cannot bring my mind to contemplate without serious misgivings as to the result.

"The question which now so unhappily agitates Scotland, is not, as far as I understand it, one of 'Doctrine'; but solely arising from an alleged interference of the Courts of Law with the Ecclesiastical Jurisdiction of the Church. Now, let me ask you; is it worth your while on such grounds, to separate yourselves from the Establishment, and plunge yourselves and others into a sea of difficulties, from which it will be no easy matter to escape.

"Take my advice, therefore; and if I may use a homely phrase, 'Stick to the ship.' By this course you will have a better chance of gaining the harbour than by trusting yourselves to an open boat. I tender you this advice on the purest and most disinterested motives, though I may thereby expose myself to the charge of interfering in matters wherein I have little concern. But such is not the view I take of the subject, for it is my earnest desire you should pause before committing yourselves irrevocably and without due consideration to so hasty, and it may prove, disastrous a step.—With my best wishes for your welfare, believe me your sincere friend and landlord,

(Signed)   LOCHIEL."
"Denton Park, Otley, May, 1843."

PRESENT RENTAL AND OTHER INTERESTING DETAILS.

The present rental of Lochiel in the counties of Inverness and Argyll is about £10,000, of which £3500 may be taken as sporting rent. The number of crofters is considerable, but much fewer than in 1846, and with holdings of less value. In 1845-46, out of a total rent of £6709 13s 7d, exclusive of a good deal then in the proprietor's natural possession, and shootings, no less than £1414 2s 1d was paid by crofters, as follows:—

	£	s	d
Corpach and Banavie Crofts	439	17	2
Achintore do.	295	11	9
Ballachulish do.	193	1	3½
Corrybeg do.	83	11	0
Drumarban do.	96	6	0½
Inchree do.	23	16	0
Bunree Mill do.	17	17	0
Kinlochiel do.	75	2	9
Murshellach do.	71	19	9
Onich do.	116	19	4
	£1414	2	1

When Colonel Donald Cameron of Lochiel died at Toulouse, on the 14th of September, 1832, Achnacarry was still unfinished, and it cost his son over £1500 to complete it. This was well done in 1836-7 under the superintendence of a superior clerk of works from the south, sent by Mr Burn, architect, Edinburgh. About 1840, a demand for forests and shootings set in, but Lochiel was very unwilling to let, his views being expressed in brief thus—"letting Achnacarry at all goes against the grain."

Lochiel was singularly fortunate in his shooting tenants, and so far as he could, he favoured as tenants for his farms those of his own clan, and on the 9th of January, 1839, when John Cameron was preferred to the farm of Drumsallie, it was because Lochiel "should have felt with regret he should have lost as a tenant the son of one of the oldest, the most worthy, and I firmly believe, one of the most attached followers of the family. The young man may rest assured, I will do all I can to make his residence at Drumsallie as easy and comfortable to him as I can."

In describing past misdeeds, I blame no one now living for them. Indeed, it is but the barest justice to the present Lochiel, who had to bear the brunt, to state that in a few years he restored the reputation of his family, absentees practically from Lochaber for upwards of a century, to a higher position than ever, and, personally filling positions of credit and honour not hitherto attained by any of his predecessors, stands out very prominently among the Highland chiefs of the first rank of this age.

The original tenants were substantial, kind-hearted, and exceedingly clannish. A crofter in Crew, named Cameron, was able to promise no less than £80 in tocher with one of his daughters. Not having paid up, the son-in-law, a Macdonald, naturally applied to Coll Barisdale to help him. As soon as Barisdale interfered, the father-in-law, equally naturally applied to his clansman, Donald Cameron of Clunes, who readily engaged in the fray, which was carried on with determination, Clunes, however, being no match far Barisdale in a legal fight.

I give the annexed letter from old Clunes as a specimen of his kindly disposition, dated the 18th of June, 1787, as also another from Ewen Cameron of Erracht (brother of Sir Allan), likewise a good specimen of the old Cameron Highlander, dated the 30th of March, 1798—

"Clunes, 18th June, 1787.

"Sir,—As Mackay would not take any security for John Cameron at Sallachie but to deliver himself upon the very day appointed, other ways to run the risque of paying the penalty; therefore I hope you'l take the trouble, if it be anyways possible to keep him from going to prison, and I will deliver him to you any day you appoint. I expected to hear from you before now, for I wrote Scothouse a few days ago but had not any return as yet. You'l oblige me and take all the concern you can of John Cameron is all from—

"Sir, yours (Signed) DONALD CAMERON."

"Erracht, 30th March, 1798.

"Dear Sir,—The bearer, Charles Cameron, who had the farm of Horrichaisteal (Torcastle) with his mother and brother in tack these twenty years back, for which they had a charge of removal lately; they are the only people that is to be dispossessed in the county without the least reason for it. Now I think it is very hard for them to be dispossessed this year, as they were not warned about the beginning of the New Year; in the first place, they have no time to look out for another farm as the time is so short, and their stock of sheep they cannot get sold; also, cannot get the one half of their plowing done. Now the above Charles Cameron goes to you for your advice, and if you would give him some encouragement to stand it out, I direct him to you as active and faithfull to any business you take in hand. I will be very much obliged to you if you will give him your best advice in this business. You and I must be friends and settle our own business amicably at Whitsunday. Offer my best respects to Mrs Macdonell and family.—I am, dear sir, yours sincerely,

(Signed) "EWEN CAMERON.
"Excuse haste and the scarcity of paper." E. C."

The ladies of the time were equally kindly, while in many instances in circumstances of difficulty they bravely struggled with fortune. I have specially in view the case of Mrs Cameron of Strone, who was left the life-rent of everything by her husband, burdened with heavy bequests. As Captain Cameron died very close to the term, while his son desired the farm, Mrs Cameron was obliged to realize the stock in a hurried manner at a very considerable sacrifice. The estate thus did not turn out anything like what old Strone expected, but the widow pinched and pinched so that the bequests left by her husband should be satisfied, even to giving up her annuity under their contract of marriage, dated the 13th of May, 1820. Mrs Cameron was Isabella Cochrane, and amongst her children were Charles Cameron, merchant in Corpach, George Cameron,

Jean, wife of Captain William Cameron of Camisky; Frances, wife of Captain Ewen Ross, Killinan; and Miss Jessie Hay Cameron.

The old family of Lundavra, staunch allies of Lochiel, left the place at Whitsunday, 1818, when it was taken by D. C. Cameron, who had made money in the West Indies. He gave great offence to Lochiel by threatening to plough up, at his removal in 1837, old arable land, which had gone out of cultivation. He had the law on his side, and Lochiel had to condescend to ask him not to plough, and that he would be compensated. When D. C. Cameron became tenant, it was let "as formerly occupied by the deceased Mr Allan Cameron, and afterwards by his son," the rent being £120 with a grassum of £400. Upon his removal in 1837, Lundavra was let to Dugald Cameron, sub-tenant of Glenshelloch, and Ewen Cameron, senior and junior, residing there, at a rent of £140.

Murligan, on Loch Arkaig side, was at one time an important and rather populous place. As late as 1817 there was a public-house there. In that year it was set to Alexander and Duncan Cameron. It came afterwards into possession of Sir Alexander Cameron of Inverailort, who assigned the lease of it in 1826 to William Cameron, son of Alexander Cameron of Glendessary. This William Cameron was also tenant of Inveruisk-a-vullin, Erracht, etc., paying a rent of £420. It afterwards became part of Corrychoillie's subject.

Some days after Culloden a few Jacobites who were lurking in the neighbourhood, met at Murligan, and, inspirited by the arrival of a considerable sum of French money, resolved to continue the contest. Why, unless through the malign influence of the Foreign adventurers who had the ear of the Prince, everything was hastily thrown up after Culloden has never been accounted for.

This meeting, early in May, 1746, was attended by Lord Lovat, Lochiel, Dr Archibald Cameron, Cluny, Barisdale, old Glenbucket, and others. Secretary Murray divided what cash he had, and at the same time intimated that 35,000 louis d'ors had actually come.

"What became of this wealth has never been rightly made out, and it is idle now to form any conjecture, but it were by no means a very great stretch of liberality to suppose that a considerable share found its way into some of the leading men's purses or strong boxes."

The writer of the foregoing paragraph, the late Mr John Anderson, W.S., further says—

"About six or seven miles from Corpach at the western mouth of the Caledonian Canal, is an old burying ground; beside which is a very curious mound of earth in the exact form of a horse shoe. I came upon it suddenly one evening (1830) on my return from an excursion to the Parallel Roads of Glenroy, and in answer to enquiries was informed it was very ancient, and was constructed in that singular shape for the accommodation of attendants at funerals in the adjoining resting-place, they being seated in the curve, while the opening gave access to the servants to bring in the wine and spirits consumed on such occasions. It is still the custom to hold orgies on this spot. Some years after the '45 a peasant digging in the vicinity of this barrier, discovered an earthen pot, which he carried to Mr Butter, factor on Lochiel's forfeited estate. Mr Butter, as an old gentleman who had heard the tale in his youth gave me the tradition, sent the jar, which was found to contain a quantity of gold Spanish coin, to St. James'! But it was known in the country that Prince Charles brought seven of these over with him, which he consigned to the care of Lochiel, with directions he should hide them where he judged they would be most secure. A few nights before the battle of Culloden, Lochiel commanded the presence of a blind piper he had, at a very late hour. With this man's assistance he carried the seven jars about three miles, and then bade him dig a pit, and into it he deposited the treasure, which he himself carefully closed up. This person often afterwards told the story. He could, however, give no other clue to the spot, than that he had walked with his master three miles or so, as nearly as he could guess, from Achnacarrie House. But the Highlanders were not slow in imputing Mr Butter's success in life to this happy discovery in in place of what was a more likely cause—his own industry."

Mr Butter has not left a good name in the Highland localities over which he was factor under the Forfeited Estates Commissioners. Mr Anderson good naturedly speaks of his industry. Perhaps he was industrious. He generally farmed part of the land he ruled over, but in his relations with the estate of Lochiel he seems to have consoled himself with his brother keeping "a public" at Corpach at a rent, as stated in 1787, of £3 10s, no doubt the same place as that which was afterwards called "the Corpach cellars," a perfect sink, which the late Lochiel was long anxious to close and was ultimately successful in doing.

Hugh Cameron, of Annock, in December 1746, an officer in Lochiel's Regiment, a powerful mountaineer, 6 feet 7 inches in height without shoes, was taken in a hut about four miles from Fort-William, by a Lieutenant and party from the garrison. He was in bed when surprised about two o'clock in the morning. By the sudden irruption he was deprived of the use of his pistols, firelock, and broad sword, and was hauled quite naked out of bed, and carried in that state to Fort-William, with the utmost despatch, for fear of escape. Next day he was manacled, tied with ropes to two soldiers, and conveyed to Inverness.

Many instances of the strength and courage of the old Camerons could be given, now alas, to a great extent, either unknown or forgotten, as is perhaps Lord Byron's splendid tribute—

> And wild and high the "Cameron Gathering" rose !
> The war note of Lochiel, which Albyn's hills
> Have heard ; and heard too have her Saxon foes.
> How in the noon of night the pibroch thrills,
> Savage and shrill ! But with the breath that fills,
> The mountain pipe, so fills the mountaineers
> With fierce native daring which instils
> The stirring memory of a thousand years,
> And Evan Donald's fame rings in each clansman's ears.

THE CAMERONS OF DUNGALLON AND GLENDESSARY.

The families of Dungallon and Glendessary are descended from Donald, uncle and tutor of Sir Ewen Cameron of Lochiel; and the brothers, Allan of Glendessary, and Archibald of Dungallon, having respectively married Christian and Isabel, daughters of the famous Sir Ewen, became the leading men of the clan next the chief.

Dungallon was a wedset of part of the barony of Ardnamurchan, and of considerable extent, is thus described in a deed of 1757 :—

"All and whole the two merk half merk land of Rannoquhanastrome. The two merk half merk land of Camuscan. The three merk land of Reispole. The two merk half merk land of Balloch. The two merk half merk land of Pollock. The two merk half merk land of Ardnastaink. The two merk half merk land of Annahall, and the two merk half merk land of Strontian, with mills as well Built as to be Built on the said Lands and multures and sequels thereof, and with all and sundry Houses, Biggings, Yeards, Tofts, Crofts, Outsetts, Annexis, Connexis, Loch fishings, as well as of salmond as of other Fishes whatsoever, lying in Sunart, within the Barony of Ardnamurchan and Sheriffdom of Argyle; and likewise, all and whole the three penny half penny land of Straith or Rannachanmore. The one penny land of Duilet. The three penny lands of Renoxanstrome. The three penny lands of Camuscan and three islands belonging thereto, with the whole pertinents of the said lands ; and likewise all and whole the three penny lands of old extent of the lands of Letterlochsheill, with the Houses, Biggings, Barns, Byres, Grassings, Sheallings, Privileges of Woods for Bigging and upholding of Bigging, parts Pendicles, and universal pertinents thereof. Together likewise with the lands of Achnalia and Drimintorran lying within the Barony and Sheriffdom thereof."

Archibald Cameron of Dungallon, above mentioned, died at Glenahurich on the 19th of September, 1719, leaving by his wife, Isabel Cameron of Lochiel, at least two sons—John and Alexander, and three daughters—Jean, who married Dr Archibald Cameron of Lochiel, Mary, who married Alexander Cameron of Glen Nevis, and Christian, who married Hugh Fraser of Foyers. Mrs Isabel Cameron of Dungallon was born in 1687 and was living in 1762.

The following interesting letter from Mr Alexander Stewart, some time writer in Fort-William, whose family carried on business for seventy years, shows what a good, hospitable lady Isabel Cameron was. A shadow fell over her life from 1740, which is hinted at in the same communication :—

"Charlie,—I am surprised at your queries. The affair is now so old, and so much failed in head and hands that you cannot but expect a lame answer. As to your first query. I wrote a contract of marriage wherein the lady was provided to 400 merks but no infeftment, nor was Dungallon himself infeft, nor was his son, John, infeft or served heir, nor was he or any other confirmed exors, nor no division made of moveables. There was no debts as I mind owing to Dungallon but he was owing of debts—upwards of 12,000 merks, but to what particular persons I do not mind. The lady was born in 1687. Archibald Dungallon made no written testament. This answers your queries. The late Lochiel and the late Glendessary were in Lochbuy's house in Mull, in Skallisdale, paying a visit, and I was with them, when an express came of Dungallon's indisposition. The wind was very great and cross, we travelled the whole night and came by daylight to Glenahurich—he lived not a full hour after we came (19th September, 1719). He verbally named his lady before we came, and Donald Cameron, *alias* Macallan, his cousin, a worthy man, and Allan Cameron in Achnanellan and Evan Macallan Oig (*alias* Cameron) to be tutors and overseers to his six children. He left 360 heads or thereabout of horned cattle, and about 70 piece of horses. They employ'd me to keep their accompts and to assist in the management. We met two tymes every year at Glenahurich, to witt at Whitsunday and Martinmas, and continued so till the year 1731 or 32. The whole debts were pay'd and 4000 merks made cash more. There was some communing betwixt these managers (that I do not mind) and Sir Alexander Murray that required a legal title, for which purpose the lady was served curatrix for form's sake at Bunaw. The lady and family with a schoolmr. were allowed a vast allowance that I cannot well mind, but few articles, which were 400 stones and quarts of butter and cheese, and 70 or more bolls of meal. She was to a degree a charitable woman and keep'd a housefull of poor people and orphans. The two eldest sons were sent to Edin. to pass their time; Jean, Glendessary's daughter, being then there and very gracious to John Macfarlane employ'd him in their affairs, which put an end to my having any hand in it. So many alterations were made afterwards that I know nothing of, but that I believe their wadset rights is continued by what is called an Eik of Reversion.

"Some differrs fells betwixt John of Dungallon and me, that I did not go see him in his languishing sickness, which I indeed for his father's sake repented not to do; but his being in such able hands as John Macfarlane's that it would seem all was right enough.

"I wrote none of the daughters' contracts of marriages but the Doctor's with Jean, but does not mind the contents, but the tocher was 3000 merks. No doubt all the contracts ran with a discharge of all they could claim in common form. What effects these clauses may have in the several turns these affairs has had since syne is more than I can tell. I kept no correspondence with the late Dungallon, which with my kindest respects to Glenevas is all from.—Your father,

"12 June, 1762.   (Signed)   ALEX. STEWART."

"In the year 1740 Mrs Cameron was deprived of her intellectual faculties, by a melancholy disposition, without any interval of reason or judgment, and in this condition and situation she still continues" (1762).

Her two sons, John and Alexander, were most attentive to their mother. Alexander Cameron was Captain in the first Fraser Highlanders, embodied in 1757, and is thus referred to by General Fraser in a letter to Foyers, dated, Moy Hall, 25th September, 1766 :—

"It gave me great pleasure to see your son so genteel and promising a lad. I do assure you, I will make it my business to be of every service I can to him and all your family, who, besides my affection for them as yours, have a very strong claim to every service in my power as the nephews of my worthy friend and old intimate companion, Dungallon."

Dying without issue, John was succeeded by his brother, Alexander, who, having no lawful issue, left his whole estate, heritable and moveable, to Allan Cameron, brother german to John Cameron of Glendessary, whom failing, to John, and after him to James Cameron, eldest and second sons of the deceased Donald Cameron of Lochiel, by settlement dated, Glasgow, the 14th of November, 1757. Glendessary was Dungallon's heir male, and Dungallon dying before December, 1759, the family and affairs were broken up, and it was necessary for Lady Foyers and Lady Glenevis to see that their mother's affairs were put in proper order and her comfort seen to by being placed legally under their tutelage.

Later on, Dungallon's wadset was redeemed by the Murrays of Stanhope, superiors.

THE HISTORY OF MISS JEANIE CAMERON.

The Camerons of Glendessary are best known in modern times from Miss Jeanie Cameron of the '45 having been one of the family.

Three small portraits of Jeanie Cameron, Flora Macdonald, with Prince Charles in the centre, and the legend underneath, "How happy could I be with either," though severe, was not beyond legitimate satire. Mr Noble, bookseller, some years ago was able to secure for me a very handsome portrait of Jeanie in riding dress, with tartan coat, and drawn dagger for a switch, on which I place considerable value. An infamous production, bearing to be her history, and understood to be written by that venal cleric Henderson, is a disgrace even to that age.

By 1745 she was no longer in the springtide of youth. Bishop Forbes, on the authority of Eneas Macdonald and Duncan Cameron, says that at the raising of the standard at Glenfinnan a considerable number of both ladies and gentlemen

"Met to see the ceremony; among the rest was the famous Miss Jeanie Cameron, as she is commonly though very improperly called, for she is a widow nearer 50 than 40 years of age. She is a genteel, well looking, handsome woman, with a pair of pretty eyes, and hair as black as jet. She is of a very sprightly genius, and is very agreeable in conversation. She was so far from accompanying the Prince's Army, that she went off with the rest of the spectators so soon as the army marched; neither did she ever follow the Camp, nor was ever seen with the Prince but in public, when he had his Court at Edinburgh."

Mr Alexander Stewart speaks of her as "very gracious" soon after 1719 with the susceptible John Macfarlane, W.S. Macfarlane had married a lady of great attraction, whose affair with the Saxon John Cayley, Commissioner of Customs, formerly a Captain in the army, created a sensation in Edinburgh in 1716. There was at the time a strong ill-feeling between English and Scots, so that biassed reports appeared. From the Scottish version, it would appear that Cayley having refused to leave Mrs Macfarlane's presence, "She let fly a pistol at him and shot him through the arm, on which he attempted to draw his sword, but she prevented him by taking up another pistol and shooting him a little below the breast, of which wound he immediately dropped down dead." In another place it is said "that Cayley was accounted to be a very fine gentleman and had the respect of everybody, and the manner of his death was much regretted by all who knew him. As for Mrs Macfarlane, she has given an uncommon instance of virtue and honour, and as she was always admired before, for the fineness of her person, so she will now for the grave and resolute defence of her chastity."

The cruel statements circulated about Jeanie Cameron of Glendessary during her life continued after her death. Even the kind hearted Robert Chambers says in his *Traditions of Edinburgh*, 1825—

"Jeanie Cameron the mistress of Prince Charles Edward (so often alluded to in Tom Jones) was seen by an old acquaintance of ours, standing upon the streets of Edinburgh about the year eighty six (1786). She was dressed in men's clothes, and had a wooden leg. This celebrated and once attractive beauty, whose charms and Amazonian gallantry had captivated a Prince, afterwards died in a stair fit somewhere in the Canongate." In corroboration of this cruel fabrication it is said that a snuff seller in Edinburgh "gave a beggar who entered his shop a groat, and the snuff seller confided to a customer accidentally present in the shop, that the recipient of his charity was no man, though in man's clothes, but a woman and no other than Jeanie Cameron, Prince Charles' too ardent follower in the '45."

Her brother, Captain Allan, I find traces of as living in Edinburgh in 1770, and it is trading far too much on credulity to suppose that a gentleman in his position would permit his sister to be a street beggar. Jeanie's real history prior to her death is recorded in Ure's *History of Rutherglen*, 1793. The author of that work says:—

"In mentioning the places of note in the parish of East Kilbride, Mount Cameron should by no means be omitted. It is a small eminence about three quarters of a mile south-east from Kilbride, and on which is built a neat and commodious dwelling-house. This place, formerly called Blacklaw, takes its present name from Mrs Jean Cameron, a lady of a distinguished family, character, and beauty. Her zealous attachment to the House of Stuart, and the active part she took to support its interest, in the year 1745, made her well known through Britain. Her enemies, indeed, took unjust freedom with her good name; but what can the unfortunate expect from a fickle and misjudging world. The revengeful and malicious, especially if good fortune is on their side, seldom fail to put the worst construction on the purest and most disinterested motives. Mrs Cameron, after the public scenes of her life were over, took up her residence in the solitary and bleak retirement of Blacklaw. But this vicissitude, so unfriendly to aspiring minds, did not throw her into despair. Retaining to the last the striking remains of a graceful beauty, she spent a considerable part of her time in the management of domestic affairs. She showed, by her conversation on a great variety of subjects, that she had a discernment greatly superior to the common. But politics was her favourite topic, and her knowledge of that subject was not confined to those of her own country. The particular cast of her mind, especially during the latter part of her life, was rather melancholy. A vivacity, however, that was natural to her constitution, often enlivened her features and conversation. Her whole deportment was consistent with that good breeding, unaffected politeness, and friendly generosity which characterise the people of rank in the Highlands of Scotland. She was not remarkable for a more than ordinary attachment to any system of religious opinions or mode of worship, which is not always the case with the unfortunate. She attended divine service in the Parish Church, in which she joined with becoming devotion. Her brother and his family, of all her friends, paid her the greatest attention. She died in the year 1773, and was buried at Mount Cameron among a clump of trees adjoining to the house. Her grave is distinguished by nothing but a turf of grass, which is now almost equal with the ground."

MISCELLANEOUS.

Sir Ewen Cameron had a large family, chiefly daughters, and as they all married, his offspring became very numerous. Mr William Mackay says in his valuable History of Urquhart that Janet, who married as his second wife John, 6th Grant of Glenmoriston, at her death in 1759, aged 81, left upwards of 200 descendants, and she was but one.

The plaintive and popular air of "Lochaber no more" was composed in honour of Jean Cameron of Lochiel, as I observe from the notes of one of the Lady of Glenmoriston's descendants, Captain Grant of Inverwick.

Like other old favourites, some of the verses now in use are modern, but the following may be held as of the original:—

> "Lochaber, Lochaber,
> Lochaber, no more,
> I'll may be no return
> To Lochaber no more.
> Farewell to Lochaber,
> Farewell to my Jean:
> Where lightsome with thee
> I hae mony days been."

With the exception of Jean, all the daughters were very plain, and the composer, said to be Macgregor or

Drummond of Balhaldie, who afterwards changed his mind after being refused by Jean, and lamenting his sad state, thinking better of it, returned to Lochaber, and married an elder and plainer sister.

Miss Jean selected Lachlan Macpherson of Nuide, a singularly handsome man, who some years after, on the death of Duncan Macpherson in 1722, succeeded to Cluny, dying in the month of July, 1746.

While Sir Ewen Cameron fought almost to the death for Glenluie and Loch Arkaig he might have had, almost for the asking at the time, Sunart and Ardnamurchan, which would have given him a vast estate, peopled to a great extent by those who were in use to rally to his standard. Dungallon was already settled there, and numerous Camerons even now are there to be found. Many Macleans, north of the Sound of Mull, were out, according to the Lochgarry manuscript, under Donald Cameron of Lochiel in the '45. Sir Ewen would have saved himself much trouble had he taken the opportunity of securing a great estate held direct of the Crown.

It will hardly be credited by those who know the localities, that when the Canal was first finished, there was no bridge at Gairlochy. From time immemorial there was a ford over Lochy at Kyleross. Here Prince Charles crossed on his way south. His route was thus. On the 19th August, 1745, the standard was raised at Glenfinnan, where the Prince rested two days. Upon 22nd of August he was at Kinlochiel, from whence several despatches were sent. On the 23rd at Fassiefern, from whence he passed to Moy, and remaining there three days, crossed the ford of Lochy to Letterfinlay on the 26th of August. From thence he went by the east side of Loch Lochy to Achadrom on the 27th, and from thence to Glengarry House, where he slept that night.

Here Lochgarry, in his Memoirs, says that he had first the honour to kiss His Royal Highness's hand, and had the command of the guard that evening. On the 28th the army moved to Aberchalder, and to stop Cope, rendezvoused as early as 7 A.M. on the morning of the 29th. Meeting with no opposition, they pushed on over Corryarraick, and were at Garvamore by 12 o'clock, a wonderful march.

Cattle, conveyances, and people were in use to cross here in great numbers from the north and west on their way to Highbridge. The Canal blocked this traffic completely, and many droves, coming unexpectedly, were detained, while the farmers in the vicinity west of the Canal were sorned upon and their grass eaten up.

X. PARISH OF GLENELG.

THE MEN OF GLENELG FEROCIOUSLY ATTACK A FUNERAL PARTY.

WHILE there were hereditary differences between clan and clan, name and name, hereditary feuds also existed between district and district. Of the latter was the feud between Glenelg and Lochalsh, and it is as old at least as the period of the final disjunction of the county of Ross from Inverness.

I now give a more complete account than that given on another occasion of a serious outbreak which occurred in the month of December, 1814, in connection with the family of Barisdale.

Funerals were generally seized upon as a convenient opportunity "to have the matter out," but the occasion now chosen was rather unusual, for although Coll, 4th Barisdale, lived at Auchtertyre in Lochalsh and had invited his friends of that district to the funeral, he was by birth and property and in essential a Glenelg and Kilchoan man. The circumstances are detailed in the statement now to be quoted, which gave Barisdale the greatest annoyance. He was not in the fray, and knew nothing of it until all was over, being detained at the funeral entertainment with some of those invited, who he said in a letter of the time were "inclined to sit at the table a little longer" than such as those from Lochalsh, for instance, who had a long way before them ere they could reach home.

In a letter from Mr John Matheson of Attadale, dated the 11th of January, 1815, he, a Lochalsh man and wounded in the scuffle, says of the parishioners of Glenelg, "they from time immemorial were notorious amongst the rest of the neighbourhood for their savage deeds."

Mrs Flora Macdonell, at whose funeral the row occurred, was daughter of Norman Macleod of Drynoch, Skye, who settled in Glenelg. She married Archibald, third of Barisdale, and was a devoted wife and mother.

The witnesses for the intended prosecution for assault and battery were—1, George Jeffrey, Esq., New Kelso; 2, Archibald Macdonell, Esq., yr. of Barisdale; 3, The Rev. Dr Downie of Lochalsh; 4, Mr Roderick Maclennan, tacksman of Killilan; 5, Mr Kenneth Mackenzie, merchant, Kyleakin; 6, John Matheson, Esq., of Attadale; 7, Mr John Macrae, tacksman of Fernaig; 8, Mr Norman Finlayson at Auchtertyre; 9, Mr Peter Gillies at Auchtertyre; 10, Mr Donald Bethune, servant at Auchtertyre; 11, Mr John Macdonald at Innestown; 12, Mr Donald Macmaster, shepherd at Glenmeddle; 13, Mr Malcolm Nixon at Kirkton of Glenelg. Of these in the list the first eleven are in Ross-shire, the last two in Inverness-shire.

STATEMENT OF FACTS.—That Mrs Macdonell of Barisdale was interred at Glenelg, on Tuesday 6th December, 1814. That among several other gentlemen invited to attend the funeral were Mr George Jeffrey of New Kelso, Mr Matheson of Attadale, Doctor Downie of Lochalsh, Mr Archibald Macdonell of Glenmeddle, and Mr Kenneth Mackenzie, merchant, Lochalsh.

That the gentlemen above named met at Ardhill early on the morning of Tuesday, and proceeded in the same boat to Kirkton of Glenelg. That after landing, the boat was hauled on the shore to carry them back at night.

That after the interment the whole company adjourned to a house near the church, where they dined and sat till about five o'clock in the evening.

That after the company broke up the gentlemen named above, joined by Mr Roderick Maclennan of Killilan, proceeded towards the boat to return to Lochalsh. That John Macmaster, a servant of Mr Macdonell of Barisdale, met with them at Glenelg and was ordered by his master to go to Lochalsh in this boat. That it appears the said Macmaster before the company came out to return home had some words with Donald Maclennan, residing in Kirkton of Glenelg.

That as the whole party was proceeding towards the boat, the said Donald Maclennan followed Macmaster and seized hold of him by the breast. That Mr Archibald Macdonell of Glenmeddle, seeing Maclennan thus knocking his father's servant, asked his name, when he replied that his name was Donald Maclennan and that he resided at Kirkton. That on Mr Macdonell threatening to send him to the jail at Inverness if he ill-used Macmaster, Maclennan let go the hold he had of him, but followed the party towards the boat.

That the boat was now in the water with the stern on shore, made fast to a boat lying on the beach by a rope belonging to the latter boat. That while in this situation the whole party was embarking, Maclennan began to abuse all the people of Lochalsh in gross language, and to bid defiance to the whole crew. That on this provocation Macmaster jumped on shore after he had embarked, seized hold of Maclennan and dragged him into the sea, where he ducked him different times. That Mr Archibald Macdonell seeing this jumped likewise out of the boat and separated them. That Maclennan crying for help a number of men armed with bludgeons rushed down the beach, and before Mr Macdonell could again embark they surrounded the stern of the boat, and began to beat with their sticks in the most insolent manner every person within their reach.

That in consequence they wounded severely Mr Matheson of Attadale, giving him a deep cut in the forehead, from which a great quantity of blood immediately issued. That Mr Archibald Macdonell received a severe stroke on his head, from which the blood immediately flowed in abundance. That Mr Kenneth Mackenzie received a cut on his head to the effusion of his blood. That Doctor Downie received a severe blow with a stick on his head which the strength of his hat prevented from being cut. That Peter Gillies, one of the crew, received a dreadful wound across his skull after the loss of his hat, and has since been confined to bed, from every appearance, in imminent danger of his life. That Ninian Finlayson, another of the crew, has one of his hands torn by a stroke to the effusion of his blood, and had the other arm so bruised by repeated strokes of bludgeons that it is now much swelled and unfit for any service. That John Macdonald, another of the crew, was much bruised by repeated strokes, and his hat taken away or lost in the scuffle. That while this work of blood was going forward the end of the boat next the shore was surrounded by a crowd of people, some of whom were keeping hold of the boat, and some endeavouring to seize hold of the oars, while others were with their sticks endeavouring to knock down every person within their reach in the boat and who, being comparatively fewer in number and having no sticks, were quite unable to defend themselves. Having at last regained the possession of one of their oars which had been wrested from them, they endeavoured to push off the boat so as to get clear of this band of ruffians, but their thirst for blood not being yet satisfied, they still kept the boat close to the shore by seizing hold of the rope which had been made fast to her as already stated. That one of the crew seeing little chance of getting clear, cut the rope, on which several of those who had hold of the other end of the rope and who had been violently dragging the boat on shore fell on the beach. That the boat was immediately pushed off into water too deep for the people to follow, and when no longer able to assail the party with the sticks, there was a shower of stones from a crowd, in appearance from thirty to forty, thrown on to the boat, until she was pushed off out of their reach. One of those stones struck Mr Mackenzie of Killilan on the breast, by which he had received a severe contusion. As the boat was proceeding home the men were throwing out such of the stones as they found in the bottom of the boat, but on examining the boat next morning 18 of those bullets were found to be in her still, some of which weighed from three to four pounds, much blood too was found in the boat next morning. The night being dark and the people in the boat being little acquainted in Glenelg, it is very difficult to point out the individuals of which this crowd was composed.

The person of Maclennan, however, will be sworn to by two of the crew. One of the crew, Donald Bethune, who resided for some years at Glenelg, will make oath to two other men of his acquaintance being in the crowd, viz., Roderick Macrae, a young man residing with his mother at Kirkton of Glenelg, and Donald Buie Maclure, residing at Islandrioch.

Which statement consisting of this and preceding pages is attested to be truth, at Ardhill, the seventh day of December, one thousand eight hundred and fourteen years, by

                    (Signed)   JOHN MATHESON.
                           "   A. DOWNIE.
                           "   GEORGE JEFFREY.

A MACDONELL-MACLEOD MARRIAGE CONTRACT.

There was a great gathering at Arnisdale on the 2nd of May, 1723, at the signing of the contract of marriage between John Macdonell, second son of Æneas Macdonell of Scotus, and Janet Macleod, Arnisdale, a copy of which will now be given. The deed has no less than fourteen signatures, and does great credit to its framer, the Rev. Murdo Macleod, parish minister. Descended of this marriage is the well-known barrister and author, Macdonell of Greenfield, now in Montreal.

Prior to the sale of Glenelg, its large farmers, under the Macleods, were, and specially those of Skye extraction, perhaps the most conspicuous on the west mainland. Even in my own time Captain Reid of Eileanreach kept up a splendid hospitality, and old Cameron of Beolary was a noted, successful farmer, and I well recollect what a wrench it was for the old man when he was removed.

Long prior to Mr Cameron's time the tenant of Beolary was Mr John Murchison of the Lochalsh family of that name. I have several of his and his wife's letters. Writing on the 20th of August, 1782, Mr Murchison says—"1 had the mortification to be informed last week of the death of a second brother that I have lost by this unfortunate war. He died at Charleston on the 27th of January last, occasioned by the opening of his old wounds, which he got the day his other brother was killed at Stoney Ferry. He was a pretty loving young man. God knows their deaths is a great heart brake to me, as my affection for them was very great."

In the contract of marriage the opinions held of black cattle and sheep respectively are effectively seen, for the sheep are thrown in under the head of "small" cattle, "such as sheep and goats."

The country of Knoydart is rich and beautiful and reared, in abundance and comfort, honest men and bonnie lasses. Why it should not do so now seems inexplicable, for though the people have greatly diminished, the land is there as of old. To my misfortune I have only once been up Loch Nevis, but the kindness and stirring reception of my one night at Inverie can never be forgotten. Here is the marriage contract referred to—

"At Arnisdale, the 2nd day of May, one thousand seven hundred and twentie three years. It is minuted appointed matrimonially, agreed and ended betwixt John Macdonell, second lawfull son to Æneas Macdonell of Scottos, on the one part, and Janet Macleod, lawfull daughter to Donald Macleod in Arnisdale, with his consent and assent, and he taking burden on him for her on the other part in manner following. That is, the saids John Macdonell and Janet Macleod, with consent foresaid, hereby promises to take each other in marriage and to solemnize the said lawfull bond of marriage instantly. And the said Donald Macleod in Arnisdale, hereby binds and obliges him, his heirs, ex'ors, and successors whatsomever to content and pay to the said John Macdonell, his heirs, ex'ors, and assignees in name of tocher good, the number of threescore of cows and four piece of sufficient horse, as they are usually payed in tocher, that is to say twentie milk cows, twentie yeall cows, ten cows two years old, and ten stirks, to be payed in manner following, viz., the number of twentie-five to be payed at Whitsunday ensueing, and as many at Whitsunday, one thousand seven hundred and twentie four, and the other ten at Whitsunday one thousand seven hundred and twentie five. For the whilk causes on the other part the said Æneas Macdonell as burden taker, binds and obliges him, his heir, ex'ors, and successors to provide the said John Macdonell, his son to the sum of two thousand merks Scots money, for which he is to pay interest to his behoof from the term of Whitsunday next to come, and until it be laid out upon interest in sufficient hands upon land or otherwise.

"The said John Macdonell as pri'nl, and with, and for him, the said Æneas Macdonell as cautioner, suretie and full debitor, binds and oblidges them, their heirs, ex'ors, and successors whatsomever con'llie and severally to secure in the hands of Donald Macleod of Tallascar or any other sufficient hands the said sum of two thousand merks money foresaid in liferent to the said Janet Macleod during all the days of her lifetime and in fee to the eldest son to be procreate of the said marriage or that shall be then in life, whilk failling to the other child or children of the said marriage. And it is hereby provyded that the said Janet shall have a tearce of all the moveables that shall appertain to the said John Macdonell at the time of his decease, she then surviving, with the whole small cattell, such as sheep and goates, by and attour the just and equal half of the conquest. And the said Janet Macleod hereby discharges the said Donald Macleod her father of her portion natural and all other things she could ask or crave thro' his decease excepting good will allenarly.

In like manner the said John Macdonell hereby discharges his father of bairns part of gear excepting good will allenarly and all the said parties binds and oblidges them to perform the premisses *hinc inde* in manner above written and the party faillzying shall pay to the party observer or willing to observe the same the sum of two hundred merks Scots. And all consent to the Regran of their pritts in the Books of Council and Session or any other judicatory competent that an decreet be interponed thereto so that letters of horning on ten days and other executorialls needful may pass hereupon in form as effeirs and to that effect constitutes
their pro'rs. In witness qrof (written by Mr Murdoch Macleod, minister of Glenelg, upon stamped paper) all have subt their pritts day, place, and year of God a wrin before those witnesses, Archibald McDonnell of Barisdel, Coll McDonnell his son, Norman McLeod

of Drynoch, Mr Alexr. McLeod his son, Lachlin McKinnon of Mishness, Donald McDonnell in Glendulachan, and the sd. Mr Murdoch McLeod writer hereof.

(Signed) "JOHN MACDONELL.
,, "JANNET MCLEOD.
,, "DONALD MCLEOD.
,, "ÆNEAS MCDONELL CA'R.
,, "LACHLAN MCKINNON, wittnes.
,, "ARCHIBALD MCDONELL, wittness.
,, "DO. MCDONELL, wittnes.
,, "COLL MCDONELL, wittness.
,, "ANG. MCLEOD, wittness.
,, "NOR. MCLEOD, wittness.
,, "ALLAN MCDONELL, witnes.
,, "ALEXR. MACLEOD, wittness.
,, "ALEXR. MCDONELL, witnes.
,, "MURD. MACLEOD, wittness."

LEASES, ROADS, RAILWAYS, AND RECRUITING.

Upwards of a century ago, it was the practice to encourage tenants in Glenelg, by granting them long leases, whereby having a considerable fixity of tenure, they found that it was worth while improving. When sales afterwards became abundant, very frequently the price given, calculated at so many years' purchase, was astonishing. In my own day, I have seen forty years' purchase given, but these times are past. Mr William Tod, factor for the Duke of Gordon, asking a high price last century for lands in Lochaber instances that between the years 1770 and 1790 two estates in Badenoch, Phoness and Raits, had been sold in public market at fifty-five and seventy years' purchase of the gross rental.

The illustration of long leases in Glenelg I have in view are two, one by Macleod to John Murchison, his factor in Glenelg, of the two penny lands of Beolary as then possessed by the said John Murchison, and Ludovick Murchison, his father; the two penny lands of Arrieharachan, as then possessed by John Macleod and his sub-tenants; and the four penny lands of Achaconon, as possessed by Donald Macleod and other tenants. The tenant had power to assign one half of the subjects to his second brother

Roderick, and the other half to his brothers—Duncan, Magnus, and Donald. The endurance was for fifty-seven years, from Whitsunday, 1774 and the rent £472 Scots. Notwithstanding the favourable terms, and that Macleod dispossessed several of his clan, the lease, dated the 8th of December, 1767, did not terminate successfully. John Murchison died in 1811, survived by one brother only, the Duncan before referred to. Two others, as previously mentioned, soldiers, died in America. The other lease referred to was by General Simon Fraser of Lovat, in favour of Ewen Gillies, of the lands of Camusnabrain of North Morar for two nineteen years from and after Whitsunday, 1780, at a rent of £9 2s 8d sterling, but excluding any right to the salmon fishings on the water of Morar.

The lands of Glenelg were considered by Government and others so central and important a position on the west mainland that barracks were erected at Bernera as suitable to command the neighbourhood. They were never of much use, and have long since gone to ruin, and the site restored; reserving to the Government the right to re-acquire the premises with a considerable piece of land at any time, should this be resolved upon. The sheep farmers from Skye and outer islands found Glenelg convenient as a connection with the south, and the late Mr Telford projected a road in 1810 from Rannoch to Glenelg and gave details of the cost. It is an interesting document, particularly in view of the recent openings of the west mainland. Glenelg is very convenient of access by sea, but the reverse by land. Telford's proposed road traverses much of the West Highland Railway route until it reaches Roy Bridge. It then directed its course by the Spean to the Lochy, thence by ziz-zag courses through the northern part of Lochiel's estate, crossing Glengarry into Glenmoriston, and by Glenshiel to the sea. This was essential if Glenelg was the terminus aimed at, because if it ascended the waters of Arkaig, one would be on the way to Loch Morar. If it ascended Glengarry, Loch Hourn would be reached, and as there is no mountain or valley access to Glenelg, the road has to go first to Loch Duich, and from thence there is a steep ascent and an equally steep descent to Glenelg.

Loch Carron at the north, and Loch Linnhe at the south, from their position can be reached easily by land, but the intermediate lakes, and particularly the Bay of Glenelg, are practically inaccessible except by sea. These lakes, however, are admirably adapted for fishery purposes, which have not been fully developed, although this may be confidently expected when railway facilities are provided from Kyleakin and Mallaig. I expect the latter will become by and bye an important centre, and that when the railway is opened, that part of it facing the Atlantic will be largely taken up for building purposes by the merchants of Glasgow and other cities, who will no longer be satisfied with country quarters on the Firth of Clyde.

Macleod of Macleod and his wife stayed at Inverness in the winter of 1789, in the house of a Captain Baillie. Giving it up by them seems to have annoyed the Captain, who according to Macleod "had, he feared," again taken another pet. "I don't know how to manage in such cases. I never take pets myself." He must have been a most exemplary person!

In another letter to a gentleman at Inverness, who had taken some trouble about his affairs, Macleod writes from Golden Square, London, on the 24th of May, 1790—"Parliament will probably be dissolved about the month of June. There seems to be no avoiding a war, in which case I shall immediately get a regiment, and will probably commence recruiting as soon as I get down."

He seems to have been very attentive to his own people in the matter of patronage. A gentleman in Inverness writing to Mr William Macdonald of Saint Martins, Macleod's Edinburgh agent, making application for a situation in the Excise for a friend, gets this reply, dated Edinburgh, 6th December, 1790. "It is by no means so easy a matter to obtain a Commission in the Excise as formerly, for this reason that the salary is nearly double, and everything in Excise and Customs go by Parliamentary interest. Macleod has many claims upon him, and many to provide for of his own clan and friends which I know too well to ask anything from him in the meantime."

Recruiting became very severe, and those engaged were hard put to. Norman Macleod, Eileanreach, General Macleod's factor in Glenelg, complains that the taxes for naval services and others were excessive and that some sympathy should be shown to those like himself, who had paid a bounty, and expenses of a volunteer to Inverness, but the recruit had declined enlistment at the last moment, and either could not or would not repay anything. The Dunvegan factor, Mr Charles Robertson, writing on the 2nd of November, 1795, says—"Considering the exertions we used in the affair of the Navy Volunteers, and that we are still endeavouring to send more recruits," trusts that delay in paying the navy rates will be given.

From one class only were recruits pretty easily obtained, viz., apprentices in towns. I see Macleod got into much trouble with a carpet weaver in Elgin, who took legal proceedings against him for the enrolment of his apprentice in the 2nd Battalion of the 42nd Regiment.

It is a pity that his promises to provide for recruits or their families with a house and a bit of land, were departed from or largely restricted, as so fully brought out by the editor of the *Scottish Highlander* in that paper a few years ago.

The condition of the people did not improve under Macleod's successors.

THE FRASERS OF LOVAT AND MACLEODS OF HARRIS.

The name of Glenelg is found at an early date, it being noted in 1282 that it was part of the Kingdom of Man. It afterwards pertained to the old Earls of Ross. It consisted of two parishes, Kilchoan, mentioned in 1372, comprehending Knoydart and north Morar, and Glenelg proper.

Falling into the King's hands, Glenelg was divided into three parts, and was included in the charter to Randolph, becoming a part of the Earldom of Moray. Two-thirds became the property of the Macleods of Harris, extending to eight davochs and five pennylands, and the other third, of the Frasers of Lovat. There is some obscurity as to the origin of the Lovat title, which rather points, however, to its being an acquisition from the Morays. Hugh Fraser is served heir to the third of Glenelg on the 2nd of May, 1430, following in the narration of lands, the barony of Abertarff, comprehending Stratherrick, which undoubtedly came through the Dunbars. Naturally, the Macleods and Frasers did not agree, and the latter made various attempts to adjudicate and get charters to the whole.

In 1540 a good opportunity occurred of reuniting Glenelg. The well-known Allister "Crotach" Macleod, had a son William, of marriageable age, while Hugh, Lord Lovat, had a daughter Agnes in the same position. Accordingly a match was made up, whereby in effect the whole three parts of Glenelg was settled upon the heirs male of the marriage, the lady also getting a liferent of the thirty pennyland of Minginish. A copy of the contract of marriage will now be given, dated Lovat, the 13th of April, 1540, from which it will be seen that Allister Crotach could not write. The well-meant intentions of the parties were, however, frustrated by the death of William Macleod, within a few years of the marriage, leaving an only daughter, Mary, the famous heiress of Dunvegan, as to whose great succession and for the custody of whose person there had been several years of fighting and controversy. Follows the contract of marriage referred to:—

"At the Lovat the 13th day of April 1540 yeirs. It is appointed staited and finally agreed betwixt ane noble Lord Hugh Lord Fraser of Lovat, as taking burden upon him of Agnes Fraser his daughter on the one pairt, and Alister McLeod of Dunveagan as taking burden upon him of William McLeod his eldest son and appearand air on the other hand in manner form and effect as after follows. That is to say the said William McLeod appearand of Dunveagan, sall God willing marry and take to his wife the said Agnes Fraser and shall celebrate the haily band of matrimony with her in face of the haily kirk, betwixt the day of the date hereof and the last day of July next to come, but any further Delay fraud or Guile, and the said Alexander McLeod of Dunveagan binds and oblishes him and his airis duly and sufficiently to infeft vest and sieze the said Agnes Fraser, now in her virginity, in all and haill

his triatty penny Lands of Mid Gaines lyand within the Isle of
Sky and Sheriffdome of Inverness to be brooked by the said Agnes all
the Days of her lifetime in conjunct Fee, for the which marriage swa
to be performed the said Hugh Lord Fraser of Lovat binds and
oblishes him and his Airis and Assigneys to renounce all Just Tıttle of
right property and possession that he has had or may have to the
haill land and barony of Glenelg with the haill parts pendices
and pertinents thereof lyand within the Sheriffdom of Inverness,
in our sovereign Lord's hands, in favour of the said William McLeod,
and Agnes Fraser his futur Spouse to be brooked possest set used and
disponed be the said William McLeod appearand of Dunvegan and
Agnes Fraser his futur Spouse, and the longest liver of them two
and the Airis meal lawfully to be begotten betwixt him and the
said Agnes Fraser svrally of our sovereign Lord even as the same
is now halden be the said Hugh Lord Fraser of Lovat and that
betwixt the Day and date hereof and the first Day of July next
providing always as God forbid if it shall happen that the said William
McLeod nocht to have Airis meal betwixt him and the said Agnes;
in that case the hail rights to the said lands and barony of Glenelg
to return to the said Hugh Lord Fraser of Lovat his eiris again as well
as gif this present Contract had never been made or granted. And
baith the said parties bind and oblishes them to stand and abid herat
under the pain of four thousand mark usual money of the Realm.
And in Case this Contract be not sufficient they are baith content and
consents that the same sall be amplified be men of Law in the
most ample form that can be devised, Keeping still the substantial
heads above written. In witness whereof of baith the said partys
have subscribed their presents as follows Day year and place forsaid
before their witnesses William Fraser of Guisachan, John Schisolm of
Commar, Allan Mackintosh, Ranald Mackallan Vickrory of Muidort,
Hugh Fraser of Foyers.

> (Signed) "WILLIAM MCLEOD of Dunveagan with
> my hand.
> "AGNES FRASER with my hand.
> "HUGH FRASER of Lovat with my hand.
> "ALISTER MCLEOD of Dunveagan with
> my hand lead by a Notar under-
> written because I could noucht writ
> myself.
> "Ita est Jacobus Hay Notarius Publicus Mandate
> dicti Scribere nescien teste manu propria."

General Macleod in his difficulties in 1794 attempted to sell
Glenelg, but failed. In the advertisement of sale the estate is
said to consist of 37,000 Scots acres, and the stool of oak

wood so considerable that if properly enclosed and preserved it might bring in £10,000 every twenty years. The feu-duty is 1s 9½d sterling, and the rent at Whitsunday 1795, £1325 sterling. It was sold at Martinmas, 1810, by John Norman Macleod to Patrick Crawford Bruce, merchant and banker in London, son of the late Sir Michael Bruce of Stenhouse, Baronet, for £98,500, an enormous price, and resold a few years later to the Right Hon. Charles Grant.

The superiority having been redeemed from the Duke of Argyll in 1802 the lands came to hold of the Crown, and the valuation of the Cess Roll being £2208 Scots, afforded qualification for 5 votes. In 1826 Mr Grant's position as member of Parliament was getting risky and he gave off four qualifications to friends and connections, viz., to Matthew Norman Macdonald Hume, W.S., his agent; Dr William Frederick Chambers, London, his near connection; Charles Mark Phillips, of Gavendon Park, Leicestershire, another near connection; and William Thomas Grant, described as "residing in London," his brother. Grant's henchmen, Rothiemurchus and Glenmoriston, were in such a hurry enrolling these four, that there were two of Bruce's equally "nominal and fictitious" barons left actually standing on the roll for the very subjects on which these four claimants were admitted. Grant's then opponent, Lord Macdonald, was equally busy, for he created no less then seventeen barons on the Macdonald estates.

NORTH MORAR.

The picturesque estate lying between Loch Nevis and Loch Morar was described of old as "a very little country." It formed the southern seaboard part of the estate of Glengarry, where it met South Morar, originally part of Clanranald. The Lovats, who had been so long in Glenelg, seem, notwithstanding having parted with their third, to have kept an eye for 150 years on the neighbourhood, and in 1768, when Glengarry was brought to a judicial sale, General Simon Fraser of Lovat purchased North Morar, which still remains in the family; and to increase his strength among freeholders, about the same time acquired the superiority of South Morar. The estate was suitable to General Fraser in another way, viz., as good recruiting ground and a place to settle pensioners.

How influence and favouritism ruled after General Fraser's death may be seen from the subjoined letter of Angus Gillis, dated East Stoul, 29th of March, 1786. Angus could not write, but the person he employed wrote an excellent hand and used very correct language—

"Sir,—At the time of recruiting Captain Frazer's company of the North Fencibles, I sent a recruit at my own expense on condition that I should be entitled to the same terms promised the recruits, that is a certain portion of land on disbanding the regiment. At the time of the lett when the lands appropriated for the soldiers were given to their nearest relations to be managed for them till their discharge, Belladrum allocated my own share to me; which in the letter of tack then given to the whole country was named for the man I had recruited. I set one half to Donald MacLelan, the other to Finlay Gillis, uncle to the man I enlisted, giving under my hand a security to the ground officer for the rent. Notwithstanding all this when the tacks came to be extended the same land was, through the partiality of Gortuleg and Belladrum, included in Angus MacLelan's tack of Glasnacardoch, and all my representations to the contrary unattended to.

"Donald MacLelan has, however, still kept possession of his own part of the land in my name, but has been warned out this spring; the warning I send enclosed and desire you will draw out a petition to be laid before the Sheriff to make known all the above, and move him to protect me in my right.

"Please to observe that if Donald McLelan is allowed to remain in peaceable possession this year, we will both give up all future claims and leave the place clear to John McLelan next year; but if he will not agree to this, we will pursue the matter as far as law will allow us, and keep possession till forced out.

"Whatever expense attends bringing thro' to a conclusion will be thankfully payed by, sir your most obedient humble servant,

(Signed) "ANGUS (his X mark) GILLIS.
Tacksman of East Stoul, North Morar.

"Stoul, 29th March, 1786."

When Archibald Fraser of Lovat came into power he did not treat the North Morar people kindly, and he was in litigation with some of them at his death, insisted upon by his successor in the entail. Mr John Macdonald of Borrodale, who always befriended the Morar people, on hearing of Lovat's death, says that Archibald after "settling the affairs of the nation," alluding to his notorious meddling, has now "to render very strict account indeed of his own acts."

The estate of North Morar still remains undivided, indeed has been added to by the acquisition of the islets in Loch Morar, sometime belonging to the estate of South Morar. The latter has, on the contrary, been much broken up; first, the Camerons of Fassiefern made the earliest purchase of land by acquiring Meople, signalising their acquisition by removing 54 people between Loch Beoraik and Oban; Letter Morar, Almie, Rhetland, etc., was added to the Glenalladale estate; and the remainder of South Morar belongs to Arisaig and Mr Eneas R. Macdonell of Camusdarroch. North Morar, a twelve merks land, had no church within its bounds.

The district of Morar is rich in Jacobite reminiscences, and Mallaig, in which Prince Charles more than once found himself, together with all the country to Fort-William, after long seclusion and neglect, eventuating in depopulation and stagnation, is evidently destined again to raise itself and become the home of a prosperous and contented people.

XI. PARISH OF ARDNAMURCHAN.

ARISAIG AND SOUTH MORAR.—MODERN EVICTIONS AND LAST CENTURY RENTALS.

ARDNAMURCHAN forms one of the parishes of Inverness-shire, yet not an inch of the portion in that county formed a part of the original parish. The high-handed, uncalled for, and eccentric dismemberment of Inverness-shire by Lord Lorne in 1632, swept away to Argyleshire the whole ancient parish of Ardnamurchan, which comprehended most of a great peninsula, terminating at the point of Ardnamurchan, the western extremity of the mainland of Scotland, and commencing at a line connecting Loch Shiel and Loch Sunart, where these lochs approach nearest to each other. Ardnamurchan in Inverness-shire, as now divided, extends from Loch Shiel to Loch Morar, and was included in the Lordship of Gartmoran. Those of the original inhabitants who interest themselves in its past history love to call it and Knoydart, the "Rough Bounds" of old "Garbh-crioch," and it was possessed in especial by Clanranald, with its cadets of Morar, Glenalladale, and Kinlochmoydart, a handsome and warlike race.

Events in early life or circumstances at that period, insignificant perhaps in themselves, lay the basis for future action and conduct, and I may be pardoned for recording that to the circumstance of my visiting the Clanranald country during a memorable year much of my sympathy towards the poorer occupants of the Highlands and Islands in after life is due.

In the autumn of 1849 I, then a clerk in a law office, was sent on an errand of trust to South Morar. From the estate of Arisaig, and in particular from the Rhue, a great number of people had been evicted, who were either too late to be deported that year, or unwilling to emigrate. Mrs Macdonell, widow of Colonel Donald Macdonell of Scotos and mother of Eneas R. Macdonell of Morar, was then tenant of the farm of Traigh, South Morar, and in the extreme distress of the evicted people, allowed them to take shelter on her farm, prompted not only by her goodness of heart—for even amongst the universally hospitable denizens of the west Mainland, the Rhue family were conspicuous—but the fact that most of the people she knew thoroughly, her late father being at one time tenant of Rhue, and I rather think she was born there. I saw two things—the places from where the people had been removed, also where for a time they were sheltered, and being a makeshift in name of a temporary home, necessarily crowded, and with flimsy protection. Yet the people were so far contented, if not cheerful, blessing their benefactress, who scrimped herself and household for their relief. This I saw and do not forget, though nearly fifty years have since passed.

Another circumstance and I shall have done with personal reminiscences. On the journey in question, at the inn of Kinchreggan, the late Angus Macdonald of Glenalladale, who and his predecessors so long lived in handsome style in the fine old house and place of Borrodale, met us and insisted on our dining at his house, as we would in any case be passing his door. I need not say that we were treated with true Highland hospitality, and were not allowed to leave until late, after hearing some exquisite music—vocal and instrumental—from the ladies, and having several "turns" on the floor of the particularly handsome drawing-room. The laird was specially genial, and could hardly be persuaded to abstain from remounting his pony and giving us a bit of Highland convoy in our progress to Traigh. Alas, alas, how Borrodale has fallen! The Glenalladales had to leave, and the Valuation Roll tells the world that the House of Borrodale is sub-divided, and presently tenanted by four retainers, paying rents of £12, £8, £4, and £3 respectively.

The oldest paper among my Clanranald collections is the service of John Macdonald vic Allan vic Iain to his father Sir Donald vic Allan vic Iain of Clanranald. The Inquest was held at Inverness on the 18th September, 1627, before Alexander Paterson, Sheriff-Depute; and John Dougall, merchant in Edinburgh; James Fraser of Keithhill; James Fraser, burgess of Inverness; Andrew Fraser, merchant, burgess there; James Abraham, David Cuthbert, Thomas Robertson, James Cumming, and Alexander Abraham, all burgesses of Inverness; Robert Innes, Alexander Hood, and Patrick Hay, burgesses of Chanonry, and David Logan, burgess of Inverness, members of Inquest. The only lands on the mainland referred to, are 3 merks of Moydart, 7 merks of Arisaig, and the superiority of the 14 merks land of South Morar, all the other lands being in the Isles. The Retour shows that Sir Donald Macdonald was grandson of the famous John Macallister of Moydart (Iain Muidartach) and that Sir Donald died in the month of December, 1619. The lands in Moydart consisted of 27 merks land, and those of Arisaig seem to have been divided into portions, one of 7 merks and the other of 24 merks of old extent. All the estates appear to have been held of the Earl of Argyll, but Ranald Macdonald was enrolled a freeholder in 1767; his son John, in 1789; and Ranald George Macdonald, son of John and late Clanranald, in 1809.

About 1805 the superiorities were purchased, and Clanranald shortly after began to give off freeholds, and to split his cess valuations. No regular rental seems to have been in possession of the family until the year 1798, when Ranald George Macdonald and his tutors followed out what was then common—the plan of establishing a "Judicial Rental;" that is, witnesses and officials deponed on oath what the rents in use to be paid were. Let us take the Arisaig rent, therefore, in its order—

1. Ardnafuaran	...	...	...	...	... £100	16 0
Miln thereof	...	...	...	...	7 7	0

Change House	17	0	0

This was a four penny land. Tenants—Mr John Macdonald, missionary, and others. For the preceding three years the tenants had an abatement of £8, as part of the lands were enclosed and planted. Rory Macdonald, being a woodkeeper to Clanranald, had a farthing's worth free of rent. Donald Chisholm, tenant of the mill and of the Change House.

2. Kinloid—Donald Chisholm ... 25 4 0
3. Duchamus and Torrabaith—Lieut. Archd. Macdonald ... 20 0 0

   Leased by Ranald Macdonald, of Clanranald to John, father of Archibald. Lease 40 years from 1777. Made about a half-ton of kelp yearly, for which bound to pay a Lordship of ten shillings per ton.

4. Ardgasich—Said Archd. Macdonald, a sub-tenant of Mrs Jean Macdonald ... 63 0 0

   Made about 15 tons of Kelp.

5. Borrodale—John Macdonald ... 34 2 6

   Possessed under lease to his father of forty years from 1777. Makes but a few cwt. of kelp. "Allowed considerable deductions for ground enclosed and planted."

6. Guidale—Donald Macdonald's heirs ... 14 0 0

   Lease, 35 years from Whitsunday, 1786.

7. Sandaig—Ranald Maceachan, sub-tenant of Duncan Campbell, Coull ... 12 0 0
8. Maine and Arnapool—Alexander Cameron 45 0 0
9. Arynskill—John Boyd ... 30 0 0
10. Lower Arnapool—Angus Maceachan and others ... 18 15 0
11. Upper Polniss—Peter Maceachan and others 24 0 0

    Make half a ton of kelp.

12. Lower Polniss—Alex. Macdonald and others 18 0 0

    Make half a ton of kelp.

13. Laggan—Angus Maceachan and others ... 42 0 0

    Make 4 tons of kelp.

14. Mulichbuy—John Maceachan and others ... 9 0 0
15. Camussarie—Mary Macdonald and others ... 6 0 0
16. Feorlindow—Ewen Macdonald and others... 10 10 0
17. Penmeanach—Ranald Macdonald and others 21 0 0
18. Kinchreggan, Arian, and Essan—Angus

		£	s	d
	Macdonald, sub-tenant of Colin Macdonald of Boisdale	55	0	0
19.	Alissary—Said Angus Macdonald and Alexander Maclean ... ... Make 4 tons of kelp.	70	0	0
20.	Change House of Kinlochaylort—John Maceachan	8	0	4
21.	Druimindarroch—Said John Maceachan ...	13	6	8
	Converted services, etc.	3	5	0
	These were 2 stones butter, 2 stones cheese, 2 wedders with their fleeces 4 year old, 2 men and horses 6 days in harvest.			
22.	Slochk—Said John Maceachan	12	0	0
23.	Keppoch—Duncan Campbell, Coull ...	83	6	0
	Keppoch House—Do.	45	16	10
24.	Ranachan—Do.	11	5	0
25.	Moy—Do.	7	10	0
26.	Torrary—Do.	11	5	0
	Campbell makes 20 tons of kelp, has lease of 35 years from 1786, and is allowed £21 yearly for grounds planted, preservation of woods, and for nursery ground on Keppoch.			

This set of Arisaig is highly creditable. The tenants were all relatives of the chief, or clansmen, with one or two exceptions. The leases were long, and, judging by the rental in after years, at the time moderate. The estate at the same time was being improved and planted.

The seven merks of Arisaig, which went by themselves, apart from the "24 merks of Arisaig," comprehended Keppoch and the old mansion-house of Clanranald in Arisaig, Manie or Mainzie, Upper Arnapool, Lower Arnapool, and Torrabeith, and were joined in the cess roll with Clanranald's lands of Eigg.

MOYDART.—RENTAL OF 1798.

The rental of Moydart in 1798 was as follows:—

		£	s	d
1.	Dalilea, Langal, Annat, Wester and Easter Drumloy, Islandfinnon, Ferry, and change house thereof—Alexander Macdonald. Rent, £53 15s 2½d for the first 8 years of the lease, and for the remainder	64	5	0

Lease, 31 years from 1790. Makes 1 ton of kelp. Contents of all the farms, four pennies or 16 farthings of land.

2. Briag— Duncan Macisaac and three others   18   0   0
Makes free of Lordship, 3 tons of kelp every three years.

3. Scardosie—Donald Macisaac and four others   30   0   0
A 2½d farthing land. No kelp made. Farm is sandy, being so encroached upon by the sea that it is now barely 30 acres exclusive of rocks. Tenants unable to pay the present rent.

4. Mingarry—Rory Macvarrish and four others   30   0   0
No kelp made. Rent too high, and expect a reduction.

5. Glenuig—Angus Macdonald and twelve others   45   0   0
A 6 farthing land. 3 tons kelp made each six years.

6. Smirrasdary—Donald Macdonald and seven others   33   0   0
No kelp made. Rent too high.

7. Portavat—William Corbet and two others ...   26   0   0
A two farthings land, and make two tons of kelp.

8. Egnag—Donald and John Macdonald ...   43   0   0
Donald has 4-5ths and John 1-5th of the land, and make 26 cwt. of kelp. In place of the sea-ware used for kelp, they purchase manure from their neighbours.

9. Blain—John Maceachan and two others ...   21   0   0
A 1½ farthing land. No kelp made.

10. Island Shona—Andrew Macdonald ...   60   0   0
Being considered dear, Clanranald appointed him woodkeeper of Moydart, at a salary of £10, to help to pay the rent.

11. Salmon fishings of Shiel—said Andrew Macdonald   3   0   0
Whatever kelp he makes on Island Shona is free of Lordship.

12. Samalaman   10   14   10
A two farthing land, let on thirty-five years' lease from Whitsunday, 1786, to Bishop Macdonald and his successors in office. Occupant in 1798, Bishop Chisholm. No kelp made.

13. Irine—John Maceachan A six farthing land. Set on lease to John's father for forty years from 1781. Makes about a ton of kelp.		30 8 6
14. Change House of Castle Tyrim—said John Maceachan		2 0 0
15 Lochans and Letnacloich—Donald Macdonald A merk land. Makes a ton of kelp.		20 0 0
16. Inchrory—above Donald Macdonald A two farthing land. Lease 30 years from 1786.		25 0 0

FEU LANDS.

17. Kinlochmoydart—Mrs Margarita Robertson Macdonald. Her total rental £512 and pays cess to Clanranald of £3 3s.
18. Glenaladale—Alexander Macdonald. The rental £130, and Dalilea says the feu duty is £24 9s 5½d.

The Church of Arisaig was at Kilmarie and is now an interesting ruin. The Church-yard might be better attended to as a whole, though some parts are very neat. Here the Morar family are buried. The Clanranalds of old were interred at Eileanfinnon, afterwards in Howmore, South Uist. There is notice of Elias, Parson of Arisaig as early as 1250, and mention made of various chaplains up to the Reformation.

EILEAN TIORAM CASTLE AND LANDS.

I visited the grand ruin of Eilean Tyrim Castle in 1885, having the good fortune of such a cicerone as the late venerated and loved Father Charles Macdonald of Mingarry. His published account of the country, in which he so long lived, is most fascinating in its vivid description of places and people within the Rough Bounds. Peace to my deceased friend's ashes and respect to his memory! The Castle, said to have been built by Amie nin Ruarie, who was buried at Eileanfinnon, witnessed many a scene. The name of Eilean Tyrim for a time gave the Clanranalds their designation, and under the name of "Tenandry of Castle Tyrim" all the Clanranald lands were erected into a Barony, rendering one sasine at the Castle sufficient for the whole estate, including the outlying islands of Eigg and Canna. The Castle and a small portion of land still belongs to the family, and a good deal of the old estate could be and ought to be reclaimed by them. The walls of the Castle have been repaired and strengthened. On a voyage in 1892 from Drumindarroch in Arisaig, to Eilean Tyrim, we almost flew over the water, the wind being highly favourable. Next day, however, Morar's men had to row every yard, first to Eigg and thence to Ardvasser in Skye, the wind dead ahead and sails useless, occupying fourteen hours. Before the men, whose patience and good spirits I will never forget, could have reached their homes at Arisaig, after landing me at Ardvasser, they must have been seventeen hours at work. And yet the West Coast men are characterised as indolent and spiritless.

Ronald Macdonald of the '45 died in the autumn of 1776, and was succeeded by his son John, who did not live long, dying in 1794, leaving his son Reginald George in pupillarity. This Reginald George Macdonald had a long minority, and succeeded to a vast unembarrassed estate. The rent roll, from kelp and other sources, increased greatly, yet thoughtlessness, extravagance, and folly brought him to grief at an early age, so that by him the estates on the mainland and in the isles were sold. He will perhaps be best remembered from his controversy with Glengarry as to superiority in title, which now seems to readers so foolish, though the then combatants were desperately in earnest.

When the late Clanranald began to fall into financial difficulties, every step was taken to put up rents, and removals became common. I have not observed until about 1810 any evictions of consequence, except one in 1780 when 13 heads of families—Donald Chisholm, Kenneth Macinnes, Alexander Maceachan, Andrew Macdonald, Donald Maceachan, Angus Macdonald, Ewen Gillies, Roderick Macdonald, Ranald Macdonald and Donald Macdonald were, with the exception of Chisholm, evicted from Ardnafuaran alone.

A younger son of Ronald Macdonald of the '45 named

James was most unfortunate. In 1806 he is described as 38 years of age, having a wife and son. He would therefore have been born in 1768. Partly educated in France, he entered the army an ensign in 1783, afterwards served as Lieutenant in the 19th Regiment, and raising his quota, was appointed a Captain in the 73rd, in 1791. He served in the East and West Indies, and received a dangerous wound in the head, the ball passing through his mouth and remaining in his neck. In 1803 he became Major of the 93rd, and latterly its Lieutenant-Colonel.

In 1805, on the voyage to Europe from the East Indies, he seems to have incurred the ill-will of Colonel Monypenny and some of the other officers, and he was tried by Court Martial in 1806 upon eight charges, the seventh being for unwarrantable and insulting language to the Adjutant of the 93rd in calling him "a damned villainous scoundrel." Colonel Monypenny, the real prosecutor, did not appear, though summoned as a witness by the accused. The Court seems to have been biassed, and by a majority found Colonel Macdonald guilty. His counsel were Mr William Adam and Mr Randle Jackson. He was infamously used, for though he alleged that Colonel Monypenny's presence was essential, a bogus certificate of sickness was accepted as a sufficient excuse for his absence, and delay of the trial until his recovery was refused.

GLENALADALE AND PRINCE CHARLES.

The mainland cadets of Clanranald, Morar, Kinlochmoydart, and Glenaladale, were all strong Jacobites, and so intimately mixed up with the movements of Prince Charles from first to last that they are inseparably and most honourably connected with the Rising of the '45. Glenaladale fortunately stands stronger than ever, but it is much to be regretted that the name of Macdonald of Kinlochmoydart has but quite recently disappeared from among the landowners of Inverness-shire. The memoirs of Lochgarry state that in the capture of Edinburgh, a notable event, the attacking detachment consisted of Lochiel, Glengarry, Keppoch, and Clanranald, and while Lochiel led his own clan, Lochgarry commanded Glengarry; Tirindiich, Keppoch; and Glenaladale, Clanranald. Lochgarry mentions with satisfaction that they obtained possession witnout the stroke of a sword.

In the Prince's wanderings after the battle of Culloden, Lochgarry notes—

"That after landing from Skye, at Mallaig, in July, most of Cumberland's army was detached, and a line made of them near the coast and parties put on every pass, so that it appeared impossible he (the Prince) could get through them undiscovered. At this time, H.R.H. had sent for or accidentally met with Macdonald of Glenaladale and two or three more, and luckily made their escape through the guards in the night time. They travelled two or three days through the hills, till at last Glenaladale lost knowledge of the ground, and knew not where he was going. They were then on the hills which march betwixt Glengarry and Seaforth, when luckily they met four Glengarry Macdonalds, who had been obliged to shun the enemy and take to the hills with their wives, children, and cattle. They, notwithstanding of their Prince's disguise, knew him, though he appeared quite a different person from what they had seen him at the head of his army; and with tears in their eyes, they fell on their knees and thanked God that his Royal person was safe. They knew also Glenaladale, who told them he had lost his way and did not know where to go, and asked them which was the safest route for H.R.H. They immediately said they would abandon their wives and everything that was dear to them, and as they knew the hills, they would do what was in their power to find out for H.R.H. a safe lurking place, and bring H.R.H what provision the country can afford; upon which they conducted H.R.H. to a cave, in one of the greatest hills in Scotland, within 15 or 16 miles of Cumberland's camp at Fort-Augustus. One of these four men went day about for intelligence and necessaries for H.R.H., and so secret and cautious they were in their office that they never went near their wives and families from the minute they met their Prince, and their poor wives concluded they were either killed, or taken by the enemy. They knew well the reward declared to give for apprehending or destroying H.R.H.; but all the bribes in the world could not make them betray that trust. I believe no other nation in the world can produce common men who would do the like. H.R.H. enquired if they could send one out and bring me to him. At this time the enemy lay behind me and them, and rendered it impossible for me to cross over the waters, which were prodigiously high, by the great falls of rain about that time. There were three different attacks made upon me, as the enemy knew where I skulked. I faced them fairly every time, and beat them off, by which they lost several killed and wounded. This was but a small affair, but the only blood drawn from the enemy, after the battle of Culloden.

"The Prince had stayed between twenty days and a month in this cave, and by this time your four men who were with him got intelligence of this and where I skulked, upon which H.R.H. came directly near that place, and sent one of them for me. This was in August, I cannot remember the day of the month. I came directly where H.R.H. was, and was overjoyed to kiss his hand; it gave me new courage to see H.R.H. safe, and I really believed once I had the happiness to meet H.R.H. he would be afterwards safe in spite of his enemies. This night we had no kind of provision, but a wild deer one of your men killed near the hut. Next day Glenaladale kissed H.R.H. hand, took leave, and went home to his own house near the West Coast: H.R.H. entrusting him that in case there came ships from France, he should acquaint him, and give him a trace to find him, in case that happened."

In 1805, the total rental was, as would have been already seen, only about £130, but the Glenaladale estate is now large and valuable. From the sources of the Finnon to the march on Lochshiel side with Lord Howard, is an extensive stretch, and some of the mountains, particularly Ben Odhar mor, Ben Odhar beg, and Ben Chaoirinn, make a grand appearance, viewed on a clear autumn afternoon, from the Terraces of Torlundy.

The propriety of a late "outing" to Prince Charles' monument is open to question, but if it does good in calling attention to the renovation of the monument, it will have done some good. The needful restoration falls properly on the public, and it would be unfair to saddle this on the Glenaladales.*

I subjoin a copy of one of Mr Alexander Macdonald's letters, not that it is of the least interest in itself, but as coming from the true hearted gentleman who, 86 years ago, erected this monument, which has been visited by thousands, and oft depicted by pen and pencil. Alexander was cut off in the flower of his age, in 1814, aged 28 years—

* Since the above was written, it has been announced that Glenaladale has, much to his credit, undertaken to do what is necessary.

Drimnin House, 28th October, 1809.

"Dear Sir,—Would you have the goodness to pay the enclosed sum to the collector of the cess.

"I shall be answerable for the same amount to your order at Dalness' on demand.

"Having no convenient way of remitting the within mentioned sum to Inverness induces me to put you to this trouble.

"My mother unites in best wishes and believe me always, dear sir, your obedient servant.   (Signed)   ALEXR. MACDONALD."

XII. PARISH OF SMALL ISLES.

CANNA AND EIGG.

THE modern parish of Small Isles comprehends the four islands of Canna, Rum, Eigg, and Muck, whereof, by the will of Lord Lorne of ever profane memory, all but Eigg are in the county of Argyle. Canna and Eigg belonged to the Clanranalds, and upon these islands I desire to make some observations. In 1798 the rental of Canna was as follows :—

1. Tarbert, an 18 penny land—Hector Macneill £72 0 0
2. Corrogdan, a 7 penny land—said Hector Macneill 28 0 0
3. Keil, a 12 penny land—said Hector 60 0 0
4. Change House of Canna—said Hector ... 6 0 0
5. Heisker Island—said Hector. No rent mentioned.
6. Sandy Island—Alex. Macdonald, a 9 penny land at £5 5s per penny 47 5 0
   There being a dispute as to the number of pennies, tenant in use to pay only £42 2s 0d.
7. Upper Island, a 4 penny land—Donald Macdonald and others 21 0 0
   Macneill makes 14 tons of kelp, Alexander 3 tons, and Donald Macdonald 1 ton of kelp.

Duncan Macarthur was ground officer, and Macneill factor, of Canna. It was reputed a fertile island and, now practically uninhabited, contained in 1772 a population of not less than 220 souls, who had neither church nor school, only a catechist. It will be recollected that while at Canna, Alastair Mac Mhaighstir Alasdair composed most of his poetry, for the amusement, it is said, of the factor for the time.

The valuations on the Clanranald estates were all penny lands, sub-divided into halfpenny and farthing lands. To stock a penny land, according to Pennant's information, required a sum of £30 sterling, and it carried seven cows and two horses.

In 1745 the principal tenant of Canna was John Macdonald, who had the fifteen pennies of Tarbert and three pennies of Garistill, being no doubt the identical subject included in 1798 under the head of the eighteen penny lands of Tarbert. John Macdonald's rent was 360 merks or about £20, so that rents even in Canna were rising rapidly in the last half of the eighteenth century. This John Macdonald was in circumstances to lend in April 1745, no less than 4000 merks Scots to young Clanranald.

The island of Eigg, at one time belonging entirely to Clanranald, consisted of 30 merks land, whereof 9 merks were given off to Morar, but afterwards re-acquired by Clanranald, and thereafter possessed as one individual whole.

Eigg is rich in ecclesiastical remains. The Church stood at Kildonan, on the east side of the island, and there are wells dedicated to Saint Duncan and Saint Catharine, and cairns to Saint Martin and the Virgin Mary. Roderick of the Isles, ancestor of the Clanranalds, was owner of Eigg in the time of Robert the Bruce. Unlike Canna and Rum, the people of Eigg were not dispossessed, and if the whole lands were thrown open the people would have enough to make them contented and prosperous.

The rental in 1798 was thus:—

1. Kildonan—Dr Donald Macaskill and his mother £65 0 0
   The tenants make 1 ton of kelp.
2. Howlin—Lachlan Mackinnon, ... 40 0 0
   an 8 penny land. Makes no kelp.
3. Sandavore — Hugh Macdonald, changekeeper 21 5 0
4. The Change House, do. 4 0 0
   Sandavore, a five penny land. Makes no kelp.
5. Howlin—Ranald Macdonald, ... 25 0 0
   a five penny land. Makes a ton kelp.
6. Laig—Ranald Macdonald 41 8 9
   Makes 1 ton of kelp.

7. Galmisdale—Colin Macdonald	42	10	0
8. Gruline—said Colin as sub-tenant of Lieutenant Donald Fraser's heirs	11	11	6

Principal tenant had a lease for 63 years. Makes 2 tons of kelp.

9. Cleadale—John Macdonell	85	10	0

Makes ½ ton of kelp.

10. Sandabeg—Rev. Donald Maclean, minister of Eigg	8	0	0

Makes no kelp. The late Clanranald set the remainder of Sandabeg, after deducting the Glebe, at a rent to be fixed by Allan Maclean and others, who had fixed £8 as above.

I have been in the Island on more than one occasion, and in 1885 visited the cave, getting a very small bone, also ascending the Scuir. The day was fine, and the view, looking down upon Muck, and to the mountains of the west mainland and Mull, magnificent. I was not then in robust health; the exertion was almost beyond my strength, and I desire to tender my thanks again to the Priest and Free Church clergyman of Eigg, who not only favoured me with their company but gave me actual bodily assistance, which I much needed, for my saddle was fastened with a piece of rope.

I heard a curious circumstance connected with the people of Arisaig, to the effect that, from want of a mill, they had to send their grindable corn across the stormy seas to the mill of Eigg. On the other hand the people of Eigg have to send to Arisaig for a doctor.

Following out the plan of taking parish by parish, and having now exhausted western Inverness-shire, I shall ask the reader to accompany me next to the Isle of Skye, and afterwards to the Long Island.

THE ISLE OF SKYE.

XIII.—PARISH OF SLEAT.

THE MACDONALDS.

SIR ALEXANDER MACDONALD, though he died a comparatively young man, was held in high estimation as a man of prudence and wisdom. As will be seen by the description of his estate, he possessed great wealth. Some allowance must be made for his behaviour in the 'Forty-five. He had everything to lose by the failure of the insurrection, and except a mere title, it is difficult to see what he could have gained by joining in it. His sympathies may be presumed from hereditary associations and otherwise, and it is more than likely that he would have joined, had Prince Charles been backed up at his landing with sufficient men and money. Even Lochiel declined to move until he was taunted by the Prince in person, and had the estates, or an equivalent guaranteed to him. The elder Clanranald and Glengarry also kept at home, perhaps no great matter, seeing how well their forces were commanded by young Clanranald and Lochgarry.

By nomination, dated the 22nd of July, 1742, registered in the books of Council and Session on the 8th of July, 1747, Sir Alexander Macdonald appointed as tutors and curators to his son James—the Right Hon. Alexander, Earl of Eglingtoune; Lady Margaret Montgomery or Macdonald, his wife; James Moray of Abercairnie; Kenneth Mackenzie, advocate; Mr Alexander Munro, Professor of Anatomy in Edinburgh; John Mackenzie of Delvin, Writer to the Signet; and Alexander Macdonald of Kingsburgh, who, in terms of the statute, lodged a tutorial inventory of the pupil's estate at Inverness on the 12th of July, 1748.

From an old duplicate of this document, I make some extracts, and observe that while his rights over Barra are carefully limited to the superiority, I think that Sir Alexander's rights to the 30 merks land of Skirrieheugh and the 12 merks land of Benbecula, etc., although stated with other lands, likewise did not go beyond the superiority thereof.

PROPERTY LEFT BY SIR ALEXANDER MACDONALD.

"All and whole the twenty pound lands of old extent of Slate; the forty pound land of old extent of North Uist; the thirty merks land of Skirrieheugh; the twelve merks land of Benbecula; the one merk land of Gergriminish; the two penny land of Tallamartine; and the sixpenny land of Orinsaig; the halfpenny lands of Bainliodrieforth; the half of the lands of Hegliegeng, with castles, towers, fortalices, houses, milns, woods, fishings, parts pendicles and pertinents—together with all and sundry privileges, liberties, and immunities as well by sea as by land used and wont lying within the Lordship of the Isles and Sheriffdom of Inverness. Also all and whole the nine penny lands and island of Heisker in North Uist; the twelve penny lands of Unguab; the twopenny lands of Torrdounise; the three penny lands of Kirkibost; the one merk land of Tootertown in Illearie, in North Uist; the two merk lands of Ardinillo in Slate; and the ten penny lands of Killievaxter in Trotternish, with parts, pendicles, and pertinents. All and whole the eighty merks lands of Trotternish, with castles, towers, and fortalices, manor places, milns, multures, woods, fishings, as well of salmon as of other fishes, and as well in salt water as fresh water, hills, plains, muirs, marshes, commonties, privileges, pasturages, parts pendicles, annexis, connexis, dependencies, and servants of free tenants, lying within the island of Skye, Lordship of the Isles, and Sheriffdom of Inverness. And sicklike these two unciates of land extending to an eight merk land of the foresaid lands of Trotternish, with houses, higgings, yards, hills, muirs, commonties, pasturages, privileges, tofts, crofts, annexis, connexis, outsetts, mills, woods, fishings, as well of salmon as of other fishes, and as well in salt water, as in fresh water, parts, pendicles, and pertinents of the same.

"Together with the feu farm duty of forty pounds belonging in property to Macneill of Barra, with the right of superiority of the said lands out of which the said feu duty is paid, together with all right, title, and interest the deceased Sir Donald Macdonald of Sleat had or could pretend to the teinds, parsonage, and vicarage of the lands above written; in which lands and estate above mentioned the said deceased Sir Alexander Macdonald stood duly infeft conform to Charter of Resignation in his favour under the Great Seal, bearing date, 13th February, 1727, whereby it is expressly declared that the foresaid haill lands and estate shall in all time coming be called the Barony of Macdonald, and that one sasine taken at the Manor place of Duntulm, as the messuage of the said Barony, should be sufficient sasine for the said whole lands and estate, notwithstanding their discontiguity.

"Item. That great lodging or tenement of land, with the yard and area belonging thereto, and pertinents thereof, lying in the Canongate, disponed by Isabella and Ann Setons, and William Dick of Grange, conform to disposition by them in favour of John Mackenzie of Delvin, dated 26th March, 1743, and which was granted to the said John Mackenzie for behoof of Sir Alexander Macdonald, and which lodging was let to the Earl of Glencairn for five months, from November 1746, at ten pound sterling per month.

"Item. Two hundred pounds of principal with the interest thereof from 25th March, 1734, decerned to be paid by John Macdonald of Glengarry, conform to the decreet arbitral dated said day, pronounced by John Macleod of Muiravonside, and Kenneth Mackenzie, both advocates, in the submission to them by Glengarry and Sir Alexander Macdonald, dated 30th November, 1733, for which debt, then amounting to £342 14s, Sir Alexander had obtained on 3rd July, 1745, decree of adjudication of the lands of Knoydart and others.

"Item. Evan Murray, brother to Robert Murray of Glencarnoch, £200 sterling, conform to bill dated 3rd June, 1745, drawn by Kingsburgh for Sir Alexander's behoof upon and accepted by Evan Murray, and was guaranteed by Robert Murray, conform to his holograph missive letters.

"Item. The said Evan Murray, the sum of £40 sterling, also dated 3rd June, 1745, guaranteed as foresaid.

"Item. The said Robert Murray personally, £39 12s 6d sterling, conform to bill dated 20th, payable 29th August, 1745.

"Item by Allan Macdonald of Knock, the sum of £700 Scots, conform to a bill drawn by the said Sir Alexander Macdonald upon and accepted by the said Allan Macdonald, dated 5th July, 1743, and payable at Whitsunday, 1744.

"Item by Macleod, Younger of Raasay, the sum of £315 12s 0d Scots, conform to a bill drawn by the said Sir Alexander Macdonald upon and accepted by the said Younger Macleod, dated 8th September, 1746, and payable at Whitsunday, 1747.

"Item by John Chisholm, wright in Ostaigmore, the sum of £34 5s 2d Scots, conform to a bill drawn by the said Sir Alexander Macdonald upon and accepted by the said John Chisholm, dated 20th September, 1746, and payable on demand.

"Item by Donald Macleod in Unish, the sum of £468 13s 4d Scots, conform to an obligation granted by him to the said Sir

Alexander Macdonald for the value of cattle, dated 5th January, 1746.

"Item by the said Donald Macleod, the sum of £60 Scots as the price of ten bolls of Borreray's farm bear, at nine merks per boll, conform to an obligation granted by the said Donald Macleod to the said Sir Alexander Macdonald, dated ———

"Item by Roderick Macdonald of Bornaskittag, the sum of sixty-six pounds thirteen shillings four pennies Scots, conform to a bill drawn by the said Sir Alexander Macdonald upon and accepted by the said Roderick Macdonald, dated the 21st of November, 1745, and payable the 29th September, 1748.

"Item by Archibald Macdonald of Tarskavaig, the sum of £42 13s 4d Scots, conform to a bill drawn by the said Sir Alexander Macdonald upon and accepted by the said Archibald Macdonald, dated the 16th of August, 1745, and payable the 29th of September, 1745.

"Item by the said Archibald Macdonald, the sum of £252 Scots, conform to a bill drawn by the said Sir Alexander Macdonald upon and accepted by him, dated the 6th of September, 1746, and payable the 15th of May, 1747.

"Item by Mr John Macpherson, minister of Slate, the sum of £333 6s 8d Scots, conform to a bill drawn by the said Sir Alexander Macdonald upon and accepted by the said John Macpherson, payable at Martinmas, 1746.

"Item by James Macdonald of Dalviell, the sum of £90 15s Scots, conform to a bill drawn by the said Sir Alexander Macdonald when and accepted by the said James Macdonald, payable 15th November, 1746.

"Item by John Macdonald of Kinlochdale, the sum of £25 13 4d Scots, conform to a bill drawn by the said Sir Alexander Macdonald upon and accepted by the said John Macdonald, payable 12th September, 1745.

"Item by Ronald Macalister, factor to the said Sir Alexander Macdonald, the sum of £1689 15s 0d Scots, being arrears of rent due to the said Sir Alexander by severals of his tenants who granted bills therefor, which bills were put into the hands of the said Ronald Macalister, who is to recover and account for the same conform to an obligation granted by him thereanent dated ———

"Item by Donald Macdonald of Castletown, the sum of 924 merks Scots, conform to a bill drawn upon and accepted by the said Donald Macdonald, dated 2nd December, 1743, and payable at Whitsunday 1744.

"Item by Ronald Macdonald of Clanronald, the sum of 4800 merks Scots of principal, 960 merks of liquidated expenses and interest of the said principal sum since 17th June, 1741, and in time coming during the not payment contained in a bond of corroboration granted by the said Ronald Macdonald relative to the grounds of debt therein recited and bearing date 30th July, 1741.

"Item by Duncan Campbell, drover in Ardkinlass, the sum of £250 sterling, yet resting of the sum of £450 sterling contained in a bill drawn by, and payable to Ranald Macalister, in the Isle of Skye, dated 3rd October, 1746, upon and accepted by the said Duncan Campbell, payable 1st or 2nd December, then next, endorsed by said Ranald Macalister to the said John Mackenzie and which indorsation was really a trust for behoof of the said deceast Sir Alex. Macdonald and which bill is protested on the 20th and the Instrument of Protest registrate in the books of Session, both in the month of January, 1747, with the Lords of Session, dated 2nd July, 1747, at the instance of the said John Mackenzie against Alexander Mackenzie of Fairburn, in whose hands arrestments were used as debtor to the said Duncan Campbell.

"Item by Donald Macdonald of Castletone, factor for the said defunct upon the lands of Slate, the sum of £1697 0s 8d Scots, as the balance of his intromissions; Crops 1744-5 conform to an account of charge and discharge filed betwixt them, dated 8th November, 1746.

"Item. There was an open account depending betwixt the defunct and the said Alex. Macdonald of Kingsburgh, upon which there was a balance of £126 17s 10d Scots, due to the defunct.

"Item. The deceast John Macdonald of Kirkibost, the sum of £30 14s 11d sterling, per bill dated 2nd October, 1746.

"Item by ditto, the sum of £10 3s 10¾d for his other bill dated 26th of the said month and year.

"Item by ditto, the sum of £6 7s 2d, his third bill, dated the 30th of the same month and year. But from these three bills there falls to be £20 sterling discompted, contained in the defunct's promissory note to the said John Macdonald, dated 15th November, 1746.

"Item by Evan Macdonald of Vallay, the sum of £334 19s 10d Scots as the ballance of his intromissions as factor for the defunct over his estate of Uist for cropt 1745, conform to account filed betwixt them, dated 4th November, 1746.

"Item at the time of the defunct's death the account of the said Evan Macdonald's intromissions, cropt £1746 was depending, but by an account of charge and discharge thereof, drawn up since signed, and wherein the said former ballance is charged against the factor. It appears that the ballance due by the said Evan Macdonald amounts to £436 3s 10d Scots, besides an article of £195 6s 0d about kelp which is disputable. Ronald Macalister at Kingsburgh was factor on the lands of Trotterness, cropt 1746, and Archibald Macdonald of Tarskavaig was factor on the lands of Slate for that cropt, and the accounts of both these factors are still depending uncleared.

"Item by the said John Mackenzie, the sum of £154 12s 0½d

sterling as the ballance of account current betwixt the defunct and him at the period of the defunct's death, and which was soon thereafter applied by him in the defunct's affairs.

"The sum of £300 sterling, part of the money which was found about the defunct at the time of his death, and which was soon thereafter remitted to the said John Mackenzie.

"Item, the further sum of £222 9s 0d sterling, the remainder of the money which was found about the defunct at the time of his death, and was lodged in the hands of the said Ronald Macalister, for defraying the expense of the defunct's funerals, and which ready money lying by the defunct is instructed by a declaration signed by some of Sir Alexander's friends bearing date the 3rd and 12th December, 1746. And at the same time that the said £300 was remitted to the said John Mackenzie he was advised that £20 sterling belonged to Clanranald, £50 to Clanranald's brother, and £15 to the Laird of Barra, who were at that time all prisoners at London, and for whose use the defunct received those sums from their friends to be delivered to them at London, as appears by several missive letters adrest to the said John Mackenzie thereanent. In consequence whereof he did accordingly remit the said sums to the persons above named.

"Item, the defunct's silver plate at Edinburgh, consisting of 332 oz. 12 drops, conform to an inventory of all particulars subscribed by Dougall Gedd, goldsmith in Edinburgh.

"Item, the furniture of the defunct's house in the Cannongate, conform to an inventory thereof subscribed by Mary Smith, spouse to James Runcyman, Wright in Edinburgh, to whose care the same was intrusted.

"Item, the number of 107 black cattle, young and old, on the defunct's farm at Mugstot.

"Item, the horses and other stocking on the defunct's said farm at Mugstot, which is to be accounted for by the servants who had the charge thereof."

An additional inventory in form of "Eik" was added in the year 1752, and is as follows :—

"The sum of £1574 17s 2d Scots of principal with the interest thereof from the month of October, 1734, as the balance of £2711 13s 1d Scots of principal contained in a bond granted to him by John Mackinnons elder and younger of that ilk, and Mr Neil Mackinnon, son to the deceased Lachlan Mackinnon of Corrychatachan, dated 26th February and 18th March, 1729.

"Item by the said John Mackinnon, younger of that Ilk, the sum of 2000 merks Scots, money and interest thereof from Martinmas, 1736, contained in a bond granted by him to Archibald Macdonald of

Ostabeg, dated 22nd September, 1736, bearing interest from Martinmas 1736, and 400 merks of penalty, to which the said Sir Alexander Macdonald acquired right by assignation from the said Archibald Macdonald, dated 15th February, 1742.

"Item by the said John Mackinnon, younger of that Ilk, the principal sum of £1000 Scots with the interest thereof from the 17th July, 1733, contained in a bond granted by him to Roderick Macleod of Ullinish, bearing interest from the date, and 100 merks of penalty, and dated 17th July, 1733, to which the said Sir Alexander Macdonald had right from the said Roderick Macleod by assignation, dated the 12th September, 1741.

"Item by the said John Mackinnon, younger of that Ilk, the sum of 1000 merks Scots money of principal, 200 merks of penalty and interest from Martinmas, 1736, contained in a bond granted by him to Mr Alexander Nicolson, minister of the gospel, dated 7th December, 1736, to which the said Sir Alexander Macdonald acquired right from the said Mr Alexander Nicolson by assignation, dated 15th September, 1741, registrate in the books of session, 14th July, 1744.

"Item by the said John Mackinnon, younger of that Ilk, and the said Neill Mackinnon, son to Corrychattachan, the like sum of 1000 merks and interest, from Whitsunday, 1744, contained in another bond by them to the said Mr Alexander Nicolson, dated the 12th of August, 1729, bearing 200 merks of penalty and registrate in the Sheriff Court Books of Inverness, the 8th of November, 1737, to which the said Sir Alexander Macdonald had also right from the said Mr Alexander Nicolson, by assignation dated the 10th of December, 1744.

"Item by the said John Mackinnon, younger of that Ilk, the sum of 5000 merks of principal, 1000 merks of penalty and interest from Whitsunday, 1733, contained in an heritable bond affecting the lands of Strathardil or Mackinnon, granted by the said John Mackinnon, younger, to the said Mr Alexander Nicolson, dated the 25th of September, 1733, and registrate in the Sheriff Court Books of Inverness, the 8th of November, 1737, bearing an obligment to infeft, with procuratory of resignation and precept of sasine for that effect, upon which precept of sasine, the said Mr Alexander Nicolson, was infeft in an annual rent of 250 merks, out of the barony of Mackinnon, conform to his instrument of sasine, under the hand of Roderick Macdonald, notar, dated the 15th of April, and registrate at Fortrose, 23rd of May, both in the year 1740, and to which heritable debt and interest thereof, from Martinmas 1744, the said Sir Alexander Macdonald had right from the said Alexander Nicolson, by assignation and disposition, dated the 12th of May, 1744.

"Item by the said John Mackinnon, younger of that Ilk, the sum of £44 sterling of principal, with the interest thereof, from the 1st

October, 1741, contained in the said John Mackinnon's accepted bill, to John Macleod, dated the 5th of August, 1741, indorsed by him, to the said Sir Alexander Macdonald."

"*N.B.*—There was also an accepted bill due by the said John Mackinnon, Younger of that Ilk, dated the 28th of December, 1735, payable the 15th of May thereafter, to Martin Macdonald, late servant to the said Sir Alexander, and endorsed by him to the said Sir Alexander, but it consisting with the knowledge of the said Lady Margaret Montgomery and appearing from several other circumstances that the indorsation was only a trust in Sir Alexander's person, the said bill was returned to the said Martin Macdonald."

"Item—There being a tack of the five penny land of Kinlochnadale, part of the barony of Mackinnon, entered into betwixt the said John Mackinnon, Younger, and the said Mr Alexander Nicolson for 38 years' continuance from Whitsunday, 1734, for payment of 300 merks of yearly tack-duty and dated the 9th of August, 1733, the benefit of the said tack with the burden of the tack-duty was assigned by the said Mr Alexander Nicolson to the said Sir Alexander Macdonald by assignation dated the 5th of June, 1745. And there was another disposition made by the said Mr Alexander Nicolson to the said Sir Alexander Macdonald, dated the 10th of December, 1744, of a house built upon the same possession."

"*N.B.*—All these writs and documents of debt were in the year 1745 lodged by the said Sir Alexander Macdonald in the hands of Mr Macdonald of Glengarry, who had been casually in the Isle of Skye and was then intending a journey to Edinburgh to be delivered to the said John Mackenzie, but the rebellion and confusions coming on stopt Glengarry's journey, who being soon thereafter made prisoner himself, these writs were only lately recovered out of his possession and it is informed by the said Sir Alexander Macdonald's factors that the tack duty of Kinlochnadale has been resting and no part thereof paid by Sir Alexander to Mackinnon since the date of the assignation in his favour."

"Item—There was due by Malcolm Macleod of Raasay to the said Sir Alexander Macdonald the sums of money aftermentioned by the following bills, viz., one bill dated the 21st of September, 1742, payable three months after date, £4 sterling. Item by another bill dated the 21st of September, 1742, payable at Martinmas thereafter, £8 6s 8d sterling. Item by a third bill dated the 11th of January, 1744, payable at Whitsunday thereafter, originally due by John Macleod and endorsed by him to the said Sir Alexander, one pound six shillings one penny one third sterling. Item by another bill or note dated the 13th of April, 1745, payable the 1st of June thereafter to Roderick Macdonald and endorsed by him to the said Sir Alexander, £18 sterling. Item by another bill or note, dated the 24th of June, 1745, payable the 1st of August thereafter also to the said Roderick Macdonald; indorsed by him to the said Sir Alexander, £2 15s od sterling, and the interest it's believed is resting on the said several bills since the terms of payment."

"*N.B.*—Sir Alexander had put these several bills some short time before his death in the hands of his factor, who had been treating with Macleod of Raasay about the payment, so that it's only of late that these bills came to the hands of the Tutors."

"Item—There was resting to the said Sir Alexander by Sir Patrick Murray of Ochertyre, the sum of £11 sterling, conform to a bill dated 19th October, 1744, drawn by John Macdonald upon and accepted by the said Sir Patrick for that sum, payable 20th December thereafter, and which bill is indorsed by the said John Macdonald to the said Sir Alexander and was protested at Sir Alexander's instance for not payment, and the protest registrate in the books of Session the 5th April, 1745."

"*N.B.*—This debt was lookt on as desperate, Sir Patrick's affairs having gone into confusion. But a small part of it has been lately paid, and there is some hopes that the rest may also be recovered."

"Item—Some considerable time after the death of the said Sir Alexander Macdonald, the Tutors finding that a considerable sum had been allowed by the Government to the captains of Independent Companies which had been raised for suppressing the Rebellion, 1745, for arrears, clothing, accoutrements, etc. But a part of this money was given and meant to reimburse the charge of levying these companies, and as two of these companies, of which James Macdonald of Aird and John Macdonald of Kirkibost were captains, had been raised at the expense of the said Sir Alexander Macdonald, who had been instrumental in procuring the command of them to the said two persons. The Tutors, therefore, made a claim upon them for reimbursing Sir Alexander's expense in levying these companies and the same was transacted at £150 sterling for each of the two companies, making in all £300 sterling, which sum was by them paid in to the said John Mackenzie as Sir James's cashier, and he has been accordingly charged therewith. But the same not having been received till after the Tutorial inventories were made up, and there being no written document to instruct the same therefor, the Tutors could not enter that sum in their former inventory, which they now eik to the same by this, that it may appear hereafter that they fairly intend to hold compt for all the minor effects which should or shall come to their hands."

This concludes the Inventory of Sir Alexander Macdonald's immense estate at his death on the 23rd of November, 1746.

His hand fell heavily on the Mackinnon and Raasay estates, and the numerous business transactions in which he was engaged, may account for his hesitation in 1745 to follow the hereditary Jacobite bent of his family. Since his time the House of Sleat has undergone many vicissitudes, but they still have a good hold, and almost without exception, it may be said, every Highlander and Islander wishes the prosperity and standing of the grand old house of "Mac Domhnuil nan Eilean."

RODERICK MACDONALD, CAMUSCROSS, AND HIS SON JAMES.

Notwithstanding the position taken up in 1745 by Macleod of Macleod and Macdonald of Sleat, many of the Skye people joined in the insurrection, and none were more active and zealous than a tacksman of good descent, Roderick, commonly called Rory Macdonald, of Camuscross, parish of Sleat. He was not only well known in the field, but also, at a later period, in the law courts.

He was held in high estimation by Sir Alexander Macdonald and his son, Sir James, but fared very differently at the hands of their successor, Sir Alexander the first Lord. It did not matter where—whether in the old Macdonald possessions, the lands acquired from Mackinnon, or in North Uist, his Lordship's hand, I observe, fell heavily everywhere. I will confine myself at present to the case of Camuscross. Roderick Macdonald took a nineteen years' lease of Camuscross, Tortamanach, Oransay, Barsavaig, with the grazings of Aslaig and Teangour, in the year 1774, from Lord Macdonald, at what the tenant considered, after experience, the extravagant rent of £72, but it was the place of his birth and upbringing. He found it difficult in course of time to pay the rent, and in consequence of a conversation with Lord Macdonald, which led him to suppose a deduction would be made, Roderick went to his Lordship, with the lease, in order, he hoped, to have a deduction marked upon the back. Lord Macdonald, he alleged, "declined to give any deduction, and, by some mistake or other, took up the missive and carefully laid the same among his other papers," and Roderick thought it best to leave it in case Lord Macdonald thought better of the application, but upon a subsequent application Macdonald got neither reduction nor the restoration of his lease. Some time after, in 1789, he was served with a summons of removal to appear before Mr Sheriff-Substitute Macdonald, at the Change-House of Dunvegan, in a Court there to be holden on the 31st of March. The service copy summoned the defender, not in terms of the specific date in the libel, the sheriff-officer, having of his own will, made the date of compearance the 3rd of April.

Roderick Macdonald appeared in the Change-House of Dunvegan, stating that he had several defences, dilatory and peremptory, but confined himself to one, which was to decline the Sheriff-Substitute's jurisdiction, he, the Sheriff being his own nephew, and thereby falling within the Act of 1681, which prohibits in certain degrees all judges from adjudicating upon the affairs of their relatives. Lord Macdonald said it was a singular and ill-conceived objection to be taken by the defender to his own nephew, though it might have been different had the pursuer been the person to raise it. Rory, however, stuck to his objection, and Sheriff-Substitute John Macdonald, on the 5th of May, 1789, sustained his objection "in respect that the Act of 1681 was absolute," adding rather inconsequently to his interlocutor, "reserving to Lord Macdonald to insist before the Sheriff-Depute of the County or a Supreme Court."

Lord Macdonald acted upon the first suggestion, and got Sheriff Fraser of Farraline, not unwilling to befriend a brother landlord, to entertain the process and order pleadings. This was strenuously opposed by Roderick Macdonald, who pled with great ingenuity that as the initiatory procedure occurred in Skye it could not be removed except by way of appeal, and that not a step could be taken except at the place to which he was first summoned, the Change-House of Dunvegan. That if a man was summoned to appear at Inverness for instance, the process cannot be transferred to Aberdeen; and in explanation of the number and variety of the defender's objections, he added that "in determining the exercise of the rights of property, especially towards the depopulation of a country by removing its inhabitants, every defence was bound to be stated and to be listened to, and have as full weight as if a person were being tried for getting him banished."

The Sheriff was in a dilemma, but he assoilzied Macdonald on the ground of the alteration in the summons of the date of compearance.

Next year a determined effort was again made to remove Macdonald. His various objections were repelled; he could not get back his missive of tack, and had only some loose acknowledgments of payments of rent. Decree was passed against him in the Sheriff Court of Inverness, and an advocation followed. Mr Fraser of Gortuleg was agent for Rory and fought well, but the Justice-Clerk refused the bill. Upon 10th June, 1790, Gortuleg writes—"This morning the Court ordered a very able petition for Rory Camuscross to be answered, but those that are deemed the greatest lawyers were for refusing, viz., the President, Gardenstone, Eskgrove, and Swinton, and probably if he was present, the Justice-Clerk would be for his own interlocuter, but he was in the Outer House, and Lord Monboddo was likewise for refusing." Upon the 1st of July, 1790, Gortuleg again writes—"The majority of the Court passed the Bill of Advocation, not without struggle, for there was much weight of metal on the other side, particularly the President and Justice-Clerk, but Lords Eskgrove and Dreghorn with others made a majority." After this Rory was left in peace. One of his sons was the well-known James Macdonald, commonly called "Knock," who carried on an extensive business as a general merchant for many years, but his affairs became embarrassed, and many in the Highlands suffered heavily. Business was carried on in those days with a high hand. Norman Macleod of Eileanreach and Coll Macdonald of Barisdale, great allies, fell out grievously from having been mixed up with Knock, and some of the creditors helped themselves. Eileanreach, on the 14th of March, 1795, says—"The Macraes did on the fourth of this month, carry thirty cows from Knock in the night time, as I am informed. Certain it is that Knock himself pursued them next day, with thirty men in three boats, but did not overtake them till they ferried the cattle across Loch Duich, where, it is said, he was opposed by such formidable numbers that he sounded a retreat. Are these not pretty doings?" Eileanreach was of opinion that Barisdale either knew of or was at the bottom of this extensive lifting.

As Knock fell behind in his circumstances, his father, old Rory Camuscross was not left alone. James, on the 24th of March, 1786, says of his father, "that from old age and lingering ailment he has lost his faculties," but two years later, he writes enclosing two six hundred pounds bonds got from his father under these conditions—

"It cost me some time to get my sister decoyed from her father, in case she might be a bar in the way of his signing the bonds. At last I got her to the Minister's house, when I immediately went to Camuscross, and got my father to sign the bonds there, upon Tuesday the 17th instant, before Malcolm Macaskill, residenter in Knock, and Farquhar Martin, change-keeper in Camuscross, both in the parish of Sleat. The bonds were read to him before signing, which was not the case with regard to my sister's bond. I am informed by one of the witnesses that it was never read to him, and that he did not know what paper he was signing. My father was so poorly the night he signed the bonds that he could not sit to sign bills. There is no settled money. All that was made in my mother's time was run through in time of his last wife. Nothing now remains but his stock of cattle, which will not be worth half the sums mentioned in the three bonds."

James of Knock is also anxious to defeat some supposed schemes of a Dr Macleod to the prejudice of his and of Tanera's children.

XIV.—PARISH OF STRATH.

THE MACKINNONS OF THAT ILK.

ACCORDING to Colonel Macleod of Tallisker's letter, of which an extract is after-quoted, the Mackinnons were "a very ancient honourable family." The chiefship is disputed, and a good deal has been written of late years connected with the family, though no satisfactory record has been given even from historic times. On the 3rd of July, 1557, at Inverness, Lauchlane Macfyngone of Strathwordill is served nearest and lawful heir to the deceased Ewin Macfyngone of Strathwordill, his father, in all lands and annual rents in which the deceased was vested at the time of his death. Duncan Bayne of Tulloch is Mackinnon's attorney.

On the 4th of July, 1581, Lachlan Macfyngon is served at Inverness, nearest and lawful heir to the deceased Lachlan Macfyngon of Strathwordill, in the lands and barony of Strathwordill.

The Mackinnons had been declining prior to 1745, while their neighbour, Sir Alexander Macdonald, a man, as we have shown, of great wealth and wordly wisdom, was on the watch to extend his already extensive bounds. John Dhu Mackinnon succeeded about 1712, and, marrying a daughter of Archbishop Sharpe, had a son, John Og, who predeceased his father, dying without issue in 1737.

The circumstances under which the estates forfeited in 1715 were restored and the peculiarity of the destination, which did not contemplate that John Dhu would again marry and have a son not affected by his continued forfeiture, are well known.

Sir Alexander bought up all the debts he could on the Mackinnon estates, and this, with the impecuniosity of Mishnish, who had entered into possession as heir of provision, was too much for the Mackinnon estate, which ultimately fell into the hands of the Macdonalds.

John Dhu Mackinnon, the faithful adherent of Prince Charles, still under forfeiture, after his son's death married again in 1743 Janet Macleod of Raasay, but there being no issue for some years, Mishnish continued in possession. In 1753 Charles Mackinnon was born of this marriage, and in 1754, Lachlan Mackinnon. John Dhu died in 1755, whereupon Malcolm Macleod of Raasay, on behalf of the infant Mackinnons, his grandsons, took steps to put Charles Mackinnon into possession and to recover what had been alienated. He was successful in dispossessing Mishnish, as also in the Court of Session in reducing the sale of the large portion of land sold to Macdonald. This decision was reversed on appeal to the House of Lords, and all that ultimately fell to Charles was the estate now known as Strathaird, for some time the property of the Macallisters; and Mishnish in Mull. Charles Mackinnon, the last of the race who held land, was in difficulties all his life. He appears by his letters to have been a man of some culture, and he had been a good deal abroad. He wrote a work, now scarce and forgotten, entitled "Essays," published by Creech, Edinburgh, in 1785, and I give short excerpts, showing his, and doubtless the minister of Strath's, views about the poems of Ossian. He writes—"I heard Gaelic poems repeated, containing combats of numbers against numbers, and single combats which were certainly not composed by Macpherson." Again—"It is with a good deal of diffidence I enter upon the specimen of the original subjoined to the English copy. One who hears the language constantly, and hears little in it he can study with pleasure, may, if he is a man of habit, feel a mechanical aversion to any new thing that appears in it. I applied to a clergyman in my neighbourhood, a man of taste, who said he was also of opinion that the English copy was superior to the Gaelic." In 1789 the crisis came. Colonel Macleod of Tallisker, on the 16th of March of that year, writes—"I suppose you have by this time heard that Mackinnon has sold the little that remained of his paternal estate (he had previously sold Mishnish) to Mr Alexander Macallister, one of Macleod's feuers, for £8400, a good price for a scrimp rent of £200 a year; and there is an end of a very ancient honourable family."

The new proprietor desired to make the most of his purchase, and conditioned that Mackinnon would give possession of all except what was under lease, and the whole possessors of Elgol, Kirkibost, Upper Ringol, and Lower Ringol were warned out. No expense was to be spared in seeing that the evictions were thoroughly carried out, Mackinnon rather cynically observing, that "since the pounds have been settled the farthings should be no obstacle."

I give a list of the people warned out four years before, but apparently they had been allowed to remain, being there in 1789—

ELGOL TENANTS, 1785.

1. Donald Mackinnon.
2. Neil Mackinnon (Neil Roy's son).
3. Catharine Mackinnon (Neil Roy's widow).
4. John Macdonald, son to Donald Macdonald.
5. Hector Mackinnon.
6. John Mackinnon, son to Hector.
7. Neil Maclean.
8. Catharine Maclean.
9. Lachlan Maclean, son to Neil.
10. Neil dhu Mackinnon.
11. Ewen Mackinnon.
12. Donald Mackinnon.
13. Neil Mackinnon vic Iain.
14. Donald Macdonald.
15. Donald Fletcher.
16. Donald Mac Innes.
17. Alexander Mackinnon.
18. John Morrison.
19. Angus Mackinnon.
20. Lachlan Mackinnon.
21. Neil dhu Maclean.

CAMUSUNARY TENANTS, 1785.

22. Neil Grant.
23. Neil Mac Innes vic Conchie.
24. Lachlan Mackinnon.

25. Finlay Mackintosh.
26. Donald Mackinnon.
27. Alexander Macleod.
28. John Mackinnon, senior, vic Eachin.
29. James Grant.
30. John Mackinnon, junior.
31. Archibald Maclean (died), his son in his place.
32. Malcolm Mackintosh, Change Keeper in Aird of Strath.

The above is a list of tenants in Strath, who are to be warned out of their lands without delay.

Charles Mackinnon retired to the neighbourhood of Dalkeith, not only in poverty, but in actual destitution. In a letter dated Edinburgh, the 29th of February, 1796, it is said " I suppose you would have heard of poor Mackinnon's untimely end. He assigned as a reason for the step he took, that he was starving, and in vain applied to his friends for support." In another letter, also from Edinburgh, dated the 5th of March, 1796, the matter is thus referred to by an Inverness man—" I daresay you would have heard that the Laird of Mackinnon shot himself about the beginning of February. The reasons he assigned to Mr Macdonald in a card he wrote him about an hour before he despatched himself, was—before he would die of want, having only a little borrowed silver in his pocket. In this card he mentions that he had made known his destitute situation frequently to his rich brother (Colbecks) and his other friends without effect." He had married Alexandra Macleod of Macleod, who had a jointure of £150 a year, and had he been prudent they might have lived respectably.

Colonel John Macleod of Colbecks is unfavourably referred to in one of the preceding extracts, and is termed Mackinnon's "rich" brother. True, he was his brother uterine and seems to have been sorely tried, as seen by the annexed letter, dated Inveresk, the 1st of July, 1783, and marked on the back " John Macleod, Esq. of Colbecks." In this letter some difficulties arise, as he refers to his father and stepmother as then alive. Mr Mackenzie in his *History of the Macleods* states that Malcolm Macleod, 8th of Raasay's daughter Janet, married first John Macleod of the old

Macleod's of Lewis, with issue, John Macleod of Colbecks. She married secondly as his second wife, in 1743, John Mackinnon of Mackinnon, with issue, Charles and others. This account is generally accepted, but if so, (1) the first John Macleod must have died prior to 1743, while the son speaks of him as living in 1783; (2) Colbecks refers to his stepmother as an ill-used person, while there is no evidence that his father married, or could have married a second time while Janet Macleod lived. Had Colbecks referred to his mother and to his brother as spendthrifts there would be no difficulty. He writes—

"Mr B. Macleod called for me to-day, and told me of my poor father's distress. God knows many a day and hour's uneasiness it has given me. Let the creditors know that what can be done will be done, but it must take time, and they should set him at liberty, for was I to pay the debt now, it would have to be done over again, so I cannot interfere further, only to give such help to my poor injured stepmother as will make her and the children somewhat easy. This I will become bound for."

THE MACKINNONS OF CORRY, AND OTHERS.

The Mackinnons of Corry stood for a long time in importance next to the chief. The old place of Corry, where Johnson was hospitably entertained, has long been vacated and the site, except for a few trees, can not be made out from the surrounding muir. Until very recently there were Mackinnons in Kyle, an old Mackinnon possession. From a letter of the John Mackinnon of more than a hundred years ago I make an excerpt, as he uses a word which I do not recollect of falling in with elsewhere. Dating from Kyleakin, the 29th of February, 1786, though that year was not a leap year, Mackinnon, writing to a young dandy merchant of Inverness, says—"I have no news, but that we had a very great ball at Broadford, and regretted that, to your great loss, you were not among the many pretty young ladies, and must say you was a fouterchang going away so soon." It was no doubt in anticipation of this ball that Miss Marion Macleod of Gesto writes, in January, 1786, in a most doleful strain, that the dancing shoes she ordered from Inverness for a ball were much too large and that she must be content with her old ones.

The original Mackinnon estate stretched across Skye from east to west, and according to the weather Strathwordill is beautiful or depressing. My first acquaintance with it was under pleasing circumstances and in magnificent weather. Upwards of forty years ago I had occasion to visit the Outer and Inner Hebrides on legal business. The journey from Inverness to Skye now by rail is far from what it ought to be in the matter of speed, but in those days it was serious, and the misery and discomfort of the old three-horse coach from Dingwall, with no inside, can only be imagined. By the time Kyleakin Ferry was crossed it was dark, and then the weary drive to Broadford towards Portree was intolerable. The day had been wet all along from Dingwall, and the evening in Skye pitch dark. Next day, however, broke beautifully, and I resolved to take the opportunity of visiting the Spar cave and Coruisk, and to rejoin the main road at Sligachan. The drive up Strathwordill was delightful, and so was the sail from Loch Slappin, by the cave and to Loch Scavaig. I recollect being much amused listening to a dispute between the boatmen how much they were to charge me, they being in doubt whether I was a stranger or countryman. I of course said nothing, and it carried that I was a Saxon and would be charged double. At parting, I thanked them in Gaelic, and said, offering the smaller sum, that I presumed that that would satisfy them. The sum was taken quietly, and nothing said, but I fancy it was well discussed on their way home. I have seen Coruisk since, and been more impressed with its grim surroundings than by the loch itself. Some days afterwards at a dinner table in Stornoway an Englishwoman with some literary pretensions said that it resembled a "huge ink-pot"—a simile I have never forgotten.

A youth desirous of going to Sligachan volunteered, if I took him in my boat with me, to guide me and to carry my belongings. A more execrable track than that from Coruisk to Sligachan does not exist in the Highlands.

During the Mackinnon greatness, part of their estate was used and known as Mackinnon's forest, and lay, as I understand, between Lochs Slappin and Oynart, comprehending the surrounding mountains.

A severe contest lasting for several years took place about 1766-1770 between the Rev. Donald Nicolson, minister of Strath, and tacksman of Torrin and Kilchrist, on the one part, and James Macdonald, Change-keeper at Sconser, on the other. The minister was pursuer, and he is described as "a man of uncommon probity and goodness." Not only was there a question of kelp shore on Loch Oynart, but also of hill marches in which the ancient boundaries of the Macdonald and Mackinnon estates cropped up. John Macrae, born in 1702, said that he heard "that Altnachaoirin was the reputed march betwixt Trotternish and Strath; but he also heard that the Tutor of Macdonald insisted that the river at the head of Loch Oynart was the march, though those of Strath alleged the said burn to be the march. That he knew the forest of Strath, and that it lies south-west of the head of Loch Oynart." Many old witnesses were examined, whose evidence and hearsay went back to the end of the seventeenth century. I had often heard of the "Cro" of Kintail, but did not know that there was a district known as the Cro of Strath. One witness, born in 1719, said "that he knew the Cro of Strath and reckoned that it is composed of and includes the tacks of Corrychatachan, Swordell, Kilchrist, Kilbride, and Torrin." Alexander Macdonald of Kingsburgh and his son Allan, were both examined, the former at his own house, being valetudinarian, of great age, and unable to travel, as represented on his behalf. By 1769 the Macdonalds had ceased to be factors for Macdonald, and one Maclean was appointed.

The reverend gentleman, who is accused in the pleadings of being unduly concerned with his secular affairs, lost his case. His tack gave him a right to the kelp *ex-adverso* of his subjects on Loch Slappin, but he tried to extend the right to Loch Oynart, which was miles distant, because his predecessor in the tack, Macleod, wadsetter of Balmeanoch, had been in use to cut seaware on Loch Oynart.

Alexander Macallister, who purchased Strathaird, was of good family, though Tallisker describes him as "one of Macleod's feuers." He had before 1789 purchased the lands of Clack-hamish and Triaslane. He was treated somewhat cavalierly, not only by Lord Macdonald but also by the schoolmaster of Strath, and in 1808 he had to take steps against Macdonald of Lyndale, his neighbour, in connection with the road. Though there was a good road on the hard by the sea-shore, Lyndale was accused at his own hand of beginning to form a new straight road through Macallister's arable and green pasture lands.

It cannot be said that the condition of the people improved under the Macallisters; indeed most of those who did not leave altogether were pressed into Elgol, a place visited with a grievous epidemic in 1883. From personal observation I can say that Elgol is much congested, and while the late Sir William Mackinnon is entitled to full credit for the carriage road which he had made from Kinloch Slappin, by Kilmorie to Elgol, yet the distribution of the people is most unsatisfactory. On my last visit I was concerned that a valued friend, Lachlan Mackinnon, had recently died. His widow, a most pleasant speaking person, though I fear indifferently endowed with this world's means, received me with old Highland hospitality. Lachlan Mackinnon, and indeed all the Elgol people I have met, impressed me very favourably by their courtesy and intelligence.

The estate is again for sale, at by no means an extravagant price, and it is to be hoped that it will fall into good hands. In any case it is a matter of satisfaction that the last time I spoke in Parliament was mainly in urging the necessity of improving the congested condition of the people of Elgol, and the estate of Strath generally.

XV.—PARISH OF PORTREE.

MALCOLM NICOLSON, SCORRYBRECK.

THE former precarious position of the great body of cottars and dependents in the rural parts of the Highlands and Islands does not admit of doubt. In all parts of the country I have fallen in with deporable cases, and perhaps the greatest oppressions and hardships occurred in the Islands, far away from the protection of the law and the assistance of agents, and entirely under large tacksmen who, however litigious and quarrelsome among themselves, could be relied on to assist, or keep aloof, if the oppressed were below their class and set. Unless the circumstances were exceptional, a poor man sought in vain for protection from the superior or chief tacksman. I am of course referring to the period when men were not of their once value, and all that was looked to was increased rental. The landlord insisted on or was offered a great rise of rent, the incomer only insisting on a free hand and full possession of the land. No wonder that the naturally proud and independent spirit of the people ended in the emigration of the flower of the old tenants and occupants. Among the larger tenants in Skye at the end of the last century one particularly prominent, and in the eye of the world held in great respect, with a flattering notice at his death, was Mr Malcolm Nicolson of Scorrybreck. I willingly admit and record with pleasure the kindness of many of the large farmers and of their families who nourished and protected the people on their extensive possessions. The kindly actions of such people unfortunately was too often interred with their bones, while evil acts, by getting into the law courts and otherwise, have come down in all their vileness and oppression.

I select one case as a specimen, begun in the harvest of 1790, and lasting until the autumn of 1792, of the mischief even a man of good reputation could do to a poor cottar, illustrating a cottar's fate who fell under his master's displeasure. Mr Nicolson stated that he had sub-let to Angus Nicolson, sub-tenant of Pennifilar, at Whitsunday, 1789, at a rent of £3, but under condition of only keeping a certain limited stock; whereas Angus insisted on keeping over stock, including a vicious mare so unmanageable that it ate the pursuer's hained grass. Further, that Angus allowed part of his buildings to fall into disrepair, particularly a byre, of which he destroyed or used up the timbers, and concluding for substantial damages. Dilatory defences were given in, chiefly that the defender was summoned to Inverness during autumn recess, and to his great loss from compulsory absence in an unusually late harvest, and denying the libel generally. Decree was promptly pronounced by the Sheriff-Substitute against the defender, on the 25th of November, 1790. An appeal was sustained, and after some further procedure, a proof of his averments was given to the pursuer, to be taken on commission by the Sheriff-Substitute of Skye. An objection by the defender that he could not get any agent in Skye to appear for him, also that he did not understand English and was only able to speak in Gaelic, was overruled, and the proof renewed and taken in the defender's absence. The evidence of the four witnesses for the pursuer was meagre, and was so severely exposed by the defender's agent at Inverness that ultimately the Sheriff absolved the defender from the charge connected with the timber of the byre, and while finding that the vicious mare had eaten some hained grass, in respect that this occurred during the winter and spring seasons, and that no evidence had been adduced to instruct the amount of the damage done, restricted the same to five shillings sterling. So, after two years of keen and expensive litigation, Scorrybreck succeeded in his claim to the extent of five shillings. It may be presumed, as Scorrybreck had to pay his own and part of his sub-tenant's legal expenses, that he, from prudential motives alone, acted thereafter in a kindly spirit to those under him, and to some extent gained his laudatory obituary notice.

XVI.—PARISH OF KILMUIR.

DUNTULM CASTLE, AND THE KILMUIR CENTENARIAN.

SIR ALEXANDER MACDONALD had large transactions with Perthshire cattle-dealers, and also regularly sent stock under his own men to the English markets, but great as his handling was, as already shown under the Parish of Sleat, he is found borrowing money to carry on. I have a bond by him to Mr Alexander Nicolson, minister of the gospel, at Aird, in Sleat, for the sum of seven thousand merks, dated at Ord, 22nd October, 1744, and witnessed by Alexander Macdonald of Kingsburgh, and Donald Macdonald of Castleton.

The family at this period had already removed from Duntulm to Monkstadt. When on a previous occasion I was in Skye, I heard that a very old woman, reputed to have passed her 100th year, lived not far from Duntulm. In 1892 she came to the roadside to meet me by request, accompanied by all the women and children of her township. I found the old lady most interesting, her chief story—and on account of which she was best known—was that she had in her youth spoken to a woman who, in her 16th year, attended and danced at the last ball held in the Castle of Duntulm, where Simon Lord Lovat and several Inverness-shire and Argyleshire proprietors were present.

I am not exactly sure when Duntulm was vacated, but believe it was between 1720 and 1730. Supposing this ball occurred in 1728, my visitor had seen and conversed with a woman born in 1712, 180 years before my visit.

Duntulm Castle has been a ruin for more than 150 years, and it is greatly to be regretted that so much of it was destroyed and carried away for base purposes within the memory of many living.

In regard to the Kilmuir Centenarian I copy an entry in my Common Place Book, made 11th of August, 1892, of an event occurring on 7th of June preceding, and as the "King of Skye" told me on one occasion that it had been abandoned—he thought, about 1730—one life connected an event which had occurred at least 160 to 170 years ago. It is as follows :—

"On Tuesday, the 7th day of June, 1892, while canvassing in the north of Skye on my way from Kilmuir to Kilmaluag by Duntulm, and when passing the ruins of the Castle of Duntulm, Mr Archibald Macdonald, Garafad, who accompanied me, together with Mr Alexander Mackenzie of the *Scottish Highlander*, mentioned that there was an old woman at Kilmaluag, reported to be about 103 years of age, who possessed some information in regard to the castle when occupied. Being under the impression that the castle was vacated long before Culloden, I asked that I might have an opportunity of speaking to the old woman, and a messenger was despatched to bring her to the roadside. On coming towards Kilmaluag, we found her waiting with several others who had been attracted by the summons. Her name is Christy Macleod. She had hobbled up to the road from her own house, no great distance, with the aid of two sticks. Her clothing was very scanty. She had a nice countenance, good eyesight, not very deaf, and such teeth as remained were sound and white. Interrogated in Gaelic, she having no English, she stated that she had lived in the neighbourhood all her days, and remembered when a great deal of the walls of Duntulm was entire. She was well acquainted in her youth with a very old woman named Mary Macdonald, who married a Donald or Alexander Macdonald, who told her, and she heard her repeat it to others, that when she was 16 years of age she was an under chambermaid at Duntulm, and had danced at a ball in the Castle when the Macdonalds of Sleat were then occupying it. That Lord Lovat, Macleod of Macleod, Lochbuie, and a great number of Inverness-shire and Argyleshire gentlemen were entertained at the castle for about a week. The old woman thankfully received a half-crown piece, which she examined with deliberation, and I received her blessings. This said Mary Macdonald was afterwards married within the castle."

XVII.—PARISH OF SNIZORT.

THE necessities of the family of Macleod involved parting with much of their land. Harris was sold out and out, but the lands in Skye, in order to retain political influence were feued. Amongst the earliest lands feued in Skye was the estate of Skeabost, parted with about 1790, to James Macdonald, a successful merchant in Portree. The description of the estate from an old deed ran in these terms:—

"All and whole the lands of Skeabost with the change house and salmon fishing in the water of Snizort, and one half of the town and lands of Edinbane with the islands, rocks, shores, and the seaware and wrecks of all kinds growing, or that may at any time be thrown on said rocks, shores, or small islands in so far as Norman Macleod of Macleod had right thereto; with the milns, multures, sucken and sequels, fishings in fresh and salt waters, houses, biggings, mosses, muirs, sheillings, grazings, and universal parts, pendicles, and pertinents of the said lands, which are henceforth to be free from thirlage to the miln of Waternish, or any miln belonging to the said Norman Macleod, as the said lands and others are more fully described in the title deeds and leases of said lands."

The feu duty is stipulated at £14 odds. In 1799 the total gross rental was only £56, and the proprietor, writing by the hand of his son Alexander Macdonald, says he occupies the house, a park, and the salmon fishing himself, adding, "houses yield very little rent in this country." James Macdonald was thrice married, and had by his first wife, sister of Captain Kenneth Macdonald, a son Donald, well-known under the designation of "Tanera," who carried on a very large fish-curing and other business, finally coming to grief. Captain Kenneth Macdonald leased Skeabost and did not behave nicely to Skeabost's second wife, who in a letter dated 1st July, 1801, signed by her for her husband, thus refers to the Captain. "He and his wife lived two years under the roof of my house, and was received with the utmost hospitality and friendship, yet this monster of ingratitude domineers over my infirmities, like a tyrannical laird over a disobedient tenant." Captain Kenneth, however, had his own troubles, for on the 19th of September, 1805, he thus quaintly expresses himself in nautical phraseology. "The times bear so hard upon me between rents, taxes, and other demands that I find it very difficult to keep up square yards."

Since the present proprietor of Skeabost came into possession of the estate it has been improved, beautified, and enlarged by him into an ideal Highland residence, wanting but the facilities of a light railway, which there is every prospect will speedily be carried out. It needs no gift of prophecy to say that a new era is more than dawning on Skye, when its wonderful natural capabilities will be fully developed, and thousands rather than hundreds will be found annual and profitable visitors.

Greshornish was feued by the Macleods about the same time as Skeabost, and after passing through several hands became the property of one of Gesto's sons.

The story of the vast works carried out by the new proprietor is graphically told by Alexander Smith, who had married one of his nieces. These improvements are seen by every by-passer, over the highway from Dunvegan to Portree, with pleasure and satisfaction. The present Macleod, who has succeeded to a fine inheritance and to one of the most honourable positions in the great county of Inverness would do well to rival if not excel the great improvements on the estates of Skeabost and Greshornish.

Another of the Macleod feus in Snizort is the estate of Lyndale. The estate has been greatly developed and in the hands of a man of wealth and taste, has become ornamental and valuable. It has passed through several hands and the unfortunate proprietor in 1835, whose political sympathies were Conservative, had a poor time of it, the ladies being Grants and zealous in the extreme for Glenmoriston. To keep "John" from the poll at the expense of scalding his feet was a mild step in contemplation.

XVIII.—PARISH OF DUIRINISH.

WHILE examining the papers connected with a case already mentioned, I came upon a letter from General Macleod of Macleod, written immediately after his appointment as Lieutenant-Colonel of the 2nd Battalion just raised of the 42nd Highlanders. From being in a damp place, the concluding two or three lines of the letter have worn away and disappeared. The letter is addressed to and docquetted by Provost John Mackintosh of Aberarder, "Col Mackleod of Mackleod London, 27th September, 1779."—

"Dear Sir,—I have the pleasure to inform you that I have been appointed Lieutenant-Colonel to the 2nd Battalion of the 42nd which is going to be raised. As I cannot obtain leave to repair immediately to Scotland, I have begged my friends in Skye to begin recruiting my quota in my absence. I have lodged £700 in the hands of Mr Alexander Anderson, Lothbury, London, as a fund for this service, and I have directed Tallisker, and my factor, Mr John Macdonald, to apply for any sum they may want to you. You may draw on me at Mr Anderson's, and depend on having your bills duly honoured. Captain John Mackintosh of the 42nd is appointed major, and I am desired by Lord John Murray to spur his friends in recruiting for him. The rank of officers depend on the speedy comp——" (Here the paper becomes illegible.)

Captain John Mackintosh, above mentioned, got his majority and was the last of the Mackintoshes of Corrybrough Mor, in Lower Strathdearn, having sold the property to the Balnespick family, who still possess it.

It is well known that Skye sent out hundreds of men and scores of officers who served in the Indian and Peninsular wars, and, judging by their letters, fine fellows they were in every respect. For instance, here is a kindly letter from Lieutenant William Macleod of Glendale, dated the 23rd of March, 1787:—

"Glendale House, 23rd March, 1787.

"The bearer, a poor though honest fellow, has this moment got the enclosed summons from our ruler, your namesake. For the love of God do exert yourself on his behalf. What prepossesses one most in his favour is that he and the rest of the tenants of the farm had a tack of the lands which our factor got a reading of, and thereby made away with it. My opinion of the matter is that you should summon the person who had the tack in keeping to produce it, and he will then tell how he gave away the other people's right. This will bring things to light in the proper colours. He will pay himself what he is able to spare, and moreover, you will yourself get renown.—Yours affectionately. (Signed) " WM. MCLEOD."

One further illustration. Lieutenant John Macleod of Unish, I should fancy a retired veteran under petticoat government, sends to an Inverness merchant for a trifle for himself, and for a young boy three or four primers, both modest purchases; but for his wife 2 dozen large yellow buttons for a riding habit, a hat to the value of eight or nine shillings, with one black feather, and a pound of pins.

MACLEOD OF BAY ASSAULTED BY AN IRISHMAN.

ANY one going from Fairybridge towards Stein and Waternish will observe a tall, gaunt, roofless building at the head of the lake, the walls whereof indicate that substantial people once lived there. Why it has become a ruin, unless it was accidentally burnt, seems rather strange. Here lived a century ago Captain Alexander Macleod, natural son of Norman Macleod of Macleod of the '45, a veteran who had seen much service abroad. In 1775 he met Dr Johnson and Boswell at Dunvegan Castle, and is described as one of the influential clansmen of Macleod. He married Anne, eldest daughter of Flora Macdonald, and one of their children was the ill-fated Lieutenant Norman Macleod, who was killed in a duel by Glengarry in 1798.

In connection with this duel Sir William A. Mackinnon, K.C.B., one of Skye's most gallant sons, sends me the following information relative to an incident which occurred several years after—

Many years after the unfortunate death of Lieutenant Macleod killed in the notable duel, Glengarry went to Skye on a visit to Lord Macdonald. He appeared at Portree on a market day where there happened to be a large gathering of Skye gentlemen, including many of the Macleod Clan, among whom were several relatives of the unfortunate Lieutenant Macleod.

On Glengarry's arrival at the Market Stance, he at once had a cask of whisky placed there, where in the old Highland style drink was served all round. Thereafter the gentlemen assembled in the inn to dine, having Glengarry present as their guest. After some time, as the whisky began to have its effect on the people attending the market, and particularly among the Macleods, a cry for revenge for Lieutenant Macleod's death was raised, which was taken up by the Skyemen generally. While the dinner was going on an angry and excited crowd gathered outside the inn, and demanded Glengarry dead or alive, as they were determined to avenge Macleod's death. Lachlan Mackinnon of Corry was in the chair, at the time holding the office of Sheriff of Skye. Corry went outside and made a speech to the crowd, praying them not to forget the laws of hospitality, or so far forget themselves as to cause injury to or insult the guest of the great Chief of the Island. Still the crowd clamoured and insisted on having Glengarry at their mercy. Corry then, seeing that matters were becoming serious and that the crowd meant mischief, got Glengarry smuggled out by the back door of the inn, where a horse was ready for him, and he rode off to Kylerhea, and thence out of Skye, to which he never again returned.

The Skyemen, however had the gillies with Glengarry's stag-hounds still in their hands. They did not touch the former, but mutilated the stag-hounds by cutting off their ears and tails, and in sending away the men and dogs a message was sent to their master that if he ever came back to Skye his head would come off.

The above account was given to me, says Sir William, by my father, late minister of Strath, and my mother, Corry's sister, many years ago.

The mutilation of his dogs must have been a severe blow to the old Chief, as from his history it is well-known how much he prided himself on his stag-hounds. In old times deer were chased and run down by the dogs, and I believe Glengarry was one of the last who continued the Ossianic method.

Sir William A. Mackinnon never forgot the story, and it is probable that he is the only living Skyeman who knows the facts here narrated.

It seems singular that Captain Alexander Macleod had been an officer in Glengarry's regiment, as is seen by the following extract from the letter of a creditor of the Captain's, dated Portree, 1795, afraid of his money :—" Mr Alexander Macleod of Lochbay has joined Glengarry's Volunteers, and has left the country in my debt without informing me."

It was Captain Macleod's daughter Mary who lived at Stein, and gave so much valuable information to the late Rev. Mr Macgregor, which he utilised in his excellent work on Flora Macdonald, published by A. & W. Mackenzie, Inverness.

Stein was one of the most pretentious undertakings of the Fisheries Society, and how its officials conducted themselves towards the natives may be gathered from the letter after quoted, written by Captain Macleod, from Gillin, 30th July, 1801, and backed as from "Captain Macleod, Bay." The Captain writes—

"A most violent attempt was made upon my life by William Porter, surgeon, and agent for the British Society at Lochbay. At said place, upon Saturday, the 6th day of June last, the said William Porter, having taken a walk upon the shore of Lochbay, upon the said day, in company with his wife, was there met by me and Captain Norman Macleod of the Waternish Volunteers, and without any altercation whatever he, in the true style of an Hibernian, struck me over the head with a stick he had in his hand, at the same time grasping my face with the other, and by the appearance of my eyes afterwards, his intention was to have pulled either one or both of them out, with his fashionable talons. Not satisfied with this, he wrested a hazel stick from me, which had a heavy head carved like a man's, which he took by the small end and continued to strike me on the head, till the stick flew in shivers, and the blood ran in torrents down my shoulders. Captain Macleod's right arm, like my own being disabled, it was impossible for him to have saved me, and if people upon the beach employed in riddling sand had not interfered, there is no doubt he had taken my life, which he most certainly wished to have done,

These people declared, though they observed the Doctor strike me repeatedly, they concluded we were diverting ourselves as they always knew us to be on very good terms. When I found myself relieved by the workmen, and finding three large cuts in my head, I took up a stone and flung it at the Doctor, which did not hit him. I also acknowledge to have called him a bloodthirsty Irish scoundrel, and that none but an infamous coward would have used a man he well knew had only the power of his left hand, in the manner he had done. Captain Macleod stood all this time with his hand upon the hilt of his sword, fearing, as I was told, that one of us might pull it from him. After he had gone away, the Captain observed he struck me with his whip, and that he believed it still remained where he dropped it. I told him it was no whip but the stick he first struck me with, and which he broke over my head, in which state it appeared to him like a whip, on which I took it up and let him see it. I do not know but his using me in this manner, knowing me to be one of the Justices of Peace for this county, aggravates the crime. My holding this office he cannot pretend to be ignorant of, as he employed me more than once in that capacity. With great difficulty I endeavoured to walk home, the distance being about a short mile, and took boat immediately for Grishernish and showed Sheriff John Macdonald the situation I was in. He pretended he was sorry for my usage, but could do nothing in the case until the matter was judicially brought before him, and suggested the propriety of my applying to Livingstone, the innkeeper at Portree, his Procurator-Fiscal, and he was uncertain when he could hold a Court on account of the sickness of one of his daughters—She, being a patient of Dr Porter's, and the Fiscal distant about fourteen miles, and having despaired of any redress, I returned home the same evening. The afternoon being chilly, and getting cold, I found myself feverish, and being next morning much worse, my wife and some others who were present deemed it necessary to send an express for Dr Macaskill, who arrived Monday the 8th of June, and found my head very much swelled, and cut to the bone in three different places, and the glands of my neck so much swollen and pained, that I could hardly move my head on the pillows. Thus, I was unable to stir out of bed for eight days. I was obliged to apply last week to Dr Macaskill, who was so kind as bring some camphor and other things to reduce the swelling in my neck, which I am sorry to say does not seem to yield to his application, but rather increases and becomes worse. Since the above accident, or rather premeditated assault, I am very sensible of a defect in my sight. During four days, from the blows given, all objects appear to me red, from which I am inclined to think that the organs of sight have been impaired.

I want damages of £200, and whether the Sheriff allows so much or not, I hope he will put a stop to the arbitrary proceedings of the

British Society's agent—he like his predecessor in office, acting more like a Spanish Viceroy than a man employed to encourage the natives of this country to industry, and to direct their attention from emigrating to the States of America."

The above presents a singular state of matters among the "upper ten" of Waternish a century ago. The representative of law and order behaves like a savage ; a Captain of volunteers goes about wearing a sword which he cannot use, reminding one somewhat of the resultless duel between Lord Chatham and Sir Richard Strachan—

> "The Earl with sword full drawn,
> Stood waiting Sir Richard Strachan ;
> Sir Richard, tho' longing to be at him,
> Stood waiting for the Earl of Chatham."

It will not surprise the reader that a lady of mature charms, but well preserved, was at the bottom of the business. The Procurator-Fiscal of Skye was an innkeeper, and the Sheriff of the day used to hold Courts within the Change-House of Dunvegan.

XIX.—PARISH OF BRACADALE.

THE MINISTER OF BRACADALE AND HIS WIFE.

THERE was a good deal of litigation in Skye a century ago. Proprietors, large farmers, ministers, and others joined in conflict. One of the most famous litigants was Captain Neil Macleod of Gesto.

Many of the Skye clergy were too fond of farming, and thereby excited such ill feeling on the part of the regular farmers and crofters as to lessen their influence.

The Rev. Roderick Macleod, first minister in Harris, was licensed on the 1st of May, 1763, and settled there in 1765, being translated from Harris to Bracadale in 1768, where he remained until his death in 1812, and is described as having been "eminently zealous in the work of his Master." The letter after given was written by his clever wife, Janet Macqueen. Mr and Mrs Macleod were taken into Court by Gesto, in respect of a charge against them for falsely proclaiming him a liar at the church door of Bracadale, after divine worship. This was the ancient way of denying publicly a malicious and unfounded report, but only resorted to in grave cases. Mrs Macleod's letter to an Inverness merchant who had interested himself in their behalf is very forcible, and reflects much credit on the writer, who was an elderly woman having, however, all her wits about her. The name of the spinster, not young it may be inferred, who was too delicate or bashful to appear in Court, but could walk many miles to weddings, making a creditable appearance on the floor, is fortunately preserved. The writer died in January, 1817, leaving three daughters. The following is the letter :—

"Balgown, March 24th, 1805.

"Dear Sir,—I hope this will find you and family well, which will give me great pleasure to hear per bearer ; he sends me word he won't carry anything home, but I hope you will prevail with him to bring me 1lb. of good tea and one pound tobacco twist. I had a letter from Dalness lately ; he says Mr Horne and him have agreed to cite witnesses by sheriff-officer, but Mr McDonell from Inverness does not mention this in a letter Mr Macleod had from him lately, but I'm sure he'll do what is best in that respect as well as in other respects. Upon receipt of this, please speak to him and tell him that if its a sheriff-officer that is to cite the witnesses we would wish to know without loss of time as we would wish to summon them early in April so as to prepare them, tho' we don't mean they should be examined sooner than the last of April, that they may finish their labouring. If any messenger came to the country (upon other business) he might do the business, but I hope you and Mr McDonell will do what is proper whether the business is to be done by a messenger or sheriff-officer ; we would grudge the money given Mr Murray and his attendant Stewart very much if one did not expect Gesto would be made lyable for it and every other expense his conduct has been the occasion of since that step. MacCaskill was one of the witnesses present when John Stewart was summoned and tho' a younger man than McCaskill he was five days later at Inverness than McCaskill, so what apology he made for his delay I know not, and I hear he got more than any other. I hear Mr Murray supported his claim, but the truth is Mr Murray kept Stewart on the Road to keep himself company, however its enough to suggest this to him when he makes the next claim, and if Gesto is brought in for it I would say nothing about it. Two or three witnesses are to go again, who I'm sure will claim horse fare, but I hope Mr McDonald and you will know pointedly who has a right to get this. I'm told none has but such as pay horse tax and keeps a riding horse. We are to summon a cousin of Gesto's. Every time she finds out any thing about her being summoned she turns sick. For this reason we keep it a secret untill we can get her summoned. Whenever Mr Macpherson summoned her she sent for a doctor who refused to answer her tho' she travelled some miles to meet him, but she was going about to dance at weddings when the people went off for Inverness. Consult Mr McDonell about this witness whether she is to be summoned over again or sent off as a prisoner, as she refused to answer formerly. Her name is Florence Macleod, residenter at Totarder. If she can be brought now at her own expense so much the better, as I am sure Gesto directs her excuses. Tell Mr McDonell let us know if he has any objections against McCaskill's evidence, for he must be asked whether Mr McLeod or me ever desired him cause Malcolm McLeod proclaim Gesto a lyar or even mention Gesto's name to him on that subject one way or other, for if he desired Malcolm proclaim him a lyar it must be at the desire of some other person or to please himself, for neither of us never mentioned Gesto's name to him or the name of any other in that way to McCaskill or any other person alive. I'll expect to hear from you per bearer. Mr McDonell or you can expect no money till after the mercat, then you may be sure to hear from Mr McLeod. I hope you'll find Dr McCaskill's children good payers. Mr McLeod and Peggy joins me in respectfull compts. to Mrs Mcpherson, the young ladies, and you. Ever yours sincerely,

(Signed) J. MACLEOD.

THE LONG ISLAND.

XX.—PARISH OF HARRIS.

ST. KILDA.

WHEN the necessities of the Macleod family compelled sales, Harris, their first possession, was purchased by a clansman. Since, it has more than once changed hands, and as the Southern portion, including Rodil, the ancient place of sepulture, is now in the market, it would be agreeable to Highlanders of the present Macleod, who has lately succeeded under favourable conditions, should re-acquire the duchus of his most ancient house.

In 1805 the then proprietor of Harris had become pinched, and sold St. Kilda to a clansman who had worthily maintained the reputation of the clan in India. This was Colonel Donald Macleod, who had either bought or succeeded to the small estate of Auchagoyle, in the county of Argyll, and was intimately associated with and appointed one of his trustees by Colonel John Baillie, father of the last Baillie of Dunain.

St. Kilda in 1805 was tenanted in chief, by William Macneill in Pabbay of Harris, with numerous sub-tenants. He lived at Pabbay, and was summoned to remove by Colonel Donald Macleod as at Whitsunday 1805. For some reason Macneill was unwilling to go and fought the case pertinaciously. When there was no dispensation, or the fixing of a messuage whereat to take sasine, formerly it was necessary for the Notary to go to the grounds. Unless a proprietor were infeft, he could not remove tenants if they were there prior to his becoming owner. It was quite recently Colonel Macleod had become owner, and at that early period of the year it was unlikely a Notary could visit St. Kilda. Even to this day the Islanders see no stranger for months yearly. The summons of removal was dated on the 2nd of March 1805 and called in Court forty days before the term. After decree was extracted the whole proceedings were opened up anew, when it appeared that Colonel Macleod had been able to get a Notary to visit the island and take infeftment as early as the 19th of March, which infeftment was registered on the 3rd of April, and then Colonel Macleod's title was complete. New objections were however proponed, one being that the Notary, an elderly retired writer, was not certificated, having ceased practising or not taken out the licence without which, involving an annual payment, it was argued the Notary was exauctorate and disqualified to act. But all the defences were repelled and decree granted.

Colonel Macleod's son, John, was the distinguished East Indian official, afterwards Sir John Macpherson Macleod, who did a great deal for the comfort and better housing of the Islanders. By request of the late Norman Macleod of Macleod, Sir John agreed to re-convey the island, and it now and for some years past, is the property of Macleod.

Sir John also purchased the one half of Glendale in Skye, which has turned out an unpleasant investment for his representatives.

The description of St. Kilda from the older titles ran— "the 2½ lands of Hargiebost, and island of St. Kilda," afterwards—"the Island of St. Kilda, being part of the estate of Harris and the small islands, contiguous thereto, viz., Borera, Soa and Duvin, with the insulated rocks adjacent, all lying within the Parish of Kilbride, now Harris, and shire of Inverness." The name of St. Kilda in Gaelic is "Hirst," or "Hirsta."

While all must wish the interesting Islanders well, the future outlook, particularly as regards fuel, must shortly be regarded as serious to all concerned.

XXI.—PARISH OF NORTH UIST.

A NORTH UIST REMOVING—MACLEAN OF HOSTA, 1780.

THE great bulk of arbitrary removals of old were chiefly of small tenants, crofters, and cottars. Sometimes a largish farmer was attacked, as in the case of Mr John Maclean, of Hosta, now to be referred to. North Uist has suffered perhaps more than any other part of the Hebrides, and it speaks volumes for the good behaviour and industry of the people that they to this day bear up so well under intolerable rule.

The name of Maclean was once numerous and respected in Uist, as tenants under Lord Macdonald and Clanranald. There is in the papers after given a perfect romance in history. There was a great rise of rent, a fall in kelp, a rush to America, all within the short space from 1769 to 1773. Then followed, some few years thereafter, a revival in kelp, from the prohibition laws of the revolted Colonies. The legal steps against Mr Maclean, involving the hurrying back of the packet boat to Skye before he could write his agent at Inverness, and the undue expedition in extracting the decree of removal pronounced in absence, etc., may give a wrinkle even to the sharpest practitioner of modern times. A letter from the minister of North Uist on the subject is also given, showing the business talent, shrewdness, and legal capacity of the island clergy of the last half of the eighteenth century noted by all travellers. Readers will be glad to know that the oppressive legal proceedings fell to the ground. Here follow the papers :—

" My Lords, etc., your servitor John Maclean, tacksman of Hosta, in North Uist. That whereas I am charged to remove and threatened to be summarily ejected furth of the said lands of Hosta with their pertinents, etc., in virtue of a decree of removing, said to have been obtained against me before the Sheriff-Substitute of Inverness-shire upon the 4th day of April last past at the instance of Lord Macdonald, proprietor of the said lands, most wrongously and unjustly. Considering that the said decreet is not only in absence but also improperly stolen out against me before I had an opportunity to state my defences; For your Lordships will observe from the citation given me bearing date the 25th day of March last past, that I was cited to appear at Inverness on the 4th day of April thereafter, and from the charge given me on the decreet, it appears to bear date on the same 4th day of April, and that the decreet was extracted on the 10th, being six days thereafter, altho' the reclaiming days were not then expired, with the avowed intention of cutting me short by giving me no opportunity to state my defences; For the matter of fact is that the foresaid citation was no sooner given me than the factor of North Uist hurryed away the pacquet boat for the Isle of Sky before I had any time to write a man of business at Inverness, and the consequence was that decreet in absence went out and was extracted in manner already mentioned before my letters reached Inverness by the subsequent pacquet, so that it was entirely owing to the advantage taken by the factor and my great distance from the seat of justice that the proper appearance was not made on my part, therefore I humbly apprehend that no regard ought to be paid to the decreet in the present question, as having been improperly obtained.

"2. In the year 1769 when Lord Macdonald made a general sett of his estate in Uist and imposed considerable augmentations on his tenants, the farm of Hosta was sett in tack for 19 years from Whit. 1771, to Hugh Macdonald and John Maclean, the then possessors, at the yearly rent of £24 sterling; but soon finding themselves unable to continue their possession, they sold off their whole stock, abandoned their farm, and emigrated to America, with many more of his Lordship's tenants who were reduced to similar circumstances, at Whitsunday, 1773. In this situation Mr Neill Maclean, factor on the Island of Uist, communicated the proceedings of the tenants to Lord Macdonald requesting his lordship's directions how to proceed respecting the vacant farms, and his lordship apprehensive that they would lye waste on his hands, desired the factor to make the best he could with respect to a sett of them till his lordship should come to the country. The factor being thus instructed, he prevailed with me to take the said farm of Hosta off his hands upon the same footing that the former tacksmen held it, and as a further inducement put into my hands the foresaid lease which the tenants had delivered up to him before leaving the country, with an assurance that Lord Macdonald would not only confirm the same to me when he came to Uist, for the period yet to run thereof, but would probably make some abatement from the rent. Induced by these fair promises, I entered into possession of the farm of Hosta, and Lord Macdonald coming to the country a few months thereafter, was made acquainted with the factor's transaction respecting the deserted farms and mine in particular, when he was pleased to signify to the factor in writing his entire approbation of the measures which had been adopted to find tenants to these farms, as will appear from his Lordship's correspondence with the factor at the time on the subject. A short time thereafter I waited of his Lordship, when contrary to my expectations, he declined making any abatement from the rent, but at same time assured me that the transaction with his factor approven of by him, entitled me to possess the farm for the period yet to run of the foresaid lease granted to Hugh Macdonald and John Maclean, in the same manner as if they had assigned the lease to me with his consent, adding that his word of honor in support of the factor's agreement rendered me equally secure as if I had it under his hands ; and in terms of this agreement I continued peacefully in possession and paid my rents as tacksman till the citation was given me in the action of removing now under consideration ; but Lord Macdonald finding of late the advantage of occupying by his own servants all the kelp shores on his estate on account of the advance in the price of that commodity since the importation of pollashes was prohibited by the American Colonies, he it seems has been persuaded to attempt taking advantage of my want of a written sett or a formal assignation of the former tack, notwithstanding of the agreements solemnly entered into with his factor and confirmed by his Lordship in manner already stated ; but in this I am hopeful he will be disappointed, and that your Lordships will see cause to suspend the decreet for the following among other reasons, vizt. :—1st, The decreet was not only obtained against me in absence in manner already stated, but the citation to the action of removing was also informal and defective in so far as it did not contain a full double of the lybell and made no mention of the Act of Sederunt authorising such removings as required by your Lordship's decisions, and the practice of all the Sheriff Courts ; 2nd, from the state of facts already given, I humbly apprehend that it is not now competent for Lord Macdonald to deprive me of my possession before expiry of the foresaid lease granted by him to Macdonald and Maclean. His Lordship authorised his factor to sett the farm of Hosta in manner most advisable till his arrival in the country, when he was pleased to confirm the factor's proceedings in the transactions with me both in writing and by his word of *honor* as above mentioned, and these facts, if denied, I am hopeful to instruct not only from his correspondence with the factor, but likewise by his Lordship and the factor's oaths, so that I humbly hope this noble pursuer will be found barred from betaking himself to the plea of *locus penitentiæ* that might be competent to him in a mere verbal lease, since the delivering the lease to me, my having entered into and continued the possession and paid my rents in the terms thereof, are circumstances forming such a *rei interventus* as I humbly hope will exclude any plea founded on my not having an assignation to the foresaid lease reduced into writing. Herefore I beseech your Lordships for suspension in the premisses upon caution in common form according to justice.

      (Signed) JAMES FRASER (of Gortuleg)."
"Edinburgh, 19th June, 1780."

The bill was intimated to Mr Duncan Grant of Bught on behalf of Lord Macdonald, on the 23rd of June, as follows:—

"Sir,—Your letter of the 25th June enclosing a copy of a Bill of Suspension in favour of John Maclean, tacksman of Hosta, was returned to me from North Uist to this country, and I return you many thanks for your diligence and assiduity in the cause entrusted to your management. It was a great pity you was not properly supported to go on with it. I am sorry to inform you that the written tack granted to Mr Maclean's predecessors is not to be found. He was so stupid as, after Mr Neil Maclean, the factor, had given it to him to return it to himself again to keep as he had no proper keeping for it himself, and by letter I received yesterday from Uist I am informed that after Mr Neill Maclean had rumaged all his drawers for it he could not find it; however, I shall cause another search to be made for it how soon I go home. Enclosed is a letter from Mr Neil Maclean, the late factor to John Maclean, Hosta, which I think is a good deal in his favour; you have also a discharge for the rents of Hosta during Mr Neill Maclean's intromission. If the tack cannot be found can Lord Macdonald be obliged to give up the copy he has of it himself, or will you advise us to treat with Lord Macdonald before a discovery is made of the tacks being lost? I wrote you a letter by last post inclosing some papers that I think make for John Maclean, and two guinea notes which I hope have come safe to your hands. If nothing better can be made of this process you'll endeavour to keep it alive till we settle with Lord Macdonald.

"Any remittances required shall be made you. Direct as formerly 'by Dunvegan' as I go to Uist in a few days.

"I always am, Sir, your most obedient and humble servant.
      (Signed) ALLAN MACQUEEN."
"Isle of Skye, 25th July, 1780."

XXII.—PARISH OF SOUTH UIST.

THE MACDONALDS OF BELFINLAY, BENBECULA.

It is often a matter of regret to those delighting in the past, to find that old places and old names around which cling the halo of romance have been obliterated, some by absorption, others by wanton change.

Take Belfinlay, which sent out in the 'Forty-five one of the bravest of the warlike race of Clan Donald, so lovingly referred to by Bishop Forbes, in illustration. Search in the county rolls of Inverness-shire will be made in vain for the name, though perhaps one may have fancied it was to be found among the Outer Hebrides. Take up a map of the old Diocese of the Isles, and you find Belfinlay on the northwest of Benbecula, looking out on the mighty Atlantic, lying between Bala-mhanaich and Bala-na-Caillich—fit abode for Hebridean poet or romancist. Some of them, it is matter of congratulation, are presently coming well to the front and stand out nobly in comparison with certain Lowland ghouls who fatten on destroying the reputation of past eminent Highlanders.

Alas, how deplorable in many respects are the changes in the Long Island, between Harris and Barra, although the places are the same as, in the main, are the attractive and kindly people.

The recent publication of "The Lyon in Mourning," that grand collection, so minute, accurate, and painstaking, for which Highlanders in all ages will hold the good Bishop Forbes in everlasting remembrance, has brought freshly to notice some papers long in my possession, wrapped up in faded paper and endorsed in an old hand, "Mrs Macdonald Belfinlay's Papers."

Allan Macdonald, counted as eighth Captain of Clanranald, had three sons, Ranald, the third, receiving from his father lands in Benbecula and Arisaig, confirmed to him in 1625. Ranald was succeeded by Ranald Og, his son by a second marriage. The latter, by Papal dispensation, married in 1653 Anne, his cousin within the prohibited degrees, daughter of the tenth Clanranald. Ranald Og was succeeded by his eldest son James, described in 1686 as "of Belfinlay." James Macdonald was succeeded by his eldest son Ranald, Captain in Clanranald's Regiment, of whom the worthy Bishop says, under date, Leith, 4th of December, 1749—"Woes me for the death of the worthy Belfinlay, whose memory I revere." Upon the 9th of January, 1748, Captain Donald Macdonald, *alias* Donald Roy, brother of Balishare, called on the good Bishop, who records that,

"Captain Donald in his journey to Edinburgh had visited Macdonald of Belfinlay, who had given him a remarkable narrative in his handwriting upon the back of an old letter, and taking the paper out of his pocket book, he delivered it to me. After reading it I desired to know if I might have the liberty of transcribing it in my collection. He told me I might dispose of it as I pleased, for that he had got it from Belfinlay on purpose that I might preserve the narrative in Belfinlay's own handwriting. I then begged leave to observe an omission, which was that Belfinlay had forgot to fix a date to his handwriting, and therefore I desired Captain Roy Macdonald to inform me (if he could) at what time he received the manuscript from Belfinlay. After recollecting himself a little the Captain answered that he was in the country of Arisaig about December 20th, 1747, and to the best of his remembrance he was upon that very day with Macdonald of Belfinlay and saw him write the narrative with his own hand in the very shape in which he had just now delivered it to me."

Here follows an exact copy of the narrative, the original of which, in Belfinlay's handwriting, is to be found among my (Bishop Forbes) papers :—

"That there was a vast number of the Highlanders killed in cold blood the next morning after Culloden battle is a fact that can't be denied, and that can be likewise attested by Mr Ranald Macdonald of Belfinlay (a cadet of Clanranald's family), who was an eye witness to that tragedy. This gentleman, who was an officer (a Captain) in the Highland army, had the misfortune to be shott through the two leggs in that action, which rendered him incapable to make his escape. He lay in a field after he received his wounds, and was betwixt the fire of the English army and that of the few French troops that made some resistance after the Highlanders were routed, where showers of balls pass'd by him. He remained likewise in the field all that night, after he was stript of all his cloaths, his very shirt and breeches being taken from him. But as he was young and of a robust constitution, he lived till next morning, when he saw that cruell command coming to execute their bloody orders, and saw many of his unhappy companions putt to death in cold blood. They were just presenting their firelocks to his own breast when he was saved through the clemency of Lieutenant Hamilton, who if he remembers, belonged to Cholmondely's regiment and who took him to* a neighbouring country house. Next day he was brought along with wounded redcoats to Inverness, they cursing and abusing him all the way for a damned rebellious rascal. He lay a prisoner at Inverness, not being able to be transported with the broken bones in his legs, till the indemnity which set him free. He lives and can walk about."

Belfinlay's case seems to have made a deep impression on the Bishop, who, signing himself "Donald Hatebreeks," in his letter to Dr Burton of York, and dating from "Tartanhall," on the 19th of June, 1749, says, *inter alia*—

"Just now a limmer is busy about an original picture at my desire upon which he is to draw the following description :—Ranaldus Macdonald de Belfinlay in Benbecula, in proelio Cullodino (Ætat : suae 18) multo vulnere saucius, nudatus, sub dio circiter horas 22 restabat ; sed tandem humanitate (tune temporis admodum singulari) cujusdam Hamiltonij vicarij de legione Cholmondiyaca salvus evasit dum vulneratos commilitones (referens tremisco) consulto mactatos, miserrime jugulatos undique videbat ; adeo ut contaminata esset terra caedibus. Monstrum !—Horrendum !—Ingens ! The limmer assures me he is determined to work off a plate of it with the same inscription not to cost above a shilling sterling per copy. As it is an historical and undeniable proof of a certain barbarous and shocking scene, so I doubt not but it may circulate far and near. Pray, dear sir, be at pains to count noses and say what demand may be for such a commodity in your corner. You may have as many copies as you please."

(Signed)   "DONALD HATEBREEKS"

Whether or not the proposed engraving was ever published I cannot say. Belfinlay's end is thus noted by Dr John

* Here ended Belfinlay's handwriting, and what follows I took from the mouth of Captain Donald Roy Macdonald.

(Signed)   Robert Forbes. A.M.

Macdonald, brother to Kinlochmoydart and stepfather to Belfinlay, with the Bishop's indorsation—

"Dear Sir,—I had no opportunity before now to let you know of our arrival in the country. We had a most severe journey of it, with most excessive winds and rains which has cast poor Belfinlay so low that alas, I fear he has not many days to pass in this world, otherwise you might be sure he had embraced so fair an opportunity of letting you hear from him. His illness puts me and whole family in very great confusion, for I have quite despaired of his recovery. There is no country news but a prodigious bad season and plenty of Red Coat parties, both very bad articles.—I am, Dear Sir, your affectionate humble servant,

(Signed) "JNO. MACDONALD.

"Kinlochmoydart, Sept. 21st, 1749."

"The original of the above is to be found among my papers. I received Dr Macdonald's letter from Neil Macdonald, Maceachen's eldest brother, John Macdonald Maceachen, who, and Angus Macdonald of Millton (Miss Flora Macdonald's full brother) made me a visit. They afterwards told me that they got notice from the Highlands that Belfinlay died on 28th September."

(Signed) "ROBERT FORBES, A.M."

Upon the 4th of December, 1749, Bishop Forbes says that he was favoured with a visit from Ranald Macdonald, son to Borrodale, who gave him a letter from Major Alexander Macdonald of Glenaladale, in which, referring to Belfinlay, Glenaladale says—

"I am heartily sorry to have the account of your real well-wisher Balfinlay's death to give you, having departed on the 27th September last, much regretted by his friends, among whom he depended on you as a firm one."

The gallant and unfortunate Captain Ranald Macdonald, on his death prematurely from his wounds and barbarous treatment at Culloden, was succeeded by his son Allan, then a child. Allan was held in great estimation by the Clanranalds, not only for his father's sake, but as due to his own high character and prudent conduct. Besides Belfinlay, Allan Macdonald had the possession of Ardgaseg or Ardghasarig, in Arisaig, and was able to lend considerable sums to his chief, unpaid at his death. He married in 1768, Jean Mackinnon, daughter of Lachlan Mackinnon of Corrychatachan, a clever helpmate, who managed prudently whilst the marriage subsisted, and during her long widowhood, conducted the family affairs with discretion. Allan Macdonald died in Muidart, in September, 1784, and was survived by his wife and at least two children—James, who succeeded; and a daughter, Janet. His debts were trifling, including sums in total not exceeding five pounds, due to Donald Macdonald of Cross, James Macdonald of Borrodale, and Colin Macdonald of Traigh.

Mrs Jean was unfortunately involved in considerable litigation, from which she generally emerged successfully, notably in one case—that with Colin Macdonald of Boisdale, factor for Clanranald.

The tax on windows was a most obnoxious one, and greatly exercised the minds of those affected, specially ladies. I give one of Mrs Jean's letters, addressed to a friend in Inverness, chiefly for her remark on the Surveyor who had visited her house on his rounds, well worth recording. "But I excuse him in a manner when he viewed my house, his eyes had a cast more than ordinar," would have delighted Dean Ramsay. The letter follows :—

"Ostaig, 2nd June, 1798.

"Sir,—By last post I had a letter from Mr Fraser of Gortuleg. Concerning his attention towards the transactions betwixt my husband and the family of Clanranald, he stated that he would show all the manner of justice possible in our favours. He says that you did not send him a copy of the assignation granted by my son James in favour of his sister Jenny, and if that is the case, begs on receiving this, you will lose no time in writing to him and enclosing the said assignation.

"I now beg to acquaint you of a tax of window lights, that I think I have no right to so much as is mentioned by Mr Mackay when here, but I excuse him in a manner, when he viewed my house his eyes had a cast more than ordinar. It is not worth my while to say anything but truth concerning them, but his imposition if I have the right side of the question, I hope you will put me on the right channel only to pay for the number hereafter mentioned, that is, six windows and one small opening without glass.

"He charged me for two riding horses. I never keep one I declare, but he has seen two large labouring horses of Mr Macpherson's on his farm which marches with mine, and has taken it for granted as it was so near my house that they belonged to me.

He has charged Mr Macpherson with the same horses; my small farm had no right to such horses, being too small. He charges me with £1 3s sterling and I don't want to lose so much by imposition yearly if I can think to avoid it. You will act for me in reasoning the case with Mr Mackay, which I will cheerfully accompt with you. Concludes with compliments to my worthy friend Mrs Macdonald, and the young family in general.—I am, sir, your most obedient servant, (Signed) JEAN MACDONALD.

James Macdonald, the next Belfinlay, resided abroad for many years. Upon the 15th of June, 1791, he made over all his estate in Scotland to his sister Jean, by deed signed at Ostaig on the above date, written by Donald Macleod, late tacksman in Canna, and witnessed by him and James Beverley, schoolmaster in Sleat.

Amongst those referred to in Mrs Jean's letters are her sister, Mrs Macpherson of Sleat, her nephew Mr Mackinnon of Kyle, and Miss Annie, Tormore. The Belfinlays' connection with Uist gradually dropped away, Skye becoming their main residence. After the last sale of Waternish the family of Belfinlay, with their connections, the Nicolsons of Ardmore, became proprietors, and still continue in possession.*

The present Allan Macdonald of Waternish, son of Major Macdonald, is a resident, and prominent in the successful rearing of West Highland stock. From his residence of Fasach, there are, weather permitting, seen perhaps the finest sunsets in the Isles—across the lesser Minch to the grand outlines of the mountains of South and North Uist, bathed in gold, a dream of beauty.

Waternish possesses in the island of Rona, a holding in his original *duchus* of Uist, and as his nephew is lately happily married, all Highlanders and Islanders wish for the standing and continuous prosperity of the house of Belfinlay.

* Since the foregoing was written, I observe on the authority of Dr Kenneth Macdonald, Gesto, that a servant of Miss' Jean's, viz., Mrs Catharine Macgillivray or Kennedy, one hundred years of age, still survives (1896), and in possession of her faculties. It is quite possible, indeed probable, that she may have spoken to and been acquainted with people who knew Belfinlay of the '45. I much regret I did not know of this old lady, or would have endeavoured to see her when in Uist in 1892. C. F. M.

THE CLANRANALD IN SOUTH UIST AND BENBECULA.

When referring to Moidart and Arisaig, I gave the Clanranald rental in 1798, in these localities. The judicial rental then taken included the Isles; that portion comprehending South Uist and Benbecula follows, and may be contrasted with the present occupancy. Later on, the names of the crofters and cottars early in this century will be given, amongst whom will doubtless be found the immediate predecessors of many of the present possessors—

BENBECULA.

1. Donald Morrison, Aird £64 0 0
   consisting of eight penny lands. 3 cliticks of land, £8 p. penny
2. Donald Ferguson—3 farthings do.
3. Donald Macdougall—3 cliticks.
4. Donald Maclellan—2 farthings.
5. Angus Maceachan—2 farthings.
6. Angus Martin—3 cliticks.
7. Donald Campbell—3 cliticks.
8. Neil Macphee—1 farthing.
9. Neil Macleod—3 cliticks.
10. Donald Macaulay, senior—1 farthing.
11. Donald Macaulay, junior—1 farthing.
12. Angus Macaulay, wright—3 cliticks.
13. Donald Mor Macdonald—1 farthing.
14. Donald Macintyre—1 farthing.
15. Neil Martin—1 farthing.
16. Neil Morrison—1 farthing.
17. Donald Macdonald, senior—1 farthing.
18. John Morrison, senior—2 farthings.
19. John Morrison, junior—1 farthing.
20. Donald Morrison, junior—1 farthing.
21. Angus Macintyre—1 farthing
22. Alexander Stewart—3 cliticks.
23. Mary Macintyre—1 clitick.
24. Archibald Maclellan—1 farthing.

    Tenants manufacture 86 tons of kelp whereof one fourth made on the west shore, receiving one pound fifteen shillings per ton for east shore kelp, and two guineas for west shore. Bound to three days' service for cutting, winning, and carrying peats to Nunton. As the place is small and tenants numerous, obliged to purchase from the proprietor a large quantity of meal yearly. Lease expires at Whitsunday, 1799.

25. Donald Mackay, Ballivanich 110 0 0
A five penny land. Makes 36 tons of kelp, 3 on the west shore for all which allowed two guineas. He and his subtenants are obliged to purchase meal annually. Lease expires in 1809.

26. Malcolm Macneill, miller 14 0 0
Rent may be 28 bolls of meal. No lease.

27. Ewen MacEachen, Dunganachy 60 0 0
A five penny and one half penny land. Allowed to make kelp on the island of Morragay. Holds on 19 years tack from 1789. Has to purchase meal.

28. Donald Ferguson, Change-house of Peninloden and Linaclate 6 0 0
Thirty years lease from 1790.

29. Donald Macpherson, Liniclate and pendicle of Creagory 57 5 0
Other tenants and possessors, in all a two penny and 3 cliticks of land.

30. D. Macpherson—1 farthing.
31. Donald Wilson—1 farthing.
32. Angus Macdonald—1 farthing.
33, 34. Michael and Donald Macaulay—1 farthing.
35, 36. John Glass Macaulay—1½ clitick.
37. Angus Macaulay—1 farthing.
38. Peter Macinnes—1½ clitick.
39. John Macneill—1 farthing.
40. Allan Macintyre—1 farthing.
41. Malcolm Macpherson—1 pendicle of Creagory ... ...
42. Archibald Macphee—1 pendicle of Creagory. Each pendicle paying £2 10s of rent. Liniclate produces 4 tons p. farthing land, and Creagory 6 tons of kelp, the prices being two guineas for the west shore, and one pound fifteen shillings for the east shore. Lease for 9 years from 1790. Three days' labour for peats to Nunton.

47. Mr Patrick Nicolson, Torlum and Griminish. 100 0 0

Torlum, a two penny two farthings land
and Griminish five pennies and a farthing. Lease for 30 years from 1798.
Makes 45 tons of kelp, on the east and
west coasts, in all 90 tons.

48. John Butter, Nunton 60 0 0
A nine penny land. Manufactures 90 tons
of kelp, whereof 84 on the east coast.

49. Donald Macdonald, Drumlich and Gramisdale, together 93 10 0
Drumlich, otherwise Uachdar, is a five
penny and one halfpenny land, and
Gramisdale a penny land. Quantity of
kelp manufactured in both places, 30
tons. Lease commenced in 1790 and
ends in 1809.

This finishes the Benbecula list, but the evidence of Donald Ferguson, ground officer, may be given in regard to the meal supplied to the tenants, viz., " That he knows the whole tenants on the estate have been in use of being supplied with meal by the proprietor, as the crops raised on the estate seldom or ever prove sufficient for the maintenance of the numerous inhabitants necessary for the manufacturing of the kelp."

SOUTH UIST.

46. Alexander Macdonald, Peninirine 30 0 0
Pays also a boll of horse corn or 10s conversion money. Lease 30 years from
1789. Manufactures 9 tons kelp.

50. Roderick Macdonald, Gerrafleugh 22 4 5
Subjects were possessed by Roderick's
father on a life lease. Father, John
Macdonald, died in 1797. Widow and
family now in possession. 3 tons of kelp
manufactured all on the east shore, for
which two guineas allowed

51. Neil Macphee, Ardivacher 29 15 6
It is a two penny and one farthing land
divided thus
Macphee himself—1 farthing.

52. Donald Smith—1 farthing.
53. Angus Macphee—1 farthing.

54. John MacEachan—1 farthing.
55. John Smith, 1 farthing.
56. Donald MacEachan, senior—1 farthing.
57. Lachlan MacIsaac—1 clitick.
58. Angus Bane Campbell—1 farthing.
59. Finlay Macinnes—1 farthing.
60. John Roy MacEachan—1 clitick.

 Pay no casualties. Manufacture 18 tons of kelp, 9 tons on the east coast for which allowed £1 15s per ton, and at the rate of £2 2s for the west coast, except for the kelp on rocks of difficult access, for which they get £2 12s 6d. This rate they consider too low and look for a rise, and each year they have to purchase a large quantity of meal.

61. Archibald Macphee, Kilaulay 48 0 0
 thus divided
 A Macphee—3 cliticks.
62. Angus Macaulick—3 cliticks.
63. Ranald Macdonald—3 cliticks
64. Malcolm Macinnes—3 cliticks.
65. Lachlan Macdonald—1 farthing.
66. Angus Mac Iain Alister—3 cliticks.
67. Angus Macdonald alias Maclachlan—3 cliticks.
68. Donald Macphee, 3 cliticks.
69. Alexander Macaulay—1 farthing.
70. John Macaulay—1 clitick.
71. Angus Macaulay—3 cliticks.
72. Lachlan Macdonald, senior—1 farthing.
73. John Macdonald—1 farthing.
74. John Morrison—3 cliticks.

 A four penny and one half-penny land. They used to pay at the rate of four pounds sterling for every three cliticks, and two cliticks make a farthing land. That they formerly paid at the rate of three pounds for every farthing lands, but on account of the sand drifts and advance of the sea, they had been allowed a deduction of about one fourth their rents. That the said deduction was given them in spring, 1794, and that since then the farm has suffered considerably by sand drift. That three pennies of Machermeanach was added to their farm, and an adequate rent laid thereupon, but which lands are now entirely destroyed by the blowing of the sand drift. The tenants manufacture about 27 tons kelp.

75. John Mackinnon, Linique 59 11 0
    Thus divided
    J. Mackinnon—1½ farthings of lands.
76. John Mackinnon, junior—1 farthing.
77. Lachlan Mackinnon—1 farthing.
78. Ewen Mackinnon—1 farthing.
79. Lachlan Ban Mackinnon—1 farthing.
80. Dugald Macisaac—2 farthings.
81. John Macisaac—1 farthing.
82. Dugald Macisaac—2 farthings.
83. John Macdonald—1 farthing.
84. Donald Maceachan—1 farthing.
85. Angus Macdonald—¾ of a farthing.
86. Farquhar Campbell—1 farthing.
87. John Morrison—1 farthing.
88. Donald Mac-Coil-Vic Iain—1 farthing.
89. Donald Campbell—1 farthing.
90. Angus Campbell, 1 farthing.
    The tenants make 18 cwt. per farthing or 16 tons of kelp, for which allowed £1 15s sterling per ton.
91. Lieut. Dugald Macdonald, Balgarva ... 59 11 0
    Holds under a 21 years' lease from 1791. Lands consists of four and a half pennies. Manufactures 21 tons of kelp. Is also tenant of the pendicles of Sandaveg and Fiachkill, for which he pays £3 1s sterling and manufactures in the east shore 2 tons of kelp.
92. Ewen Roy Macmillan, Roug-Askernish ... 5 0 0
    Makes 2½ tons of kelp, for which allowed at the rate of £1 15s. Holds on a seven years' lease from 1794.
93. Donald Macintyre, sen. Kilvannan p. farthing land, thus divided being a 3 penny land whereof Donald 1 farthing. 24 or £2
94. Donald Macintyre, junior—1 farthing.
95. John Rose—1 farthing.
96. John Macmillan—1 farthing.

97. Allan ban Macdonald—1 farthing.
98. Allan Macdonald alias Mac Coil Oig—1 farthing.
99. Angus Bane—1 farthing.
100. Dugald Macaulay—1 clitick.
101. John Morrison, and his son Donald—1 farthing.
102. Ewen Macdonald—2 farthings.
103. Widow Macdonald, 1 clitick, which she possesses gratis.

    8 tons of kelp are manufactured, all being east shore. No. 93 has been tenant for 28 years, but neither he nor the others had leases.

104. Gerrinish, Lachlan Macvurrich   24   0   0

    Gerrinish is a 3 penny land whereof he possesses 1 farthing.

105. Donald Macpherson—1 farthing.
106. Murdo Macvurrich—1 farthing.
107. Duncan Campbell—1 farthing.
108. Mr Samuel Macdonald—1 farthing.
109. Alexander Macdonald—1 farthing.
110. Donald Chisholm—1 farthing.

    8 tons of kelp are manufactured, all being east shore, none made on the west; allowed £1 15s per ton. Require annually to be supplied by the proprietor with meal.

111. Grogary and Stiligarry, Lieutenant Angus Macdonald   24   17   11

    Grogary a 2 penny land and Stiligarry a 4 penny land. Succeeded to a lease held by his late father expiring in 1804. Has power of disposing of kelp by payment of 10s to the proprietor. Makes 4 ton yearly

112. Neil Macphee, Hestimal   3   9   6

    Has no lease but been in possession for 25 years. States that his father, Francis, who is still alive, was promised by Clanranald neither to be removed nor his rent increased. They make 2 tons of kelp for which allowed £1 15s.

113. John Morrison, Change-house of Kilaulay   5   0   0

    Has a lease expires 1799.

114. Donald Chisholm, Caolis Lusa   7   0   0

    Donald's brother Roderick has a lease for

19 years from 1790, and 5 tons of kelp made for which allowed 2 gs. per ton, but as some of it is cut on very difficult rocks, expects an increase of the allowance.

115. Angus Macdonald, Miltown, Kildonan, and Gerravaltas, rent 59 6 7
These lands each 5 penny lands, in all 15 penny. Lease dated 2nd February, 1774, for 24 years in favour of Angus Macdonald, the tenant's father. He and his father make on the east shore about 22 tons kelp, for which privilege they pay 10s per ton. This is Flora Macdonald's family.

116. John Macdonald, Roanaglash at Loch Einord   4 0 0
Lease for 19 years from Whitsunday, 1796. Makes 2 tons of kelp, for which allowed £1 19s per ton.

117. Rev. George Monro, Drimisdale 40 0 0
These lands are 13 single 1d lands. Holds during his incumbency, with a certainty to his heirs for 19 years from 1789 at a reduced rent to them of £25. Makes 8 tons kelp, for which allowed 3 gs. per ton. Mr Monro also possesses 3 double penny lands of Howmore 40 0 0
Holds during his incumbency. No kelp made.

118. James Currie, Change-house of Ardmichael and point adjacent 5 0 0
Holds on a 30 years' lease from 1789. Makes 5 tons of kelp for the proprietor's behoof. Proprietor obliged to lay out £100 on buildings, for which tenant has to pay at the rate of 7½ per cent.

119. James Currie, Ormiclate 80 0 0
A four penny land. Sub-divided thus, the said James Currie, one half penny, one clitick.

120. Miss Macdonald of Clanranald —1 penny 1 farthing.
121. Donald Currie—1 farthing.
122. Rory Currie—1 farthing.
123. John Macdonald—1 farthing.

124. Angus Morrison—1 farthing.
125. John Maclellan—1 farthing.
126. Rory Macisaac—1 clitick.
127. Angus Macintyre—1 farthing.
128. Allan MacCormick—1 clitick.
129. Neil Macisaac—1 farthing.
> Tenants have no lease. Make of black and cast ware 25 tons of kelp, for which allowed £2 2s per ton, but complain as far too low, considering the difficulties in making and distance of carriage to place of shipment.

130. Alexander Maceachen, Howbeg 60 0 0
> A 3d land. Holds on lease of 25 years from 1789 Makes from cast seaware about 4 tons of kelp, for which allowed at the rate of three guineas. By missive from the late Clanranald, dated 9th September, 1789, is allowed £3 for preserving the fishing on the River Hough.

131. Donald Robertson, Mill of Howmore ... 30 0 0
> Possesses since 1787, so long as he serves the thirl with satisfaction. The thirl extends from the ford of Benbecula to the water of Roe Glass.

132. Lauchlan Currie, Lower Bornish 90 0 0
> Holds on lease for 25 years from 1793. Makes 34 tons of kelp, whereof from cast ware east coast 15 tons, remainder from cast and black ware.

133. Kenneth Beaton, Stoneybridge 80 0 0
> A four penny land, whereof he holds one farthing.

134. Angus Macdonald—1 farthing.
135. Donald Lyn—1 farthing.
136. Neil O'Henley—1 farthing.
137. John Macintyre—1 farthing.
138. John Macintyre, junior—1 farthing
139. Malcolm Macisaac—1 farthing.
140. Neil Macintyre—1 farthing.
141. John Macdonald—1 farthing.
142. Lachlan Mackinnon—1 farthing.
143. John Macisaac—1 farthing.
144. Malcolm Smith—1 farthing.
145. Allan Smith—1 farthing.

146. John Walker—1 farthing.
147. John Mackelaig—1 clitick.
148. Angus Macdonald—1 clitick.
149. Donald Macinnes—1 farthing.
    Make 30 tons of kelp from black and cast ware, for which allowed at the rate of two guineas, which owing to difficulty in cutting, making, and carrying to market, considered too small.

150. John Macdonald of Bornish. Feu 160 merks, and in lieu of commuted customs in all   24   9   5
151. Captain James Macdonald, Garrahellie   ...   25   0   0
    Occupies Drimore, under tack in 1789 to Donald Macaskill, surgeon in Uist, assigned to him. Is allowed to manufacture kelp for his own behoof, but only makes 1 ton on the east shore, except one year when he made 5 tons.
152. Mrs Macdonald, Garrahellie   25   0   0
    Her son Captain James, manages for her, and succeeds to the farm, if the lease, expiring in 1808, falls in by her death prior to that date. Seldom or never makes any kelp.
153. Hugh Macdonald, Killipheder   100   0   0
    An 8 penny land. Lease 15 years from 1788. Pays in addition to his rent 1 boll horse corn. Allowed two guineas per ton for his kelp.
159. The said Hugh Macdonald, Daliburgh   ...   70   0   0
    A double four penny land. Pays 1 boll horse corn. Possessor under tack in favour of his deceased brother Alexander Macdonald. On expiry of current lease, it may be prorogated for 12 years at an additional rent of £30—including both farms. Makes 70 tons of kelp for which allowed two guineas per ton—40 tons made on east coast, and remainder on west shores.
160. Colonel Alexander Macdonald, younger of Boisdale, Askernish, and the two Frobosts   80   0   0
    Twenty-two single penny lands. Holds on missive from 1786, during his father's

life. Some years makes no kelp, in other years a few tons.

161. Colin Macdonald of Boisdale 31 8 10
In name of feu-duty and public burdens. Roderick Chisholm, ground officer for South Uist, confirms the foregoing rental, and adds that the small tenants require a considerable supply of meal from the proprietor to support them while manufacturing the kelp.

Ranald George Macdonald of Clanranald, who succeeded to his great estates when a child, was brought up with an exaggerated idea of his importance and wealth. Bad management, inefficient supervision, and above all the fall in the value of kelp, proved fatal, and one after another of his great estates had to be sold, until nothing remained but Castle Tyrim and a few acres in Moidart. He lived to a great age, and at least on one occasion, when an octogenarian, visited the north and spent some days in Inverness. Within no great distance of each other live in the great Metropolis, the representatives of the once great houses of Glengarry, Clanranald, and Maclean, and worthy representatives they are, but alas, whose are their lands?—occupied by "the sons of little men," to use the words of Ossian.

THE MACDONALDS OF BORNISH.

The family of Bornish is described in the Old Statistical Account as the only resident heritors in South Uist. They, like Clanranald and Boisdale, have in turn disappeared. There were two Bornishes, Upper and Lower. Lower Bornish belonged to Clanranald, while Bornish Uachdar was feued out by Donald Macdonald of Moidart, Captain of Clanranald, to Ranald Vic Coil, by charter dated the 16th May, 1672, registered in the Books of Session at Edinburgh, on the 29th November, 1760. Infeftment followed on the 2nd December, registered in the General Register of Sasines at Edinburgh, on the 28th of August, 1683. The feu duty and casualties, latterly commuted into a fixed money payment of £24 5s 9d, originally consisted of 160 merks Scots, twelve ten stones butter, and five stones of cheese; and the entry of heirs and successors is fixed at two hundred merks Scots.

A century later brings us to John Macdonald, a stirring man in his day. By his first wife Bornish had Ranald Macdonald, who succeeded and was the last Bornish, also Dugald, Archibald, Christian, and Marion. His second wife was Catharine Macdonald, and there was serious litigation between her stepson, Ranald Macdonald, and herself. John Macdonald died very early, I think in January, 1803, leaving by his settlements, dated 8th December, 1802, only £20 per annum to his relict and certain allowances by way of furniture and stocking. John Macdonald seems to have entertained doubts as to the steadiness of his son, for he leaves considerable money provisions to his younger children, in the event that Ranald should dispose of his heritable property to a stranger, or sell the same, or allow it to be evicted by his creditors.

The disputes ended in Court, and protracted and ruinous litigation carried out, I fear, by pretended friends. Real friends in the country met and got matters referred to Major James Macdonald of Askernish and Mr Robert Brown, Clanranald's factor. These gentlemen, aided by mutual friends in the country, endeavoured to arrange differences, but ineffectually, and the Edinburgh lawyers had the business in hand from 1809 to 1814, terminating in the defeat and ruin of Ranald Macdonald, who, however, struggled on till 1837, when he is still found as the only resident heritor in South Uist. By 1845 Bornish, with all South Uist, had fallen into the hands of the unlamented Aberdonian Colonel Gordon, who wished to turn the island into a convict settlement, and was ready to dispose of it as such to Government, no doubt, in the meantime, clearing off the whole population, as was done in Clanranald's other islands of Rum and Canna, after their sale.

Mrs Macdonald appears to have had no relative or willing friend in Uist, except Major James Macdonald of Askernish, whom Bornish accused of initiating and keeping up the ill-feeling between him and his stepmother. The names of the Rev. Ranald Macdonald, priest at Bornish; Ranald Macdonald, shepherd; the Rev. William Arbuckle, minister of the Gospel in South Uist; Dugald Macdonald at Bornish; Hugh Macdonald, late at Killipheder; Malcolm Morrison, tenant in Bornish; Captain James Maclean, at Penmore of North Uist; Alexander Maceachin, tenant in Howbeg; John Macdonald, tenant in Lower Bornish; Neil Maclellan, tenant there; Angus O'Henley, tenant there; and Christian Macdonald, his wife, appear in course of the proceedings.

Old Bornish left £2 per annum to each of the two parish priests of South Uist and Benbecula for the use of the poor of their respective parishes, and nominated Hector Macdonald Buchanan, W.S., Captain James Macdonald of Askernish, Rev. Alexander Maceachin of South Uist, and James Macdonald of Borrodale, to be his executors and as tutors and curators to his daughter Marion during her pupillarity and minority.

The estate, which extended to about 1600 acres, is thus described in the old titles:—"All and haill the Town and lands of Bornish Uachkar, extending to seven pennies and a half lands of old extent; with houses, biggings, yards, woods, fishings, sheallings, mosses, muirs, parts, pendicles, and pertinents thereto belonging."

THE MACDONALDS OF BOISDALE.

The family of Boisdale only ran through four generations, but in the time of Colin Macdonald, the second, it attained great importance on the Clanranald estates and in the Isles. The first of the family was Alexander Macdonald, son of Donald Macdonald of Benbecula, afterwards of Clanranald, by his second marriage. He may have been in possession of Boisdale previously, but the charter in his favour by Ranald Macdonald, designed Younger of Clanranald, is dated the 26th of July, 1758, on which he was infeft in the same year. The description of the lands and mill thirlage, is in these words—

"All and whole the twenty penny lands of Boisdales, Smerclet, Kilbride, Eriskay and Lingay, with the corn mill lately built on the said lands, with grazings, sheillings, mosses, muirs, meadows, woods, fishings, islands, rocks, and whole parts, pendicles and pertinents of the said lands of Kilbride, Boisdale, Eriskay, Smerclate, and Lingay and miln aforesaid ; together with the teinds of the said lands so far as the said Ronald Macdonald of Clanranald had right thereto, with the mill lands, multures and sequels thereto belonging, and payable out of the lands lying between the Sound of Barra, and the water called Ryglass, particularly after-mentioned, viz., the lands of Kilpheder, Dalibrugh, Garryhualach, Askernish, South Frobost, North Frobost, Garryvaltos, and Milntown, belonging in property to Clanranald, together with the services performable by the tenants and possessors of the said lands to the mill, all lying within the parish of South Uist and shire of Inverness."

In some of the titles Boisdale is described as a five merk land of old extent, called Beustill or Boisdale.

The first Macdonald of Boisdale, forsaking the ancient faith, became a Protestant, and showed his zeal by driving his tenants to church with a staff of foreign importation, of yellow colour, hence the nickname applied to the new religion, "the religion of the yellow stick." Boisdale's unhappy persecution of his tenants ended, as is well known, in the expatriation of many of the flower of the Clanranald people, headed by John Macdonald of Glenaladale, who sympathised with them in their sad fate.

Alexander must have died early in 1768, perhaps before that year, for a precept of clare constat is granted in favour of Colin Macdonald, as eldest son and heir of Alexander Macdonald of Boisdale, on the 28th of May, 1768.

In the time of this Colin, second of Boisdale, the family had attained its height, he being almost supreme over the great Clanranald estates. Colin had numerous sisters and brothers, his father having married three times, and was himself married first to Margaret Campbell of Airds, and secondly to Isabella Campbell of Glen-Falloch. Miss Margaret Campbell's portion was 9000 merks. Colin died between 1799 and 1800, leaving a large family, of whom may be mentioned Hector, a Writer to the Signet, who feathered his nest handsomely through the love of litigation or imbecility of some of the island proprietors, and who assumed the additional name of Buchanan on his marriage with a Dumbartonshire heiress; Reginald, of Staffa, who succeeded by special destination to the baronetcy of Allanton, and, by marriage, to the Seton-Touch estates. "Old Staffa," as he was called, was well-known in Edinburgh society in its palmiest days, during the times of Sir Walter Scott and others. Margaret Macdonald, Boisdale, became the wife of Flora Macdonald's nephew, Angus of Milton. Their contract of marriage is dated the 10th of March, 1783.

Colin Macdonald was succeeded by his eldest son Alexander, third of Boisdale, afterwards a Lieutenant-Colonel. He married, contract dated 11th June, 1783, Marion Maclean of Coll. Before his father's death Boisdale was in difficulties, and the heavy provisions to his numerous brothers and sisters proved so burdensome while his father's trustees were in possession of the estate, that he had to place himself under trust, first in 1813 to William Dallas, W.S., and at a later period to Alexander Maclean of Coll, Hugh Macdonald, his eldest son, and Messrs Mackintosh and Macqueen, Writers to the Signet. He died in 1818 and was succeeded as representative of the family, but not in the estate, by Hugh Macdonald, fourth of Boisdale, who went to England, married, and, since the estate was sold to the Gordons, lost sight of.

Alexander Macdonald, third of Boisdale, besides his family burdens, was engaged in several litigations, particularly one with his uncle, Major James Macdonald of Askernish. There was also a keenly fought question with some of the Barra people about rights of fishing, which, as they related to the historic isle of Eriskay, may be briefly noticed here. The southern part of South Uist, including Eriskay, formed of old a part of the property of the MacNeills of Barra, and though the lands had long passed to the family of Clanranald, yet the Barra people continued to fish around and land their boats on Eriskay.

In 1809 Colonel Alexander Macdonald makes an application in the Court of Session against, among others, Ewen Ban Macdonald, grieve to MacNeil of Barra; Peter Robertson, schoolmaster of Barra; Finlay Mackinnon, ground officer there; Angus Macmillan, John O'Henley, Alexander Macneil, Neil Macinnes, and Neil Maclean, all in Barra, to prevent them from encroaching and roaming abroad upon Eriskay at pleasure, and injuring Boisdale's cattle and disturbing them, as also from fishing upon the banks adjacent to his islands. The respondents are said to admit Boisdale's right of property, but plead certain rights of use and wont, which Boisdale characterises "as savouring more of ancient depredations, than of the modern civilization of the Highlands and Islands of Scotland." He goes on to say that Eriskay lies in the channel between Barra and that part of South Uist belonging to him, but much nearer to South Uist, and through his predecessor's toleration, the Barra people were permitted to fish close inshore at Eriskay, the fish there being more numerous and of better quality. The sea around the island subsides greatly at ebb, leaving a considerable beach, which the Barra people utilised by hauling up their boats and taking sand worms for bait. Indeed they went so far as to kindle fires and pluck up grass by the roots, to prevent their lines from intertwining, and even erected huts.

Further, Boisdale contended that the Barra people had no right to fish nearer Eriskay than the mid channel with Barra, and stated that he was Depute-Admiral over the coasts of his own estate. He further stated that the respective fishing banks should be distinctly defined, for the present state of matters frequently ended in a fray and riot, and the loss of fishing tackle; and that in order to secure a kind of preference for the season South Uist and Barra began to set their lines in the favourite banks, two months before the season opens, taking them away from the cultivation of their lands.

It came out in the procedure that the old occupiers of Eriskay had emigrated, and those remaining knew nothing of its ancient history, or the old manner of possession.

Fishing seasons vary, but it may be said with truth that there will always be considerable fishing *ex adverso* of the old Boisdale lands and those of Barra. A new era for these long neglected localities will commence when the Mallaig line is opened, while the names of its unpatriotic opponents will be held in merited obloquy.

PRESENT AND PAST DISTRIBUTION OF LAND IN SOUTH UIST.

Men were of value in the islands of old as a fighting body, and consequently cherished by the proprietors. Later, in the palmy days of kelp, they still continued of use, but evil days came when the old proprietors were ruined, and new-comers looked for mere returns.

In other parts of the county sheep farming played havoc with the people, but in the isles, chiefly in the outer Hebrides, men had to make way for large cattle farms. The black cattle of the islands were not only pleasant to look at, but fetched high prices, hence the finest land became absorbed in a few large black cattle farms. Many of the people emigrated, doubtless the most active and energetic, while the sluggish and spiritless were planted either in poor near places, or amongst people already bordering on congestion. In South Uist the best lands face the Atlantic, and the west side of it was the first to suffer.

I will take Ormiclate, which has long been a large farm possessed by a single tenant, by way of illustration. In 1810 there were removed from it no fewer than 16 heads of families, perhaps 100 souls, viz., Ned Macisaac, Donald Curry, John Macdonald, Angus Morrison, Roderick Macdonald, Ranald Maceachin, Duncan Macisaac, James Maclean, Alexander Maclean, John Maclennan, John Macphee, John Maclean, John Macdonald, piper; Roderick Curry, James Curry, and John Macintyre. It will be observed that the place was the home of a piper.

There is now in Lower Bornish one tenant, but in the same year, 1810, no fewer than 26 tenants, or about 150 souls, were removed from Lower or Clanranald's Bornish, viz., Roderick Macdonald, Lachlan Curry, Angus Macmillan, John Maclellan, Roderick Macmillan, Neil Macintyre, Donald Macmillan, Donald Macdonald, senior, John

Morrison, Donald Macisaac, Angus Macisaac, John Macdonald, — Macintyre, John Macdonald, Donald Macdonald, junior, John Macdonald, junior, Archibald Maclellan, Widow Curry, Roderick Buie, Donald Maceachan, Roderick Maclellan, Angus Mackintosh, John Mackintosh, Angus Macintyre, John Macmillan, and Donald Maclellan.

In Kilaulay and Linique there appears to be now in all 11 occupants, while no less than 35 were removed in 1810, viz., John Mackinnon, Ewen Mackinnon, Lachlan Mackinnon, Widow Dugall Macdonald, Roderick Macisaac, Alexander Maceachin, Farquhar Campbell, John Morrison, Angus Campbell, Donald Mackinnon, Donald Macisaac, John Macphee, Alexander Maceachin, senior, William Burke, Alexander Macdonald, Roderick Macisaac, senior, Donald Macisaac, Neil Macphee, Angus Macdonald, Ranald Macdonald, Allan Macdonald, Malcolm Macinnes, Lachlan Macdonald, Alexander Macaulay, Lachlan Macaulay, John Macdonald, Donald Macdonald, senior, Donald Macinnes, Donald Macdonald, second, Neil Macphee, junior, John Mackinnon, Alexander Macdonald, Neil Macphee, senior, Donald Macphee, and John Macphee.

The townships of Liniclate and Balgarva are much as they were in the beginning of the century, numbering 41 at present, as compared with 44 in 1810; Balvannich and Dungannich numbering 31 against 32 in 1810.

Stoneybridge is notoriously congested, having at present 37 tenants against 18 in 1810, while the lands have been curtailed, and added to Ormiclate.*

In 1810, Lieutenant Angus Macdonald of the 91st Regiment, Colin Macdonald, at Garryvaltos, sons of the deceased Captain Angus Macdonald of Millton; Margaret Jane, Penelope, and Isabella Macdonald, their sisters, are summoned out of Millton; but this historic family were not actually dispossessed until a few years later.

Two great improvements have been carried out since

* It is a matter of great satisfaction to observe (November 1896) that the sadly congested holding of Stoneybridge receives considerable enlargement of holdings from the Crofters Commission out of this Ormiclate.   C. F. M.

South Uist was sold, the one being the shutting out of an inlet of the sea which practically made two islands of South Uist. This very desirable improvement in banking and draining was of the greatest importance, not only adding to the producing area, but ridding considerable tracts from sea water which came in with every tide. It is to be feared that this great operation has not been well attended to of late years, nor has the efficient keeping open of certain valuable main drains. The other improvement, also it is feared now getting neglected, was the planting of bent on the west coast machars, which not only gave considerable sustenance, and added greatly to the beauty of the coast, but effectually stopped sand drifts. In 1794, the sea had encroached so far that a reduction of rent was made, while the ancient road by the Atlantic shore, from Nunton to Ormiclate, had become in part obliterated.

As I previously said, in the Outer Hedrides all the best land faces the Atlantic, to which it slopes gently with a south-western aspect from the mountains to the sea.

With security of tenure, a better distribution of the good land, the opening up and developing of the fisheries, the speedy access to the southern markets by the Mallaig Railway, which last has been so villainously impeded during the last four years, a new era of comfort and prosperity ought and will doubtless arise for the long suffering but lovable and orderly inhabitants of the Isles.

A SOUTH UIST CENTENARIAN.

I may mention that in 1892 when in South Uist, I saw Neil Maceachin at Howbeg, who said that his age then was "five twenties and one," though those about him made out that he was only ninety-seven. Neil was well acquainted with Margaret Macdonald, sister of Clanranald of the '45, commonly called "Miss Peggy Ormiclate," whose father was born as far back as 1692. It was to verify statements to this effect that I called at Neil's bothy, and I had it from himself. He was not only well up in the Clanranald history but in that of Flora Macdonald's house of Millton. It was this Neil who gave my friend, Father John Mackintosh of Bornish some of the verses on the sad death by drowning of Captain Angus Macdonald of Millton, which will be found in one of the volumes of the *Transactions of the Gaelic Society of Inverness.*

I select the following from my note-book, taken down at the time :—

"On Tuesday, the 28th of June, 1892, I attended a meeting in course of my canvass at Howmore, in South Uist. Recollecting that I had papers showing that Miss Margaret Macdonald, sister of the young Clanranald of the '45, was living at Ormiclate as late as the year 1825, whose father Ranald Macdonald, in his youth styled "of Benbecula," was born as far back as 1692, I told Father John Mackintosh of Bornish, if there was any old person in the district who had seen Miss Margaret, that I should like to have an interview with such person. He enquired of people assembled at the meeting, when a middle-aged man named Macdonald came forward and stated that he believed his mother was acquainted with Miss Macdonald, whom he described as "Miss Peggy Clanranald." His house was some miles distant but not far from the high road, and in case he might not be there before my arrival, he described the situation. Upon driving up to the house I took to be the one indicated, I saw at the door a person who did not look old enough to be Mrs Macdonald, and the place altogether looked inferior to what I would expect as the residence of my well-dressed and intelligent informant. I asked her if she was Mrs Macdonald and she said "No," but pointed to an inner room, upon entering which I saw a very old man, sitting alone by the fireside, who seemed very much astonished at my appearance.

"I saw then that I was in the wrong house, but the man being apparently very old, I thought I would question him. He gave his name as Neil Maceachin, and that he was 101 years old. At this stage the woman contradicted him and said he was only 97, upon which he stated, striking his staff on the floor (all the conversation being in Gaelic) "No, no, five twenties and one." Stated that he had been in "South Uist all his days." Did he know Miss Peggy Clanranald who lived at Ormiclate? Answered, "Perfectly; she was an old woman when I was a comparatively young man, but I have seen and spoken to her frequently. She was an active energetic person whom I used to see constantly going about and very much thought of as the only member of the Clanranald family who remained and constantly resided in Uist." By this time the apartment had become full of people, who all seemed to be acquainted with my name. I gave the old man five shillings, with which he was very pleased, and he attempted, with the aid of his staff, to rise while thanking me, but failed in the attempt. On going outside, Macdonald came up breathless to say that he had seen his mother, who had told him that she recollected Miss Peggy quite well, and wished me to go with him to his house, but as his mother was described as only 87, and as I had already got the connecting link of information I wished—time also being pressing—I was obliged to continue my journey, though probably losing some interesting fragments of Clanranald and South Uist story."

XXIII.—PARISH OF BARRA.

THE MACNEILLS OF BARRA AND ITS PEOPLE.

THE modern description of the estate of Barra as contained in the last MacNeill's titles ran thus—

"All and whole my lands and estate of Barra, comprehending the particular lands and others following, viz., the Island of Barra comprehending the rooms and lands of Skirsall, Oligarry, Killbar, Keil, Vaslinclead, Grin, Quire, Allistill, Balnacraig, Buron, Tangistill; with the Islands of Watersay, Passay, Mingilay, Sandray, Bernera, and Friday; also haill other little islands thereto belonging, with milns, miln lands, multures and sequels thereof, and tiends, parsonage, and vicarage of the said lands, so far as the proprietor had right thereto, and with woods, fishings, grazings, sheillings, mosses, muirs, meadows, and hail parts, pendicles, and pertinents of the said lands whatsomever, all lying within the parish of Barra and Sheriffdom of Inverness."

This description may be contrasted with an ancient one which ran thus, establishing that the MacNeills at one time also possessed the southern part of South Uist, viz.—

"All and whole the lands of Barray, Watersay, Sandray, Phappy, Migillay, Berneray, the Isles of Ferray and Killigilt, and hail remanant lands and islands adjacent to the said Isle of Barray, called the Pennicle Isles of Barray; and all and whole the lands called Tirrung of Degastill, lying in South Uist, and of old occupied by Macniel of Barray, Tirrungs of Finday, Kilbarry, Niclein, Grangeburrow, the Tirrung of Kelles and Hannugastill, with the Castle of Keismill; and all and sundry other castles, towers, fortalices, manor places, mills, woods, fishings, tofts, crofts, muirs, marshes, islands, lochs, pasturages, parts, pendicles, annexis, connexis, and pertinents thereof whatsomever, pertaining to the said Isles of Barray and remanent isles above specified, or possessed by the said Macniel, all lying within the Sheriffdom of Inverness, and now united, annexed, and incorporated in ane haill and free barony called the barony of Barray."

The MacNeill family are of great antiquity, allowing largely for such ridiculous exaggeration, such as that there were 33 Roderick MacNeills in succession. The first known as having a charter was named Gilleonan, found in 1427, but his father's name Roderick, and grandfather's Murdoch, are also recorded. Besides making a good appearance in the field as fighting men, the MacNeills were, as might be expected, quite at home on the sea and a terror to all their neighbours. In 1745 the chief would have joined Prince Charles were he not led and dominated by his superior, Sir Alexander Macdonald of Sleat. Barra's sympathies however were so well known that he was kept in confinement for some time in London. Sir Alexander's letter to the effect that he had no wish Barra should commit himself, involving forfeiture, is much to his credit, seeing that as superior the estate might fall into his own hands.

This MacNeill, or his son Roderick, was a Captain in the Fraser Highlanders and was killed at Quebec in 1759.

The superiority of Barra, some £40 Scots, still forms, I understand, part of the Macdonald estates.

Sir Walter Scott in one of his poems, referring to the Highland and Island chiefs, couples the MacNeills with the Mackintoshes—

"Macneil of the Islands, and Moy of the lake,
To honour, to justice, and vengeance awake."

The people, if the land, including all the islands, extending to 22,000 acres, were evenly distributed, are not in excess, but at present, were it not for occasional good fishing seasons, many are ill off, and the east coast fishermen who frequent Castlebay and other parts, carrying with them as they do their labour and sustenance, spending little or nothing, do not contribute to the well-being or prosperity of the people. It may be hoped, however, that when a regular market all the year over is opened by the Mallaig railway, the people by their fishing, including lobsters, cockles, and other shell-fish, will be permanently benefitted.

The MacNeills, like the Clanranalds, were ruined by the supercession of kelp. The last of them, who failed in almost every scheme he undertook while proprietor, distinguished himself as a soldier after the sale, which took place about 1838. He was, however, singularly kind to the people, and his and his family's name are held in reverent respect to this day. A good illustration of this has fallen under my personal observation and deserves to be remembered. My devoted friend and supporter, Mr Michael Buchanan, accepted my invitation to London chiefly that he might with his own eyes see the house where General MacNeill lived, and died in 1863.

A very interesting account of the Barra family by that talented clergyman, the Rev. A. Maclean Sinclair, of Prince Edward Island, shows that Roderick MacNeill, residing at Vernon River in that island, a tall, good-looking, and pleasant man, father of six sons, in good circumstances, now represents Barra. He is a son of Lachlan, who died in 1892, aged 73, son of Rory Og, who died in 1850, son of Roderick, styled of Brevaig, which Roderick, then an old man, emigrated in 1802. Brevaig was a son of Gilleonan, younger son of that Roderick Macneill of Barra who obtained a Royal charter of Barra in 1688.

I look back with pleasure on my visits to Barra, and my intercourse with its interesting people, not the least being a visit to Eoligarry and its worthy occupants of the kith and kin of Clan Chattan.

I must now leave the Isles and take a long stride to Badenoch, and Strathspey.

BACK TO THE MAINLAND.

XXIV.—PARISH OF LAGGAN.

LAGGAN, the largest of the Badenoch parishes, made, probably from its altitude, until within the last 25 years, less progress perhaps than any other parish in the county. This was further to be expected, considering who were the former leading owners. These, fortunately for the prosperity of the district, have disappeared, unhonoured and unlamented.

The Comyns, the oldest possessors of whom there is authentic note, grudged even the trifling portion assigned to the Church.

In 1260, however, a compromise is finally made whereby Walter Comyn grants to the Bishop of Moray a davoch of land, thus described—" One davoch of the land of Logy Kenny, to wit Edenlogyn, and also both Abyrcarden and the land on which is situated the Church of Logy Kenny, which land lies between two streams, to wit Kyllene and Petenachy." These lands were afterwards known as the four ploughs or davoch of Aberarder, and continued with the Bishops until shortly before the Reformation, when acquired by the Grants, who had an eye far and near for any Church lands going. The boundaries of the Church lands can only be arrived at through the adjacent properties, viz., Kyleross to the south-west, and MacCoul to the north-east. The streams Kyllene and Petenachy are not now known as such, but there are several falling into Loch Laggan on the west side.

The subsequent ownership of Aberarder, in Laggan, may be given in brief. After remaining with the Grants for about 150 years, the three wester ploughs were feued in or about 1698 to Macdonald of Achnacoichan, with a feu of £3 15s to the laird of Grant.

Shortly after, they were acquired by Lachlan Mackintosh of Mackintosh, proprietor of MacCoul to the north-east, also of the whole lands south of Loch Laggan facing Aberarder, and were *inter alia* gifted by Mackintosh to the Macphersons, under return, in the event of failure in certain acknowledgments and services which, by the forfeiture of Cluny after the 'Forty-five, were swept away by the House of Lords reversing the Court of Session as inconsistent with the times. Restored in 1788, the lands of Aberarder still remain part of the Cluny estate, but the Mackintoshes received neither pecuniary price for them nor the equivalent stipulated. Such was the act of the Hanoverian Government. The person who continued loyal was deprived of his property, while the attainted's descendants got an ordinary unrestricted right in place of one burdened, restricted, and qualified.

The other quarter of Aberarder was also feued by the Grants to the Macdonalds of Gellovie, and afterwards acquired by Cluny, who possesses the whole four ploughs of Aberarder, a very beautiful estate, though narrow, with the great natural curiosities of the Loch, the Posts, and the Window of Corrarder.

While under the Forfeited Estate Commissioners there occurred that frightful depopulation of Aberarder, the full particulars of which I detailed in the *Celtic Magazine*, No. XXXIII., Vol. II., p. 418, many years ago. All I then wrote I now re-affirm, merely adding that the several scattered green oases of former cultivation so striking amid the vast extent of heather, as seen from Ardverikie, are still prominent, and remain a standing protest against the infamous removal of the people.

The name of Ardverikie has been prominent in Laggan for the last fifty years, but originally it was a pendicle of the great davoch of Gellovie, which davoch, including MacCoul and Inverwidden, stretched along the whole east side of Loch Laggan, from the Gulbin to the Pattaig, and on the west side from the Pattaig to Camuskillen, or rather the stream which falls into the lake at the inn of Loch Laggan.

By planting, building, and draining, this davoch of Gellovie has been immensely improved, beautified, and increased in value since it came into the possession of Sir John Ramsden in 1870.

Lachlan Mackintosh, younger son of Malcolm the tenth Mackintosh, commonly called Lachlan Badenoch, acquired the lands of Gellovie in the latter part of the fifteenth century, and his son Malcolm received a precept from Alexander, second Earl of Huntly, as son of Lachlan Mackintosh, in the following terms:—

"George Gordoune, Earl of Huntlie, and Lord of Baidzenach, To our well beloved Alexander Gordon of Muldare, Alexander Mackintosh of Rothiemurchus, John, Donald Mackintosh's son, Donald, Angus Mackintosh's son, and Alexander, John Reid's son, and either of them conjointly and severally our baillies in that part irrevocably constituted. Greeting—We command and charge you that on sight hereof ye immediately give and deliver state and heritable sasine of all and sundry the lands of Gallovie with the pertinents to Malcolm Mackintosh, as son of the late Lachlan Mackintosh, according to the tenor of his charter, by delivery of earth and stone as use is. For the doing whereof to you and either of you conjointly and severally by the tenor hereof, we commit our irrevocable and full power, saving the rights of everyone. And in token of such sasine delivered by you, append your seal to these presents in the second tail after our seal. Given under seal at Newark upon Spey, on the twentieth day of April, in the year of our Lord, one thousand four hundred and ninety-two."

Malcolm Mackintosh was infeft on the 28th of September, the same year, by William de Duffus, Presbyter of the Diocese of Moray, Notary Public, by Imperial authority— Finlay vic Keir, William Charteris, Gillechrist vic Aonas, John Duff, John, Alexander's son, Donald, Angus' son, Farquhard, William's son, Donald vic William, John Maclean's son, and Patrick, William's son, Mair, with others being witnesses. Dying without issue, Malcolm was succeeded by his brother William, afterwards of Mackintosh, the superiority of the lands remaining with the family of Mackintosh to this day, and now the oldest possession for which there is an unbroken series of title in Badenoch.

The names of some of the possessors of Gallovie nearly 300 years ago may be given and, perhaps later on, those of the whole heads of families, lairds, tenants, cottars, and dependants in Badenoch generally. At the period in question, surnames were not generally used—Lachlan Mackintosh of Borlum, principal tenant of Benchar, Clune, and Gallovie; Ewen Vic Allan Roy there, Neil vic Robert there, Dugald vic Neill vic Coil there, Dugald vic Neill in Kinloch, William Dhu vic Coil there, Donald Our vic Coil there, Duncan vic Ewen there, John Vic Coil Roy there, John vic Conchie vic William, in MacCoul; Allan vic Conchie vic William there, Angus vic William vic Coil there, and John Macphail there.

For a very long period there were no people living towards the head of the Spey beyond Garvamore. By the authority after quoted it would, however, appear that there were in 1637 at least one family living at Mealgarbh, at the foot of Corryaraick, who carried on business as wood merchants in the Brae of Lochaber. It is understood that Braeroy is well adapted for planting, but Sir John Ramsden's attempts above Garvabeg and elsewhere in Glenshiero have not hitherto been entirely satisfactory. Want of drainage and sheep grubbing have well nigh deprived the lands of profitable use—

"We, George Marquis of Huntlie, Earle of Enzie, Lord Gordoun, and Badenoch, gives our full power and Commission to our lovite William Mackintosh of Torcastell, to attach, take and apprehend all and whatsoever tymber of whatsoever kynd, sort, or qualitie, cuttit in my wood of Lochaber, or in any part thereof, found with whatsomever person or persons dwelling upon any part of our land, within the Lordship of Lochaber or any part of the same, carrying and transporting the same, either by water, or land, to brugh or mercat (excepting such as be's found with our men of Sliesgarve, called Donald, John, and Allan vic Aonas Vors, who has our warrant already for cutting of wood, and carrying off the same, to burgh or market upon their own proper horses and no otherwise), In witness whereof we have subscribed these presents with our hand at Huntlie the twenty-six day of September, 1637.   (Signed)   "HUNTLYE."

From this it would appear that there was considerable wood on the Gordon Lochaber estates and a market therefor in Badenoch and elsewhere.

In the parish of Laggan there is a good deal of the highest land in Scotland, some peaks rising over 3700 feet in height, while its waters flow east, west, and south, finding their way into the sea at Speymouth, Fort-William, and Dundee. The office of forester was at one time much appreciated, and, like that of bailie, often led to better things. Questions of great hardship arose in Atholl and Aboyne in especial, in connection with rights of forestry, as is well known to the readers of old legal Court decisions.

Ben Alder was a very ancient forest and, not thriving under sheep, has reverted to its former occupancy. The east portion of Gallovie, known as Garryvounuck, adjoining as it did the old Ben Alder forest, naturally fell into similar use.

As I have not observed the original sasine to Macpherson of Cluny, I do not know its date, but have concluded that the original grant, certainly after 1600, of the three ploughs of Cluny also included the extensive grazings on Ericht side, extending from Dalinlongart to the Perthshire march.

Cluny having these grazings would naturally wish to extend his borders and rights. Though Ben Alder forest, properly so called, lay adjoining, and did not belong to Cluny till 1791, yet some right or interest in Garryvounuck was highly desirable, even though of a temporary nature. So Cluny was glad to accept the dignified office of forester to Mackintosh by a written grant, as may be seen by a perusal of the following attested document, dated 31st of May, 1678. Allan Macdonald, sometime possessor or wadsetter of Gallovie, apparently wished to include Garryvounuck, which lay immediately to the east, within his possession, and the matter was referred by Mackintosh and Gallovie, to William Mackintosh in Blargie, Lachlan Mackintosh of Balnespick, John Macpherson of Shirrobeg, and John Macpherson, in Kinloch, as arbiters. The arbiters, with the exception of Macpherson, Kinlochlaggan, met at

Dunachton on the 31st of May, 1678, and these notes were taken by a Notary Public :—

"At Dunachton, the last day of May, 1678, anent the reference referred by the Right Honourable Lauchlane Mackintoshie of Torchastell, and Allan Macdonald, sometime of Gallovie, on the one and other parts, of the date the   day of   1678 years, to William Mackintosh in Blairagie, Lachlan Mackintosh of Balnespick, John Macpherson in Shirobeg, and John Macpherson in Keanloich to declare what sheillings and grazings did belong to the tenants, residenters, and inhabitants and residenters of the half davoch of Gallovie, sometime possessed by said Allan Macdonald, who had passed minute of the wadset right of Gallovie with the said Lachlan thereanent, as at length specified in the said minute.

"Compeared the said William Mackintosh in Blairagie, Lachlan Mackintosh of Balnespick, and the said John Macpherson in Shiro. The said John Macpherson in Shiro deponed on solemn oath, as he who hath passed three score ten years, that he did never see a tenant or possessor of the half davoch land of Gallovie, sometime possessed by the said Allan, to have sheilled on the sheilling called Loupvain since his memory, neither heard formerly any in Gallovie claim right thereto but the said Allan; and that he remembered above 40 years since that William Mackintosh of Strone and Angus, his brother, who lived in Gaskinloan, to have sheilled on the said sheilling called Loupvain, and that by the permission of the deceased Andrew Macpherson of Clownie, as he who had power of Frosterrie (sic) from the laird of Mackintosh to be froster (sic) of the forest of Gairvouneig, and thereafter did see Donald MacAonas, vic Iain Dhu, who possessed Inverwidden, sheal on the said sheilling, and that he also heard that the sheilling of Ailtan Dhu-na-Creallein did belong to the forest foresaid.

"William Mackintosh of Blaragie compearing thereafter, being sworn, deponed that since he had memory, remembered his father and uncle to have sheilled on the said Loupvain, as also heard that others was by the permission of the said deceased Andrew Macpherson of Clunie, as being froster to the Laird Mackintosh of the forest of Gairvouneig, to which forest Ailtean Dhu-na-Creallein did belong.

"Lachlan Mackintosh of Balnespick being interrogate, answered that he was not old, nor nothing known to him of the said sheillings as to his own knowledge, but depones that he heard from this present Duncan Macpherson of Clunie that he had as yet in his custody a power of frosterie, which was granted by one of the Lairds Mackintosh to his Guidshir Andrew, as a forester of Gairvouneig, and that he heard the like report from others.

"This deponed day, month, and place foresaid in presence of John Macpherson of Dalraddie, Thomas Macpherson of Killyhuntly, and me David Cumming, writer hereof, and several others that were present who could not write.   (Signed)   "L. McKINTOSHE.

"John Macpherson in Shiro, and William Mackintosh in Blargie with our hands at the pen led by the Notar under written. Ita est David Cumming, Notarius Publicus mandatis scribere nescien teste manu propria sub."   (Signed)   "D. CUMMING,
"Notarius Publicus ut Asserunt."

By the marriage of William, son of Lachlan Mackintosh of Gallovie, commonly called "Lachlan Badenoch," with Isabella Macniven, the heiress of Dunachton, the possessions of the Mackintoshes were much enlarged. Later on, through the murder of William Mackintosh at Strathbogie, Lachlan Mor, his son and successor, received a great increase of estate from the Earl of Huntly in form of assythment.

This occurred in 1568, and thereafter Mackintosh was owner of Gallovie, Dunachton, Kincraig, South Kinrara, Dalnavert, part of Glenfeshie, Benchar, Clune, etc. Another Mackintosh, ancestor of the Balnespicks, possessed the three Gasks in Laggan, being the only heritors, besides the Gordons and Bishops of Moray, in all Laggan prior to 1600.

Lachlan Mor Mackintosh, assisted by his clever and energetic spouse, Agnes Mackenzie of Kintail, raised the family of Mackintosh to great power and influence, all of their seven sons being provided in landed estate, and each of the five daughters making good marriages.

The Gordon family could not endure to see the rising power of the Mackintoshes, neither, it may be well supposed, did the Mackintoshes bear any good feelings to Huntly.

In 1572, the Gordons were again forfeited, and their opponents were glad of the opportunity of crippling their power. Lachlan Mackintosh, after the death of the Earl of Huntly, from whom he had received the assythment lands, and to whom he had to give his bond, saw his opportunity, and made a bold stroke for supremacy in Badenoch. He had powerful friends and succeeded in obtaining from the Regent Morton a gift of the 60 davochs of Badenoch, which unfortunately, did not pass the Seals, and fell to the ground. After this the Mackintoshes and Gordons were, with rare intervals, bitter and hereditary opponents.

In fairness it must be admitted that in the view of the Gordons the Regent Morton gift was a deep offence, and the present Lord Huntly is really to be admired when, considering that his own family was passed over in favour of an heir female, he in his book of Aboyne criticises Mackintosh in this business.

Modernizing the old spelling, the gift, which is endorsed by the single word " Macyntoshie," is in these words—

"Our Sovereign Lord, with advice, consent, and authority of his right trusty cousin, James, Earl of Mortoun, Lord of Dalkeith, etc., Regent to his Majestie, his realm and lieges, ordains a charter to be made under his Great Seal in due form; To his loved Lachlan Mackintoshie of Dunachton, his heirs and assignees, of the heritable gift in feu farm of all and sundry the lands underwritten. That is to say, Garvamore, Garvabeg, Killarchill, Crathiecroy, Crathiemor, Shirromore, Shirrobeg, Tirladoun, The Ord and Strathmashie, Blargiebeg, Blargiemor, Gasklone, Gaskbeg, Gaskmor, Catclack, Breackachie, Pitgoun, Clony, Owie, Cowothilly, Nessintullie, Croubinbeg, Croubinmore, Daleanach, Pressmuckerach, Ettridge, Invernahaven, Foyness, Noidmore, Noidbeg, Biallidbeg, Biallidmor, Ye Strone, Ballachroan, Pitmain, Kingussie, Ardbrylach, Ruthven, Killyhuntly, Invertromie, Corrarnstilbeg, Corrarnstilmor, Countellaive, Farletter, Invereshie, Invermarkie, Raitbeg, Raitmor, Raitmeanach, the two parts of Pittourie, Pitchern, Dalraddie, Kinraramor, Gortan na Creich, Lynvuilg, Garlinmor, Dellifour, Lynvuilgmor, Rewymor, and the two Tullochs, with the milns, multures, woods, fishings, towns, fortalices, manor places, outsetts, parts, pendicles, tenants, tenandries, and service of free tenants of all and sundry the said lands, and all the pertinents lying within the Lordship of Badenoch and Sheriffdom of Inverness. Which all and sundry lands above written, with the milns, multures, woods, fishings, towns, fortalices, manor places, outsetts, parts, pendicles, tenants, tenandries, and service of free tenants thereof, and all the pertinents, pertained to George, some time Earl of Huntlie, Lord Gordon, and Badenoch, heritable of before, holden by him immediately of our Sovereign Lord, and now pertains to His Majesty, and are vacant in his hands by reason of escheat, through process and doom of forfeiture orderly led against the said George, some time Earl of Huntlie, for certain crimes of treason and leze-majestie committed by him of the which he was convicted in Parliament, as in the process and doom of forfeiture orderly led and deduced against him thereupon at more length is contained – To be holden and To Hold all and sundry the lands above specified, at length to be mentioned and engrossed in the precepts and charter to pass hereupon, with all and sundry milns, multures, woods, fishings, towns, fortalices, manor-places, outsetts, parts, pendicles, tenants, tenandries and services of free tenants thereof, and all the pertinents, to the said Lachlan Mackintosh, his heirs, and assignees, of our sovereign lord and his successors, in feu farm and heritage for ever; By all rights meiths and divisions as the same lie in length and breadth in woods, plains, etc., mills, multures, etc., halking hunting, fishing, with Court plaint, herezeld, bluidwitt, and *mercheta muilerum*, unlaws, amerciaments, and escheats of said Courts, with common pasture, free ish and entry; and with all and sundry other commodities freedoms, etc., freely, quietly, etc, without any revocation etc., Payand therefor yearly the said Lachlan Mackintosh, his heirs and assignees, to our Sovereign Lord and his successors, the sum of two hundred pounds usual money of this realm, at two terms in the year Whitsunday and Martinmas in winter by equal portions, and also the heirs of the said Lachlan Mackintosh doubling the said feu farm, the first year of their entry to the lands above written with the pertinents as use is, of feu farm allenarlie; and that precepts be directed orderly hereupon. Subscribed by the said Lord Regent at Edinburgh ye 18th day of December, the year of God 1572 years."

(Signed) "JAMES, REGENT, GRANTS."

On the same day, Mackintosh's lands of Benchar, Clune, Kincraig, Dunachton's Kinrara-na-choille, Dalnavert, Coignafearn, Essich, Duntelchaigs, Tordarroch, and Bochrubin, formerly held of the Earl of Huntly, are by a warrant from the Regent Morton to be held in future direct of the Crown.

The Gordon rental in the parish in 1677, amounted, as hereafter detailed, to 2675½ merks, or under £150 sterling. This may be contrasted with the rental when these lands were offered for sale in 1829.

By 1677, some of the lands had been feued on a money payment, attour services. The Chamberlain then was Duncan Macpherson of Cluny, who had succeeded Coll Patrick Grant, tutor of Grant. There were two mills in Kingussie Parish, at Kingussie and at Nuide, one in the parish of Alvie, at Dalraddy, but none in the parish of Laggan. There was a mill at Gallovie at an early date, and after 1677 mills at Strathmashie, Crathy, Cluny, and Aberarder.

	M.	S.	D.
Garvamore pays yearly at Martinmas one hundred and thirty merks	130	0	0
Crathiemore and Garvabeg	420	0	0
Shirromore	135	0	0

Shirrobeg	75	0 0
Tirfadoune	189	0 0
Druminord	90	0 0
Stramashie and Iosal an Ord	200	0 0
Blaragiebeg	75	0 0
Blaragiemor	95	0 0
Gergask	107	6 8
Ovie paid yearly 235 merks, and the possessor thereof complaining to the Noble Marquis that he would not possess the same unless he got a consideration and courtesie, the land not being worth the said duty, whereupon the said Noble Marquis ordained certain gentlemen to visit the said land what it was able to pay, which accordingly they did, and esteemed the said lands of Ovie not to be worth of yearly rent but 200 merks	200	0 0
Breackachie	150	0 0
Crubenmore and Presmuckerach	220	0 0
Crubenbeg...	130	0 0
Nessintullich possessed by Donald vic Soirle his son	105	0 0
The other half of Nessintullich possessed by Soirle	110	0 0
The half davoch of Kylarchill possessed by Cluny ought to pay yearly	80	0 0

FEUS.

Cluny pays yearly for the lands of Clunie and Gaskinloan, with the plough of Kylarchill	164	3 4
Merks	2675	10 0

The following significant docquet to the rental may be given :—

"It is to be remembered that there is noted that Cluny possesses the half davoch of Kylarchill which ought to pay four score merks yearly which sum is included in the total of the above specified rental, yet Cluny never paid the said four score merks to Arradoull, or me the said Lieutenant-Colonel Grant while I was Chamberlain, which the entering Chamberlain is in like manner to consider."

        (Signed)   "PK. GRANT.
                "   "D. MCPHERSON."

By this date the Macphersons began to show up. Cluny

will pay nothing for Kylarchill, and Ovie, apparently with justice, complains of being over-rented.

The following is the rental in 1829 when the Gordon estates in Badenoch came into the market:—

	£	s.	d.
Moy and Kyleross...	185	0	0
Garvamore...	100	0	0
Garvabeg, Shirrabeg, Kylarchill and Crathiecroy	600	0	0
Shirramor and Sheallings	100	0	0
Hill grass in Drummin which formerly belonged to Ovie and Achmore	60	0	0
Dalchully, Tirfadoune, and Blargybeg...	250	0	0
Crathiemor and Mill, Balmishaig and Coul	197	0	0
Blargymor, Island Dhu, Croftcarnil, and Croftcroy	120	0	0
Gergask	60	0	0
Gaskbeg	30	0	0
Gaskmore	90	0	0
Corriebuie Hill, common to the three last places	—		
Balgoun and Shealling of Aultdearg	120	0	0
Strathmashie, Druminord and Mill	295	0	0
Ovie and Achmore without Drummin Grazings	100	0	0
Breackachie, Coraldie, and Corrachie...	210	0	0
Little Dalwhinnie...	20	0	0
Shauval	55	0	0
Nessintully...	90	0	0
Crubinmor...	75	0	0
Crubinbeg...	75	0	0
Pressmuckerach and Druminlaggan, with the whole hill grazings in Drumouchter, divided as sheallings among these and the six preceding farms...	165	0	0
Cockburn Croft being a small piece of hill grazing on the Athole march lying on the east side of the military road	10	10	0
Total	£3057	10	0

Thus the rental had increased twenty fold since 1677, but what did that matter? At Duke Alexander's death, he owed one creditor, the Royal Bank of Scotland, the enormous sum of £450,000.

I now give a list of the heads of families in Laggan in 1679, and perhaps some of the few Macphersons now in Laggan may discover therein traces of their ancestors—

Cluny.—Duncan Macpherson of Cluny, James Macpherson there, William vic Iain vic Andrew there, Dougal Oig there, John Macgillivray there, Donald Mac Coil Oig there, John Miller there, John Miller his son there, Allister Macgillivray there, Kenneth Mor there, Angus Mac Ian Mor there, William Mac Ian vic William there, William Mac David, tailor there, Allister Maclennan there, Duncan Mac Coil Oig there, Donald Mac Ewen Dhu vic Keir there.

Ovie.—Ewen Macpherson of Ovie, Malcolm Macpherson there, William Mac Coil there, Allister Mac Hamish vic Lachlan there, Allister Mac Coil Kier there, John Mac Coil Oig there.

Druminord.—Angus Macpherson in Druminord, Angus bain Maclachlan there, Duncan Mac-a-Gowin there.

Strathmashie.—Donald Macpherson in Strathmashie, John bain Mac Hamish vic Iain Ban there, Donald Mac Coil Oig in Heave (?), William Macpherson there, Allister reoch vic Iain ban vic Allister reoch there, Finlay Mac Iain vic Mhurich there, Finlay Macpherson in Strathmashie, Donald Macpherson there, Murriach Macpherson there, John Macpherson there, Donald ban Mac Soirle vic Quian there Allister Gow there.

Tirfadoun.—Malcolm Mac Ewen in Tirfadoun, John Mac Gillechallum there, Duncan ban Mac Soirle there, Donald Mac Finlay vic Homas there, John Mac Coinneach Roy there, Duncan Mac Coinneach his son there, Allister dhu Mac Phail there.

Shirrobeg.—John Macpherson in Shirrobeg, Finlay ban Mac Aonash vic Gilliephatrick there, Allister ban Mac Iain there, Ewen Mac Rorie vic William there, John Roy Mac Iain vic Gilliephatrick there.

Shirromore.—John Roy Mac Vurrich in Shirramore, Paul Macpherson his son there, Murroch Macpherson his son there, Dougall Mac Gilliechallum there.

Gaskinloan.—Thomas Macpherson in Gaskinloan, Donald dhu vic Coinneach there, John dhu Mac Homash, Mac un taillor there, Dugald Mac Homas Roy there, William Mackintosh there, Finlay Mor Mac Coil vic Finlay there, Duncan Mac Ewen vic Homas there, Donald Mac Ewen vic Finlay there.

Catlodge or Catti"eck.—Donald Mac Eachen vic Iain Roy there.

Breakachie.—Malm Macpherson of Breackachie, Iver Mac Finlay vic Phail there, Dnald Mac Ferquhar vic Phail there, William Macpherson there, Allister Mac Iain there, John Mor Mac Iain reoch there, Ewen Cattanach there, Thomas Mac an Taggart there, John Mor Mac Coil vic Soirle there, Paul Moukiter there, Donald Roy Mac a Greasich Vor there.

Garvabeg.—Malcolm Mac Soirle in Garvabeg, Ewen Mac Soirle vic Ewen there, John Mac Soirle vic Ewen there.

Garvamore.—Allan Mac Iain Gromach in Garvamore, John Mac Iain Gromach there, Ewen Roy vic W.rrich there, John Mac Coil vic Ruarie there, John Mac William vic Phaill there, Duncan Mac Iain vic William vic Phaill there, Ewen Mac Iain vic Coinneach there, Angus Mac Gillespie there, Donald Mac Gilliephatrick there, John dhu Mac (illegible) there, John dhu Mac Finlay oig there, Ewen Mac Aonas vic Ewen there.

Kylarchill.—Duncan Mac Iain dhu in Kylarchill, Duncan Mac Ewen Roy there, Duncan ban Mac Soirle there, John Mac Ewen vic Iain there, John Mac Ewen vic Finlay there, Donald dhu Mac Ewen vic Kenneth there.

Crathiecroy.—John Macpherson in Crathiecroy, Paul Macpherson there, Ewen Gow there, John Fraser there, John dhu vic Coil vic Allan there, John ban Mac Aonas vic Coil ban there, Angus Mac Bean dhu vic Aonas there.

Crathiemor.—Angus Mackintosh in Crathiemor, Alexander Mackintosh there, John Mac Aonas mor there, John Mac Iain reoch dhu there, William Mac Iain reoch dhu there, John Mac Iain reoch dhu there, Ewen Mac Coil vic Iain dhu there, James Dearg there, Arthur Forbes there, Donald Forbes his son, Rorie Charles there, John Mac Ian dhu vic Aonas there, John ban Mac Ewen-a-Gowin there, Alexander Mac Iain dhu vic Aonas there, Angus Mackintosh there, Allister Allan Mac Allister vic Allan there, Angus ban Mac Soirle there.

Blargymor.—Angus Mackintosh in Blargymore, John Mac Raild vic Allan there, Ferquhar Mac Ferquhar vic Iain there, Allister Mac a Greasich there, Donald Mac Finlay oig there.

Gergask.—Robert Mackintosh in Gergask, Donald dhu Mac a Greasich there, Angus Mac Coil oig there, Duncan Mac Gillie Glass there.

Gaskmore.—James Mackintosh in Gaskmore, John Mackintosh there, James Mackintosh there, Allan Mackintosh there, Finlay Mac Gill Andreis there, John Mac Iain ban there, Donald Macpherson there.

Pitgown.—William Fraser in Pitgoun, Donald Mac Cill Andrish there, William Mac Coil ban there, Aonas Mac Gill Andrish there.

The name of Macpherson, so common in Laggan, is not to be found among its landowners until about the middle of the seventeenth century. Andrew Macpherson, who fought at Glenlivat, and was alive in 1648, sometimes styled "of Cluny," was latterly designed "of Grange" in Banffshire, and is so described in his son Ewen's contract of marriage with Anna, daughter of the first Duncan Forbes of Culloden, dated the 16th of November, and the 2nd of December, 1641. In this contract Ewen is designed of Cluny, and as only son of Andrew Macpherson of Grange.

The bride's tocher was 5000 merks, the cautioners for Cluny's obligations being John Macpherson of Nuide, Donald Macpherson, his eldest lawful son and apparent heir, Ewen Macpherson of Brin, Paul Macpherson of Dalraddie, Dougal Macpherson of Ballachroan, and Alexander Macpherson of Essich, the principals at the time of the name.

By a document dated at Inverness, the 26th day of May, 1643, Cluny discharges all Culloden's obligations, having received full payment, in presence of David Paton, burgess of Inverness, Ewen Macpherson in Gaskinloan, and others.

For assisting Montrose Ewen and his father Andrew are prosecuted by the clergy. Ewen makes apology at Elgin, the value of which may be estimated by his having asserted, according to the latest clan historian, that he was in command of the Clan Chattan, a statement confuted at the moment by several Mackintoshes who declare that they were in arms under "the guid man of Stron," and Angus Mackintosh, portioner of Benchar, second son of Borlum. Andrew Macpherson's personal presence was dispensed with on account of his age and feebleness. Ewen Macpherson and Anna Forbes had at least two sons, Andrew and Duncan.

Andrew Macpherson succeeded, a youth of metal and courage. His portrait has been preserved and is now at Cluny. He was contracted in marriage with one of the Calder ladies in 1665, but died suddenly before the marriage.

An elegy composed on the occasion has been preserved, and though of no poetic value, is yet an interesting memorial, and will, I hope, gratify such Macphersons as may read it.

> Ane elegy upon the Laird of Cluny who died betwixt his contract and the time designed for his marriage, ye year 1665.
>
>> Might these sad lines but as pathetic be
>> As those tears real I bestow on thee,
>> Then should my grief more tragic make my hearse,
>> Then greater still in elegiac verse—
>> But drown'd in floods of tears can I yet live
>> And after such a fatal stroke revive,
>> Or shall my grief, swol'n quite glutted with sorrow
>> By emptying of itself a new life borrow?
>> No; language thou'rt too narrow and too weak
>> To ease us now, or our great woes to speak.

Nor can we in this dearth of words express
A loss which all bemoan, none can redress,
For destiny hath with this fatal blow
Marr'd more at once than all the world can show.
Yet know we not what this our loss to call,
But say in losing him we have lost all,
For what was either brave, wise, fair or good,
Might his qualities be understood.
The greatest linguist could not speak his due,
And would but praise what he compared him to—
The highest praise to him being but a stain,
And to say it was, he does more which may contain,
Then if we should our suburb wits extend,
And what we all admire strive to command.
But this may sparingly our loss speak forth,
He was the seat of beauty and of worth,
His sweetness was all love, his boldness, spirit,
And all he did did admiration merit.
Yet were those fair buds in his youth did bloom,
But promises of greater things to come,
We scarcely knew how glorious he us made.
Till his loss taught us ; and his being dead
Maketh us now with mourning groans to fill
The empty air that with alasses still
Hath echoed since thou, O dear, thou art gone,
Who did enrich these worthier parts alone,
These parts to which thou all their lustre gave,
Which now with thee lies buried in thy grave,
So that to all who knew thee, they but seem
A cask where a rich jewel late has been.
Let sorrow now itself find words to show
Thy Mother's anguish and thy sisters' woe.
In thee their hopes and comforts were begun.
And now with thee their joy and all is gone.
But, ah ! compared to hers all grief is small,
Who was his love, his life, his joy, his all,
His bliss, his comfort, and his better part,
Nay was himself, for both had but one heart.
Death had not acted here a tragedy
If both had lived or had he made both die ;
But she must live his obsequies to mourn,
And his late conquest (her heart) proves his urn.
A widow's name embittering that life
That never knew the happy state of wife
Fain would she think some rival framed this lie

Who did her too, too happy state, envy,
But all she merits with mournful silence show
What they are loth to tell, she feared to know.
Then to some solitary place she goes
Where all she sees are emblems of her woes.
Then over-pressed with grief, stupid with sorrow,
A flattering joy doth from a deep sleep borrow,
And there she fondly dreams he's come, and he
For his long absence makes apology.
Now means she him in her fair arms to hold,
Tells him what sad lies on his death were told,
And fearing he should go perforce, him kisses,
Bashful at this awakes and then all misses.
But carried by grief's torrent all this while
Can aught be found that may our ways beguile.
Yes, yes, a real joy we here may see,
Man being at the first ordained to die,
And so made purer should we then repine
That he who blaz'd on earth in Heaven should shine.
No this may from our private griefs us raise,
His change was for his Maker's greater praise,
So we reflecting on his happy state
No longer mourn but do congratulate,
While fame shall so preserve his memory
That even on earth he shall immortal be.

. . . .

Non est mortale quod opto,

Duncan Macpherson succeeded his brother Andrew, and reigned about 60 years. He had an only daughter, Anna, and at her marriage with Archibald Campbell, son of Sir Hugh Campbell of Calder, the Macphersons, fearing that the estate and representation would be taillied away to a stranger, met and subscribed the patriotic protest in favour of Macpherson of Nuide, the heir-male, which is recorded at page 377 of the Book of the Thanes of Cawdor, published by the old Spalding Club, and printed in 1859. This protest, which was signed at Benchar on the 14th of March, 1689, by sixteen Macphersons of standing, is too well known to require any particular description. The only point worth consideration is, were the circumstances such as to justify or cause general alarm to the Macphersons? No doubt the story of alienation was current, and from the known hereditary character of the Campbells the Macphersons were wise to be on the alert. That the parties to the contract got alarmed and modified its terms is probable, but the finale as embodied in the contract, dated at Cluny, the 15th day of March, 1689, a day after the protest, leaves the matter in obscurity. The contract is signed by Sir Hugh Campbell and his son, by Cluny and his daughter, before these witnesses—John Macpherson of Dalraddie, John Macpherson, younger thereof; Malcolm Macpherson of Breakachy, Colin Campbell, son to Calder; Lachlan Campbell, Chamberlain of Ila; Mr Thomas Macpherson, minister of Alvie; Lachlan Macpherson of Dellifour, and John Campbell, servitor to Calder.

Upon a perusal of the contract as signed, the only clause which bears on the point is in these terms, and readers can determine for themselves whether the words in italics justified the energetic protest by and in favour of Nuide, the heir-male—

"And further it is hereby provided and declared that the said sum of six thousand merks money foresaid promised to be paid as dote and tocher good foresaid, shall be detained by the said Sir Hugh in the first end of the sums contained in his bond granted to the said Duncan Macpherson and paid to the said Archibald to the effect and behoof foresaid. Providing always that the said sums shall be paid to Cluny himself for redeeming the wadsets which now lies on the lands of Cluny, the said Duncan Macpherson *giving the said lands to the said Archibald upon the terms and conditions they are now wadsetted and possessed by the present wadsetters and possessors thereof.*"

Duncan Macpherson steered his way carefully through the Revolution troubles. He is very intimate with Lord Dundee, and has the good opinion of Mackay; signs the address to George I.; and in his latter years is only known by his hostility to the heir-male; and neither going out himself in 1715, perhaps incapacitated by age, nor suffering Nuide to do so.

After the death of William Mackintosh of Borlum in 1717, long the Gordon Chamberlain of Badenoch, the Gordons resolved to appoint a stranger and one of their own name as most likely to be depended on. Accordingly that gallant warrior John Gordon of Glenbucket, born in 1672, was appointed, and getting a wadset of Strone, made it his residence. This step greatly increased the irritation of the Macphersons, who had chafed under the rule of the Borlums. Steps were taken to poison the Duke of Gordon's ears, but being ineffective, bolder courses were resolved upon—nothing less than slaying Glenbucket. The circumstances are narrated by Burt, always on the alert to pick up anything unpleasant about Highlanders of note ; by the Lord Advocate on the trial of Stuart of Acharn ; and by the Dowager Lady Mackintosh in her very curious memoirs of events in her life.

Burt's account briefly is in these terms—

"Whereupon the tenants came to a resolution to put an end to his suit and new settlement in the manner following. Five or six of them, young fellows, the sons of gentlemen, enter'd the door of his hut ; and in fawning words told him they were sorry any dispute had happened. That they were then resolved to acknowledge him as their immediate landlord, and would regularly pay him their rent. At the same time they begged he would withdraw his process, and they hoped they should be agreeable to him for the future. All this while they were almost imperceptibly drawing nearer and nearer to his bedside, on which he was sitting, in order to prevent his defending himself (as they knew him to be a man of distinguished courage), and then fell suddenly on him ; some cutting him with their dirks, and others plunging them into his body. This was perpetrated within sight of the Barrack of Ruthven. I can't forbear to tell you how this butchery ended, with respect both to him and those treacherous villains.

"He, with a multitude of wounds upon him, made shift in the bustle to reach down his broad sword from the tester of his bed, which was very low, and with it he drove all the assassins before him. And afterwards, from the Duke's abhorrence of so vile a fact, and with the assistance of the troops, they were driven out of the country and forced to flee to foreign parts."

Old Glenbucket, born as just stated in 1672, had been out in 1715, took part in the Rising of 1745, and his appearance, from the effects of the savage attack nearly 30 years before, is described as incapacitating him to sit erect on horseback. The gallant veteran escaped, first to Norway, then to France, and lived comfortably, until June, 1750, on a pension of 1200 livres. I possess certain papers signed by him while Chamberlain of Badenoch, and also some relative to his posterity, the latest referring to John Charles Gordon, residing at Tomintoul in 1812.

As the Glenbuckets intermarried with the Glengarrys, I may publish these papers some day, including the appearance made, early in the 'Forty-five, by the people of Badenoch at the request of Lord Lewis Gordon.

The Duke of Gordon was naturally furious at the attack on his chamberlain, and not only threatened vengeance and extirpation on the Macphersons, who held their whole lands of him, but took some active steps in the matter. In their distress, the Macphersons, under their new chief, Lachlan, whose mother was daughter of Lachlan Mackintosh of Kinrara, bethought themselves of a reconciliation with Mackintosh, and becoming independent to a certain degree of the Gordons. Mackintosh fell into the snare, foolishly thinking that the Macphersons, who had deceived his predecessors so often, had changed their skin and spots, while his wife in her memoirs appears to have seen clearly the folly of having any dealings with them. Mackintosh's desires for the consolidation and unification of Clan Chattan were highly praiseworthy. To make the Macphersons *quasi* independent, and particularly of the Gordons, Mackintosh granted them Gallovie and Aberarder, upwards of 40,000 acres, under certain conditions, of which the forfeiture of Evan Macpherson of Cluny and the passing of the Jurisdiction Acts deprived him, and of the equivalents stipulated.

In the whole deplorable record of Crown robberies arising out of the forfeitures of 1715 and 1745 there is perhaps no greater wrong than that inflicted on the Mackintosh family in connection with those lands in Laggan. The loyal subject was punished, while the insurgent family benefitted.

As I have not the slightest desire to be enrolled among the Stevenson-Lang ghouls, the sordid detractors of prominent Highland gentlemen of the past, I will say but little more at present upon this very tempting subject.

The Cluny rental was so beggarly that Evan Macpherson, a man of great strength and activity, was in his father's time obliged to become a Captain of the Watch, a business not taken up except by those in a secondary position. Sir Walter Scott in depicting Fergus Macivor (the prototype of old Glengarry, a chief of the first rank) makes a ridiculous blunder in assigning to him the office of Captain of Thieves. The following docquetted "Discharge of Watch money payable to Clunie, 15th June, 1745," shows that he was still engaged in the business very shortly before the landing of Prince Charles—

"Forres, June, 15, 1745.

"Received from Sir Robert Gordon of Gordonstoun the sum of four pounds 16s 3d sterling, as his whole proportion of the Watch money payable to Evan Macpherson of Cluny, at the rate of half a crown out of the hundred pound of his valued rent p. me.
(Signed) "JOHN DUFF, junr."

A month later Lord Advocate Craigie writes to Lord Tweeddale, whereby it would seem Government relied on Cluny as its supporter—

"Edinburgh, 11th June, 1745.

"My Lord,—I have the honour of yours of the 6th July, and you may believe the particulars you mention of the situation of our affairs in Flanders, tho' not altogether such as could have been wished yet being much better than was believed from the former accounts gave me a sensible pleasure, and as I thought it was of service to the Government to encourage his Majesty's real friends and to discountenance disaffection I hope you'll approve of my not keeping your intelligence a secret and even the mentioning your authority, which I don't choose to do upon other occasions.

"We have all got up our spirits here with an exception of those who are in anxiety about their friends who were engaged in the late action near Ghent, and this anxiety will continue until we have the particulars of those that perished and escaped in the action.

"Sir John Cope communicated to me the copy of the letter you sent him touching Cluny's management with respect to the shire of Banff. I am persuaded from all I have heard of Cluny's conduct from people of all sides that the insinuations made against him will be found to be groundless. His character is to be a perfect enemy to thieves and thieving. Last year he protected the adjacent country at a very small expense in spite of the opposition that was made to him by those from whom it would not have been expected. Your Lordship knows he wished to have been employed by the Government, but that he did not succeed in his application. That the character he acquired last year procured him more numerous applications this season, and it is not to be wondered at, because though commissions were issued for these companies some time ago, yet they are but now raised, and it's very lately that two of them got their arms, and the third is still without arms, and none of them are as yet stationed for the protection of the country, and at the time referred to in the letter transmitted to you, Cluny had no notice of his commission. This is what occurs to me and I have no doubt that Cluny will be able fully to justify himself.

"Sir John Cope sends you by this post Inveraw's opinion with respect to the French recruiting in the Highlands. I own I believe he speaks what he knows, but I think he is too lately come from Argyllshire to be able to discover what is passing in the recruiting countries.

"The Duke of Atholl is in town and intends to wait for the Duke of Argyll's arrival. He is expected here Monday next. I have the honour to be with great truth and respect, my Lord, your Lordship's most obedient, and most faithful humble servant.

(Signed) "ROB. CRAIGIE."

Further to support him, Mackintosh allowed young Cluny as he did Keppoch, an annual present, or "gratuity" as it is termed, of one hundred merks, as may be seen by the following document, which is holograph of Cluny:—

"I, Evan McPherson, younger of Cluny, grant me to have received from Angus Shaw, factor to the Laird of Mackintosh, the sum of one hundred merks, and that as the Laird of Mackintosh's gratuity to me payable Martinmas last, seventeen hundred and thirty-six years. In witness whereof I have written and subscribed their presents at Cluny the twentie-second day of January, one thousand seven hundred and thirty-seven years. (Signed) "EV. MCPHERSON."

Conceive a "Chief" of the great Confederation of Clan Chattan granting such an acknowledgment.

This same "Chief" appears to have by himself or his men lifted and eaten poor William Robertson's cow—

"William Robertson in Badenoch, declares young Cluny came to his house and ordered 20 cows and 6 horses to be taken from him, and otherwise threatened him, and upon consenting to go, they were all restored except one cow which was killed.

"WM. (his X mark) ROBERTSON."

A great deal is made of Evan Macpherson's son, Duncan Macpherson. I have met with several people who knew him well, and the concurring report was that he was an insignificant looking little man, entirely ruled by his clever wife, Catherine Cameron of Fassifern.

Lord Adam Gordon thus writes of him in 1769 to the Marquis of Granby—

"Prestonhall, 25th December, 1769.

"As to some promotions I hope I may name to you for a company Captain Macpherson on the half-pay, who has undertaken to find forty recruits provided he gets on full pay. I thought it a handsome offer and am certain he can make it good. He is a very pretty young man and who, *for reasons of policy*, should be kept in the service. He is a nephew of Colonel Fraser's and has been educated under the eye of Dr Robertson, the historian, who does him great justice."

The italics are mine.

The following most interesting letter of General Simon Fraser's should be perused with care, showing as it does, how Duncan Macpherson was brought up, and how his surrounding Macphersons behaved :—

"Oporto, 16th August, 1770.

"It happens luckily that your letter of 12th July found me here and more so that there is a ship just ready to sail for London by which I send this, for I am uneasy every moment that I lie under the least suspicion with my worthy friends the Laird and Lady Mackintosh, and as I am allowed now no more time than is necessary for this letter, I desire you may immediately, upon receipt of it, send to Lady Mackintosh a copy of what relates to this business to clear me in the meantime till I have an opportunity of writing her, which I am told I shall have in a week's time by another ship from this place.

"In the first place it hurts me not a little that the words of any man or set of men should be taken by Lady Mackintosh against me without some proof. She has known me about 20 years and I flatter myself in all that time has had no instance of any unfair or underhand dealing in me. When my prospect in life was at the worst I defy the world to tax me with unfairness or ingratitude. It's not then likely that I should begin now to expose myself and that for another to an imputation that I never would put to the least hazard to promote my own affairs. I should think myself so much obliged to the Laird and Lady Mackintosh that I would sooner cut my tongue out than I would speak, or my hand off than I would write, anything directly or indirectly to their prejudice. If I could to-morrow get these lands for the asking to myself, I protest to God I would not ask them nor any other, that they had any pretentions to, far less for my nephew. Since the world began there never was an imputation so void of foundation. What I thought myself to blame for, turns out to be lucky—that is that from my leaving England in 1766 I never wrote a syllable to my nephew or any of the name of Macpherson except an answer to a letter from Breackachy's son informing me of his intention of marrying my niece and my letter to him was simply upon that matter of his marriage, without a syllable on any other business whatever. Judge then how I could have been consulted or advised upon the application in question. My nephew's coming to Portugal was not only not at my desire but it was without my knowledge, the first notice that I had of it was from Simon Fraser, Borlum, telling me of his being embarked. I have still the letter wrote by James Macpherson and some others of his friends in which they mention the purpose of his coming being to show himself to me, and to have my advice for his future plan of life, which they proposed to begin by purchasing a company, and the real view was clearly pointed out to be their expectations that I would advance the money for that purchase, but they did not mention any other business, far less drop a hint of any intention of an application for the lands.

"When he came I found him a fine looking boy, but not enough broke to start in the world, and therefore I thought it would be of great use to him to spend some months in France, which I proposed to him and agreed to be at the expense of a couple of hundred pounds for that purpose, and after staying about three months with me at Lisbon he set sail for Rheims, where he has been since the beginning of June. As I was myself upon the wing I had very little time to speak to him about business while at Lisbon, and I found that he knew very little of his own affairs. He told me that Mr James Macpherson had said to him that he meant to make an application for him to the Treasury, but he could not give me an account about what, and as you wrote me of the application for Killihuntly's debt I took for granted it was that ; and altho' he is a clever lad it's surprising how little he attended to or knew of his own affairs ; his friends, I should rather say his relations, kept him supplied with money and in such ignorance that it looked as if done on purpose. He referred me for every thing of that sort to letters they were to write me and which I have never received, and I sincerely believe he knew nothing of the application for the gift when he left Lisbon, which was in the month of May, and as to myself I solemnly declare before God and by all that's sacred that I never directly or indirectly advised, encouraged, or consented to any such application being made and knew no more of it than the Great Mogul till I received your letter, and that what I have here set forth is all I know of my nephew's affairs except some letters that I have received within this month about their absurd disputes for the Tack of Cluny, to which I made no answer. As he had accounts of his uncle's death at Lisbon, I foresaw those disputes, and proposed to him to leave me a Procuration to act for him, which he did, but I have never made the least use of it, nor even mentioned it to any body till now, and as to my corresponding with those people I might have done it, and it was natural I should on my nephew's account, but I am happy to be able to say that I not only never exchanged word or wrote on the subject of the lands, but that except the letter upon his marriage to young Breakachy, I have not put pen to paper to anyone of the name of Macpherson these 4 years. If all this is not enough, I don't know what will be enough to satisfy Mackintosh, but let the Lady herself say what she will have me to do to satisfie her and the world of my affection and gratitude towards her and her family, and I will do it; and if it will be of the least use I am ready to write to the Lord Privy Seal my total ignorance of my nephew's application, and that my wishes are for Mackintosh in preference even to my nephew. She must allow that this is a proposal inconsistent with any consciousness of guilt of the imputation laid to my charge, and I hope will immediately restore me to that share of her esteem which I have all my life put such a value upon, and will rest assured that it is only with my life that my attachment and gratitude to her and Mackintosh will end."

From whence did the surrounding Macphersons get the cash which seemed so abundant? I have an idea which wild horses will not drag from me. The pleasant tradition that young Cluny got his Commission so early, that he was a Major while still eating his matutinal porridge, is contradicted by Lord Adam Gordon's letter showing that he was only a Captain on half-pay about the time he arrived at full age.

After the restoration of the Cluny estates, these were well administered by Lachlan Macpherson at Ralia, afterwards in Breackachie, predecessor of the present Glentruim. His services to the family were truly great, having circumvented the clever William Tod, Gordon Chamberlain, very handsomely in a great adjustment of marches about 1791, and getting nearly 20,000 acres in the heart of the forest of Benalder in exchange for a plough of Kylarchill and certain grazing rights in the Braes of Spey. His family certainly did not deserve to be treated in the contemptuous way Mrs Macpherson of Cluny expressed herself when it was rumoured that one of Ralia's sons was likely to become purchaser of the estate of Glentruim. She would not give him a capital letter. No; the poor man in the numerous letters I have of hers is always "ralia." The same depreciatory spirit is shown by her horror on hearing that one Allan

Macpherson in the east end of Kingussie, by the assistance of a relative in the West Indies, was to purchase a good slice of Gordon land then in the market, the feeling towards Allan being instantly changed on hearing that the purchase was intended for Ewen, her own son. She also fought very shy of the shrewd George Macpherson-Grant, rapidly building up that position in Badenoch which placed his family territorially at the head of the Macphersons. She cannot understand him or his designs, but fears,

> "Why it is, I cannot tell,
> Thee I like not, Doctor Fell."

The Macphersons did not fare well at her hands after she had the control on her husband's death. The bitter persecution begun in his time of Colonel Duncan Macpherson's son, Cluny's near relative, continued briskly after his death, but young Barclay Macpherson was vigorously and successfully defended by his other near relatives, Mrs Mackintosh of Borlum and her only daughter, Margaret Mackintosh. By the marriage of the latter with Mr John Macpherson, latterly at Gallovie, a doughty foe of the Clunys came to the rescue, who for years when at Cluny Mains was a thorn to the Cluny family. Colonel Duncan Macpherson of Bleaton and his son, afterwards General Barclay Macpherson; John Macpherson, Cluny Mains; Ewen Macpherson, MacCoul; and other Macphersons of note, were in turn forced into litigation and another serious burden fell upon the tenants more exacting and severe than I have noticed on any other estate. This was, on getting a new lease, the giving of a present to the lady. In the case of Cluny, large sums frequently exceeding £100, were given, and taken by the lady, during her active management, which, notwithstanding the son's affection for his mother, he felt compelled when settling up with her, to call in question. She did not deny these presents but pleaded a "voluntary custom" in regard to them.

Such estates as fell under the control of the lady's brother suffered, and in several cases sunk. When Colonel Duncan Macpherson of Cluny married Miss Catharine Cameron of

Fassifern, the estates were held in fee simple, and destined by the contract to the eldest son of the marriage. This did not suit or satisfy the lady's friends and advisers, and in defiance of the contract of marriage, which by the Scots law over-rides all obligations, an entail was made out which cost Ewen Macpherson of Cluny a deal of money to set aside, and apparently was one of the leading causes which piled up the debt on the property, necessitating ultimately a sale of some fifty thousand acres of the Cluny estates.

There is perhaps no place in Badenoch at the present day better known, or rather more frequently referred to, than "Cluny Castle." It is a modern assumption, having no basis of time in its support. Colonel Duncan Macpherson, it is only right to say, did not call his house a castle, and never ! assumed the title of Chief or Captain of Clan Chattan. He knew better, and those about him at his death did not I understand (for I have not been within the grounds) place this baseless designation on his tombstone. Those who succeeded Colonel Duncan Macpherson made their first step of assumption in the month of June or July, 1828. Lady Cluny's letters prior to the 12th of June are all dated "Cluny House." By the 5th July, 1828, they bear to be from "Cluny Castle," the good lady on one or two subsequent occasions seeming to have overlooked the newly-fledged dignity by dating from "Cluny House," as was her wont.

I must now allude in brief to another modern assumption, viz., that of "Craigdhu" as the war cry of the Macphersons. The two things which appear to throw simple Macphersons into a state of ecstatic adoration are the contemplation of Ewen of the 'Forty-five and the hill of Craigdhu. A certain native of Scandinavian Scotland, where there is no Gaelic, is particularly possessed. What does all this mean? The war cry of historic clans, when a locality, indicated that it was centrical and the sole undoubted possession of the clan, such as "Tullochard," "Craigellachie," "Loch Moy," "Loch Sloy," etc., etc. Let this rule be applied to Craigdhu. It is very true that the whole mountain since about 1830 belongs exclusively to Cluny. But did it when clanship was active and gatherings common?

Craigdhu lies in the Parishes of Laggan and Kingussie, having several distinctive and nominative summits, whereof the waters of the western portion slope to and run into the Calder, and on the east to the Spey. The three ploughs of Cluny, the first heritable property of the Macphersons of Cluny, do not nearly extend to the higher summit. The highest summit from the south was part of the Duke of Gordon's Ovie and Achmore, which remained with them until the final dispersion sixty years ago. The only part to the east of the Cluny property which approached, if at all, to the summit, was the hill of Biallid Beg; then came Biallid Mor and Coronach, all facing the Spey, feued to Borlum in 1637, and latterly again the Gordon property.

The whole of the west side of the mountain sloping to the Calder belonged to the Borlums, being that part of the hill grazings of Benchar called Tullichero. Thus at the most, while clanship and clan cries were in vogue, the Macphersons could only claim, if even to that extent, a third of Craigdhu, or so much as followed Biallid Beg.

When Mr John Macpherson was tenant of the mains of Cluny the shootings were let apparently for the first time on rent, to the Peel family. In 1816 Mr William Peel and his nephew, afterwards the distinguished statesman, came north. Being on bad terms with the estate authorities John Macpherson took steps to interdict the sportsmen and all others. The petition is well drawn, and proceeds upon the allegation that he, Macpherson, had the lands let to him exclusively, that the reports of shots and roaming of dogs disturbed his sheep, preventing them from pasturing quietly, and was likely to lead if not to their loss, at least to their harm. I am not sure whether any decision was pronounced by the Sheriff, as the Peels compromised matters so well that Mr Macpherson speaks highly of their behaviour. After this landlords took good care in their leases of sheep and arable farms to reserve game and power to lease it separately. In time this reservation was in many cases pushed to extremities, but public sentiment having been aroused better feeling prevailed, and the grievance of two rents from the same subject, and in especial that of fostering rabbits where hill grounds for grouse are scarce, is now much modified.

THE MACPHERSONS OF BREACKACHIE.

The Breackachie family long held a good position in Badenoch, but latterly they unfortunately incurred the deep-seated hostility not only of their own Chief, but also that of Mr Tod, the well-known Gordon factor.

Mr Donald Macpherson of Breackachie, himself closely connected with Cluny, and whose son, Colonel Duncan, had married Margaret, one of Evan Macpherson of Cluny's daughters, was with his son evicted from Breackachie, in 1773, to be succeeded by another Macpherson—Lachlan of Ralia. The removal was defended vigorously, but the defences failing, it was effected, breaking the heart of old Donald Macpherson, who had possessed under leases granted in 1735 and 1752. His latter years were spent with his daughter, Mrs Mackintosh of Borlum, and the last letter I have of his dated, Raits, the 24th of July, 1777, in a tremulous hand, is a strong appeal to William Mackintosh of Balnespick to cease persecuting "the poor remnant of the Borlums and their estate," represented by his daughter.

Donald Macpherson was succeeded as representative of the family by his son, Colonel Duncan Macpherson, who at one time was very well off, being owner of Wester Gask in Strathnairn, and Bleaton at the foot of Glenshee. Colonel Duncan, who had seen a good deal of service, must, judging by his letters, have been an accomplished gentleman, but unhappily getting mixed up with the notorious "Black Captain," John Macpherson of Ballachroan, lost both his estates and died in comparative poverty. He is said to have built the first house in Kingussie towards the east end on the upper side of the road, I believe still standing.

Colonel Macpherson was also proprietor of Callag Etterish, or Catlodge, which had to be sold, and was purchased by Cluny. The place occupied by several sub-tenants was given by him for 29 years from 1787. He died early in the century, and was succeeded by his son Barclay, afterwards General Barclay Macpherson, in the lease of Catlodge and the house in Kingussie.

At Whitsunday, 1816, the lease of Catlodge fell out, and for some reasons which I have not been able to ascertain, Colonel Duncan Macpherson of Cluny, uncle of Barclay, then Colonel, and abroad with his regiment, commenced certain vindictive and outrageous legal proceedings connected with the outgoing from Catlodge.

In Colonel Barclay's absence, his paternal aunt, Mrs Mackintosh of Borlum, and her daughter, Mrs MacEdward, looked after his affairs, but without any written authority. The rent of Catlodge was only £18, and it had 8 sub-tenants. Cluny's first step was, before Whitsunday, to present a petition to have the biggings valued to ascertain the pejoration. An ex-parte report was got fixing them at over £200, a monstrous sum, seeing that the meliorations payable by Cluny were not to exceed £30. The proceedings were directed against Colonel Barclay, then abroad, but he was neither served personally nor summoned edictally, and it was by accident that Mrs Mackintosh heard of them. The next step on the part of Cluny was to raise a summons for £2000 in name of damages, before any damages had either been ascertained or legally fixed, while arrestments were laid in the hands of all the sub-tenants. Whitsunday had now arrived when the rent had to be paid, and Mrs Mackintosh, on applying to the sub-tenants to put her in funds, was for the first time informed of the arrestments, and of all these outrageous proceedings. But Cluny, or those advising him, were not yet satisfied, for no sooner was the rent unpaid, really in consequence of the arrestments used by himself, than sequestration was applied for. Mrs Mackintosh and her daughter bestirred themselves vigorously for their relative, and got one of the ablest lawyers in Inverness to appear. Some of his allegations for Colonel Barclay are scathing even in legal warfare, while Mr Alexander Shepherd, who appeared for Cluny, after doing his best, had to yield, and finally Cluny got nothing but his rent, which had always been at his disposal.

Colonel Barclay Macpherson, the last of the Breakachies, an honourable and high-spirited man, took no legal steps for redress, but took such a dislike to Badenoch that after his retirement he ceased almost all connection with it, dying in Stirling. He left £100, the interest to be allotted for keeping up the burial place in St. Columba's Churchyard, and being satisfied that Ewen Macpherson of Cluny, a child at the time of these proceedings, had no concern in them, and indeed had afterwards expressed his regret that such had taken place in his name, nominated him one of the Trustees to administer the above fund, and if I mistake not substituted one or two of the Cluny family to succeed to the house in Kingussie, failing the institute. So much regarding the three last Macphersons of the good old family of Breackachie, one of whom, John, is mentioned in 1609 as concurring in the Bond of Union among the Clan Chattan.

The Breackachies were not the only Macphersons of standing who incurred the hostility of the restored owners. Ewen Macpherson, tacksman of MacCoul, had, through Ballachroan, got rather behind, and in 1811 was sequestrated at the instance of Colonel Duncan Macpherson of Cluny. Ewen's rent was £100, and his subject was worth £700. The rent due was forehand, yet a sequestration was applied for and granted on the 25th of January, 1811, and a warrant of sale for ready money applied for and obtained on the 6th of February, the sale to take place at Kingussie, 20 miles distant, on the 16th of February. To carry out a sale at that period of the year, the weather being very inclement, when there was no demand for cattle because no keep, and for a forehand rent, was so oppressive that MacCoul and his trustee, for he was sequestrated as a bankrupt by the Court of Session, came forward and obtained an interdict. Bad as the factors of the forfeited estates were, I fancy the tenants in Badenoch or some of them would, I should say, have been glad to see them back.

THE MACPHERSONS OF OVIE AND MACCOUL, ETC.

Another respectable family in Laggan was also oppressed and dispossessed about the same time, namely, the Macphersons of Ovie. Hugh Macpherson had the temerity to cross Factor Tod, and was ejected neck and heel, to make way for James Shaw, from the parish of Alvie. Shaw was foolish enough to offer a rent of £42 instead of the former rent of £27, and not getting possession for months, in consequence of the outgoing tenants retaining violent possession, his plans fell through; he could not pay his rent, and was in turn ejected like Ovie.

No more interesting place exists in Laggan than Crathy, where there is at this day the only cluster of small tenants in all Badenoch. Long may they hold their place, and send out strong men and strapping lasses to supply those services so much needed in the parish.

Crathy was threatened with extinction in 1806, but it has happily survived while the extirpators have themselves been long since extirpated. The following were in that year summoned to remove but maintained their place, viz.:—James Mackintosh, Donald Macdonald *alias* Macgillivantich, John Mackintosh, Alexander Kennedy, Donald Mackillop, Angus Cattanach, Alexander Macpherson, Angus Macdonald, and Alexander Macdonald. I hope to see the day when the lands from Crathy Mor and Crathy Croy to Gaskmore and Gaskbeg will be peopled as of old by Mackintoshes, that the ancient burial place of Kylarchill will be enclosed and beautified, and the Brae of Spey and of Roy opened up by railway.

THE "GENTLEMEN" OF BADENOCH.

The "Gentlemen" of Badenoch was the honoured designation of many of the larger farmers, particularly in Laggan. In the palmy days of sheep farming there flocked down to the Inverness Wool Fair, where they kept "the crown of the causeway," Garvamore and Garvabeg; Shirramore and Shirrabeg; Tullochcrom and Aberarder; Gallovie and

Kinlochlaggan ; MacCoul and Brae Laggan ; Druminord and Iosal an Ord ; Dalchully and Strathmashie ; Crathiemor and Crathiecroy ; Gaskmore and Gaskbeg, and several others, fine seasoned vessels, who never shirked their glass, and could well hold their own with the choicest stalwarts of Lochaber.

The family of MacNab, terminating in the last Dalchully, were long influential in Laggan, and to them chiefly falls the credit of erecting on Tirfadoun, the pretty Roman Catholic Chapel so picturesquely situated, guarding the pass into the Brae of Spey and the famous Corryaraick. The natural beauty of the locality has been much enhanced by Sir John Ramsden's plantation of the Dun.

The Macdonalds, long wadsetters of Gallovie, nourished by the Mackintoshes, were dispossessed by the Macphersons, who in 1790 got possession of the lands of Innisnagaul on Loch Laggan side. The last of the Gallovie Macdonalds who had any hold in Laggan was Ranald Macdonald, tenant in Strathmashie. Judging from the paper after quoted, Ranald inherited the pugnacious instincts of his predecessors without the opportunities which they possessed of indulging in them. By 1810 the King's writ ran, even in Laggan, though the relaxations of the "Gentlemen" were rather startling.

Counsel did not see his way to recommend any legal steps in the case to which the document refers, the evidence being too scrimp, and Dalchully had to put up with the assault, which must have been particularly galling to him when it is recollected that according to the veracious Aytoun, with four exceptions, "Of all the Highland clans, MacNab is the most ferocious." The document is entitled—

"Memorial for Donald MacNab, Esq., at Dalchully, in the District of Badenoch and County of Inverness," dated the 2nd of November, 1810.

"The memorialist feels it to be a duty which he owes to himself as at the head of a family as well as for the sake of public example not to pass in silence an atrocious attack lately made upon his person by a neighbour, who has been hitherto held in the estimation of a gentleman, and is a Justice of Peace in the county ; but before proceeding to any legal measures, he is desirous of having the best advice, how far, from the occult nature of the assault, and the deficiency of evidence consequently attending it, he will be able to establish a claim of reparation in a court of law, on account of the injuries he has already suffered ; and what steps he ought to adopt for the safety and security of his person and property in the future. With this view the consideration of the learned counsel is requested to the following statement.

"The memorialist holds, as sub-tenant, the farm of Dalchully, and Mr Ranald Macdonald rents that of Strathmashie, both in the close vicinity of each other, and separated by the water of Mashie, which forms the march between them. About three months ago, the memorialist was informed from good authority that Macdonald was making application to the Duke of Gordon, the proprietor of both farms, for part of the farm of Dalchully to be attached to that of Strathmashie at the next sett. As the memorialist was a good deal interested in a measure of this kind, and being on a perfectly good footing at that time with Macdonald, he enquired of him if the report was true, which after some evasion he admitted, and added that right or wrong he would persist in his application. This produced some hasty words between the parties, which ended in a formal challenge to fight by Macdonald to the memorialist—but the quarrel was amicably settled by the interposition of friends, and the memorialist thought no more about it; tho' he at the same time made a counter application to the proprietor and principal tacksman respecting Dalchully, and received every assurance that Macdonald's views would be disappointed, and so the matter rested.

"An application had also been made some time before by Macdonald to the memorialist for payment of certain mill dues or multures which he said were due to him, in answer to which the memorialist addressed a letter to Macdonald, alleging that the demand was unjust to the extent called for, and that it would not be paid. In short, the terms of the memorialist's letter were perhaps in some degree harsh and unpalatable to Macdonald. But whether (as Macdonald afterwards alleged) that the origin of their recontre was the view he had of asking an explanation of this letter, or, whether some grudge rankled in Macdonald's mind respecting the proposal about Dalchully, or, if both circumstances gave rise to a determined hostility on the part of Macdonald towards the memorialist, cannot be ascertained, but so it is that for some time he had meditated revenge against the memorialist. Accordingly on Tuesday, the 16th ultimo, Macdonald resolved on carrying his plan into effect. The memorialist had after breakfast taken a walk to that part of his farm opposite the house of Strathmashie, where he has some hay stacks. He had not been long there when he saw Macdonald (who had been out of doors and must have seen the memorialist) suddenly enter his house, and with equal haste come out carrying something in his hand like a bludgeon, and then walk away in the direction likely to be taken by the memorialist on his return home. The memorialist after remaining some time where he was, proceeded homeward, and when he had advanced a considerable way (at least a mile's distance), and was in a private part of the road, Macdonald crossed the water, and commenced his attack by knocking down the memorialist with a large bludgeon. The memorialist received no less than eleven cuts and blows on the head and face, which must have appeared sufficient to extinguish life. After some time, however, the memorialist recovering his senses a little, saw Macdonald, and two men along with him at some distance. The memorialist from his situation only knew one of these men, to whom he called aloud, with the little exertion of which he was capable, to keep in memory what he had observed, when both the men immediately sneaked away. It has been since understood that they were father and son. While the memorialist lay on the ground, he recovered his senses so far as to ask Macdonald if he intended to murder him, whose answer was, " I do, by God, you scoundrel," which words were accompanied by another dreadful blow a little above the temple, which again deprived the memorialist of motion and sense—and there the bloody scene ended. The memorialist having been conveyed home, a medical man was sent for, who found him in a state of the most imminent danger, and declared that if some of the blows had been an inch and a half lower they must have killed a much stronger man instantly. The same medical man continued to attend the memorialist constantly, and reside in his house for several days—so late as the 20th ulto. the memorialist was so ill as to be pronounced by no means out of danger. The only evidence which can be adduced to prove this assault is the statement given by Macdonald himself, in a letter to the Rev. Mr Macintyre (a copy of which is herewith laid before counsel), and the depositions of the two men who were in company with Macdonald, whose depositions, however, cannot be relied upon, as it seems they are poor dependents and cottars of Macdonald's and will swear to whatever suits his purpose. Two circumstances operate strongly against Macdonald, namely, that the attack was made in a private and unfrequented path, after having crossed the water purposely to get at the memorialist, and that Macdonald himself holds the situation of a Magistrate, being a Justice of Peace for the county. It is alleged by Macdonald, in his statement, that the memorialist was the aggressor. If so, it appears extraordinary that Macdonald should carry no marks of injury on his person, as the memorialist had a stick in his possession, which he certainly would, in this case, have used—but the assertion is totally false, and to account for the appearance of blows about him, Macdonald pretends that the memorialist pulled him to the ground and commenced the assault by seizing his neck-cloth.

Upon the whole, counsel will be pleased to give his opinion what proceedings it would be proper in the memorialist to follow forth with the view of protecting himself, his family and property from the future violence of this outrageous man, and also in obtaining reparation for the injuries which he has already sustained; counsel will further say, whether the circumstances, and the evidence are such as would justify the memorialist in endeavouring to make the case the subject of a public prosecution, and what steps he is to adopt for that purpose."

XXV.—PARISH OF KINGUSSIE.

RUTHVEN CASTLE—ITS ANCIENT AND MODERN POSSESSORS.

RUTHVEN CASTLE, latterly used as barracks, now long a ruin, stands out imposingly, commanding an old passage over the Spey. The Chartulary of Moray contains a graphic account of certain great doings at the Standing Stones of Raite, and within the chapel and the great chamber behind the hall, in the Castle of Ruthven in October, 1380, connected with the disputes between Alexander, Seneschal and Lord of Badenoch, known as the Wolf of Badenoch, on the one hand, and Alexander, Bishop of Moray, on the other. Reference is made to free "tenants of Badenoch, and others who owed suit, following, compearance, or service, attached to the Court of Regality of Badenoch," who were summoned to attend by John Gray, "Mair" of Badenoch. A translation into English of what occurred will be found on pages 80, 81, and 82 of *Invernessiana*, whereby it will be seen that the Bishop was victorious all along the line.

The Stuarts did not long maintain possession of Badenoch, which, reverting to the Crown, was re-granted to the Gordons. In the first half of the seventeenth century, the Gordons began feuing in Kingussie chiefly to Macphersons, and the present representative of the Gordons possesses of the original 60 davochs of Badenoch, only three, namely, the lands known as North Kinrara in Alvie. The Castle and a few acres adjoining were either reserved from the original grant to the Gordons, or afterwards assumed by the Crown for use as a fortified place to overawe the people and compel obedience. Ruthven in 1746 I need not advert to, as it is frequently noticed, but soon after Culloden it fell into disuse, and formed merely an excuse to maintain some dependent of the Crown as barrack-master, the last being John Macpherson, styled "of Inverhall."

Dissatisfied with their immense possessions in Badenoch the Gordons could not endure to see these few acres in the hands of others; and there being a question with the Crown as to Fort-William in the year 1787, they seized their opportunity. The Fort-William matter having been referred to David Young of Perth, and Angus Macdonald of Achtriachtan, to fix the amount payable by the Board of Ordnance, the wily Gordon factor, Tod, saw a likely way to acquire the Ruthven barrack grounds without payment. The circumstances are explained by Captain Rudyard's letter to the Duke of Richmond, Master-General of Ordnance, dated Edinburgh, the 5th of November, 1787, sending the Fort-William report. Mr Young, he narrates, by "particular request of Mr Tod, steward to the Duke of Gordon, went to visit the barracks at Ruthven of Badenoch, belonging to Government, as Mr Tod considered it highly probable that the Duke of Gordon, would expect the site of that ruin in part of the compensation for the grounds to be ceded at Fort-William, and in order to give your Honours a view of its value, I have enclosed Mr Young's report as to Ruthven also, and hope his going there, tho' not directed by me, will for the reasons recited meet your approbation."

So far Mr Tod had his own way, the next step being to get the barracks, by this time generally known as "St. George's Castle," for nothing. The two arbiters declined reporting on any sum for Fort-William, merely fixing the extent and boundaries. Their not naming a sum, probably on the astute Tod's suggestion, left it open to him to ask 40 years' purchase of the rental. Of course, Government kicked at this figure, when it was graciously reduced by Mr Tod to 30 years' purchase, on condition that the barracks should be thrown in, or to use the Duke of Gordon's own words, 3rd of December, 1787—"I hope your Grace will not think it unreasonable that I should expect that the barrack hill of Ruthven shall be restored to my family." So it was ultimately arranged, and a disposition having been prepared, the Duke of Gordon was infeft in it on the 31st of October, 1792.

The report of Mr Young, who is described as "a man of superior judgment and abilities, being an author on agriculture," is as follows, and is of value as showing the exact state of matters 109 years ago —

"At the desire of Mr William Tod, steward to His Grace the Duke of Gordon, I viewed the ruins of the barracks belonging to His Majesty at Ruthven of Badenoch.

"This was formerly the castle of the Comyns, then Earls (?) of Badenoch, who had very extensive possessions in the Highlands, perhaps more than any nobleman since possessed—which castle after having decayed was taken down and made into barracks for the military in the year 1727. It was burnt by the rebels in the year 1745, and is just now a complete ruin.

"This hill upon which the barracks are built is perhaps as remarkable as any to be met with in Scotland, being evidently an artificial mount, containing 2 acres and 10 falls, raised 40 feet high above the surrounding plain, having only access to it from the south, by reason of a morass, containing 2 acres 2 roods and 19 falls, which surround it nearly in the form of a square, which has been intended for a ditch that was to be kept always full of water in order to strengthen the place. This mount being surrounded by the morass, damped, as I am informed, the barracks very much, so that the military stores could not be kept from rusting, and even their linens would be so damp that they were obliged to have them conveyed to another place, in order to save them from rotting. This evil might be remedied by cutting a deep drain to communicate with the River Spey, which after being partly filled up with stones and a sluice put on, so as to let the water in and out at pleasure, might be converted to draw up and down. Upon my first view of this mount, I considered that it was artificial, and I was confirmed in my opinion by being afterwards told that after the military had dug a well forty feet deep for the supply of the garrison, they met with piles of wood that had been put there to support the earth. It appears to me that to erect any new building on this mount would be both difficult and expensive to get a proper foundation, being so unequal, as it would require a very great number of piles of wood to be driven in and long planks in order to make a firm foundation. The present ruins seem to prove this, as many of the walls are rent from top to bottom.

"Notwithstanding these inconveniences the temptation for building is very great, as it has a very extensive prospect both of the surrounding hills and plains.

"The whole of the grounds, belonging to Government, forms an oblong square, containing 5 acres 1 rood and 19 falls, divided as follows :—

	AC.	R.	F.
The Hill or mount	2	0	10
Formerly garden ground	0	2	30
The marsh which surrounds the mount	2	2	19
Total belonging to His Majesty	5	1	9

"The above measurement is taken off His Grace the Duke Gordon's plan of his estate in that neighbourhood.

"The whole is set just now by Mr John Macpherson, barrack master, at 40s yearly rent for pasture.

"Ruthven of Badenoch, 20th, October, 1787."

OLD POSSESSORS AND RENTALS IN THE PARISH.

'The householders in the parish in 1679 were as follows :— James Macpherson of Ardbrylach, James Mac Neill there, Donald Mac Allister reoch there, Allister Mac Coil-Chrom in Glengynack, Ewen Mac Coil-Chrom there, William Mac a Mair there. John Macpherson of Ballachroan, James Macpherson, his son, there, William Mac Coillie there, John Mac Gillie dhu there, William Mac Coil there, — Mac Iain vic Conchie, younger, tailor there, Donald roy Mac Willie there, John Mac Gillie Challum vic Coil there, Murriach reach there, Finlay Mac Conchie vic Chotter there, Donald Mac Coil-Chrom there, Thomas roy Mac Challum vic Coil there, John Mac Hamish vic Aonas vic Allister reoch there. Lachlan Macpherson of Pitmain, Donald Mac Allister there, Paul Mac Iain vic Allister vic Homas there, John Mac Allister dhu vic Allister mor there, Donald Mac Willie there, John Mac Homas vic Allister there, John ban Mac Andrew vic Clerich there. John Macpherson of Invereshie, John reoch Mac a brabiter there, Allister reoch, his son, there, Allister Oig there, Donald Glassich Mac Ildonich there, James Mac Iain vic Hamish vic Aonas there, John Mac-a-Bhuie there. Thomas Macpherson, elder of Killyhuntly, Thomas Macpherson, younger, there, Thomas Mac reoch vic a brabiter there, Allister Mac Coinnich mor there, Malcolm Macpherson of Phoness. Donald Mac Iain Glas in Dallanach, Donald Mac Iain mor there, Donald Mac

Allister vic Iain reoch there, Donald Mac Allister mor there. Thomas Macpherson of Etteridge, John Macpherson, his son, there, John Taillour there. James Macpherson of Invernahaven, William Macpherson in Corrarnsdale, Donald dhu Mac Iain vic Iver there, John Macdonald Mac Shan Gruer there, Duncan Mac Conchie mor there, James roy there, Angus Mac Ildonich there. Angus Mac Iain Oig in Corrarnsdale beg. Malcolm Macgregor vic Conchie vic Allister in Tomfad, Allister Mac Conchie vic Allister there, John Macpherson, there, John Mac intaillor in Contalood, John, his son, there, Allister Mac Ildonich there, Adam Smith, there, Archibald Macdonald in Farletter, Malcolm Macpherson there, William Macpherson there, Ewen Mac Durririch (?) there, William Mac Aonas mor there, John Mac Andrew vic Iain buie there, John Mac Coil vic Shader there, John Mac Allister vic Thomas there, Donald Mac Iain, his son, there. Allister mor Mac Shan-Taillor in Inveruglass, Donald, his son, there, Allister Mac Soirle there, William Mac Soirle, his brother, there, James Mac Iain Oig there, James Mac Conchie there, James Mac Andrew, miller there, Donald Mac Soirle Roy there. William Macpherson of Nuide, Finlay Mac Angus ban there. Allister Mac Hamish ban there, Duncan Clerich there. James Macpherson in Laggan of Kingussie, Donald Mac Vurrich vic Ewen in Kingussie mor, James Mackay gald, there, Duncan Miller there, and John Mac Vurrich vic Ewen there.

The Gordon rental by the set of 1667 was thus in Scots money:—

LANDS.

	Merks	Scots.	
Dallanach	80	10	0
Corronach	100	0	0
Biallidmor, possessed by Finlay Mac Hamish vic Finlay	115	0	0
Pitmean	200	0	0
Kingussie mor	220	0	0
A plough of Kingussie beg, called Garline	90	0	0
A quarter of Kingussie beg ought to pay	80	0	0

Laggan of Kingussie	80 0 0
Summa of Parochin of Kingussie	965 merks

FEUS.

	Merks.
Nuidmore and Nuidbeg	133 0 0
Phoness	16 8 8
Etterish	33 3 4
Invernahaven	16 8 8
Ballachroan	66 6 8
Ardbrylach	62 10 8
Invereshie	299 3 4
Invertromie	66 6 8

MILNS.

The Miln of Kingussie	90 0 0
The Miln of Nuide	103 6 8

In all 1851 merks odds, or about £100 0s 0d sterling.

This may be contrasted with the rental at the intimation of sale, say crop 1828:—

Ballachroan	£215 0 0
Pitmain and Inn	152 10 0
Ardbrylach	33 0 0
Village of Kingussie	363 12 0
Garline	13 0 0
Boatman's Croft	12 0 0
Meal Mill	10 0 0
Breakery	24 0 3
Kerrowmeanach	54 9 0
Laggan	35 0 0
Drumgalvie	40 0 0
Knappach	60 0 0
Ruthven, and croft including Barrack Hill	100 0 0
Brae Ruthven and Mill	80 0 0
Gordonhall	118 0 0
Gaick	150 0 0
Biallidmor and Corronach, and half davoch of Biallidbeg, with the hill grazings annexed to it, on the North side of Loch Erricht, possessed by Lieutenant Macpherson	140 0 0
Shootings of Delinlongart, at Loch Erricht side, possessed by Mr Baird of Newbyth	10 0 0
Cockburn croft, being a small piece of grazing on the Athole march, east side of the military	

road 10 0 0

£1620 11 0

The whole public burdens of Badenoch, including rates, stipends, and salaries, amounted to £331 4s 7d, whereof payable by the tenants £211 3s 3d, leaving to be paid by the landlord £120 1s 4d for the three parishes.

The rental of the parish of Kingussie had increased from £100 in 1667, to £1620 odds in 1829. The rise, in proportion to Laggan, was not so great, on account of the greater number of feus in the parish, which of course remained fixed.

I now give a list of some of Mackintosh's tenants in Kingussie parish in 1635 :—Bessie Innes (widow of the first Borlum), in Benchar; Angus Mackintosh there (one of her sons), ; John Mac Andrew vic Clerich in Clune; John Mac Coil dhu vic Allister there; Finlay Mac Iain Roy there; Donald Mac Iain vic Clerich there; Donald Roy Mac Iain vic Fionlay there; Duncan Mac Iain vic Clerich there; George Mac Iain mor vic Ewen there.

It will be observed there are no fewer than three Clarks in the above list, from one of whom descended Mr Alexander Clark, the well-known writer in Ruthven, grandfather of my late lamented friend and early patron, Mrs Robertson, formerly of Benchar, whose death the other day at a venerable age, without issue, closed a singularly useful life, also an ancient connection betwixt the Clarks—an important branch of Clan Chattan—and the parish of Kingussie.

THE MACPHERSONS OF PHONESS.

In 1853 there died at Kingussie intestate, without father or mother, wife or child, brother or sister, Mr Eneas Peter Macpherson, the last of the ancient and honourable house of Phoness. This family had been decaying for some time before the sale of the estate in 1788, but Eneas Peter Macpherson, an indolent, weak man, succeeded to considerable property, after attaining middle age, through an uncle, Peter, who had long expatriated himself, settling, before the French Revolution, as a jeweller in Paris, where he died. His nephew and namesake was not forgotten, and thus it happened that Eneas Peter Macpherson, who never earned a penny, died in comfortable circumstances, carefully tended by his attached natural sister, Anne Macpherson.

The last Phoness was buried with all honour, the funeral being attended by the "Gentlemen" of Badenoch in great force, with Cluny at their head. After the funeral, they met at the Duke of Gordon Hotel, and a minute, drawn up by the late Mr Donald Macrae, writer, as clerk, bearing to be of "the gentlemen of Badenoch" was made out and signed by Cluny as chairman and by the clerk. They were all Macphersons, and invited to say whether or not they claimed to be minuted as heirs of Phoness. Amongst others Colonel Gillies Macpherson, son of the Black Captain of Ballachroan, was mentioned. A poor man, giving a lengthened pedigree, stated that he was descended of Alexander of Phoness, who lived 200 years before, in which at least two Gilliecallums, two Donalds, and other such names appeared. Towards the close of the meeting, Cluny called for any further claimants, when, after a pause, the late Major Duncan Macpherson, some time at Drummond, of the Ralia family, stood up, and stated with much solemnity, that having heard all that had been said, he was satisfied that he, and he alone, was the nearest heir to Phoness, and he intended to make his claim good, sitting down amid applause and to the consternation of the Gilliecallum claimant, who for the time collapsed. Who was ultimately declared executor dative, and my own connection with the case, will be mentioned hereafter.

Lieutenant William Macpherson, father of the above-mentioned Eneas Peter, and last Laird of Phoness, on one occasion records, with proper pride of ancestry, but great inaccuracy, that his father "was the 17th heritor who sat in Phoness," a charming expression, being a literal translation of an old Gaelic idiom, now in disuse.

The first Phoness of whom I have any note was Allister Roy, whose son Donald signs the Bond of Union amongst the Clan Chattan in 1609 for himself and as taking burden upon him for Iain vic William in Invereshie, and for the remanent of his kin of that race and house. Donald could not write, and it is to be noted that the Macphersons were divided under three heads—Cluny for himself, and for Brin and Breackachie ; Thomas vic Allister vic Homas for Pitmean and those of that house ; and Phoness as above.

Another Donald Macpherson of Phoness, probably a grandson of Donald of 1609, is a party to the bond, titled " Band be certain of the name of Clan Chattan to their Chieffe, 19th November, 1664," and stands fifth on the list, headed by Brin, with Invereshie coming third. This bond, in favour of Lachlan Mackintosh of Torcastle, is signed by nine Macphersons, five Mackintoshes, four Farquharsons, three Macgillivrays, two Macbeans, two Shaws, one Macqueen, all leading men. At what time Phoness was acquired in property I have no note of. Even the name of the tenant is not given in the Gordon rental of 1603, but I am satisfied the Phoness family had a title at the time of this Donald of 1664. The extent of the land was a half davoch, and in the time of Alexander, son of Donald, who is found from 1689 to 1712, the family stood at its height, for he is found lending considerable sums of money.

The next proprietor was Malcolm, born about 1690, referred to in 1774 as in his 84th year. He had at least one brother, named Donald, of whom afterwards.

This Malcolm managed his affairs so foolishly that he was known as "Callum Gorach," and ran through his means, which included a wadset of Nessintullich. He entered the army, and even in his old age served in America and France, acquiring great popularity. Henry Davidson of Tulloch befriended him in London more than once. Here follows a letter—Phoness to Tulloch :—

" Honoured Sir,—You'll please deliver the bearer hereof, Mr Lachlan Mackintosh, Shanval of Badenoch, or his order, Lieutenant Macpherson of Captain Ludovick Grant's Independent Company's acceptance of fifteen pounds sterling. He will deliver you your obligation to me for the same, as also pay the five guineas advanced to me at Cromarty. I was in great straits after my coming from Ireland, and was obliged to take up money from this gentleman for the balance of this bill, and

I am with most respectful compliments to you and worthy lady, and ye may believe me your poor friend willing to serve you,
(Signed)   "MALCOLM MCPHERSON.
"Addressed to "Henry Davidson, Esq. of Tulloch, at his house in London."

Malcolm Macpherson appears to have had a pension, but his memory giving way it was not regularly uplifted, hence on a particular occasion Invereshie and Balnespick, junior, as neighbours and Justices, kindly interfered and signed the following declaration :—

"These are certifying that Malcolm Macpherson of Phoness, through the infirmities incident to old age, has been for some years past incapable to manage his own affairs. This made him neglect to go to Inverness where Chelsea men were ordered to attend there, by which means he has been struck off from the list of Chelsea pensioners. As the poor old man has no means to support himself, it would be a most charitable action to get him reponed to his Chelsea, and as he is totally unfit himself even to manage that trifle properly, to order his Chelsea to be paid to a friend upon presenting a certificate of the old man's being alive. Inneressie, 3rd June, 1776. The above is certified by me,
(Signed)   "WILL. MCPHERSON, J.P,
"And likewise by me at Invereshie of the same date.
(Signed)   "LAU. MCKINTOSH, J.P."

Malcolm's son Donald had, it appears, been put in possession of the estate before his father's death. He seems to have led an idle useless life, though receiving some legal training in the writing chambers of John Macbean, Sheriff-Clerk of Inverness-shire, in 1736. Donald married, first, Isobel, daughter of Ludovick Grant of Knockando, and widow of Donald Macpherson of Corronach, and secondly, Margaret Macpherson, who, after his death, married Mr John Stewart. Dying without issue, about 1766, Donald was succeeded by his brother Angus.

Angus Macpherson, describing himself "of Phoness, Lieutenant in General Marjoribank's regiment, in the service of the States of Holland," on the narrative that he was to join his regiment, nominates as his Commissioners, George and William Macpherson, elder and younger of Invereshie, and Lieutenant John Macpherson (Ballachroan), of the

Battalion of Highlanders, lately commanded by Major James Johnston, by deed dated at Edinburgh, on the 25th of May, 1767. He married Elizabeth, only daughter of James Macpherson of Killyhuntly, and having returned home by 1771 writes the following letter to his law-agent at Inverness :—

" Sir,—You'll please without loss of time, serve my wife heir to her father, James Macpherson of Killyhuntly, and send up the Edict here, to be published in the Parish Church. Being in haste, I remain your most obedient servant, (Signed) "ANGUS MACPHERSON.

"Phoness, 20 March, 1771."

" P.S.—Be sure to return the Edict by this very post, as there is a sum of money in the Exchequer, which lies there without interest, and cannot be paid until the service is expede. The money is a balance of debt due by the late Evan Macpherson of Cluny, to James Macpherson of Killyhuntly. The Barons is willing to accept a confirmation upon ten pounds of the subject. To this you'll advert and send the Edict accordingly."

Lieutenant Angus Macpherson died about 1779, survived by his widow, and by at least two sons, the eldest of whom, Lieutenant William Macpherson, succeeded, and was the last Macpherson of Phoness.

The estate was sold to Mr James Macpherson, about 1788, who by this time had also acquired Etteridge and Invernahaven, east of Spey, Raitts in Alvie, and shortly afterwards Clune and Benchar, all west of Spey.

Lieutenant William Macpherson had married a worthy lady, who strove hard to keep up the family's credit before her husband's death about 1826, and thereafter for her son's sake. She and her son resided in Brae Laggan, and I have several of her letters to a rather exacting creditor, John Macpherson, Gallovie, which do her great credit.

After his mother's (Jean Macpherson) death Eneas Peter lived in obscurity at Raitts, of little use in the world while a trouble to no one, until all of a sudden, by the death of the Paris jeweller, he succeeded to a competency, indeed wealth, and retired to Kingussie, most carefully looked after by his natural sister, Anne.

The details of the fight for the Phoness succession in 1853-54 are too long, and I am hardly the person to give particulars of what occurred in my professional career. Suffice it to say that an old man, Mr Donald Ferguson, from Pitlochry, my client, was ultimately successful. He had not a scrap of writing, merely floating family tradition, to instruct his claim. Two ladies of the best type of the old school of Highland gentlewomen, the late Misses Robertson of Kindrochit, supported Mr Ferguson; and through them the late Mr Robertson of Banchor, their relative, interested himself. The active opposition was latterly reduced to Colonel Gillies Macpherson of Ballochroan, who after a lengthened absence re-appeared in Badenoch, but was ineffective; as though nearly related to the Phoness family through his mother, the paternal or legal connection was almost as remote as the Gillie Callum claimant. Having had to make minute and laborious searches, in this case lasting over several months, my inclination for antiquarian and genealogic subjects received a great impetus. By the greatest good fortune I discovered a paper referring to Donald Macpherson, Mr Ferguson's ancestor, in which Donald 'was referred to as "brother to Phoness," in 1737. The late Mr Skene was examined, amongst others, as to the proper interpretation of the expression, and ultimately my client was successful. My late lamented friend, Mrs Robertson, Banchor, with her husband, exerted themselves greatly, and entertained the Kindrochit ladies at Banchor, and at Kingussie for several days when they came to give evidence before the Commissary Depute, Sheriff Colquhoun.

On behalf of the successful claimant, I gave a great dinner in the Duke of Gordon Hotel to the Sheriff, the agents, witnesses, and all interested or concerned, and, as one present said, he had not seen such a festive gathering in Kingussie since the days of the Duke of Gordon's occasional visits at rent collections.

THE OSSIAN MACPHERSON PURCHASES AND EVICTIONS.

In consequence of the spread of the burgh of Kingussie, the population in the parish has been increasing in marked contrast with Laggan and Alvie. The country parts, excepting Kingussie and Newtonmore, have however become greatly depopulated, and in especial those parts bordering on the river Truim. The opening of the railway has neither removed nor checked the sad state of matters. Mr James Macpherson of Ossianic fame, who acquired Phoness, Etterish, and Invernahaven, began this wretched business, and did it so thoroughly that not much remained for his successors, though they followed his example in doing their little worst up to the comparatively recent clearings in Glenballoch and Glenbanchor.

Take the case of Dallanach as an illustration. The very name is now practically lost. Yet as late as 1763 there were eight well-doing heads of families, namely, Andrew Macpherson, who lived at Inishlea of Dallanach, Andrew Clark, Alexander Clark, William Macpherson, Donald Macpherson, Thomas Macpherson, Donald Macpherson, and Angus Macpherson, say 50 souls. Every place James Macpherson acquired was cleared, and he had also a craze for changing and obliterating the old names. The first attempt, namely, to suppress Phoness, Etteridge, and Invernahaven, and call the whole Glentruim, was stopped by the Duke of Gordon, who owned one side of the Truim towards its foot, and both sides higher up. Another attempt of Mac Ossian's was more successful—changing Raitts into Belville. This last seems of late undergoing a further change into Balavil, perhaps to emerge in time, even in English, into Palaville. Upon this point it may be noticed that Mac Ossian, in making an entail and calling four of his numerous bastards in the first instance to the succession, declares an irritancy if any of the heirs use any other designation than that of "Macpherson of Belleville."

There is not a single inhabited house, I rather think, on the estate of Invernahaven at present, but it was once a rather important place, possessed and occupied by people in fair circumstances as heritors. Dalwhinnie, as its hill grounds, at one time pertained to Invernahaven. Captain Alexander Clark, one of Mac Ossian's nephews, was long tenant of the place. Here is one of his letters, illustrating a gross case of oppression by one of the "gentlemen" of Badenoch, who, according to the well-known Gaelic saying, swarmed in every town, and was

ONE OF THE "THREE CURSES" OF BADENOCH.

Writing from Invernahaven on the 12th of April, 1808, Captain Clark says—

"Andrew Macpherson, tacksman of Biallidbeg, was on Saturday last served with a summons to the Sheriff Court of Inverness at the instance of Mr Lachlan Macpherson, tacksman of Biallidmor, and the nature of the complaint, you as a Highlander, will easily comprehend. In the beginning of March last Andrew Macpherson went to Biallidmor to ask the liberty of kiln-drying some corn in Mr Macpherson's kiln, and not finding him at home, sent his grieve or foreman with his compliments to Mrs Macpherson, requesting the use of the kiln, which Donald Macrae the grieve, said his mistress granted. That Andrew then had none of his own horses at home, and finding two of the petitioner's horses at his door and in his grass, he supposed for the distance he might use the liberty of sending the little corn he had to the kiln with these horses. The defender lives on the next farm to the pursuer, besides you must know that it is a common practice in the Highlands to get the neighbours and their horses to assist in sending to kiln and miln. I only regret for the sake of the community how little they have been troubled in that way this season. That Andrew denies his having used Mr Macpherson's horses in any bad way, or over-loading them in the least. That John Macpherson in Crubinbeg, brother of the pursuer, assisted in loading the horses, and the beforementioned Donald Macrae and Donald Mackintosh, two of the pursuer's men servants, assisted in unloading the horses, and that Mackintosh at the time said that the cart fitted the pony remarkably well. From these circumstances it will clearly appear that there was no intention of using the horses ill. That when Andrew was in the act of kiln drying his corn, Mr Macpherson came home and locked the door of the kiln, and would not for the space of three days allow to proceed with the drying which the corn wanted, neither would he give him a sack of it for the use of his family. By this interruption the meal produced from the corn was much injured. Andrew from the very first offered to submit all he did to the decision of any two gentlemen in the county, or the Justices of the Peace."

This is a good illustration of Biallid's churlish disposition. Let us take an instance of his violence. Mr John Macpherson at Cluny Mains, afterwards at Gallovie, writes on 24th January, 1816, transmitting information for

"Donald Macpherson, one of my neighbours, against my neighbour Captain Macpherson, Biallid. It is a well founded complaint, for upwards of 12 months since Biallid attempted to lay hands on him on my own farm. In consequence, the complainer was afraid to attend to his duty near the march. Biallid is known to be the most turbulent man in the county, and has within the last few years committed many acts of violence, so much so that one poor man's life was for a long time despaired of, and after he summoned Biallid before the Sheriff Court for redress, his funds failed him, the doctor's fees taking all he had. He had applied by petition last April to the Justices, at least to two of them, but Biallid had the ear of them, so they refused a deliverance."

Wrong doings were not confined to the "gentlemen." Ralia writes wrothfully from Breackachie on the 15th of April, 1794, of another Macpherson thus—

"This covers a bond of caution by Captain Charles and myself for the persons complained of in the Process of Lawburrows. I am such a stranger to legal operations that I do not know whether it is competent to counteract Letters of Lawburrows. If such a step is known in law, there never was a better field for it than the present. The infamous man, who I cannot better describe, since his discharge from the Duke of Gordon's First Fencibles, has made it his study to foment quarrels, and form parties on public and private occasions to attack persons unguarded from liquor, or alone, ever since. He did so on the occasion for which he now sues Lawburrows. The persons complained of, who are as industrious, decent men as any this country produces in their sphere, came to see the anniversary of their children at cockfighting annually observed. In the evening with the master of the school they withdrew to a whiskey house adjacent to take some refreshment to themselves. This William Macpherson, in his usual manner, who bore no good will to any of the parties, thrust himself upon the company after they were something flustered (being fasting) with liquor, and after being told his company was disagreeable, withdrew with a confidant of his, who prudently counselled him not to join the company any more, upon that occasion, as they seemed to dislike his association, which he then promised. The reverse he acted. He withheld himself from the company until they became stupid with the excess of drink, and collected from different farms in the neighbourhood, a parcel of unwary people. He then came and attacked them in a state of insensibility, beat and bruised them most cruelly, broke two ribs in the side of one of the persons complained of, dislocated the thumb of another, and with his teeth bit a third. He then withdrew, but terrified that such rascally behaviour would not be overlooked, took this mode of protecting himself. The persons concerned being of the first character in this country in their own line, scorn to apply for a similar defence, yet they and their friends consider themselves greatly injured."

I turn to a more agreeable subject and give a really creditable contract of marriage, written by a country lad, James Macpherson at Coraldie, dated Etterish, the 2nd of February, 1737. Endorsed on the back is an acknowledgment of the loan of a book, " Kennet's Roman Antiquities" (much in repute at one time, but now superseded), indicating considerable erudition on the part of some of the ancient residenters in the valley of Truim—

"Etrish, 2nd February, 1737.

"Sir,—Seeing that your sister Margaret and I by God's assistance resolve to marry again to-morrow, and the time being so short and the want of stamp paper, that she cannot be secured effectually in the hundred merks she is to have of my effects free out of this house in case she did survive me, by and attour her division as law provides her. I do assure you and promise by these to grant and give to her my obligations on stamps at or before my receiving of the bill resting by Duncan Macpherson in Crubinbeg and John Macpherson his brother, payable for her behoof, for 270 merks Scots. So that you need not scruple to allow the marriage to go on. And being a favour done to me who am and resolve to be your affectionate brother.
(Signed) " JAMES MACPHERSON.

"Addressed to Mr John Macpherson, son to the deceased Thomas Macpherson some time in Garvabeg."

"Nessendullie, November 19th, 1750.

"There received by me, Donald Macpherson, son to Ewen Macpherson of Laggan, from Nessendullie, the " Roman Antiquities" by Kennett, which I oblige myself hereby to return when demanded.
(Signed) " DONALD MACPHERSON."

I conclude this part by giving the terms of arrangement of separation between Evan Macpherson, schoolmaster of Ralia, and Margaret Macpherson his wife, also Isobel Macpherson, her mother, which has in all seven signatures—

" In presence of Captain John Macpherson of Ballachroan, Bailie Macpherson in Glentromie, Captain Alexander Macpherson of Biallid and Captain Alexander Clark in Knappach. We, Mr Evan Macpherson in Ralia, Isobel Macpherson, his mother-in-law, and Margaret Macpherson, his spouse, have come to the following agreement :—That Mr Evan shall yearly from his salary allow five pounds sterling yearly for the aliment of his mother-in-law and wife, over and above the annual rent of the money in Invernahaven's hands, which Mr Evan is to make up to fifty pounds sterling. This settlement to stand from the date hereof till January, 1786. This principal of fifty pounds to be lodged with Invernahaven is to be conceived in fee to Mr Grant's children, and in life-rent to his mother-in-law, and after her demise to his wife. In case the above designed women do not agree long in one family, we agree that the foresaid aliment shall be divided equally between us. Moreover, if Mr Evan's salary is reduced, we promise to suffer our income to be reduced in proportion. It is to be observed that if Mr Evan cannot at the first term add what is requisite to make up fifty pounds as above, in that case he is to be allowed one pound sterling of the foresaid aliment to help him. If Mr Evan's salary is reduced to very little and that he cannot spare any, in that case, as the interest of the fifty pounds cannot support both the women, they shall be allowed to draw ten pounds from the capital, but the forty pounds always to remain in fee for the children. In testimony that we are willing to abide by the above settlement, we subscribe these at Muirhouse, 29th July, 1785, before and in presence of the above gentlemen.

     (Signed) "EVAN MACPHERSON.
        " "ISOBELLA MCPHERSON.
        " "MARGARET MACPHERSON.
        " "JOHN MACPHERSON, Witness.
        " "D. MCPHERSON, Witness.
        " "ALEX. MCPHERSON, Witness.
        " "ALEX. CLARK, Witness."

INVERTROMIE, ETTERISH, INVERNAHAVEN, ETC.

Invertromie, originally feued in 1638 to Donald, son of Macpherson of Noidbeg, consisted of a davoch of land. When sold in 1795, it was, and had for sometime, with that curious perverseness for changing ancient names, been called Inverhall. The seller, Hugh Macpherson, became involved, like many in Badenoch, with the Black Officer of Ballachroan, and though his private debts were insignificant —only a few hundred pounds—a sale had to be made. The description, as will be seen, was couched in an inflated style worthy of Robins. Still it was a beautiful place and a valuable sporting ground. This is the advertisement which appeared in the Edinburgh newspapers—

"An Estate in Badenoch, with excellent shooting quarters, for sale. To be sold, by public voluntary roup, within the Old Exchange

Coffee-house, Edinburgh, on Monday, the 16th day of June next, between the hours of five and six afternoon,

"All and whole, the Lands and Estate of Inverhall or Invertrommie, with the whole Sheillings, Pasturages, and Pertinents thereof, lying in the lordship of Badenoch, parish of Kingussie, and county of Inverness. These lands hold feu of the Duke of Gordon, for payment of 50 merks Scots, with some small customs and services, which are all converted. The yearly rent is at present only £110 sterling, but, as there are no leases on any of the lands, a very considerable increase of rent may reasonably be expected, and has indeed been offered, on granting leases for a moderate endurance.

"There is not perhaps in the Highlands of Scotland a more beautiful or picturesque spot than that now offered to sale. It lies in the very heart of Badenoch, along the banks of the Water of Trommie, and is also bounded by the River Spey, at the junction of the Trommie with that river. It is interspersed and skirted with birch and other brushwood; extends four or five miles from the strath or middle of the country, due south, up the Glen of Trommie; and the proprietor has a right of pasturage to the very source of Trommie, several miles farther up.

"In the low part of the estate, or at Invertrommie, there is a large field of fine arable land, of the best quality in the country. There is also an extensive meadow or morass, adjoining to the arable land, along the banks of the Spey, and yielding great crops of fine natural hay. Trommie and Spey afford great plenty of salmon, and trout of different kinds, in the greatest perfection. There are several falls of the waters of sufficient force to drive mills or machinery of any extent, and constantly supplied with water. The estate is well supplied with moss of the best quality. It contains a slate quarry, and it is believed there is also plenty of lime stone. It is in every respect capable of the highest improvement.

"In the middle of Glentrommie, there is a residence which has for several years been occupied as a shooting quarter, by different gentlemen of rank and fortune, and here the proprietor has built a substantial house of several apartments, superior to most shooting quarters. Fancy can scarcely figure a more pleasant or romantic situation than the place affords. It is close by the river, surrounded with natural woods of great beauty and considerable value on both sides. There are large fields of fine natural grass round the house by the river side. For a sportsman, there cannot be a more eligible station; as, around the residence, there is a range of four or five miles of the best shooting ground in the Highlands; the game is in great abundance, and frequently within twenty yards of the house—and trout and salmon in the river running past the door. There is also a carriage road to the shooting quarters, leading from the high road from Edinburgh to Inverness.

"The whole estate and particularly the glen, is also well calculated for a sheep walk, and having the water on one side of it, and the whole being well supplied with stones, may easily be enclosed at little expense.

"There is no mansion-house on the estate, but many delightful situations for building on, particularly at Invertrommie, where, besides having a view of that part of the estate, there will also be had a complete view of the country of Badenoch for many miles up and down, the beauty of which is well known to every person who has travelled the Highland Road. Belville House (a new modern and elegant building) immediately fronts this part of the estate—the ruins of the Barracks of Ruthven, the Parish Church, the Place of Gordonhall, and many other beautiful objects are all in the immediate neighbourhood. There is also a view of Loch Inch, and the River Spey for several miles of its course through that delightful country. The whole forming one of the finest landscapes in Scotland.

"In short, there can seldom occur an estate for sale situated like the present, fitted alike to gratify the pleasures of the sportsman and the man of taste, who may choose to reside in the country ; and, at the same time, affording every possible encouragement to the purchaser in a mercantile view merely, as a proper subject for improvement.

"The title-deeds, which are perfectly clear, are in the hands of James Robertson, writer, Castle-hill, Edinburgh, to whom intending purchasers may apply for further information ; or to Captain Charles Macpherson, at Gordonhall, near Ruthven, who will also show the estate, and either of whom have power to conclude a private bargain."

The first feu of Invertromie was included in the charter by George, Marquis of Huntly, with consent of Lady Ann Campbell, his spouse, and George, Lord Gordon, his son, in favour of Donald Macpherson, eldest lawful son of John Macpherson of Nuide beg, who also received with it, described as a davoch of land, the town and lands of Nuide mor. This charter is dated at Huntly, the 28th of April, 1638, and confirmed by the Crown on the 5th of March, 1642. Six years later Invertromie belonged to Captain Thomas Macpherson, from whom it passed to Lachlan, who is found in 1683. Lachlan was succeeded by his son, Duncan Macpherson, found in 1697 and 1698. In 1711 there is notice of Thomas, son of the deceased Angus, son to the also deceased Lachlan Macpherson of Invertromie before mentioned. Duncan of Invertromie, also before mentioned, was succeeded by his son, Alexander, found in 1723. A break in my notes here occurs until 1787, when Hugh Macpherson, described of Inverhall, gets a charter from the Duke of Gordon as heir of his father, John. This was the Hugh who became involved with the Black Officer of Ballachroan, and had to sell the estates. They were advertised in 1794 for public sale, but no sale being effected, though several were after it, a sale by private bargain was made to the Duke of Gordon on behalf of his illegitimate son, Major George Gordon of the 11th Dragoons. Major Gordon was infeft in 1796, and was well-known as "*The Duke's* George," so called by the Duchess of Gordon to distinguish him from "*My* George"—her son, George, Marquis of Huntly. Major Gordon was a great sportsman, for whom was also purchased Dalwhinnie hill grounds, as popular in his own way as his distinguished brother. Major George Gordon later became Inspector General of Foreign Corps, and sold Invertromie to George Macpherson Grant of Invereshie, who was infeft in 1835 in "the davoch town and lands of Invertromie, with the grazings, sheillings, and pasturages thereof, and outsetts of the same in Glentromie, called Kinchraggan, Linacloich, Lynmore, with the sheillings in Riechraggan, parish of Kingussie." The feu duty originally stipulated remains on the lands, passing with the Badenoch lands sold to the Baillies.

The earliest proprietor of the davoch of Etteridge that I have note of was John Macpherson, found in 1627. The descent I do not propose to trace but merely note the following names—John found in 1677, Thomas in 1683, Murdo in 1697, another Murdo found in 1760, who was father of John of Etteridge found in 1781, while in 1787 James Macpherson is infeft by the Duke of Gordon. The Etteridge family had a grazing on Loch Errocht—west side, called Catlag-Etterish to distinguish it from Catlag, or Catlodge-Cluny. The last-mentioned James Macpherson of Etteridge sold the estate to his namesake, Mac

Ossian, whose heir of entail presently possesses the place.

The Macphersons of Invernahaven long occupied a creditable position in the parish. The earliest I have noted was James Macpherson, found in 1679, 1683, and 1711. James Macpherson was succeeded by his son Alexander, found in 1712; then there is a break to 1781, when John Macpherson is found proprietor of Invernahaven. He made a settlement in favour of his son James, who sold to Mac Ossian.

In a letter to one of James' creditors, Captain Charles Macpherson of Gordonhall, on the 15th of September, 1799, writes of him—"He has for many years been a resident in the West Indies, but is expected home about Martinmas, when his few creditors who have claims against his estate will be satisfied." His mother or step-mother was then living. James Macpherson left no issue—a title to Drumouchter, or the Dalwhinnie hill lands, all that remained of the Invernahaven estate, being made up in 1801, by Captain John Maclean of the 93rd, and Jean Macpherson, his aunt, spouse of Lieutenant John Macpherson of Blargie, as heirs portioners to John Macpherson of Invernahaven, their grandfather and father respectively, who on precept by the Duke of Gordon were infeft 14th August, 1801.

Captain Maclean, arranging with his aunt, became sole owner, and in 1819, then Colonel Sir John Maclean, K.C.B., sold Drumouchter to the Marquis of Huntly.

Drumouchter now belongs to Glentruim.

XXVI.—PARISH OF ALVIE.

THE INVERESHIE FAMILY.

THE family of Invereshie is one of the few old Highland families showing an almost unbroken line of prosperity, at present standing higher than ever. Putting aside for the moment his Ballindalloch holding, Sir George Macpherson-Grant stands head and shoulders territorially over all other Macphersons both in acreage and rental. By origin Sir George is descended of the two houses of Macphersons of Dalraddie, and Grants of Rothiemurchus, being of Invereshie originally by purchase, and of Ballindalloch by destination. Invereshie alone falls within the scope of these papers, and I pass at once over the fabulous origin given by Douglas and the asserted connection with the old Invereshies, and mention the first Macpherson of Dalraddie, properly so termed, viz., Paul, whose name and designation in the original charter of Dalraddie is stated thus, "Paul Macpherson, son lawful of Donald Macpherson in Dalraddie." This charter, or rather disposition and feu contract, is granted by George, Marquis of Huntly, Earl of Enzie, with consent of Lady Anna Campbell, his spouse, and George, Lord Gordon, his son, dated 12th October, 1637, and registered in the books of Council and Session at Edinburgh, 24th July, 1767. The lands conveyed are thus described—

"All and whole, the town and lands of Dalraddie, extending to a davoch of land, comprehending therein the seats and town following, viz., Kynintachar, Knockcaillich, Lynanruich, and Balavullin, which are parts and pendicles of the said davoch lands of Dalraddie, with all and sundry their houses, biggings, yards, tofts, crofts, woods, fishings, multures, mosses, muirs, outsetts, insetts, parts, pendicles, and other pertinents whatsoever, as well not named as named, together with the sheillings, grazings, and pasturages in Teavorer, Teriuchneck, and Badabog, and other parts used and wont, and as the tenants and possessors of the said lands were in use of before, lying within the parish of Alvie, Lordship of Badenoch, and the Sheriffdom of Inverness."

I have no note of Paul's son, but in 1683 John of Dalraddie, his grandson, appears, and in 1691 Angus Macpherson, also described as grandson of Paul, is found. This John, third of Dalraddie, had a son, also called John, married to Isobel Cuthbert, daughter of Provost Cuthbert of Inverness, of the Castlehill family. Of this marriage there were two sons—John, fifth, who succeeded, and married to one of the Cluny ladies, leaving no issue, was succeeded by his brother George, sixth.

I now turn to the Macphersons of Invereshie, which by this time had been acquired by Dalraddie. The first Macpherson who acquired the heritable right to Invereshie was Angus Macpherson, by disposition and feu contract by the forenamed George, Marquis of Huntly, his wife, and son, in his (Angus') favour, dated 22nd October, 1637, registered in the Books of Council and Session on said 24th July, 1767. The following is the description of the subjects :—

"All and whole the lands of Invereshie, Countilate, Corarnstilmor, with houses, biggings, yards, tofts, sheillings, grazings, and whole parts, pendicles and pertinents whatsoever, with the liberty of the woods and pasturages in the whole foresaid lands as well in property as in commonly used and wont, all extending to a davoch land of old extent. The lands of Farletter, Corarnstilbeg, with houses, biggings, yards, and whole other pertinents thereof, extending to a davoch land, with the fishing of salmon upon the Lake of Loch Insh and the water Spey, running through or by the same, commonly called the fishing of Farletter. The land of Inveruglass and Clauchan with the mill thereof, formerly upon the water of Dallishaig, now upon the water of Tromie, extending to the half of a davoch land of old extent. The lands of Dell of Killyhuntly with the croft thereof, extending to a davoch land of old extent. The lands of Invermarkie with the mill thereof, comprehending the lands of Achnisuchan, *alias* Auch Guisachan, with the mill croft of Invermarkie :—all extending to four davochs and a half davoch of lands, with houses, biggings, yards, tofts, crofts, woods, fishings, sheillings, grazings, and whole pertinents thereof used and wont, lying within the Lordship of Badenoch, parishes of Kingussie and Insh, late Regality of Huntly, and Sheriffdom of Inverness."

Angus Macpherson, first heritor of Invereshie, was a few years after he became owner, killed in one of Montrose's battles, and left a son John, very young, whose estates were managed by the Tutor, also called John Macpherson. John Macpherson, second of Invereshie, was succeeded by his son Gillies, but commonly called Elias Macpherson, who falling into serious pecuniary difficulties sold his estates to Macpherson of Dalraddie. Elias afterwards became a soldier, and died abroad without issue, about 1697. His uncle, Sir Eneas Macpherson, left no male issue, but he had at least one daughter, who married Sir John Maclean of Duart. The premier male line of Invereshie thus terminated, but it is understood there are male descendants in existence of Angus before mentioned, the first heritor of Invereshie.

I now revert to George, sixth of the Dalraddie line, who possessed Invereshie and Dalraddie for upwards of 60 years, and being a man of great prudence and thrift, bordering on penuriousness, placed his family on a very secure footing, and by his marriage brought the fine estate of Ballindalloch ultimately to them. He purchased the very convenient adjoining estate of Balnespick. Before this purchase, although Invereshie extended to the Perth and Aberdeen marches, the frontage to the Spey, only from the flat near the church of Insh to the Feshie was insignificant. I rather think that it was he who managed to secure for a trifle the Glebe of Insh, but this may have been managed before George's time. Some of the ancient residenters in and about Insh have inherited curious stories of his penuriousness. Be that as it may he preserved and added to his estate, and has the credit of making the first fir plantation in Alvie, viz., "Baddan Shonat," a piece of planting not far from the home farm of Invereshie, so called from a clever strong country woman, Janet, who carried the plants on her back from Ballindalloch, after George Macpherson's marriage. Naturally, Alvie grows the finest fir, but it has not been the worse of the handsome and thriving plantations of recent years made on the plains of the Mackintosh and Invereshie estates. In old times these two families were not only near neighbours, but close and hereditary friends. Here is a letter from Invereshie to Mackintosh of Balnespick on behalf of the Laird of Mackintosh, dated Invereshie, 17th May, 1779—

"I am favoured with yours just now, with respect to my casting and using divots for my houses on the Muir ground west of Lagganlia and Croftbeg. It was by an indulgence which we had from Laird Lachlan Mackintosh, and his successor, Laird William, during their pleasure. I never pretended to have any title of using any property upon said ground, but by permission, and when that permission is withdrawn I will always be thankful for past favours. If it is continued I shall give as full an acknowledgment as may be desired in these terms. As to my milner or others of my people, if they have encroached in casting divots or peats upon Mackintosh's property, I shall notify to them to stay for the future. All here joins me in compliments to you and Mrs Mackintosh.—I ever am, dear sir, your affectionate humble servant, (Signed) GEORGE McPHERSON."

The first break in this hereditary friendship occurred towards the end of last century, when Mackintosh found it necessary to embank the turbulent Feshie for some distance from its inver into the Spey. The Iosal of Dalnavert being situated below Invereshie, received naturally the first and bulk of the Feshie when in flood, and as a great part of the farm was becoming useless, Mackintosh resolved to make on his side a straight and powerful embankment, which was carried out at the enormous expense in those days of over a thousand pounds sterling. This did not at all suit Invereshie, whose lands were thereby every winter flooded from Loch Insh to the Feshie, but it was a matter that could not be stopped, and only mitigated in part by an additional cut made by Invereshie for surplus river Spey water. In later years march differences in Glenfeshie occurred, and a well-meant effort of final settlement by excambion failed. As the whole of Glenfeshie has been for several years let as one forest, difficulties have been, for a time at least, overcome.

George Macpherson was succeeded by his son, William Macpherson, who did not marry. George's second son, Captain John Macpherson, a man of sterling character and cultivation, far beyond his turbulent or dissipated neighbours, predeceased the elder brother, William, on whose death the succession opened to his nephew, George, afterwards Sir George Macpherson-Grant, who had succeeded prior to his uncle William's death, to the estate of Ballindalloch. Sir George, first Baronet, may be considered as the real founder of the family. Shrewd, ambitious and determined, party and men were made subservient to his wishes, and he was steadily successful. He bought up at great expense all the ridiculous but burdensome stipulations in his Gordon charters, finally acquiring not only the freehold of Invereshie, but the lands of Invertromie, and also a great slice of the Gordon Kingussie lands. He was succeeded by his son, Sir John, whom I cannot more fitly describe than as a fair-minded, scrupulous, and honourable gentleman, whose promising life was unhappily cut short after a too brief career. His son, the present Sir George, is so well known that I need but say that he, like the present Lochiel, has, by zeal, industry, and thought, in course of a long reign, strengthened and added to the best traditions of his house, and shown what a great Highland proprietor can and ought to be.

THE GORDON RENTALS AND REMOVALS.

The rental of the Gordons in 1667, was as follows, and it may be mentioned that from the large holdings of Mackintosh and Invereshie acquired early the Gordon rental was smaller in Alvie than in the other parishes of Badenoch :—

	Merks	Scots.	
1. The two parts of Pittourie	194	6	8
2. Kinrara and Gortanchrive	180	0	0
	374	6	8

It is to be remembered that the wadset right of Easter Lynvuilg, possessed by Borlum ought to pay yearly 12 merks money, which he rests till he clears himself by discharge.

FEUS.

1. Borlum for the three davochs of Raitts ...	186	0	0
2. Dalraddie	62	0	0

3. Invereshie, for his whole lands in Alvie, Insh,
   and Kingussie 299 3 4
4. The miln of Dalraddie pays yearly 12 bolls
   farme at £5 the boll, inde 4 score 10 merks   90 0 0

                                                  ─────────
                                                  637 3 4

Total, 1,011 10s 0d merks or about £60 sterling.

The rental when sold by Duke Alexander's trustees was thus, say crop 1828—

1. Pitchern, lease expires in 1832 ... ... £82 18 6
2. Pittourie 77 3 6
3. Dellifour 84 0 0
                                              ─────────
                                              £244 2 0

A four fold rise only in 150 years, not including,
however, Kinrara, and Lynvuilg.

Here follows a list of some of Mackintosh's tenants in the parish of Alvie in 1635—Angus Macqueen, principal tenant of Meikle Dunachton; John Mac Coil vic William there; Angus Mac Conchie there; John Roy Mac Allister vic Fionlay there; William Roy Mac Huistean there; Donald Mac Coil vic Iain Dhu there; Andrew Miller there; Donald Mac Conchie vic Gorrie there; Allister Mac Fionlay vic Ewen there; —— Mac Fionlay Dhu there; Kenneth Mac Fionlay Mor there; James Gow there; Duncan Mac Gorrie there; Ferquhar Dhu there; Donald Dhu Mac Gorrie there; James Shaw in Dunachton beg; Soirle Mac Fionlay vic Ewen there; Finlay Mac Allister vic Fionlay vic Ewen there: Katharine nin Donald Roy there; William Mac Allan Roy there; Gillespie Mac Coil vic Gorrie there; John Mac Hamish vic Aonas there; Alexander Roy in Pittourie; Lachlan Mackintosh of Stron, principal tacksman of Kincraig; Finlay Mor there; Alister Dhu Mac Fionlay there; Soirle Mac Allister vic Fionlay there; Allister Mac Fionlay there; Hugh Macqueen there; James Shaw in Dalnavert; William Shaw, his son, there; Thomas Mac Iain vic William there, William Miller there; Donald Mor Mac Allister there; John Mac Hamish, tailor, there; Angus Macpherson of Invereshie, principal tacksman of the croft of Dalnavert, bewest the water of Feshie.

I next give a list of several of the tenants and occupants of Alvie generally in 1679:—Lachlan Macpherson of Dellifour; Leonard Macpherson, his son, there; Duncan Dow there; Ewen Mac Coil there; Angus Mac Coil vic Phail there; John Macrae there; Allister Mac William vic Iain Mor there; Allister Macpherson there; Donald Macpherson in Pittourie; Donald Mac Phail vic Coinich there; Patrick Macpherson there; Thomas Mac Griasich Chotter there; Allister Macpherson of Pitchern, there; John mor Mac a ghillie rioch there; William Mac Iain vic Gillandrish there; William Gow there; Donald Macpherson in Pitchern; Allister Mac Allister vic Muriach there; Ewen Oig there; Allister Mac Coil Reoch there; John Macpherson in Dalraddie; Finlay Mac Ewen there; John roy Mac Coil vic Eachen there; William Mac Gillie Michael there; Allister Mac Hamish vic an Taillor there; Donald Mac Phadrick mor there; Donald Gordon there; Thomas Dow there; John Mor Mac Iain vic Thomas there; Donald Maclean of Wester Lynvuilg; Donald Mac Conchie vic Phail there; Hucheon Rose there; James Mac Iain vic Iier there; James and Angus Macpherson there; Angus Macferquhar there; Donald Mackenzie there; John Mac Gillie Phadrick vic Iain there; Donald Maclean there; John Mac Phail vic Coinich there; John Oig Mac Ferquhar there.

After his marriage Alexander, fourth Duke of Gordon, brought Jane Maxwell, the new Duchess, to the north, and they visited all his estates. She was not taken with Gordon Castle, but so much struck with Kinrara that she at once made up her mind that it should become her Highland residence, and she stuck to it to the last, ordering that her remains be there laid.

Both Kinraras, Gordon's and Mackintosh's, are beautiful, and nowhere in Badenoch are the hills more set off with birch than at North Kinrara. But, alas, at the beginning the Duchess' wishes were carried out by the removal of a numerous and contented people. Even yet after the lapse of more than a hundred years green oases on the sides of the wooded Tor Alvie showing ancient cultivation, are to be found—and it is a great satisfaction to me that ere matters have fallen into utter oblivion, never to be recalled, I record the woful events which occurred in 1770, in connection with the clearing of North Kinrara. Upon the 20th of February, 1770, the Duke signs in London a precept agreeable to the ancient Scottish form, to warn out Patrick Grant of Rothiemurchus, principal tenant, and the following people, in the personal occupation of the lands of Kinrara and Dellifour:— 1, Donald Grant, in the boat house of Knappach ; 2, Peter Grant, in Easter Kinrara ; 3, John Grant there ; 4, John Shaw there ; 6, James Grant, in Wester Kinrara ; 7, Anna Forbes there ; 8, James Grant, in Balnacruick ; 9, James Cameron, in Sloch ; 10, Alexander Macdonald, senior, in Gortnacreich ; 11, Peter Macdonald there ; 12, Alexander Macdonald, junior, there ; 13, Donald Grant, in Abban ; 14, Alexander Cameron, in Croftgown ; 15, Robert Cameron there ; 16, Annie Grant there ; 17, Mr William Gordon, minister of the Gospel there ; 18, Peter Grant, in Dellifour ; 19, James Grant there ; 20, John Campbell there ; 21, Alexander Cuthbert there ; 22, Alexander Cameron there ; 23, Christian Macpherson, Mailander there ; 24, Malcolm Macdonald, Altnagown, probably over one hundred souls, doubtless poor enough, but honestly paying the whole rent exacted by the Gordons, while allowing a neighbouring laird to sit free for the best part of the possession. Great precautions were taken that the services were legally complete. Patrick Grant seems to have then resided at Dell of Rothiemurchus, but the house was shut up, and copies were not only left in the lock hole, and stuck on the church door of Alvie, but also a copy left in a cloven stick on the grounds of Kinrara and Dellifour.

Retiring from the great Metropolis the Duchess statedly and for long periods lived at Kinrara, nearly always accompanied by her daughter Georgina, afterwards Duchess of Bedford. Lady Georgina was passionately attached to Badenoch, but unlike the others, the steady close friend and protector of all poor people far and near, and her name to the present day is deservedly held in the warmest affection.

DUCHESS JANE'S INSCRIPTION.

As I said, Duchess Jane, who died in London in April, 1812, is interred at Kinrara, with an absurdly inflated incription about her descendants, quoted by Banker Macpherson, page 82 of his *Old Church and Social Life in the Highlands*. At page 81 Mr Macpherson makes this statement, "*She had herself prepared* the inscription to be placed on the monument." If Duchess Jane prepared the inscription, as Mr Macpherson alleges, then she had among her many undoubted gifts one hitherto unknown, no less than the second sight, or more properly that of foretelling futurity.

The descendants of her five daughters are given nominatim on the monument, and under the head of Lady Georgina, fifth daughter, above referred to, who married John, Duke of Bedford, there are mentioned four sons and two daughters, viz., Lady Georgina Elizabeth Russell, and Lady Louisa Jane Russell, the present Duchess Dowager of Abercorn. It is to the last venerable lady, who not long since celebrated her 80th birthday, surrounded by over one hundred descendants, I have to refer. Peerage authorities tell the public that Lady Louisa Jane Russell was born on the 8th of July, 1812, three months *after* her grandmother, Jane Duchess of Gordon's death. How could Duchess Jane, if *she* prepared the inscription, know that an unborn child of her daughter Georgina, would be a girl and named Louisa Jane, perhaps Mr Macpherson, if he stick to his text in any new edition, will explain and clear up.

The end of the inscription runs thus—"This monument was erected by Alexander, Duke of Gordon, and the above inscription placed on it at the particular request of the Duchess, his wife." I quite admit an ordinary reader, who perhaps never heard of any Duchess but Duchess Jane, might be misled by this. Mr Macpherson ought to know, but seems to have overlooked that Duke Alexander was married a second time, after Jane Maxwell's death, to Mrs Christie, who had been in the first Duchess's service, and was much attached to the Gordon children. The inscription, although obscure in its latter part, can by no possibility have been prepared by Duchess Jane.

THE OSSIAN MACPHERSONS.

A pretentious erection, said to have been originally designed by the architects of The Adelphi, London, was erected by Mr James Macpherson after he became purchaser of Raitts in 1788 and had removed most of the old possessors. These under the Borlums were very numerous, and mainly removed by the first James, while a total clearance was made by the second James Macpherson, who leased the Mains of Raitts and a considerable part of the estate in 1809 to Thomas Dott, feuar in Hilton Hill, near Cupar-Fife, at an enormous rise of rent, viz., £360 forehand. A list of the people removed by Macpherson in 1809 will be found as an appendix.

To Croftmaluack was assigned the name of Chapel Park, and having called a series of bastards to succeed as heirs of entail, he departed, securing, by payment, interment in Westminster Abbey!

Macpherson's works, other than the Ossian fabrications, have fallen into oblivion. He was deeply imbued with the atheistic cant so fashionable in the second half of last century and gave free rein to his views in the *Introduction to the History of Great Britain and Ireland*, a publication scathingly reviewed and exposed in a scarce pamphlet called "Remarks" on the "Introduction," published in London in 1772.

For some years he resided in a certain locality, in London, near the Houses of Parliament, long since swept away, which locality is so graphically described by Dickens in "Nicholas Nickleby" that, though somewhat lengthy, I transcribe it—

"Within the precincts of the ancient city of Westminster, and within half a quarter of a mile or so of its ancient sanctuary, is a narrow dirty region, the sanctuary of the smaller members of Parliament in modern days. It is all comprised in one street of gloomy lodging-houses, from whose windows, in vacation time, there frown long melancholy rows of bills, which say, as plainly as did the countenances of their occupiers, ranged on Ministerial and Opposition benches in the session which slumbers with its fathers, "To Let," "To Let." In busier periods of the year these bills disappear, and the houses swarm with legislators. There are legislators in the parlour, in the first floor, in the second, in the third, in the garrets; the small apartments reek with the breath of deputations and delegates. In damp weather, the place is rendered close by the steam of moist Acts of Parliament and frowsy petitions; general postmen grow faint as they enter its infested limits, and shabby figures in quest of franks flit restlessly to and fro like the troubled ghosts of complete letter writers departed. This is Manchester Buildings; and here, at all hours of the night, may be heard the rattling of latch-keys in their respective keyholes: with now and then —when a gust of wind sweeping across the water which washes the Building's feet, impels the sound towards its entrance—the weak, shrill voice of some young member practising to-morrow's speech. All the livelong day there is a grinding of organs and clashing and clanging of little boxes of music; for Manchester Buildings is an eel-pot which has no outlet but its awkward mouth—a case-bottle which has no thoroughfare, and a short narrow neck—and in this respect it may be typical of the fate of some few of its more adventurous residents, who after wriggling themselves into Parliament by violent efforts and contortions, find that it, too, is no thoroughfare for them; that like Manchester Buildings it leads to nothing beyond itself; and that they are fain at last to back out, no wiser, no richer, not one whit more famous, than they went in."

THE DR JOHNSON CORRESPONDENCE.

It was while in Manchester Buildings that Macpherson and Dr Johnson had the famous tussle. A few years ago, at the cost of a few shillings, I became possessed of several papers, copies of some of which follow. Nos. 1, 2, 3, 4, and 5 are in Macpherson's handwriting. What appears in italics are underlined by him:—

No. 1. "*Private.*

"Dear Sir,—Upon mature consideration I have sent the enclosed *ostensible letter.* However unwilling I may be *at this time especially* to do anything that may create noise, I find I cannot pass over the expressions contained in Dr Johnson's pamphlet. I desire therefore that you will use your endeavours with *that impertinent fellow,* to induce him to soften the expressions concerning me, though it should occasion the delay of a few days in the publication. If he has a grain of commonsense I suppose he will see the impropriety of the words, and prevent further trouble. You may show to him the enclosed but to none else, and take care to keep it in your own hands.—I am, dear sir, Yours affectionately

(Signed) "J. MACPHERSON."
"Manchester Buildings."
"Jany. 14th 1775."

(Addressed) "To William Strahan, Esq., New Street, Fetter Lane, Fleet Street," and endorsed by Mr Strahan, the publisher, "J. Macpherson."—

No. 2.

"Dear Sir,—A friend of mine this moment put into my hands, a sentence extracted from a work entitled 'A Journey to the Western Islands of Scotland' which I am informed is written by Dr Johnson expressing his incredulity with regard to the authenticity of the Poems of Ossian. He makes use of the words *insolence, audacity,* and *guilt.* To his want of belief, I have not the smallest objection. But I suppose you will agree with me that such expressions ought not to be used by one gentleman to another, and that whenever they are used, they cannot be passed over with impunity. To prevent consequences that may be at once disagreeable to Dr Johnson and to myself, I desire the favour that you will wait upon him, and tell him that *I expect* he will cancel from his Journey the injurious expressions above mentioned. I hope that upon cool reflection he will be of opinion that this expectation of mine is not unreasonable.—Dear Sir, Your most obedient, humble servant

(Signed) "J. MACPHERSON.
"Manchester Buildings."
"Jany. 15th 1775."

(Addressed) "William Strahan, Esq."

Macpherson seemed in a great hurry for a reply in the form of an apology, and again writes Mr Strahan, probably the same day, but there is no date—

No. 3. "*Private.*

"Dear Sir,—I expected to have had Dr Johnson's final answer to my, I think, very just demands at seven o'clock. I beg leave to enclose to you the *purport* of such an advertisement as would satisfy me. As I am *very serious* upon this business, I insist that you will keep it to yourself, for were it not the present circumstances of an affair in which *you,* as well as I are concerned, I should before this have *traced out* the author of the *Journey* in a very *effective* manner. Unless I have a satisfactory answer I am determined (indeed it is necessary) to bring this business to a *conclusion* before I begin any other.—Dear Sir, Yours, etc., etc., (Signed) "J. MACPHERSON."
"Past 4 o'clock."

No. 4.   "*To the Printer of the 'St. James Chronicle.'*
            Advertisement."

"The author of the *Journey to the Western Highlands of Scotland*, finding when it was too late to make any alterations, that some expressions in page   and   had given offence to the gentleman alluded to, he takes this mode of informing the public, that he meant no personal reflection ; and that should this work come to a second impression, he will take care to expunge such words as seem, though undesignedly, to convey an affront. This is a piece of justice which the author owes to himself, as well as to that gentleman."

No 5.   "*Private.*

"Dear Sir,—Something like the enclosed may do. Will you transcribe it carefully, as it would be highly improper anything in commendation of the *work* should go in the hand of the author. I can easily trace the malignity of the Johnsonians in the "Plain Dealer." Such allegations, though too futile to impose on men of sense, may have weight with the foolish and prejudiced, who are a great majority of mankind. I think, therefore, it were better no such things should appear at all if that can be done.—Dear Sir, your's affectionately
                                (Initialed)   "J. M."
      Addressed to "Mr Caddell, bookseller, opposite Catharine
                                Street, Strand."
"½ past 4 o'clock."

No. 6.

"Mr James Macpherson,—I received your foolish and impudent letter. Any violence offered to me I shall do my best to repel, and what I cannot do for myself the law shall do for me.

"I hope I shall never be deterred from detecting what I think a cheat by the menaces of a ruffian.

"What would you have me retract ? I thought your book an imposture. I think it an imposture still. For this opinion I have given my reasons to the publick, which I here dare you to refute. Your rage I defy. Your abilities since your Homer, are not so formidable ; and what I hear of your morals induces me to pay regard not to what you shall say, but to what you shall prove. You may print this if you will.
              (Signed)   "SAM JOHNSON."

It is quite possible that Mr Caddell never sent the prepared apology. In any case no apology was made, nor the contemplated steps, if any were really intended, taken by Macpherson.

THE OSSIANIC ORIGINALS.

I shall next refer to the original Ossian papers which Mr Macpherson said he had deposited for exhibition. No one apparently did examine them, and when the Highland Society, years after Macpherson's death, took up the matter of their authenticity, no papers could be found. His representatives, at least those called as heirs of entail, professed they could find none, and it was contended and has been generally thought that Macpherson had destroyed them before his death, huffed at their being questioned, and that when he offered exhibition no one appeared. By accident, however, reading over some legal proceedings connected with Macpherson's succession and estates I found, not long since, a distinct reference showing that as late as 1807 these Ossian papers did exist, and I now give the verification.

Mr Alexander Macdonald, merchant, of Thames Street, London, aged 25 years and upwards, deponed on oath on examination before a Commissioner in 1807 that Mr John Mackenzie, late of the Inner Temple, was one of James Macpherson's executors, and George Mackenzie, late surgeon 42nd Regiment, was administrator of John Mackenzie's estate. That the said George Mackenzie, previous to his leaving London in autumn, 1803, deposited with the deponent all the books, papers, and documents found in the repositories of the said John Mackenzie at his chambers, Fig Tree Court, Temple. Depones that by the authority of the said George Mackenzie he, Macdonald, had delivered the papers to Mr Alexander Fraser, solicitor of Lincoln's Inn, London. That the said John Mackenzie by his memorandum showed that he, one of James Macpherson's executors, received these Macpherson papers in autumn, 1796, from Sir John Macpherson, another of the executors. Depones that there were a great variety of books and papers, contained in an iron chest and two or three tin boxes, sent to Mr Fraser, but the deponent had no means of knowing to what subjects they related, save and except that the contents of the iron chest were composed chiefly of the manuscript of the poems of Ossian, that having been pointed out to him by the said George Mackenzie, by whose directions he acted.

Here then certain Ossian papers are clearly traced to the custody of Mr Alexander Fraser of the Leadclune family, in 1807, who lived on to about 1832, as I think, but I have no note of his death. What became of them is hard to say, and though some of them have no doubt disappeared for ever many may exist. The Macvurrich manuscript, which had been entrusted to Macpherson, has fortunately turned up after many vicissitudes. People have made up their minds that no poems such as those given by Macpherson ever existed, but that he had collected a number of valuable manuscripts does not admit of any doubt, and it may be hoped that at least some of them may yet be recovered and given to the world, as has been so handsomely done by the present Clanranald in the case of the Macvurrich MS.

JAMES MACPHERSON'S MORALS, SUCCESSORS, AND FORTUNE.

It will have been noticed that Dr Johnson had no high opinion of Macpherson's morals, a well-founded view, for rarely even in the profligacy of last century has it been more flagrantly flaunted than by him. The eldest natural son, James, according to his tombstone in Kingussie Churchyard, was born in 1765, and the name of his third, though not the youngest, is there found, born in 1778, so that the business is found at least running over a period of 20 years. But what could not wealth and wordly success surmount? A detestable, cringing, and apologetic tone has been used by several writers from whom better things might be expected that cannot be too severely censured. Let me just for a moment refer to his manner of life in his later years. A certain woman, Margaret Macpherson, deponed at Edinburgh on the 14th of December, 1808—

"That her name was Margaret Macpherson, otherwise Bain, and that she was wife of Walter Bain, mason in Dundee. That she was about twenty years in the service of the late James Macpherson of Belville, and that she acted during the last 14 years in the capacity of housekeeper. That she was with Mr Macpherson, both when he resided at Belville and in England. That Mr Macpherson was in the habit of talking much to the deponent confidentially on matters of business, especially during the latter part of his life. . . . Depones that Mr Macpherson has shown her several letters from the Colonel (Colonel Allan Macpherson of Blairgowrie), some of which she read herself, and others that were read to her by Mr Macpherson, and as far as she recollects the general purport of them was to solicit Mr Macpherson not to take infeftment upon the estate of Blairgowrie, as it would bring the Colonel to disgrace, and break his wife's heart."

Is it any wonder that no respectable woman ever entered the doors of Belville, although from some hints by Mrs Grant of Laggan, that good lady was not disinclined to gratify a rather prurient curiosity by doing so, of course paying her respects to the "housekeeper."

By means of the gold and jewels of the Nabob of Arcot, a determined enemy of Britain, Mr Macpherson sat in Parliament for Camelford, afterwards disfranchised by and through its utter corruption, amassed a considerable fortune, his allowance being 12,000 pagodas annually from the Nabob. From Macpherson's accounts against the Nabob, I excerpt the following as specimens. " H—— of C——" means House of Commons, and a pagoda was worth perhaps 3s to 4s according to the exchanges :—

	Pagodas.
To small acknowledgments made as from the Nabob, in rings and East Indian manufactures, to persons who gave their aid, countenance, and support to His Highness' service	3049 0 0
To secret service money for obtaining of information, copies of papers, dispatches, etc., from the time of my being employed to 1st January, 1793...	7685 0 0
To H—— of C—— expenses from the 1st of September, 1780, to 1st January, 1793 ...	37,500 0 0

Further—oh the shame of it—he was able to buy a tomb in Westminster Abbey. It is to be hoped that the day may not be far distant when such monuments as those of

Macpherson's, and of frauds like Sir Cloudesley Shovel's, will be swept out of the national Walhalla.

Macpherson educated and sent his eldest natural son, James, to India, introducing him to a friend in these terms, by letter, dated London, 12th of July, 1782 :—

"This, I trust, will be delivered to you by James Macpherson, who is appointed a cadet on your establishment. Mr Macintyre will probably have informed you what and who he is. I shall therefore only introduce him to your countenance and protection."

This son James was a poor extravagant creature who did little in India, as may be judged from the following personal account given by himself under date :—

"Camp, Shur Gur, 30th November, 1786.

"I assure you I have entirely laid aside my extravagance and steadfastly resolved to be as economical as my station will allow of, nor can I fail to act up to this resolution, having continually such good examples as the Marrattas before me."

Upon being called as heir of entail at his father's death early in 1796, he came home, making no figure further than removing the people and raising his rents. He had, it is true, to encounter tremendous litigation in connection with his father's intricate and involved affairs. He came out as a great Whig in politics, being dominated therein by Ballindalloch, and in his estate affairs by that objectionable politician, Sir David Brewster, who, posing as patriot, as placeman feathered his nest handsomely at the public expense; ruling for years at Belville as if it were his own. James Macpherson, the son, though married had no family. The next in succession was one of his natural sisters, Miss Anne Macpherson, who was not likely to marry, and indeed did not even live in Scotland, so the Brewsters reigned, and the estate seemed within their legal grasp. This James Macpherson, dying without issue in 1833, the next heir of entail, Miss Anne Macpherson, succeeded. She, a stranger to the north, and from the misfortune of her birth, had hitherto led a retired but thoughtful life, having considerable firmness of character. Miss Macpherson found it necessary to free herself of the Brewsters, who tried to continue supreme as in James Macpherson's time, and she at last had to turn the key of her door on Sir David. His desire to outlive Miss Macpherson, who at her accession was rather delicate in health, and well over 50 years of age, was not to be gratified. She got stronger, while age was fast creeping over Sir David, and the chances were that she would survive him. To add to his vexation Miss Macpherson regularly recorded improvements under one of the Entail Acts, constituting these a debt on the entailed property. His latest appearances in Inverness were to scrutinize the vouchers recorded in the Sheriff Court books, through a magnifying glass, to discover, if possible, erazures, vitiations, or imperfections which might thereafter be the ground for setting aside the charges as affecting the succeeding heirs of entail. But he was called away, while Miss Anne Macpherson, known as the "Miss dubh," lived honoured and respected until 1862, reaching the age of 84, when she was succeeded by her sister Juliet's son, the late Colonel Brewster, who assumed the additional name of Macpherson in terms of the deed of entail.

I pass over at present some of the cruel aspersions by some of the Brewsters on members of the Borlum family and its connections, although I deeply resent them, as these can be dealt with more properly in a work for which I have been gathering materials during the last 40 years, and hope to be able to publish some day, after visiting the New England States and Georgia, to verify some important points, and to be called *Annals of the House of Borlum in Great Britain and America*.

THE MACKINTOSHES, AND THE DUCHESS OF BEDFORD'S GLENFESHIE HUTS.

The family of Mackintosh is connected by property with the parish of Alvie for over 600 years, by authentic writings, and at present the largest heritors are able to say that they were there prior not merely to the Gordons but to the Wolf of Badenoch, and even to the Comyns. I have said so much about them in the little work, *Dunachton Past and Present*, published in 1866, that I do not incline to say much here in addition. But I would point, in evidence of antiquity, to Dalnavert, and that curious wooded eminence on the Iosal of Dalnavert, latterly known as Keppoch, but of old "the Shian," where as far back as the 13th century dwelt Ferquhard Mackintosh, son of Shaw, or Seth, as it is written. The superiority of that part of Alvie parish, including Invermarkie, was in 1336 part of the Earldom of Ross. I might also say much about Mackintosh's part of Glenfeshie, formerly Rie Aitchacan, Rie-na-Bruich, and Achleam-a-choid, now all forest, and unfortunately of late years dependent on the greater Glenfeshie belonging to Sir G. Macpherson-Grant. The place which Lady Georgina Gordon, Duchess of Bedford, was so fond of, sometimes called "The Island," sometimes "Georgina," was the favourite residence of the Duchess of Bedford, and her "huts" were visited by the highest in Great Britain. Mrs Fraser, wife of James Fraser, sometime forester in Glenfeshie, who died lately at Lynchat, was a favourite servant with the Duchess, and Mrs Fraser, who could hardly restrain her tears when referring to her late loved mistress, has often told me that the Duchess was in the habit of saying that she loved her huts in Glenfeshie over and above every spot in the world. The huts were mere turf walls, bottomed with stone, and by and over each door rowans were planted and trained, carrying out the ancient view that they kept away witches. In the memoirs of Charles Matthews there is a graphic description of the locality and of crossing the River Feshie in flood. Above the fireplace in the dining-room hut, was a fine picture of a stag on the rough plaster, by Sir Edwin Landseer. The whole needed the greatest care from the severity of winter weather. The Duchess' chief residence was at the Doune of Rothiemurchus, but she spent much of the season at the huts. After her death both sides of the Feshie were rented by the same sporting tenants, and the houses opposite the huts being built of wood were dryer, and consequently became the principal residence of unhardy Southrons. The late

Alexander Mackintosh, twenty-sixth of Mackintosh, was on such friendly terms with the Duchess—a splendid tenant in every respect—that latterly no conditions were inserted in her leases, the result being that the huts fell into ruins, particularly in the time of the Duke of Leeds, over whom the Mackintoshes had no control, nor was he there even with their consent. Mark the ill consequences. Her Most Gracious Majesty rode on one occasion from Balmoral, through Glenfeshie, and to the Spey, and records her surprise and regret to see the state of ruin in which the huts had fallen, through the vandalism of the owner. I think, but not having the Queen's book by me as I write cannot verify it, that she was guided by Lord Alexander Russell, who is still alive, and who ought to have known all about the place in which his mother so frequently stayed. He did so himself, for a hill road still known as "Lord Alexander's Road," is called after him. He did not, however, know the truth, for he allowed Her Majesty to believe that the ruin lay at the door of the Mackintoshes. The real truth was that Mackintosh had nothing to do with it, could not interfere, and knew nothing about it, the wrongdoer being Her Majesty's own "cousin and Councillor," that notorious Duke of Leeds, of whom the well known story is related as to his treatment of guests invited to the forest.

He was so selfish that he could not endure any visitor killing a stag. Upon one occasion a young gentleman was invited to Glenfeshie, to whom the Duke showed so much attention as to attract the notice of Watson, the head stalker. Next morning early, Watson, to make sure, knocked at the door of his Grace's bedroom, and asked if Mr So-and-So "was to have a *stalk*, or the *walk*" in use to be given to visitors. The Duke was deafer than usual, and the query had to be repeated in tones sufficiently loud to be overheard by others, as also the gruff reply, "A walk." To the credit of the young gentleman, who either heard the colloquy or was told of it by others, he left the place immediately and told the story, which circulated in every club, sporting and political, making it so disagreeable for the Duke that he either ceased renting forests, or would not be accepted as a tenant, and had to purchase Applecross.

When I had charge of the Mackintosh estates the late Alexander Æneas Mackintosh, twenty-seventh Mackintosh, authorised the dining-room to be restored as far as possible, and a pretty wooden hall of the finest Glenfeshie wood, with handsome windows, was erected, with the old gable on which was Sir E. Landseer's picture properly enclosed and incorporated. As to its present state I know not, not having been in the Glen for many years. I desired that Lord Alexander Russell should be called on to explain the true position of matters to Her Majesty, but the late Mackintosh thought, as it had become ancient history, it was not worth while stirring up a matter which was passing into oblivion, so it was dropped for the time. It has, however, always rankled in my mind and I welcome this opportunity of letting the truth come out.

I pass from Alvie with regret, endeared as it is and ever will be to me, not only from old family ties but happy personal reminiscences of times and people gone for ever, leaving naught but that

"Fond memory which brings the light
Of other days around me."

XXVII.—PARISH OF ROTHIEMURCHUS.

THE MACKINTOSHES, SHAWS, AND GRANTS.

THE name of Rothiemurchus is found as early as 1226, when the lands were granted by Alexander II. to the Bishop of Moray. In 1476 Alexander Mackintosh or Shaw, gets a judicial transumpt of the charter of 1226 made, but whether the original charter or transumpt is still in existence I do not know—the oldest document in my possession not going back farther than 1572.

In the MS. History of the Mackintoshes it is recorded "that the estate departed from the Mackintoshes or Shaws, after it was possessed by them for nearly 360 years."

Lachlan Mor Mackintosh, according to the Grant History, had made a pathetic appeal to the laird of Grant to allow him to re-acquire for the family their ancient Duchus. This was not only refused by Grant, but a later connection with that family involved the loss, not only of many of the Mackintosh papers, but the almost crushing loss of Glenlui and Loch Arkaig. Charred skins of parchment presently existing bear witness to the Grant doings after the battle of Culloden in attempting to destroy the Mackintosh writs and titles, stolen furth of the Isle of Moy. There is indeed a heavy score yet to settle between the Mackintoshes and the Grants.

> "The clan that would hang its chief,
> And the chief that would hang his clan."

—*Ancient Highland toast, not unknown of old in Strathspey and neighbourhood.*

Long before the fight at the North Inch of Perth in 1396, the Mackintoshes had become possessors of Rothiemurchus, and in course of time settled it on one of the family named

Shaw, which Shaw, called "Corr-Fiaclach," led at that famous battle. Holding of the Bishops of Moray as superiors, Shaw's descendants were some times called Shaws and sometimes Mackintoshes. The history of the Shaws has been given by the late Rev. Mr Shaw of Forfar, and others, so fully that I will merely give the names of some of the owners, jotted down at different times. At the battle of Harlaw, 1411, James Mackintosh of Rothiemurchus fell in command of one of the companies of Clan Chattan. In 1500, is found John Mackintosh, the epithet "Kier" becoming hereditary. In 1521, Allan Kier Mackintosh is entered in Rothiemurchus as heir of his father, John Kier. In 1542, James Kier Mackintosh, son of Allan is found. In 1536, the above Allan Kier wadsets half of Guislich and the Hacnach (?) to John Grant of Culcabock, for one hundred merks, and thereafter assigns his right of reversion to George Gordon of Baldornie, Constable of Badenoch. As Patrick Grant of Glenmoriston, son and representative of John Grant of Culcabock, declined taking the wadset money, George Gordon took the necessary legal steps to redeem, and summoning Patrick Grant to the choir of the Parish Church of Inverness, where consignation was appointed to be made, he, on the 23rd of October, 1572, deposited the amount in the hands of James Paterson, Provost of Inverness; Sir William Anderson and William Cumming, notaries public, being witnesses; and Sir Alexander Clark, Procurator. In 1567 the Gordons appeared to have bargained with the Grants, and in 1568 Duncan Grant of Freuchie is absolute owner. In 1574, Patrick, the laird of Grant's second son, receives Rothiemurchus from his father. In 1581-86 the Mackintoshes are busy harassing Patrick Grant in his lands of Rothiemurchus, Balnespick, Ard Inch and Laggan, but without avail, and in 1586 they finally gave up the struggle. Except one fight as to marches between Rothiemurchus and South Kinrara, the Mackintoshes and Grants have for over 300 years been excellent neighbours.

The noted and picturesque ruined castle—Loch-an-Eilean—goes back to the time of the Shaws, when most of the stormy events that still cling around the castle occurred. There is one Grant incident, however, which may be mentioned, and is thus recorded in the Farr Collections—"During the troubles in the year 1688-9 the family of Rothiemurchus and some of the neighbours were obliged to take refuge in the castle of Loch-an-Eilean, their own property. During their residence there they were attacked from the shore, while a smart fire of musketry was kept up from the castle on the enemy, which it required all the men then in the castle to carry on. Grizel Mor, the Lady Rothiemurchus, daughter of William Mackintosh of Kellachie, who was a clever, active woman, was busily employed all the time of the attack in casting leaden balls for the defence."

The history of the Grants is neither eventful nor startling, but like all old Highland families they have their stories and traditions. Some regarding Patrick Grant (MacAlpine) may be repeated, one being that during the Civil War he declined to take any side, his view being—

"Upon the banks of the Spey,
Lies my Duchus,
Who e'er may be King,
I'll be Rothiemurchus."

Patrick was so much troubled with law suits, and demands for medicine and medical aid, that in despair he exclaimed—

"God keep us
From law and leeches."

The burial ground of both the Shaws and Grants lay in the lower part of the Churchyard of Rothiemurchus near each other. Patrick Grant ordered his body to be interred in the very highest ground of the churchyard, and being asked why, replied that by doing so, he on the Great Day would be ascending the hill of Torbane by the time the Shaws (his abhorrence) could only be having the flags over their graves removed, and thus have a clear start of them.

Perhaps the best story of Patrick is that concerning his treatment of his ancient mother, Grizel, before named. "Grizel Mhor, on account of her great size, lived to a very advanced age. Patrick MacAlpine had to pay her a small sum annually out of the estate as her jointure, and which sum in these times pressed so hard upon him that he was thinking very long to be free of the burden. It at last struck him that the Almighty might have forgotten her, and so he had her carried up to the top of a hill near Rothiemurchus, so that she might in his opinion be nearer Heaven than she ever was before." This outing and exposure does not seem to have inconvenienced the old lady, for it is recorded that "she lived for many years afterwards."

Another story about Grizel Kellachie may be given. Quite unexpectedly two great men, one Catholic, the other Protestant, accompanied by their chaplains, arrived at the Doune to dinner. Grizel was at her wits' end which of the chaplains, to avoid offence, should be asked to say grace. The difficulty was solved by her saying grace herself, and in Gaelic, but unhappily her words, probably unique, are not recorded.

There is a fine painting of Grizel Mhor and her two sons, Patrick and William, at the Doune, which was specially pointed out to me in 1868 by the late William Patrick Grant of Rothiemurchus.

Under 1732 I have note of James Grant, Younger of Rothiemurchus, and in 1787 Patrick Grant was proprietor. He executed an entail which has preserved the estates to the family, though at great suffering for many years to the two next heirs who succeeded.

The most noted of the later owners was John Peter Grant, advocate, nephew of Patrick the entailer, who, with James Grant of Corrimony, were two of the ablest and most successful pleaders in the Criminal Circuit Courts held in the north.

Rewarded for his politics and removed to India, knighted, and placed at the head of a legal Court, Sir John's legal career was not a success. Admirable as a pleader or counsel, he was unbearable and unsatisfactory as a judge. He was summoned before the Privy Council, under charges detailed in a print of the time. I have been informed by an East Indian that the two minor judges composing his Court were specially selected so as to muzzle as far as possible the head of the Court. Meantime the estate of Rothiemurchus was put under trust, grossly mismanaged by Edinburgh leeches, while the magnificent timber, unequalled, in the Highlands, was not merely cut but slaughtered. The administration, like that on many other Highland estates, was everything it should not be, resulting in the fact that while tens of thousands of pounds worth of wood were sold, the creditors were glad, after years of waiting, to accept a dividend in 1841, of 5s 6d per pound.

Better times dawned. The last Sir John Peter Grant was a most honourable and useful public servant, and able in his old age to live at the Doune as long as he liked or found it convenient to do so.

The estate of Balnespick is held in feu of Rothiemurchus.

The Doune, for many years, while tenanted by the Duchess of Bedford, was visited annually by many of the highest and most renowned of the age. The Duchess in particular was as much attached to it as to Glenfeshie, and secretly erected a monument, with suitable inscription, in honour of her husband near their favourite walk on the Ord Hill. To this, all unconscious, the Duke was led, and to the surprise of the Duchess said very little in appreciation of the compliment. But the Duke, though he said little, thought much, and the following season he led his wife to a monument in her honour, and with suitable inscription.

The last time I was on the hill I visited these monuments, most interesting memorials of peoples and times gone for ever, around which cling the halo of romance.

Rothiemurchus, as also Tullochgorum, are very difficult words to rhyme. Both were tried, I think, by Sir Alexander Boswell—

"See the Grants of Rothiemurchus
Ever ready for to dirk us,
. . . .
Lo the Grants of Tullochgorum!
Proud the mothers are that bore 'em."

XXVIII.—PARISH OF KINCARDINE AND ABERNETHY.

THE STUART BARONS, JOHN ROY, AND THE COUNT OF MAIDA.

THIS interesting parish, now given up almost entirely to sport, was once the centre of poetry, song, and activity.

I have note of a very early charter, without date, but from the names of the witnesses, circa 1296-1307. It is a conveyance, in very loose description, of lands which appear to read "Corncarn." The original was communicated on the 11th of August, 1815, to the well-known antiquarian collector, General Hutton, by "Lieutenant-Colonel Gordon, Inverness-shire," no doubt of Invertromie, and as it is included among Inverness-shire charters, I have concluded that it applies to the ancient barony of Kincairn or Kincardine, and was part of the Gordon muniments.

It is right to say that I have noticed a farm to let a century ago called "Corncairne," in the county of Banff, but being merely a farm, I do not suppose it is identical with the lands in this ancient charter. It is granted by Sir William de Soulis to Sir William of Abernethy of "all and whole his lands of Corncairn, also his other land which he held in exchange from Sir Thomas de Colville, videlicet, the lands some time held by Sir Walter de Umphraville of and under two Kings of Scotland," and are not further described, by parish or county. The witnesses are Robert, Bishop of Glasgow, Sir John, Abbot of Jedburgh, Sir Alexander de Ballo, Sir Thomas de Colville, and Hugh de Scoresby.

Kincardine was afterwards possessed by the Wolf of Badenoch, and descended to one of his illegitimate sons.

The Stuarts of Kincardine were Free Barons, and ruled in Abernethy for about 300 years, when, according to Shaw, a weak proprietor sold it, or rather was cozened into selling it to the first Duke of Gordon.

As the names of the various owners are given in Stuart's genealogies, I merely note the names of such as I have myself observed.

In 1520 there is notice of Donald, Baron of Kincardine; in 1544 John is served heir to his father Donald, and is living in 1561. To this John succeeded Walter; and in 1602 John of Kincardine, eldest son of Walter, appears. In 1642 Duncan, son of John is found; his brother Patrick is served heir to his brother Duncan in 1657, and I rather think that it was this Patrick, styled "of Kincardine" in 1661, who parted with the estate.

A branch of the Stuarts settled at Inverness, and was represented in 1745 by Bailie John Stuart, a noted Jacobite, frequently referred to in the Jacobite histories. The Bailie's grandson, I understand, was Lieutenant-General Sir John Stuart, Count of Maida, a most distinguished officer, regarding whom the following notice appeared in the *London Gazette*:—

"Whitehall, May 14, 1813.

"His Royal Highness the Prince Regent has been pleased, in the name and on the behalf of His Majesty, to grant unto Lieutenant-General Sir John Stuart, Count of Maida, Knight Companion of the Most Honourable Military Order of the Bath, His Majesty's royal license and permission, that, in compliance with the desire of His Majesty Ferdinand the Fourth, King of the two Sicilies, he may accept, and that he and his descendants may bear the following honourable armorial augmentation, viz., in chief of his and their arms the Royal Sicilian Eagle, with the royal cypher, ensigned with the Crown of his Sicilian Majesty on the breast thereof; 'and as a crest the same Eagle charged as aforesaid'; the said distinction having been granted by His Sicilian Majesty to the said Sir John Stuart, as a signal mark of his royal favour and esteem, and in order to perpetuate in his family and to posterity the remembrance of the great, important, and highly distinguished services rendered by him to the Crown of Sicily on divers occasions whilst commanding the British Army, serving in defence of his dominions, and particularly in the year 1810 (an era to be ever memorable in the annals of Sicily) when a most formidable attempt upon that Kingdom, by a powerful enemy, was repelled by the valour and firmness of the British forces in co-operation with the faithful and zealous exertions of His Sicilian Majesty's own brave and loyal subjects; the said armorial distinctions being first duly exemplified according to the laws of arms, and recorded in the Herald's Office."

Though long disconnected with Kincardine it is understood that there are several representatives of the family in existence, including the gallant Sir Donald Stuart, and it is hoped that Mr William Mackay, who has had the matter before him, will find time to write a full and suitable account of this ancient family. So much has been written about Colonel John Roy Stuart that there is not much new to say; but though somewhat lengthy, relating as they do to the 'Forty-five, events of never-dying interest to Highlanders, I give certain extracts from the collections of the late Mr John Anderson, W.S., made from personal researches and observations, written down about seventy years ago—

"On the morning of the battle of Culloden, John Roy was exceedingly anxious that the army should take up a position at Dalmagarrie, several miles to the south of the River Nairn, and beyond a pass where cavalry and artillery of the enemy would be useless. Lord Elcho, who commanded a party of Life Guards, even went to the Prince to solicit that the command on that day be conceded to John Roy Stuart, and that his plans should guide them. The Prince's answer was to this purport—'He had given his word that he would fight where he was, and it could not be violated; moreover, he had promised Lord George Murray that *he* should lead the battle, and he had too many men, besides ten pieces of cannon, to cause him to be slighted. Stuart himself asked that nobleman what was to be the upshot of opposing the English to such disadvantage. His words were—'You'll soon see Stuart, we'll make short work of it,' a reply which subsequent events led the Highlanders, and especially John Roy, to believe smacked of treachery. Lord Elcho afterwards found the Prince in a cabin beside the river Nairn, surrounded by Irishmen, and deaf to his entreaties to rally the fugitives and again to make head. Hence the muster at Ruthven on the 18th and 19th of 9000 Highlanders came to nought. John Roy Stuart took refuge in a wild cave near Rothiemurchus. A natural son of his, by name Charles Stuart (afterwards an officer in the English army) brought him his victuals daily to the cave, in front of which ran a mountain stream. Coming on one occasion early in the morning on his usual errand, he met a party of soldiers, headed by a Lieutenant, making for his father's place of concealment. With instinctive sagacity he at once guessed their purpose, and picking up acquaintance with a little drummer, who could hardly drag his weary limbs along under the weight of his drum, he offered the boy some of the food which, he said, he was carrying to the hills for his own breakfast whilst he tended his master's cattle if he would tell him what sort of an instrument that was he carried. The poor lad, glad to relieve his hunger at so cheap a rate, twisted round his drum and beat two or three flourishes on it. This was all young Stuart wanted. The officer in command in a hasty tone chid the little musician, and said he had spoiled their labour, for the game was scared! And so it was: on the first stroke John Roy leapt at one bound out of the cave to the opposite side of the burn; there crouching under a tree whilst he firmly grasped his broadsword he awaited the soldiers' approach. But they had turned back, rightly conjecturing that the cave was empty. Stuart dislocated his ankle in the leap, but with great personal strength and acute pain reset it, tearing off his shirt to make a bandage. Then crawling through the water he ascended to his eyrie. It was whilst lying under a tree, his wounded foot dangling in the water, that he composed the prayer in Gaelic, so much admired in the Highlands in the last age, which goes by his name."

Other localities, it is right to say, claim the spot of John Roy's concealment. I follow Mr Anderson, who was a careful observer with trained intellect, who wrote at a comparatively recent date and free from bias, whether as regarded peoples or localities. Another recent Collector says—

"Upon another occasion word was brought to this gallant soldier that his mother had died in Rannoch. Bent on personally beholding the last rites paid to her remains, he assumed the long gown and the limping gait of one of the privileged Bedesmen who then roamed from place to place. As he came through the forest of Drimochter he encountered two English officers. With a feigned tale of distress he demanded charity of them, the better to keep up his assumed character. One of them cursed him for a Highland rascal and passed on; but the other gave him a trifle, which he was in the act of pocketing when his gown, raised too high, disclosed part of his broadsword. 'We have got a rebel here,' shouted the officer to his companion in advance, 'let us take the villan.' 'That you never shall,' retorted Stuart, as drawing a pistol from his belt he shot the speaker dead. His friend hastened to revenge him, but he met more than his match and called for mercy, which Roy granted on condition that he reported to the Duke of Cumberland he owed his life to him."

"John Roy was a famous poet and composer of music, much of both being repeated and sung at the time, and the reel 'John Roy Stuart' is one of the finest reels which is now played. He added much to the music of Strathspey, and gave it such a character that it will now stand for ages." (*Farr MS. Collections*, 1834.)

THE ABERNETHY REMOVALS.

The Parish of Abernethy was latterly possessed by two proprietors. Kincardine began to suffer from the moment it became the property of the Gordons. Wood grew there naturally to magnificent proportions, and the desire to convert it into money brought about the settlement of hard and unsympathetic Southrons, who deemed it much to their advantage to get rid of the inhabitants. Further, the people were Roman Catholics and, with the zeal of converts or perverts, the Gordons having changed themselves, persecuted the people by the conditions in their leases against papists! Then followed considerable depopulation by large sheep farmers, culminating in the Barony being ultimately converted into a deer forest. The Valuation Roll for 1896-97 gives a total rent of £1678 19s 6d from 18 subjects, whereof not less than £1310 is for forest rent alone.

The Grants have treated their part of Abernethy in no better spirit. First, the area for timber growing has been much increased at the cost of the agricultural occupants, while, worst of all, the occupants have in many cases, such as Tulloch and Garten, been removed to make room for a deer forest. By favour one may drive up from Nethy-Bridge towards the northern slopes of the Grampians and cross over into the Glenmore or Kincardine forest, coming out at Rothiemurchus. A finer drive cannot be imagined, nor can grander pines be seen in Strathspey; but alas, along this beautiful line of road the traveller passes much arable land of considerable extent, going back yearly to sour pasture, with the ruins of houses, I might say townships, standing out gaunt and bleak, guilty memorials of the destroyer.

These ruined localities, given up to sport of an isolated and selfish character, were once the abode of a cheerful and happy people, imbued with the romance of their magnificent surroundings, breaking out into song and poetic feeling, as may be evidenced by the mere name, which I preserve from extinction, of one little streamlet of water, "*Ruith bhrist cridhe*"—The run of the broken heart.

The life and prosperity in and about Nethy-Bridge testify most strongly as to what could be done if the whole district were permitted to be opened up. Is it to be, and by whom?

XXIX.—PARISH OF DUTHIL.

JOHN BEG MACANDREW AND SOME OF HIS EXPLOITS.

THE greater part of this parish lay within the lordship of Badenoch and was, and I believe is, held in feu by the Grants, of the Gordons.

The upper part of the strath of Dulnan is very beautiful, but for a long time, from its inaccessibility, little known. The highest dwelling presently is at Eil, while at one time, people lived as high up as the lands behind Dellifour and Raitts hill grounds. When the railway through Duthil, Strathdearn, and Strathnairn is made, I anticipate that Strath Dulnan will be opened up and become an important fishing centre, and the whole country wakened up from the torpor following upon the virtual disuse by strangers of the Highland Road between Inverness and Kingussie.

Glencharnich is the cradle of the Grants, and broad as their borders extend, it is still essentially their duchus.

The caterans of the west returning from their forays went by the valleys of the Dulnan or Findhorn, as they found most convenient, and the remains of their tracks, "Rathaid na mearlach," can still to some extent be traced.

In the Commissary Court Records are to be found names of some of the family of John Beg MacAndrew, Dalnahatnich, establishing that this person, regarding whom so many startling traditions, chiefly connected with the Lochaber raiders, existed.

I cannot do better than give a fuller account than perhaps has yet appeared of one of the bloodiest and latest of these affrays, as written about a hundred years ago, when the story was a common one among the dwellers along the banks of the Findhorn and Dulnan.

The last creach or the lifting of cattle to any extent which occurred in the county happened prior to or about 1670, and was committed by Macdonell of Achluachrach, in Lochaber, and a party of twelve men. It was then the custom in the Highlands that a man of any consequence, before his marriage, should take a creach, or commit some other equally daring deed. Achluachrach was engaged to be married, and accordingly he set off with a party to carry one of these attempts into execution. They fell upon the lands of Kilravock and drove away the cattle of the Baron and his tenants, in the course of one night. The low country people rose in a body and pursued, but being overcome by fatigue they obtained the assistance of those of the Braes of Strathnairn and Strathdearn to follow up the pursuit, headed by William Mackintosh of Kellachie, commonly called "William Maclachlan," who at that time was the Captain Freiceadan, or Captain of the Watch, from the march of Lochaber to the River Spey, and he was accompanied by his faithful attendant on such occasions, John beg MacAndrew, in Dalnahatnich, on Dulnan-side, an active man, of small stature, and an excellent bowman.

The robbers had settled for the night in a small hut or bothy in the heights of Strathdearn and the Glen of "Croc-lach." Here they had lighted a fire and killed one of the cattle for provisions. One of them, the Gille Maol Dhu, was picking the shoulder blade, and, observing by the light of the fire drops of blood in the bones, he remarked to his companions that he was sure their followers would soon be up on them and that they would all be killed. They did not, however, attend to his prediction, but so strongly was he impressed with what he had seen that he made his escape. They had left the hide of the animal killed by them outside the hut.

Kellachie and his party, suspecting that the robbers would take shelter here, made for the place, and having seen the cattle near it, they prepared their plan of attack. John Mac Andrew placed the hide (which was in a bundle) with the hairy part towards the ground, at the door of the bothy, with the side towards the flesh facing upwards. An arrow was then thrown into the hut. Achluachrach came out, and falling upon the hide, which was slippery, instantly received an arrow from Mac Andrew, which killed him. Kellachie killed the next that came out, and then by a shower of arrows poured into the hut at the door, window, and some holes, all the band were killed. And the Gille Maol Dhu, who escaped, was the bearer of the news to the bride, who must have been waiting with anxiety the return of her betrothed. The stolen booty was thus redeemed and restored to the Baron of Kilravock. The dead bodies were afterwards buried by their own countrymen, who came for the purpose, and the graves are still to be seen. It is said that one of the Strathdearn men went next day to the scene of action and saw one of the robbers who had crawled out of the bothy, half dead in quest of water. He asked the man as a favour to give him a drink either in his bonnet or in his shoe, but such was the spirit of revenge that, as the Strathdearn man was handing him the water, he attempted to stab him with his dirk.

In general there was an understanding amongst those who pursued these marauders that their names should not be mentioned upon any occasion when within hearing of their opponents, but more particularly in a night attack. This precaution was necessary for the purpose, if possible, of preventing the robbers or those of them that might escape, or their friends, from afterwards coming and attacking in revenge any of the pursuers (in their houses when unprotected), at that time a common practice with Highlanders.

Upon the above occasion Kellachie forgot the usual precaution, and when Achluachrach was killed by Mac Andrew he called out, on account of his dexterity, "Well done John Mac Andrew in Dalnahatnich," and when Kellachie had killed another John said, "Well done William Maclachlan of Kellachie, your hand is equally sure when you have the opportunity." This was to show the Lochaber men that John had a good protector. But some of Achluachrach's friends soon came after poor John, when he made a singular escape at his own door, through the cleverness of his wife.

John beg Mac Andrew, who resided at Dalnahatnich, on Dulnan side, was a man of low stature, but uncommonly active and of a bold and daring mind. He was an excellent marksman, particularly with the arrow, and William Mackintosh of Kellachie, while Captain of the Watch of the whole land from the borders of Lochaber to the River Spey at Fochabers, seldom would go to the field against the foe, without the assistance of his faithful friend John, their principal expeditions being the guarding of the country people against the invasion of the Lochaber gentry.

Always on these occasions it was a necessary precaution for the pursuers never to mention their own names in cases of night attacks upon the freebooters, as should any of the latter be killed, the attacked would not know by whom the deed was done, and thereby the friends of the deceased could not show their revenge by coming after them.

John's name, however, was discovered on several occasions, and thus in such constant danger that at night he generally betook himself to a very large fir tree, which grew near his house. Here he had a kind of bed made of its branches, his bed-fellows being his bow and arrows. Shortly after his return from one expedition, where the Lochaber men suffered, particularly by his hand, three of their number and friends came upon the "Toir" or Search after John, in order to be revenged for his killing their kinsmen. These three men entered John's house and asked his wife "if John MacAndrew was at home." Her answer was, "that he was not far away, and that if they would sit down it would not be long until he came back." She knew well the errand they were upon, and appearing as if in a rage she said in Gaelic to a little figure lying upon the bed, "Get out you little rascal and see that the cattle are put out ere your master comes home." This was no other than John himself, who had a red plaid wrapped round him, and although he passed the men in the house on his way towards the door, they never took him to be the object of their journey. John having got safely out, he went to a small window or aperture in the west end of the house, and his wife, being there waiting, handed out to him his bow and arrows. Without loss of time John took possession of his favourite tree and prepared for the future. One of the men soon came outside to see if he could observe John coming home, when he was instantly killed by an arrow. The others coming out to see what detained their companion were also shot down.

It is said that on another occasion John killed seven men, and as none of these seven, or of the three previously mentioned, ever returned to tell tales, John was afterwards left at peace by the Lochaber men, dying in his bed, fortified by the approval of the church.

XXX.—PARISH OF MOY AND DALAROSSIE.

THE population of this parish has been dwindling for some years, but it may be reasonably expected that with the opening of the railway to Aviemore, so unhappily delayed for so many years, a new era of life and prosperity will arise.

The parish has been essentially Mackintosh, the Chief alone having nearly 70,000 acres, including not only the upper and highest portion of the Findhorn and its tributaries, where the four parishes of Laggan, Boleskine, Kingussie, and Dalarossie meet, but also both sides of the Findhorn downwards, where the counties of Inverness and Nairn meet.

I will deal first with the small estate of Pollochaig, long the possession of a branch of the Macqueens of Corrybrough. The Macqueens were not only great sportsmen, but were supposed to be on familiar terms and intimate with witches and fairies. "Macqueen's candles" are old acquaintances of Strathdearn children. The following story about the origin of the decay of the Macqueens may be given :—

"John Dhu Macqueen of Pollochaig, generally called Iain Dhu vic Coul (son of Dougal) was a famous sportsman and excellent marksman. It is said that he was upon a friendly footing with all the witches, fairies, and warlocks of his day, but more especially those in his own neighbourhood. He lived in the beginning of the 18th century, and had married Anne, sister of Laird Lachlan Mackintosh.

"At one time John went out to enjoy his favourite sport with the view if possible of killing a deer or mountain roe, and had gone a considerable way before he fell in with any. At last a roe appeared within easy shot. John fired, and down came the object of his day's work. He quickly went up to the spot where the roe fell but it could not be found. Tho' he searched for several hundred yards round the place, the supposed dead roe was nowhere to be seen.

"When John got home in the evening he told at his fireside what had happened him, and the hearers marvelled much, John being confident that he had killed the animal. Next morning he set off again to search at the place for the dead roe, but when at the very spot he met an old woman, who at once said to him, speaking in Gaelic, 'Black John, son of Dougall, take the lead out of my foot which you put into it yesterday.' This he did accordingly and then asked her for a wish or blessing, which she pronounced in Gaelic, translated thus—'Your best day will be your worst day, and your worst day will be your best day.' Naturally disappointed, John asked for another, but she said she could not alter it. Had he requested it before he took out the lead it would have been different. It is said that no sooner had she finished than she vanished into air, and that it was one of the fairies or witches who had turned into the shape of a roe that John shot at and thought he had killed.

"From that time the family of Macqueen of Pollochaig began to fall off in their circumstances, and writing in 1820 a writer records that it is not long since they sold the estate, the paternal inheritance which had been in the family for nearly 300 years. Pollochaig, it is further noticed by the same writer, is a pretty Highland place. It lies at the top of the Streens on the river Findhorn, and from 3 to 5 miles below the inn of Freeburn. Some of John's successors are still alive (1820), and tell the story."

At one time the whole of Strathdearn in Inverness-shire was possessed by members of Clan Chattan, excepting Daltomich, belonging to the Earl of Moray, but even it was wadsetted to the Kellachie family.

The upper portion of Strathdearn, the home of the famous "pipers," even in these modern days, is occasionally tuned up with shrill effect. The great davoch of "Schevin," commonly called "Coignafearn," or the "Monalia," runs at the back of the parishes of Alvie, Kingussie, and Laggan, and of old the habitat of the red deer, famous when most modern forests were unknown, has again become a forest. It was let at the end of last century to the Black Officer of Ballochroan for fifty shillings of grazing rent. The last Duke of Gordon, when Marquis of Huntly, Lord Saltoun, and Fraser of Culduthel rented Coignafearn at £80 as shooting quarters. This nowadays would be laughed at, but at the time (1824) it exhilarated Alexander, then laird of Mackintosh, so much that he exclaimed in Gaelic, "A big rent for hens." The present rent of Coignafearn is £1000 per annum.

Strathdearn since the Highland road has been practically closed remained stagnant, with its population decaying, but is now certain to awake to vitality and prosperity. It is full of romance and interesting story, on which I do not at present enlarge. With the exception of Pollochaig, all Mackintosh's great possessions in the parish hold of the Crown properly, or as in the right of the Bishops of Moray. The rest of the parish holds of the Earl of Moray, Lord of Stratherne and of Petty.

The following anecdote, relating to one of the Borlums connected by marriage with Strathdearn, shows that expatriation did not quench the "native fires." Benjamin Mackintosh, natural son of Brigadier Mackintosh, emigrated with his wife, daughter of Mackintosh of Holm, and his family to America, where he became a distinguished officer, and conducted himself highly and honourably in the service of some of the American States. At one time he had occasion to go against a party of Red Indians, who annoyed Georgia. The Indians made their appearance at the edge of a wood, ready for the attack. Being much more numerous than Benjamin Mackintosh and his men, his negro servant called out, "Massa, massa, run or you will be killed by these savages." Benjamin Mackintosh merely said in reply, "You may run, but I come of a race that never ran." Assistance coming, the Indians decamped.

A further anecdote connected with Dalarossie. On one occasion eleven Camerons were passing down Strathdearn on a thieving expedition, travelling on the south or east side of the river Findhorn. The valley at this spot is narrow, and the sides of the river and neighbouring haughs were then covered with wood. A man named Mackintosh, living at Daltomich, on the north or west side of the river, an excellent bowman, observed them going along on the opposite side, and having a grudge against them for a previous injury, went down to the wooded haughs near the river and killed three of them with the arrow at Craig Allister, and the survivors could not see, with the wood, from whence the arrows came, he being on the north side of the river. He fired his arrows generally through every opening in the wood he could find, and in this manner he alone killed the whole eleven. The last fell at a small well in the bank of the river below the new house of Dalmigavie, since known by the name of "Fuaran Cameronich." All were killed within the space of two miles.

XXXI.—PARISH OF DAVIOT AND DUNLICHITY.

THIS once important and busy parish has long been declining in population, while most of the ancient owners have disappeared. There is a certain fictitious excitement no doubt during the sporting season, followed by stagnation. The fine old possessions of the Mackintoshes of Aberarder, including Brin, and Glenmazeran in Strathdearn, were occupied by an independent and stirring race. The family is descended from Duncan, fifth son of Lachlan Mor Mackintosh of Mackintosh, and it is recorded that no fewer than four sons of William Mackintosh, second of Aberarder, fell at or immediately after the fight at Mulroy in 1688. Among them was Lachlan, the eldest son, who was succeeded by his son William, bred an advocate, and served heir to his father in 1692. William Mackintosh married Isabella Rickhart, and dying between 1723 and 1729, left two sons; the elder, also Lachlan, dying unmarried very shortly after his father, was succeeded by his brother William. Of this William there are even yet many floating traditions. He it was who built the pleasant and comfortable old house of Aberarder, standing the last time I was in the locality, but whether it has disappeared, like the old house of Dunmaglass, I cannot say. Connected with the old house there is this story. When William married in February, 1729, Isabella, daughter of Lachlan Macpherson of Cluny, on their home-coming across the hills of Badenoch to Strathnairn, as the bride was entering the doorway, the mantel stone—a very large one—of the dining-room broke and rent in twain, which either occasioned or revived the old saying that a Mackintosh and a Macpherson could never agree. That they did not agree in this case will be seen presently. An old chronicler says he saw the rent stone, but good naturedly concludes that it may have arisen from extra heating of the fireplace in welcome of the party after their long and bleak ride across the Monalia in the month of February.

The disputes between the young couple became so violent, that the aid of the law was invoked by the lady. Simon Lord Lovat was then (1735) Sheriff-Depute of Inverness and exerted himself to settle matters extrajudicially, in which he was assisted by that honourable and clear-headed man, Lachlan Macpherson of Cluny, the lady's father. Matters were patched up, but broke out with greater violence, and in the procedure Lady Aberarder depones to very violent acts on the part of her husband, whom she had finally to leave. She had a capital income out of the estate and her treatment, like that of Lady Rothiemurchus, does not seem to have disagreed with her, for she outlived her husband, son, and several of her grandchildren. She executed her last will and testament, declaring herself as sound in judgment, though weak in body, at Catlodge of Laggan, on the 6th of January, 1783, leaving among other bequests, to her sister Christian Macpherson for her very great care of and attention to her for forty-five years, thirty pounds; to defray her funeral expenses, thirty pounds sterling; ten pounds sterling for enclosing the chapel or burying-place at Cluny, in which she decrees her body may be decently interred ; to her nieces, Mrs Colonel Macpherson and Mrs Mackintosh of Borlum, five pounds sterling each, to buy mournings.

John Mackintosh, eldest son of William Mackintosh and Isobel Macpherson, who succeeded in 1743, died unmarried in apparency about 1747, and was succeeded by his brother William, who in 1756 married Mary Falconer of Drakies, and died in 1763. William Mackintosh left issue—one son, Captain William, and one daughter, Mary. William, fourth in succession of this name, entered the army and was killed in Holland, in October, 1799. Being unmarried, and his sister Mary, who had married Provost John

Mackintosh, also dead without issue, the succession opened by destination to Miss Jane Mackintosh, only daughter of William Mackintosh who died in 1743. She did not live long after her succession, and there being no relative, male or female, of the family of Lachlan Mackintosh, third of Aberarder, killed as aforesaid at Mulroy in 1688, except herself, she destined the estate by deed executed 3rd March, 1800, to Provost John Mackintosh, of the Kellachie family, who had married her niece Mary. This gave rise to a great legal struggle. Provost John had to defend himself from a claim at the instance of the redoubted Campbell Mackintosh, afterwards of Dalmigavie, Town Clerk of Inverness, who claimed that Aberarder was either entailed or held under limitation to heirs male, and that he as son of Robert, son of William, son of James Mackintosh, wadsetter of Mid Craggie, and second brother of Lachlan killed at Mulroy, was entitled to the estate. After a severe contest Provost John Mackintosh was successful and took the title of Aberarder. By his second wife, daughter of Provost Chisholm of Buntait, he left two sons—William, who died without issue, and Charles Mackintosh, who succeeded and was the last Mackintosh of Aberarder. Old Aberarder, as he was called even in my younger days, was a well-known figure in Inverness for many a year; his easy going disposition led him to neglect his affairs, whereby they fell into hands who cared for nothing but to feather their own nests.

The present position of Aberarder is deplorable. A bank and insurance company are entered in the Valuation Roll as owners or managers, and while nothing is expended the last shilling is extracted from the occupants. These naturally have dwindled to a low figure, twelve in all. The total rental is £1032 18s, whereof £500 is shooting rent, and about £350 in the proprietor's hands, leaving less than £300 for ordinary tenants, the only Mackintosh on the estate paying one shilling of rent, four other tenants paying £1 10s, £1, £2 7s, and £2 respectively.

Let this lamentable state of matters be contrasted with

the year 1797, when there were no fewer than forty-three tenancies, as under—

RENTAL OF ABERARDER ESTATE, 1797.

Knocknacrousaig.—1, Finlay MacChandy; 2, Andrew Smith; 3, Charles Maclean.

Balnaboch.—4, Donald Fraser, weaver.

Brinbeg.—5, William Macbean.

Tork.—6, Donald Fraser.

Brinmore.—7, Archibald vic Ali Homas; 8, John MacChandy; 9, Donald Macbean.

Tomintoul.—10, Donald Mackenzie; 11, William Macgillivray.

Milton of Brin.—12, Alexander Shaw.

Achvraid of Brin.—13, John Smith; 14, Donald MacChandy.

Croftgorm.—15, Donald Macpherson.

Tynallan.—16, Duncan Forbes; 17, Charles Macbean.

Easter Croachy.—18, James Davidson; 19, John Shaw.

Wester Croachy.—20, Charles Mackintosh; 21, Alexander Smith.

Duhallow.—22, Farquhar Smith; 23, Duncan Macgillivray; 24, Donald vic Ali Homas.

Millton of Aberarder.—25, John Mackintosh; 26, Duncan Smith; 27, Widow Duncan Macqueen; 28, William Smith.

Glenbeg.—29, John Smith; 30, Finlay Smith; 31, Donald Smith; 32, James Macpherson; 33, Widow John Macdonald.

Achvraid.—34, John vic Ali Homas.

Pollochy.—35, William Macbean.

Braevullin—36, William Mackintosh; 37, Robert Shaw; 38, John Forbes Miller.

Mains of Aberarder.—39, James Rose.

Gortannagour.—40, William Rose.

Tynrich.—41, Charles Rose; 42, Duncan Mackintosh; 43, James Mackintosh.

One or two of the above form part of the present estate of Brin, and are thus disjoined from Aberarder proper.

Like Strathdearn, Strathnairn was essentially Clan Chattan. On both sides of the river, from head to foot, within the county of Inverness, Macgillivrays, Mackintoshes, Macphails, Macbeans, Shaws, flourished, reigning supreme as owners. The old lairds, with two exceptions, have disappeared, but many of the people of the good old stock remain waiting for the return of brighter times.

XXXII.—PARISH OF CROY.

THE DALLASES OF CANTRAY, ETC.

THE family of Dallas long held a good position in the Counties of Inverness and Nairn. Descended of the Dallases of that Ilk in Moray, they finally settled in Cantray in the fifteenth century, William Dallas of Cantray, not the first owner, being on record in 1492.

He was succeeded by his son Henry, and the latter by his son, Alexander Dallas, found in 1522-1566. This Alexander was one of the leading men of his day, and owned the lands of Lopan Durris, with its mill, lying in the parish of Dores, now part of Aldourie. He also possessed the Barony of Lairgs in Strathnairn. In 1567 notice is found of Henry Dallas, nephew to Alexander, and in 1569 of John Dallas of Cantray, brother to Henry. In 1582 Marjory Dallas is served heir to her great-grandfather, Alexander Dallas of Cantray. In the same year Alexander Dallas is served heir in a wadset of Cantray to John Rose, burgess of Nairn, his great-grandfather. From the time of William Dallas, found in 1630, and married to one of the Cawdor ladies, the line is distinct down to William Dallas, a mariner, who, from necessity and the amount of debt on the estate, sold the estate about 1768 to Mr David Davidson, born on the Cantray estate, who made his fortune in London.

James Dallas of Cantray, one of the officers of the Regiment of Clan Chattan, fell at Culloden, much regretted by all who knew him. He was a man of fine appearance and polished manners, held in much favour by Lady Mackintosh, to whom, while raising the clan for Prince Charles, he offered his services and was appointed a Captain. He married Margaret Hamilton, and had a brother Walter, burgess of Nairn, father of Mr Alexander Dallas, merchant, London, afterwards in Nairn, who married Miss Ophelia Phipps, of the Mulgrave family. A charming miniature of this lady, also her silver cream jug, have come into my possession by bequest of Miss Elizabeth Jane Dallas, who died some years ago at her house in Church Street, Nairn. Miss Dallas was much esteemed, not only as the last of the Dallases resident in the north, but for her great genealogical acquirements. To Miss Dallas, my relative through a marriage between the Dallases of Cantray and the Macleans of Dochgarroch, I was indebted in early life for much valuable old world story. The present Duchess of Portland is descended of Cantray, and there are others in high positions scattered over the world. One correspondent, Mr Dallas of Exeter, another Mr A. J. Dallas, of Florida, are accomplished genealogists, and take much interest in their family history.

The Dallasses of Budgate long held a good position, their connection with Budgate ceasing 200 years ago. Several of them settled in Ross and occupied a fair position, notably Hugh Dallas, Commissary Clerk of Ross; Dallas of St. Martins, author of a legal work on styles once in great repute.

Miss Anne Dallas, sister of Cantray of the 'Forty-five, married Duncan Mackintosh, being great-grandfather of the present Mackintosh of Mackintosh. The three families of Cawdor, Kilravock, and Cantray were long supreme, and the two former still hold great sway. The Dallas family at Inchyettle have been tenants of the place for about 250 years.

Much of the old barony of Dalcross lay within the parish of Croy. But bit by bit the large possessions of the Lovats passed from them. It is a matter of great interest to those who take up such matters, that the old Castle of Dalcross, erected by Simon Lord Lovat 300 years ago, and long a ruin, is being restored in a reverent and becoming manner. Long may the restorer enjoy the occupancy of a place unrivalled in the north in extent and grandeur of hill and dale, sea and mountain, woods and fields—an extensive and imposing panorama.

Dalcross, once a parish, has, with its church and burial ground, long been in absolute ruin and disuse. The latter is but an insignificant corner of land, which the late Mackintosh planted at my suggestion to prevent its possible incorporation at any future period with the surrounding fields. I certainly never contemplated that anyone could be found so utterly lost to the fitness of the surroundings as to suggest that the crowded state of the Croy church-yard might be met by utilising the few square yards representing the site of old Dalcross chapel and burial ground. Within the parish lies the field of Culloden, never more an object of pilgrimage than at the present day. When the new line of railway is opened, with its station near the Cumberland Stone, it will become more and more a place of resort. The ground reserved from plantation, supposed to indicate the place of battle, strikes every visitor as small and contracted, but this is found to be the case with all the sites of ancient and renowned battles. Culloden relics are not uncommon, but I place a high value on two swords, whereof the authenticity is undoubted—one, that of Donald Mackintosh na Brataich who saved the colours of Clan Chattan; and the other, turned up by the workmen of the late Mr John Rose of Kirktown in course of his extensive reclamations, given to me by one of his sons, my late old and valued friend, Mr Hugh Rose, solicitor, Inverness. It will ever be to me a subject of gratification that I paid my first visit to the field in 1846, one hundred years to a day, after the event, and drank to the memory of the immortal dead and a warm corner to the Butcher.

"The deil was working in a neuk,
Rieving sticks to roast the Duke."

The three Leys, Easter, Mid, and Wester, were detached from the parish proper, and of old presented, like the famous Maol Bhuie, in spring an extensive show of broom and whins in blossom, extending for miles, as I have been told, in one stretch. Plantations and reclamations have replaced ancient wilds, and it is as well it should be so, and that we see now snug farm-houses, squared fields, and altogether a pleasant landscape. Possibly, however, some may say with regret that like the exile in distant lands—

"They canna see the broom
Wi' its tassels on the lea."

XXXIII.—PARISH OF CAWDOR.

THERE never was much of this parish in Inverness-shire, and that little has been transferred to Nairn.

Yet it is full of past interest, with only three predominant families during the last 700 years, viz.—the Roses, Calders, and Campbells. No Highlander wishes ought but well to the Roses, both of Kilravock and Holme, while the behaviour of the Campbells for many a long day has wiped out their original and arbitrary intrusion.

The history of the Campbells of Cawdor has been so well and fully given by the late Mr Cosmo Innes and others as to be familiar to most people. As I happen to possess several genealogies brought down to 1750 and many curious papers, I select a few extracts.

The first, from an anonymous compilation made about the beginning of the century, is not without interest. The compiler, under the head of John Campbell, the first Lord Cawdor, so created in 1796, says of the estate—

"When Lord Cawdor visited Cawdor Castle in 1804 he was much struck with the great extent of waste lands and useless wood lands on the estate. For 25 years previously Scotland had made such rapid strides in planting and agriculture that the change was most apparent, and the contrast between his estates and many others, was notorious and frightful. He therefore gave orders to enclose and plant the hills of Urchany and Budgate; adding such other enclosures as his quick and penetrating eye saw absoutely necessary for their improvement. There was particularly one bleak and barren spot between Campbelltown and Nairn, of great extent, and of no value but for planting. This land tho' partly planted is still a great eyesore to travellers who inquire whose wastes and wilds are those that lie so much neglected?

"The pernicious system of leases for lives is here most apparent; which was granted to Mr James Macpherson, the factor who succeeded Mr White.

"His Lordship was much hurt at the destruction of the noble wood at Cawdor, and chiefly around the hermitage, one of the most interesting objects of the estate. He saw that the beautiful old birch trees, so ornamental with their weeping branches and rugged stems (which years like grey hairs render so venerable) were all cut down near the hermitage. They had attracted the notice and admiration of visitors, and that of the justly celebrated Jean, the late beautiful Duchess of Gordon, who had seen this fine scenery while on a visit to Kilravock Castle. She had complimented his Lordship on their possession and hoped they would be preserved. But what was his mortification to find they had all been cut down and sold. It will take ages to fill up the blank thus made in the wood.

"The place was planted with some fine young oaks, which show the hand of man at work, where nature lived formerly undisturbed, and where the hermit could sing —

> "Nymph of the grot whose sacred fount I keep;
> And to the murmur of whose waters sleep;
> Ah, spare my slumbers, gently tread the cave,
> Or wash in silence, or in silence lave.

"Had Linnæus seen the furze or whins about the romantic waterfalls of Cawdor before he fell down in adoration to his Maker upon seeing their blossoms on Blackheath, what would he say? For Sweden like the west coast of Scotland produces no whins. Lord Cawdor, however, wisely ordered their destruction and their place to be supplied by the beautiful young wood now so thriving. He rebuilt the hermitage and made a neat safe path to it from the castle enclosures along the west bank of the burn, where he showed his taste and knowledge of mechanics by a small ingenious bridge thrown over the same, one end of which is supported by the branch of a fine old birch tree. The enclosing of the romantic scenery to the south-east of Budgate and the manse, and adding it to the wood would add to the grandeur of the place, as well as beauty to the woods, which it is easier to anticipate than express. He was fully aware of the rich inheritance which these improvements, in a few years would give his heirs."

The family of Cawdor, after a severe contest with that of Moray, secured the superiority of the barony of Strathnairn. The feu to Lord Moray was trifling compared with the sub-feus or heritable tacks by the latter to the actual possessors. Yet, as holding of the Crown, the Cawdor family had the political influence in the baronies of Strathnairn and Durris. The first Lord Cawdor sold all his superiorities about the beginning of the century, except that over Dunmaglass, for considerable sums, while their over superiority did not fall to

Lord Moray until a later period. He is now Crown vassal and superior of all Strathnairn in Inverness-shire, with the exception only, as I think, of half of Tullich and Elrig, Tordarroch, and that part of the old barony of Lairgs, consisting of Lairgindour and Mid Lairgs.

Sir Archibald Campbell of Clunes, second son of Sir Hugh Campbell of Calder, married in 1688, Anne Macpherson of Cluny, as mentioned in a former chapter. Sir Archibald has recorded no less than five poetical tributes both in English and Latin to her memory. Even one of them is too long for quotation, but I give an old conceit in form of acrostic.

"To the Memory of the Honourable pious and truly virtuous, The Lady Clunes, who died the 24th day of January, 1727.

"*Ane Accrostick.*

"ANNE MACKPHERSON.

"A—vessell for the Master's use made meet,
N—ow leaving Earth, in heavenly places set,
N—o cause she hath at all the change to rue,
E—ach day this was the hope she did pursue.

M—irror of Piety, for manners bright
A—dorned with virtues rare—a shining light,
C—omely in person, handsome mien and height,
K—ind to her friends, to great and small discreet,
P—rudent and just in conversation sweet,
H—umble and civil, even in her walk,
E—xact in her affairs, of modest talk,
R—etired in her devotions, always chaste,
S—ure in her promise, once her word she passed,
O—bliging still to all, yet never mean,
N—eat in her dress, and in her conscience clean.
Vivet post funera virtus."

Sir Archibald Campbell's eldest son married Miss Trotter of Morton Hall, with issue—an only child, Elizabeth, understood to have been betrothed to the ill-fated Lieutenant-Colonel Alexander Macgillivray of Dunmaglass killed at Culloden, 17th April, 1746, and to have died of a broken heart within four months thereafter. Elizabeth Campbell was very much admired, and is particularly referred to in a letter by Simon, Lord Lovat, quoted in the book of the Thanes of Cawdor.

I give a letter to one of her aunts, dated Clunes, 22nd October, 1743—

"The unexpected promise I was obliged to make my Lord Lovat of waiting Lady Clunie home, has hurried me so that I must leave the country in a very confused manner. I attempted seeing you oftener than once when at Muirtown, as Miss Taylor can tell you, but was so undetermined about my time of leaving that place, and knew that I could not command one day. I came here from Moyhall, Friday last, and engaged to return there again Monday next and from that to Castle Downie. As 26th of this month is what was fixed upon for joining Lady Clunie home, we meet Miss Farquharson at Moy who goes along'st with us to Clunie, and I go straight from thence to Edinburgh. As I have no time to ask your commands, if you send me them they shall be cheerfully obeyed.—Your affectionate niece and humble servant. (Signed) ELIZ. CAMPBELL."

XXXIV.—PARISH OF ARDERSIER.

THE history of this small parish has been destitute of interest ever since it became the exclusive property of the Campbells of Cawdor.

The Mackintoshes, who were in the ascendant in the neighbouring Parish of Petty at an early period, were ousted by the Campbells, after the lapse of a liferent conceded to the last Mackintosh possessor. The Templars at one time had a good hold, and under them were Mackays.

The possession up to the time of the sale to the Crown for the erection of Fort-George and the sustenance of the garrison was of little value to the Campbells. From the Crown was obtained a much larger sum than was originally paid for the whole of Ardersier.

The erection of a Fort attracted a considerable population, and the foundations of the two settlements of Stewarton, so called, on the Moray estate, and of Campbelltown on the Cawdor estate. A ditch dividing the estates of these two potentates, draining a large extent of land, has through neglect become a public nuisance, reflecting little credit on the wealthy owners of the lands adjoining.

The clergyman of Ardersier of old sat in the Presbytery of Chanonry, and ministerial inductions, judging from the mass of papers concerning them, created more interest with the estate managers and owners than the weal of the inhabitants.

The Crown has been curtailing its interest in Ardersier by parting with the lands of Hillhead, and if the Fort itself disappeared, with its name, the public would not regret.

The present inhabitants of Campbelltown have shown their public spirit by the erection of a substantial pier, which it is hoped may satisfy the wishes and objects of the promoters. By Fort-George is an old highway to Ross-shire and the Northern Counties, and if a light railway from the present Fort-George station to the sea were made, and an efficient system of ferryage established, prosperity would follow.

The further scheme of adapting the Fort into bathing quarters for the Inverness people and others who, in the summer and autumn, pour into Nairn and other places on the Moray Firth, has much to recommend it to public favour.

XXXV.—PARISH OF PETTY.

GREAT material progress has been made in this parish within the last twenty years, as testified by the neat and handsome farm houses and offices everywhere to be found.

Nearly the whole parish belongs to the Earls of Moray, who rounded off their possession some years ago by the acquisition of Bracklich. It is now a silent quiescent parish, though at one time torn by warfare.

The bounds of the old lordship of Petty cannot now be distinctly defined. After the forfeiture of that Earl of Douglas who married the heiress of the Dunbar Earls of Moray, the lands were in continuous dispute. Mackintoshes, Ogilvies, the Little Earl of Moray of the Stuart line, all contended. These disputes are so well known that it would be superfluous to give any account here, suffice it to say that the Mackintoshes were ultimately expelled, and have not a foot of its land other than a distinct place of sepulchre within the old church of Petty. What Mackintosh reminiscences the Parish has? Halhill, where so many Ogilvies were slaughtered ; Termit, where in 1609, the biggest Clan Chattan muster ever took place. Connage then comprehended almost the whole of the Parish, lying between the long hollow whence water flows west to the bay of Castle Stuart, and east to the burn or ditch dividing Campbelltown on the one side, and the sea on the other.

As this great hollow in winter and floods, before drainage works were known, filled with water it sometimes gave Connage the appearance of a long island, and is indeed sometimes described as an island.

I desire to refer, being little known in history, to that part of Petty, lying at its south or west, and adjoining Inverness, known as Alturlies.

This small estate, long the property of the Culloden family, was Templar ground, and given off in feu about three hundred years ago. The first owners of whom I have note were named Wincester. After Mackintoshes and Cuthberts, the estate was divided into two portions, and the distinction of halves is still kept up in the titles. In 1687, John Cuthbert of Alturlies sold the estate in halves, one half to George Cumming, the other to Robert Rose. Some time thereafter, Cumming sold his half of the property and superiority to John Forbes of Culloden, about 1727. Robert Rose's family possessed the other half, until 1757, when the Rose half was sold judicially to William Fraser of Balnain. Balnain, shortly after the purchase, feued his half to Culloden, and the latter family thus hold half of Alturlies direct of the Crown and the other half of Balnain's heirs. The old feu was eight merks for the whole, and the estate, including small fishings, though so small, had the high valuation of £301 15s, Scots. The estate presents many opportunities for being opened up and developed in form of villas, and for boating and yachting and fishing purposes, whereby the people of Inverness could almost at their own doors obtain all they have now to seek for in summer and autumn at considerable distances.

It is to be hoped that Castle Stuart, so long uninhabited though restored, will, like its neighbour of Dalcross, be again regularly inhabited, and its old amenities revived, restored, and augmented,

ADDENDA ET CORRIGENDA.

PAGE 163.

Mr Alexander Macdonald of Upper South River, Antigonish, Nova Scotia, has sent me the following interesting account of the respectable family of Bohuntin. My correspondent say, that the story that Angus Mor, third of Bohuntin, had only one son, both deaf and dumb, is incorrect—

THE MACDONALDS OF BOHUNTIN.

I. JOHN MACDONALD of Bohuntin, the son of Ranald Macdonald, VI. of Keppoch, was a renowned warrior. He is said to have been conspicuous by his stature, strength, and personal beauty, and in skill in the use of arms and in daring courage to have had few equals and no superior. At the feud of Boline, when Alastair the eldest son of Raonull Mor was wounded, Ian Dubh had to take his place.

JOHN MACDONALD, first of Bohuntin, married a daughter of Donald Glas Mackintosh, with issue—

1. Alexander, his heir, progenitor of the elder branch of Bohuntin.

2. Donald; 3. John; 4. Ranald. Those three brothers, Donald, John, and Ranald, were treacherously put to death by the unprincipled Alastair nan Cleas of Keppoch.

5. Angus, progenitor of the younger branch of Bohuntin; that is, the Macdonalds of Tulloch, Aberardair, Crenachan, Dailchoisnie, and others.

II. ALEXANDER MACDONALD, second of Bohuntin, who married a daughter of Macdonald of Glencoe, by whom he had one son,

III. ANGUS MACDONALD, known as "Aonghas mor Bhothuntainn," who married a daughter of Cameron of Strone, with issue—

1. John, his heir.

2. Angus, known in the Braes as "Aonghus Mor a Bhocain," and of whom hereafter.

3. Alexander, known as "Alastair na Rianaich."

Aonghus Mor, third of Bohuntin, was succeeded by his eldest son,

IV. JOHN MACDONALD, who married a daughter of Cameron of Glenmallie, with issue—

1. Alexander, his heir.

2. Donald, known as "Domhnull Donn Mac Fhir Bothuntainn."

3. Donald "Gruamach."

They were men of good poetic talents.

John, fourth of Bohuntin, was succeeded by his eldest son,

V. ALEXANDER MACDONALD, who by his wife, had issue—
1. Angus; 2. Alexander; 3. Ranald; 4. "Ian Og," who succeeded his father; 5. Donald Glas.

Angus, Alexander, and Ranald died of pleurisy within a few weeks of one another, about 1720.

Alexander Macdonald, fifth of Bohuntin, was the author of several poems, but they have nearly all perished.

VI. JOHN OG MACDONALD, sixth of Bohuntin, and Donald Glas, his brother, were transported to South Carolina for taking part in the Rising of 1745. They were both married, and their descendant are still in the United States.

Angus Mor "a Bhocain," second son of "Aonghas Mor Bhothuntainn," married a daughter of Macgregor of Glencearnaig, with issue—

Alastair Mor, who for killing a number of the King's troops at the battle of Mulroy was transported to Holland, where he died of yellow fever in 1688. He married a daughter of "Fear Mhurlagan," with issue—

1. Angus, who married Nighean Mhic Aonghais Oig, the poetess.

2. Alastair Ban, who married "Nighean Ghilleasbuig Mhic Dhomhnuill Ghuirm Chliathanaig," with issue—1. Angus, who married Catherine Mackintosh, with issue. 2. Alexander, who married Mary Campbell, with issue—three sons and five daughters. He emigrated to America with his family, in 1816. When his wife, who outlived him thirty years, died in 1860, she left descendants to the number of two hundred and fifty.

PARISH OF SLEAT.

PAGE 272.

The following curious incident, communicated by Sir W. A. Mackinnon, K.C.B., connected with the visit of Marshal Macdonald, Duke of Tarentum, to the Isles, is a reminiscence little known. Sir William says—

"When Marshal Macdonald visited the Highlands after the French War, he paid a visit to the Lord Macdonald of that day at Armadale Castle, Skye. My father, the Rev. John Mackinnon, was then minister of Sleat, and was staying with Lord Macdonald at Armadale. Lord Macdonald was much exercised in his mind as to how he could give the Marshal the salute he was entitled to, as there was only one old carronade available, and no one knew how to load and fire it properly. At the time there were extensive building and quarrying operations going on in the vicinity of the Castle, and the idea suggested itself to my father that the blasting of the rocks might be utilised for the purpose of saluting the distinguished Field Marshal with the number of guns his rank required. Accordingly the number of blasts equivalent to the number of guns for a Field Marshal's salute had been prepared and let off at intervals, with excellent effect, so much so that Marshal Macdonald, until informed next day, thought his salute was fired by artillery, and he was greatly amused when the method of saluting was explained to him. It will be remembered that the Marshal's father, Neil Mac Eachen from South Uist, went to France as an exile with Prince Charles."

PARISH OF PORTREE.

PAGE 285.

In a pamphlet of eleven pages, printed at Edinburgh in 1782, entitled "A letter concerning the state of arms in Scotland, addressed to the Earl of Haddinton (sic) occasioned by the remarks of a county gentleman on the proposed laws for establishing a militia in Scotland," lent to me by Sir W. Mackinnon, there is the following reference to an intended French landing at Portree in harvest, 1780:—

"In the year 1780, on the   day of August, which is the day of the fair for black cattle in the Isle of Sky, there was at Port Rey a great show of cattle, and no small concourse of people. About the height of the market, a large vessel appeared standing in the bay. She hoisted out two boats, and having manned them with as many musketeers as they could hold, the seamen began to row towards the shore. The Highlanders seeing this immediately got together. There were about six or seven hundred men, old and young, but there was not one firelock or sword among them all; however, they instantly pulled down a hut or two, and shouldering the poles made of the beams and rafters, marched down like a battalion to the shore. The Frenchmen, seeing this resolute body, never imagined that they had no arms but staves and stones, and not liking their countenance, rowed back again to their ship; and Captain Fall (for it was he) steered another course with his vessel."

PARISH OF SOUTH UIST.

PAGE 310.

The following corrections of the text are necessary:— Line 35, for "Miss" read "Mrs." Allan Macdonald of Belfinlay had four sons and one daughter. The eldest, James, died in America without issue; Ranald, second son, also died without issue, in Prince Edward Island. The third son, Allan, entered the army in 1799, having received a commission in the 55th Foot, which regiment shortly afterwards embarked for the West Indies. In 1808 he was sent with the flank company on an expedition to St. Domingo, and on the termination of hostilities there, was placed in command of the 2nd West India Regiment. In 1813, having rejoined the 55th, ordered to the Netherlands, Allan Macdonald, then Captain of Grenadiers, was second in command at the storming of Bergen-Op-Zoom, where he was severely wounded. He served with the 55th until he became Major, when he retired.

Major Macdonald sold his estate in Arisaig and purchased Waternish, which became the permanent residence of the Belfinlay family.

PARISH OF BARRA.

PAGE 332.

I am informed by my friend and intelligent correspondent, Mr Michael Buchanan at Borve, that the late General Macneill purchased the superiority of Barra.

PARISH OF ALVIE.

PAGE 399, LINE 15.   For 1809 read 1801-1806.

SAME PAGE.

The following is a list of some of the evictions carried out by James Macpherson, the younger, in 1801, 1802, and 1806:—

1801.
1. John Macpherson, Tillysoul of Raitts.
2. Ewan Macdonald, Easter Raitts.
3. Duncan Robertson, Midtown of do.
4. John Macpherson, Achacha.
5. Donald Davidson, Acharunach.
6. Jas. Mackintosh, Croftroy.
7. John Mackay, Croftduach of Benchar.
8. Alexander Gordon, Newtown.

1802.
Donald Gallovie, Torgarve of Phoness.
Alex. Macpherson, Etterish (2).

PHONESS 1803.

1. John Macpherson, Wester Phoness.
2. Alex. Macpherson, do.
3. Malcolm Macpherson, do.

BENCHAR.

4. Duncan Macdonald, Tullichero of Benchar.
5. Duncan Mackintosh, do.
6. Neil Macpherson, do.
7. Donald Macdonald, Croftdraulin of do.
8. Wm. Kennedy, Dalchimmor of do.
9. Elspet Anderson, do.
10. James Macintyre, do.
11. Duncan Macbean, Dalchirnbeg of do.
12. John Mackintosh, Millton of do.
13. John Mackintosh Mac Coil, do.
14. Wm. Mackintosh, Croftcoinack of do.
15. Wm. Davidson, Croftcoinack of do.
16. Alex. Warren, Croftduack of do.
17. Alex. MacEdward, do.
18. Jas. Davidson, Croftroy of do.
19. Alex. Maclean, Lurg of do.
20. Alexander Mackay, Lurg.
21. John Mackintosh, Lurg, Clune.
22. John Kennedy, Craggan of Clune
23. Duncan Cattanach, Clackernach of Clune
24. Wm. dhu Cattanach, Croft of Clune.
25. John Macpherson, Knock of Clune.
26. Jas. Cattanach, Shanval of Clune.
27. Donald Mackintosh, Mosshouse of Clune
28. John Mackenzie, Newton of Clune.
29. John Gordon, do.
30. Lachlan Mackintosh, do.
31. Donald Maclean, do.
32. Janet Macpherson, do.
33. Alexander Roy Cattanach, do.

RAITTS.

34. Duncan Macbean, Wester Raitts.
35. John Macpherson, do.
36. John Gordon, do.
37. Evan Macdonald, Midtown of do.
38. Patrick Macdonald, do.
39. Lachlan Macdonald, do.
40. Elspet Stewart, do.
41. Donald Davidson, do.
42. John Cattanach, do.

43. Wm. Macbean, Easter Raitts.
44. Wm. Macpherson, Tigh-na-cairne.
45. Donald Stewart, Tullysoul House.

1806—PHONESS.

1. Elspet Macpherson, Mains of Phoness
2. Evan Macgregor, Wester Phoness.
3. Malcolm Macpherson,   do.
4. Elizabeth Macgregor,   do.

ETTERISH.

5. John Macpherson, merchant, Easter Etterish.
6. James Macdonald, Torgarvebeg.
7. Anne Macintyre, Torgarvebeg.
8. Elizabeth Cameron,   do.
9. Malcolm Macintyre, Easter Etterish.
10. Katharine Macpherson, Wester Etterish (warned in 1802).
11. Nelly Robertson,   do.
12. James Macpherson,   do. (warned in 1802).

BENCHAR.

13. Margt. Macintyre, Dalchirnmore.
14. Anne Cattanach, Millton of Benchar.
15. Winnie Macpherson,   do.
16. Margt. Cattanach,   do.

CLUNE.

17. Alex. Cattanach, Craggan of Clune.
18. Margt. Maclean,   do.
19. Janet Cattanach,   do.
20. Elizabeth Cameron,   do.
21. Anne Warrand,   do.
22. Katharine Macpherson, do.
23. Mary Macpherson, Clackernach.
24. John Mackay, Croftroy of Benchar.
25. Donald Maclean, Newtown of Clune.
26. Alexander Gordon,   do.
27. Samuel Macpherson,   do.
28. Lachlan Mackintosh,   do.
29. John Mackenzie,   do.
30. Anne Macpherson,   do.

RAITTS.

31. John Macdonald, Upper Raitts.
32. Christian Cattanach, Baldhu of Raitts.
33. Duncan Robertson,   do.
34. Marjory Macdonald   do.
35. Isobel Gordon, Kerrow of Raitts.

36. Jean Cruikshank, Strathinlea of Raitts.
37. Christian Macbean, Tyravoan of Raitts.
38. Alexander Gordon, Achavourich of Raitts.

INVERNAHAVEN.

1. Capt. Alex. Clark.

PHONESS.

2. John Macfarlane, Mains of Phoness, Tynallan.

WESTER PHONESS.

3. Alex. Macpherson, Wester Phoness.
4. John Macpherson,   do.
5. Donald Kennedy,   do.
6. John Kennedy,   do.
7. Margt. Kennedy, Torgarve of Phoness (warned out 1802 under name of Mary K. or Guthrie).
8. John Guthrie,   do. (warned 1802).
9. Donald Mackinnon,   do.
10. John Anderson,   do.

ETTERISH.

11. Donald Macpherson, Easter do. (warned in 1802).
12. Evan Macpherson, Wester do.
13. Thomas Macpherson, Culreach.
14. John Macpherson,   do.
15. James Macpherson, Drumree.
16. John Macpherson, Phoness.

CLUNE.

17. Duncan Macdonald, Tullichero.
18. Donald Macpherson.   do.
19. Neil Macpherson,   do.
20. Donald Macdonald, Croftdraulin.
21. James Macintyre, Dalchirnmor.
22. William Macdonald,   do.
23. William Kennedy,   do.
24. Duncan Macbean, Dalchirnbeg.
25. Evan Mackintosh,   do.
26. John Mackintosh, Lurg.
27. Alexander Maclean, do.
28. Alexander Mackay, do.

BENCHAR.

29. John Mackintosh, miller, Milltown of Benchar.
30. John Mackintosh, Milltown of do.
31. William Mackintosh,   do.
32. Alexander Mackintosh, do.
33. William Mackintosh, Croftcoinack.

34. William Davidson, do.
35. John Macpherson, Revack of Clune.
36. John Kennedy, Craggan of do
37. Angus Kennedy, do.
38. Wm. Cattanach, Croft of Clune.
39. James Cattanach, Shanval of Clune.
40. Duncan Kennedy, Clachernach.
41. Charles Warrand, Croftduack.
42. Alex. Kennedy, do.
43. Samuel Davidson, Croftroy.
44. Donald Mackintosh, Muirhouse of Clune.
45. Donald Cattanach, Newton of Clune.
46. John Gordon, do.
47. William Gordon, do.
48. Alexander MacEdward, do.
49. Alexander Macpherson, Knock na Coileach.

RAITTS.

50. Alex. Macpherson, Upper Raitts.
51. Ewen Macpherson, do.
52. Donald Davidson, do.
53. Duncan Macbean do.
54. John Gordon, junior, do.
55. John Gordon, senior, do.
56. Wm. Macpherson, Tynacairn of Raitts.
57. Lachlan Macdonald, Baldhu of Raitts.
58. Donald Davidson, do.
59. Evan Macdonald, do.
60. Peter Macdonald, do.
61. Elizabeth Stewart, do.
62. Alex. Macpherson, do.
63. John Cattanach, do.
64. Robert Warrand, Kerrowdhu of Raitts.
65. Paul Macbean, Tillysoul of Raitts.

Total heads of families in 1806, 103, probably 500 souls.

PARISH OF DAVIOT AND DUNLICHITY.

PAGE 434, at the end.

There are two names connected with the parish in later times that should not be overlooked in these days when the Gaelic people, their language and literature, have come so well to the front, viz., those of the Rev. Duncan Mackenzie, the respected Episcopal clergyman at Tullich, and Mr John Rose, schoolmaster at Croachie, who, at a very depressed period of Celtic literature, earned by their labour and learning, a high name in their day, and are at present, looked upon with the respect, affection, and admiration of Highlanders. That I had the honour of the acquaintance of both is a matter of great satisfaction.

INDEX.

INDEX.

NAMES OF PERSONS.

A

Aberarder Estate, rental and names of tenants in 1797, 434
Aberdeen, Duchess Dowager of, 398
Abernethy, Sir William of, 416
Alexander, Lord of the Isles, 162, 174
Alexander II., King, 411
Alvie, List of evictions in 1801, 1802, 1803 and 1806, 450, 451, 452, 453, 454
— Names of Mackintosh tenants in 1635, 395
— Names of tenants and occupants generally in 1679, 396
Ardersier, Clergyman of, 142
Argyll, Duke of, 114, 115, 175, 192, 202, 207, 245, 250, 354
— Archibald, 2nd Earl of, 17, 18
— Colin, 3rd Earl of, 18
Atholl, Duke of, 175, 354

B

Badenoch, "The Gentlemen" of, 364, 365
— Alexander, Seneschal and Lord of, "Wolf of Badenoch," 369, 416
Bailleul, De, 31
— Renaud De 31
Baillie, Alexander, first of Dunain, 31
— Alexander, seventh of Dunain, 31, 32, 33, 34, 40, 41, 46
— Alexander of Dunain, 36, 37, 46, 47
— Alexander, second of Dochfour, 35, 36, 41, 50, 57
— Alexander, son of Alex. 2nd of Dochfour, 36, 37
— Alexander, illegitimate son of Alexander 2nd of Dochfour, 37
— Alexander, fourth of Dochfour, 33, 36, 37
— Alexander, of Davochfour, 34
— Anne, of Dunain, 53
— Captain James, 32
— Colonel John of Dunain, 31, 33, 37, 58, 299
— David, 1st of Dochfour, 33, 37
— David, son of Alex. 3rd of Dochfour, 36
— Duncan M., Custom House, Fort-William, 190
— Duncan, son of Hugh, 2nd of Dochfour, 36
— Evan of Abriachan, 36, 37, 57, 101
— Evan of Dochfour, 33, 37

Baillie, Evan, writer, Inverness, 58
— Hugh, 3rd of Dochfour, 35, 36
— James, son of Alex., 2nd of Dochfour, 36
— James, son of Hugh, 3rd of Dochfour, 36, 37
— James Evan Bruce, M.P., of Dochfour, 37
— Janet, sister of William Baillie of Dunain, 99
— John Dhu in Lagnalien, 32
— Peter of Dochfour, 37
— Rev. Robert, 36
— Sir William of Lamington, 31
— the late Evan, of Dochfour, 37, 44
— William in Davochfour, 32
— William in Davochnacraig, 32
— William of Dochfour, 34, 46
— William, son of Alex. 2nd of Dochfour, 35
— William of Rosehall, 36
— William of Dunain, 42, 44, 46
Baird, James, of Camusdoon, 133
Baliol, John De, 31
— King John, 31
— Sir Alexander De, 31
Ballo, Sir Alexander De, 416
Barbour, John, of Aldourie, 66, 67
Bayeux, Bishop of, 31
Bedford, John, Duke of, 398, 415
— Lady Georgina, 397, 398, 408, 409, 415,
Belford, Mr, factor, 210, 213
Belladrum, family of, 2
Belot, Guillame, 31
Beverly, George, 82
Blair, Mr, advocate, 140
Bohuntin, Macdonalds of, 447, 448
Bonicastle, Major, of the Royal Engineers, 137
Borlum, Names of those fit to carry arms and act as drivers in 1798, 70, 71
Boswell, James, 63, 291
— Sir Alexander, 415
Brae-Lochaber, Names of tenants, cottars, and dependents in 1655, 162, 163, 164
Brewster, Sir David, 406, 407
Brodie, George, Governor of Fort-Augustus, 76, 84, 85
Bruce, King Robert, 261
— Mr, Glenelg, 154
— Patrick Crawford, merchant and banker, London, 245
— Sir Michael of Stenhouse, baronet, 245
Bryce, Professor, of Winnipeg, 130
Buchanan, Mr Michael, Barra, 333, 450
Buidhe, Alister, 176
Burnett, Alexander of Kinchyle, 69
Burt, Edmund, Esq., 102
Butter, Henry, estate factor, 208

INDEX.

C

Cameron, Alexander, tenant of Invergueeran, 142, 143
— Alexander of Glendessary, 222
— Alexander of Glen Nevis, 225
— Allan of Clunes, 205
— Allan of Glendessary, 224, 226, 227
— Archibald of Dungallon, 224, 225, 226
— of Beolary, 237
— Captain, Alexander of Dungallon, 227
— Captain John, 212
— Peter, 216, 221
— William of Camisky, 222
— Charles at Culchenna, 198
— Colonel, of Clifton Villa, Inverness, 204, 205
— Colonel Donald of Lochiel, 217, 219, 263
— Donald Mor Og, 171
— Donald, yr. of Lochiel (1745) 207
— Donald of Lochiel (1784) 208, 210, 211, 212
— Donald, the late, of Lochiel, 212, 213, 227, 231
— Donald, elder of Erracht, 207, 208, 211, 212,
— Dr Archibald of Lochiel, 222, 225
— Dugald, tenant in Boline, 126
— Evan of Lochiel, 202, 203
— Ewen, at Erracht, 220, 221
— General, Clunes, 216
— George, of Letterfinlay, 171
— Hugh, of Annoch, 224
— Jessie of Glendessary (of the '45) 225, 227, 228, 229, 230
— John, "Corrychoillie" 214, 215, 216, 222
— John of Dungallon, 226
— John, yr. of Glenmore, 214
— Lieutenant Allan, of Lundavra, 208, 211, 212
— Lieutenant Colonel John of Lienassie, 212
— Miss of Fassifern, 358
— Miss Jean of Lochiel, 230, 231
— Mrs Isobel of Dungallon, 225 226
— Sir Alexander of Inverailort, 222,
— Sir Allan, 220
— Sir Duncan, 217
— Sir Duncan of Inverlochy, 182
— Sir Duncan of Fassifern, 210 211
— Sir Ewen, 176
— Sir Ewen of Fassifern, 210

Cameron, Sir Ewen of Lochiel, 224, 230, 231
Campbell of Glendaruel and Dochfour, 36
— Alexander, brother german to Calder, 64
— Alexander, minister of Croy, 149
— Archibald, of Calder, 349, 350
— Captain Neill, 79th Regiment, 138, 139
— Colin, of Calder, 350
— Elizabeth of Clunes, 440, 441
— Janet of Calder, 13
— John, 1st Lord of Cawdor, 438, 439
— Lachlan, Chamberlain of Ila, 350
— Lord Archibald, 67
— Mrs Cameron, 182
— Pryse, yr. of Calder, 68
— Sir Archibald, of Clunes, 440
— Sir Hugh of Calder, 65, 66, 349, 350, 440
— Sir John of Calder, 60, 61, 62, 64
Carrach, Alexander, 1st of Keppoch, 159, 174
Castleleathers, minister of Boleskine and catechist of Dores, 36
Caulfield, Governor of Fort-Augustus, 84
Cawdor, Earl of, 53
Celestine of the Isles, 160
Chambers, Robert, 229
Charles, I, 41
Chevalier St. George, 66
Chisholm, Agnes, daughter of Alex. Chisholm of Comar, 48
— Alexander of Comar, 21
— Alexander of Kinnairies, 22
— Allister Mor, 24
— Colin, late, Inverness, 22
— John of Comar, 21
— John of Kinnairies, 21, 22
— Mrs Colonel, of Fasnakyle, 157
— Provost, of Buntait, 433
— The (1569), 21
— The (1837), 137
— Thomas of Kinnairies, 22
Clanranald, Captain of, 113, 114
Clark, Alexander, writer in Ruthven, 375
— Captain Alexander, 381, 382, 384, 385
— Rev. Alexander, Inverness 27, 28
— Thomas, vintner at Fort-Augustus, 72, 79, 81, 82
"Cleirach," Bean, 14
Clerk, Sir John, Bart., Baron of Exchequer, 102
Cluny, Lady, 441
— of the 'Forty-five, 222, 335
— Macpherson of, 169, 338
Collingwood, Governor of Fort-Augustus, 84

INDEX. 459

Colquhoun, Ludovick of Luss, 101, 102, 103
— Sheriff, Commissary Depute, Inverness. 380
Colville, Sir Thomas De, 416
Comyn, Walter of Laggan, 334
Cope, Sir John, 353, 354
Craig, Robert, advocate, 101
Craigie, Lord Advocate, 353
Cromwell, Oliver, 180
Cumberland, Duke of, 85, 420
Cuming, James, Keeper of the Lyon Records, 116
Cumming, Alexina or "Lexy," Inverness, 47
— George, 445
— James of Delshangie, 46
— James writer and messenger, 47
— James yr. of Delshargie, 49
— The Red, 63
Cumusunary, Skye. Names of tenants in 1785, 279
Cuthbert, John, of Alturlies, 445
— Provost, of the Castlehill Family, 391
— William, Burgess of Inverness, 176.

D

Dallas of St. Martins, 436
— Alexander, 51
— Alexander, of Cantray, (1522-1566), 435
— Alexander, of Cantray (1582), 435
— Alexander, merchant, London, 435
— Anne, sister of Cantray of the '45, 436
— A. J., of Florida, 436
— Christina, wife of John Maclean, IX. of Dochgarroch, 51
— Henry, of Cantray, 435
— Henry, of Cantray (1567), 435
— Hugh, Commissary Clerk of Ross, 436
— James, of Cantray, an officer of the Regiment of Clan Chattan, 435
— John, of Cantray (1569), 435
— Marjory, of Cantray (1582), 435
— Miss Elizabeth Jane, Nairn, 436
— Mr, of Exeter, 436
— Mr, schoolmaster, Fort-Augustus, 78, 85
— Walter, burgess of Nairn, 435
— William of Cantray, 51
— William, of Cantray (1492)), 435
— William, of Cantray (1630), 435
— William, of Cantray, a mariner (1768), 435
Dallonach, Heads of Families, in 1763, 381

Dalrymple, George, Baron of Exchequer, 102
Davidson, David, Cantray and London, 435
— Donald, Inverness, famous fiddler, 147
— Henry of Tulloch, 377, 378
— Rev. Thomas, minister of Kilmallie, 217
Dawson, Helen, of Graden, Roxburgh, 154
— Mr, of Graden, Roxburgh, 154
Devorgilla of Galloway, 31
Donald Dhu vic Homas vic Allister in Badenoch, 176
Donaldson, Robert, Writer to the Signet, 72
Douglas, Earl of, 444
Doun, John, 6th of Glenmoriston, 99
Downie, Rev. Dr, of Lochalsh, 234, 235, 236,
Drummond, William, of Balbaldie, 103
Duff, John Archibald, 72
— Major Alexander, 72
— Mrs Hugh Robert, of Muirtown, 138, 139
— William, 73
Dunbar, David, proprietor of Durris in 1569, 60
— Sir Alexander of Westfield, Hereditary Sheriff of Moray, 60
Duncan Caum, son of Iain Mor a Chaistell, third of Glenmoriston, 112
Dundass, Robert, His Majesty's Solicitor General, 92, 93, 188
Dundee, Viscount, 157, 174, 350

E

Eachin, Farquhar vic, 32
Edward, Seneschal of Lochaber, 158
— Sir David, 18
Elcho, Lord, 418
Elgol, Tenants in 1785, 278
Elias, Vicar of Bona, 25
Enzie, Countess of, 31, 32, 41, 42, 46
— George, Earl of, 31, 32, 34, 41, 62 65, 337
Erskine, Mr, advocate, 140
— Sir Charles, Lord Lyon King at Arms, 116
Eva, Heiress or Mother of Clan Chattan, 159, 179

F

Fairweather, Sir Walter, 18
Fall, Captain, 449
Fentons of Ogill, 18
Fenton, Alexander, of Ogill, 18,
— James, of Ogill, 18, 19

INDEX.

Fenton, Janet, 2
— Thomas, of Ogill, 18
— William, of that ilk, 2
Ferguson, Donald, of Pitlochry, and of Phoness, 380
Ferquhar, Seneschal of Badenoch, 158
Ferquhar vic Allister, 61
Forbes, Bishop, 62, 228, 305, 306, 307, 308
Forbes, Duncan George, of Culloden, 30
— Duncan, 1st of Culloden, 346, 307
— John, 2nd of Culloden, 42, 43, 65
— John, of Culloden, 445
— John, of Tollie, 176
— Will., Writer to the Signet, Town Agent in Edinburgh, 92, 93, 95
Foster, Mrs. Beaufort Buildings, London, 120
Flemying, Nigel, Secretary to Earl of Ross, 161
Flyter, Mr. lawyer, Fort-William, 186, 187
Fraser, of Erricht, 96
— Agnes, of Struy, 40, 46, 47, 48
— Alexander in Eskadale, 6
— Alexander, son of 13th Lord Lovat, 8
— Alexander, son of Malcolm Fraser of Culduthel, 35
— Alexander, son of Colonel Hugh of Kinnairies, 56
— Alexander, of Reelig, 57
— Alexander, of Torbreck, 62
— Alexander, of Culduthel, 82, 428
— Alexander, alias "Ucky," 84
— Alexander, of the Leadclune Family, 404
— Allister vic Homas, 20
— Andrew vic Coul, 20
— Archibald, of Lovat, 246
— Captain Hugh, of Eskadale, 6, 104
— Captain Simon of Foyers, 104,
— Captain Thomas, J.P., of the Leadclune Family, 70
— Colonel Hugh, 1st of Kinnairies, 22, 56
— Colonel James, VII. of Belladrum, 57
— Dr James, of London, 97
— General Hastings, 86
— Hon. Archibald, 8, 9, 82
— Hon. Colonel Archibald Campbell, 11
— Hugh, of Belladrum, 2, 3, 22, 23, 43
— Hugh, of Aigais, "Old Father Aigais," 8
— Hugh, in Muilzie, 6
— Hugh, of Fraserdale, 8
— Hugh, of Achnacloich and 8th of Eskadale, 9, 11
— Hugh of Culbokie, 22, 23

Fraser, Hugh, in Struy, 42, 43
— Hugh of Bochrubin, 68
— Hugh, yr. of Foyers, 94, 95, 97, 225
— James vic Allister, 20
— James, of Belladrum, 3
— James, in Glendo, 84
— James of Gortuleg, Writer to the Signet, 97, 138, 274, 304, 309
— James in Inchlair, 6
— James in Polmon, 6
— James of Reelig, 57
— James, viutner in Inverness, 98
— James, in Foyness, 115
— James, 1st of Phopachy, 2
— John of Farraline, 14
— Major Andrew, Chief Engineer for North Britain, 181
— Major Archibald, 104
— Major, of Castle Leathers, 47, 98
— Miss Jean, daughter of Bailie William Fraser, of Inverness, 92, 95, 96, 97, 98
— Rev. Donald of Kilmorack, daughter of, 6
— Robert, of Aigais, 9, 10, 11
— Robert, tenant in Wester Muilzie, 5, 6
— Simon, in Inchlair, 6
— Simon, son of 13th Lord Lovat, 8
— Simon, sometime Commissary at Gibraltar, 68
— Simon, of Kinchyle, 69
— Sir William, 111
— Thomas, 6
— Thomas, of Moniack, 20
— Thomas, of Struy, 21, 46
— Thomas, 1st of Strichen, 25, 26
— Thomas, of Garthmore, 96
— Thomas Alexander, of Lovat, 105
— William, of Balnain, 445
— William, progenitor of the Frasers of Struy, 13, 14, 15, 21
— William, merchant in Fort-Augustus, 85, 86, 92, 93, 94, 95, 96, 97, 98, 99

G

"Gaelmore," Tenants in 1797, 173
Gairdner, Thomas, merchant in Edinburgh, 184
Galda, Ranald, 114, 115, 119
Garve, Mr. inspector of Roads and Bridges, 87, 89
Gellovie, Names of possessors in, 300 years ago, 337
George I., King, 350

INDEX. 461

James III., King, 155
— IV., King. 147, 164
Gibson, Henry, 127
— Sir John, parson of Urquhart, 176,
Gillespie, Thomas, 127
— Thomas, of Ardochy, 213
— Thomas, at Glen-Quoich, 82
Gillies, Angus, tacksman of East Stoul, North Morar. 246
Glasgow, Lord Provost and Magistrates of. 50
— Robert, Bishop of, 416
Glencairn, Earl of, 265
Glenelg, Lord, 105, 106
— John Macleod, Lord of, 160
Glengarry, 104, 108
Gollan, Barbara, 83
Gordon, Alexander of Biramoir, Rute-Master of Horse, 48
— Alexander, Duke of, 344, 351
— Alexander, 4th Duke of, 396, 398
— Charles, Esq. of Cluny. 181
— Colonel of South Uist, 321
— Duchess of, 187, 190, 191, 195
— Duchess of (Jane Maxwell) 396, 397, 398, 399, 439
— Duke of, 9, 39, 169, 171, 177, 180, 181, 187, 193, 194, 197, 239, 366, 370, 371, 372, 380, 381, 387, 388, 390, 428
— George, of Baldornie, Constable of Badenoch, 412
— Jean, wife of Lachlan Mackintosh, of Mackintosh, 18, 19, 20
— John Charles, in Tomintoul, 352
— John, of Glenbucket, 351, 352
— Lieutenant-Colonel, of Invertromie, 416
— Lord Adam, 188, 354, 357
— Lord Lewis, 352
— Major George, of 4th Dragoons, 388
— Rentals in 1650, 169, 170
— Rentals in 1667, 394, 395
— Rentals in 1828, 395
— Sir Robert of the Glen, 18
— Sir Robert of Gordonstoun, 353
Gow, Thomas. Nottar, 176
Graham, Dr Robert of Stirling, 184
Granby, Marquis of, 354
Grant, Alexander, minister of Glenurquhart, 47
— Alexander, yr. of Craskie, 111
— Allan, son of John Grant of Glenmoriston, 111, 112
— Angus, of Dalldragon, 111
— Captain, of Inverwick, 230
— Donald, Aberchalder, 78, 79, 81
— Duncan, of Bught, 304
— Duncan, of Freuchie, 412
— George Macpherson, 358
— James of Ardmill, 23
— James, of Corriemony, 414

Grant, James, yr. of Rothiemurchus, 414
— James, of Sheuglie, 47
— John, of Culcabock, 412
— John, elder of Corrimonie, 49
— John, of Freuchie, 23
— John, of Glenmoriston 40, 46
— John, 6th of Glenmoriston, 100 101, 102, 110, 111, 112, 230
— John Patrick, Tutor of Grant, 342, 343
— Laird of, 35, 98, 99
— Ludovick Grant of, 56
— Ludovick of Knockando, 378
— Margaret, 40
— Marion, daughter of Rev. Edward, vicar of St. Lukes, Jersey. 54
— Marjory, daughter of Sir Ludovick Grant of Dalvey, 124, 125, 128, 129
— Mary, daughter of Alex. Grant, in Milltown of Ballachastrell, 35
— Miss Anne Grant of, 15
— Miss Maria H., 106
— Mrs, of Laggan, 89, 90, 91
— Patrick, 7th of Glenmoriston, 100, 104, 111, 112
— Patrick of Rothiemurchus (Macalpine), 413, 414
— Patrick of Rothiemurchus, 397
— Rev. James, of Laggan, 83, 90
— Rev. Patrick of Boleskine, 128
— Robert in Buntait, 50
— Right Hon. Charles, 245
— Sir Alexander, 137.
— Sir George Macpherson of Ballindalloch, 388, 390, 394, 408
— Sir James Grant of, 57, 58
— Sir John Macpherson, 394
— Sir John Peter, advocate, 414,
— Sir Ludovick, of Dalvey, 124
— William, advocate, 101
— William Patrick, of Rothiemurchus, 414
— William, yr. son of Corriemonie, 49
Gray, John "Mair," of Badenoch, 369
Gwyne, Captain Mark, 90, 91, 92
— Family, 89

H

Haddinton, Earl of, 449
Hamilton, Captain, Commander of Revenue Cutter, 190
— Duke of, 107, 175
— Margaret, 435
Head, Mrs. of Inverailort, 155
Hector vic Allister in Davochcairn, 32
— Coil vic Ferquhar, 40
Henderson, Elizabeth, wife of William Maclean of Dochgarroch, 54
Hepbourn, Robert, Custom House, Edinburgh, 188

INDEX.

Horne, James, W.S., 138
Hossack, Provost John, Inverness, 92, 93
Huntly, Alexander, 2nd Earl of, 336
— Earl of, 29, 61, 114, 161, 162, 174, 175, 179, 340, 341
— Family of, 26, 31
— George, Marquis of, 337, 341, 387, 390, 391
— Lord, the present, 341
— Marquis of, 31, 32, 41, 42, 48, 133, 389, 428

I

Iain-a-Chraggain, 6th of Glenmoriston, 99, 101
Innes, Baillie Hugh, Inverness, 53
— Thomas, 25
— Cosmo, 438
Inshes, Lady, 32
Irving, Washington, 107
Irwine, Master John, Rector of Benholme, 18

J

James, III, King, 44
— IV, King, 18
— V, King, 18, 114
— VI, King, 16, 20, 21, 23, 24
— VII, King, 50
James vic Coil Glass, of, Gask, 176
Jansen, Commodore Dirck, of Ship "Campbelltown," 184, 185
Jedburgh, Sir John, Abbot of, 416
Jeffrey, Mrs, of New Kelso, 154
— George, New Kelso, 234, 236
John, Bishop of Sodor or the Isles, 39
— The Tutor, son of Iain Mor Abhaisteil, 3rd of Glenmoriston, 112
— Third and last Lord of the Isles, 159, 161
— vic Horkil, 13
Johnson, Dr Samuel, 63, 90, 280, 291, 400, 401, 402, 404
Johnston, Major James, 379

K

Kennedy, ——, Dancing Master, Fort-William, 183
— Allan, borther of Angus Bàn Kennedy, 140
— Angus, commonly called Angus Bàn Kennedy, at Invervigar, 140
— Archibald Bàn in Greenfield of Glengarry, 168
— Donald, in Maryburgh, 193, 194
— John, of Kirkland, tenant in Annat, 212

Kennedy, Rev. James, Inverness, 27
— Thomas, Esq., Baron of Exchequer, 102
— Widow, Lochiel Estate, 130
Keir, John, Burgess of Inverness, 176
Kincardine, Barons of, 417
Kingussie, Gordon Rental in 1667, 373, 374
— Householders in 1679, 372, 373
— Mackintosh's Tenants in 1635, 375
— Rental in 1828, 374, 375
Kinnaird, Mrs Jean, Inverness, 92, 95

L

Laggan, Gordon Rental in 1829, 344
— List of Heads of Families in 1679, 344, 345, 346
— Rental in 1829, 344
Landseer, Sir Edwin, 408, 410
Lauder, Sir Robert De, Knight, 56
Lee, Baillie Alexander, Inverness, 53
— Barbara, Inverness, 53
— Jean, Inverness, 53
Leeds, Duke of, 409, 410
Leo XII., 136
Leslie, Bishop, 113
— Mr, the "strong" minister of Moy, 52
Lochiel, 161, 162, 182, 192, 193, 197, 198, 202, 205, 206, 207, 214, 215, 216, 217, 218, 219, 220, 222, 223, 224, 226
— Allanson Ewen of, 174
Lockhart, Mary, 52
Lom, Iain, Bard of Keppoch, 166
Lorne, Lord, 201, 248, 260
Lovat, Alexander, 6th Lord, 13, 14, 15, 16, 113
— Family of, 76, 82, 100
— General Simon Fraser of, 7, 68, 71, 103, 124, 227, 240, 245, 246, 255
— Hugh, 1st Lord, 2
— Hugh, 3rd Lord, 44, 60
— Hugh, 5th Lord, 13, 15, 16, 18, 19, 56, 113, 114, 115, 117, 118, 119, 120, 243, 244
— Hugh, 7th Lord, 13, 14, 20
— Hugh, 9th Lord, 26
— Hugh, 10th Lord, 3
— Lady, wife of Hugh, 5th Lord, 4, 113, 118
— Master of, son of Hugh 5th Lord, 4, 13, 15, 113, 114, 118, 119
— Simon, 8th Lord, 2, 3, 22, 23, 61
— Simon, 13th Lord, 5, 7, 8, 35, 47, 58, 93, 94, 95, 100, 102, 103, 222, 286, 287, 432, 436, 441
— Thomas, 12th Lord, 100

INDEX. 463

Lovat Trustees, 57
Lyndsay, Sir David, of Beauford, 17

M

Malmesbury, Earl, 216
Man, Lieutenant Colonel Miles, Deputy Governor of Inverness, 43
Mains of Borlum, tenants in, 69
Marjoribanks, General, 378
Mary, Queen, 180, 181
Matheson, John, of Attadale, 233, 234, 235, 236
Matheson, Sir Kenneth, 4
Matthews, Charles, 408
Midtown, tenants in, 69
Mitchell, Mr, Aberarder Farm, 167
Monro, Archbishop, 39
Montgomery, Sir James, 141
Montrose, Duke of, 347
Moray, Alexander Bishop of, 56, 369
— Bishop of, 334, 411
— Countess of, 60
— Earl of, 26
— Earl of, 444
— George, Bishop of, 25
— James, Earl of, 46, 60
— John, Bishop of, 56
— Lord, 439, 440
— Regent, 60, 175
— The Little Earl of the Stuart line, 444
Morton, James, Earl of and Regent, 340, 341, 342
Munro, Alexander, Commissary of Inverness, 101
Munro, Annabella, of Daar, 47
— Mr James, Lochaber, 199
Mulmoire or Myles vic Bean vic Coil Mor, 64
Murchison, John, of the Lochalsh Family, 237, 239, 240
Murray, Lord George, 192, 418
— Sir Alexander, 223

MAC

Macallister, Alexander, of Strathaird, 283
— Mor, Donald, in Cullachy of Abertarff, 171
Macandrew, John, solicitor, Inverness, 147, 148
— John Beg, Dalnahatnich, 422, 423, 424, 425
Macbean, Angus, 1st of Kinchyle, 64, 65, 66
— Angus, minister of Inverness, 66
— Angus, writer in Inverness, 66
— Captain Forbes, of the Royal Artillery, 68

Macbean, Donald, 7th of Kinchyle, 68
— Effie, goodwife of Easich, 45
— Eneas or Angus, 5th of Kinchyle, 67, 68
— Gillies, 64
— Gillies, 6th of Kinchyle, 67
— John, 2nd of Kinchyle, 65
— Lieutenant Alexander, 68
— Paul, 3rd of Kinchyle, 65, 66
— Rev. Alexander, of Inverness, 68
— William, Attorney-at-Law, London, 68
— William, 4th of Kinchyle, 65, 66, 67, 68
Macdonald, Alexander (Alister nan Cleas) of Keppoch, 176
— Alexander, of Glencoe, 178, 214
— Alexander, author of Gaelic Dictionary, 194
— Alexander, of Glenalladale, 258, 259
— Alexander, of Kingsburgh, 282, 286
— Alexander, 1st of Boisdale, 322, 323
— Alexander, of Upper South River, Antigonish, Nova Scotia, 447
— Allan, of Kingsburgh, 282
— Allan, 8th Captain of Clanranald, 306
— Allan, of Belfinlay, 308, 309
— Allan, of Waternish, 310,
— Allan of Gellovie, 338, 339
— Angus, son of Alex. Carrach 1st of Keppoch, 174
— Angus, of Achtriachatan, 181, 370
— Angus, of Glenalladale 249, 257, 258
— Angus of Keppoch, 176
— Archibald, Garafad, 287
— Archibald Dhu, 144, 145
— Archibald, in Tullochcrom, 171
— Captain Angus, of Milton, 324, 327, 329
— Captain Donald, alias Donald Roy, 306
— Captain Kenneth, of Skeabost, 288, 289
— Captain Ronald, of Belfinlay, 306, 307, 308
— Colin, at Garryvaltos, 327
— Colin, 2nd of Boisdale, 322, 323, 324
— Donald, son of Donald Gorm of Sleat, 14
— Donald, of Castleton, 286
— Donald, of Cairngoddy, 78, 79, 84, 85
— Donald, of Benbecula, 322
— Donald, of "Tanera," 288

INDEX.

Macdonald, Donald, of Moidart, Captain of Clanranald, 320
— Dr Alexander, son of Charles Macdonald in the Clachlan of Aberfoyle, 184, 184 ; patients of, 185
— Dr Alex., *alias* Maceachin, called the "Doctor Roy," 184-185
— Dr Donald, of Fort-Augustus, 108, 139, 140, 141
— Dr John, Fort-William, 188
— Dr John, Kinlochmoydart, 308
— Dr Kenneth, Gesto, 310
— Ewen, son to Glencoe, 119, 154, 173, 174
— Father Charles, 155, 156, 157
— Flora, 138, 227, 291
— Hector, W.S., of Boisdale, 323
— Hugh, 4th of Boisdale, 324
— James, of Knock, 224, 275
— James, merchant, Portree, 288
— James, Changekeeper of Sooneer, 292
— James, of Belfinlay, 306, 309, 310
— John, in Torgulbin, 167
— John, of Borrodale, 247
— John of Glenalladale, 323
— John, of Bornish, 321, 322
— Lachlan, of Tor Castle, 202
— Lachlan, of Skeabost, 289
— Lord, 448
— Lord of Sleat, 129, 272, 273, 283, 291, 301, 302, 303, 304
— Lieutenant Angus, of Milton, 327
— Lieut.-Colonel James, 256
— Lieut.-Colonel Alexander, 3rd of Boisdale, 324, 325
— Major, 138
— Major Alexander, of Glenalladale, 308
— Major Allan, of Arisaig, 450
— Major James, of Askernish, 331, 332, 324
— Margaret, of Clanranald, "Miss Peggy Ormiclate," 328, 329, 330
— Marshall, Duke of Tarentum, 449, 449
— Mrs Coll, of Knock, 154
— Ranald, of Bornish, 321
— Ranald yr. of Clanranald, 322, 323
— Ranald, of Gellovie, 171
— Ranald, of Strathmashie, 365, 366, 367, 368

Macdonald, Ranald George of Clanranald, 320
— Reginald George, 255
— Ronald, of the '45, 255
— Roderick, Camuscross, 272, 773, 274, 275
— Ronald Mor, 8th of Keppoch, 174, 175
— Sir Alexander of Sleat, 263, 264, 265, 266, 267, 268, 269, 270, 271, 272, 276, 286, 332
— Sheriff John, 294
— Sir Donald of Sleat, 264
— Sir Donald vic Allan vic Iain of Clanranald, 250
— Sir James of Sleat, 263, 272
— Sir, Reginald of Staffa, "Old Staffa," 324
— William of St. Martins, Clerk to the Signet, 129
Macdonell of Achluachrach, 423, 424, 425, 426
— of Greenfield (Montreal) 286
— of Lochgarry, 191, 192, 193
— Æneas of Morar, 191, 247, 249
— Æneas of Scotos, 236, 237, 238
— Alexander, "Blarour" of Glenturret, 172
— of Glengarry, 120, 121, 122, 123, 124, 126, 191, 193
— Alexander, at Kinloch, factor for Glengarry, 140, 142
— Alexander, of Lochshiel, 158
— Alexander, of the Scotos Family, priest, afterwards Bishop of Kingston, 128, 130, 131, 135, 136, 137
— Alexander, tacksman of Tulloch, 167, 168
— Alexander, 16th of Keppoch, 177
— Alexander of Wester Aberchalder, 120
— Allan, of Cullachie, 120
— Angus, of Greenfield, 120, 139
— Angus, *alias* "Inmore," 85
— Angus, of Muirlaggan, 164, 165, 166
— Angus, of the Family of Keppoch, 178
— Archibald, 1st of Barrisdale, 156
— Archibald, 3rd of Barrisdale, 126, 152, 156, 224, 238 ; wife of, 234
— Archibald, 5th and last of Barrisdale, 155, 156, 193
— Archibald, of Glenmeddle, 234, 235
— Archibald, in Tulloch, 166, 167

INDEX. 465

Macdonell, Archibald, tenant in Moy, 167, 168
— Captain, of Faichem, 87, 89
— Captain James, 156
— Captain James, of Glenmeddle, 120
— Captain Ranald, of Glenturret, 172
— Coll, 2nd of Barisdale, 152, 155, 156
— Coll, 4th of Barisdale, 126, 152, 153, 154, 155, 156, 193, 233, 238, 274, 275
— Coll, of Dalness, C.S., 139, 140
— Coll, of Inch, 213
— Coll, of Keppoch, 171
— Coll, 15th of Keppoch, "Coll of the Cows," 176, 177
— Colonel Alexander, of Glengarry, 108, 128, 129, 130, 131, 137, 138, 139, 140, 141, 142, 143, 144, 145, 146, 147, 148, 149, 150, 151, 154, 156, 197, 198, 291, 292, 293
— Colonel Donald, of Scotos, 249
— Donald, of Daldundearg of Tulloch, 166
— Donald, of Lundie, 99, 122, 125, 126
— Donald, alias MacAllister-vic-Aonas-Roy, 172
— Donald, in Tulloch, 166, 167, 168
— Donald, tacksman of Farm of Auchcar, 193, 194
— Duncan, of Glengarry, 120, 124, 125, 127, 128, 129, 134
— Eneas Ronaldson, of Glengarry, 133, 147
— Father Ranald, of Leek, 172
— Gorrie, of Glenturret, 172
— Isabella, 120
— John, of Ardnabi, 97
— John, of Drynachan, 112
— John, of Glengarry, 111, 112, 120, 191
— John, junior, piper to Glengarry, 140
— John, of Inveroy, 171
— John, of Keppoch, 178
— John, of Leek, 120
— John, second son of Æneas of Scotos, 236, 237, 2·8
— J. A., of Greenfield, 135, 136
— Juliet, the Keppoch Poetess, 196
— Lieutenant-Colonel Angus, 120, 191
— Lieutenant-Colonel Donald, of Lochgarry, 191
— Lord, and Aros, 129, 171
— Major Alexander, of Keppoch, 177, 178
— Miss, of Slaney, 156
— Ranald, of Keppoch, 177
— Ranald, of Lethindrie, 172

Macdonell, Ranald, of Shian, 112
— Ronald, of Scammadale and Crowlin, 155, 156, 157, 158
— Ronald, of Scotos, 104
— Ronald, tacksman of Glenbuie, 140
— Ronald, tenant in Moy, 167
— Ronald, of Clionavaig, 171
— Shiela, the Keppoch Poetess, 196
MacEachin, Neil, South Uist, 449
MacEachin, Neil, at Howbeg, centenarian, 328, 329, 330
Macfarlane, John, Writer to the Signet, 103
Macfyngone, Ewin, of Strathwordill, 276
— Lauchlane, of Strathwordill, 276
Macgillivray, Lieutenant Colonel Alexander, of Dunmaglass, 440
Macgillivray, Wm., of Dunmaglass, 68
Mac Gillie Callum, Dugald Mor, 17, 18
Macgregor, Rev. Alexander, of Inverness, 293
— Sir Evan Murray, 164
Macintyre, Dr, in Kilmonivaig, 199
Mackay, Alexander, Inspector of Taxes, Inverness, 86
— John, messenger-at-arms at Innis-na-cardoch, 71, 72, 73, 74, 75, 78, 79, 80, 81, 85, 86, 87, 88, 89, 139, 141
— William, solicitor, Inverness, 38, 110
Mackenzie, Alexander, the Highland Clan Historian, 133, 207, 208, 279, 287
— Colin, of Kincraig, 3
— Colin, junior, of Kincraig, 3
— Isobel, daughter of Roderick Mackenzie of Redcastle, 67
— Rev. Dun., Episcopal Clergyman at Tulloch, 454
— Sir George, of Tarbat, 3
Mackinnon, Charles, of Strath, 277, 278, 279, 280
— John, of Corry, 280
— John Dhu, of Strath, 276, 277, 280
— John Og, of Strath, 276
— Lachlan, of Corry, Sheriff of Skye, 292
— Lachlan of Corrychatachan, 308
— Lachlan, Elgol, 283
— Lachlan of Strath, 277
— Lachlan of Strathwordill, 30
— Rev. John, minister of Sleat, 448
— Rev. Mr, minister of Strath, 292
— Sir William A., K.C.B., 283 291, 292, 293, 448, 449
— William, Sheriff-Clerk Depute at Fort-Augustus, 86, 87, 89

466 INDEX.

Mackintosh (1633-1637) 201, 202, 203, 204, 205, 206
— Alexander Æneas, 27th of Mackintosh, 410
— Alexander, 20th of Mackintosh, 409
— Alexander of Connage, 43
— Alexander, son of Kellachie and Aldourie, 61, 65
— Allan Kier, of Rothiemurchus, 412
— Angus, 6th of Mackintosh, 63
— Angus, Portioner of Benchar, 347
— Benjamin, of Borlum, 429
— Brigadier, of Borlum, 52, 429
— Campbell of Dalmigavie, Town-Clerk of Inverness, 433
— Captain Alexander, 52
— Captain John, of Corrybrough Mor, 290
— Captain William, of Aberarder, 432
— Charles, last of Aberarder, 433
— Donald, brother-german of Farquhar Roy, 17
— Donald, na Brataich, 437
— Duncan, 436
— Farquhar Roy, 17
— Father John, of Bornish, 329
— Hon. Lachlan, Captain of Clan Chattan, 164, 165, 177
— James, of Rothiemurchus, 412
— James Keir, of Rothiemurchus, 412
— Janet, of Holme, 49
— Jean, daughter of Donald Mackintosh of Kellachie, 66
— John, of Aberarder, 432
— John, in Easter Bohuntin, 173
— John, of Rothiemurchus, 412
— Lachlan, 3rd of Aberarder, 433
— Lachlan, brother to the Laird of Mackintosh, 43
— Lachlan, of Balnespick, 338 339, 378
— Lachlan, of Gallovie, "Lachlan Badenoch," 366, 340
— Lachlan, of Dunachton, 16, 18, 19, 61, 175, 176, 177, 335, 427
— Lachlan of Kinrara, 352
— Lachlan, of Knocknageal, 52
— Lachlan, of Mackintosh, 20, 21
— Lachlan, Shanval of Badenoch, 377
— Lachlan, of Strone, 172
— Lachlan, of Torcastle, 339, 340, 377

Mackintosh, Lachlan Mor, of Mackintosh, 340, 341, 342, 411, 431
— Lady, 435
— Malcolm Beg, 10th of Mackintosh, 17, 159, 160, 161, 336
— Marie, daughter of Lachlan Mackintosh of Knocknageal, 52
— Miss Jane, 433
— Mrs, of Borlum, 358, 361, 362
— of Mackintosh, (the present) 436
— of Mackintosh (the late) 436, 437
— 7th of Mackintosh, 64
— of Mackintosh, William, 61, 174, 175
— Provost John, of Aberarder, 290
— Provost John of the Kellachie Family, 432, 433
— Rentals in 1650, 169, 170
— Right Hon. Lachlan, of Torcastle, 172
— Sir Eneas, 164, 177
— Sir Lachlan, of Torcastle, 20, 21, 22, 23
— Sir James, of Kellachie, 68, 71
— The 158
— William, 2nd of Aberarder, 431
— William, of Balnespick, 361
— William, in Blargie, 338, 339, 340
— William, of Borlum, 50, 350
— William, of Borlum, son of Lachlan Mor Mackintosh of Mackintosh, 61, 62, 63, 64, 65, 67
— William, son of Duncan Mackintosh, 50, 52
— William, of Gallovie, 340
— William, son of Donald Mackintosh of Kellachie and Aldourie, 66, 413, 423, 424, 425
— William, 15th of Mackintosh, 19, 20
— William, 433
— William, of Torcastle, 337
Maclachlan, Archibald, writer in Fort-William, 143
— Lachlan, 26, 27
— Rev. James, of Moy, 27
— Rev. Thomas, 27
Maclean, Agnes and Marion, Prioresses of Iona, 39
— Alexander of Coll, 324
— Alexander, of Dochgarroch, "Allister-vic-Coil-vic-Ferquhar, 38
— Alexander, 5th of Dochgarroch, 39, 40, 41, 42, 43, 44, 45, 46, 47

INDEX. 467

Maclean, Alexander, 7th of Dochgarroch, 48, 49
— Alexander, son of John, 8th of Dochgarroch, 50, 52
— Allan, son of Alexander, 7th of Dochgarroch, 48, 49
— Allan, 13th of Dochgarroch, 53
— Allan, 14th of Dochgarroch, 54
— Allan Mackintosh, son of Allan, 14th of Dochgarroch, 54
— Captain James, at Penmore of North Uist, 322
— Charles, 1st of Dochgarroch, 38
— Charles, 10th of Dochgarroch, 52
— Colonel, of Dochgarroch, 30
— Colonel Sir John, K.C.B., 389, 392
— C. J., Treasurer of the Clan Maclean Association, 50
— David, son of John, 8th of Dochgarroch, 50
— Donald, 4th of Dochgarroch, 39, 45
— Donald, Hector's son, apparrent of Kingairloch, 40
— Donald, merchant burgess in Inverness, son of John, 6th of Dochgarroch, 49
— Donald, son of John "Og," 50
— Donald, son of John, 8th of Dochgarroch, 50
— of Drummine, 192
— Elizabeth, of Rochester, 53
— Farquhar, Bishop of the Isles, 39
— Farquhar, 3rd of Dochgarroch, 39
— Farquhar, in Kinmylies, son of John, 6th of Dochgarroch, 49
— Hector, 2nd of Dochgarroch, 38
— Hector, in Dochnalurg, son of John, 6th of Dochgarroch, 49
— Janet, daughter of John, 8th of Dochgarroch, 50, 52
— John, 6th of Dochgarroch, 40, 42, 45, 47, 48, 49
— John, son of Alexander, 7th of Dochgarroch, 49
— John, 8th of Dochgarroch, 49
— John, 9th of Dochgarroch, 49, 50, 51
— John, 11th of Dochgarroch, 52, 53
— John, of Hosta, 301, 302, 303, 304
— John, in Leys, son of John, 6th of Dochgarroch, 49
— John, " Og," 50
— John, Vice-President of the Clan Maclean Association, 50

Maclean, Lachlan, son of John, 8th of Dochgarroch, 50
— Lieutenant Alexander, 50, 51
— Lieutenant-Colonel Charles, son of William, 12th of Dochgarroch, 53, 54
— Marcella, of Pennycross, 172
— Margaret, daughter of John, 8th of Dochgarroch, 49
— Neil, land surveyor, 144, 145,
— Sir Charles, 29
— Walter, President of the Clan Chattan Association, 50
— William, 12th of Dochgarroch, 52, 53
— William, son of John, 9th of Dochgarroch, 52
— William, son of William, 12th of Dochgarroch, 53, 54
Macleod, Alexandra, of Macleod, 279,
— Allister, " Crotach," of Dunvegan, 243, 244
— Captain Alexander, of Lochbay, 291, 293, 294
— Captain Donald, of St. Kilda, 299, 300
— Captain Neil, of Gesto, 296, 297, 298
— Captain Norman, of Waternish Volunteers, 293, 294, 295
— Christy, Kilmuir Centenarian, 286, 287
— Colonel, of Tallisker, 276, 277
— Janet, Arnisdale, 236, 237, 238
— Janet, of Raasay, 277, 279
— John, of Lewis, 280
— John Norman, of Glenelg, 245
— Lieutenant John, of Unish, 291
— Lieutenant Norman, 130, 138, 291, 292
— Lieutenant William, of Glendale, 290, 291
— of Macleod, General, 241, 242, 244, 290
— of Macleod, the present, 289, 299
— Malcolm, 8th of Raasay, 277, 279
— Miss Marion, of Gesto, 280
— Norman, of Drynoch, 239
— Norman, General, Eileanreach, Macleod's factor, 242
— Norman, of Eilean Reach, 154, 274, 275
— Norman Macleod of, 95, 96, 97, 272, 287, 288, 291, 300,
— Rev. Murdo, parish minister of Glenelg, 236, 238
— Rev. Roderick, of Bracadale, 296
— Sir John Macpherson Macleod, 300
— Torquil, Lord of the Lewes, 160

468   INDEX.

Macleod, William, apparent of Dunvegan, 243, 244
— William, apparent of Macleod, 15
Macnab, Donald, of Dalchully, 365, 366, 367, 368
— Donald, in Inverlair, 167
Macneill, Captain Rod. of Barra, 332
— General, of Barra, 333
— Roderick, Vernon River (of Barra), 333
— William, in Pabbay of Harris, 299
Macniven, Isabella, heiress of Dunachton, 340
Macphail, Angus vic Phoil vic Gillies Macbean, 61
Macphee, Ewen, "Outlaw of Glen Quoich," 215, 216
Macphersons of Dalraddie, 390, 391, 392
Macpherson, Alexander, of Essich, 347
— Alexander, factor for Cluny, 116, 117
— Alexander, of Invertromie, 388
— Alexander, of Phoness, 377
— Alexander, writer, 71, 125
— Allister Roy, of Phoness, 376
— Andrew, of Cluny, 339, 346, 347
— Angus, 1st of Invereshie, 391, 392
— Angus, of Invertromie, 387
— Anne, of Belleville, 406, 437
— Anne, of Phoness, 376, 379
— Bailie D., in Glentromie, 384, 385
— Bailie Donald, of Inverness, 71
— Captain Andrew, of Biallidbeg, 382, 383, 384, 385
— Captain Charles, of Gordonhall, 389
— Captain John, 393
— Captain Mungo, 42nd Highlanders, 164
— Captain Thomas, of Invertromie, 387
— Catharine, in Daltochy of Ardclach, daughter of John Maclean, 6th of Dochgarroch, 49
— Colonel Alexander, of Blairgowrie, 405
— Colonel Duncan, of Breackachie, 358, 361
— Colonel Duncan, of Cluny, 356, 359, 360, 361, 362, 363, 376
— Gillies, son of the "Black Captain," 376, 380
— Donald, of Breackachie, 361
— Donald, apparent of Nuide, 347, 385, 387
— Donald, of Corronach, 378
— Donald, brother of Malcolm, 377
— Donald, of Phoness, 376

Macpherson, Donald, of Phoness, grandson of above Donald, 377, 378
— Dougall, of Ballochroan, 347
— Duncan, of Cluny, 171, 339, 342, 343, 349, 350
— Duncan, of Invertromie, 387, 388
— Duncan, Kingussie, 164
— Eneas Peter, of Phoness, 375, 376, 379
— Evan of Cluny, 352, 353, 354, 359, 361, 379
— Evan, schoolmaster of Ralia, 384, 385
— Ewen, of Brin, 347
— Ewen, of Cluny, 346, 347, 363
— Ewen, in Gaskinloan, 347
— Ewen, of MacCoul, 358, 363
— Fiscal, 171
— George, of Dalraddie and Invereshie, 392, 393
— George, of Invereshie, 378
— General Barclay, 358, 362, 363
— Gillis or Elias, 3rd of Invereshie, 392
— Hugh, of Inverhall, 388
— Hugh, of Ovie, 364
— Iain vic William, in Invereshie, 377
— James, of Beleville, son of "Ossian," 406, 407
— James, of Coraldie, 384
— James, factor, 438
— James, of Invernahaven, and descendants, 389
— James, of Killybuntly, 379
— James, of Phoness, Etteridge, Invernahaven, Raitts, etc., "Ossian," 379, 381, 389, 399, 400, 401, 402, 403, 404, 405, 406
— John, of Breackachie, 363
— John, of Cluny Mains and Gallovie, 358, 366, 379, 382
— John, of Dalaraddie, 339, 350
— John, Younger of Dalraddie, 350
— John, of Etteridge, and descendants, 388
— John, in Kinloch, 338, 339
— John, "of Inverhall," 370, 372
— John, of Invereshie, 66
— John, 2nd of Invereshie, 392
— John, of Nuide, 347, 349, 360, 387
— John, of Pitmean, 66
— John, of Shirrobeg, 336, 339, 350
— Lachlan, of Biallidmore, 382
— Lachlan, of Cluny, 431, 432
— Lachlan, of Dellifour, 350
— Lachlan, of Invertromie, 387

INDEX.   469

Macpherson, Lachlan, of Ralia, 337, 361, 383
— Late Ewen, of Cluny, 116
— Lieutenant, 377
— Lieutenant Angus, of Phoness, 378, 379
— Lieutenant, of the Ovie Family, 71, 72, 73, 74, 75
— Lieutenant William, of Phoness, 376, 379
— Malcolm, of Breakachy, 350
— Malcolm, of Phoness. "Callum Gorach," 377, 378
— Major Duncan, of Drummond and Ralia, 373
— Miss, of Lonnie, in Petty, 68
— Murdo, of Clune, Depute-Steward, 161
— Paul, of Dalraddie, 347
— Peter, of Phoness, jeweller in Paris, 375
— Rev. Thomas, minister of Alvie, 350
— Robert, tacksman of Lonnie, 68
— Sir Eneas, 392
— Thomas, of Killybuntly, 339
— William, of Dalraddie and Invereshie, 393, 394
— William, of Invereshie, 151
Macqueen, Allan, 304
— Elspet, in Inshes, daughter of John Maclean, 6th of Dochgarroch, 49
— James, Younger of Corribrough, 165, 166
— John Dhu, of Pollochaig, 427, 428
— Lachlan, in Glenmoriston, 84
— William Mac Eachan, of Corriebrough, 176
Macra, Dr John, Ardintoul, Kintail, 107
— Parson Rory, 153
Macrae, Alexander, sheep farmer and innkeeper, Cluny, 86, 87, 88, 89
MacRonald, Allan, of the Leys, 16
MacVicar, Duncan, barrack-master, Fort-Augustus, 90

N

Nicolson, Angus, sub-tenant of Pennifiler, 285
— Malcolm, Scorrybreck, 284, 285
— Rev. Alexander, at Aird, 286
— Rev. Donald, minister of Strath, 282
North Laggan, tenants in, 150

O

Ogilvie, Alexander, styled of Farr, 60

Ogilvie, Catharine, wife of Alexander Grant, in Milntown of Ballochastell, 35
— James, 60
— James, of Cardale, laird of Findlater, 19
— Margaret, 19
O'Neill, Lord, 147
Orme, Alexander, Writer to the Signet, 120

P

Paton, David, Burgess of Inverness, 247
Paterson, Janet, daughter of William Paterson, wife of David Baillie of Dochfour, 35
Peel, William, 360.
Phadrig, Alexander vic, in Davochnacraig, 32
Phipps, Miss Ophelia, of the Mulgrave Family, 435, 436
Polson, David, of Kinmylies, 56
Portland, Duke of, 85
Porter, Dr Wm., Lochbay, 293, 294, 295
Prince Charles Edward, 71, 95, 155, 156, 157, 158, 179, 191, 192, 205, 207, 211, 223, 227, 229, 231, 256, 257, 258, 263, 277, 332, 353, 418, 435, 449

R

Ramsay, Lady, 137
Ramsden, Sir John, 33, 58, 336, 337, 355
Ranald, John vic, 13
Randolph, Sir Thomas, 60
Reid, Captain, of Eileanreach, 237
— David, Custom House, Edinburgh, 188
— Robert, Bishop of Orkney, Abbot of Kinloss, and Prior of Beauly, 107
Richmond, Duke of, Master General of Ordnance, 370
Riddell, Sir James of Ardnamurchan, 187
Robertson, Hugh, Lochiel's Factor, tenant in Moy, 212
— Hugh, wood merchant, 198
— Misses, of Kindrochit, 380
— Mr, of Banchor, 380
— Mr Charles, factor, Dunvegan, 242
— Mrs, of Banchor, 375, 380
— Roderick, of the Isles, ancestor of the Clanranalds, 261
Rolland, Adam, advocate, 58
Rose, John of Kilravock, 15
— John, schoolmaster at Croachie, 454
— Late Hugh, solicitor, Inverness, 437
— Late John, of Kirktown 437
— Robert, 445
Ross Captain Ewen, Killinan, 222

INDEX.

Ross, Earl of, and Lord of the Isles (Alexander of Yle) 159, 160
— Janet, Lady Dowager of Lovat, 13, 14, 15, 16
— John, last Earl of, and Lord of the Isles, 38
— Rev. Dr Thomas, of Kilmonivaig, 139, 172
Rothes, Earl of, 3
Rothiemurchus, Lady "Grizel Mor," 413, 414
Roy, Andrew, of Kirkhill, 119
— Andrew vic Homas, 13
Roystoun, Lord, 93
Russell, Lady Georgina Elizabeth, 398
— Lady Louisa Jane, 398
— Lord Alexander, 409, 410

S

Scoraby, Sir Hugh de, 416
Scott, John, tenant in Brunachan, 172
Scott, Sir Walter, 48, 90, 324, 332, 353
Seafield, Earl of, 58
Seaforth, Earl of, 1
— George, Earl of, 3
— Proprietrix of, 86
Selkirk, Earl of, 107, 108
Sharpe, Archbishop, 276
Shaw, Angus, factor to the laird of Mackintosh, 165, 166, 167
— James, of Ovie, 364
Shovel, Sir Cloudesley, 405
Simpson, William, "Reader," 25
Sinclair, Alexis, student, 199, 200
— Rev. A. Maclean, Prince Edward Island, 333
Soulis, Sir William de, 416
Stark, Alexander, Fort-Augustus, 78
Stevenson, Captain Robert, of Greenock, 136
Stewart, Alexander, writer in Edinburgh, 72
— Alexander, writer in Fort-William, 225, 226,
— Alexander, "The Wolf of Badenoch," 58
— David, Procurator-Fiscal for Lord Moray, 46
— Dr Alexander, of Nether-Lochaber, 199
— James, 107, 112
— James, schoolmaster of Urquhart, 49, 50
— Janet, widow, 11
— Sir John, of Gartentullich, 176
Strachan, Master Gilbert, 19
Stuart, Alexander, Earl of Mar, 172
— Bailie John, Inverness, 417
— Colonel John Roy, 418, 419, 420

Stuart, Lieutenant, of the Invalids, 83
— Lieutenant-General Sir John, K.C.B., Count of Maida, 417, 418
— James, "The Little Earl of Moray," 19

— James, in Tillyfourie, 176
— Jessie, of Appin, 177
— John vic Andrew, of Inverchynachan, 176
Sutherland, Earl of, 100

T

Telford, John, engineer, 149, 210
Tempest, Sir Henry Vane, 147
Thomas vic Hamish, 13
Thornton, Colonel, 169
Tod, Will., factor on Gordon Estates, 74, 187, 191, 239, 357, 361, 364, 370, 371
Trapaud, Governor of Fort-Augustus, 79, 83, 84, 85
Tweeddale, Lord, 353

U

Upper Cullairds, tenants in, 69
Urquhart, George, public carrier, Inverness, 86, 87, 88

V

Victoria, Her Most Gracious Majesty Queen, 409, 410,

W

Wade, General, 61, 168, 171
Walker, C., of Ness Castle, 62
White, Mr, factor, 438
William, King, 176, 180
— the Conquerer, 31
— vic Angus vic Phoil in Kinchyle, 63
"— vic-Homas in Inchlochell," 3
Williamson, Angus of Termit, or "Angus of the Brazen Face," 16

Y

York, Duke of, 47
Young, David, of Perth, 181, 370, 371
— John, of the "Inverness Journal," 63

NAMES OF PLACES.

A

Aboyne, 41
Aberarder, 334, 335, 433
Aberchalder, 108, 109
Abernethy, 416, 417, 420
Abertarff, 25, 75, 76, 108, 115
Abriachan, 25, 26, 34, 51, 55, 57, 59
Achluachrach, 173
Achmony, 110
Achnabat, 62
Achnacarry, 207
Achnacroich, 16?
Achnagairn, 22
Achnasoul, 206
Achterawe, 106
Aigas, 2, 3
Aird, 2, 5, 7, 14, 17, 18, 20, 21, 22, 44
Aldourie, 61, 62
Altdearg or Ault Dearg, 29, 59
Altdochcairn, 29
Alturlies, 445
Alvie, 380, 390, 391, 392, 394, 397, 407, 410, 428, 450
Annat, 212
Antfield, 62
Applecross, 410
Ardchuilck, tenants in 1767, 5
— tenants in 1803, 10
Ardersier, 442, 443
Ardgour, 201
Ardhill, 236
Ardnamurchan, 187, 188, 189, 190, 201, 225, 231, 248
Ardochy, 36
Ardverikie, 335
Arisaig, 248, 249, 251, 255, 306, 450
Arisaig, Rental in 1798, 250, 251
Armadale Castle, Skye, 448
Arnisdale, 236, 237
Auchtertyre, in Lochalsh, 126
Aultdearn, 64
Aviemore, 427

B

Badenoch, 31, 33, 71, 177, 359, 363, 364, 369, 371, 375, 380, 382, 385, 386, 387, 394, 396, 422, 431
Balblair, 60, 61
Baliol College, Oxford, 31
Ballachulish, 182
Ballimore of Dochgarroch, 5, 54
Ballindalloch, 62, 63
Ballindarroch, 54
Balmacaan or Balmaceachainn, 38
Balmoral, 409
Balnacruik, 35, 54

Balnafroig, 62
Balnagriassichean, 59
Balnain, 61
Balnespick, 415
Balvanich and Dungannich, townships of, 327
Banavie, 199, 201, 211
Bannockburn, Battle of, 159, 160, 161, 162, 163, 164, 165, 166, 167, 168, 169, 170, 171, 172, 173, 174
Banquhar, Barony of, 26, 29
Barra, 331, 332, 333
Battle Abbey, 31
Beandcher, 32
Beaufort, 9, 18, 20, 23, 24, 94
Beauly, 2, 13, 23, 120
— Inhabitants of, in 1803, 12
Belfinlay, 305
Belladrum, 24, 57
Benbecula, List of tenants in 1798, 311, 312, 313
Benchar, 349, 450, 452, 453
— Barony of, 2
Bencharan, tenants in 1767, 5
— tenants in 1803, 10
Bencharran, 2
Benchor, 380
Bergen-Op-Zoom, 450
Bernera, 240
Blackfold, 45
Blarnahinven, 172
Blar-nan leine, Battle of, 4, 113, 116, 205
Bochasky, 173
Bochrubin, 61
Bog 'o Gight, 31
Boisdale, 322, 323
Boleskine, 25, 60, 71, 75, 76, 427
Bona, 25, 25, 44, 54, 57, 62, 65, 71, 72
Bonach, Barony of, 56
Borlum, 27, 44, 60, 61, 62, 69
— Castle of, 62
Bornish, Lower, tenants removed in 1810, 326
Bracadale, 296
Bracklich, 444
Braeroy, 337
Brahan, 3
Breakachie, 383
Brewling, 3
Brighton 54
Broadford, 280, 281
Budgate, 348
Bunachton, 61, 65
Bunchrew, 22
Bunoich, 82
Buntait, 2

C

Caiplich, 25, 26, 37, 46, 57, 59

Calder, 65
Calicut, 52
Callaig Etteridge, or Catlodge, 361, 362
Camelford, 405
Campbelltown, 190, 442, 443, 444
Canna, 221
— Rental of, in 1798, 260
Carsdale, Barony of, 60
Carn Dearg, 30
Carriencoir, 23, 24
Castlebay, 332
Castle Dounie, 5
Cawdor, 438
Clachnahalig, 32
Cladh Uradain, 30
Cluanie, 98
Clune, 452, 453
Clunemore, 98
Clunes, 206, 211, 441
Cluny, 89 350, 360
Connage. 444, 445
Corpach, 196, 231, 211
Corriecharrabie, 4, 9
Corrimony, 110
Corrichulachie, 58
Corryarraik, 83, 837, 365
Corryfoness, 56
Cradlehall, 36
Cragaoh, 19, 21, 22, 23, 24, 42, 44
Craigaig, 20
Craigcailleoch, Battle of, 17
Craigdhu, 359, 360
Crask of Durris, 62
Crathie Croy, 31
Crathy, 364
— List of tenants summoned to remove in 1806, 364
Cromarty, 377
Crowlin, 156
Croy, 435, 436, 437
Cruachan, 88
Culbokie, 24
Culnakirk, 98
Cullachy, 71
Cullairds, 60, 52
Culloden, 5
— Battle of, 67, 71, 126, 145, 157, 178, 191, 222, 223, 257, 258, 287, 306, 308, 369, 418, 435, 437

D

Dalarossie, 61, 527, 429
Dalcattaig, 98, 99, 101, 102, 103, 104, 105, 106
Dalcrag, 14
Dalcross, 13, 14 436, 437
— Barony of, 19
Dalchully, 365, 366
Dalkeith, 20
Dallanach, 381
Dalmigavie, 61, 430
Dalnahatnich, 425
Dalnavert, 408
Dalraddie, 390, 391
Daltomich, 428, 429

Dalwhinnie, 169, 381, 388
Darnaway 19
Davochcairns, 32
Daviot and Dunlichity, 431
Deanie, 11
— tenants in 1803, 10
Delchapple, 106
Dingwall, 281
Dochcairn, 25, 26, 32, 33, 34, 35, 36, 37, 54
Dochfour, 25, 28, 29, 33, 34, 35, 37, 44, 54
Dochgarroch, 25 26, 27, 29, 39, 34, 37, 38, 40, 41, 42, 43, 44, 48, 54, 55
Dochnacraig or Davochdearg, or Davochnacraig, or Lochend, 25, 26, 27, 28, 29, 30, 31, 32, 33, 34, 37, 44, 58
— tenants in 1799, 54
Dochnalurg, 41, 42, 43, 44, 45, 48, 54 55
Dores. or Durris, or Daars, Parish of, 60, 61, 62 63
— church lands of, 61, 62, 64, 69, 71, 439
Dounie Castle, 5
Drumchardiny, 20, 22 23 24
— Barony of, 19
Drummond, 60, 61, 64
Drumouchter, 389
Duirinish, 290
Dulnan, 422
Dunachton, 339
Dunain, 26, 28, 32, 34, 37, 38, 42, 43, 53, 57, 58, 99
Dunballoch, 5
Dundee, 338
Dunkeld, 176
Dunlichity, 61
Dunmaglass, 61, 439
Duntelchaig, 61
Duntulm, 286, 287
Dunvegan, 295
Duthil, 422

E

East Indies, 6, 112
Easter Abriachan, 56, 58
— Brewlin, tenant in 1769, 5
"Easter Dowinsche," 62
— Kinchyle, 66
— Muilzie, 4, 5
Edinbane, 288
Edinburgh, 17, 18, 23, 24, 39, 41, 53, 74, 92, 103, 120, 137, 140, 141, 160, 164, 190, 191, 228, 229 241, 256, 279, 320, 353, 370, 379, 390, 404, 449
Eigg, Rental in 1798, 261, 262
Eilean-'ic an Toisich, 204
Elgin, 46, 74, 128, 174, 242, 347
Elgol, 283
Englishton, 22
Eriskay, 324, 325
Erricht, 61, 96, 97

INDEX.

Errogie, 61
Eskadale, 104
— Easter, 19, 21, 22.
Essich, 27, 62
Etteridge, 452, 453
Etterish, 384

F

Faicham of Glengarry, 71
Faillie, 64
Falkirk, 120, 191
Farraline, 61
Fassifern, 201
Fochabers, 190, 425
Forestry of Brewlin, 2
Fort-Augustus, 61, 75, 76, 77, 78, 81, 82, 83, 84, 86, 88, 89, 90, 91, 108, 114, 115, 140, 141, 195
Fort-George, 74, 138, 442, 443.
Fortrose, 54
Fort-William, 73, 130, 143, 147, 166, 169, 177, 179, 180, 182, 183, 184, 186, 187, 188, 189, 190, 195, 198, 224, 247, 338, 370
Freicharrie, 32
Fuaran-na-Baintighearna, 45

G

Gairlochy, 198
Gallovie, 335, 336, 337, 339, 365
Garmouth, 74
Garryvounack, 338
Gartallie, 49
Garvabeg, 337
Garvamore, 337
Gibraltar, 74, 75
Glac-na-madaidh of Borlum, 55
Glasgow, 195, 227
Glaster Glen, 165, 172. 173 ;
Glen Affric, 11
Glenballoch, 381
Glenbanchor, 381
Glencannich, 11
Glencharnich, 422
Glenconventh, 14
Glendale, 300
Glenelg, 14, 88, 154, 233, 234, 236, 238, 240, 242, 243, 244, 245
Glenfeshie, 393, 408, 409, 410, 415
Glenfinnan, 179, 201, 228, 231
Glenfintaig, 210
Glengarry, 7, 82, 115, 120, 121, 124, 128, 133, 134, 147, 152, 240, 245,
— County, Ontario, Canada, 130, 136
— Estates, Rental of the lands in 1762, 121, 122, 123, 124
— Rental in 1802, 131, 132
— Tenants, crofters, and cottars warned out in 1785, 127, 128
— Tenants warned out in 1786 and 1787, 128

Glengarry, Tenants warned out in 1803, 1804, 1806. and 1808, 132, 133
Glenglory, 195, 196
Gleninchlochell, 11
Glenlivat, 45, 175, 346
Glen Loyne, 98
Glenlui and Loch Arkaig, 205, 231, 411
— Names of tenants in 1642, 202, 203
— Rentals of, in 1642, 203
— Rental in 1738, 208, 209
Glenmoriston, 7, 82, 91, 98, 102, 104, 106, 110, 111, 240
Glenroy, 172, 196
Glenshee, 361
Glenshiel, 98. 240
Glenshiero, 337, 338
Glenstrathfarar, 1, 2, 3, 11, 12
Glentruim, 357, 381, 389
Glenturret, 172
Glenurquhart, 5, 43, 57, 98
Gordon Castle, 74
Gortan-nan-gour, 54, 55
Gortuleg, 61, 94
Greenock, 190
Grenada, 52
Greshornish, 289, 294

H

Hallbill, 444
Harlaw, Battle of, 64, 412
Harris, 288, 299
Head of Auldynak, 42
Hillhead, 443
Holm or Holme, 19, 21, 22, 23, 24, 42, 44, 61
Huntly, 387

I

Inch, 178
Inchberry, 17, 18, 22
Inchlochell, 3, 11
Inchvallagon, 3
Inchvlair, tenant in 1803, 10
Inchvuilt, 2, 3,
— tenants in 1803, 10
Inchyettle, 436
India, 157
Innisnacardoch, 86, 89, 106
Inshlaggan, 136
Inver, 99
Invereshie, 151, 390, 391, 392, 393, 394
Inveresk, 279
Inverfarigaig, 61
Invergarry, 111, 143, 145, 149, 216
Inverhall or Invertromie, 385, 386, 387, 388
Inverie, 205, 237
Inverlair, 173
Inverlochy or Inverlochie, 31, 64, 115, 172, 175, 180, 182, 195, 196
Invermoriston, 65, 145
Invernahaven, 381, 382, 452

INDEX.

Inverness, 1, 3, 5, 6, 14, 20, 25, 26, 27, 29, 35, 39, 41. 43. 46, 49, 55, 57, 59, 63, 73. 74, 89. 94, 96, 98, 129, 137, 145, 147, 148, 149, 152, 157, 175, 194, 241, 263, 281, 297, 301, 302, 307, 347, 378, 379, 407, 417, 422, 433, 443, 445
— Castle and Castle Lards of, 18, 29, 30, 30, 32, 62.
— Parish of, 61, 62
Iona, 51
Island of Canay, 189
Isle Ornsay, 189

K

Keanpoul, 66
Keppoch, 174, 177, 178
Kilaulay and Lungie, tenants removed in 1810, 327
Kilbride, 229
Kilchoan, 188, 189, 190
Kilichuiman, now Fort-Augustus, 14, 90
Killichoan, 157
Killicrankie, Battle of, 49, 156, 157
Killin, 11
Killionan, 59, 129, 134
Kilmallie, 179, 182
Kilmallie, Rental, in 1677, 182, 201
Kilmalusg, 287
Kilmonivaig, 113, 181, 193, 196, 197, 198
Kilmuir, 286, 287
Kilpheder, 45
Kilravock, 1, 2, 17, 22
Kiltarlity, 3, 13, 17, 19, 20, 21, 22, 104
Kincairne, 66
Kincardine, 416, 418, 420
Kinchyle, 60, 61, 62, 64, 65, 67
Kingairloch, 201
Kingillie, 19
Kingston, Canada, 137
Kingussie, 169, 361, 362, 363, 369, 375, 379, 380, 381, 422, 427, 428
Kinloss, 13
Kinmylies, 22, 26, 34, 35, 56
Kinnairies, 19, 21, 22
Kinrara, 396, 397, 398, 412
— and Dellifour—Names of tenants warned out in 1770, 397
Kintail, 7
Kirkhill, 17, 19, 20, 44, 57
Kirkton, 17, 18, 22
— of Pharnaway, 14, 16
Knock, 154
Knockie, 106
Knoydart, 104, 133, 134, 136, 144, 155, 157, 184, 186, 237, 248
Kyleakin, 280
Kyle Rea, 66

L

Lachline, Canada, 136
Laggan-a-bhan, 83

Laggan Achindrom, 205, 206
Laggan, 334, 338, 346, 352, 364, 365, 380, 427, 428
Lagnalien, 24, 42, 59
Lairgindour, 440
Lairgs, Barony of, 435, 440
Leachkin, 59
Leadclune, 61
Leckroy, 168, 171, 195, 196
Leith, 93, 184, 185, 306
Lentran, 19, 57
Letterfinlay, 115
Lewis, 1
Leys, 14
Liniclate and Belgarva, townships of, 327
Little Ballichernoch, 60
"Little Inverness," 96, 97
Little Portclaire, 102, 103
Lochaber, 31, 63, 115, 158, 177, 195, 197, 199, 201, 204, 205, 210, 213, 337, 365, 423, 425
Lochaleb, 233
Lochan bhanval, 43
Lochend, 25
Lochiel, 201
— Barony of, Rental in 1788, 208
Lochy, 14
London, 9, 74, 107, 137, 147, 332, 333, 355, 377, 378, 396, 398, 399, 403, 453
Lopan, 60
Lopan Durris, 435
Lovat, 2, 14, 15, 57, 243
Luibreoch, 11

M

Mallaig, 247
Mam-Cha, Battle of, 45
Mamore, 195
— Rental in 1788, 201
Maryburgh, or Gordonsburgh, or Duncansburgh (Fort-William), 180, 181, 182, 190, 191, 194
Meikle Ballichernoch, 61
Meikle Portclair, 100, 101
Merkinch, Island of, 22
Mid Craggie, 433
Mid Lairgs, 440
Milltown, lands of, 63
Milton, 62
Milton of Helmc, 61, 62
Moidart, 320
Monar, Shielings of, 4
Moniack, 22, 42, 44
Monkstadt, 286
Montreal, 136
Morar, 9, 158
Moray, Bishopric of, 56
— Earldom of, 60
Morven, 201,
Moy, 212
Moy and Dalarossle, 427
Moydart, Rental of in 1798, 252, 253, 254

Moyhall, 165, 207
Muidart, 115, 309
Muilzie, 3
Muilzie nan-Clach. tenants in 1803, 10
Muilzie-Reoch, 4, 5
Muilzie-Reoch. tenants in 1803, 10
Mu'roy, 431, 433
Murligan, 165, 173

N

Nairn, 435, 436 439, 443
Netherlads, 450
Nether Cullairds. 52
Nethy-Bridge, 420, 421
New England, 7
— States, 125
Newton, 19, 57
Newtonmore, 381
North Carolina, 91
North Inch of Perth. 411
North Morar, 8, 124, 129, 144, 245, 247
North Uist, 301, 302, 303, 304
Nova Scotia, 183
Nunton, 328

O

Oban, 190
Ochtero, 2, 3
— tenants in 1767, 5
Oich, 82
Oporto, 355
Ormiclate, 327 323
— tenants removed in 1810, 226, 329
Orrin, 11
Ostaig, 309, 310

P

Paris, 136
Perth, 147
Peterhead, 128
Petty, 442, 444, 445
Phones, 377, 379, 450, 451, 452
Phopachy, 22
"Poll an Laggan." 43
Pollochaig, 427, 428, 429
Portclair, 98, 99, 101, 104, 106
Portree, 281, 284, 293, 449
Prestonhall, 354
Prestonpans, Battle of, 157
Prince Edward Island, 449

Q

Quebec, 130, 136, 332

R

Raasay, 39, 45
Raitts, 361, 381, 422, 451, 452, 454
Rannoch, 240, 419
Reelig, 44, 57
Relig Orain nan Braithrean, 51
Rhinduie or Rhindowie, 19, 21, 23

Rome, Court of, 19
Rothiemurchus, 411, 412, 413, 414, 415, 418, 420
Roy Bridge, 196, 240
Ruielachnagrane, 32
Rui-ic-Gillie-Chrom, 34
Rui-na-ceardarioh, 34
Ruinachorrie, 32
Rui-na-Clerich, 34
Rui-na-Gunderrie, 34
Ruinataink, 32
Rum. 321
Ruy-Sluggan, 57
Ruthven, 369, 370, 371, 372, 418

S

Saratoga, 71
Scammadale, 155, 156
Scaniport, 62, 63, 71
Scotos, Estate of, 104
Selkirk, Earldom of, 107
Sheuglie, 110
Skeabost, 288, 289
Skye, 263, 281, 284, 283, 290, 291, 301
Sleat, 448
Sliesgarve of Glengarry, 109
Sliesmore, 109
Sligachan, 281
Small Isles, Parish of, 260, 261, 262
Snizort, 288, 289
South Morar, 144, 245, 246, 247, 248
South Uist, 305, 320, 321, 324, 325, 326, 328, 331, 449
— List of Tenants in 1796, 313, 314, 315, 316, 317, 318, 319, 320
33, 35, 55
Spiritane or Spiritual, Castle, 29, 30, 32,
Spyne, Lordship of, 56
St. Domingo, 450
St. Kilda, 299, 300
Stein, 293
Stewarton, 412
Stirling, 363
Stoneybridge, 327
Stornoway, 281
Strathdearn, 422, 423, 424, 428, 429, 431, 433
Strath Dores, 61
Stratherrick, 14, 95, 104, 107, 108
— Bailieship of, 14
— Barony of, 60, 61
Strathfarar, 4, 7, 8, 9, 11
Strathglass, 5, 11, 104
Strathmashie, 169
Strathnairn, 361, 422, 423, 431, 433, 439, 440
Strontian, 190
Sunart, 201, 231

T

Tarbat, 1
Tarradale, 2
Teary, near Forres, 68

Terce of Aigais, 13
Termit, 444
Tigh Corriecharrabie, 11
Tirchurachan, 60
Tobermory, 187, 189, 190, 191
Tomcon, 59
Tomatin, 64
Tom-na-choin, or the Greyhound's Hillock, 66
Torbreck, 62
Tordarroch, 440
Torlundy, 194, 195, 196
Tor, Mill of, or Dunain Mill, 36
Tormore or Hill o' Tor, 43
Torrankenlia, 6
Treachory, 58, 59
Trotternish, 39
Tullich, 440
Tulloch, 173

Uchanro, tenant in 1803, 10
Urchany, 438

"Uchterache," 2
Urquhart, 7, 25, 56
— Barony and Regality of (in Moray), 64
— Priory lands of, 61
Urquhart and Glenmoriston, 110, 114

Virginia, 7

Wardlaw, 3
Waternish, 310, 450
West Indies, 91
Wester Abriachan, 56
"Wester Dowinsche," 62, 63
Wester Eskadale, 104
Wester Muilzie, tenant in 1767, 5
Wester Phoness, 453
Woodend, 31

www.ingramcontent.com/pod-product-compliance
Lightning Source LLC
Chambersburg PA
CBHW021424300426
44114CB00010B/629